Y0-DUV-621

# LEARNING FROM JESUS

# The Bible Study Textbook Series

## NEW TESTAMENT

| | | |
|---|---|---|
| New Testament & History<br>By W. Wartick & W. Fields<br>Vol. I - The Intertestament<br>Period and The Gospels | The Gospel of Matthew<br>In Four Volumes<br>By Harold Fowler | The Gospel of Mark<br>By B. W. Johnson<br>and Don DeWelt |
| The Gospel of Luke<br>By T. R. Applebury | The Gospel of John<br>By Paul T. Butler | Acts Made Actual<br>By Don DeWelt |
| Romans Realized<br>By Don DeWelt | Studies in Corinthians<br>By T. R. Applebury | Guidance From Galatians<br>By Don Earl Boatman |
| The Glorious Church<br>(Ephesians)<br>By Wilbur Fields | Philippians - Colossians<br>Philemon<br>By Wilbur Fields | Thinking Through<br>Thessalonians<br>By Wilbur Fields |
| Paul's Letters<br>To Timothy & Titus<br>By Don DeWelt | Helps From Hebrews<br>By Don Earl Boatman | James & Jude<br>By Don Fream |
| Letters From Peter<br>By Bruce Oberst | Hereby We Know<br>(I-II-III John)<br>By Clinton Gill | The Seer, The Saviour, and<br>The Saved (Revelation)<br>By James Strauss |

## OLD TESTAMENT

| | | | |
|---|---|---|---|
| O.T. & History<br>By William Smith<br>and Wilbur Fields | Genesis<br>In Four Volumes<br>By C. C. Crawford | Exploring Exodus<br>By Wilbur Fields | Leviticus<br>By Don DeWelt |
| Numbers<br>By Brant Lee Doty | Deuteronomy<br>By Bruce Oberst | Joshua - Judges<br>Ruth<br>By W. W. Winter | I & II Samuel<br>By W. W. Winter |
| I & II Kings<br>By James E. Smith | I & II Chronicles<br>By Robert E. Black | Ezra, Nehemiah<br>& Esther<br>By Ruben Ratzlaff<br>& Paul T. Butler | The Shattering of<br>Silence (Job)<br>By James Strauss |

| | | |
|---|---|---|
| Psalms<br>In Two Volumes<br>By J. B. Rotherham | Proverbs<br>By Donald Hunt | Ecclesiastes and Song of<br>Solomon — By R. J. Kidwell<br>and Don DeWelt |
| Isaiah<br>In Three Volumes<br>By Paul T. Butler | Jeremiah and<br>Lamentations<br>By James E. Smith | Ezekiel<br>By James E. Smith |
| Daniel<br>By Paul T. Butler | Hosea - Joel - Amos<br>Obadiah - Jonah<br>By Paul T. Butler | Micah - Nahum - Habakkuk<br>Zephaniah - Haggai - Zechariah<br>Malachi — By Clinton Gill |

## DOCTRINE

| | | | |
|---|---|---|---|
| The Church<br>In The Bible<br>By Don DeWelt | The Eternal Spirit<br>Two Volumes<br>By C. C. Crawford | New Testament<br>Evidences<br>By Wallace Wartick | Survey Course<br>In Christian Doctrine<br>Two Bks. of Four Vols.<br>By C. C. Crawford |

| | | |
|---|---|---|
| New Testament History—Acts<br>By Gareth Reese | Learning From Jesus<br>By Seth Wilson | You Can Understand<br>The Bible<br>By Grayson H. Ensign |

BIBLE STUDY TEXTBOOK SERIES

# LEARNING FROM JESUS

by

Seth Wilson

College Press, Joplin, Missouri

Copyright © 1977
College Press Publishing Company
Second Printing . . . . . 1979

Printed and bound in the
United States of America
All Rights Reserved

BT
299.2
.W48
1977

Library of Congress Catalog Card Number: 77-155407
International Standard Book Number: 0-89900-056-8

ACKNOWLEDGEMENTS

A compilation of published and unpublished materials.

Many of these essays have been rewritten from articles which appeared in *Christian Standard* and *The Lookout*, publications of Standard Publishing of Cincinnati, Ohio. Some of the articles appear in this book essentially as they appeared in these publications.

Permission has been secured from Standard Publishing for the use of the following copyrighted materials:

"Matthew and the Prophets," *Standard Lesson Commentary*, 1975-1976, ed. by James I. Fehl. Copyright 1975, pp. 115, 116.

"God's Law Is For Our Good Always," *Standard Lesson Commentary*, 1972-1973, ed. by James I. Fehl. Copyright 1972, pp. 341, 342.

"What the Kingdom Is Like," *Standard Lesson Commentary*, 1965, ed. by John M. Carter. Copyright 1964, pp. 5-7.

"Law or Grace," *Standard Lesson Commentary*, 1960, ed. by John M. Carter. Copyright 1959, pp. 3, 4.

"The Ground of Our Faith," *Standard Lesson Commentary*, 1958, ed. by John M. Carter. Copyright 1957, pp. 338-341.

"Why John Wrote His Gospel," *Standard Lesson Commentary*, 1954, ed. by John M. Carter. Copyright 1953, pp. 6, 7.

"He Lives," *Standard Lesson Commentary*, 1959, ed. by John M. Carter. Copyright 1958, pp. 3-5.

*Excerpts From:*

"The Gospel of John," *Standard Adult Bible Class*, Jan.-Mar., 1961. John W. Wade, ed. Copyright 1960.

Some of these essays originally appeared in *The Compass*, published at Joplin, Missouri, by Ozark Bible College. Several essays and charts are published here for the first time.

Generally quotations of scripture are taken from the American Standard Version (1901).

## FOREWORD AND DEDICATION

A few words must be included to acknowledge the work of Lynn Gardner in producing this book. It would be impossible to overstate my appreciation for his efforts.

He and brother Don DeWelt originally urged the publication of this collection of studies. Brother Gardner undertook the work of assembling, organizing and editing the entire book. He has freely given an incredible amount of time and labor to this project, doing everything he could to make it as complete and usable as possible. His constant kindness, cheerfulness and spirit of good will have made it especially easy and pleasant for all concerned to work with him.

He encouraged and directed Mrs. Carla Scott, Mrs. Debbie Johnson and Mrs. Nancy Page in the big task of typing reams of pages. Mrs. Page did much additional work on the indexes. Many thanks go to these sisters, also to Mrs. Barbara Gardner for all the ways in which she helped her husband to complete this production. Don DeWelt has been very helpful and spent valuable time from his very busy life to make these studies available in as usable form as they are.

Lynn Gardner was one of my most perceptive and devoted students in the study of the Gospels. He continued his studies until now he has become an outstanding teacher in this subject and related fields of study. I appreciate having him as a colleague in the same department and often draw upon his superior scholarship. With humility and a genuine desire to serve, he has always been a good and beloved brother who strengthens and encourages others.

*I gratefully dedicate this book to Lynn Gardner as one who most appreciates and exemplifies in his own life the truths studied herein.*

—Seth Wilson

# PREFACE

Our Lord Jesus invited, "Come unto me, all ye that labor and are heavy laden, and I will give you rest. Take my yoke upon you, and learn of me: for I am meek and lowly in heart: and ye shall find rest unto your souls. For my yoke is easy, and my burden is light" (Matthew 11:28-30). Seth Wilson has written this book to help the reader learn more fully to know and trust Jesus as the Christ, the Son of God and to submit to His will and authority.

These practical studies set forth in everyday language the important truths about Jesus: who He is, what He taught, what He accomplished and how we should respond to Him. They are not technical academic essays filled with difficult theological terms nor are they superficial off-the-cuff type of lessons. This book represents a lifetime of careful serious study and effective preaching and college teaching of the Life of Christ.

Many will find this book profitable. Any person who wants to study and understand the Gospels better can find guidance and inspiration in these pages. The man who wants to preach Christ more effectively will find valuable sermon-building material. The Sunday School teacher will find here a resource book and study guide for practical help in teaching the Life of Christ. It will be useful to college teachers and students as a text or collateral reading text for courses in the Gospels and Life of Christ.

These studies are not just factual analyses of the Gospel passages. Every effort is made to correctly understand the author's intended meaning in each passage studied. Also the leading principles are applied personally and practically to the reader's life.

Seth Wilson teaches and serves as Academic dean at Ozark Bible College, Joplin, Missouri. He has served in these capacities since 1940 in Ozark Christian College, Bentonville, Arkansas and continued in Ozark Bible College as it moved to Joplin, Missouri in 1944. He has taught many subjects with the major emphasis being in Life of Christ, Hermeneutics and Greek.

As dean he has been the key man in shaping the philosophy of Ozark Bible College as a school committed to training a ministry for the church. Emphasis has been given to teaching students why they can believe in God, Christ and the Bible; how to understand the Bible; the basic content of the Bible; and tools for effectively proclaiming the Christian message.

In his teaching ministry, Mr. Wilson has been a motivator and teacher of preachers, teachers, missionaries and Christian workers now serving all over the world. Many of his students look back to their study of the Life of Christ under Seth Wilson as a life-changing experience. They came to realize they were saved by grace not by law. They came to see in a personal way the truth Paul expressed: "I have been crucified with Christ; and it is no longer I that live, but Christ liveth in me" (Gal. 2:20). Some of his best sermons were spontaneous outpourings of his soul in the classroom. Such times manifested real depth because of the hours of study he had put in the night before as well as the years before.

Studies in the Gospels at The Cincinnati Bible Seminary in Cincinnati, Ohio under R. C. Foster developed his interest and disciplined his mind in his early training. His knowledge of the subject has grown while teaching the Life of Christ in the college classroom for thirty-six years.

He has communicated his faith outside the classroom through preaching, teaching in Christian workers' and youth camps, speaking in conferences and by conducting hundreds of clinics on church leadership. His concern for people is evident in the time he takes to personally answer letters and to give wise counsel to individuals and churches.

Mr. Wilson has written extensively, primarily short articles and essays such as those collected in this book. He wrote the weekly lesson for the *Christian Standard* during the years 1944-1948. Since 1954 he has contributed weekly the background for the lesson in *The Lookout.* Many of the articles in this book originally appeared in the *Christian Standard, The Lookout* or *The Bible Teacher and Leader,* all published by Standard Publishing of Cincinnati, Ohio. These articles have appeared at various times over the last thirty years. Many have been revised and duplicated in mimeographed form for extensive classroom and general distribution.

As a student at Ozark Bible College, I received over forty semester hours of classroom instruction under Seth Wilson. I confess a deep indebtedness to him for the better understanding I gained of Christianity through the study of the Life of Christ under his teaching. Now as a fellow teacher at Ozark Bible College I have been privileged to organize and to edit the essays, outlines and charts in this book. I am responsible for the selection of the books listed under "For Further Study" after each essay.

Seth Wilson practices one of the mottos of his life: "The Word of Christ taught in the Spirit of Christ." This book is presented with the prayer that "the word of Christ [will] dwell in you richly" (Col. 3:16). "That Christ be formed in you" (Gal. 4:19) and that you "may grow up in all things into him, who is the head, even Christ" (Eph. 4:15).

Lynn Gardner
July, 1977

# TABLE OF CONTENTS

## LEARNING FROM JESUS

# *Part One*

# INTRODUCTION

## 1

## THE GROUND OF OUR FAITH

The Gospel records of the life of Jesus are the focal center of the entire Bible; and they are the chief foundation of our assurance that the Bible is from God. If these accounts are true, they confirm the Old Testament and guarantee the divine inspiration of the New Testament. If Jesus actually said what these report He said, then indeed He spoke as never man spoke. If He did what these say He did, His works bear witness of Him that He is from God, for no one could do these things except God be with Him. If He died for us and rose again as they testify, He is the Conqueror of death and the Lord of all. If what they say is true, He came forth from God, was born of a virgin, and ascended back to God's throne; then the Son of God has visited us, and we can know whom we have believed, and can trust Him completely to do whatever He has promised.

According to these accounts, Jesus has all authority in heaven and on earth; He will raise all the dead and judge all men; He is the Way, the Truth, and the Life, and no one can come to God except through Him (John 14:6): no one knows God unless he learns of Him from Jesus Christ (Matt. 11:27); if we do not believe in Jesus, we walk in darkness, we will die in our sins, the wrath of God abides upon us, and we will be condemned (John 8:12, 24; 3:18, 36; 12:46-48; Mark 16:16); if we do believe in Him and obey Him, we will have eternal life with Him in glory. Our eternal destiny depends upon what these records say. They had better be right. It is of utmost importance for us to know whether or not they are true and reliable.

### *Truthfulness and Trustworthiness of the Gospel Accounts*

Some men say the important thing is that the story of Jesus inspires us to nobler attitudes and better deeds, whether it is historically true or not. There are religious leaders who insist that we should simply take the samples and sentiments of the New Testament as a pattern for our lives, and not believe the supernatural claims and events recorded in the Gospels. They even claim that the Gospels present sublime principles in an oriental style of personifying and illustrating ideals in the form of exaggerated accounts of real events or stories of imaginary incidents. They say it does not have to be true history to be great religion. *But that is not true.* Beware of such a delusion! Christianity is not mere sentiment stirred by fiction. It is not noble feelings and ideals based on the psychological effect of examples, real or imaginary. Christianity is living under a contract with God, faithfully following His definitely revealed will for us.

The Gospel is not primarily a set of ideals for conduct. It is first a message of facts—real, true, unique facts of what God has done for us and made known to us. It is, of course, a message to be believed, and that faith is to be genuine and deep enough to control our lives. We are to know these things so that we may act accordingly. But the gospel story cannot adequately affect our lives unless we are convinced that it is true.

Furthermore, it certainly cannot bring us the gifts and helps from God which it promises, unless it is true. We cannot change the basic nature of our sinful hearts, or bear the fruit of a divine spirit of righteousness, without regeneration and the coming of the Spirit of God to dwell within us. The righteousness taught in the New Testament is not something that can be embodied in a set of impersonal rules or described in abstract principles, but it is a personal relationship with the living Christ. (See Rom. 8:1-17; II Cor. 5:14-17; Gal. 2:20, 5:6; Phil. 3:8-11; Col. 1:27, 2:6-23, 3:1-17; Rom. 14:17; I Cor. 16:22). The person of Christ the Son of God must be real, must be known, must be relied upon with complete trust, must be loved. Any religion that could exist without faith in the truth of the New Testament message is not the Christianity described in the New Testament—that is sure!

There is nothing the world needs as much as a clear, decisive faith in the Christ of the New Testament. We need the kind of firm conviction that makes us eager to follow wherever He leads, obey whatever He commands, and trust Him whatever befalls us. Faith is not holding to an idea regardless of the evidence, but it is trusting the reliability of the Lord regardless of the consequences. We need a solid foundation of facts and good reasons to show that the New Testament is the Word of Him whom we can trust for all of life and eternity.

The Gospel accounts of the life of Jesus furnish that foundation. John stated the purpose of His writing, and it fits all four Gospels: "These are written that ye might believe that Jesus is the Christ, the Son of God; and that believing ye might have life through His name" (John 20:31). *"Believing"* means being convinced that it is true, so that we act upon it, with our consciousness, desires, and will controlled by it.

There is plenty of evidence to convince any reasonable person that the Gospels are true—evidence both within the books themselves, and outside the books concerning them and their contents.

*We Have In The Gospels the Surest Kind of History*

1. *Credibility of the witnesses.* Here are enough good witnesses to establish any fact. They tell their story with serious purpose, factual details and stedfast consistency. Their writings show that they were intelligent men. They were prepared by extensive and close association with the things of which they speak. Early Christian writers declare, without a dissenting voice, that our four Gospels were written by Matthew and John, who were apostles of Jesus, and by Mark and Luke, who were companions of the apostles. Many direct testimonies and incidental references in numerous writings of the first three centuries unite to show that these four Gospels were written in the apostolic age, were handed down to the succeeding generations as authoritative Scriptures, and were in widespread general and public use at least from the beginning of the second century. Thus our four records are the work of men who were qualified as eyewitnesses and close associates of eyewitnesses who were constantly engaged in proclaiming these facts. And the facts which were written by them did not originate at the writing, but had been preached for several years by other eyewitnesses, and had been accepted by vast multitudes of people of whom many had opportunity to know personally or to inquire directly concerning the circumstances involved. These witnesses were men of good character, having reverence for God, love for the truth, and zeal for righteousness. They lived as believers in their own testimony, and spent years in labors and hardships to propagate this message, which meant no gain to them unless it was true. Their sincerity is sealed by their martyrdom and the persecutions which they were willing to bear for the sake of the truth and their love for the Lord.

2. *Agreement of the Testimony.* The accounts in the four Gospels are so similar that they have been accused of copying. Yet they are so independent and different in telling many details that they are sometimes accused of contradicting one another. They make no attempt to explain the differences or to prove agreement, in what they say. On close study they are seen to agree perfectly, but not with the kind of surface agreement that would appear if they were made up to agree. R. A. Torrey observed concerning their testimony of the resurrection of Jesus:

> These accounts must be either a record of facts that actually occurred or else fictions. If fictions, they must have been fabricated in one of two ways—either independently of one another, or in collusion with one another. They could not have been fabricated independently of one another; the agreements are too marked and too many. It is absolutely incredible that four persons sitting down to write an account of what never occurred independently of one another should have made their stories agree to the extent that these do. On the other hand, they cannot have been made up, as we have already seen, in collusion with one another; the apparent discrepancies are too numerous and too noticeable. It is proven that they were not made up independently of one another; it is proven they were not made up in collusion with one another, so we are driven to the conclusion that they were not made up at all, that they are a true relation of facts as they actually occurred.[1]

3. *Support of Archaeology, Geography, and History.* The Gospel testimony is confirmed by agreement, not only with one another, but also with many other writings and with all available facts of the land of Palestine, the rulers, the parties, coins, customs, etc. Gospel writers have been accused of error, but they have never been proved false. When the facts have been brought to light, in every instance the Gospels have been shown to be accurate history: e.g., the account of Quirinius (Cyrenius) and the enrollment in Luke 2:2. Everywhere their testimony can be checked it proves to be sound.

4. *Support of Old Testament Prophecies.* By far the most important outside information to confirm the Gospels is found in dozens of passages in the Old Testament which give many scores of items of information about the Christ, His life, character and work. Matthew makes many references to the testimony of the prophets; and all the Gospels quote Jesus' appeal to the prophets in support of His claims and for explanations of His life and sufferings. This testimony from the Old Testament has special quality and value, because obviously it reports not things as seen understood by men, but truths as known and revealed by God.

5. *Evidence of Miracles.* Miracles wrought by the apostles confirmed their testimony to the hearers who saw and knew them, and their confirmation has been relayed to us by many witnesses, both Biblical and

---

[1] R. A. Torrey, "The Certainty and Importance of the Resurrection of Jesus Christ" in *The Fundamentals,* Vol. II, ed. by R. A. Torrey, A. C. Dixon, and others (Grand Rapids, Michigan: Baker Book House, reprint 1972 [1917]), pp. 301-302.

traditional. Their miracles are not mere unexplained wonders, but are given clear meaning as credentials of their message (Heb. 2:4). They tell plainly that Jesus gave them the miracle-working power to support the message, and that He also gave them inspiration of the Holy Spirit to aid them in remembering what He taught and to guide them in revealing the truth. Miracles were a reasonable accompaniment to their message, for it was all concerned with the facts of God's revelation to man and His supernatural intervention in the affairs of the world.

6. *Claims of Divine Inspiration.* An integral and indelible part of the apostles' testimony is found in their repeated claims of supernatural aid and inspiration from God to guarantee the accuracy and Divine authority of their message. This claim extends to some who were their co-workers like Mark and Luke (See Matt. 10:1-20, 40; 16:19; Mark 13:11; 16:20; Luke 24:45-49; John 14:26; 15:26; 16:13-15; 20:21-23; Acts 1:4-8; 2:1-4, 16, 17, 33; 4:8; 5:12-26; 8:6, 13-18; 13:1-4; 15:6-12, 28; I Cor. 2:6-16; 12:8-11; 14:37; Gal. 1:8-12; Eph. 3:2-5; I Thess. 2:13; II Tim. 1:6; I Pet. 1:12; II Pet. 3:15-16). If they are men of truth, these claims are true. In any case, such claims demand from us a strong and decisive verdict either for or against them. Such claims are either very significantly true or they are monstrously false. They mean that the apostles cannot be treated indifferently, but must be considered either deliberate liars, deluded maniacs, or completely dependable messengers of God. There can be no middle ground, no supposition of general good intentions, partial reliability, and innocent mistakes. If they are not the worst of frauds, they are the truest of witnesses, and vice versa.

7. *Incredibility of Fraud.* The charge of fraud is answered by their consistent and extended witnessing, by the agreement of their lives with their testimony, by the success of their proclamation among people to whom many of the facts were known, by their endurance of persecution and death for the Gospel. Furthermore, it is absolutely incredible that the matchless life and character of Jesus could have been invented by deliberate liars, or dreamed up by lunatics, or formed in the popular imagination over any period of time. It is almost as incredible that anyone who invented such a character could have made other men to believe him to be real and to join in the proclamation of the fraud without having any evidences of His reality. The almost irreverent words of Theodore Parker have a strong element of truth in them: "It would have taken a Jesus to forge a Jesus." Another has said, "If Jesus is not the living Lord, then the man who invented Jesus deserves our worship." It is a shocking and repulsive

thought; but it is true—if the Bible is not true, then there is no true God known to man, and we have nothing more admirable and helpful to man than the lies about Jesus. Just try to imagine how fiction, forgery, and fraud could produce the teachings of Christ, the converting power of the Gospel, and the actual establishment and spread of Christianity—just think of the magnitude of the imposture, the difficulty of contriving the mighty features and the many details of such a system, the sharply contradictory types of skills and cunning and character that would be required in the fabricators—and you will see how anyone who faces the facts must believe that the Gospels are true. It is necessary for any normal mind to believe that every effect has an adequate cause.

We do not have to prove all the facts of the record, if we can be sure of the reliability of the author. If the Gospel record is not only good and honest human testimony, but also written by men inspired of the Holy Spirit, then we can and must believe it whether we can verify it or not. It becomes more than a collection of ideas to be tested; it is a source of truth to be trusted. It is also the solid ground on which we rest a faith that is reasonable, helpful and honest—a faith that knows whom it believes and why he is deemed trustworthy. After we know the evidence that Jesus is the Son of God, we can quite reasonably say, "If Jesus says it, I believe it, and that settles it." When we know the facts of His life which manifest His love and goodness, as well as His wisdom and power, we follow Him with loving confidence and are content to say:

> "And so I go on not knowing; I would not know if I might.
> I would rather walk with Him by faith, than to walk alone by sight;
> I would rather walk with Christ in the dark, than to walk alone in the light."

For Further Study:

Anderson, J. N. D. *Christianity: The Witness of History.* Downers Grove: InterVarsity Press, 1969. A British lawyer sifts the evidence and makes a positive case for the life, death and resurrection of Jesus Christ.

Bruce, F. F. *The New Testament Documents: Are They Reliable?* 5th ed. Grand Rapids: Wm. B. Eerdmans Publishing Co., 1960. Presents internal and external evidence for the reliability of the New Testament books. His acceptance of the two-source theory weakens the book.

Montgomery, John W. *Christianity and History.* Downers Grove: InterVarsity Press, 1964-1965. A defense of the truth of Christianity on the basis of reliable historical records showing us a divine Christ.

Wartick, Wallace. *New Testament Evidences.* Joplin: College Press, 1975. Updating of J. W. McGarvey's classic work, *Evidences of Christianity.*

# 2

# Divine Truth

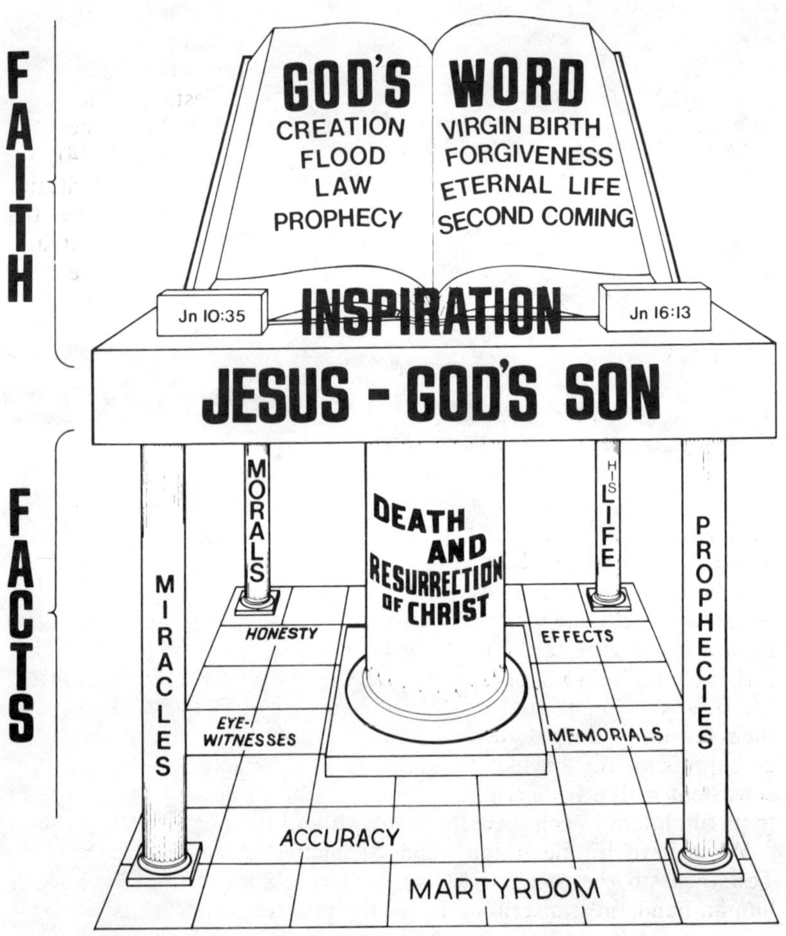


## Grounded in Human History

# 3

## A STATEMENT OF FAITH[1]

Christianity is a matter of faith. It has doctrines and practices simply because Christ taught and commanded. Those who believe Christ believe what He taught, and those who accept Jesus as Lord obey what He commanded. Our Christian faith is faith in Christ and the divine revelation of which He is the source and the center. Because He put His stamp of approval on the Old Testament and declared that it could not be broken (John 10:35) and that none of it shall pass away until all be fulfilled (Matt. 5:18; Luke 24:44), we believe that the Old Testament scriptures are inspired, authoritative and divinely dependable. Because Jesus promised the apostles the Holy Spirit to guide them in remembering all that He taught and in revealing all truth (John 14:26; 16:12-14), we believe the New Testament scriptures to be inspired of God and possessed of divine accuracy and authority. Many facts of the record and claims of the New Testament writers confirm this faith.

We believe Christ—and all His appointed spokesmen. Christ said it; we believe it; that settles it, on any subject of which the New Testament plainly speaks.

We believe that the words of the apostles are the words of Christ and are full of compelling authority unto the end of the age. When Paul gives inspired advice concerning marriage, we do not explain it away as his personal and fallacious opinion. His modest reminder in I Cor. 7:40—"and I think also that I have the Spirit of God"—certainly should not be taken as an expression of doubt about His inspiration in view of the positive assertions in the same letter (I Cor. 2:10-13; 14:37) and in others (Gal. 1:12; I Thess. 2:13; II Thess. 3:14). We believe we must find the intended meaning of the apostle in all their teachings and abide by them. We do not disregard any of it as expressing the bias of Paul against women, or any of it as inconsistent with other Scriptures. But we seek to heed every statement to its full intent in complete harmony with all the rest.

We believe in the unique and distinctive authority of the New Testament to the extent that we deplore all the changes made by human hands in transcribing it, all the misstatements of its meaning

---

[1] This statement appeared in the *Compass,* official organ of Ozark Bible College, to explain the basic faith of the men who taught at this college. Seth Wilson is Dean of Ozark Bible College.

in translating it, and all the mishandling of it by men interpreting and applying it. We do fervently desire to have the original inspired word in the purity and fullness of its original meaning and we have no interest in preserving the traditional corruptions of it in any manuscript, translation or commentary. Therefore, we are interested in weighing carefully all reliable evidence for correcting our interpretations, our commentaries, and our Bible versions whether they be new or old, at every point of error, although they are minor points.

We rejoice that God has so written His word and so preserved it that the fundamentals of salvation have been preserved in all versions and copies of it for those who will diligently study it and find its truth in spite of the errors and inconsistencies of its translators. But we believe that when errors in any version are found they should be rejected, rather than perpetuated as part of this divine truth; for, of course, they did not belong to it originally.

This we believe and teach.

# 4

# MATTHEW AND THE PROPHETS

It is generally agreed that Matthew wrote as a Jew, addressing his account of the life of Jesus especially to Jews, both believers and non-believers. Although he did not write to Jews exclusively, his purpose was to present Jesus clearly as the Messiah, the true fulfillment of the Old Testament.

At least seventy-one passages from the Old Testament are quoted or paraphrased in Matthew. About seventeen of these are freely adapted from its language.

At least ten records of events are referred to, without any quotation being made.

## *Jesus' Use of the Prophets*

This kind of use of the Old Testament certainly did not originate with Matthew. He ascribes most of it to Jesus. Sixty percent (642) of the 1071 verses in Matthew's Gospel contain his quotations of Jesus' sayings and sermons. In these quotations there are fifty-four places in which Jesus used the language of the Old Testament directly or loosely. Perhaps fifteen of these are so brief and so loosely quoted that they may not be intentional quotations. They at least show His familiarity with Old Testament and inclination to use its language.

Matthew, Mark, Luke, and John report the sayings of Jesus in the style of direct quotation rather than indirect; yet they do not always agree exactly in wording the same sayings. Thus we see that Matthew may have summarized or altered slightly the original words of Jesus; but we cannot assume that he put quotations from the Old Testament into the mouth of Jesus. Yet Matthew chose (being led by the Holy Spirit) to record especially those teachings of Jesus in which He used the Old Testament. This fits Matthew's purpose to show that Jesus is the Messiah and fulfillment of the entire revelation which God has made.

Jesus (as reported by Matthew alone) quoted from fourteen different books of the Old Testament. At least six times He introduced quotations by the phrase "it is written," a well-established form of referring to the canonical authority of the Scriptures. He mentioned Isaiah, Moses, David, and Daniel as authors through whom God spoke.

Jesus cited at least twenty passages of the Old Testament as commands of God to be obeyed; at least eleven as statement of historic fact or truth; and at least twenty-one as prophecies fulfilled in His life or circumstances of His time. He spoke of the prophecies as needing to be fulfilled, probably meaning that any predictions made by God will inevitably come true (Matthew 26:54, 56).

Of the laws or duties which Jesus cited from the Old Testament, He quoted five of the ten commandments, on at least three different occasions: in the sermon on the mount (5:21, 27), in argument with Pharisees (15:4), and to the rich young ruler (19:18, 19). He used Deuteronomy three times in His answers to Satan's temptations (4:4, 7, 10), as stating rules from God which bound His own conscience and conduct. The history which Jesus used as true and important included accounts of creation, Adam and Eve, Noah and the flood, Abraham, Sodom and Gomorrah, Moses and the law, David and the showbread, the Queen of Sheba, Jonah in the fish, and the murder of both Abel and Zachariah.

All of the above facts are from Matthew's account of Jesus alone. The other Gospels add more statements and figures to show Jesus' emphasis upon the testimony of the law and prophets. "These are they which bear witness of me" (John 5:39). "If ye believed Moses, ye would believe me; for he wrote of me" (John 5:46). "All things must needs be fulfilled, which are written in the law of Moses, and the prophets, and the psalms, concerning me" (Luke 24:44). See also Luke 24:25-27 and 45-47.

The sermons and letters of the other apostles show much of this same emphasis. Peter's sermon in Acts 2 uses prophecies as its main evidence and for more than half of its total contents. Even in preaching to Gentiles he said, "To him bear all the prophets witness" (Acts 10:43). Paul before King Agrippa described his ministry as "testifying both to small and great, saying nothing but what the prophets and Moses did say should come; how that the Christ must suffer, and how that he first by the resurrection of the dead should proclaim light both to the people and to the Gentiles" (Acts 26:22, 23). Their chief method of persuading men to believe was by use of the prophets (Acts 3:18, 21, 24; 8:30-35; 13:27, 40; 24:14; 26:27; 28:23). They also emphasized them in strengthening the faith of believers (Romans 1:2, 17; 3:21; I Peter 1:10-12; 2:6-8; II Peter 1:19-21; 3:2).

As John wrote "that ye may believe," and John the Baptist came "that all might believe through him" (John 20:31; 1:7), so also the prophets wrote that men might recognize the Christ when He came, and might expect Him before He came. They did cause a general expectation all over the East that someone from Judea should become ruler of the world. Prophecies like those in Daniel 2:44; 9:25-27; and Micah 5:2-15 could account for that. Remember the long career of Daniel in high offices in the Babylonian and Persian empires, and the coming of the wisemen from the east at Jesus' birth.

Preaching the gospel of Christ is not presenting His teachings for men to evaluate with human wisdom or to test by experimentation. It is identifying Jesus for all men to accept, trust, and follow Him, obeying Him as God and only Source of life.

Many scholars and churches of Christendom in the last two hundred years have greatly erred, not knowing the Scriptures or the power of God. They have tried to judge the message of the Bible or modify it by the wisdom and wants of men, putting too much confidence in new conclusions from insufficient discoveries. They have been too much like Aladdin, trading the true wonder-working lamp of God for a shiny new-made thing of brass; because they have not listened to the witnesses who gave God's testimony to His own Son. They have not proclaimed the identity and unique authority of Jesus the Son of God and only Savior of the world.

Jesus' high regard for the Old Testament (Matt. 5:17, 18) was shared or learned by the apostles, and they followed His practice of making effective use of it. Should not all of His disciples today similarly learn from Him?

### *Matthew's Use of the Prophets*

Matthew's use of the prophets is not so different from that of the other apostles, except for the quantity of citations accumulated in his more extensive quotations of Jesus' teaching and his own repetition of his favorite clause for introducing a prophecy. He also reports the fact that the scribes of Jerusalem quoted the prophecy of Micah about the birth of the Christ at Bethlehem (2:6).

Exactly ten times Matthew quotes the Old Testament in his own narrative to point out the fulfillment of a passage. One other time (in 2:23) he quotes a prediction that apparently is not written in the Old Testament: "that he should be called a Nazarene."

Eight times Matthew uses the same form of expression to introduce a prophecy: "that it might be fulfilled which was spoken through the prophet" or "spoken by the Lord through his prophet." Here they are. Jesus was born of a virgin (1:22, 23). God's Son was taken to Egypt and back to Nazareth (2:15 and 23). Jesus ministered in Galilee (4:14-16). He healed the sick (8:16, 17). He avoided unnecessary strife and concentrated on positive ministry to the need of persons (12:15-21). He used parables (13:34, 35). He rode an ass into Jerusalem while being acclaimed king (21:4, 5).

In this expression Matthew probably did not mean to say that these things were deliberately done for the purpose of making the prophecies come true. It does contain the form of grammar which usually expresses purpose; but in the New Testament Greek it also is used to express a result in John 9:2; Romans 11:11; I Corinthians 7:29; I Thessalonians 5:4; I John 1:9; Galatians 5:17; Revelation 13:13; Mark 5:23 and Luke 1:43. It may not even be recognizable in these passages, because it should not be translated too literally. Did Matthew mean to say that either Joseph or Herod purposely acted to fulfill the words of Hosea 11:1, 2? Did John mean, in a similar statement, that the soldiers at the cross gambled for Jesus' robe, or pierced His side instead of breaking His legs, for the purpose of fulfilling prophecies? Matthew's form of introduction to prophecies does not require us to believe that these things happened just because they were predicted; they were predicted because God knew they were going to happen.

In two other places Matthew says, "Then was fulfilled that which was spoken through the prophet": about the sorrow for Bethlehem's babies (2:17, 18), and about Judas' betrayal money and what was done with it (27:9, 10). Once he says, "This is he that was spoken of through Isaiah the prophet" about John the Baptist (3:3).

### *Matthew's Use of Prophets Limited*

Matthew did not try to use all the prophecies he could. He omitted many dozens of impressive ones. But like the other apostles, he wanted to show that the ministry of Jesus, of which he was writing so briefly, was indeed "according to the scriptures" (see I Corinthians 15:3, 4).

Matthew used the prophets modestly, with restraint, just enough to keep us conscious of the fact that Jesus did not come in His own name or contrary to God's plan. He used them most in recording how Jesus used them, and then to show that the Scriptures had foretold many of the very things about Christ which his people did not expect of the Messiah. Such things as: His being God with us by virgin birth (Isaiah 7:14), His life being threatened by Herod and saved by a stay in Egypt (Jeremiah 31:15; Hosea 11:1), His lowly service to the people and in despised provinces (Isaiah 9:1, 2; 42:1-4; 53:4). Even John the Baptist found such actions contrary to his expectations of the Messiah and sent a question about it to Jesus (Matthew 11:2-6).

But why didn't Matthew argue vigorously from such strong and obvious prophecies as Isaiah 9:6, 7 and 53:5-12? Matthew was not making a case for Christ from prophecy. He was reporting the simple facts as the Spirit of God guided him. By the same divine wisdom he was caused to cite some Scriptures which foretold or prefigured them.

Some "scholars" allege that "Matthew twists the Scriptures" to apply them to Christ. I deny the allegation and in all good humor I defy the *allegator* (especially the reptile really responsible for this blindness—II Corinthians 4:4; 11:14, 15; Revelation 12:9). Careful study of Matthew's quotations will reveal that some of them are taken from the Septuagint (the Greek version of the Old Testament which was common among the Jews), although it was not exactly like the original Hebrew in meaning. Some of the passages quoted by Matthew were plain predictions directly fulfilled in the life of Christ. But some of them were spoken originally of another matter, yet in language which finds again fulfillment in the facts of Christ: for example, the sorrow over the Babylonian captivity expressed in Jeremiah 31:15 happens again in the slaughter of the infants of Bethlehem and the surrounding area.

Hosea 11:1, cited at Matthew 2:15, is part of a statement about the history of Israel expressed in such a figure of speech that it fits even better the facts of Jesus. One can easily suppose that the Spirit of God used the language of Hosea to put another line in the Old Testament portrait of the Messiah, of whom more than three hundred details are given in the entire Old Testament.

It is not unreasonable that the inspired writers of the New Testament should state the facts more fully or specifically than the predictions do, or be able to determine meanings which were not evident to the uninspired reader. For example, even if it could be shown that Isaiah 7:14 used a word which meant a young woman, Matthew is competent to tell us that God intended to predict the birth of a son to a virgin, just as Paul can tell us in Galatians 3:16 that the ambiguous word "seed" in Genesis was really intended to apply to Christ as a singular term.

The purpose of predictions and foreshadowing types is not to give details of history in advance, but to identify a plan and its Author, to build a faith in the Author of revelation who knows the end from the beginning. A study of prophecy should give all of us a greater appreciation of the facts of Christ's coming and ministry on earth, when we realize God's long-range planning, His control over the ages, His faithfulness to the promises and purposes of His grace.

For Further Study:

Fowler, Harold. *The Gospel of Matthew,* Volume I. Joplin: College Press, 1968, pp. 81-86. Studies how Matthew used the prophecies with attention to Matthew's use of the word fulfill.

Gundry, Robert. *A Survey of the New Testament.* Grand Rapids: Zondervan Publishing House, 1970, pp. 90-93. Itemizes the New Testament quotations of fulfilled Old Testament passages.

Nicole, Roger. "New Testament Use of the Old Testament" in *Revelation and the Bible,* ed. by C. F. H. Henry. Grand Rapids: Baker Book House, 1958. Pp. 137-151. Excellent essay on this topic.

R. V. G. Tasker. *The Old Testament In the New Testament,* rev. ed. Grand Rapids: Wm. B. Eerdmans Publishing Co., 1954. Pp. 41-48. Brief discussion of Matthew's use of the Old Testament.

# 5

## WHY JOHN WROTE HIS GOSPEL

Every writing has a purpose of one kind or another. And every book or sentence is best understood in the light of the purpose for which it is written.

### *Stated Purpose*

Many writings have purposes so insignificant, or even frivolous, that we pay no attention to them. But John's story of the life of Jesus has a purpose so vital to all of us that it is more than an academic question of aid to interpretation. His purpose is worthy of our special consideration and appreciation.

John states his purpose in the plainest terms in 20:30, 31:

> "Many other signs therefore did Jesus in the presence of the disciples, which are not written in this book: but these are written, that ye may believe that Jesus is the Christ, the Son of God; and that believing ye may have life in his name."

The contents of the fourth Gospel seems clearly to indicate that this author was familiar with the books of Matthew, Mark and Luke and that he supposed many of his readers would know these other books. He seems to have designed his account to supplement the others in giving a greater knowledge of the first year of Christ's ministry, a more explicit view of the chronology of the whole of Jesus' public work and additional emphasis upon the teaching of his deity. But it was not John's purpose merely to relate more miracles or more parables such as the earlier accounts had recorded. He designed rather to give a deeper understanding of the significance of the words and deeds of Jesus. While John's Gospel is in full harmony with the others, and at the same time bears a reasonable relationship to them as the earlier accepted and approved accounts of the same general subject, still the question whether to repeat incidents which they had told is only incidental to his main purpose. That purpose is to produce the greatest possible conviction and understanding about the person of Jesus—the greatest possible faith in Jesus—in all his readers, whether they have read the other Gospels or not. To John the issue was faith versus unbelief, and he emphasized it by quoting much more of Jesus' discussions concerning Himself and the necessity of faith in Him. Take a look at the following passages in John: 3:11-

15, 16-21; 4:10, 25, 26, 39-42; 5:24, 37, 38, 43-47; 6:29, 35, 40, 62-64; 7:17, 37, 38; 8:21-25, 31, 45-47; 9:35-38; 10:3-5, 25, 26, 34-38; 11:25-27; 12:31-43, 44-50; 13:19, 20; 14:6, 7, 8-12; 16:27-31; 17:8, 20; 18:37; 19:35; 20:25-31; 21:24.

John sought to bring to his readers a positive testimony of fact—the clear evidence of an eyewitness—giving the utmost assurance of the great truth of the deity of Jesus Christ. In doing so he claims to be an eyewitness (1:14 and 19:35) and tells many incidental details with the perfect familiarity of one who has participated in the events of which he writes.

John lays great stress upon the "truth" and things that are "true." He expects us to accept Jesus for the reason that the testimony about Him is true and entirely sufficient to convince all who love the truth. To bring out the full emphasis and meaning of 19:35 we might translate it thus: "He who has seen has borne witness (and his witness is of a nature to be thoroughly competent, and he knows that he speaks accurately) in order that you may believe." It is strange how much this Gospel has been accused of being "theology," "unhistorical," "an interpretation of later views of the church," or even "speculative" while it is filled with insistence upon concrete fact and objective truth supported by the most direct testimony and authoritative witnesses.

### *John Tells Who Jesus Is*

All that is in the fourth Gospel has been chosen to produce a definite result. Every part of it is told in order to make us understand that the eternal Word of God, who was in the beginning with God and who was God, became flesh and dwelt among us, and that he lived and died and rose again that we might have eternal life. In the most concrete and concise manner, *John is telling us who Jesus is:*

1. He is the Word of God, the perfect expression of the Father (1:1, 18).
2. He is the Creator of all things (1:3).
3. He is the true light (1:9).
4. He is the Son of God (1:18; 3:16, 35), one with the Father (10:30, 36; 14:9), who came forth from God and returned to God (13:1, 3; 17:8, 13), who is in the Father and the Father in Him (14:10; 17:21; 10:38).
5. He is the Lamb of God (1:36), the divine sacrifice and the only sacrifice that can take away the sin of the world.
6. He is the promised Christ of the Old Testament, the King of

Israel (1:45, 49; 4:25, 26; 18:33, 36, 37; 6:69; 11:27; 12:12-15; 17:3; 19:19; 20:31).

7. He is the Lord of nature (2:3-10; 6:5-21).
8. He is the Lord of the temple of God (2:13-20).
9. He is the Savior of the world (3:14-17; 4:42).
10. He is the true witness (1:18; 3:11, 32, 33; 7:16-18; 8:26, 45; 12:49, 50; 17:8; 18:37, etc.) who speaks always exactly and only the words of God.
11. He is the Lord of life (5:21, 25-29), the "resurrection and the life" (11:25, 26; 8:51; 6:40, 54, 57, 68).
12. He is the Judge of all (5:22, 27, 30; compare 9:39).
13. He is the Bread of life (6:35-58).
14. He is the Water of life (7:37).
15. He is the Light of the world (8:12; 9:5; 12:35, 46).
16. He is the author of liberty (8:31-36).
17. He is the good Shepherd (10:11, 14-18).
18. He is the door to safety and the way to God (10:7-9; 14:6).
19. He is the humble Master and the perfect example of love (13:1-17).
20. He is the Truth (14:6).
21. He is the sender of the Spirit of truth (14:26; 15:26; 16:7, 13-15).
22. He is the true Vine, the actual source of spiritual life and fruit in those who abide in Him (15:1-8).
23. He is the greatest friend (15:13-17), who brings the actual love of God into the experience of men.
24. He is the risen Lord (20:19-29).
25. He is the one who is coming to receive His own unto Himself to share His eternal glory (14:3; 16:16, 17, 19, 22; 21:22).

### *John Tells How We Know Who Jesus Is*

Out of a very great abundance of facts and experiences (21:25) John selected those which would produce the deepest conviction about Jesus. That conviction was to be twofold—that Jesus is the Christ of Old Testament prophecy, and that He is the Son of God—the representative of God, the expression of God, and the gift of God to all mankind. This conviction was to be for a specific purpose; namely, to enable the reader to have life (eternal life, free from sin and condemnation) in Jesus' name. John does not affirm such things about Jesus merely for the sake of variety or wonder, but because they are true; and he frequently emphasizes the authority and validity of the witnesses from whom we receive such statements about Jesus. For *John is also telling us how we can know who Jesus is:*

1. By the witness of Jesus himself, in His constant claims and the accompanying fitness of His whole life.
2. By the voice of the forerunner prophet, John the Baptist.
3. By the testimony of God.
4. By the witness of the law and the prophets.
5. By the demonstration of supernatural power in the miracles worked by Jesus as "signs" of His relation with God.
6. By the testimony of His disciples, particularly as witnesses of the resurrection of Christ.
7. By the testimony of the Holy Spirit, both as a fact in their lives demonstrating the dependable power of His promises, and as a revealer and guarantor of further testimony through the apostles in convincing the world that God did send Jesus.

When men reject the message of John's Gospel, they do not reject merely the ideas of John, but they reject all these witnesses named above.

To put it briefly and directly: John wrote this book to preach Christ. He wrote it to save souls through faith in Christ. He wrote it because he knew the true nature and power of Christ. He knew whereof he spoke and in whom he was trusting. John was fully convinced and deeply impressed with the reality of the goodness and power of God manifested in Christ. And to John it was not merely the power of an idea to influence the kind of life as we live here in the flesh, but it was actually the power of God to deliver us from sin and death and to give us life anew with Christ, both now and forever. John really believed that "God hath given us eternal life, and this life is in His Son. He that hath the Son hath life; and he that hath not the Son of God hath not life" (I John 5:11, 12). We need to be as convinced of it as John was; and then we need to remember throughout all the lessons on the content of John's Gospel that we are to teach them with the same purpose in mind that John had when he wrote them.

A misconception of John's Gospel and its purpose is apparent in much of the use that is made of it today. It is a mistake that has serious consequences, even though it is committed by well-meaning believers in the deity of Christ. It is the mistake of speaking and acting as if the Book of John clearly gave us the full instructions for manifesting our faith and receiving salvation in Christ. Terms of pardon explicitly stated elsewhere in the New Testament are not mentioned by name in the Book of John. The Book of John should not be used as if it were a substitute for all the rest of the New Testament. And when it is used to teach salvation without repentance, confession, or baptism, it is being misused. The Gospel according to John did not stand alone in the day in which it was written, and it does not stand alone today. It well supports the authority of Jesus and the authority of the word spoken by the apostles under the guidance of the Holy Spirit. An intelligent and humbly obedient faith in the message of John will go on and act upon the commandments elsewhere recorded in the New Testament.

John shows in his own epistle (I John) that he certainly did not believe and teach a salvation by faith without the obedience of faith. See I John 1:6, 7; 2:3-5; 2:15; 2:24; 3:10; 3:15, 23, 24, etc. Yet he teaches that love and obedience are grounded in faith and are the outgrowth and manifestation of a real faith making open confession that Jesus is the Son of God.

For Further Study:

Guthrie, Donald. *New Testament Introduction,* 3rd ed. Downers Grove: InterVarsity, 1970. Pp. 271-282. Survey of various theories on the purpose of John's Gospel.

Hendriksen, William. *New Testament Commentary: The Gospel of John.* Grand Rapids: Baker Book House, 1954. Pp. 31-35. Examines the reasons and purpose of this Gospel.

Morris, Leon. *Lord From Heaven.* Grand Rapids: Wm. B. Eerdmans Publishing Co., 1958. Pp. 93-102. Studies the claims and credentials of Jesus as presented in the Gospel of John.

Morris, Leon. *The New International Commentary: Gospel of John.* Grand Rapids: Wm. B. Eerdmans, 1971. Pp. 35-40. Brief statements of various theories of John's purpose and then the author's affirmation of John's stated purpose.

# 6

## DO YOU HAVE IT IN YOUR HEART?

God's word is powerful seed, when sown in good and honest hearts (Luke 8:5-15).

If we had a dollar for every time anyone has said—"I wish I could remember . . ."—we would be rich. But we can be even richer if we will store up in our hearts the precious and useful gems of God's word.

Memory is a most priceless power, given to us by God. It is the means of accumulating and using all knowledge. Watts wrote: "Without memory the soul of man would be a poor, destitute, naked being, with an everlasting blank spread over it, except the fleeting ideas of the present moment." Thank God for this treasury of the mind which makes us rich by preserving the results of our studies and experiences. We can deposit there vast treasures at no cost, and with but little effort.

*Power of the Remembered Word*

When J. Russell Morse was 15 months in a Chinese Communist prison, he endured severe tortures and terrific strain supported chiefly by his memory of the Bible. He testifies that the promises and precepts of God's word came to him in memory and gave strength, wisdom, and hope which were sorely needed. Therefore he urges all his brethren to fill their memories with that living and powerful word.

An unknown author has written:

> This book contains the mind of God, the state of man, the way of salvation, the doom of sinners, and the happiness of believers. Its doctrines are holy, its precepts are binding, its histories are true, and its decisions are immutable. Read it to be wise, believe it to be safe, and practice it to be holy. It contains light to direct you, food to support you, and comfort to cheer you. It should fill the memory, rule the heart, and guide the feet. It is given you in life, will be opened in the judgment, and be remembered forever.

However, much of the light and power of the Scripture is lost because it is not remembered at the time and place where it should be applied. God's word should furnish us all with guidance in everyday life, with protection in time of temptation, with hope and inward peace, with the message of life by which to bless and save others. It was not intended to be a mere subject of Sunday discussion and cermony, but was given to be applied by everyone in conduct, in decisions, and in attitudes. If it is to be so applied, *it must be brought to mind.*

The Scripture bears witness to its own power and value. "Man shall not live by bread alone, but by every word that proceedeth out of the mouth of God" (Matt. 4:4). It is "able to build you up, and to give you the inheritance among all them that are sanctified" (Acts 20:32). It is the seed of the Spirit by which we are born anew: see James 1:18; 1:21; I Pet. 1:23; Luke 8:11; John 6:63. But before that good seed can bear fruit it must take root in the soil of human hearts—its meaning must become a part of the thinking of men.

Then, what a difference it makes! The greatest difference between men is not physical size, strength, age, ancestry, possessions, or the circumstances which surround them; but it is in the thoughts and motives that rule their lives. The essential difference between a communist and a Christian is what a man thinks. As a man thinks, so he is. "Sow a thought, and reap an act. Sow an act, and reap a habit. Sow a habit, and reap a character. Sow a character, and reap a destiny!" "Let the word of Christ dwell in you richly" (Col. 3:16a). How great, how well furnished is the life of the man whose mind is *filled with the thoughts of God!*

### *You Can Remember!*

Don't say, "I can't memorize." You can. Don't rob yourself of the great profit that comes with just a moderate effort in the right way. There is no need of constantly forgetting. The memory can be trained, and there is no known limit to its capacity. We may not be able to duplicate the amazing feats of memory that some have performed; but we certainly can improve our use of such powers as we have. A little training and practice, even a little confidence and cheerful effort, can work wonders.

H. H. Halley, author of the *Bible Handbook,* was 39 years old, with only an ordinary memory, when he began using his time on long train trips to memorize prominent verses from the Bible. In a few years he could recite more than one third of the entire Bible. I know several students who objected at first that they could not memorize, but who went on to learn all of the book of Romans or of Hebrews. Age is no barrier. A man past 74 years of age learned a large portion of the New Testament. A friend of mine about that age brightens his days and inspires his associates in a rest home by memorizing and reciting the words of grand hymns he can no longer sing.

Practical rules for general improvement of memory are simple and easy to apply. Get *sufficient sleep* regularly. Be *thankful* to God for the powers and opportunities that are ours. Take a *cheerful* and *hopeful attitude,* expecting to accomplish something worthwhile and to enjoy it. Seeing what others have done, *be confident* that you can too. A strong *purpose*, incentive and enthusiasm will help. When you have enough *interest* you do not have to memorize most things. Love and hate always remember.

If you want to make the most of memory, *practice daily,* at the *same hour;* take pleasure in your study; and *expect to remember forever.*

To memorize a Scripture passage:

1. Give it full attention; get a clear, strong impression of both the thought and the wording of it.
2. Especially try to understand it as fully as possible. In the long run, to know the true sense is much more important than to know the exact words. Get the thought in order to learn the words.
3. Picture it in the mind. See the thought, filling in details with the imagination. Then write down a word picture of the way you visualize it. Make the most of your natural tendency to remember by sight.
4. Repeat it aloud. This combines hearing and activity with sight, while it speeds up the recollection. But avoid monotony! It kills interest and dulls the attention. Mere repetition is a very poor substitute for wide-awake interest. Analyze the passage: take it apart and put it back together an idea at a time. Give attention to the subject matter, not to the process of learning. We remember best, not things we have labored to "memorize," but the things we see so vividly, with such understanding and interest, that we do not realize we are memorizing them. Recall and reuse the quotation frequently.

The interest of others helps to lighten any work and to make more enjoyable any hobby. A Bible School Class memorizing together or sharing with each other choice passages memorized each month can greatly stimulate and aid its members. Passages chosen for a definite purpose and related to each other or to regular lessons will be easier to learn.

### *What To Learn*

Learn passages that state key facts of Christianity, like the well-known John 3:16 or John 14:6—"I am the Way, the Truth, and the Life; no man cometh unto the Father, but by me." Add Rom. 1:16, 17; 6:23; 3:23, 24; I John 5:11, 12; I Cor. 15:3, 4. Be prepared to urge non-Christians to believe and accept the Saviour.

Learn the initial commands of the way of salvation: Acts 2:38—"Repent ye, and be baptized every one of you in the name of Jesus Christ unto the remission of your sins; and ye shall receive the gift of the Holy Spirit." Acts 17:30—"The times of ignorance therefore God overlooked; but now he commandeth men that they should all everywhere repent." Acts 22:16—"And now why tarriest thou? Arise, and be baptized, and wash away thy sins, calling on the name of the Lord." Add Mark 16:15, 16; Matt. 28:18-20; Rom. 6:4, 5; Gal. 3:26, 27; Rom. 10:9, 10; Titus 3:5; I Pet. 1:22, 23; 3:21.

Learn the great principles of the Christian life: Col. 3:17—"And whatsoever ye do in word or in deed, do all in the name of the Lord Jesus, giving thanks to God the Father through him." Gal. 2:20—"I have been crucified with Christ; and it is no longer I that live, but Christ liveth in me: and that life which I now live in the flesh I live in faith, the faith which is in the Son of God, who loved me, and gave himself up for me." Add Rom. 12:1-2; I Cor. 6:19, 20; II Cor. 5:14, 15; Gal. 5:22-25; 6:14; Eph. 4:1; 5:11; James 1:27; Acts 2:24; I John 1:6, 7; 2:5; 3:23; Heb. 12:14.

Learn the solemn warnings of the Lord: I Cor. 10:12—"Wherefore let him that thinketh he standeth take heed lest he fall." Gal. 6:7, 8; I Cor. 6:9, 10; I Pet. 5:8; 2:11; I John 2:15-17; II Pet. 2:1, 21; 3:10, 11; I John 4:1, II John 7-11; Rom. 16:17; Eph. 5:5, 6; Col. 2:8, 9.

Treasure the promises. They have a special purpose and peculiar power to strengthen the Christian life. II Pet. 1:4—"Whereby he hath granted unto us his precious and exceeding great promises; that through these ye may become partakers of the divine nature, having escaped from the corruption that is in the world by lust." Add Matt. 6:33; Phil. 4:19; I Cor. 10:13; Matt. 10:32; Mark 10:29, 30; Eph. 3:20; Phil. 3:20, 21; James 1:12; I John 1:9; 3:2; II Pet. 3:13, 14; Rev. 3:5, 21; 21:4, 7.

One should go on from such short selections as these to learn some longer passages, whole paragraphs of great importance and power, such as: Rom. 8:1-14; 6:1-11; 3:21-31; 12:9-21; I Cor. 13; Col. 3:1-17; II Pet. 1:3-11; Eph. 4:1-6; or 11-16; 6:10-18.

There are also many precious gems in the Old Testament, which may very profitably be memorized after careful study to determine to whom they were spoken, for what purpose, and how what they were actually intended to say applies to us who live under Christ and not under the law. Every bit of it is instructive and valuable if it is correctly understood and properly applied, but one must beware of misapplying the laws and promises of the old covenant which are not intended for us today.

For Further Study:

Lucas, Jerry. *Remember the Word.* Los Angeles: Memory Ministries, 1975. A memory expert utilizes principles of association with special study pictures in this Bible memorization system.

Schoenhals, G. Roger. "Tuck Away a Verse a Day," *Christian Life* (January, 1975), pp. 18-19, 50-1. Also reprinted in *The Christian Reader* (January/February: 1976), pp. 70-76. Practical suggestions on regular Scripture memorization.

Smith, Wilbur M. *Profitable Bible Study,* rev. ed. Grand Rapids: Baker Book House, 1963. Mr. Smith discusses the spiritual benefits of Bible study (pp. 7-26) and the value of meditation on God's Word (pp. 62-65).

Wilson, Ben. "Thy Word Have I Hid In My Heart: An Exhortation to Christian Workers to Memorize God's Word." An unpublished mimeographed essay available from Ozark Bible College Bookstore, Joplin, MO.

# 7

## LIFE OF CHRIST — TIME PERIODS

| Period | Span | Event | Reference | Ministry |
|---|---|---|---|---|
| *PREPARATION* | *30 yrs.* | Birth in Bethlehem | Luke 2 | |
| | | Flight to Egypt | Matt. 2:13-23 | |
| | | Home in Nazareth | Luke 2:40 | |
| | | In temple, 12 yrs. | Luke 2:41-50 | |
| | | Youth in Nazareth | Luke 2:52 | |
| | | BAPTISM | Mt. 3; Mk. 1; Lk. 3 | |
| | *few mo.* | Temptation | Matt. 4:2 | |
| | | Winning first disciples | John 1 | |
| | | Wedding feast at Cana | John 2:1 | |
| | | Not many days at Capernaum | John 2:12 | |
| **1st PASSOVER** | | | (April, AD 27) | *Jn. 2:13* |
| *FIRST YEAR* | *8 mo.* | Cleansing the Temple | John 2 | EARLY JUDEAN MINISTRY |
| | | Nicodemus / Disciples / Baptizing | John 3 | |
| | | TO GALILEE (At Jacob's Well, 4 mo. till harvest) | | GREAT GALILEAN MINISTRY |
| | *4 mo.* | 2 days in Samaria | John 4:35 | |
| | | Beginning Galilean Ministry | Matt. 4:12 | |
| | | First Tour of Galilee | Matt. 4:23 | |
| **2nd PASSOVER** | | | (April, AD 28) | *Jn. 5:1* |
| *SECOND YEAR* | *& whole 2nd year* | Healing lame man at pool | John 5 | |
| | | Sermon on the Mount (Apostles named) | Matt. 5; 6; 7 | |
| | | 2nd Tour of Galilee | Luke 8:1-3 | |
| | | 3rd Tour of Galilee (12 sent forth) | Matt. 9:35—11:1 | |
| **3rd PASSOVER** | | | (April, AD 29) | *Jn. 6:4* |
| *THIRD YEAR* | *6 mo.* | Feeding 5,000: Climax & Close of Galilean Ministry | | |
| | | Travel to Tyre & Sidon Decapolis (4,000 fed) | Matt. 15 | DECAPOLIS (PEREA) MINISTRY |
| | | Confession - Transfiguration Cross - Church | Matt. 16; 17 | |
| | | FEAST OF TABERNACLES | (Oct., AD 29) | *Jn. 7:2* |
| | *3 mo.* | Sermons & growing controversy | Jn. 7; 8; 9; 10:1-39 | LATER JUDEAN MINISTRY |
| | | (70 helpers sent out) | Lk. 10; 11; 12; 13 | |
| | | FEAST OF DEDICATION | (Dec., AD 29) | *Jn. 10:22* |
| | *3 mo.* | Perean Ministry | Lk. 13; 14; 15; 16; 17 | LATER PEREAN MINISTRY |
| | | Raising Lazarus | John 11 | |
| | | Last busy journey | Mt. 19; 20; Mk. 10 | |
| **4th PASSOVER** | | | (April, AD 30) | *Mt. 21; Mk. 11; Lk. 19; Jn. 12* |
| | *43 days* | CRUCIFIXION and RESURRECTION | | |
| | | 40 days appearances | Acts 1:3-11 | |
| | | ASCENSION | Lk. 24; Acts 1 | |

# Part Two

# BACKGROUND

## 8

## BETWEEN THE TESTAMENTS

### *History of the Interval*

Although no Old Testament books record the history of this period, there were Jewish writings during the time. Some of these are the "Apocrypha," about fourteen books, or portions, to be added to the Old Testament books, which have been "canonized" as a part of the Old Testament by the Roman Catholic church. Of these, the first Book of Maccabees is the most valuable as history. Josephus, a Jewish historian who was born in the decade after Jesus' crucifixion, wrote two important works—*The Antiquities of the Jews* and *The Jewish Wars*—which give an account of the Jews from 170 B.C., through the destruction of Jerusalem by Titus, in A.D. 70. The history of the empires of the world during this period between the Old and New Testaments is well covered by Greek and Roman historians. Moreover, this period is pictured with amazing accuracy, prophetically, in the Book of Daniel (Dan. 2:36-45; 7:3-8, 17; 8:3-22; 11:2-45). This history of the Jews in these times may be divided into six periods:

1. *The Persian Period* (538-332 B.C.). The return from Babylon took place under Persian rule (Ezra 1). Under the Persians, the Jews were usually governed by their own high priest, subject to the Syrian satrap, or governor. Persian rule was usually mild, and often very favorable toward the Jews (e.g., the stories of Zerubbabel, Ezra, Nehemiah, Esther, Daniel). The Samaritans and renegade Jews caused the most trouble in this period. The Samaritan temple on Mt. Gerizim was built about 432 B.C., a seat of degenerated Judaism that continues until today.

2. *The Greek or Macedonian Period* (332-323 B.C.). The Persian rule was broken by the world-sweeping conquests of Alexander the Great, out of Macedonia. Alexander showed consideration for the Jews, and did not destroy or plunder Jerusalem. His short but brilliant career had far-reaching results in the introduction of Greek language over Palestine and all the Mediterranean area.

3. *The Egyptian Period* (323-198 B.C.). On the death of Alexander,

his empire was divided among four of his generals. Seleucus ruled Syria, and Ptolemy ruled Egypt. Palestine, between them, was claimed by both of them. The Ptolemies early attached Palestine to Egypt. They extended privileges to Jewish settlers on the Nile. Alexandria became the center of a large Jewish population and a seat of Jewish learning. It was, for the most part, a century of prosperity for the Jews. The most important event was the translation of the Old Testament into Greek at Alexandria. The Greek version is known as the Septuagint (meaning "seventy"), from the traditional number of translators.

4. *The Syrian Period* (198-167 B.C.). The Seleucidae (Greek kings of Syria) finally recovered Palestine from Egypt.

> The period of Syrian rule was the darkest yet most glorious in the whole four hundred years. The Seleucidae were dissolute tyrants. Antiochus Epiphanes (175-164 B.C.) was the most notorious of them all. Returning on one occasion from defeat in Egypt, he vented his vengeance on Jerusalem. He massacred forty thousand of its population, stripped the temple of its treasures and outraged the religious sense of the Jews by sacrificing a sow on the altar and sprinkling the interior of the temple with the liquor in which a portion of the unclean beast had been boiled. He sought by every means to stamp out the Hebrew religion and spirit and transform the nation into Greeks. He shut up the temple and, on pain of death, prohibited the Jewish religion. Multitudes heroically sacrificed their lives rather than their faith.[1]

5. *The Maccabean Period* (167-63 B.C.). A heroic revolt against such violence and sacrilege was led by a family of priest-patriots known as the Maccabees. An old priest, named Mattathias, and his five sons, in turn, led the Jews in a war for independence, which was finally gained after thirty years of struggle. Judas Maccabeus (166-161 B.C.) led in a remarkable series of victories and re-opened, cleansed and rededicated the temple in honor of which the feast of dedication continued to be kept (John 10:22). Judas fell in battle; but his brothers (first Jonathan, then Simon) fought on, and, taking advantage of political deals with rivals for the Syrian throne, obtained, in turn, the dual office of governor and high priest, recognized

---

[1] B. S. Dean, *An Outline of Bible History,* Rev. ed. (Cincinnati: Standard Publishing Co., 1912), p. 105.

by Syria. Simon lived his last days in peace and made a league with Rome. He was succeeded by his son, John Hyrcanus, who was subdued by the Syrian ruler for a time, but found opportunity to throw off the yoke and went on to conquer much additional territory. His change from the Pharisee party to the Sadducees caused much bitter strife at home. His son was ambitious and murderous, took the title of king, ended the glory of a great family, started it on its decline, a period of 60 years filled with intrigue and barbarous civil war.

6. *The Roman Period* (63 B.C., through the New Testament period). Pompey captured Jerusalem in 63 B.C. The plots and murders of the different members of the Maccabee family continued to curse the land. Antipater, of Idumea (Edom), and his infamous son, Herod, took part in the rivalries and the deals with Rome until Herod finally conquered Judea, amidst shocking atrocities, in 37 B.C. He destroyed the rest of the Maccabee family, including his wife, Mariamne. This Herod rebuilt the temple (larger than Solomon's and much richer than Zerubbabel's), and slaughtered the babies of Bethlehem in an attempt to murder the Messiah (Matthew 21). He gave to the kingdom the greatest external splendor it ever knew, save in the reigns of David and Solomon. Yet the moral and religious quality of his reign was deplorable. Despite the outward splendor, Israel chafed under the yoke of subjection to Rome and under the crimes of Herod's regime. "The tabernacle of David was, indeed, fallen, and the elect spirits of the nation, the 'Israel within Israel,' looked and longed for him who should raise it up again and build it as in the days of old (Amos 9:12)."[2]

There arose a party of *Herodians* who favored the rulers of the Herod family and their collaboration with Rome. An opposite party of *Zealots* worked "underground" to bring violent action against all such. The *Sadducees,* a small but influential party mostly of priests, became political opportunists, conniving at wrongs and losing faith in the scriptures. The *Pharisees,* who began as faithful upholders of the law against all Gentile influences, became self-righteous and hypocritical formalists, seeking public acclaim and political influence. Even devout believers among the common folk became political-minded and materialistic, and found it hard to accept the spiritual nature of the kingdom of Christ as the fulfillment of Israel's hopes.

---

[2] Dean, *op. cit.*, p. 107.

*Preparations for the Coming of Christ*

Throughout this dark period God was working His own plan for Israel. Several developments in these centuries helped to bring about the "fulness of time" for the Messiah to come.

1. *The Dispersion of the Jews.* Many more were scattered abroad throughout the empire than lived in the homeland, yet everywhere they remained Jews. Thus they became world-wide missionaries of the knowledge of the true God and of a message of hope in a hopeless world.

2. *The Synagogue,* which probably arose to meet the needs of the exiles in Babylon, became the center of worship for many of them who were too far separated from the temple and the place of instruction for all. The reading in the synagogue every Sabbath fixed the eyes of Israel more firmly on their Scriptures and the promised Messiah. Thus the synagogue everywhere became the great missionary institute, imparting to the world Irael's exalted Messianic hopes. Then after the gospel of Christ was given, synagogues became key places to begin its proclamation, and they furnished prepared persons for leadership and oversight in the new church.

3. *The Spread of Greek* prepared the world for the Word of God.

4. *The Septuagint Translation of the Old Testament,* spread throughout the world by the Jews and their synagogues, prepared the world for the gift of God, in His Son. "The Septuagint thus is a distinct forward movement in the fulfillment of the Abrahamic promise (Gen. 12:3; 18:18)."

5. *Rome made of the world one empire,* and Roman roads made all parts of it accessible, while Roman stress on law and order made a comparatively high degree of peace and safety, which encouraged travel and communication.

6. *The Jewish Messianic Expectation.* H. E. Dosker summarized this hope:

> The Jews themselves, embittered by long-continued martyrdoms and suffering, utterly carnalized this Messianic expectation in an increasing ratio as the yoke of the oppressor grew heavier and the hope of deliverance grew fainter. And thus when their Messiah came, Israel recognized Him not, while the heart-hungry heathen humbly received Him (John 1:9-14). The eyes of Israel were blinded for a season, 'till the fulness of the Gentiles shall be gathered in' (Rom. 9:32; 11:25).[3]

---

[3] H. E. Dosker, "Between the Testaments" in *The International Standard Bible Encyclopedia* ed. by James Orr, (Grand Rapids: Wm. B. Eerdmans, 1939), Vol. I, p. 458.

7. *The Silence of Prophecy for Four Hundred Years,* immediately preceded by the clear prediction of the coming of a great messenger like Elijah (Mal. 3:1; 4:5, 6), put dramatic emphasis upon the message of John the Baptist. It strongly accented every inspired utterance that announced the coming of the Christ.

For Further Study:

Bruce, F. F. *New Testament History.* Garden City: Doubleday and Company, Inc., 1969. Pp. 1-204. Surveys the Intertestament period and sets the life of Christ in its political, religious and social background.

Ferguson, Everett. "A History of Palestine From the Fifth Century B.C. to the Second Century A.D." in *The World of the New Testament* ed. by A. J. Malherbe. Austin, Texas: R. B. Sweet, 1967. Pp. 37-67. Readable, reliable essay. Other essays in this book illustrate the religious and social background.

Tenney, Merrill C. *New Testament Times.* Grand Rapids: Wm. B. Eerdmans Publishing Co., 1965. Pp. 3-178. Useful presentation of the Roman, Greek and Jewish contribution to the world to which Christ came.

Wartick, Wallace and Wilbur Fields. *New Testament History: The Christ and the Inter-Testament Period.* Joplin: College Press, 1972. Wilbur Fields' revision of William Smith's *New Testament History,* (Book one).

# 9

## FEAST DAYS OF THE PEOPLE OF ISRAEL

The word translated "feasts" means appointed times, and includes the Day of Atonement which was observed by fasting, as well as those appointed times which were actually feasts. "These are the set feasts of Jehovah, which ye shall proclaim to be holy convocations" (Lev. 23:37). They include even the Sabbath of every week (Lev. 23:2, 3).

Three great annual feasts required the presence of every able male Israelite at the tabernacle or temple "before the Lord" (see Exod. 23:14-17; 34:22, 23). These were the feasts of Passover, Pentecost, and Tabernacles.

*Passover* was in the last of March or in April, and occupied eight days, including the feast of unleavened bread and the offering of first-fruits of the barley harvest.

*Pentecost* was fifty days, or seven full weeks, after the Sabbath of passover week, and occupied, according to the original commandment, one day. It is also called the feast of weeks (e.g. II Chron. 8:13). The name "pentecost" comes from the Greek word for fifty.

*Tabernacles* came in October (six months after passover) and occupied eight days. It is also called the feast of ingathering.

The first and last days of unleavened bread, the Day of Pentecost, and the first and last days of the feast of Tabernacles are particularly called "holy convocations."

Other occasions called holy convocations, but not requiring the pilgrimage to the national center of worship, are the Day of Atonement, the Feast of Trumpets, and the Sabbath. The Day of Atonement was five days before the Feast of Tabernacles. The Feast of Trumpets was ten days before the Day of Atonement, on the first day of the seventh month of the religious calendar, and the first day of the new civil year. The Jewish months always began with each new moon and hence did not correspond to our months. Each new moon, or the first day of each month, was to be observed with special sacrifices and the blowing of trumpets (Num. 28:11-15 and 10:10). Although the new moons are not specifically mentioned in the law as holy convocations or as times of ceasing from labor, Amos 8:5 indicates that trade and craftwork were stopped on them.

In the New Testament *The Feast of Dedication* is mentioned (John 10:22), but it was not commanded in the law. It was added to commemorate the purification of the temple by Judas Maccabaeus about 165 B.C., after it had been robbed and desecrated by Antiochus Epiphanes. Another feast, called "Purim," was added to commemorate the deliverance of the Jews from the plot of Haman in the days of Esther.

### *How They Were Kept*

The term "holy convocation" would indicate an *assembly* of people "called together," but the law does not command the people to come to the central sanctuary for the Sabbath, the Day of Atonement, or the Feast of Trumpets. On every day of holy convocation "servile work" was forbidden: that is, all *ordinary labor such as belonged to one's worldly calling must stop.* The preparation of food was allowed (Exod. 12:16). But on the Sabbath of each week and on the Day of Atonement it was not lawful to do work of any sort, not even to kindle a fire (Exod. 35:3; Lev. 23:28, 30).

Each special day had its *special offerings and sacrifices.* Many of them were marked by the *blowing of trumpets.* They were times of special reverence and realization of God. They emphasized the remembrance of His great works. They furnished impressive forms of worship. They led the worshipper to seek God's mercy through the appointed sacrifices. Some of the feasts were times of special rejoicing. The Day of Atonement was a day on which everyone was to "afflict your souls." This means *fasting* (abstaining from all food throughout the day) together with the contrite spirit and attitude of soul that should befit men seeking pardon for sin.

In the case of the Passover Feast, *special foods* marked its observance. The roasted yearling lamb of the Passover meal was eaten in the night with many particulars of ceremony. The unleavened bread was eaten at all meals, and no leaven allowed in their houses for seven more days.

The Feast of Tabernacles is so named because it was to be observed by *living for seven days in booths or tabernacles* made of boughs of trees. This is considered to be a dramatic remembrance of the hardships of the wilderness, to stimulate thanksgiving for the land which God had given them (Lev. 23:42, 43).

In connection with the Passover the very first sheaf of barley harvest was to be cut and waved as an offering before Jehovah, and meal offerings of fine flour mingled with oil to be presented. At Pentecost a portion of the wheat harvest was to be baked into cakes with leaven and salt and offered. At Tabernacles the fruit of goodly trees with branches of trees were to be used or displayed, in rejoicing over the ingathering of all the fruits of the earth.

*Significance And Value Of The Feasts*

God originated and established the nation of Israel. It was God who designed all their institutions and dictated their laws. He prescribed these feasts for their good and as part of the mission of Israel in preparing a blessing for all the families of the earth. When they failed to keep them faithfully they were charged with disobedience to Jehovah. The Old Testament is not an accumulation of pious frauds and misrepresentations; hence these feasts must be taken as it represents them, as the provisions of the all-wise God for His people, and not as the natural development of national ceremonies. Jehovah commanded these feasts, imposed them upon a people who seemed never too willing to keep them all properly, but His commandments are "for our good always" (Deut. 6:24).

> There are similar feasts and ceremonies in other religions. In our Bible the feasts tie in with historical facts, great ideas, and educational objectives to a degree not known in other faiths. In other religions they are rather isolated and miscellaneous and are largely an accumulation, while in the Jewish economy the feasts are integrated and organized into an effective process. . . . These colorful feasts and appointed seasons found in Leviticus constituted Jehovah's great program of visual education.[1]

In these feasts, indeed, are combined several different advantages to the people. *They served to unify the nation.* Drawing the separate tribes from their separate homes, they brought them together in the celebration of the things which made them one nation and which looked forward to their common destiny. The people were given occasion and leisure for developing mutual acquaintance, and were made to have an interest beyond themselves which would produce loyalty to one another and to the nation. Here was opportunity for interchange of ideas and experiences which must have stimulated improvement of their arts and crafts. These things would be incidental. More important than these were the religious values of the feasts.

They gave instruction to the people; for they were connected both with the law which commanded them and with significant items of

[1] W. R. White, *Broadman Comments* (Nashville: Broadman Press).

history which they commemorated. The scriptures were read and knowledge of great works of God were renewed at the feasts. The Passover, especially, was to keep alive the memory of the deliverance from Egypt. Such observances perpetuated the knowledge of their unique origin, their special relationship to God, and their high destiny.

They furnished worthy and definite forms for the worship of God, which *aided the real spirit of worship.* They were expressions of joy and gratitude to God for the produce of the land. At each of the three major feasts—Passover, Pentecost, and Tabernacles—much attention and ceremony was given to recognition that the fruit of the land was from God and the first and best of it was to be offered back to Him. A sense of dependence upon God was promoted, and would naturally be connected with desires to be faithful and pleasing unto Him. Men always need reverence for God and realization of His superintending Providence.

All the feasts promoted love and respect for God, but *deepest reverence and repentance were especially kindled by the Day of Atonement* with its most solemn and awe-inspiring ministrations by the high priest in the Holy of Holies, while all Israel, whether gathered at the sanctuary or in their dwellings, afflicted their souls. It taught the lesson of the need of reconciliation, and pointed out the prospects of complete redemption through acceptable sacrifice. Thus it proclaimed both the wrath and the mercy of God.

Very probably Israel did not always realize any typical significance in the feasts, but certainly *one of the greatest purposes for them was that they should be prophetic patterns and promises of "good things to come"* (Col. 2:16, 17; Heb. 10:1). All the plan of the nation of Israel was made to look to the future with expectancy and preparation for the great manifestations of God to come. Therefore the Old Testament scriptures are "able to make thee wise unto salvation, through faith which is in Christ Jesus" (II Tim. 3:15).

The new moon, or the first day of each month, was to dedicate each month to God. The feast of trumpets was one of these. It was also New Year's Day. It had more ceremonies attached to it than the first days of the other months, and served to sanctify also the whole year.

### *Special Days In The New Testament*

Only one set feast of reverence, love and devotion is prescribed in the New Testament. That is the Lord's Supper every first day of the week. It combines most of the best features of all the old feasts. Let us keep it faithfully and worthily and we will not forget God, or His great works in bringing us to our inheritance, or our special relationship to Him and our high destiny.

None of these Old Testament feasts or special days are binding upon Christians. No new set fasts or annual celebrations are instituted. No calendar dates or suggestions are given to encourage us to sanctify Christmas or Easter. But if a man esteems one day above another, and does it devoutly unto the Lord, it is his privilege (see Rom. 14:5, 6). However, set days legalistically regarded are dangerous (see Gal. 4:10, 11; Col. 2:16-20). They cannot be kept as forms of obedience, for they are not commanded. They are of absolutely no merit formally observed. Their only value will be in the true spirit of reverent and loving devotion with which they are kept.

Special seasons of thanksgiving, of rejoicing and praise, of commemoration, of fasting and repentance, of faith-filled conventions with multitudes of like precious faith giving intensive attention to the things of God, are good for all of us to lift us up out of the hum-drum life of too much attention to petty and selfish things. But let them be kept unto God in the spirit; and let them make ordinary days not less holy, but more holy.

For Further Study:

Alexander, David and Patricia Alexander, eds. *Eerdman's Handbook of the Bible.* Grand Rapids: Wm. B. Eerdmans Publishing Co., 1973. Pp. 110-115; 180-181. Chart on the Jewish calendar. Notes on the feasts.

Edersheim, Alfred. *The Life and Times of Jesus the Messiah,* 2 vols. Grand Rapids: Wm. B. Eerdmans Publishing Co., 1956 (reprint of 1886 ed.). See index on specific feasts. This converted Jew gives valuable information on the Jewish background of the life of Christ.

Lewis, J. P. "Feasts," the Zondervan Pictorial Encyclopedia of the Bible, Vol. II, pp. 521-526. Grand Rapids: Zondervan Publishing House, 1975.

Tenney, Merrill C. *New Testament Survey,* rev. ed. Grand Rapids: Wm. B. Eerdmans, 1961. Pp. 95-99. Brief explanation of each of the Jewish feasts.

# Part Three

# PERSON OF CHRIST

## 10

## JESUS, THE SON OF GOD

### *What The Gospels Teach About Jesus*

There is no Christ other than the Christ of the Bible. Some men talk of Christ while they deny the Biblical account of Him, but the Christ of whom they talk is the product of their own imaginations—a mere idol. The facts about Jesus are given in the reliable testimonies of the Bible, or there is no knowledge of Him available to man. What is more, if the manner of testimony given by the Biblical witnesses is not reliable, there never can be any such thing as historical knowledge, for by every test the testimony of the Bible writers is equal or superior to any other testimony anytime, anywhere, on any subject.

The fact of Jesus' person or true identity is the most important matter that will ever be considered in the minds of men. His divine sonship is the essential fact and central message of the New Testament, and consequently of Christianity.

In all His teaching about the kingdom, Jesus directed the people to faith in himself and made actual participation in the kingdom a matter of such faith. Thus, appropriately, the work of John the Baptist, announcer of the kingdom, was to prepare the way for the King and to bear witness of Him "that all might believe through him" (John 1:7). See John 1:30-34; 3:28-36. Thus, Jesus' ministry and teaching were planned to make himself known to men (John 17:3-8). All the preaching of the apostles and prophets of the first century was designed to establish in men's hearts the truth and importance and fruits of the fact that He is the Son of God. (See Acts 2:36; 9:20; and everywhere that message is recorded.) See also the stated purpose of the written Word in John 20:30, 31.

### *"Who Say Ye That I Am?"* (Matthew 16:15)

The confession that Jesus is the Son of God was made to Him by the apostles on different occasions (John 1:49; Matthew 14:33; John 6:69). But as the time approached for His death and for their great responsibilities, they had to be brought to a distinct understanding of His deity. What any man thinks of Christ is an all-important matter. Jesus was especially concerned about these apostles that they should be prepared to endure the trial of His crucifixion and prepared for their lifework of preaching this faith. The former confessions made in time of excitement or enthusiasm must be quietly and thoughtfully reaffirmed. So we who have once confessed Him publicly under favorable circumstances and inducements need to restate our faith soberly in the face of special trials of faith.

The announcement that Jesus was about to make of His coming death was contrary to all their ideas about the Messiah. In order to receive it they needed to be conscious of the faith they had in Him personally. We, too, must prepare ourselves to believe Him and follow Him even though our natural minds cannot understand. Jesus knew the difficulties and the misunderstandings of all the people. He sometimes avoided telling them that He was the Christ when He knew that the word Christ or Messiah would arouse in their minds only false hopes and misconceptions. But He never left any doubt about His claim to come from God and to speak with all authority for God (Matthew 10:40; John 5:30; 8:26-29). He always identified one's doing the will of God with believing and following His words (Matthew 7:22-27). He repeatedly used expressions about himself that could be said only of deity:

"The Son of man hath authority on earth to forgive sins" (Mark 2:10).

"The Son of man shall send forth his angels, and they shall gather out of his kingdom" (Matthew 13:41).

"All things have been delivered unto me of my Father: . . . neither doth any know the Father, save the Son" (Matthew 11:27).

"He that descended out of heaven, even the Son of man" (John 3:13).

"Before Abraham was born, I am" (John 8:58).

"I am the resurrection, and the life" (John 11:25).

"I am the way, and the truth, and the life: no one cometh unto the Father, but by me" (John 14:6).

"I am the bread of life . . . he that believeth on me shall never thirst" (John 6:35).

"I am come down from heaven" (John 6:38).

"I am the good shepherd . . . I came that they may have life" (John 10:14, 10).

"I am the true vine . . . apart from me ye can do nothing" (John 15:1, 5).

"I and the Father are one" (John 10:30). "He that hath seen me hath seen the Father" (John 14:9).

"All authority hath been given unto me in heaven and on earth" (Matthew 28:18).

"The Son of man shall come in the glory of his Father with his angels; and then shall he render unto every man according to his deeds" (Matthew 16:27).

In John 5:17-29 Jesus called God His Father, "making Himself equal with God," called himself "the Son of God," said that He would raise all the dead and execute judgment upon all.

Three times Jesus directly said, "I am the Son of God" (Mark 14:62; John 9:37; John 10:36). That He claimed to be the Son of God was commonly recognized by the people, by the rulers, by the devil, and by the soldiers who crucified Him (Matthew 27:40, 43, 54; John 19:7; Matthew 4:3, 6; 14:33).

More citations than this page could hold could be listed. But these should show that one must worship Jesus as God or reject Him as a fraud. Jesus said that in order to work the works of God men must believe on Him, whom God sent (John 6:29). He said, "I am from above . . . not of this world . . . except ye believe that I am he, ye shall die in your sins" (John 8:23, 24). He is asking us today. "Who say ye that I am?"

His claims are sustained by:

1. His divine birth (Luke 1:30-35).
2. The fulfillment of the prophecies of the Old Testament (John 5:39, 46; Luke 24:44).
3. The divine, sinless life He lived.
4. The divine quality of His teaching.
5. The miracles He worked.
6. The manner of His death.
7. His resurrection from the dead.
8. His divine influence throughout the ages.
9. The testimony of inspired men before and after His earthly life (Isaiah 9:6; Psalm 110:1; Hebrews 1:1-4; Colossians 1:14-17; John 1:1-18; Mark 1:1).
10. By the testimony of His enemies, His disciples, Pilate, Judas, demons, angels, a Roman centurion.

*"Him the Father, even God, hath sealed"* (John 6:27)

"Flesh and blood hath not revealed it unto thee, but my Father who is in heaven" (Matthew 16:17). God had revealed the person of Christ through His words and works (John 5:36, 37; John 3:34, 35). God was in Christ revealing himself and reconciling the world unto himself. God also bore direct testimony to Him in word at His baptism and on the Mount of Transfiguration, although Peter probably did not hear the former and heard the latter one week after this confession. Should we form our idea of Jesus from the opinions of the crowd, from our "inner consciousness" (which is our own selfish heart), or from the revelation and record that God has given us? Why?

### *"Every spirit that confesseth . . . Jesus Christ"* (I John 4:2)

Confessing Christ is not just saying words that are soon to be forgotten. It is making a public expression of a wholehearted conviction that affects everything else. The Lord is not arbitrary or unjust in judging us according to what we think of Jesus. For, what we think of Him, and what we do about it, is the key to our whole attitude toward truth and authority and guilt and pardon. We may hear of the midnight sun in polar regions and admit that it is a fact, but, although we suppose it makes some difference to some people there, it doesn't affect our lives. But when we hear of Jesus manifested to the world in Palestine two thousand years ago it is not distant or indifferent matter to us to admit that is a fact! That is a decision that cannot be forgotten without being denied.

If our Creator has appointed a Master and Teacher over us who will also be our Judge, and has commanded all men to acknowledge His lordship, then we cannot safely ignore Him. "Hear ye him" (Matthew 17:5). Believing on Him, we accept all that He teaches. We bow to His authority in all things. Confessing Christ as the divine Lord means a submission that accepts not only His authority, but also that which He delegates, and those whom He appoints. Accepting Him, we accept the New Testament. He is our creed, but the whole New Testament becomes our rule of faith and duty. His Word becomes the final authority on any subject as far as He speaks expressly on that subject. Religion may seem to be a big problem, and to contain many problems in it, but there is really only one question to be settled: "What think ye of the Christ?" (Matthew 22:42). That is the question that settles all others that really have to be settled. God has given us abundant evidence upon which to settle that. Since divine grace offers pardon and salvation and eternal life to all who accept and obey Him, we certainly need to confess Him, and cannot be indifferent to the issue. Confession is unto salvation (Romans 10:10), and denial unto damnation; for to deny Christ is to refuse God's help and to defy God's government.

*"He That Denieth Me"* (Luke 12:9)

Let Him state for himself (and through His apostles) what He thinks of those who will not believe on Him and confess Him: "Him will I also deny" (Matthew 10:33). See II Timothy 2:12. "This is the deceiver and the antichrist (II John 7). See I John 4:2, 3; 2:22. "He that believeth not God hath made him a liar; because he hath not believed in the witness that God hath borne concerning his Son" (I John 5:10). They "shall die in [their] sins" (John 8:24). "The same hath not the Father" (I John 2:23). "The wrath of God abideth on him" (John 3:36). They are "false teachers" of "destructive heresies, denying even the Master that bought them, bringing upon themselves swift destruction" (II Peter 2:1).

It is possible (and all too common) to profess to know Him, but by works to deny Him, being disobedient (Titus 1:16).

"He that is not with me is against me" (Matthew 12:30).

For Further Study:

Lewis, C. S. *Mere Christianity.* New York: The MacMillan Company, 1954. Pp. 54-56.

Lewis, C. S. *God in the Dock.* Grand Rapids: Wm. B. Eerdmans Publishing Company, 1970. Essay "What Are We To Make of Jesus Christ?" Pp. 156-160. Lewis, in other of the above, makes it very clear that Jesus is either a liar, a lunatic or Lord and God.

Machen, J. Gresham. *Christian Faith in the Modern World.* Grand Rapids: Wm. B. Eerdmans Publishing Company, 1936. Pp. 131-187. Clear-cut defense of the deity of Christ.

Stott, John R. W. *Basic Christianity,* rev. ed. Grand Rapids: Wm. B. Eerdmans Publishing Company, 1971. Pp. 21-34. Sets forth clearly Jesus' direct and indirect claims to be God in the flesh. Outstanding chapter.

# 11

## THE MAN WHO IS GOD

It is vitally important to examine the claims of Jesus Christ and come to a rational decision about Him. A decision is demanded by what Jesus says about himself. Acceptance of His claims demands unconditional surrender to His person in absolute faith and obedience. If we do not consent to unqualified commitment to Him, we do not accept His claims, and thus we are condemning His teaching about himself. His claims allow no middle ground of accepting Him *merely* as a good teacher.

*Jesus claimed to be the Son of God:* "For this cause therefore the Jews sought the more to kill him, because . . . he called God his own Father, making himself equal with God" (John 5:18). Jesus said, "Say ye of him, whom the Father sanctified and sent into the world, Thou blasphemest; because I said, I am the Son of God?" (John 10:36). Lazarus' "sickness is not unto death, but for the glory of God, that the Son of God may be glorified thereby" (John 11:4). On oath He declared that He was the "Son of God" (Matthew 26:63, 64).

*Jesus refers with unmistakable clarity to His pre-existence with God:* "For I am come down from heaven" (John 6:38). "Before Abraham was born, I am" (John 8:58). "Ye are from beneath; I am from above: ye are of this world; I am not of this world" (John 8:23). "I and the Father are one" (John 10:30). "And now, Father, glorify thou me with thine own self with the glory which I had with thee before the world was" (John 17:5).

*Jesus claimed divine supremacy in both worlds:* "The Son of man shall send forth his angels, and they shall gather out of his kingdom" (Matthew 13:41). "When the Son of man shall come in his glory, and all the angels with him, then shall he sit on the throne of his glory" (Matthew 25:31). "Then shall the King say unto them on his right hand, Come, ye blessed of my Father, inherit the kingdom prepared for you" (Matthew 25:34). He claimed, "All authority hath been given unto me in heaven and on earth" (Matthew 28:18). "And no one hath ascended into heaven, but he that descended out of heaven, even the Son of man" (John 3:13). John heard Jesus say, "I have the keys of death and of Hades" (Revelation 1:18). "I will give unto each one of you according to your works" (Revelation 2:23).

*Jesus claimed indisputable power in dealing with every moral duty and destiny:* In His Sermon on the Mount, He said, "Ye have heard that it was said . . . but I say unto you . . ." (Matthew 5:21, 22, 31-34, 38, 39, 43, 44). At the conclusion of the sermon He claimed to be the solid rock on which wise men are to build (Matthew 7:24). Other inspired teachers appealed to the law and to the testimony (Isaiah 8:20), but Jesus claimed an inherent power to apply perfectly or to supersede the law in righteousness (Matthew 12:3-8). He charged His disciplies in His name to teach "them to observe all things whatsoever I commanded you" (Matthew 28:20). John said Christ claimed to be "he that holdeth the seven stars in his right hand" (Revelation 2:1). "He that overcometh, I will give to him to sit down with me in my throne" (Revelation 3:21). "Be thou faithful unto death, and I will give thee the crown of life" (Revelation 2:10) are statements by Jesus to the churches.

*Jesus asserted full possession of the power to forgive sins:* "But that ye may know that the Son of man hath authority on earth to forgive sins (then saith he to the sick of the palsy), Arise, and take up thy bed, and go unto thy house" (Matthew 9:6). "And he said unto her, Thy sins are forgiven" (Luke 7:48). "If therefore the Son shall make you free, ye shall be free indeed" (John 8:36).

*Jesus claimed the power to raise His own body from the grave, and to raise all the dead at the last great day:* "Destroy this temple, and in three days I will raise it up . . . but he spoke of the temple of his body" (John 2:19, 21). "I have power to lay it down, and I have power to take it again" (John 10:18). "Every one that beholdeth the Son, and believeth on him, should have eternal life; and I will raise him up at the last day" (John 6:40). "All that are in the tombs . . . shall come forth; they that have done good, unto the resurrection of life; and they that have done evil, unto the resurrection of judgment" (John 5:28, 29).

*Jesus claimed to be the source of life that is real and eternal:* "But the water that I shall give him shall become in him a well of water springing up unto eternal life" (John 4:14). "For as the Father raiseth the dead and giveth them life, even so the Son also giveth life to whom he will" (John 5:21). "I am the bread of life" (John 6:35). "For this is the will of my Father, that every one that beholdeth the Son, and believeth on him, should have eternal life" (John 6:40). "Except ye eat the flesh of the Son of man and drink his blood, ye have not life in yourselves . . . he that eateth this bread shall live for ever" (John 6:53, 58). "And I give unto them eternal life; and they shall never perish" (John 10:28). "I am the resurrection, and the life: he that believeth on me, though he die, yet shall he live;

and whosoever liveth and believeth on me shall never die" (John 11:25, 26). "I am the way, and the truth, and the life: no one cometh unto the Father, but by me" (John 14:6). "As the branch cannot bear fruit of itself, except it abide in the vine; so neither can ye, except ye abide in me" (John 15:4). "Glorify thy Son . . . that to all whom thou hast given him, he should give eternal life. And this is life eternal, that they should know thee the only true God, and him whom thou didst send, even Jesus Christ" (John 17:1-3).

*Jesus declared he had power to do all His Father's works:* "My Father worketh even until now, and I work" (John 5:17). "What things soever he doeth, these the Son doeth in like manner" (John 5:19). "I do always the things that are pleasing to him" (John 8:29). "If I do not the works of my Father, believe me not. But if I do them, though ye believe not me, believe the works: that ye may know and understand that the Father is in me, and I in the Father" (John 10:37, 38).

*Jesus claimed to know the Father uniquely:* "Neither doth any know the Father, save the Son, and he to whomsoever the Son willeth to reveal him" (Matthew 11:27). "I know him; because I am from him, and he sent me" (John 7:29). "Ye have not known him: but I know him" (John 8:55). "O righteous Father, the world knew thee not, but I knew thee" (John 17:25).

*Jesus claimed to reveal the Father flawlessly:* "And he that beholdeth me beholdeth him that sent me" (John 12:45). "Have I been so long time with you, and dost thou not know me, Philip? he that hath seen me hath seen the Father" (John 14:9). "He that hateth me hateth my Father also" (John 15:23). "That they may all be one; even as thou, Father, art in me, and I in thee" (John 17:21).

*Jesus claimed to obey the Father perfectly:* "I can of myself do nothing: . . . because I seek not mine own will, but the will of him that sent me" (John 5:30). "For I am come down from heaven, not to do mine own will, but the will of him that sent me" (John 6:38). "But now ye seek to kill me, a man that hath told you the truth, which I heard from God" (John 8:40). "I speak the things which I have seen with my Father" (John 8:38). "For I spake not from myself; but the Father that sent me, he hath given me a commandment, what I should say, and what I should speak . . . the things therefore which I speak, even as the Father hath said unto me, so I speak" (John 12:49, 50b). "The words that I say unto you I speak not from myself: but the Father abiding in me doeth his works" (John 14:10).

*Jesus unequivocally demands faith in himself:* "I said therefore unto you, that ye shall die in your sins: for except ye believe that I am he, ye shall die in your sins" (John 8:24). "If therefore the Son shall make you free, ye shall be free indeed" (John 8:36). "If a man keep my word, he shall never see death" (John 8:51). "I am the door; by me if any man enter in, he shall be saved, and shall go in and go out, and shall find pasture" (John 10:9). "And whosoever liveth and believeth on me shall never die" (John 11:26). "Believe in God, believe also in me" (John 14:1). "Every one therefore who shall confess me before men, him will I also confess before my Father who is in heaven" (Matthew 10:32).

Such claims must be taken seriously, as either true or false. Jesus must either be obeyed as the Lord of all, or be rejected as a blasphemous impostor. He could not be a good man and be only a man.

He could not make such sweeping claims and still profess to be meek and humble, unless He does have the authority of God, and did take upon himself the place of a lowly servant in revealing God and bringing us to salvation. In His lesson to the disciples in John 13 on humility, He states that because He is their Lord and Master, His washing of their feet is an act of humility. If he were a mere man, it would hardly be an act of humility to tell others, "If I then, the Lord and the Teacher, have washed your feet, ye also ought to wash one another's feet" (John 13:14).

Have you considered how strange it was that a man could stand in front of others and claim to be the only one who knew about God, the only one who could satisfy the needs of all men, and say at the same time, "I am meek and lowly in heart" (Matthew 11:29)? In the midst of His strongest claims, "If a man keep my word, he shall never see death" (John 8:51), He says, "I seek not mine own glory" (John 8:50).

He commanded the hearts of men and demanded absolute submission and allegiance to himself with as much authority as any absolute monarch. Yet, at the same time He admitted being homeless as a beggar, not having a place to lay His head (Luke 9:57-62).

It seems impossible for such extremes to combine with any harmony in one person. Yet, in Jesus this combination is possible because of the uniqueness of His divine nature and the grace of His human condescension. The only way to understand Him is as the humble incarnation of the divine Lord, the eternal Word. This is what He wants us to understand because this is what He really is. For this reason we should love and appreciate Him, both for His majesty in eternity and His ministry to earth for us.

An honest inquirer must conclude that Jesus Christ is the Lord of life and death, the Lord of heaven and earth, and that He holds in His hands the destiny of every soul. The man who knows Christ, then, ought to do His will out of joyous obedience to one who "existing in the form of God, counted not the being on an equality with God a thing to be grasped, but emptied himself, taking the form of a servant" (Philippians 2:6, 7).

His commands are for the purpose of making us "partakers of the divine nature" (II Peter 1:3). With this in mind, Jesus demanded absolute faith in himself: "Except ye believe that I am he, ye shall die in your sins" (John 8:24). He required men to make an abrupt turnabout of allegiance from themselves to himself when He said, "Except ye repent, ye shall all in like manner perish" (Luke 13:3). He made clear the need for a life of courageous confession of Him as Lord before mankind in the statement: "Every one therefore who shall confess me before men, him will I also confess before my Father who is in heaven" (Matthew 10:32). He provided remission of our sins when He "humbled himself, becoming obedient even unto death, yea, the death of the cross" (Philippians 2:8), and He asks us to demonstrate our death to sin by a symbolic burial and resurrection to new life in the act of baptism. "He that believeth and is baptized shall be saved; but he that disbelieveth shall be condemned" (Mark 16:16). He unmistakably links faith and trust in Him to obedience in baptism for the remission of sins, as a demonstration of our faith and commitment to Him.

As His followers we will be distinguished by our love for Him and each other, "By this shall all men know that ye are my disciples, if ye have love one to another" (John 13:35). Because Christ lives in our hearts, by His power we will have a forgiving spirit toward our brother (see Matthew 6:12; 18:21-35; Luke 17:3, 4). Our lives will be characterized by good works, "For we are his workmanship, created in Christ Jesus for good works, which God afore prepared that we should walk in them" (Ephesians 2:10). We have been directed to follow Paul's admonition "Present yourselves unto God, as alive from the dead, and your members as instruments of righteousness unto God" (Rom. 6:13).

Because we are His new creation we will put to death the sins listed by the apostles of Jesus in their Sprit-inspired writings: for example, Galatians 5:19-21; Ephesians 2:2, 3; Colossians 3:5-9; James 3:1-16. We will surely be bound to live by the principle of life given in Colossians 3:17: "And whatsoever ye do, in word or in deed, do all in the name of the Lord Jesus, giving thanks to God the Father through him," with all its implications of a wholehearted desire to please the Lord Jesus in every area of life.

When one has reached a conclusion about this Jesus of Nazareth, action is demanded: either the action of full faith and obedience because He is the reigning Lord of glory, or the action of complete rejection because He is a shameful imposter.

For Further Study:

Bruce, F. F. and William J. Martin. "The Deity of Christ" in *Christianity Today,* IX (December 18, 1964). Pp. 283-289. Careful study on the New Testament teaching on the deity of Christ. Exposes the misinterpretations of those who deny the deity of Jesus.

Henry, Carl F. H. ed. *Jesus of Nazareth: Savior and Lord.* Grand Rapids: Wm. B. Eerdmans Publishing Company, 1960. Scholarly defense of the New Testament picture of Christ in answer to the subjectivizing of modern theology.

McDowell, Josh. *Evidence That Demands a Verdict.* San Bernardino: Campus Crusade For Christ, International, 1972. Pp. 91-112. Clear presentation of the claims of Christ and the necessity of decision on our part concerning his claims.

# 12

## THE WORD . . . DWELT AMONG US (JOHN 1:1-18)

The Old Testament begins: "In the beginning God created the heavens and the earth," (Genesis 1:1). Then it tells how man was made in the image of God to rule God's creation, how men fell into sin and separation from God, how God chose the family of Abraham to be His instrument through which to reveal himself and to prepare a great salvation for all the families of men.

John, the fisherman of Galilee, was one of the descendants of Abraham. He had learned from the Old Testament about God and His promises to Israel. When John the Baptist came prophesying in the Jordan Valley and baptizing people in preparation for the promised kingdom of God, the fisherman John and his brother James left their fishing business for a while to go hear the prophet. There they saw Jesus. They heard the prophet point Him out as the "Lamb of God, that taketh away the sin of the world" (John 1:29).

They began that day to follow Jesus, and for more than three years they lived with Him and were among His closest friends. They saw His miraculous signs. They heard His teachings that revealed who He was—the Son of God who was before Abraham (John 8:58), who had glory with God before the world was (17:5), who came into the world that men might have life (10:10), the light of the world (8:12), the resurrection and the life (11:25), the only way of life eternal for every man (6:53; 14:6). What a wonderful person to know and serve! They also saw Jesus rejected and crucified; then they saw Him repeatedly after He arose in triumph from the dead.

By all these experiences their faith and understanding were increased. But human understanding, even with such experiences, was not enough. They, with all the apostles, were given the power of God's Holy Spirit to bring to memory all that Jesus had taught them and to guide them into all truth. Thus John gained such clear and sure knowledge, even of things beyond human experience, that he was able to tell us about Jesus, that "In the beginning was the Word . . . And the Word became flesh, and dwelt among us (and we beheld his glory . . .)" (John 1:1, 14).

The first eighteen verses of the first chapter of the Gospel according to John are an introduction to John's account of the events in Jesus' earthly life and ministry. This prologue or introduction sets forth the theme for the whole book, and attracts the mind of the reader to the exceptional importance and solemnity of the book's contents.

All Christians would do well to memorize and meditate upon this precious gem of divine revelation. It is simple in its form and wording, but very profound in meaning. We know almost too easily what it means to say in a general way, so that we do not realize the force and significance of these tremendous truths. In very simple language it declares:

1. The eternal existence of Jesus Christ—"In the beginning was the Word" (v. 1).
2. His deity—"the Word was with God, and the Word was God" (vv. 1, 2).
3. His relation to the world as Creator—"All things were made through him" (v. 3).
4. His relation to the needs of man—"In him was life; and the life was the light of men" (v. 4).
5. His forerunner, John the Baptizer—"a man sent from God . . . that he might bear witness of the light" (vv. 6-8, 15).
6. His tragic rejection by men—"He came unto his own, and they that were his own received him not" (v. 11).
7. His redemption and regeneration of those who did believe on Him—"To them gave he that right to become children of God . . . who were born . . . of God" (vv. 12, 13).
8. His incarnation and sojourn with men—"The Word became flesh, and dwelt among us" (v. 14).
9. His revelation of the glory, grace, and truth of God, and His revelation of God himself (vv. 14, 16-18).

These are supremely significant truths of Christianity. Other religions, at their very best, are capable only of showing man's seeking after God. Christianity is the result of God's seeking after men! Other religions show man's need of God. Christianity offers God's help for man. If religion were, as some conceive it, only a collection of the best wisdom of men for ordering our personal lives and social relationships, it would probably be, even then, of some value for our short life on this earth. But Christianity is far more and better than that. Christianity is not merely the experience of our fathers preserved for us; it is the wisdom and power of God present with us—God with us and in us for our perfection and preservation here and hereafter, now and forever! Our religion is not a philosophy to be experimentally confirmed or disproved, revised or refined; but it is a matter of facts faithfully witnessed, things done and forever unchangeable, divine truths unerringly revealed.

This Scripture records the coming into the world of the greatest thing that has ever been in the world: life, light, glory, grace, and truth, all embodied in the person of Jesus Christ.

Here is told briefly but plainly

1. Who came,
2. Why He came,
3. How He was received, and
4. What He accomplished.

### *The Word and God*

John is writing of the life and nature of Jesus Christ. In telling who it was that came, John uses a title for Him that is used only in John's writings—"The Word." The Word was in the beginning. The Word was with God. The Word was God; that is, the Word was deity, and had the nature of God. The Word became flesh and dwelt among us, and we beheld His glory. See I John 1:1, Revelation 19:13.

The Greek word used in these expressions is *logos*, which means much more than merely a word as a unit of speech. If often means a saying or extended utterance, the faculty of speech, instruction, a matter under discussion, a reason, an act of reasoning, or power of reason. The Greek language has another term for a mere word as a thing spoken or a unit or language; it is *rhema,* which is the "word" used in Hebrews 11:3 and at least 66 other times in the New Testament.

The words of a man are a most important expression of his character. The Christ is the supreme expression of God's character. He was much more than mere actions of God; He was and is a person, but in His whole personality and life He is the perfect expression of what God is and does. As John says in 1:18, He "declared him." That is, He expressed plainly to human senses the nature and the will of God, whom no man had seen or known adequately. Jesus was such an adequate manifestation of God that He was able to say, "He that hath seen me hath seen the Father" (John 14:9), and "I and the Father are one" (John 10:30). He well deserves the title "Word."

God is a person. That is, He is a Spirit Being, having will and power of choice, capable of personal relations with others such as feeling love or obligation, being pleased or displeased, showing goodness or judgment, and the like. Since God *is* a person, a perfect revelation of God must be made in the life and character of a person. The only one who can be the kind of character and live the kind of life that will manifest the supreme being adequately must himself be equal with God in the possession of divine attributes.

John makes plain the fact of the personal, eternal existence of the Word from the beginning with God and like God, and acting in the creation of all things. But our understanding of such a grand truth, so beyond human reason and experience. is helped by other statements in divine relvelation. Genesis says God created the world; but it also uses a plural word for God and quotes God as saying, "Let us make man in our image" (Genesis 1:26). John in verse three declared that not even one thing was made without the Word. Christ's pre-existence in the form of God and on equality with God is expressed in Philippians 2:5-8. See also John 8:58; 17:5, 24; Revelation 1:8. He was not a created being, but is eternal and uncaused, like God. His work as Creator is affirmed in Colossians 1:16, 17 and in Hebrews 1:1-4. His deity and glory with God before coming to earth are stated or implied in John 17:5, 24; 6:62; Isaiah 9:6; and Micah 5:2. The following works of divine power and scope are attributed to Him:

1. Creation of all things,
2. The work of upholding and holding together the universe,
3. Raising the dead,
4. Eternal judgment of all men,
5. Forgiveness of sins,
6. Regeneration or renewal of those who were dead in sin,
7. Bestowal of the gift of eternal life,
8. Transformation of the bodies of the redeemed.

The deity of Christ is not a matter of cold, stale, abstract theology that has no practical importance to us. Rather, it is a truth of the greatest importance for us, for it is a matter of knowing whom we have believed and being fully persuaded that whatever He has promised He will do.

### *Life And Light*

"In him was life; and the life was the light of men" (John 1:4). All life originated with Him, and He is the power that sustains life in the universe. As John proceeds with His account, it becomes plain that he is thinking of the spiritual and eternal life that is offered to men in Christ, and only in Christ. Life manifests itself in many forms, but in man it becomes intellectual and moral light, reason and conscience. All the light of men came from Christ the Creator even before He came into the world as Jesus.

The light of moral truth and God's revelation of Himself has been shining into the darkness of human sin and folly through the ages. Before Jesus came, a measure of divine light had been given to man in his moral nature, in the original knowledge of God, in the progressive revelation in the Old Testament. When the light was manifested the darkness did not understand it or did not overcome it (John 1:5). The Greek verb can be translated either way. Either of these meanings expresses what is true, and each may fit the context. Men in the darkness of sin did not receive and appropriate the light as they should have; nor on the other hand, did the darkness overpower the light.

All the real light that any man receives comes from Christ. Through His life and His gospel Christ furnishes light for all men, although some may not receive it, and many love the darkness rather than the light (John 3:19; 12:35, 36, 46). Christ was the true light coming into the world. He is the "light which enlightens every man." When Jesus came in the flesh, the world knew not that He was the Creator and Lord of all. Some came to know Him, but most did not. The original language helps us understand verse eleven. John says, "He came unto His own things and His own people received him not." The first "own" is neuter, suggesting things, and the second "own" is masculine, suggesting people. The Jews, who had been chosen and prepared to know God and to serve Him, were peculiarly His own people. There is pathos in this simple statement.

"But as many as received him, to them gave he the right to become children of God, even to them that believe on his name" (John 1:12). Not all rejected the Lord; a few were believing and appreciative. Though most Jews rejected, many Gentiles have received Him. The original word means "authority" rather than "power." God does not give the believers ability or force to become sons of His by their own efforts; but He gives the authorization or right to come into Christ by His grace.

Some persons have used John 1:13 to refer to the virgin birth of Jesus. Jesus was born of the virgin Mary but this verse does not affirm that fact. John here states that believers become children of God, not by natural descent or ordinary birth and not by the efforts of their own will, but by being born anew from God. This is a birth of water and the Spirit (John 3:5; Titus 3:5; Romans 6:4-11). It is accomplished through believing and obeying Christ. Thus we appropriate His life and light.

## *Unique And Incomparable*

God came to us in human flesh and for a brief time lived among men, showing in His life and works the goodness and truth of God. In Him men saw the glory of God, unique and incomparable. John plainly identifies the eternal Word in His earthly sojourn as Jesus Christ. In many versions, we read in John 1:14 of "the only begotten of the Father," and in John 1:18 we see "the only begotten Son." The word translated "only begotten" is *monogenes.* It does not necessarily refer to begetting, but may mean "the only one of his kind." Thus it is used in Hebrews 11:17 to describe Isaac, who was not literally the only begotten son of Abraham. Ishmael was begotten by Abraham before Isaac, and six brothers were begotten by Abraham after Isaac. But Isaac was indeed Abraham's unique son of miraculous birth and divine choice.

Applied to Jesus, the word *monogenes* seems not intended to emphasize the fact that He was the begotten Son among others who were adopted, though that is true. But the word refers to His unique relationship with the Father in all eternity, *before He was begotten in the flesh* as well as after. No one else had such a relationship; He was the one and only. He not only was with God; He also *was* God. So John 1:18 tells us that no man has known God face to face, but one who is of the nature of God has come from the heart of God to us. In some of the oldest and best Greek manuscripts we find in John 1:18 the reading *monogenes* God instead of *monogenes* Son. This represents a difference of only one letter in the way manuscripts were copied. This would express not the sonship but the deity of the one who has come in the flesh to expound the invisible Father (Col. 1:15; 2:9).

Jesus is not important simply because His teachings are superior and effective; but His teachings are supremely important because He is in reality *God with us,* speaking the eternal truth of God! Because He is God with us, His death is more than an example of self-sacrificing meekness; it is rather the accomplishment of a divine plan of redemption with power to save the lost and purge the sinful.

We need also to realize that the God revealed by Jesus is the only God there is. There is no God but the God and Father of our Lord Jesus Christ, and we must have no other gods beside Him. If we make any philosophy about God that considers Him to be different from the character and purposes and teachings of Jesus, we make an idol as surely as if we carved one out of wood.

Therefore, also, if we would pay any respect to God or serve Him, we must do it through Christ and according to God's will as revealed in Christ. We cannot know God or serve Him while rejecting or disregarding Jesus Christ. Beware of all those occasions on which men claim to honor God or to teach His will while they bypass Jesus and include in their ceremonies men who deny Christ. "He that honoreth not the Son honoreth not the Father that sent him" (John 5:23).

### *Christ Among Us And In Us*

Try to imagine what significance it would have if the apostle Paul were to come to preach among us for three months! What if he were with us to correct our concepts of Christian teaching, to direct our emphasis in Christian work, and to demonstrate what real faith and holy zeal are like? But how much more wonderful than even that would be is the fact that the very Son of God came and lived among men for thirty-three years as a perfect demonstration of God's love, wisdom, purposes, and holiness! He showed us, throughout an entire lifetime, the way of righteousness, the glory of service, the power of love, the life of prayer, and the victory of complete trust in God.

His earthly life was perfect in godliness, but it was truly human at the same time. For our sakes He came to be really one of us, to be tempted in all points as we are, yet without sin. For having suffered being tempted, He is able to help those who are now being tempted. He lived a very real and complete human life, as a helpless babe, as a growing boy, as a working youth, as a man of sorrows, serving and saving humanity. His humanity is not to be denied any more than His deity is (see I John 4:2; II John 7). He became one of us that He might represent us as our priest before God. He even suffered our death, that through it He might free us from the sentence of the second death and the fear of the first one.

His coming to dwell among us is especially significant when we let Him come and dwell within us. For the Word of God not only dwelt *among men* nineteen hundred years ago; He will *dwell in our hearts* today through faith. This is the real purpose of the incarnation and the teaching of the Gospel—to bring Christ into the lives of all men, to be their life and righteousness and their hope of eternal glory (see Col. 1:27; Gal. 4:19). When we really accept Him as Lord, and His death as the death our sins deserve, we are baptized into His death and are counted as "crucified with Christ." Henceforth, the life of faith in Him is not our own life, but Christ living in us (Gal. 2:20 compare Rom. 6:1-11). This is the divine purpose and the abiding glory of the Word becoming flesh and dwelling among us.

For Further Study:

Butler, Paul. *The Gospel of John.* Joplin: College Press, 1961. Comments on John 1:1-18 (Pp. 19-34). Special study on the Greek word translated "only begotten" (Pp. 125-128).

Foster, R. C. *Studies In the Life of Christ.* Grand Rapids: Baker Book House, 1971. Pp. 223-230. Explanation of John 1:1-18.

Hendriksen, William. *New Testament Commentary: The Gospel of John.* Grand Rapids: Baker Book House, 1953. Pp. 69-91. Comments on John 1:1-18.

Morris, Leon. *New International Commentary: Gospel of John.* Grand Rapids: Wm. B. Eerdmans Publishing Company, 1971. Pp. 71-128. Explanation of John 1:1-18 and special discussion on the meaning of the word, *logos.*

# 13

# THE PURPOSE OF MIRACLES

Why did Jesus heal? The New Testament states plainly the main reason for the miracles wrought by Christ and the apostles.

Jesus said, "The works which the Father hath given me to accomplish, the very works that I do, bear witness of me, that the Father hath sent me" (John 5:36). "The works that I do in my Father's name, these bear witness of me" (John 10:25; see also 37, 38). Even to the apostles at the last supper Jesus offered the same evidence: "The Father abiding in me doeth his works. Believe me that I am in the Father, and the Father in me: or else believe me for the very works' sake" (John 14:10, 11).

## *A Demonstration*

A very clear case is given in Mark 2:4-12. When the paralyzed man was let down through the roof for Jesus to heal him, Jesus said, "Son, your sins are forgiven." Scribes who were in the crowded house thought Jesus was blaspheming in claiming to forgive sins.

Jesus answered their thoughts: "Why do you reason these things in your hearts? Which is easier, to say to the paralytic, 'Your sins are forgiven,' or to say, 'Arise, take up your bed and walk'? But so that you may know that the Son of man has authority on earth to forgive sins (He said to the paralytic), 'I say unto you, Arise, take up your bed and go to your house.' " And he did!

## *Signs That Bear Witness*

The book of Hebrews reports that this great salvation, "having at the first been spoken through the Lord, was confirmed unto us by them that heard; God also bearing witness with them, both by signs and wonders, and by manifold powers, and by gifts of the Holy Spirit, according to his own will" (Heb. 2:3, 4).

John regularly called Jesus' miracles "signs." In the twenty-one chapters of his Gospel, he refers to them fourteen times as "signs." As Nicodemus saw, and as Jesus said, they were signs that God was with Jesus and was doing His works in Him (see John 3:2).

Peter preached on Pentecost that Jesus was "a man approved of God unto you by mighty works and wonders and signs which God did by him in the midst of you, even as ye yourselves know" (Acts 2:22).

When the apostles worked miracles in Jesus' name, they gave evidence that Jesus was at the right hand of God (Acts 2:33), evidence of the power of His name (Acts 3:16), evidence that God was with them and their message was from God (Acts 13:9-12). Their miracles gave boldness and strength to the new witnesses faced by overwhelming opposition (Acts 4:29-33; 5:12-16). Their miracles gave to their persecutors more convincing evidence than they were really willing to admit (see Acts 4:16; 5:17-24, 33-39; 6:7).

Miracles gave proof that the Gentiles were to be accepted in Christ through obedience to the gospel, the same as Jews (Acts 10:9-16, 44-47; 11:15-17; 15:8, 9, 12). They were the evidence, even to the elders and the church at Jerusalem, that the preaching of Paul and Barnabas among the Gentiles was according to God's will (Acts 15:12-22).

The great miracles of God, wrought through the apostles and some on whom they laid their hands, were so clear and so certain that even sorcerers and people who practiced magical arts saw the proof of real truth and gave up their superstitions and trickery (Acts 8:6-13; 19:11-20).

### *Miracles Not Always for Compassion*

The miracles of the Bible taught God's power and authority, sometimes His love and goodness, sometimes His righteous and fearsome judgments.

Consider the death of Uzzah, who touched the ark (II Sam. 6:6, 7); of Nadab and Abihu, the sons of Aaron who offered strange fire (Lev. 10:1, 2); and of Ananias and Sapphira, who lied about their offering (Acts 5:1-11). Consider the leprosy of Gehazi, the servant of Elisha who coveted Naaman's gifts (II Kings 5:20-27); and of Miriam, the sister of Moses, when she questioned Moses' leadership (Num. 12:1-15). Consider the blindness of Elymas (Acts 13:8-12), or of the Syrian band (II Kings 6:18-20); the destruction of armies (27,000 Syrians killed by the falling walls of Aphek—I Kings 20:30; and 185,000 Assyrians smitten by an angel outside Jerusalem—II Kings 19:35; Isa. 37:33-38), or of the cities of Sodom and Gomorrah (Gen. 19:24, 25) and Jericho (Josh. 6:20).

Although such miracles as healing and feeding people did show the merciful goodness of God and did express the compassion of Jesus, the accounts show that they were not worked merely to relieve suffering.

Physical healing, material blessing, or the prolongation of this earthly life are not the real purposes of God's grace toward us. He did these things sometimes as visible examples of His power and loving goodness, to encourage faith.

But miracles have always been limited to few and special cases. Never have they been used impartially to relieve suffering or prolong this life for all of God's people. Their benefit was usually temporary and only a demonstration to engender and support an abiding faith.

All who were delivered from sickness or affliction had other times to suffer and to die. All who were raised from the dead had to die again. Once and again Peter was delivered from prison and from persecutors; but another time he was left to die, when God was no less compassionate and Peter was no less believing. So it was also with Paul.

Some received no miraculous deliverance here, but a better resurrection for the life hereafter (Heb. 11:35-40). John the Immerser, greatest of the prophets, worked no miracles, nor was he miraculously delivered from prison and death (Matt. 11:7-11; 14:8-12; John 10:41).

Jesus could have healed all the sick or raised all the dead. But he did not and would not. Many were healed by Paul (Acts 19:11, 12), but Trophimus and Timothy were not (II Tim. 4:20; I Tim. 5:23). A multitude of sick and afflicted lay by the pool at Jerusalem, but Jesus healed only one man (who did not know Him or ask Him to) and then hid himself from the others (John 5:3, 5-9, 13). But later He sought the healed man again to teach him and to meet the debate which the Sabbath miracle had aroused with the Pharisees.

Miracles form part of the foundation of our faith, being divine demonstrations witnessing to the origin of the message we have believed. But they are not an inherent part of the faith and its practice in the lives of obedient believers. The miracles wrought by the messengers of God while the faith was being "once for all delivered to the saints" are still effective evidences to establish the truth and authority of that faith.

### *Modern Miracles*

Miracles claimed by preachers today do not clearly confirm the message of ancient apostles and prophets; they seem instead to have the opposite effect. They are not the conclusive and undoubtable kind that established the faith in the beginning. They are claimed by men whose message does not altogether agree with the sure Word of God as given in the Bible.

We should not hastily suppose that anything we cannot explain must, therefore, have been done by God. The mere fact that something marvelous or apparently miraculous has happened does not necessarily attest a divine religion or indicate a revelation from God, not in the same way that Bible miracles prove that the Bible is from God. There are false miracles and misleading wonders (Matt. 24:24; 7:22; II Thess. 2:8-10; Rev. 13:14; 16:14; 19:20; I John 4:1-6).

Bible miracles were a part of a coherent combination of many miracles and messages to which they were significantly related. They were closely connected with the message that explained them, and thoroughly consistent with it in character. Satan tempted Jesus to work miracles, which He would not do because they were not consistent with the purpose of God. The whole body of Biblical miracles verify and explain each other. Any unexplained wonder here or there must be tested by its coherence with that undeniable body of complete evidence which is found in the miracles and prophecies of the Bible. The certainty, the extent and the quality of miracles and revelations by the apostles and other Bible writers are different from the many various "miracles" and "prophecies" that have been claimed since the days of the New Testament.

Even if true miracles were worked today by men who taught the truth of God's Word, they would add little or nothing to the proof of that divine revelation. In fact, they would make men tend to depend upon continual miraculous demonstration rather than upon the unchanging authority and veracity of God. When miracles are reported or claimed today, they tend to make men overly eager for physical and material aid, more than they are concerned for spiritual and eternal salvation or for faithfulness to God by knowing and obeying His Word.

The spiritual transformation of a sinner through birth of water and the Spirit and the reality of Christ dwelling in him through faith is a greater work than even the mightiest miracles wrought by Jesus in Galilee. Miracles in the spiritual realm are greater than miracles in the physical realm. They have a more significant quality and a more lasting consequence. Making real saints out of sinners is a greater work than turning water into wine. This is surely what Jesus meant by John 14:12: "Greater works than these shall he do; because I go to the Father." Surely no greater miracles in the physical realm have ever been worked by anyone. But the humblest believer by the power and instrumentality of God's Word may convert a sinner and produce the fruit of the Spirit, and so participate in a new creation (II Cor. 5:17) which shall shine as the stars forever to the eternal glory of God (study Eph. 1:12-14; 2:19-22; 3:10, 11, 17-21; 4:13, 22-24; and 5:26, 27). Pray that we may.

For Further Study:

Hoover, Arlie. "The Case For Christian Miracles" in *Pillars of Faith,* ed. by H. Wilson and M. Womack. Grand Rapids: Baker Book House, 1973. Pp. 109-125. Excellent defense of the reality of Christ's miracles.

Little, Paul. *Know Why You Believe,* rev. ed. Downers Grove: Inter Varsity Press, 1968. Pp. 59-68. Helpful discussion of the nature and purpose of Christ's miracles.

Ramm, Bernard. *Protestant Christian Evidences.* Chicago: Moody Press, 1953. Pp. 125-162. Scholarly defense of the miraculous verification of Christianity. Answers objections raised against miracles.

Smith, Wilbur M. *The Supernaturalness of Christ.* Boston: W. A. Wilde Company, 1940. Pp. 109-162. Essay on "The Nature and Testimony of Christ's Miracles."

# Part Four

# BIRTH OF CHRIST

## 14

## THE BIRTH AND CHILDHOOD OF JESUS

### *Matthew and His Book*

The Gospel of Matthew does not name its author, but there is abundant testimony of very early Christian writers (beginning with Papias who was a student of the apostle John) that it was written by Matthew the Apostle.

Very little is known about Matthew's life before and after the ministry of Jesus, of which he was an eyewitness. Jesus called him from the "receipt of custom" or "place of toll," for he was a tax-collector (Matt. 9:9-13; Mark 2:14-17; Luke 5:27-32). He was also called Levi, and he is named in every list of the Twelve (Matt. 10:3; Mark 3:18; Luke 6:15; Acts 1:13).

> The only word that Matthew has about himself is that he was a 'publican.' Publicans were collectors of Roman taxes, ordinarily extortioners, and generally despised. Luke tells us that Matthew made a great feast for Jesus, and forsook all to follow Him. But Matthew does not even give himself credit for that. He loses sight of himself utterly in adoration of his Hero. We love him for his self-effacing humility.
>
> . . . . . . . . . . . . . . . . . .
>
> Tradition says that Matthew preached in Palestine for some years, and then traveled to foreign countries; that he wrote his Gospel originally in Hebrew, and some years later, probably about 60 A.D., issued a more complete edition in Greek . . . The widely-held but unsubstantiated, present-day hypothesis that Matthew copied from Mark's Gospel is, on the face of it, absurd. It is not at all certain that Mark even knew Jesus. Why should Matthew have to copy from one who had not been an eyewitness accounts of things which he himself had seen with his own eyes and heard over and over with his own ears?[1]

---

[1] Henry H. Halley, *Halley's Bible Handbook*, 24th ed. (Grand Rapids: Zondervan, 1965), pp. 413-414.

The special emphasis of Matthew's Gospel is on showing that Jesus is the Messiah predicted in the Old Testament. He seems to write especially for Jewish readers and quotes frequently from the Old Testament.

In keeping with this purpose Matthew begins his account of Jesus with the genealogy, which shows that Jesus was qualified by birth to be the "seed of Abraham" (Gen. 12:3; Gal. 3:16) and the "Son of David" (II Sam. 7:12-16; Ps. 89:3, 4, 19-37; Isa. 9:6, 7; 11:1). This genealogy seems to give the lineage of Joseph, and that in Luke 3 the lineage of Mary. Thus Matthew records Jesus' line of legal inheritance, and Luke His line of blood relationship (cf. Rom. 1:3).

### *Brevity of the Records of Jesus' Childhood*

All the Bible is wonderfully concentrated, limited to the essentials that accomplish its divine purposes. This characteristic is most plainly seen in the biographies of Jesus and especially in the accounts of His childhood. Only Matthew and Luke tell anything of His birth and youth. In them we find none of the usual descriptions of personal appearance or of childhood incidentals. All that they tell is what is needful to establish our faith in Jesus as the eternal Son of God, fulfillment of the prophecies, and the Son of man, having actually come in the flesh and being made in all things like unto His brethren.

Luke tells of Jesus' consciousness of His unique Sonship and life-mission at twelve years of age, and also gives a general statement of His manner of life and development in the Nazareth home (Luke 2:40-52).

Matthew tells only of His birth and His earliest childhood, not things that He did, but things that befell Him in the first months of His earthly life.

Now since the wisdom of God has so designed these inspired records, should we not conclude that these things contain important lessons for us? Should we not look for the meaning of the things revealed and not speculate on the things about which the record is entirely silent? These chapters tell so little, why tell anything at all? What should we see here?

### *His Identity*

The most important things set forth in these accounts are the marks of identification of Him who was born. All of Christianity is the acceptance of Him as Lord and Saviour. All the proclamation of Christianity is the preaching of Jesus as "Lord and Christ," the tidings of a "Saviour, who is Christ the Lord." Anything disconnected from His Person, anything that can stand independent of His saving power and ruling authority is not distinctly Christian; for His Church is built upon that rock (Matt. 16:18) and without Him we can do nothing (John 15:5).

As the genealogies tell His human parentage and inheritance, so the angel, announcing the miraculous birth, tells His divine parentage: "conceived of the Holy Spirit" and "Son of the Most High."

His deity is declared in the name given Him in the prophecy of His virgin birth (Isa. 7:14); "Immanuel" means "God with us." The citation of Isaiah's prophecy naturally points to the further description of the "Son" in Isa. 9:6, 7, where He is called "Mighty God" and "Everlasting Father."

The Wise-men's coming and worshipping Him points out His deity; for no man merits worship. No righteous man will permit himself to be worshipped (Acts 10:25, 26); neither will an angel (Rev. 22:8, 9). Indeed angels worshipped Him at His birth (Luke 2:10-14 and Heb. 1:6).

Matthew, in chapters one and two, cites at least four Messianic prophecies fulfilled: concerning His birth of a virgin, His birth at Bethlehem, His being brought out of Egypt, and His being called a Nazarene. He says that the events fulfilled words (not necessarily predictive) of Jeremiah about the mourning for lost children. This history shows that the prophecies were not only such as could be applied after the events, but that there were prophecies of His coming which were so clear that such a birth was expected and the place was definitely known. Apparently without disagreement or hesitation the scribes told Herod that the Christ would be born at Bethlehem. The coming of the Wise-men is proof of application of prophecies or, at least, of some special revelations to them. It is most likely that they applied the Old Testament prophecies.

Josephus (an unbelieving Jew), Tacitus and Suetonius (pagan Roman historians) bear record of a general expectation in those times. Suetonius says: "There had been for a long time all over the East a prevailing opinion that it was in the fates that at that time some one from Judea should obtain the empire of the world."[2] All the three named agree upon the time when the person should appear, the place where he should arise, the greatness of his dominion, and

---

[2] Suetonius in Life of Vespasian quoted by Alexander Campbell, *The Christian Preacher's Companion.* (Joplin: College Press, n.d.), p. 43.

the widespread nature of the expectation. Philo, Appian, Sallust, Plutarch, Cicero and Virgil are all said to have referred to predictions or expectations of the birth of a great conqueror or king fairly close to the time of Jesus birth.

> In the Jewish prophets, . . . generally read all over the East, various express and clear predictions are written, fully warranting the expectation so often alluded to by all the reputed writers of that age. So early as the time of Jacob, it was intimated that Shiloh, of the tribe of Judah, would have the scepter and allegiance of the world . . . Gen. 49:10. The prophets afterwards mentioned the exact place where he should be born, . . . Micah 5:2. Daniel, as well as other prophets, also foretells the time of his nativity: 'From the going forth of the decree to restore and build Jerusalem' (7th year of Artaxerxes Longimanus—Ezra 7:21) 'unto the Messiah the Prince, shall be seven weeks and three score and two weeks' (of years—Dan. 9:24, 25). But the same prophet, in his interpretation of the dream of the Chaldean monarch, positively and unfiguratively asserts 'that in the days of the last kings (the Roman emperors) the God of heaven would set up a kingdom,' which should finally engross all the empires of the world, which kingdom would stand forever.'[3]

The star, the angels, the several revelations to Zacharias, Elizabeth, Mary, Joseph, Simeon, Anna, Shepherds, Wise-men, and again to Joseph—all these miracles surrounding the birth of Jesus point to Him as the Son of God and the promised One.

### *His Relation to the Old Testament*

Matthew makes the connection between the old and the new covenants and shows the new unfolding out of the old. Jesus "came not to destroy the law or the prophets, but to fulfill" (Matt. 5:17). Any attempt to discredit the Old Testament is an attack upon the foundations of Christianity. Still, it is as if all the Old Testament were made to focus on Him and surrender its glory to Him. Though He comes after it He is not its follower but its Leader and Goal. What light it had was by reason of Him for whom it furnished a series of beacons to point through the darkness to "the true light, coming into the world."

---

[3] Alexander Campbell, *Ibid.*, pp. 43-44.

### *His Reception*

As John said, "He came unto His own, and they that were His own received Him not" (John 1:11). Jerusalem had all the advantages over the rest of the world for knowing when and how and where He should come. Yet when He did come they knew nothing about it until they were told by Gentiles, and when they were told, they were troubled. There was no room in the inn for Him to be born—a symbol of cold indifference. Herod determined that there should not be room in the land for Him to live and grow—a symbol of the world's violent opposition to Him, already raising the cry, "Away with him!" Yet He was received by some poor shepherds, by holy and faithful individuals full of the Spirit, by strangers from a far country who believed the prophets.

### *His Father's Care of Him*

God chose for His only begotten Son a humble home with parents who would reverence such a son and heed the instructions of the heavenly Father. Notice how promptly Joseph obeyed every command, though it meant disgrace, or excitement and sadness, or a long hard journey and indefinite exile.

God's care is shown in the supernatural warnings and directions given though angels to Joseph and in the providential supply of means for the sojourn in Egypt through the gifts of the Wise-men.

### *His Childhood Journeys*

When Jesus was about six weeks old He was presented in the temple at Jerusalem. Sometime after that wisemen from the east followed the star to the house in Bethlehem where He was. Then, according to an angel's instructions, He was taken to Egypt till Herod's death. When Joseph and Mary returned from Egypt they apparently planned to go back to Bethlehem, but hesitated upon hearing of Archelaus, the son of Herod, upon the throne. Joseph was told in a dream to go and dwell in Nazareth, where they had lived before Jesus was born.

Nazareth is about 65 miles, in an air line, north of Jerusalem, but it is nearly 100 miles from Jerusalem by the usual pilgrim route around Samaria and down the Jordan valley. Nazareth is in the southern edge of the hills of Galilee, about 1000 feet above the plain of Megiddo (or Esdraelon) through which the trader's caravans passed on their way to lands east of the Jordan.

At the age of twelve Jesus was taken to Jerusalem for the Passover

(Luke 2:41-51). The Passover was commanded by God through Moses as an annual commemoration of the great and miraculous circumstances of the deliverance of Israel from Egypt (See Exodus 12:14-20). All the men of Israel were required to go for the Passover (and for two other feasts each year) to the central sanctuary, which was the temple at Jerusalem (Exod. 23:17; 34:23). Hundreds of thousands of pilgrims thronged the roads to and from the city, traveling in large companies. It was easy for a boy to be lost from sight, especially since the men walked in one group and the women in another.

According to Jewish custom boys became "sons of the law" at 12 years of age and were then obligated to go to the feasts. But since Joseph and Mary "went every year," Jesus possibly had gone often before He was 12.

For Further Study:

Edersheim, Alfred. *The Life and Times of Jesus the Messiah.* Grand Rapids: William B. Eerdmans Publishing Company, 1956 (Reprint of 1886 ed.). Pp. 180-234. A study of birth and childhood narrative in the light of context of Jewish social religious life and Roman political influence.

Foster, R. C. *Studies in the Life of Christ,* Grand Rapids: Baker Book House, 1971. Pp. 231-294.

Fowler, Harold. *The Gospel of Matthew,* Vol. I. Joplin, MO.: College Press, 1968. Pp. 31-86.

Harrison, Everett. *A Short Life of Christ.* Grand Rapids: William B. Eerdmans Publishing Company, 1968. Pp. 32-65. Chapters on "The Birth" and "The Infancy and Boyhood."

Hendriksen, William. *New Testament Commentary: Gospel of Matthew.* Grand Rapids: Baker Book House, 1975. Pp. 130-193. Careful comment on the birth and childhood narratives.

# 15

## LESSONS FROM THE GENEALOGIES AND BIRTH ACCOUNTS[1]

I. The genealogies show:

1. God always keeps His word, what He promised Abraham and David came to pass.
2. The sinfulness of human nature. Grace and goodness does not necessarily run in families. Human heritage could not account for Jesus.
3. How great was the mercy and the grace of our Lord Jesus! He was "not ashamed to call them brethren." He actually shared human nature and had fellowship with sinners, although He was sinless.

II. The recorded genealogy serves to establish and emphasize the following lessons:

1. That Christ was truly human, with a true close relationship with men.
2. That the past leads up to Him, and looked forward to His coming.
3. He is not accounted for by His ancestry.
4. He surpasses all the glories of the past, and sums up the best to be found in it.
5. The coming of Jesus was carefully planned and prepared for.
6. His coming fulfilled God's promises to Abraham, to Jacob, to Moses, to the nation, to David, to Isaiah and all the prophets.
7. His coming was appropriately in the kingly line, with the right to rule; but it was lowly and in keeping with His purpose to serve, to save and to restore.

### *Christ's First and Second Comings Compared*

1. Both were prophesied.
2. Purpose of each: the first to be a Savior; the second to be Judge of all men, while perfecting the salvation of those who received Him as Savior.

---

[1] I am indebted to persons and sources no longer remembered for many of these points.

3. He came "in the fulness of time" (when God knew everything was the best for the purpose); and He will come when God wants Him to, in the "fulness of time."
4. Many were not prepared for the first coming, and did not want it to happen. Many are not ready, and will not be ready, for the second coming. "Watch, and be ready."

*Miraculous Nature of His Birth and Its Importance*

1. Notice that His birth was accompanied by miraculous demonstrations and announcements, and that it was divinely extraordinary in the virgin conception.
2. This was in keeping with His divine nature and pre-existence.
3. He became man, but He was not an ordinary man; He was also God, the Son of God.
4. He was not born of a virgin because normal marriage is sinful or to avoid contamination with original sin; but to show that He came from God.
5. His life and ministry are entirely in keeping with His miraculous birth as the unique Son of God, and they are unexplainable without that divine nature.
6. No one can believe the New Testament is a reliable record and not believe in the fact of the virgin birth. The only record we have of His birth says it was a miraculous, virgin birth. The records are clear and unmistakable in meaning. If they are false, in this matter, they cannot be trusted in any other. There is nothing to account for such stories arising and being written in the New Testament, if they were not the truth.

*Example of the Wise-men*

1. It is wise to seek Christ.
2. They followed a divine guide, not feelings or nature or human wisdom.
3. The need of following all the way
4. It is wise to worship and give the best to our Lord.

For Further Study:

Fowler, Harold. *The Gospel of Matthew.* Joplin: College Press, 1968. Pp. 11-31. Basic comment on Matthew's genealogy of Jesus.

Geldenhuys, Norval. *Commentary on the Gospel of Luke.* (New International Commentary). Grand Rapids: William B. Eerdmans Publishing Company, 1951. Pp. 150-155. Very helpful brief explanation of genealogies.

Hendriksen, William. *New Testament Commentary: Gospel of Matthew.* Grand Rapids: Baker Book House, 1973. Pp. 105-129. Deals with purpose of genealogies and the alleged contradictions.

Machen, J. Gresham. *The Virgin Birth of Christ.* N.Y.: Harper and Row Publishing, 1930. Pp. 202-232. Valuable defense of the virgin birth. Full discussion of the genealogies. Machen holds both accounts trace descent of Jospeh.

Robertson, A.T. *A Harmony of the Gospels.* New York: Harper and Row Publishing, 1922. Pp. 259-262. Deals with the problems of reconciling the two accounts and concludes that Matthew gives the descent of Joseph and Luke gives the descent of Mary.

# 16

## GOD'S GREATEST GIFT

"Every good gift and every perfect gift is from above, coming down from the Father of lights, with whom can be no variation, neither shadow that is cast by turning" (James 1:17). The earth and all that it contains is the Lord's. All we are and have has come from Him. But by far the greatest gift from God is His only begotten Son, given for our redemption. The other gifts reveal God's creative power and ownership of all things, but the gift of Christ reveals His love for us in the most impressive manner, Jesus, the Son, is God's greatest gift because in Him God gave of Himself and not of the things of His creation.

### *Christianity's Special Message*

"For God so loved the world, that he gave his only begotten Son, that whosoever believeth on him should not perish, but have eternal life" (John 3:16). This is the special message of Christianity. No wonder John 3:16 is called the Golden Text of the Bible. All that went before was to prepare for the coming of Christ; all that follows His coming has been to make Him known and effective in the lives of all men, and to look forward to His coming again. Christ is God's gift to *all* men. It is altogether fitting that this text has been translated into more languages than any other message. It is published in more than 1,600 tongues.

This Golden Text of God's Word (John 3:16) bears witness to a surprisingly large amount of gospel doctrine:

1. That God is, and is good and loving.
2. That Jesus is the Son of God, specially sent into the world.
3. That Christ is the atonement for men's sins.
4. That faith in Him is the necessary condition of pardon and salvation.
5. That there is eternal reward or punishment awaiting every man.

This one verse emphasizes especially these four things: 1. *The sublimity of the gospel,* its sublime basis and source—"God so loved the world." 2. *The severity of the gospel,* its great cost, its stern realism—"that he gave his only begotten son." 3. *The simplicity of the gospel,* its simple all-transforming requirement to accomplish regeneration of men and to overcome the world, the flesh, and the devil—"that whosoever believeth on him." 4. *The security of the gospel,* its assurance of the gift of everlasting life to all who flee to Christ for refuge from the wrath to come—all who escape perishing shall partake of unlimited life with God—"should not perish, but have everlasting life."

The value of Christ as a gift to man is beyond all measurement, though it be considered from every point of view by which things are priced. His worth should be measured by the need of man to be saved from total loss and eternal despair because of sin, multiplied by all the men of all the ages, to whom there is no other help or hope but Christ. Add the value of His enlightenment and enrichment of this life for individual, home, and nation, plus the life eternal as children of God and joint-heirs with Christ. Estimate, if you can, what the gift cost the giver; evaluate the fact that it lasts forever without depreciation, ever increasing in preciousness to us. What can be compared with Him for rarity, purity, beauty, as a source of security, of joy, and of deep satisfaction? What can approach this personal, imperishable, powerful gift as an expression of the loving favor of Him who gave it?

"Herein was the love of God manifested in us, that God hath sent his only begotten Son into the world that we might live through him. Herein is love, not that we loved God, but that he loved us, and sent his Son to be the propitiation for our sins" (I John 4:9, 10).

"He that spared not his own Son, but delivered him up for us all, how shall he not also with him freely give us all things?" (Rom. 8:32). He "is able (and has proved Himself more than willing) to do exceeding abundantly above all that we ask or think" (Eph. 3:20). "Fear not, little flock, it is the Father's good pleasure to give you the kingdom" (Luke 12:32). "His divine power hath granted unto us all things that pertain unto life and godliness, through the knowledge of him who called us by his own glory and virtue" (II Pet. 1:3).

This is the gospel—that Christ left His heavenly glory, became flesh and dwelt among us on earth, ministering unto men, even giving His life as a ransom for sinners, in order that we might know the love of God and be reconciled unto the Father, trust and serve Him, and receive the fullness of the benefits of His power and love both now and forever! This is the good news of divine truth—not a philosophy and not a dream.

When will men open their needy hearts to receive such a gift? Isn't it strange, and tragic, that of all the Christmas gifts, ill-fitting or useless, or hypocritically given, nearly all are received and appreciated except the one greatest gift of all and the cause of all Christmas giving. God's gift is commonly rejected, scorned by blind and ungrateful men who need Him more than they need anything else.

### *How Shall We Celebrate His Coming?*

How can we express appreciation for such a gift? Surely it was loving appreciation and gratitude that started the celebration of Christmas. Although no one knows the date, or the season, or, indeed, even the year, in which Jesus was born, this season has been set by tradition and custom as the one in which His birth is celebrated; and we naturally think of His coming as the gift of God's love more at this season than at others. But we should not turn our thoughts to praise of His coming only once a year. Moreover, the celebration of Christmas has become so corrupted with commercialism, irrelevant traditions, pagan symbolism and even debauchery, that it is a poor and unworthy celebration of *the greatest gift of God.* How few there are, comparatively, who really exalt Christ worthily in their Christmas celebration! And those who do are those who exalt Him throughout the year in their worship and in their lives.

The Lord has made no provision and no request for any celebration in remembrance of His birth. But He has given the Lord's Supper and the special request that we keep it in remembrance of His death for our sakes. We should proclaim and praise the love of God and the coming of His Son in the flesh to save us, "in season and out of season." If we are moved, however, to sing His praises at the remembrance of His birth, we should certainly be happy to proclaim His death till He come, by keeping the Lord's Supper every Lord's Day. The only Christmas tree the Lord designed was the tree on which He Himself was hanged. As some poet has said:

> "Rude and crude, it stood on a hill.
> (In memory's fancy I see it still.)
> Its festoons were nails—its streamers were blood;
> The gift on that tree—the dear Son of God.
>
> "Thanks to God for His unspeakable gift,
> Who came from glory to heal the rift
> Between man and God, that sin had made—
> Our Lord on that tree the price fully paid."

"To obey is better than sacrifice" (I Samuel 15:22). The best way to honor the "Teacher come from God" is to hearken to His teaching. The best way to exalt the Lord is to obey Him. The best appreciation of God's gift is to receive Him as Savior with love and lasting devotion.

In appreciation for His love, it is fitting for us to show love and to give gifts of love. True love is always giving. "Beloved, if God so loved us, we also ought to love one another" (I John 4:11). We owe thanks unto God. "Thanks be to God for his unspeakable gift" (II Cor. 9:15). Notice the connection in which Paul makes this statement. Read II Corinthians eight and nine, and see that our gratitude for God's gift to us should lead us to give continually and liberally to His work and to the glory of His name. Too much of our Christmas giving is not in Jesus' name, but for our own glory in the eyes of men.

The Lord gave Himself to us. Surely the most fitting response is for us to give ourselves to Him for His glory and joy forever. We needed Him and not merely the things of His creation. He wants us and not merely the things we temporarily possess which, after all, are really His.

### *Christ Dwelling In Our Hearts*

In Ephesians 3:14-19, Paul expressed his prayer that Christ might dwell in our hearts through faith. It was a great thing that the Son, eternal and powerful and equal with God, should "become flesh and dwell among us" even for His extraordinary life of about thirty-three years on earth. But it is a much greater thing to be realized and appreciated that He will dwell in our hearts throughout our lives and in all the generations of men (see John 14:23; 17:23; Revelation 3:20; Galatians 2:20).

The apostle prays that Christ may dwell in us in order that we may be firmly established and rooted fast in a foundation of love, and in order that we may be prepared to grasp the surpassing magnitude of Christ's love for us, and that we may know the knowledge-surpassing love of Christ and be filled with all the fullness of God. The perfect comprehension of the love of Christ is not possible to us, but we *can* have a *real* knowledge of that love which in its fullness surpasses knowledge. The realization of divine love is in store for the Christian who grows strong by means of His Spirit in the inward man. After the apostle's example, let us also pray earnestly for ourselves and our brethren in Christ, that we may increase in the power of spiritual perception and in participation in the spirit of Christ, until we may know by experience a real conception of the immeasurable love of God revealed and ministered in Christ—the love which sought us and bought us and seeks now to bless us above all we ask or think. "Behold, what manner of love!"

For Further Study:

Lambert, G. 'Christmas' *Zondervan Pictorial Encyclopedia of the Bible,* ed. M. C. Tenney, Vol. 1, Grand Rapids: Zondervan Publishing House, 1975.

Smith, Wilbur M. *Great Sermons on the Birth of Christ.* Boston: W. A. Wilde, 1963. Collection of sermons on the birth of our Lord by famous preachers.

# 17

# THE MESSAGE OF CHRISTMAS

There is perennial interest in the never-too-well-known story of the birth of Jesus, our Saviour. It really never grows old or loses its charm for the believer. Though the world grows old, this story is still unique; it is still "glad tidings of great joy"; it is still "to all the people." Though familiar, it is fresh; not merely because it is a rare idyll of rare beauty, but because of the deep and practical meaning that it always has for the present time for all people, and for the most significant things of life.

*"What Mean These Stones?"*

When Joshua led the tribes of Israel across the Jordan, while God held back the rushing waters and allowed them to walk over on dry ground, he took stones from the river bed to set up a monument on the bank. It was to cause the people to remember the great miracle, and to cause their children to ask, "What mean these stones?" Then they could tell the wonderful story of the faithfulness of God's promises, and of His great works in bringing them into the land. (Read Josh. 4). The celebration of Christmas is a monument to even greater works of God, sending His Son into the world to "bring many sons to glory." Christmas is especially adapted to make children ask, "What does it mean?" "Why do we have it?" We ought to keep it as a monument full of meaning!

I suppose that God is pleased if we celebrate, in sincerity, the coming of His Son into the world. However, He did not preserve for us a record of the day, or month, or even the year of that event. (Dating history from the birth of Christ was not invented until more than five centuries after, and did not come into general use for another five centuries. The monk who calculated the year of Jesus' birth made a mistake of at least five years, and the exact number can not yet be settled.) We simply agree to keep the traditional date, December 25, which has been commonly accepted since the fourth century. It is as good as any other. The Lord made no request or suggestion that we should celebrate the birth of Jesus, either at any particular time, or in any particular way, or at all. But the singing, rejoicing and worshipping done by Zacharias, Elizabeth, Mary, Simeon, Anna, the shepherds, angels, and Wise-men, in connection with the announcements and events of Christ's Nativity, are suggestive and somehow infectious. When we think seriously of the great unequaled event, we want to join in the psalms, carols, and adoration, and even in the prophetic dreams of what it will yet mean to the world of men that God's Son came to be one of us, born of a woman.

But, brethren, when we think of commemorating Christ's birth appropriately—when we consider whether Jesus Himself is pleased with Christmas—remember this: Jesus left a monument by which He did want to be remembered. He provided for a meaningful and solemn commemoration of His death in the "Lord's Supper." (See Matt. 26:26-29; Mark 14:22-25; Luke 22:14-19; Acts 20:7; I Cor. 11:23-28.) He was born to die—to be the Saviour of men (Matt. 1:21; 20:28; John 12:23-28, etc.). If we are sincere in our desire to hallow a special day or season to the memory of His birth we should neither refuse nor neglect to keep the memorial which He Himself consecrated to His death. We do not know that God wants us to keep Christmas; but we know for sure that He wants us to keep the feast of the communion of the body and blood of our Saviour (I Cor. 10:16). Since we do keep Christmas, let us make it a memorial of honor to Him and of meaning to our children—and ourselves.

*Christmas Speaks!*

Christmas does have a message for the world; let it speak clearly. It speaks of the love of God for man (John 3:16). Man at his best is dependent on God; but in his sin he is utterly helpless and hopelessly lost. The glorious thing about the birth of Jesus is the way it brings help from on high and shows that man's sad condition matters to God.

> There is considerable disposition today to treat Jesus as but a teacher, a prophet, a social leader. Let it be noticed that the Christmas message of the New Testament is clearly built around the essential fact that the Christ, or Messiah, is a Savior from sin. Joseph was clearly told that the name was to be Jesus, because He was to be a Savior from sin (Matt. 1:21), and He was announced to the shepherds as a Savior (Luke 2:11). The Christmas message is evangelistic.[1]

The old priest, Zacharias, in his inspired psalm at the birth of John, said: God "hath visited and wrought redemption for his people, and hath raised up a horn of salvation for us in the house of his servant, David." He also said that John would go before the face

[1] *Christian Standard,* (Dec. 23, 1933), p. 3 (1023).

of the Lord "to give knowledge of salvation unto his people in the remission of their sins" (Luke 1:68, 69, 77).

Christmas proclaims that God is faithful to keep His promises, which were made through the Old Testament prophets (Micah 5:2-4; Isa. 7:14; 9:6; 11:1, etc.). Notice how the decrees of heathen rulers and the deeds of men unconscious of God's purpose work together to fulfill His Word and the providential plan.

Christmas announces the coming of Immanuel, meaning "God with us" (Matt. 1:23), answering the cry of Job for a mediator (Job 9:33) and his desire that he might see God and settle with Him (Job 23:3 and 31:35), and bringing God's infinite power and wisdom to the aid of man with mercy equal to His righteousness. This means that we can now know God in the person of His Son who is the "brightness of his glory, and the very image of his substance" (Heb. 1:3), so that he who has seen the Son "hath seen the Father" (John 14:9). No less than a divine Savior can answer man's needs. His coming in the flesh gives us (1) the fixed certainty of historic facts of supernatural character as the basis for our faith, (2) absolute confidence in the covenant and the promises that He brings and offers to us, and (3) boldness to draw near to Him who has come so far to be near and helpful to us. We have great need of such a faith with firmness unto the end. The special information in the accounts of Jesus' birth that is worthy of space in the very brief accounts of His life is this: That Jesus is the only begotten Son of God, conceived of the Holy Spirit and born of a virgin.

The record of the exceedingly humble circumstances of Christ's birth emphasizes to us the great condescension of the Lord, becoming really human, subjecting Himself to the afflictions and temptations of the flesh. We know He was a man, but we realize more fully that He shared the flesh with us when we know He was a baby, too. Those same circumstances also proclaim eloquently that physical surroundings and such things as good housing, financial "security" and freedom from physical want are not everything in life, are not even necessary to greatness and glory undimmed. God can use the poor and humble when they that trust in riches, in worldly wisdom, and in political contrivance, can not be reached. The Christmas story warns us that the Lord Himself may be shut out of our lives by our being preoccupied with those other things. R. A. Torrey observed:

> It was not that the inn was hostile, it was simply preoccupied. That is the trouble in men's hearts today. They should have made room in the inn for Jesus, even though every one and everthing

else must be turned out, and we should make room for Him, no matter what else or who else has to go. They would have made room for Jesus had they known who He was. We do know, and yet we do not make room. Why not? (Jer. 17:9; John 15:24; Rom. 8:7).

Part of the Christmas message is the work and the interest of angels in accomplishing our redemption (Cf. Heb. 1:14 and I Pet. 1:12). Angels of heaven stood on earth with men and rejoiced at the works of God for the salvation of men. They also rejoice when one sinner repents (Luke 15:10).

The message that the angels brought began: "Fear not." All men, being defiled with sin, have great fear in the presence of the righteous power of God or holy messengers from heaven, ever since Adam was afraid and hid himself. God is trying to reconcile us unto Himself, to take away our sin and to take away our fear. We do need to reverence Him, and the reverent "fear of the Lord is the beginning of wisdom," but we need also to trust Him. "Fear not, little flock, it is the Father's good pleasure to give you the kingdom" (Luke 12:32).

It is "good tidings of great joy" that Christmas angels bring. They know that it is not for their salvation, but for us; yet they rejoice greatly to see the goodness of God (Cf. Heb. 2:16.) How ought men to rejoice! At the coming of Jesus for our redemption we should have greater joy than men being released from a prison camp, greater than the joy of a blind man receiving sight, greater joy than that of a battle-weary soldier at the coming of peace, joy that exceeds all these, because the coming of Jesus to earth means all this to us and much more. The best good news the world will ever hear is this ancient gospel, the story of Jesus, a Savior who is Christ the Lord. O that all were as humble and believing as those lowly shepherds.

It is a message of peace. "The angels invoke blessing on God and peace upon men, peace between God and man, and ultimately peace between man and man. The love of God is shed abroad upon all, even the vilest of sinners (Rom. 5:8; I Tim. 1:15); but this peace comes upon those who have accepted His Son, and in whom He is therefore especially well pleased (Rom. 9:11)."[2]

For Further Study:

Geldenhuys, Norval. *Commentary on the Gospel of Luke.* (New Inter-

---

[2] J. W. McGarvey and P. Y. Pendleton, *The Fourfold Gospel.* (Cincinnati: Standard Publishing Co., n.d.), p. 31.

national Commentary), Grand Rapids: W. B. Eerdmans, 1951. Pp. 99-115. Comments on Luke 2:1-20.

Arndt, William F. *The Gospel According to St. Luke.* St. Louis: Concordia Publishing House, 1956. Pp. 71-88. Comment on Luke 21:1-20 with special notes on "The Census of Cyrenius" and "The Date of Jesus' Birth."

Edersheim, Alfred. *The Life and Times of Jesus the Messiah,* 3rd ed. Grand Rapids: Wm. B. Eerdmans, 1956 reprint of 1886 ed. Vol. 1, pp. 180-190. Good information on the Jewish background on this text.

Geldenhuys, Norval. *New International Commentary: Commentary on the Gospel of Luke.* Grand Rapids: Wm. B. Eerdmans, 1951. Pp. 99-115. Comment on Luke 2:1-20.

Plummer, Alfred. *International Critical Commentary: The Gospel According to St. Luke,* 10th ed. Edinburgh: T. & T. Clark Publishing, 1914. On Greek text.

## *Part Five*

# EARLY MINISTRY

## 18

### WHY JESUS CAME

"God, having of old time spoken unto the fathers in the prophets by divers portions and in divers manners, hath at the end of these days spoken unto us in his Son" (Heb. 1:1, 2). The voice of God unto the fathers in the prophets ceased with Malachi and remained silent four hundred years. Then the silence was broken by the angel Gabriel announcing the birth of John and of Jesus. Various inspired and prophetic utterances accompanied the birth and babyhood of John and Jesus. Then "came John the Baptist," "in the spirit and power of Elijah," "a prophet and much more than a prophet," "preaching in the wilderness" "make ye ready the way of the Lord."

*"After John . . . Jesus Came"*

John was the forerunner to herald the coming of the Christ, as predicted in Isaiah 40:3, 4 and Malachi 3:1; 4:5, 6. He was born about six months before Jesus, and apparently started his public ministry about six months before Jesus did. But the imprisonment of John was not the beginning of Jesus' ministry, only of His Galilean ministry. While John's ministry was at its height of popularity, Jesus was baptized by John, endured the forty days' fast and temptations in the wilderness (Matt. 3:13—4:11), returned to John, called disciples, went into Galilee to the wedding at Cana (John 1:29—2:2), and with His disciples and family made His abode in Capernaum "not many days" (John 2:12). John was still preaching during Jesus' early ministry in Judea, which began with the cleansing of the temple at the Passover (John 2:13), brought Jesus' popular following to exceed John's (John 3:26, 30; 4:1) and ended with the journey through Samaria eight or nine months after the Passover—"four months till harvest" (John 4:35).

*He came in fulfillment of the Old Testament promises.* All of the events and records of the Old Testament were to prepare for the coming of Christ. He is the "seed" of Abraham in whom "all the nations of the earth shall be blessed" (Gen. 22:15). He is the "Shiloh" or the coming one to whom the ruler's staff belongs (Gen. 49:10). He is the "prophet" (Deut. 18:15-18); the "shoot out of the stock of Jesse" (Isa. 11:1-5, 10); the Son of David (Ps. 89:3, 4); Jehovah's anointed (Ps. 2:2); Jehovah's Son (Ps. 2:7); the "priest for ever after the order of Melchizedek" (Ps. 110:4); the "Wonderful Counsellor, Mighty God, Everlasting Father, Prince of Peace" (Isa. 9:6); the suffering Servant (Isa. 53); the "ruler in Israel" (Micah 5:2); the King that cometh (Zech. 9:9); the "most holy" and the "anointed one" (Dan. 9:24, 25); the "Branch" (Jer. 33:15; Zech. 3:8). Indeed, this was He "of whom Moses in the law, and the prophets, wrote" (John 1:45). The hopes and the struggles, the judgments and the forbearance of the centuries are justified in Him (Cf. Rom. 3:25).

*He came as no other ever came.* Only He was ever born of a virgin; the eternal God was His Father. Only He ever came voluntarily from a previous existence. Only He was sent into the world as He was sent (John 5:36-38; 8:42; 17:8). Only He came down from heaven to earth, from glory to suffering, from Lordship to obedient service. No other ever came accompanied by a choir of angels, preceded by such ages of preparation and longing, faced with such a heavy assignment.

"Think not that I came to destroy the law or the prophets: I came not to destroy, but to fulfill" (Matt. 5:17). Jesus did come to keep the promises of God, but those promises were made because He was coming; He did not do His works merely to follow the suggestions of a literature expounding a national dream.

### *"To Do . . . the Will of Him That Sent Me"*

"For I am come down from heaven not to do mine own will, but the will of him that sent me" (John 6:38; 5:30). It is the world's salvation that He perfectly fulfilled this purpose. Every act of His was instituted of God and approved of God. Every promise He makes will be performed by the power of God. His many words approving of the Old Testament are the certifications of the God of truth.

"I am come a light into the world, that whosoever, believeth on me may not abide in darkness" (John 12:46). See also John 3:19-21; 8:12. It is still true that the "darkness apprehended it not." After nineteen hundred years of light, men still blindfold themselves because they love darkness rather than light.

"To this end have I been born, and to this end am I come into the world, that I should bear witness unto the truth. Every one that is of the truth heareth my voice" (John 18:37). He came to preach the coming kingdom; He came to make known the standards of divine righteousness. Thank God, He proclaimed the *good news* of mercy, release and redemption! For He preached not only the rule of divine authority over the affairs of men, and not only the law of perfect righteousness, but He proclaimed pardon and redemption for all men, an expression of divine love undreamed of.

### *"A Ransom For Many"*

"The Son of man came not to be ministered unto, but to minister, and to give his life a ransom for many" (Matt. 20:28). He labored day and night, going about "doing good," showing the love of God for the needy and the power of God to save. He set a perfect example of the kind of greatness which He preached in contrast to the world's twisted ideas of greatness (Mark 10:42-44; John 13:1-15).

"I came not to judge the world, but to save the world" (John 3:17; 12:47; Luke 5:31, 32). "For the Son of man came to seek and to save that which was lost" (Luke 19:10). See I Tim. 1:15. "Not wishing that any should perish" (II Pet. 3:9), "God was in Christ reconciling the world unto himself" (II Cor. 5:19). Sin separates men from God, dooms them to eternal punishment in the lake of fire, Jesus knew the terrible punishment of sin, and in order to save men from it He was even willing to take their sin upon Himself. After He had shown Himself free from all sin and worthy to be the ransom, He bore the unfathomable punishment of the cross and "gave his life a ransom for many."

"God sent forth his Son, born of a woman, born under the law, that he might redeem them that were under the law, that we might receive the adoption of sons" (Gal. 4:4, 5). The great bondage of the Hebrew nation was not to foreign empires, but to their sins (John 8:31-36) which, through the responsibility which the law placed upon them, made even the law and covenant of God to be a "ministration of condemnation" (II Cor. 3:4-11). A knowledge of right is not enough to save! The knowledge of the Word of God is able to make one wise unto salvation only through the faith that is in Christ Jesus (II Tim. 3:15).

"Whom God set forth to be a propitiation, through faith, in his blood, to show his righteousness . . . that he himself might be just, and the justifier of him that hath faith in Jesus" (Rom. 3:25, 26). He fulfilled the requirements of the law and of all holy and righteous standards in His personal life, then He satisfied all the requirements of justice in giving Himself as a ransom, in bearing in Himself the penalties from which He would set free those who come in faith to receive the gift of His mercy.

*"Taste of Death for Every Man"*

"That by the grace of God he should taste of death for every man" (Heb. 2:9). "For this cause came I unto this hour" (John 12:27). "The Son of man must suffer . . . and be killed" (Mark 8:31; Luke 24:26). Jesus came into the world to die. He faced the temptation to avoid it and by the word of God overcame. He succeeded in His assignment; He finished His work, for He sanctified Himself in death to give life to you and me. He seeks that we should remember His death above all the works of His life (Luke 22:19).

"I came that they may have life, and may have it more abundantly" (John 10:10). "The wages of sin is death; but the free gift of God is eternal life in Christ Jesus our Lord" (Rom. 6:23). "And the witness is this, that God gave unto us eternal life, and this life is in his Son. He that hath the Son hath the life; he that hath not the Son of God hath not the life" (I John 5:11, 12). "Man's life consisteth not in the abundance of things which he possesseth" (Luke 12:15). God would give life, not merely things. It is a shameful blasphemy that men would so pervert Jesus' statement of His benevolent purposes that they turn this verse to application to things of this world. No matter what abundance of things a man may call his own, he is poor, wretched and blind—an object of pity that breaks God's heart—until he receives the Son of God and His righteousness. "Work not for the food that perishes, but for the food that abideth unto eternal life, which the Son of man shall give you: for him the Father, even God, hath sealed" (John 6:27). Jesus will restore us to the paradise of God where is the tree of life.

"For judgment came I into this world, that they that see not may see; and that they that see may become blind" (John 9:39). "Think not that I came not to send peace, but a sword" (Matt. 10:34-36; Luke 12:49-53). He said he did not come to judge the world, that is, not to judge and to impose a sentence upon all the works of men. He will come again for that when the day of mercy is past, but He did come with a burning issue that divides sharply between the subjects of God's kingdom and the aliens. It is an issue that will never cease or fade in importance—the sides of it will never be compromised until He comes again to receive His followers into the kingdom of eternal peace and to destroy those who are not willing that He should reign over them. He will fully triumph over evil.

For Further Study:

Morgan, G. Campbell. *The Crises of the Christ.* New York: Fleming

H. Revell Company, 1903. Pp. 84-94. Chapter considering the meaning, value and purpose of Christ's mission to earth.

Smith, Wilbur. *Therefore Stand.* Grand Rapids: Baker Book House, 1939. Pp. 45-53. In answering a liberal view on the purpose of Jesus' coming, Mr. Smith points out the Biblical teaching.

Warfield, B. B. *Biblical Doctrines.* New York: Oxford University Press, 1929. Pp. 255-324. An essay on Jesus' mission according to His own testimony.

# 19

## PREPARATION FOR MINISTRY

### *Son of God—Son of Man*

Jesus had grown up as a son of man, "subject to" Mary and Joseph. His development was normal according to the true human ideal—"Jesus advanced in wisdom and stature, and in favor with God and men" (Luke 2:52)—but also unique, "filled with wisdom, and the grace of God was upon him." At twelve years of age He revealed His awareness of Sonship to God and special mission in life. His foreknowledge of His ministry and of its climax on Calvary greatly affected the meaning of His baptism and His temptations which marked the beginning of that ministry. Still He was baptized and tempted as a son of man.

### *The Baptism of Jesus*

It is very fitting that Jesus began His public life with an act of obedience to the Word of God through His forerunner. He came as one of the people to obey God's messenger. It was an act of humiliation that seems to us hard to harmonize with His divine birth and sinlessness.

John, a kinsman of Jesus (Luke 1:36), though he had lived apart from Jesus (Luke 1:80) and "knew him not" (John 1:33), still knew enough about Him (whether naturally or supernaturally) to hesitate to baptize Him. John's baptism was "of repentance unto remission of sins" (Mark 1:4), and ordinarily the people came "confessing their sins" (Matt. 3:5). When the Pharisees and Sadducees came without repentance and confession of sins, John, by miraculous insight, knew their hearts, condemned them for their pretense and demanded "fruit worthy of repentance." But when Jesus came without any sins to confess or to repent of, John said, "I have need to be baptized of thee, and comest thou to me?" (Matt. 3:14).

Jesus did not disclaim the holiness and superiority John ascribed to Him. Jesus did not insist that perhaps He had some hidden fault that needed forgiveness. He indicated the very opposite and showed the true reason for His baptism in His reply: "Suffer it now, for thus it becometh us to fulfill all righteousness" (Matt. 3:15). "Now" He was as one of Israel; the time would come when His person and perfection would be made known. Meanwhile, even a perfectly righteous man must obey God in order to remain righteous.

The baptism of Jesus puts the stamp of divine authority upon John's ministry, while John bears witness to the sinlessness of Jesus.

The baptism of Jesus marked a turning point in His life—not a turning from sin to do the will of God, but a turning from quiet home life at Nazareth to take up the burden laid upon Him as Messiah. This is emphasized by the descent of the Holy Spirit upon him "in bodily form as a dove," and by the testimony of God's voice, saying, "Thou art my beloved Son: in thee I am well pleased" (Luke 3:22).

The descent of the Spirit upon Jesus has been compared with the anointing of the priests who began their service at thirty years of age. But exactly what it brought to Him is a puzzle to us when we remember that He was born of the Spirit and was in His own nature divine. Even John was "filled with the Holy Spirit even from his mother's womb" (Luke 1:15). Jesus was not without the Spirit before His baptism. Only one purpose of this visible appearance of the Spirit is stated in the Scripture; i.e., to identify the Christ to John (John 1:32-34). However, it is likely that it meant much to Jesus; such as the full restoration to Him of divine powers and foreknowledge of which He "emptied himself" in becoming a babe. Jesus worked no miracles before this (John 2:11). The temptations that immediately follow this are closely connected with His consciousness of miracle-working power and with the foreseeing of the cross.

### *The Temptations of Jesus*

The Spirit took charge of Jesus and led Him forcibly into the lonely wastes to be tempted. In order to help us when we are tempted, and in order to represent us before God, He was tempted as a man "in all points like as we are" (Heb. 2:18; 4:15).

*He was tempted of the devil.* God may try us with clear issues, but He does not tempt anyone (James 1:12, 13). The devil tempts with deceit and would ensnare us with hidden traps. The devil really exists and we must suffer his attacks (I Pet. 5:8, 9); hence, Jesus submitted to his worst blows that He might become a perfect Savior for us (Heb. 2:18; 5:8, 9). The devil came to Him, probably not in any visible form, but as he comes to us—with inward suggestions of falsehood and wrong in the guise of truth and right. It is not a sin to be tempted, but we should pray that we enter not into temptation (Matt. 26:41).

*He fasted forty days.* Luke says, "He did eat nothing." It has been suggested that, as an athlete trains up to the peak of his strength for a contest, Jesus trained *down* to meet the devil under the most adverse conditions, making the victory more conclusive.

Most temptations of serious weight have more than one hook by which to catch us. These temptations were designed to trap the greatest mind and the best heart that ever was tempted. They seem to be made to lure Him in several ways at once and to hide the real sinfulness of the acts suggested. If we can't see fully and exactly how they enticed Him to do wrong, it is not surprising. We can learn this one major lesson: that Satan is very subtle and we can be safe from his lies only by following closely the Word of God. But further study will be richly rewarded. Many valuable lessons can be learned from them, in addition to those suggested here.

*The temptation to make bread* was to throw Jesus' will out of gear with God's will. It was an urge to distrust God's care and to act independently in looking out for Himself. While every cell in Jesus' body cried out for food, the devil said to Jesus, in effect: "You are the Son of God with miraculous power. You need not suffer so. You are the Creator of nature. Just command nature to serve you." It was a temptation to be not a son of man, but to fall back on miraculous power in meeting the tests of men. And if He had, what calamity for us! But Satan's deceits coupled with the pangs of starvation, could not wrench Jesus' will from His Father's will. This was He who later said, "My meat is to do the will of him that sent me." All the bread in the world is not life without God. Bread is not a necessity of life, but to obey every word of God is.

*The temptation to jump off the temple.* The devil can quote Scripture, or misquote it. Here he tries to make a conditional promise appear unconditional. Here he tries to turn Jesus' trust into presumption. It is as if Satan said:

> Yes, you are the favored Son of God for whom the Father will not fail to care. You may count on all His angels to serve you. You may go without food and not starve. Just show your complete confidence in His promises. Test and attest your trust in God. Cast yourself down from the height of the temple and show the people the proof of your Sonship.

But Jesus could not be enticed to tempt God in an exhibition of false "trust." *Obedience is the only real expression of trust in God.*

> To go before God is to go without God, and to go without Him is to go against Him; and as to the angels bearing Him up in their hands, that depends altogether upon the path and the errand. Let it be the divinely ordered path, and the unseen convoys of

> heaven will attend, a sleepless, invincible guard; but let it be some forbidden way, and the angel's sword will flash its warning, and send the foot of the unfaithful servant crushing against the wall.[1]

*The temptation to rule the world*

> was an appeal to reveal Himself in the fulness of His power and authority as above generals, princes, kings . . . An appeal to obtain by physical rather than by spiritual power; by the short-cut path of policy rather than by the long road of suffering and martyrdom. Jesus came to obtain the kingdoms of the world . . . He must reign until He puts all His enemies under His feet, and until all the kingdoms of the world become His kingdom. Satan's way to obtain this kingdom differed from God's way.[2]

If Satan could not prevent the kingdom of Christ, he would, if possible, change its character—from kingdom of heaven to kingdom of earth, from regeneration to regimentation. It was a many-sided appeal. It looked like a way to *avoid the cross.* It offered easy and quick results. How many reforms He could accomplish immediately with power over the nations and all their resources. Alas, how often the churches have fallen for this bait, and how many men have! "Many parents, in encouraging their children to seek earthly glory and distinction, unconsciously assist Satan in urging this temptation."[3]

But Jesus was not led to do wrong for the price of power and reward, nor for "the good He could do" thereby. Moreover, He didn't argue with Satan the relative merits of methods; He just kept God in sight and God's Word in mind and the love of God in His heart. All was settled without argument when God had spoken. "It is written, Thou shalt worship the Lord thy God, and him only shalt thou serve." "No other gods." It is all the same whether we worship Satan, or mammon, the gift that he offers.

Jesus overcame by the *sword of the Spirit* and the *shield of faith.* In Him was truly fulfilled the saying, "Thy word have I hid in my heart, that I might not sin against thee" (Ps. 119:11).

This momentous contest means much to us. Our champion was

---

[1] Henry Burton, *The Gospel According to St. Luke: Expositor's Bible* (New York: A. C. Armstrong and Son, 1902), pp. 125-126.

[2] J. W. McGarvey and P. Y. Rendleton, *The Fourfold Gospel* (Cincinnati: Standard Publishing Co., n.d.), p. 97.

[3] *Ibid.*

victor. The temptations overcome were representative. We see in them "the world, the flesh and the devil." They were physical, intellectual and spiritual. He was tempted in the first as a man, in the second and as a divine Son and in the third as the Messiah. He was asked to use power over nature and coerce stones; over the angels and coerce God; over the world and coerce men—all for self. Yet He overcame them all by a simple reliance upon God's Word rightly applied. For us there is with every temptation the same way of escape (I Corinthians 10:13).

For Further Study:

Foster, R. C. *Studies in the Life of Christ.* Grand Rapids: Baker Book House, 1971. Pp. 314-337. Discusses the Biblical accounts of Jesus' baptism and temptations and answers questions relating to these events.

Fowler, Harold. *The Gospel of Matthew,* Vol. I, Joplin, MO: College Press, 1968. Pp. 111-153.

# 20

## JESUS DEMONSTRATES HIS AUTHORITY (John 2)

When Jesus was about thirty years old, He was baptized by John in the Jordan River, down near the Dead Sea. The Holy Spirit descended upon Him in a visible form like a dove, and the voice of God spoke from heaven to approve Him and to acclaim Him God's own Son.

Then He went into the wild and barren regions nearby and fasted for forty days, being tempted by Satan. He was victorious over all the temptations and returned to where John was baptizing.

John the Baptist pointed out Jesus as the one about whom he had been making predictions. John told his disciples that Jesus was the Lamb of God that takes away the sins of the world, that He was the one who would baptize in the Holy Spirit and in fire, and that He was the Son of God. John told how he knew these things by a special message from God and by the visible sign of the Holy Spirit coming down and abiding upon Jesus (John 1:29-37).

Two of John's disciples followed Jesus and spent most of the day with Him. One of them was Andrew, who then found his brother Peter and brought him to Jesus. The other seems to have been either John, the writer of this Gospel, or his brother James; and it is implied that he also brought his brother to Jesus. Then Jesus called Philip, and Philip brought Nathanael. These six men were probably the disciples who went with Jesus to the marriage feast at Cana.

Following His first miracle in Galilee, when Jesus was in Jerusalem for the Passover feast He cleansed the temple, the first great public act of His ministry. In these two events at the beginning of His ministry He dramatically demonstrated His authority as the Son of God.

### *The Miracle At The Marriage in Cana* (John 2:1-11)

Cana was the home town of Nathanael. It was only a few miles from Nazareth, where Jesus grew up. It was not more than twenty miles from Bethsaida and Capernaum, from which the other disciples came. Jesus and His disciples were invited to the marriage. Perhaps Mary was more an assistant at the feast than a guest. She evidently felt a need to do something about the shortage of wine. It is not strange that she was bold enough to be on the verge of telling Him what to do. Her words to Him, "they have no wine," seem to be taken by Him to mean that she expected Him to do something about it.

The idioms of His reply sound strange to us and are likely to be misunderstood. His word of address, "Woman," was not disrespectful, or harsh, or rude (see John 19:26; 20:13; Luke 13:12). "What have I to do with thee?" is the common meaning of an idiom which says literally, "What is it to me and to thee?" It is used in Mark 1:24; 5:7; Matthew 8:29, and Luke 8:28 idiomatically, but here in John it may mean "What is it to us?" Then He said, "Mine hour is not yet come," which apparently means that the hour for a public and miraculous display of His powers as Messiah had not yet come. Certainly it implies that something more significant was contemplated by Mary and Jesus than merely leaving the feast, or making some other humble human attempt to relieve the embarrassment of the host. The whole answer of Jesus was probably intended to suggest to Mary that she had no right to dictate to Him what He should do. He was directed by God; and He showed no favoritism toward His family or His home town (Matt. 12:46-50). Jesus came to do God's work in God's way, at the time and place that God would direct. It was not yet time for Him to make a public display of His supernatural power. Jesus' ministry was conducted in keeping with God's timetable (John 7:6, 8; 7:30; 8:20; 12:23; 13:1; 17:1).

Nevertheless, Mary was not totally discouraged. Somehow she so trusted in His ability and in His readiness to help that, although she did not try to persuade Him, she prepared the servants with her words of wonderful faith in the Master, who had been her son: "Whatsoever he saith unto you, do it" (John 2:5). Mary had complete faith in Jesus' ability to do whatever was best to do. While she was completely willing to leave to Him the decision about what He should do she had sensed in His answer to her that He was ready to act at the proper time. She communicated her faith to the servants so that they would be ready to carry out instructions that might seem strange and out of order, coming from a guest.

Certainly Mary was not accustomed to seeing Jesus work miracles to relieve His family and friends of need or embarrassment. John distinctly says that this miracle at Cana was the beginning of Jesus' signs. If she did expect a miracle (and it seems hard to avoid that conclusion) it must have been some demonstration or announcement of His Messiahship, such as Jesus was not ready to make at that time. The fact is, He did go ahead and work a miracle; but it was one which was known only to the servants and the disciples (John 2:9).

Jesus told the servants to fill the waterpots to the brim. These waterpots for ceremonial washings held twenty to twenty-five gallons each. The servants gave a sample of this newly created wine to the ruler of the feast. He was the chief waiter, one in charge of the banquet, or a master of ceremonies. Evidently the ruler of the feast was not in the same room as the waterpots when Jesus had them filled. Jesus did not attract attention of anyone except the servants that drew the water and the apostles. The ruler of the feast was surprised. He does not affirm that anyone was drunk at this feast, but only that men usually serve the good wine first; then when people have had plenty to drink, they serve what is not so good. The verb may mean either to be intoxicated or to have drunk freely. This verse certainly does not say that Jesus made intoxicating wine, but it indicates that what He made was of exceptional quality.

No one should neglect the good things in this lesson to argue over the kind of wine Jesus made. John, writing as directed by the Holy Spirit, did not consider it necessary to explain what kind it was. A discussion about it is fruitless because of the lack of facts to settle it. Moreover, the question usually arises from the desire either to excuse selfish indulgence or to judge rather than to edify a brother. Either motive is legalistic and unworthy of a Christian. Wine was regularly an important food item in those times. Grapes were the third most important fruit of the land. Jesus ate and drank in a normal manner, in contrast to John the Baptist. He was even abused for it (Matt. 11:19; Luke 7:34). Their wine was not always strongly intoxicating, and seems to have been called wine when it was not intoxicating at all. But when it was intoxicating its use was restricted or forbidden; excessive drinking and drunkenness were definitely condemned (Lev. 10:9; Prov. 23:29-32; 31:4, 5; I Cor. 6:10; I Tim. 3:3, 8). Surely Jesus would not approve the modern liquor traffic with its terrible results. New Testament teaching is firmly against all the selfishness, irresponsibility, lawlessness, and associated evils involved in the use of alcoholic beverages. Drunkenness could not be more clearly condemned (I Cor. 6:10; 5:11; Gal. 5:21; Eph. 5:18). The New Testament teaches the Christian out of love to have nothing to do with anything, though it be a liberty, that causes so many to stumble and fall into sin (I Cor. 8-10; Rom. 14 and 15).

The first "sign" apparently was (1) a work of kindness to a friend who had invited Him and His followers to a feast although the provisions were quite limited; (2) an answer to the unwavering and reverent faith of Mary; (3) a sign for the benefit of the disciples and for all of us to whom it has become known; (4) but not a great public display at that time. This beginning of miracles showed His great power over nature, the power to create, His goodness in the use of His power, His wisdom, self-restraint, and perfect mastery of the situation. His disciples had indicated and expressed faith in Him before this. But seeing the miracle made their faith in Him much more than the acceptance of words the meaning of which they could not fully grasp.

### *Cleansing the Temple in Jerusalem*

Jesus really began His public preaching and manifestation of Himself at Jerusalem at the Passover feast, just three years before His crucifixion. He drove the grafting merchandisers from the temple courts twice—at both the first and last Passovers of His ministry (John 2:13-15; Matt. 21:12, 13). It was an outrage to turn the house of the righteous God, built for worship in repentance and contrition, into a place of greed and robbery.

This was a bold assertion of His authority in the affairs of the nation and in the things of God. Jesus spoke with authority on the right use of God's temple. Although the meetinghouse of a church should be a house of prayer, and certainly not a den of graft, still no church building of today is really equivalent to the temple in Jerusalem. The New Testament gives us no precedent of any special building set apart for church and worship purposes. God's temple in the Christian age is not made with hands (Acts 17:24). It is the body of the individual Christian (I Cor. 6:19, 20; II Cor. 6:16) and the whole congregation of believers (I Cor. 3:16, 17; Eph. 2:20-22). Let us not destroy the holiness or strength of our bodies with drugs, indulgence, or any corruption. Let us not strain at gnats such as eating in a "church" basement while we swallow camels, like destroying the congregation's fellowship and effectiveness with envy, pride, and parsimony, or using a church to exalt men rather than God.

When Christ comes into our lives as He did into the temple and puts out everything selfish and unsuitable to the service of God, it is no intrusion, but it is His natural right to do so.

### *Authority*

Both the miracle at Cana and the cleansing of the temple reveal Jesus' authority. Christ's authority is supremely important. *Jesus means nothing to us unless we acknowledge His authority.* Christianity is essentially authoritarian. It is not to be denied, of course, that between man and man Christianity promotes mutual respect and brotherliness, hence democracy in the affairs of men; but Christ's church is not a democracy. The church is not a society of men; it is the kingdom of Christ, and He is head over all things pertaining to it (Eph. 1:22).

Jesus' life and ministry were full of gentleness, love, lowliness, and self-sacrifice. He "came not to be ministered unto, but to minister, and to give his life a ransom for many" (Matt. 20:28). But at the same time He constantly asserted unlimited authority. He claimed and exercised authority over the temple of God, over the realm of nature (John 2:19; Matt. 8:27), over the forgiveness of sin (Mark 2:10, 11), over the lives of all men (Matt. 7:22, 23; 10:32, 33; 12:30; Luke 9:59; John 5:22-29; 8:24), over death and the grave (John 5:25-29; 10:17, 18; 11:43, 44), over demons and angels (Luke 4:36; 9:1; Matt. 26:53). He "taught as one having authority," indeed (Matt. 7:29). *In fact, He claimed all authority in heaven and on earth!* (Matt. 28:18). *If He did not actually have supreme authority unquestionable, then He was not a good man, but a usurper, an imposter, and the world's biggest liar.*

Jesus' authority was not assumed; neither was it delegated; it was inherent in His person. All who believe that He is the eternal Son of God must acknowledge His authority. So Mary, the mother of His human flesh, knowing well His supernatural origin and character, expressed her confidence and respect toward Him in her words to the servants at the marriage: "Whatsoever he saith unto you, do it" (John 2:5).

The fishermen of Galilee set us a good example. When Jesus came by in the morning after they had washed their nets to put them away for the day, and told them to put out into the deep for a catch, Peter answered: "Master, we toiled all night, and took nothing; *but at thy word I will let down the nets*" (Luke 5:5). Their deference to His authority was amply rewarded. The modern scientific spirit would have said: "We have experimented. What you say to do will not work; for we have tried it." Experiment is necessary where all parties concerned are ignorant. But faith is able to reach far beyond the limit of human observation and experiment when it has a teacher with authority in whom to put confidence safely. Peter recognized in Jesus an authority greater than his experience.

For Further Study:

Butler, Paul. *The Gospel of John.* Joplin: College Press, 1961. Pp. 63-84. Helpful comment on John 2:1-22.

Foster, R. *Studies in the Life of Christ.* Grand Rapids: Baker Book

House, 1971. Pp. 352-365. Discussion of the wedding feast in Cana and the cleansing of the temple with answers to unbelieving critics.

Geldenhuys, Norval. "Authority and the Bible" in *Revelation and the Bible* ed. by Carl Henry. Grand Rapids: Baker Book House, 1958. Pp. 371-386. Shows that respect for the authority of Christ leads to respect for the authority of the Bible as well.

Taylor, William. *The Miracles of Our Savior.* New York: Harper and Row, Publishers, n.d. Pp. 28-45. Explanation of the miracle of changing water into wine, John 2:1-11.

# 21

## THE NEW BIRTH (John 3)

Bible readers overlook the extent and significance of Jesus' early ministry in Judea, which occupied nearly one-fourth of His entire public career. Only John tells of it, and he gives but a brief summary.

After the wedding at Cana, Jesus moved to Capernaum, then went to Jerusalem for the Passover. There He really began His public ministry with the cleansing of the temple. During the eight or nine months Jesus was in Judea He worked many miracles and drew many disciples to Him (John 2:23; 3:2, 26). During the same time, John the Baptist was still preaching and baptizing multitudes about forty miles northeast of Jerusalem. People who believed and repented at Jesus' preaching were baptized by His disciples, and they became more numerous than those being baptized by John (John 4:1, 2).

The ruling Pharisees and Sadducees had looked with disfavor upon the early popularity of John (John 1:19-28; Matt. 3:7-12). Their opposition to Jesus was aroused by His cleansing of the temple because that injured their prestige and disturbed a profitable monopoly. Jesus' increasing ministry near Jerusalem caused their hostility to grow. Therefore, when John was imprisoned by Herod, Jesus went into Galilee.

### *"Nicodemus . . . Came To Him By Night"*

In the early part of this Judean ministry, Nicodemus, one of the ruling Pharisees and one who had seen Jesus' miracles, came to Jesus by night, saying, "Rabbi, we know that thou art a teacher come from God; for no one can do these signs that thou doest, except God be with him" (John 3:2). As a Pharisee, he was part of the elite ruling class. Pharisees were firm believers in the Old Testament and were strict in their observance of many traditional regulations. They believed in life after death and in the coming kingdom of the Messiah. Nicodemus was a member of the Sanhedrin, a body of seventy men which was the supreme court and senate of the Jews (John 7:45-53).

Nicodemus rightly judged that Jesus' miracles were evidence of the power of God working through Him, yet Nicodemus feared men. He received a wonderful opportunity that night. He heard words of infinite wisdom from the divine teacher. But Nicodemus seemed to want to investigate Jesus from a distance, as it were, semi-officially and impersonally, rather than to submit himself to Jesus in faith, to learn by experience in following Him, and to receive the full light and power of His divine teaching by following it step by step. We do not know why he came at night: perhaps to have more time with Jesus when there was no crowd, perhaps to avoid criticism.

Two and a half years later, Nicodemus was still in the Sanhedrin, among the enemies of Jesus, daring only to suggest that Jesus should receive a fair trial before He was condemned (John 7:50). Finally, after the crucifixion, Nicodemus appeared the third and last time in the Bible records (John 19:38-40). He helped Joseph of Arimathea, another secret disciple, to bury Jesus, and he furnished a large quantity of costly spices or perfumes. We do not know whether he ever entirely overcame his timidity or desire for the favor of men and really became a fruitful Christian.

### *"Except A Man Be Born Again, He Cannot See The Kingdom."*

Of the most interest to us is what Jesus taught Nicodemus concerning the necessity of a new birth for all men. The Kingdom of God is the reign of God, the realm in which God's rule is recognized and obeyed and in which the blessings of His grace are enjoyed. To see the kingdom is to have part in salvation and eternal life. No one can be a part of that kingdom without a spiritual change, without beginning a new life with and in Christ.

Jesus' deity is shown in the uniqueness and superiority of His ideas. His purposes were eternal, universal, worthy of God. His understanding was perfect. He "needed not that any one should bear witness concerning man; for he himself knew what was in man" (John 2:25). Jesus *solved* problems no philosopher had been keen enough to see. The idea of reforming or renovating men by regenerating them was a superior and original idea. The fact that Ezekiel (36:26-31) and Jeremiah (31:33) has mentioned the making of a new heart and a new spirit in men only emphasizes that it was a divine purpose; and the fact that they did not carry out the idea, but predicted it as an ideal, emphasizes the truth that such regeneration could be accomplished only by the divine Son and Savior.

Jesus' teaching on the new birth well illustrates His divine ability to put the most profound meanings into available form with simple approach. He is the wisdom of God to every one that believeth.

Our lives have been broken, condemned, forfeited, lost by sin. But Jesus came to give us life. We sold ourselves into the grip and under the doom of sin. Jesus came to release us from the grip and redeem us from the doom. He had to settle the matter of that old life with its ingrained sin and its obligations incurred by sin. He had to establish the new—to bring forth life that is not under the dominion and the curse of sin—life that is subject to God so that God can maintain it and sustain it eternally.

Therefore, the gospel of Christ has a twofold function. It puts to death, and it brings to life. Read Romans 6:2-14; II Corinthians 5:14-17, and Galatians 2:20. Now look over Colossians 2:20—3:17, noting such expressions as these: "If ye died with Christ, . . . If then ye were raised together with Christ, . . .For ye died, and your life is hid with Christ in God. . . . Put to death therefore your members . . . put off the old man . . . put on the new man."

If Christ is to save us from the just condemnation and inherent weakness of our Godless lives, then we must die in Him and He must live in us. Does that sound mysterious? But it is not impossible. Jesus said it another way: "If any man will come after me, let him deny himself, and take up his cross, and follow me (Matt. 16:24).

He died not His death, but ours. His death as a sacrifice is offered a standing offer to us to be reckoned our death (of the old man and his condemnation) if we will accept it. To accept it is to give consent that my life—my private life, my alien-to-God life—is done for. It is condemned, and that condemnation is laid upon Jesus, my Friend. But I must join in that death, the pain of which He bore for me. My pride, my desire, my will must perish from the earth. And the life that I live (because He died for me), the life that is left by mercy unto me, must be His. His Spirit must supplant mine. I must be a branch of Him, the vine, and receive my life and bear my fruit in Him. I must be inseparable from Him, a member of His body. I have life only because He died for me, and my life is sustained only because and while He lives in me.

". . . The whole world lieth in wickedness" (I John 5:19, KJV. ASV has "in the evil one."). The whole world is guilty before God and under sentence to die (Rom. 3:19; 6:23). The state of man in sin is such that it repenteth God that He hath made man. A comprehensive contemplation of man in his sins makes us to say, "Why doesn't God wipe out this sin-degraded race and make a creature that is not subject to sin's dominion and seduction? Why doesn't He make a *new race of men* that will do His will?" That is *exactly* what He is doing! Thank God that He was not willing to lose what could be saved out of the burning! Thank God that *we* have an opportunity through Christ to *choose* to be of that new creation; to cut off the old man voluntarily and let the Lord of life remake us. Thank God that He has designed to use this life and this race as the seed bed for the new; and that we may sow this life, that out of its perishing a new and fruitful one may grow by the grace of Jesus who hath life and immortality in Himself.

### *"Be Born Of The Water And Of The Spirit"*

Nicodemus evidently did not understand what Jesus meant. He was thinking only of the impossibility of being born again in the same way that one is born the first time. When Jesus said, "Verily, verily, I say," He meant to show that He was speaking with all authority and assurance. He did not expect Nicodemus to understand these things by logic or experience but to take them as a matter of divine revelation to be accepted because their Teacher came from God.

If it all sounds very deep and mysterious; if we cannot understand how we are born again, just remember this: It is God's work to bring us forth as new creatures unto eternal spiritual life; it is our part to follow step by step where He leads. It is for us by faith to receive what He offers and submit ourselves to His loving power to remake us. It is easier for us to understand these words than it was for Nicodemus, because we have the whole New Testament to help us. Jesus was indicating the spiritual nature of the kingdom by saying that it requires a new birth of all who enter it. He said the new birth was one of water and the Spirit, not a second physical birth, as Nicodemus was thinking. A physical birth produces a new physical body, but Jesus was talking about a birth that produces a new spirit in the same physical body (verse 6). This is mysterious, but so is much in the natural realm (verses 7 and 8).

The full instructions and practices of the apostles show us the meaning of "Born of water and of the Spirit." When Jesus sent the apostles to preach in all the world, He said "He that believeth and is baptized shall be saved" (Mark 16:16). On Pentecost, Peter preached, "Repent, and be baptized every one of you in the name of Jesus Christ unto the remission of your sins; and ye shall receive the gift of the Holy Spirit" (Acts 2:38). Paul wrote, "He saved us, by the washing of regeneration (new birth) and renewing of the Holy Spirit" (Titus 3:5).

We are begotten of the Spirit when we believe that Word that comes from the Spirit. That Word has the life of the Spirit in it. In the parable of the sower Jesus explained, "The seed is the word"

(Luke 8:11). "It is the spirit that giveth life; . . . the words that I have spoken unto you are spirit, and are life" (John 6:63). Paul says "For in Christ Jesus I begat you through the gospel" (I Cor. 4:15). James adds, "Of his own will he brought us forth by the word of truth" (James 1:18). Peter writes, "Having been begotten again, not of corruptible seed, but of incorruptible, through the word of God" (I Pet. 1:23). See also Acts 11:14; 20:32; I John 5:1. We must be born of the Spirit; the Spirit begets us through the Spirit's word. There is no true experience of this new birth that leaves out the Word of God.

Obedience to that Word brings forth new creatures, even as it brings us into Christ. When the Word is believed, the mind is changed. When the truth of the Word is felt in the heart, the desires and emotions are changed. When, through faith in the Word, we become willing that Christ should possess and rule our lives, the volition is changed. When, by overt obedience, we are buried in baptism, and we come forth from that watery grave, even our physical nature is changed in its relationship to Christ. When in the spirit of repentance we give Christ consent that He should come into our lives and rule them, the first command He gives is that we should be baptized. And in that baptism the old man is buried with Him into death, and the new creature is brought forth to begin the actual existence and activity of the new life (II Cor. 5:17). We must be born of the water (John 3:5), and out of the waters of baptism we come forth to live in newness of life (Rom. 6:4, 11; Col. 2:12, 13). "According to his mercy he saved us, through the *washing of regeneration and renewing of the Holy Spirit*" (Titus 3:5). "Christ loved the church, and gave himself up for it; that he might sanctify it, having cleansed it *by the washing of water with the word*" (Eph. 5:25, 26).

In answer to Nicodemus' wondering question: "How can a man be born when he is old?" Jesus explained just enough to identify the birth He meant—"be born of water and of the Spirit," and "that which is born of Spirit is spirit." Later in the same chapter He says that whosoever believeth should not perish but have eternal life (John 3:16, 36). He is not there speaking of some other salvation outside the kingdom, or apart from the new birth. The new birth will be accomplished in all who believe in Him with all their hearts and obey His Word, as faith demands they will.

At the close of His earthly sojourn, Jesus gave the commandment to the apostles to preach the gospel to every creature, and "he that believeth and is baptized shall be saved" (Mark 16:15, 16). Surely

Jesus was not changing His requirements, but was speaking of the same thing as the new birth, only in different words. Actually, faith in and obedience to the Spirit-inspired gospel brings forth life in us that is new, life that is spirit, life that Jesus lives in us. (See Rom. 8:1-15; Gal. 3:27; II Cor. 5:17; Gal. 5:16-26; 2:20).

To be begotten of the Spirit is equal to believing.

To be born of water is equal to being baptized.

To be in the kingdom of God is equal to being saved.

For Further Study:

Butler, Paul. *Gospel of John.* Joplin: College Press, 1961. Pp. 91-115. Comment on John 3.

Campbell, Alexander. *The Christian System.* Cincinnati: Standard Publishing Co., n.d. Pp. 153-240. Thorough study of the New Testament teaching on the plan of salvation.

McGarvey, J. W. *Sermons.* Cincinnati: Standard Publishing Co., n.d. Pp. 44-121. Sermons concerning God's plan of salvation.

# 22

## CHRIST FOR ALL PEOPLE (John 4)

When Jesus had been for some time working miracles and preaching repentance in the region of Judea, the Pharisees were informed "that Jesus made and baptized more disciples than John (although Jesus himself baptized not, but His disciples)" (John 4:1, 2). Then Jesus departed from Judea and started for Galilee. It seems probable that Jesus left Judea to avoid arousing at this time the strenuous opposition of the rulers until He had ministered among the common people in the other provinces. Later, He came back and faced to the showdown the bitter antagonism and hatred as well as the burning issues of right and wrong that raged between Him and the rulers, and that finally caused them to put Him to death. His ministry was planned and timed by infinite wisdom. Jesus had His time to avoid persecution and His time to face it.

Another factor in Jesus' trip into Galilee was the imprisonment of John the Baptist by Herod, the ruler of Galilee (Matt. 4:12; Mark 1:14; and 6:17-20). Therefore, Jesus left Judea and went to Galilee also to help John's followers avoid any rash action that might involve them in serious conflict with the Pharisees. In John 4:35 Jesus speaks as if it were then four months till the harvest. Since the harvest began between Passover and Pentecost, it would indicate that Jesus was returning to Galilee eight or nine months after coming to Jerusalem for the Passover at which He began to show Himself as a prophet and public teacher.

### *Samaria and Samaritans*

Samaria lay between Judea and Galilee. Jesus had to go through Samaria or take three or four days longer going around it. Because of the hatred between Jews and Samaritans, many Jews would go from Judea to Galilee by going eastward and crossing the Jordan and then going north through Perea. Jesus made another trip through Samaria (Luke 9:51-56). Josephus said that Galileans often passed through Samaria on their way to and from the Jerusalem feasts (*Antiquities,* xx, 6, i).

This territory of Samaria had once been the very center of Israel, inhabited chiefly by the tribes of Ephraim and Manasseh. Just after the death of Solomon, the northern tribes were separated from Judah under Rehoboam (931 B.C.). When the northern kingdom was carried away by the Assyrians in 722 B.C., Gentiles were brought in and settled in the country (read II Kings 17:6, 23-41; Ezra 4:2, 10). These Gentiles mixed with the remaining Israelites. After the Jews returned from Babylon to rebuild Jerusalem, further enmity developed between them and the mixed people of Samaria (Ezra 4; Neh. 4 and 6). About 400 B.C. the Samaritans built a temple on Mount Gerizim, a rival to the one at Jerusalem. They had a copy of the Pentateuch (the five books of Moses), and they claimed it as the basis for their religious system and their only sacred book. Even though they claimed to follow the law, their religion was never true and scriptural.

In 128 B.C. John Hyrcanus of Judah extended his reign to Samaria and destroyed the temple on Gerizim. From generation to generation for many centuries the traditional hatred between Jew and Samaritan was handed down and was buttressed by many local incidents arising from it. In Jesus' day the Jews generally had no dealings with the Samaritans (John 4:9). Among the Jews it was a first-class insult to call a man a Samaritan (see John 8:48). The Samaritans claimed that the Jews were all wrong in worshiping at Jerusalem, that they themselves were the true upholders of the law, that Gerizim was the place where Abraham sacrificed Isaac, that Gerizim was the highest mountain in the world and the only mountain not covered by Noah's flood, etc. The Samaritans have continued to worship on Mount Gerizim, and to this day they have a small group that keeps the annual Passover feast there, following old custom.

Although Jesus knew well the sins and false traditions of the Samaritans, He did not share the hatred and prejudice of the Jews toward them. He knew also the sins and failings of the Jews. He did not refuse to teach on that ground. He did not make it a matter of indifference whether or not one obeyed the law, but He dealt with individuals according to their ability to receive His mercy, not according to a prejudicial attitude toward a race, class, or nation. While His short ministry was concentrated upon the Jews to lay a foundation for sending the gospel to all nations and peoples, He did not reject the believing pleas of Gentiles or Samaritans (Matt. 8:5-13; Mark 7:25-30; Luke 17:16; John 4:40).

### *"Salvation Is From The Jews."*

As Jesus traveled across Samaria, He came to Jacob's well in the plain beside Mount Gerizim. Here He met a Samaritan woman, whom He surprised by asking for a drink of water. In the ensuing conversation Jesus informed her that He would give her living water;

one drinking it would never thirst again, and it would become a spring of everlasting life. She said, in effect, "O.K., give me this water." She was perhaps flippant, calling the bluff of a boastful Jew. Jesus said, "Go, get your husband." Evading Jesus' command, she answered, "I have no husband." To her surprise, Jesus said, "You have had five husbands and the one you have now is not yours. You have told the truth." At that she became serious and said, "You are a prophet." Then she brought up the old argument between Jews and Samaritans, whether it was lawful to worship at Jerusalem or on Mount Gerizim.

Jesus did not evade the question or refuse to "take sides." He did not hesitate to tell her that the Samaritan worship was not according to knowledge, and that "salvation is from the Jews" (John 4:22). Under the Old Testament law, God required sacrifices and services of the priests for all the people to be performed at one central location. Jesus explained that the day was soon coming when His own death would put an end to sacrifices, and God could be approached through faith in Him by anyone at any place. Even Jerusalem would no longer be God's special dwelling place. Jesus took issue with false religion. Worship at Jerusalem followed God's law, while Samaritan worship did not. God sent the Savior through the people who obediently worshiped at Jerusalem. It is notable that Jesus did not say to her that God is the Father of all, anyway, and cares for all men the same, regardless of customary standards and traditional forms of worship. Jesus offers to all men *opportunity* to become the children of God; He does not give to all *approval* as being already such unconditionally.

Jesus pointed out to the woman that then, and always, true worship is in the heart (in spirit) and in obedience to God's word (in truth). God wants individuals to worship Him sincerely. There are formal actions that express the right spirit according to God's revealed will; but the actions alone without the spirit are not acceptable worship. Psalm 51 may be read as a good commentary on this principle. "God is a Spirit: and they that worship him must worship in spirit and truth" (John 4:24). The necessity for spiritual worship is grounded in the nature of God. He is not simply a force to be controlled at a certain place or by ceremonies and charms. God is a person. He is the source and maker of the human spirit. To worship Him we must have the right personal relationship with Him.

"The woman saith unto him, I know that Messiah cometh (he that is called Christ): when he is come, he will declare unto us all things" (John 4:25). Messiah is a Hebrew word meaning "anointed one." The more familiar word "Christ" is the Greek translation of it. Prophets, priests, and kings were anointed in ancient Israel. The Messiah or Christ was to be the supreme prophet, the eternal king, and priest over all. His coming was prophesied in many ways in the Old Testament. The Samaritans did not have all the Old Testament and consequently had less understanding of the Messiah than did the Jews; but they shared the expectation of His coming. In Deuteronomy 18:15-19, God foretold the coming of the great prophet, saying "I . . . will put my words in his mouth; and he shall speak unto them all that I shall command him." The Samaritan woman may not have known just where she got this idea, but apparently she began to desire His coming to bring more knowledge of God's will on the matter of worship.

Jesus answered, "I that speak unto thee am he" (John 4:26). Now Jesus could announce himself to her because she had begun to feel the need for the word of God and to express faith in the promise of the coming great messenger of the Lord. Still, no doubt, she was surprised at His announcement, but His manner of speaking and His miraculous insight into her life made it easier to believe His words than to deny them. Salvation came from the Jews because the Messiah and Savior came through the Jews.

### *Jesus and Gentiles*

When Jesus sent out His chosen apostles to preach of the coming kingdom, He commanded them strictly not to go to any city of the Samaritans or of the Gentiles "But go rather to the lost sheep of the house of Israel" (Matt. 10:5, 6). When He planned the course of His three packed-full years of ministry on earth, He concentrated almost exclusively on the people of Israel. But this did not arise from any lack of love for the rest of the world. It was rather the plan of wisdom to complete the preparation and revelation of the long-promised blessing to all the nations (cf. Gen. 12:3; 18:18; Gal. 3:8, 14).

When Gentiles sought His help with prayers of faith, Jesus praised and rewarded their faith (Matt. 8:5, 13; Mark 7:25-30). He responded to their needs and desires at least enough to make it plain to us that he did not exclude them just because they were Gentiles. When the Samaritans besought Him to abide with them, He gave them two days of His busy life. His personal ministry and His *first* commission to the apostles were limited to the house of Israel, not at all in the way of favoritism, but in the way of laying a foundation, or of making a blueprint, or of preparing an instrument for work to come. Jesus often spoke of the "other sheep . . . not of this fold" (John 10:16), or of the many from the east and the west who would come and sit with Abraham, Isaac, and Jacob, in the kingdom of heaven (Matt. 9:11; Luke 13:29). Jesus did give the *great commission*, sending the full love and saving power of the gospel unto every creature.

As the maker of all men He was keenly interested in the redemption and regeneration of all. If He ministered especially to relatively few, it was to teach them to minister to all. He gave His life a ransom for all men of all races, classes, and times. He was not willing that any should perish, wishing that all should come to repentance (II Pet. 3:9; I Tim. 2:4). He is "no respecter of persons: but in every nation he that feareth him, and worketh righteousness, is accepted with him" (Acts 10:34, 35). *We need to learn that those whom we despise are as dear to the heavenly Father as we are; and that we are not true to Christ and His will if we do not minister to all with impartiality.*

### *Christ and Women*

When the disciples returned from Sychar "they marveled that he was speaking with a woman." Such conduct was surprising because it was contrary to the etiquette and attitudes of the time. The rabbis contended that "a man should not salute a woman in a public place, not even his own wife," and daily thanked God that He had not made them women. The disciples marveled, but said nothing, being convinced that whatever Jesus did was right and wise. One of the true marvels of Jesus' life and ministry was His free and graceful, but entirely blameless and dignified relationships with women. His dealings with women show the perfect purity and total impartiality of His heart. Women were among His most faithful disciples. They ministered unto Him of their substance (Luke 8:2, 3). They shared in His miraculous healing and feeding, and in His teaching. They became bold to ask for His help (Matt. 15:22-28; John 11:3, 20). They anointed His feet, they wept over His agony, they followed Him to the cross, they were early at the sepulcher. Their faithfulness was rewarded with the first appearances of the risen Christ. They received a place in the church, both giving and receiving of its fellowship of love. Some of them shared miraculous powers of the Spirit (Acts 21:9). In Christ "there is neither Jew nor Greek, there is neither bond nor free, there is neither male nor female: for ye are all one in Christ Jesus" (Gal. 3:28). Christ's saving blood, His sustaining grace, His everlasting love are given alike to all that will receive Him. He does not, however, make all to have the same personal qualifications nor the same duties in His service. We are all members of one body, but have not all the same office (Rom. 12:3-8; I Cor. 12:12-27). He has made us all brethren and has forbidden us to lord it over one another, but He has given to some the responsibility of oversight, and to others the obligation to be subject to them willingly and with love (Heb. 13:7-17; I Pet. 5:1-7; 3:1-7). He did not remove the divine order in the divine and human families (I Cor. 11:3). He did not choose any women for apostles, nor did His Spirit permit in the church women to serve in authority over men as overseers or teachers of the church (I Tim. 2:8-15).

### *Savior and All Mankind*

When the disciples returned from town the woman left her waterpot and went into the town. Either she was so excited by the wonderful news that this was the Christ that she forgot the waterpot, or she left it purposely to make a quick trip to tell the news and to return. "Come, see a man, who told me all things that ever I did: can this be the Christ?" (John 4:29). She urged the people to come and see for themselves. She exaggerated, but she conveyed the right idea—that Jesus knew all and could tell all that she ever did. In the Greek the form of her question indicated that she expected a negative answer: "This is not the Christ, is it?" Her actions show that she was convinced that Jesus was the Christ, but she tactfully suggested that others could judge better than she could. Some believed on the basis of her report; many more believed when they saw and heard Jesus for themselves. They concluded, "This is indeed the Savior of the world" (John 4:42).

The universality and impartiality of the gospel of Christ, and of the entire Bible, as well as of Christ himself, is a striking evidence of divine authorship. The Bible is everybody's book. This is true to a surprising degree, in view of the fact that it is so largely written about one nation of people that are very distinct from others and very little understood and appreciated by others. But in every part it is God's book. Even so, Christ, while limiting His earthly ministry to Jews, was and is everybody's Savior, everybody's ideal man, and everybody's manifestation of God. He was perfectly true to the essentials of human nature, as man is made in the image of God.

How completely Christ fulfills the needs of all men! In Him they of every time and place that believe on Him find such a supply of the water of life that they need never thirst. He not only offers himself to all men, but He is perfectly adapted to every kind and condition of man, and perfectly sufficient for all their needs.

For Further Study:

Coleman, Robert E. *The Master Paln of Evangelism*, 2nd ed. Old Tappan, New Jersey: Fleming H. Revell Co., 1964. Sets forth Jesus' plan and principles of evangelism.

Edersheim, Alfred. *The Life and Times of Jesus the Messiah*. Grand Rapids: Eerdmans, 1954 (reprint of 1886). Pp. 404-421. Good background information and insightful comment.

Tenney, Merrill C. *John in The Gospel of Belief*. Grand Rapids: Wm. B. Eerdmans Publishing Company, 1948. Pp. 91-99. Interesting explanation of the events in John 4.

# *Part Six*

# DISCIPLES AND FRIENDS

## 23

## ANDREW BRINGS MEN TO JESUS

Andrew was one of Jesus' original twelve apostles, and the brother of the well-known Simon Peter. Sometimes we feel as if we knew rather much about all the apostles, because we have a fairly extensive knowledge of the lives of some of them and of the call and commission and authority given to all of them as a group. Perhaps we seldom realize how little definite information we have concerning the lives of some of the men in that group. Andrew is neither among the best known, nor is he the least known of them.

### *An Early Disciple*

His first association with Jesus was near the Jordan River, as he listened to the preaching of John the Baptist. In fact, Andrew is called a "disciple" of John (John 1:35-37), which seems to imply that he was more than a casual listener. Certainly he was an interested and believing hearer of John's predictions of the coming Messiah. He was one of those who were waiting for the appearance of the Hope of Israel.

Andrew and Peter were working men who made their living by fishing in the sea of Galilee. But they were also the kind of men who would leave their work to go more than a day's journey from their home (at Bethsaida on the northwestern shore of the sea of Galilee) down the Jordan valley to where John the prophet of God was announcing the immediate approach of the kingdom of God.

Andrew had the privilege of being one of the first to hear and see Jesus pointed out as the Lamb of God that takes away the sin of the world. He and one companion were the first two men to follow Jesus. The other man is not named, but it was almost certainly the apostle John, the son of Zebedee. It was about ten o'clock in the forenoon when John the Baptist pointed out Jesus, and Andrew and John followed Him. Jesus asked what they sought, and by their answer they indicated that they really wanted to know Jesus and to be associated with Him. "They abode with him that day." We would like to know what discussions took place that day; but we only know that

Andrew came back with the conviction that he had found the Messiah indeed, and with the desire to tell his brother Peter (John 1:37-42).

### *Ready To Do the Will of God*

Andrew was a man ready to do the will of God; he believed in the Christ at the first testimony he received; he followed Jesus the first time he saw Him; and he brought his brother to Jesus at the first opportunity. Thus he attained the distinction of being the first man to believe in Jesus as the Christ and to bear witness of that faith to others (aside from the inspired, prophetic witness of John the Baptist).

When Jesus went from the Jordan to Cana of Galilee, to the marriage feast, the disciples went with Him (John 2:1, 2). With His disciples He moved to Capernaum and abode not many days (John 2:12). His disciples were with Him (at least intermittently) in an extended ministry in Judea, from Passover until four months before the harvest—a period of eight or nine months (John 2:17, 22; 3:22; 4:2, 8, 27-38). Surely, John intends for us to understand that these were, or at least included, the same disciples he had introduced in his first chapter. Often it is overlooked or forgotten that Peter and Andrew had known Jesus and traveled with Him for some months before the day when Jesus called them by the seashore to leave their nets and follow Him. When Jesus and His disciples returned to Galilee through Samaria just after the imprisonment of John the Baptist (Mark 1:14; John 4:1-45), the group probably included Peter, Andrew, James, and John, who seem to have returned to their homes and their work of fishing for a time, while Jesus visited again Cana and Nazareth (John 4:46-54; Luke 4:16-30), and perhaps other places.

### *Called to Be An Apostle*

Jesus came again to Capernaum. As He taught a multitude by the sea He borrowed Peter's boat from which to teach the people. Then He caused the fishermen to cast their nets and gave them a great, miraculous catch of fish. Then He called them to become fishers of men, and they left all and followed Him (Luke 5:1-11; Mark 1:16-20).

Still a greater stage of responsibility and intimacy with Christ was attained a few months later when out of a large body of disciples the twelve were chosen to be "apostles" (Mark 3:13-19; Luke 6:12-16). A disciple was any learner, especially a believing and faithful follower. An apostle was an ambassador sent out with authority and responsibility. A few months after naming them apostles, Jesus gave them miraculous powers and a commission to go two by two and preach the coming kingdom (Matt. 10).

It was at the close of that campaign that Jesus took the apostles away from the excited crowds around Capernaum to the other side of the sea of Galilee in a boat. But the people ran around the lake, until there were five thousand men, besides women and children, who spent the day with Him without food (Mark 6:30-38; Matt. 14:13-21; John 6:2-14). When Jesus desired to feed the people He told the apostles to find what food they had. It was Andrew who found and reported to Jesus a lad with five loaves and two fishes. Jesus asked that they be brought, and He fed the multitude with them.

*Considerate of Others*

The only other instances of special mention of Andrew are in connection with two incidents in the week of Jesus' crucifixion. The first was when Andrew, with Peter, James, and John, came to Jesus and questioned Him concerning the destruction of Jerusalem and the end of the world (Mark 13:1-4). The other was when Philip was approached by certain Greeks who had come to the Passover, and wanted to see Jesus. Apparently, Philip was undecided about taking Gentiles to Jesus; hence he first went to Andrew and talked it over with him (John 12:20-22). Philip had sought Nathanael to bring him to Jesus (John 1:45, 46); but bringing a devout Jew like Nathanael was then a very different thing from bringing Gentiles. Philip probably had sympathy for the Greek inquirers and was not displeased that such men should inquire after Jesus; but he knew how completely Jesus concentrated His ministry upon "the lost sheep of the house of Israel" (see Matt. 10:5, 6; 15:24, 26), and he naturally would feel what a new and revolutionary thing it would be to bring the Greeks to Jesus, even if they were proselytes to Judaism. He may have feared that the bitter opposition to Jesus among the rulers in Jerusalem would be stirred up to violent action if Jesus should be seen to be friendly with Greeks. Witness what happened to Paul in that same city several years later (see Acts 21:27-36). Therefore, Philip hesitated to act upon his own judgment, and took the matter to his brother-disciple and fellow-townsman Andrew. Their consultation resulted in both of them taking the matter to Jesus. At least they felt it was safe to tell Him, and leave Him to do as He pleased about it. The record does not tell whether the Greeks were granted an interview with Jesus, but it does tell some of the very significant and far-reaching statements with which Jesus answered the announcement, showing that He was deeply moved by it.

Andrew must have been habitually unselfish and considerate of others. He lived in the same house with his brother, who was married and had a mother-in-law there (Mark 1:29). He and Peter were partners in the fishing business. When he found the Christ he thought first of bringing Peter to the Lord. In nearly every incident in which he is specially mentioned he is bringing some one to Jesus. Andrew evidently considered the privilege of being a follower of Jesus as a gift from God to be shared with others. He sets a good example under one of the basic principles of Christianity, which is the secret of its growing and leavening power from nation to nation and from generation to generation: that is, that every one who is brought to Christ should bring others. We are saved to serve. When the treasures of the Christ are given to one of us, they are labeled for delivery to every one else, and we become indebted to all men until we make to them the same offer of divine grace which we have received. The educational principle expressed in the slogan, "Each one teach one," is as old as Christianity, and is still the best way to spread the blessing to every one. It is also one of the very best ways to stabilize the faith and to insure the growth of those who receive the word.

### *Seeker of the Right Things*

The Lord's first words to Andrew, "What seek ye?" suggest an important key to his character and secret of his success. He *sought* the right things. He did not wait until some one forced such matters upon his attention. He was out there in the wilderness of the Jordan *seeking* the message of God through the prophet John. Many people seem to avoid the company of Christ, but Andrew *sought* the companionship and teaching of the Lord. Having found the object of his yearnings toward God, he *sought* his brother to share it with him. He sought and found the lad and his lunch for Christ to use to feed the multitude. He took the lead in helping other earnest seekers after Christ.

"Seek, and ye shall find," is the Lord's gracious promise; but it is also a kind of threat. For if our yearnings and efforts are expended for the wrong things, what we find will not be good. What we sow we shall also reap. How can we answer the Lord's question, "What seek YE?"

"Seek ye first the kingdom of God and his righteousness (Matt. 6:33)." Having found that for ourselves, then our chief aim in the world as Christians is to seek the conversion and salvation of all men by bringing them to believe in Christ and to obey His gospel. If we partake of the Spirit of Christ our Savior, we, too, will be impelled to "seek and to save the lost."

For Further Study:

Barclay, William. *The Master's Men.* Philadelphia: Westminister Press, 1959. Pp. 40-46.

LaSor, William S. *Great Personalities of the New Testament.* Westwood, New Jersey: Fleming Revell Company, 1961. Pp. 50-59.

Lockyer, Herbert. *All the Apostles of the Bible.* Grand Rapids: Zondervan Publishing House, 1972. Pp. 46-56.

Robertson, A. T. *Epochs in The Life of Simon Peter.* Grand Rapids: Baker Book House, 1974 reprint. Pp. 4-15.

# 24

# FOLLOWING JESUS

Jesus calls all men to repentance, to higher living, and to eternal life; He calls some to special fields of service, to works of great importance in His kingdom and to intimate fellowship with Him; but we must respond to His call. His election is not unconditional. He sets before us glorious opportunities the fulfillment of which depends upon our response to them. The greatest invitation is of no benefit if it is not accepted. The vital point in Christianity is what we do about it (James 1:22). Therefore, it is well for us to make the most of this lesson based on the example of men who respond to Jesus' personal invitations and ministrations in the days of His flesh.

## *The Fishermen*

Mark gives a brief account of Jesus' call of four of the best known of His disciples (Mark 1:16-20).

> And passing along by the sea of Galilee, he saw Simon and Andrew the brother of Simon casting a net in the sea; for they were fishers. And Jesus said unto them, Come ye after me, and I will make you to become fishers of men. And straightway they left the nets, and followed him. And going on a little further, he saw James the son of Zebedee, and John his brother, who also were in the boat mending the nets. And straightway he called them: and they left their father Zebedee in the boat with the hired servants, and went after him.

See the parallel accounts in Matthew 4:18-22 and Luke 5:1-11. Mark tells nothing of the earlier association of these same men with Jesus. John 1:29-51 shows that Peter and Andrew had been associated with Jesus as disciples nearly a year before He called them from the boats on the Sea of Galilee. Soon after Jesus' baptism and temptation He was pointed out by John the Baptist as "the Lamb of God that taketh away the sin of the world," and two of John's disciples followed Jesus. One of them was Andrew, and it is very likely that the other was either James or John (John's entire narrative never mentions his name or that of any of his family). Andrew found Peter and brought him to Jesus. Philip and Nathanael were added to the group. From that time on Jesus' disciples are usually mentioned with Him—at the wedding feast in Cana (John 2:2); moving to Capernaum (John

2:12); cleansing the temple in Jerusalem at the Passover (John 2:13-22); baptizing multitudes in Judea (John 4:2); journeying through Samaria back to Galilee eight or nine months after the Passover, "four months until the harvest" (John 4:8, 27, 35-37). Matthew, Mark, and Luke begin their accounts with the Galilean ministry of Jesus, omitting nearly all of the first year's events; hence the first thing they tell of these disciples is the call by the sea.

Those earlier experiences of the fishermen with Jesus help to explain why they responded so quickly to such an abrupt call. This, of course, was not the first invitation of Jesus to them to be associated with Him, but it was the significant occasion in which He challenged them to leave all else and to come and commit their whole lives to following Him. Before, they had been with Him as learners and seekers of their own accord. Now Jesus suggests a special work or office to which He will appoint them: "I will make you fishers of men." The *unhesitating, cheerful, and self-sacrificing compliance* with Jesus' call is no less remarkable in this light.

Peter and Andrew showed the deepest respect, even reverence, toward Jesus in all things. *His summons was felt by them to be authoritative and binding upon them.* When He asked for their boat to use in teaching, it was granted (Luke 5:3). That might have been only a courtesy. But when He told them where and when to cast a net after they had fished all night with no result, and had washed the nets, it was no ordinary courtesy which caused Peter to say, "Master, we toiled all night, and took nothing; but at thy word I will let down the nets" (Luke 5:5). In answer to Jesus' call they made no objection, no condition, not even an inquiry; but *in contented obedience they left their equipment, their occupation, their families, readily giving up all that they might follow Jesus. Surely their immediate and definite decision was based upon confidence in Him personally, not upon agreement with His plans and program.*

### *The Gadarene Demoniac*

The Gadarene demoniac's response to Jesus is of quite a different nature (Mark 5:18-20). This man was a lunatic, possessed of many demons, living in the tombs, and no man had strength to tame him or to bind him. Jesus cast out the demons, permitting them to enter a large herd of swine. The swine rushed into the sea and were drowned. The people around were amazed that the man was healed, clothed and in his right mind; but they asked Jesus to leave. As He went, the man who had been possessed wanted to go with Him.

Naturally, he would be grateful to Jesus and would feel that the company of Christ and the apostles was safer and more congenial than that of the people of his own town. But Jesus had a work for him to do: "Go to thy house unto thy friends, and tell them how great things the Lord hath done for thee" (Mark 5:19). The fine thing is that the man *willingly obeyed* and did a good and fruitful work in bearing the testimony which Jesus commanded him. *His response was obedience to what Jesus wanted, whether it was what he himself wanted or not.*

### *The Blind Beggar*

A close comparison of Mark 10:46-52 and Luke 18:35-43 reveals that blind Bartimaeus heard a multitude with Jesus pass by as Jesus went into Jericho. He followed after them crying for help and healing. He must have had difficulty reaching Jesus then, and he went around the little town to be directly on Jesus' way as He came out of Jericho going on to Jerusalem. Again with loud and persistent cries he called for mercy that he might receive his sight. Jesus gave him sight. He received his heart's desire, but he did not go away and use it selfishly. He continued to follow Jesus, "glorifying God." We do not know how long he followed Jesus or what later service he may have rendered to the Lord; but it is good to see that he not only sought after Jesus in need and desire to receive his sight, but he also followed Jesus in gratitude and devotion to give glory to God.

### *The Taxgatherer*

Matthew was sitting at "the place of toll"—small shelters were placed on the roads entering a city and attended night and day by men who collected a tax on the produce brought into the city. Mark seems to connect it with the seaside (Mark 2:13, 14). Anyway, it would be on a public thoroughfare and it was at Capernaum, affording every likelihood that Matthew had often seen and heard Jesus, and had begun to have faith in Him. Jesus knew men's hearts. He knew what kind of man Matthew was and when to call him.

Matthew was a busy man; moreover, he was busy in a work of collaboration with the hated Roman rule, and in a work that tended to the evils of greed and extortion. Nevertheless, Jesus' words and works were sufficient to produce faith and transformation in the heart of any who would sincerely heed them. When the call of Jesus came: "Follow me," Matthew was ready without delay to leave all and follow Jesus. "He forsook all, and rose up and followed him"

(Luke 5:28). Again it was a case of personal confidence in and attraction to Jesus, of obedience to His commands above everything else.

*Our Response to Christ's Call*

The essence of Christianity is to follow Jesus. No amount of social science and institutionalism can in any wise equal the Christianity which is simple faith and devotion toward Jesus, who causes all who abide in Him to "bear much fruit." We must recognize Him as the Son of God, duly honor Him, and yield ourselves to His commanding leadership. He is the only hope of redemption of lost sinners. He is the last word on the ways of righteousness. He is the greatest source of security—the surest insurance in calamity. He is the truest teacher, the strongest helper, the kindest friend, the most challenging leader in noble and worthwhile things—the Alpha and Omega, in whom dwelleth all the fullness of the Godhead bodily—the end of man's search for the highest, the best, and the permanent—he that comes to Him shall not hunger, and he that believes on Him shall never thirst.

Forsake all for Jesus, certainly, instantly, and completely. When He teaches, it is ours to learn. When He calls, it is ours to respond. When He commands, it is ours to obey. No boats, no business, no associates, no aims and ambitions must stand in the way of complete consecration to Christ and His cause. No other life is worth living. Leave all at Christ's call.

(1) *Await specific instructions from the Lord. 'Come ye after me.'* (2) *Start where you are.* 'By the sea . . . casting a net . . .' (3) *Begin the moment the call comes.* 'Straightway . . . straightway.' (4) *Abandon the good for the best.* 'They were fishers . . . to become fishers of men.' (5) *Make any sacrifice Christ requires.* 'They forsook their nets . . . they left their father.' (6) *Win family and neighbors to Christ.* 'Go home to thy friends, and tell them.' (7) *Believe and receive sight and strength for service.* 'Thy faith hath made thee whole.' (8) *Follow Jesus wherever He leads.* (9) *Do the nearest duty without delay.* (10) *Aim for Christ and attain with Christ.*[1]

*Must one "leave all" to follow Jesus?* Let Jesus answer: "If any

[1] Hight C. Moore, *Points of Emphasis.*

man would come after me, let him deny himself, and take up his cross, and follow me" (Matt. 16:24). See also, Luke 14:33.

*Did any one ever turn down Jesus' invitation: "Come follow me"?* Yes, the rich young ruler (Mark 10:21, 22). He was moral, legally religious, seeking eternal life, and seeking it from Jesus; still he refused to follow Him, because he was not willing to deny himself.

*How can we follow Jesus?* He is not here in the flesh for us to follow as Matthew did, but we can give ourselves and all that we have to Jesus. We can forsake all selfish purposes and purely worldly pursuits. We can receive His words of instruction. We can give unquestioning and unhesitating obedience to His commandments.

For Further Study:

Barclay, William. *The Gospel of Matthew,* Vol. I. Philadelphia: Westminister Press, 1956. Pp. 70-74; 336-342. Barclay is untrustworthy in some of his views in his books.

Bruce, A. B. *The Training of the Twelve,* 3rd ed. New York: Harper and Brothers, n.d. Pp. 11-28.

Fowler, Harold. *The Gospel of Matthew,* Vol. I. Joplin: College Press, 1968. Pp. 163-173.

Fowler, Harold. *The Gospel of Matthew,* Vol. II. Joplin: College Press, 1972. Pp. 95-128; 146-176.

Hendriksen, William. *New Testament Commentary: Mark.* Grand Rapids: Baker Book House, 1975. Pp. 58-62; 196-198; 416-422.

# 25

## JESUS AND THE TWELVE
(Matthew 10)

In Matthew 10 we find the first mention of the Twelve in Matthew. Matthew has told of the calling of the four fishermen (Matt. 4:18-22) and of himself (Matt. 9:9); also of the offers some men made to follow Jesus, in response to which Jesus' words seem to indicate that something was lacking in their courage or resolve (Matt. 8:19-22). Luke 6:12-16 tells us that, before the Sermon on the Mount, Jesus had "continued all night in prayer," and in the morning called His *disciples;* and he chose from them twelve, whom he also named *apostles.*" A disciple (Greek: *mathetes* from *mathein*—to learn) is a learner. Jesus had many of them. An apostle (*apostolos* from *apostello*—send away with commission) means one sent forth with orders.

### *Compassion*

*We* might suppose that Jesus sent the Twelve on this first and limited mission primarily to train them and to try them, or as a step to an over-all plan to establish His kingdom's organization, but Matthew 9:36-38 shows that uppermost in Jesus' mind was the need of the common people to know the supreme goal of life and to be guided to that goal. With so many straying sheep, the good Shepherd needed more shepherds. Lest they should think of themselves and of dignity of position, etc., and serve like hirelings (see John 10:11-13) He taught them to see the need and to pray for laborers. Jesus wanted them to have a true shepherd's compassion for the "lost sheep of the house of Israel." Preachers and pastors (a New Testament word for elders, which means shepherds; I Pet. 5:1-4; Acts 20:28-35) who pity themselves had better learn to pity the multitudes. Were men all over the world ever more like "sheep without a shepherd" than they are today?

Before Jesus sent His disciples to preach, He taught them to pray for God to send leaders to the people. A church that does not pray for missions does not raise up missionaries. Blessed is that community whose preachers really earnestly pray that God will gather His flock, and then feel called to be used by God in the work that has become their heart's expressed desire. Some one has said: "You can do *more* than pray *after* you have prayed, but you *can not* do more than pray *until* you have prayed."

### *A Limited Mission*

This commission must be clearly distinguished from the Great Commission (Matt. 28:18-20; Mark 16:15, 16; Luke 24:47-49; John 20:21-23) given after the resurrection. The first mission of the Twelve (like another special mission of seventy disciples, Luke 10) was carried to completion under Jesus' personal direction during the preparations for the crucifixion, resurrection and Great Commission. Consequently, it had suitable limitations which do not apply to the universal commission now in force. It was to be only temporary, and only to the Jews. The time would come when the preparatory covenant would have fulfilled its mission, the law would be nailed to the cross, the distinction between Jew and Gentile blotted out, and the gospel preached to "every creature" in "all the world." Now they are still laying foundations in Israel alone. The kingdom was still future but drawing near. It actually came somewhat over a year later on the day of Pentecost (cf. Acts 1 and 2; Col. 1:13).

The burden of the apostles' preaching was the simple announcement, "The kingdom of heaven is at hand," but probably more than this was to be said about the kingdom in carrying out Jesus' words: "What I tell you in the darkness, speak ye in the light; and what ye hear in the ear, proclaim upon the housetops" (Matt. 10:27).

Most of the instructions given the apostles at this time concern their use of the power to work miracles and their methods and manners among the people.

### *He Gave Them Authority*

It seems that Jesus had imparted no miraculous powers to any one before this. Even John the Baptist "did no sign" (John 10:41). Notice that the apostles did not reach a degree of faith that produced miraculous powers, but it was given to them, all of them, at one sudden pronouncement. It included even power to raise the dead, and was to be freely exercised. At one occasion (at least) after this, nine of them failed in an attempt to cast out a demon. They asked Jesus why they had failed, and He told them that they lacked faith and prayer to use the power which had been formerly given to them and exercised by them (Matt. 17:16, 19, 20; Mark 9:29).

Some good people doubt that the apostles worked miracles at this time, because they were not baptized in the Spirit, but Jesus would not have told them they could and should if they could not. Mark

6:13 says they did, and Luke 10:17 plainly states that the seventy on a similar mission did. Miracles, then, are not necessarily dependent upon baptism in the Holy Spirit.

Jesus gave them the powers needed to do the work assigned. For the work He has given us to do, He has also given "the power of God unto salvation" which is the gospel (Rom. 1:16). The original announcement of a supernatural message required supernatural evidences. The miracles the messengers worked were to be the signs of the divine authority of their announcement of the coming kingdom. Therefore whoever received them and their word received Christ and God (Matt. 10:40). And whoever did not receive them shall fare worse in the judgment than will Sodom and Gomorrah (Matt. 10:15). Even so it is today with all who receive or reject God's authorized apostles. Would you accept Jesus' word if He preached His kingdom and His salvation to you in person? Then accept His word as preached by the apostles in the New Testament!

### *The "Wise" and the "Babes"*

When Jesus had received from the imprisoned John a question of doubt, when He had discussed the perversity of the people who rejected both John's and His own call to repentance of the cities in which He had done most of His miracles, judging them in the light of their great opportunity Jesus' reaction was an outpouring of thanksgiving to God for the fact that the ways of life are hid from the wise and prudent and revealed unto babes.

In our own generation and nation with all its learning and "wisdom" the genuine worth of Jesus Christ and His kingdom are not perceived and received. The truth is not accepted because we have too much confidence in our own progress, and in our own ability to apply wisely certain things we learn from Jesus' teachings mixed with our own folly. The majority of Americans believe in God (some way or other), rationalize their conduct, make shrewd explanations, and think they are "pretty smart." *But they do not recognize the most important fact ever revealed*—that God has delivered all things unto His Son Jesus, and no one can know or serve or honor God without accepting Jesus as first and supreme in everything.

Who can say he knows life when he knows not God, the author and sustainer, the source and goal of life? Who can say he lives wisely and well, apart from Jesus who alone can supply the real necessities?

"These things"—truth, righteousness, life and fellowship with God—were "revealed unto babes" (the simple and unsophisticated, the lowly and least honored of men, Matt. 10:25) in that they received Jesus and believed what He said. The whole nation was expecting a kingdom, deliverance from foreign oppression, and establishment of a great age of divine glory. The whole nation was seeking some favor with God by keeping the forms of the law. But then, when the kingdom was announced the sinners and publicans, who had made no show of faith in expectation, recognized their sinfulness, appreciated the mercy of Jesus and loved Him and followed Him; on the other hand, those who were most certain they understood the kingdom and most confident of their getting what they expected, rejected Jesus in disbelief. Thereby they threw away the key to understanding, and "these things" were hidden.

God's method of revealing is through His Son, Jesus Christ. All who are too proud or too "wise" to accept Him have the wisdom of life hid from them. All who are babes enough to lean on Him and learn from Him and follow Him have the eternal truth.

God said, "This is my Son. Hear ye him!" God appointed Him to lead us and to save us. God gave Him all authority and power to do it. (Read Matt. 28:18; John 3:35; 13:3; 17:2; I Cor. 15:7; Eph. 1:20-23.) What could be plainer? These claims are either true or false! He is either the door to heaven and the only door, or He is the world's worst imposter and most unconscionable liar. But God approved Him and attested His appointment by voice at the baptism and the transfiguration (Matt. 3:17 and Matt. 17:5); by "mighty works and wonders and signs which God did by him in the midst of you as ye yourselves know" (Acts 2:22; cf. John 5:36; 10:37, 38; 14:10-12); by prophecies (John 5:39, 46); by the resurrection from the dead (His own and others—Rom. 1:4). "No one cometh unto the Father but by me," (John 14:6) and "no one knoweth the Father save the Son and he to whom the Son willeth to reveal him" (Matt. 11:27). Either we take Jesus for our God or we make our own god and trust in an idol of our own creation!

How marvelous is the patience and the mercy of God! How gentle and personal is the appeal of Christ! He had preached the kingdom, exalted its blessedness, its purity, its unspeakable riches, and urged all to enter in by the strait gate. But in spite of all He can say, these things are hid from them. Their hearts are hard. But He does not rant; He does not continue to upbraid. He opens His heart of love to them. He forgets everything but their misery and woe, and tenderly entreats His beloved: "Come unto me, all ye that labor and are heavy laden, and I will give you rest" (Matt. 11:28). Christ says His yoke is easy, and no one ever tried it and found it otherwise.

For Further Study:

Bruce, A. B. *The Training of the Twelve,* 3rd ed. New York: Harper and Brothers, n.d. A study of the disciples, their personalities, their progress in the kingdom of God, and the teachings they received from Jesus, based on a study of the gospel records.

Coleman, Robert E. *The Master Plan of Evangelism,* 2nd ed. Old Tappan, New Jersey: Fleming H. Revell Co., 1964. Sets forth in plain language the principles of evangelism Jesus used in teaching the disciples.

Geldenhuys, Norval. *Supreme Authority.* Grand Rapids: Eerdmans, 1953. Pp. 45-122. Strong defense of the authority of Christ delegated to the apostles and their teaching and writings.

Ridderbos, H. N. *The Authority of the N.T. Scriptures.* Philadelphia: Presbyterian and Reformed Publishing Co., 1963. Pp. 13-47. The authority of the New Testament Scripture must be accepted if we accept the authority of Jesus and the validity of the promises he made to the apostles.

Stewart, John David. *The 12.* Austin, Texas: R. B. Sweet, 1963. Convenient summary of N.T. information on each of the apostles and an assessment of the traditions about each.

# 26

# WORKING WITH CHRIST

In the growing Christian life there must be at least three departments steadily developed in the right relation to each other: 1. worship. 2. separation. 3. active service for the Master.

We are very much inclined to neglect one or another and to be satisfied if we can point to one or two of them in our lives.

The Christian life is not only in what we *do not* do, but what *we do* do. We are not very good if we are good for nothing. When we accept Jesus as our Savior we also accept Him as Lord. We receive from Him the magnificent gifts of pardon for sin, eternal life, light for darkness, peace within, etc.; but we also surrender to Him all that we are and have and are able to do. He said, "Come unto me and I will give . . . . Come learn of me . . . . Take my yoke upon you" (Matt. 11:28-30). Let us "be not idle nor unfruitful unto the knowledge of our Lord Jesus Christ," but rather give diligence to make our calling and election sure (II Pet. 1:8-10); for "every branch in me that beareth not fruit, he taketh it away" (John 15:2).

In this essay we study, as an example and a challenge to us, the early service of the twelve apostles and seventy other disciples whom Jesus sent out campaigning for Him, two by two. The twelve were sent out at one time and the seventy at another time (Mark 6:7-13; Luke 10:1-20). Another and fuller account of the mission of the twelve is to be found in Matthew 10:1-42. The only record of the seventy and their work is in Luke 10:1-20. These passages should be read carefully and in full in order to gain a proper understanding of this study.

## *Points in Which the Twelve Apostles and Seventy Disciples Are Examples for Us*

1. They first followed Jesus to learn and receive for themselves. The most vital thing they had to learn was loyalty and obedience to Jesus, submission of personal desires, ambitions and opinions to His divine plans and purposes. They had to learn to deny themselves and to be willing to take up the cross and follow Jesus.

2. They went when and where Jesus told them to. We are told to go into all the world, and we ought to do as commanded.

3. They preached what He told them to. This mission was before the cross; they were to preach a message somewhat different from

that given to us, but we should obey as they did, and not devise our own message.

4. They had faith in His authority and promises, and did not devise their own methods and powers for casting out demons, etc. They knew that they were not able and were not expected to do all His work by their own power and wisdom. While we have not exactly the same assignment of work to do, we should realize that God furnishes the power for our work (that which is necessary beyond our faithful work and testimony), and we are not expected to regenerate men, to redeem and transform them, by our own skill and influence alone. The power of God to save is in His word of the gospel (Rom. 1:16) which is alive and working (Heb. 4:12), and which is the seed of the kingdom (Luke 8:11), through which we are begotten by the Spirit (I Cor. 4:15; I Pet. 1:23; John 3:5). His words are Spirit, and they are life (John 6:63). The life and power of God in the words of the gospel believed and witnessed in a faithful life may seem mysterious and unreal to some; but I say it is not so incomprehensible and incredible as the vitality and productivity of vegetable life hidden in the little dry seed that holds it while waiting for suitable soil in which to germinate.

### *Points of Difference To Be Observed Between Their Work and Ours*

1. This was preparatory work, before the cross and before the origin of the church. They themselves were given a later commission with different terms by Jesus in person (Matt. 28:18-20).

2. Their message was different on this first mission; it was not the full gospel, but only "Repent; for the kingdom is at hand."

3. Their chief assignment was to work miracles, while that is not an essential part of the Great Commission and our work today.

4. They were to go only "to the lost sheep of the house of Israel" (Matt. 10:5, 6), while we are commanded to "go into all the world" (Mark 16:15).

When we carefully note such elements in which the Scripture indicates that these early commissions were essentially different from ours, we may draw comparisons between those disciples' work and ours which are instructive for us.

### *Two Other Points of Comparison*

1. When the seventy returned they were rejoicing in the great work they were enabled to do for Christ. Yes, there is joy in Christian

service—but Jesus said to them, "Nevertheless in this rejoice not, that the spirits are subject unto you; but rejoice that your names are written in heaven" (Luke 10:20). When we have done all, we are still unprofitable servants (Luke 17:10). We can not brag on what we do for the Lord, because He has done so much more for us. We are still liabilities to Him, not assets, when all is reckoned. Hence the fact that He saves us is more wonderful than all the special or miraculous works we may perform by His grace.

2. Some time after the twelve had received their endowment with power to work miracles and their first commission, nine of them tried to cast out a demon and failed (Matt. 17:14-20; Mark 9:14-29). They suffered embarrassment before the heckling scribes, before the multitude, and before Jesus Himself. When they asked Jesus why they could not cast out the demon, Jesus answered: "Because of your little faith." Christ had given them the divine power to command diseases and demons, but they needed faith to use it. Faith alone will not in itself create miracle-working power; the power to work miracles is one thing (given by God), and the faith to use it is another (in men). Now Christ did not give to us of all generations the commandment to work miracles, and did not give us the power for that purpose; but He did command us to make disciples of all the nations. The power of God to save men through Christ, and to transform them through faith, has been given to us (Rom. 1:16). *We must have faith to use it!* If we were to ask Christ the reason for our failure to win much more of the world than we have, would He not say, "Because of your little faith"?

*Working for Christ Today*

Working for Christ is:

1. Commanded by God, a strict obligation.
2. Necessary for the salvation of the world.
3. Necessary in order to save ourselves.
4. Most rewarding, both in present benefits and in hope for the future (I Cor. 15:58; Mark 10:29, 30; I Tim. 4:8).
5. Work that is challenging, important, ennobling, and glorious in its results. *Let's do it with diligence and endurance!*

Work for Christ may take several different forms; for in the body of Christ we are many members and not all have the same office; i.e., not the same abilities and duties (Rom. 12:4-8; I Cor. 12:12-30). Our own share of the work will be determined by: (1) The need we see; (2) the commands of Christ we realize and acknowledge; (3) the ability we have to fill the need and obey the command, and (4) to some extent by the common consent of the brethren in Christ (that things may be done decently and in order). Work for Christ may include: preaching, teaching, or oversight (Eph. 4:11-16); responsible office in church or mission; benevolence and hospitality, etc. (Matt. 25:31-46; Gal. 6:6-10; II Cor. 9); financial support of the preaching (I Cor. 9:11, 14); blameless living and faithfulness to every duty in whatever condition we find ourselves (Eph. 5:22—6:9; Tit. 2:1-15), etc. But regardless of how our talents and opportunities may vary and cause the specific forms of our service to vary, Christian service must involve the surrender of our lives and energies to Christ in such a manner that it is "not I that live, but Christ that liveth in me" to do His will (Gal. 2:20).

*Wholehearted Surrender Involved*

We must renounce allegiance to family and personal interests, that Christ and His interests may have the unrivaled devotion of our hearts and absolute command of our services—just as a foreigner seeking citizenship in the United States of America must not only swear allegiance to the United States, but must also renounce allegiance to his former homeland.

> Now there went with him great multitudes: and he turned, and said unto them, If any man cometh unto me, and hateth not his own father, and mother, and wife, and children, and brethren and sisters, yea, and his own life also, he cannot be my disciple. Whosoever doth not bear his own cross, and come after me, cannot be my disciple. (Luke 14:25-27)

> Hating loved ones is very drastic. It was an Oriental way of expressing complete renunciation of all things, including the tenderest ties, for Christ. Sometimes this is required in a literal way, but the basic idea of making Christ absolutely first is meant. Our love for relatives will actually deepen through primary devotion to Christ. . . . Jesus was not interested in superficial discipleship. Multitudes were following Him. He deliberately discouraged them by making exacting demands and predicting the high cost of discipleship. Men were to despise any tie or possession in favor of unconditional surrender to the will of God. Of course, no real value or legitimate tie would suffer, but would gain in the long run by complete discipleship. There is no real

Christianity without a cross.[1]

### *Help Wanted!*

Jesus still calls for laborers. The fields are still white unto the harvest—as much or more than ever. He points out the challenge of the field, and calls to all who are willing to do what He wants done. The laborers are few. Pray the Lord of the harvest that He send forth laborers into His harvest (Matt. 9:38). Then accept the call yourself and help that much to answer your prayer.

For Further Study:

Foster, R. C. *Studies in the Life of Christ.* Grand Rapids: Baker Book House, 1971. Pp. 615-622; 842-849. Studies on sending out of twelve (Matt. 10) and the sending out of the seventy (Luke 10).

Fowler, Harold. *The Gospel of Matthew.* Vol. II. Joplin: Collge Press, 1972. Pp. 262-429.

Geldenhuys, Norval. *New Testament Commentary: The Gospel of Luke.* Grand Rapids: Eerdmans, 1951. Pp. 298-305. Comment on the mission of the seventy disciples.

---

[1] W. R. White, *Broadman Comments* (Nashville: Broadman Press, 1945).

## 27

## JAMES AND JOHN LEARN GOOD WILL FROM JESUS

James and John were Galilean fishermen and partners of Peter and Andrew (Luke 5:10). Their father, Zebedee, was in business with them and had hired servants (Mark 1:20). A comparison of Matthew 27:56; Mark 15:40, and John 19:25 seems to indicate that their mother was named Salome, and that she was a sister of Mary, the mother of Jesus. From their father's activity in fishing, and the long life that John lived after the ministry of Jesus, we may infer that James and John were young men when they were called by Jesus. James and John with Peter became the three apostles most closely associated with Jesus—the only ones permitted to be with Him at the raising of Jairus' daughter (Mark 5:37; Luke 8:51), at the transfiguration (Matt. 17:1-8; Mark 9:2-8), and at the agony in the Garden of Gethsemane (Matt. 26:36-46; Mark 14:32-42).

In John's account of the life of Jesus he never mentions by name himself or any of his family; hence we can not tell for sure whether James and John were associated with Jesus and John the Baptist at the Jordan River as Peter and Andrew were. But in telling how Andrew found his "own" brother, John uses an emphatic and unnecessary word which may indicate that the man with Andrew (John 1:40, 41) was either James or John, who likewise found his brother.

In view of the rebukes given John by Jesus in Mark 3:14-17; Luke 9:49-56, it is interesting to note that John always called himself the disciple whom Jesus loved. James and John thought that they stood especially close to Jesus, and even presumed upon their intimacy with Him to the extent of asking for the chief seats on either side of Jesus in His kingdom (Mark 10:35-45). According to Matthew, their mother joined with them in this request (Matt. 20:20-28).

The title "Bonanerges," meaning Sons of Thunder, which Jesus applied to these young men is not explained anywhere in the Scriptures; but it is usually considered to be an indication of the stormy, intolerant attitude of which we have two examples recorded in Luke 9:49-56. In our attempt to fill in from reason and imagination what is lacking in the account, it is well for us to remember that Jesus chose them, not that they chose Him, and that in giving them the name "Boanerges," He gave no sign of disapproval of them or any traits implied in the name.

### *Unknown Miracle Worker*

Jesus sent His apostles out two by two into all the cities and villages where He Himself was about to come. He gave them power and authority to heal all manner of sickness and to cast out demons. (See Matt. 10:1-8). At a later time He sent out seventy disciples with similar powers and a similar commission (Luke 10:1-20). But at some time between those two campaigns, when the disciples knew of no one authorized to do mighty works in Jesus' name except themselves, they came upon a man casting out demons in Jesus' name who followed not with them. When they saw this man, Jesus was not with them, and they took it upon themselves to forbid him. John later told Jesus about the incident, but he does not say what other apostles were with him at the time it happened. Sometimes John alone is accused of the exclusive and jealous attitude shown in forbidding the unknown miracle-worker, but it may be that John told Jesus about it because he perceived the force of Jesus' teaching about humility and really questioned the rightness of the action of the group.

How did this independent worker come to be casting out demons? We can not be sure. Jesus could have commissioned him at some time when He was campaigning separate from the Twelve. Some expositors assume that the man had observed the power of Jesus' name and simply appropriated it in the place of the Jewish rituals of exorcism. But that kind of thing did not work so well for the seven sons of Sceva, at Ephesus (Acts 19:13-19). J. W. McGarvey observes:

> If the man had been an enemy of Christ, using his power in opposition to the truth, it would have been right to forbid him; but, according to John's own statement, he was casting out demons in the name of Jesus, and this proved him to be a friend. Moreover, John should have known that no man could cast out demons in the name of Jesus unless Jesus had given him the power to do so; and if Jesus had given him the power it was his privilege to exercise it.[1]

The apostles probably thought that they had good reasons for silencing the man that companied not with them; this is surely indicated in the fact that they told the Master what they had done and were willing to receive His instruction. John, at least, seemed to

---

[1] J. W. McGarvey, *A Commentary on Matthew and Mark* (Delight, Arkansas: Gospel Light Publishing Co., n.d.), p. 321.

want to know whether it was right or wrong. Still, no doubt, it was partly jealousy of their official relationship to Jesus that made them test a man simply by whether or not he was with them.

> The offense of the stranger, if it were an offense, was not against Jesus, but against the disciples, whose rights and privileges were presumably infringed upon.[2]

> This passage hits hard at officialism, which has been one of the curses of Christianity. Someone secures a place of power by politics or violence; an organization is formed and worshiped as the center of their entire religious life. Everyone is outlawed who does not bow to the human authority or work through the human organization. But Christ pointed out that no one person has a monopoly on Christian service. We should all seek to serve humbly and rejoice in the success of all who are true to Christ and His Word.[3]

This incident reminds one of the similar one recorded in Numbers 11:24-30. There, Moses' correction of the attitude of Joshua clearly shows the fault in the attitude of Jesus' disciples. Read it as part of this study.

Jesus' appraisal of the apostles' action is unmistakable; He said, "Forbid him not." Luke 9:50 records one reason given by Jesus—"for he that is not against you is for you." Mark 9:39-42 records also other reasons:

> for there is no man who shall do a mighty work in my name, and be able to speak evil of me. For he that is not against us is for us. For whosoever shall give you a cup of water to drink, because ye are Christ's, verily I say unto you, he shall in no wise lose his reward. And whosoever shall cause one of these little ones that believe on me to stumble, it were better for him if a great millstone were hanged about his neck, and he were cast into the sea.

Reflect on all of these.

Notice that Jesus did not rebuke the disciples for forbidding the stranger on the ground that they should have fellowship with and

---

[2] H. D. M. Spence, *The Pulpit Commentary: Gospel of Luke* (Grand Rapids: Eerdmans, 1962 reprint), p. 243.

[3] R. C. Foster, *Studies In the Life of Christ* (Grand Rapids: Baker Book House, 1971), p. 763.

give encouragement to any and every kind of person and religion, but rather on the ground that he was not a denier of Jesus, but was really with the apostles in the work. We are not to forbid a good work merely because it is not "authorized" by us or contributing to our pride; but, on the other hand, this lesson should not be perverted into advocating that we should give consent and fellowship to every one regardless of his relation to Jesus. A man's relation to us may not matter, but his relation to Jesus certainly does. See Matthew 12:30: "He that is not with me is against me." God has sent His Son into the world as both Lord and Christ, has commanded all men everywhere to hear and obey Him, and will judge us according to what we do with Jesus. To be righteous before God a man must accept Jesus as Lord, must join his life and heart to Jesus; but all men are not under any similar obligation to accept me and join my company.

The same John, aged, mellowed, fully *inspired and enlightened* by the Holy Spirit, who wrote, "Let us love one another," also wrote, "If any one cometh unto you, and bringeth not this teaching, receive him not into your house, and give him no greeting," (II John 9-11). We need to give heed to both. The same apostle and the same Spirit that wrote I Corinthians 13 also wrote I Corinthians 16:22; 5:4-11; II Corinthians 6:14-18; Romans 14:1-4; 16:17; Galatians 1:8-10; 5:22—6:5; Ephesians 4:31, 32; 5:6-11.

### *Unfriendly Samaritan Village*

When James and John suggested calling down fire from heaven, doubtless they supposed themselves to be moved by pure and righteous indignation and to be exalting the Christ. But Jesus "turned and rebuked them." It is all too likely that they really were guilty of unholy irritation against men who would not receive *them* and *their* Master. No matter how evil men vex the righteous heart, our hearts' desire should be for their repentance and pardon rather than for their punishment.

W. Clarkson wisely comments:

> Not extinction, but reformation; not the infliction of death which is due, but the conferring of the life which is undeserved; not the rigorous exaction, but patient pity; not the folded fist of law, but the open hand of helpfulness, is the Christian thing. When we find ourselves giving way to wrath and proposing punishment, we do well to ask ourselves whether we are sure we know the

'spirit we are of,' and whether there is not a 'more excellent way' for Christian feet to tread.[4]

The following phrases in the King James Version, in Luke 9:54-56; "as Elijah did," "Ye know not what manner of spirit ye are of," and "For the Son of man is not come to destroy men's lives, but to save them," are omitted from enough of the oldest and best manuscripts and versions of Luke that it is probable that they were not part of the original book, but have been added. However, they are true and fitting remarks in these places, and are based on passages elsewhere which are unquestionable parts of the inspired Scriptures. Truly, Jesus did not come to destroy men's lives, but to save them. Oh, that we might have the greatest zeal for truth and righteousness; that we might abhor evil even as God hates it (Prov. 6:16-19; Amos 5:21; Zech. 8:17; Rev. 2:6, 15, etc.); and still so love and long to save the souls of men that, while we could never compromise with or condone evil, we would work always in all ways not to destroy men, but to heal them and to save them, overcoming evil by the blood of Christ and by forgiveness, both divine and human, rightly conditioned!

For Further Study:

Bruce, A. B. *The Training of the Twelve,* 3rd ed. New York: Harper and Brothers, n.d. Pp. 29-40, 230-249. Shows the growth in character of James and John.

Robertson, A. T. *Epochs in the Life of the Apostle John.* Grand Rapids: Baker Book House, 1974. Brings together the information we have on the Apostle John.

---

[4] W. Clarkson, *The Gospel of Luke* (*The Pulpit Commentary*) (Grand Rapids: Eerdmans, 1962 reprint), p. 263.

# 28

## SIMON BECOMES A ROCK (PETER)

The study of Peter's life and development is profitable for both the noble examples and the warnings it contains, and especially because of its outcome through the victory of faith.

We do not have any extended biography of Peter (except the ones by men discussing the few facts recorded in the New Testament). Although only a few incidents in his life are mentioned in the Bible, they are more than are told of any other apostle except Paul, and enough to give a very interesting picture of his character.

### *New Testament Facts About Peter*

Peter and Andrew were disciples of John the Baptist, and among the very first to follow Jesus. They heard John's testimony, and from the very first considered Jesus as the Messiah (John 1:35-42).

Although not named in the accounts, they were probably in the company of disciples that went with Jesus to Cana (John 2:1-11), to Capernaum (2:12), to the passover at Jerusalem (2:13-25), baptizing in Judea (3:22-30) till they returned to Galilee through Samaria about eight months later (4:4, 35).

It seems that on returning to Galilee, Jesus went alone to Nazareth (Luke 4:16-30), and the disciples revisited their homes. In a short time Jesus came to the sea where they were fishing and called them to leave all and follow Him. A miraculous catch of fish in Peter's boat caused him to worship Jesus in reverential fear (Luke 5:1-11).

Peter was chosen as one of the twelve apostles and is the first named in every list of them. With James and John he was permitted to be near Jesus at such times as the raising of Jairus' daughter (Mark 5:37), the transfiguration (Matt. 17:1ff), and in Gethsemane (Matt. 26:37-45). With all the apostles he received miracle-working power and a part in preaching the coming kingdom (Matt. 10:1-7; Mark 6:7-13).

One night Jesus came walking on the water near the disciples' boat, and Peter said, "Lord, if it be thou, bid me come unto thee upon the waters." He did walk on the water, but began to doubt and to sink; the Lord lifted him up and said, "O thou of little faith, wherefore didst thou doubt?" In the boat all the disciples worshiped Jesus, saying, "Of a truth thou art the Son of God" (Matt. 14:22-33).

The next day Jesus preached the sermon on the Bread of Life.

The great crowd forsook Him and many disciples walked no more with Him. Jesus said to the twelve, "Would ye also go away?" Peter answered, "Lord, to whom shall we go? thou hast the words of eternal life. And we have believed and know that thou art the Holy One of God" (John 6:60-69).

A few months later, Jesus sought to prove the faith of the twelve and to prepare them for His crucifixion, and he asked: "Who say ye that I am?" Peter spoke for them: "Thou art the Christ, the Son of the living God." Jesus pronounced His blessing upon this confession, and declared that He would build His church upon its truth, promising the keys of the kingdom to Peter (Matt. 16:13-20; Mark 8:27-30; Luke 9:18-21).

Jesus spoke plainly of His coming death, and Peter dared to rebuke Jesus, but received a severe rebuke himself: "Get thee behind me, Satan." From the time he first heard of it, Peter tried to stop the crucifixion, but he continued to believe and follow Jesus until he came to say, "We must obey God rather than men," in spite of pain and death (Matt. 16:21-23; Mark 8:31-33; Acts 5:29). The transfiguration of Jesus was to help the disciples believe that Jesus' predicted death was in keeping with the Old Testament, the good pleasure of God and the glory of Christ. Peter was thrilled at the scene and spoke up to suggest building dwelling places there. He was rebuked by God's voice telling him to listen to Jesus (Mark 9:2-7).

Other situations in which Peter spoke up are found in Matthew 17:24-27; 18:21; Luke 12:41; Matthew 19:27-30; Mark 10:28-30; 11:21; John 13:2-11.

Especially in the night before Jesus' death, Peter was expressing both his devotion to the Lord and his self-confidence: "Lord, whither goest thou? . . . Lord, why cannot I follow thee even now? I will lay down my life for thee" (John 13:36-38). Jesus then predicted that Peter would deny Him thrice before morning, but pointed hopefully to his repentance (Luke 22:31-34). Peter said that others might forsake Jesus, but he would never (Matt. 26:30-35; Mark 14:26-31). When the mob came to arrest Jesus, Peter drew a sword and cut off a man's ear, but Jesus rebuked him. Jesus had to submit to suffering and death, though He could have called legions of angels (John 18:10, 11; Matt. 26:52-54). Peter followed at a distance, and with John even entered the open courtyard around which the high priest's house was built. While he was there, three different persons charged him with being one of Jesus' disciples, but he denied persistently and vehemently. The cock crew and Jesus looked at him, and Peter realized how untrue and cowardly his supposed bravery and devotion had been, and he went out and wept bitterly (Matt. 26:58, 69-75; Mark 14:54, 66-72).

In the exciting events of the resurrection day Peter shared an important part. Read these Scriptures in this order: John 20:1, 2; Mark 16:5-8; John 20:3-10; Luke 24:12; 24:34; I Cor. 15:5; Luke 24:36-49, and John 20:19-23.

After the ascension, Peter was spokesman and leader of the apostles (Acts 1 and 2). He and John became outstanding leaders in the church. They suffered imprisonment, scourgings and the threat of worse things; but they rejoiced to suffer for Christ, and obeyed God rather than men.

These are almost all the facts given about Peter. Consider them fully. Students of the character of Peter need to study the facts in the New Testament rather than the traditional theories about him, which are largely imaginary. Surely so much more is told of him than of others because of the value of these things as examples for our admonition. Peter was often not so different from the other disciples as we assume. He reacted first and most expressively to Jesus' words and deeds; and he was the one to speak up first in almost every situation, but that the others shared his attitudes the accounts often state.

### *The Character of Peter*

The characteristic reactions of Peter indicate his impulsiveness—not that he lacked fundamental stability of conviction or constancy of character, but that he made decisions quickly, said what he thought immediately, often before he thought it over much.

Peter is often called weak and vacillating in character, as if he were a man of little conviction, determination, and devotion. I think some accounts have been badly misinterpreted, and others ignored, in order to sustain this supposition. It is charged that Peter had given up all hope and faith in Jesus and deserted the apostleship to go back to fishing, or, what is worse, that having seen and accepted the risen Lord, Peter still loved fishnets and boats more than he loved Christ and the kingdom. It is certain that Peter had seen and talked with the risen Christ at least twice, and very probably a third time, before that night in Galilee (John 21). He had the testimony of more than a dozen others who had seen Him also—the women, the two who walked to Emmaus, the other apostles and still others (Luke 24:33). After the first day of Jesus' resurrection appearances there is never any suggestion that Peter disbelieved in the resurrection of Jesus; and Peter believed that Jesus was the Christ from the first.

Jesus had commanded the apostles to go to Galilee to meet Him there; Peter and the others were on the shore of the lake by appointment! How long they were to wait was uncertain. There was no demand for *idle* waiting. They probably needed food; why beg when they could work for it themselves? It seemed good to all seven of them to fish; and when Jesus appeared He certainly did not rebuke their fishing, but rather aided it miraculously! Peter, instead of loving fishing more than the Lord, dropped the net full of fish and jumped into the lake to swim and wade a hundred yards to Jesus.

Jesus asked Peter if he loved Him more than the rest of the apostles did, because Peter had stoutly professed that he did. Jesus' questions now were to humble Peter and to prepare him for the prediction of the martyrdom which he must yet suffer for Christ. The fact is, Peter was willing to accept the assignment of suffering and death for his Lord; but he still thought in terms of comparing his service and devotion with that of John and the rest. He still had to learn—"What is that to thee? follow thou me."

Peter appears vacillating simply because he was a man of two convictions to which he was determinedly devoted, and the two were contrary. One was that Jesus was the Son of God and Messiah of the Old Testament who would bring in the promised kingdom; the other was Peter's own preconceived notion of what the kingdom would be and how the Messiah must triumph. The latter conviction had to yield to the other, but before it did it caused Peter to rebuke Jesus for predicting His death. It caused him to refuse the plain meaning of many of Jesus' statements. It caused him, with great determination, to try to stop the crucifixion by fighting in the garden, by following into the court of the high priest and denying knowledge of Jesus in order to stay in there and to keep himself from arrest.

Every time Peter got ahead of the Lord's leading, he went in the wrong direction; every time he spoke or acted on his own judgment with reference to Christ and the kingdom, he did the wrong thing, because he minded "not the things of God, but the things of men." But it is to Peter's everlasting credit that every time he made such a mistake he yielded to Jesus, humbled himself in faith, and continued to follow and to learn.

For Further Study:

Griffith-Thomas, W. H. *The Apostle Peter.* Grand Rapids: Eerdmans, 1946.

Lockyer, Herbert. *All the Apostles of the Bible.* Grand Rapids: Zondervan Publishing House, 1972. Pp. 126-152.

Robertson, A. T. *Epochs in the Life of Peter.* Grand Rapids: Baker Book House, 1974 reprint. Extensive study of the life of Peter by a noted New Testament scholar.

# 29

## THOMAS LEARNS IN THE SCHOOL OF FAITH

Thomas was one of the twelve apostles whom Jesus chose from among His disciples after a night of prayer in the first half of the second year of His public ministry (Luke 6:12ff). Nothing is told of Thomas' former association with Jesus, but he may have been among the disciples from the beginning. Nothing is known of his origin, occupation, age, or background. In most of the lists of the apostles, he is mentioned with Matthew in the fourth pair (Matt. 10:3; Mark 3:18; Luke 6:15). This might suggest that he and Matthew worked together when the twelve went two by two. He was one of the seven apostles who were fishing on the Sea of Galilee one night after the resurrection and Jesus appeared on the shore (John 21:2). From this it is guessed that he was a Galilean, but such conclusions are very uncertain.

In fact, Matthew, Mark, and Luke merely name Thomas; all that we know of him is from the Gospel according to John. The full extent of John's record is to mention that he was called "Didymus," or "Twin," and to quote four short sentences which Thomas spoke on four different occasions.

Of course, any judgment of his character upon such slight information is highly speculative, especially since men do not always speak or act characteristically. But Thomas' four utterances have a noticeable conformity and consistency with one another, and are all serious commitments of himself regarding his attitude toward Jesus. Nothing shows a man's character like his attitude toward Jesus, especially under trying circumstances.

### *Willing to Die With Jesus* (John 11:1-16)

It was only a month or two before the crucifixion that Mary and Martha sent word to Jesus in Perea that Lazarus, His friend, was very sick in Bethany. Bethany was less than two miles from Jerusalem, and Jesus had recently left Jerusalem because of the efforts of the rulers to seize Him. For as long as two years some had been seeking to kill Him (John 5:18). At the two most recent feasts Jesus had attended they had become more determined and definite in their plots (John 7:1, 13, 19, 25, 30, 32, 44, 45-52; 8:20, 40, 59; 10:31, 39), even sending officers to arrest Him and openly taking up stones to stone Him.

When Jesus prepared to go to Bethany to raise Lazarus, the disciples sought to dissuade Him because of the danger there. He told them that when one travels by the light of day he need not stumble, but that a man walking at night would stumble. He meant that if He walked in the will and plan of God no harm could befall Him, but if He forsook the pathway of duty marked out for Him, He would surely fall into trouble. Jesus told them Lazarus was dead, and He was going to raise him for the glory of God and that they might believe. Thomas saw that Jesus was determined to go to Bethany, and he knew that the rulers were determined to kill Jesus, so he spoke a challenge to his fellow-disciples: *"Let us also go, that we may die with him,"* (John 11:16).

Thomas certainly was devoted to Jesus in this. He had followed Jesus this far; he would follow Him even in death. From this statement of Thomas' it is often inferred that he was naturally gloomy and melancholy, looking for the worst to happen. But all the disciples feared and expected the same thing. They knew how old and how fierce the opposition at Jerusalem was. If they were at fault, it was in considering only the human plans and forces involved while failing to trust fully enough that God will provide for and protect those who are doing His will. Their calm boldness in the face of persecution at a later time shows how they learned even this lesson. (See Acts 4:5-31 and 5:17-33, 41, 42.) As someone has said, "Resistance and rocks did not deter Jesus. He followed the line of duty regardless of what might be before Him. Stephen and Paul caught the same spirit."

### *Asking About the Way* (John 14:5)

At the last supper, Jesus said He was going to the Father to prepare a place for the disciples. "And whither I go, ye know the way. Thomas saith unto him, *Lord, we know not whither thou goest; how know we the way?*" Isn't such a question natural enough? It shows that Thomas was interested, if, perhaps, he was not as sharp a listener as he should have been. Jesus was going to the Father by the way of His cross and death; the same way is the way we all must go if we come to the Father—*He is the way*—we must go by *His* cross and follow on, bearing our cross daily!

Some think Thomas was despondent here again, not asking for information, but excusing ignorance and belittling the evidence they had received, in the attitude of "How in the world could anybody be expected to know?" But I object that this interpretation is imposed upon the account out of the imagination of men who have a theory about Thomas' "gloomy skepticism."

### *Refusing to Believe the Report of the Resurrection* (John 20:25)

On the day of His resurrection, Jesus appeared to Mary (John 20:11-18), to other women (Matt. 28:1-10), to Peter (Luke 24:34), to two going to Emmaus (Luke 24:13-22), and that night to the apostles and some others who were with them (Luke 24:33; John 20:19-24), but Thomas was not with them. When the other apostles told Thomas they had seen the Lord, he said, *"Except I shall see in his hands the print of the nails, and put my finger into the print of the nails, and put my hand into his side, I will not believe."* That was a very strong demand for evidence to come from a man who had heard Jesus predict plainly His own death and resurrection, and in the face of the testimony of his fellow-disciples. For it we have called him Thomas, the Doubter.

But remember that when the other ten apostles were told by the women that the risen Christ had been seen, they regarded it as an idle tale (Mark 16:11; Luke 24:11). Moreover, when they had heard the whole story of the two who went to Emmaus and the report of the appearance to Peter, they still disbelieved (Mark 16:13, 14; Luke 24:34, 35, 41); and even when Jesus Himself appeared among them they were frightened, believing Him to be a spirit, disbelieving their eyes until He ate fish before them to prove that He was there in a body. Thomas did doubt the word of the apostles, but he believed as soon as he saw Jesus. Jesus did not rebuke Thomas for unbelief as He did the others (Mark 16:14). Yet we call Thomas "*the* Doubter."

Many kinds of accusations have been thrown at Thomas for being absent when Jesus first appeared to the company of apostles, but they are gratuitous. No one can possibly know why he was not with them. The Lord left us no suggestion that Thomas was blamable for that fact, or that it in itself indicated any doubt or disinterest. There is no real indication that Thomas was inclined to doubt the supernatural, to be a rationalist, or to demand direct evidence of his own senses before he would believe *anything.* In fact, it does not seem that the Gospel accounts mean to represent that his doubt of the resurrection was any greater or essentially different from that of the other apostles. They all had to learn in the school of faith. They all were severely disturbed in mind by the crucifixion, having had their hopes set on something entirely different, and not realizing the place that sacrifice must have in the divine plan of redemption and in the ministry of the Christ.

*Worshiping In Full Faith* (John 20:26-29)

When Jesus appeared a second time to the company of apostles, Thomas was with them. Jesus, of course, knew what Thomas had said. The others were now believing. Hence, when Jesus had greeted them He immediately addressed Thomas: "Reach hither thy finger, and see my hands; and reach hither thy hand, and put it into my side: and be not faithless, but believing."

> Will Thomas still insist on applying his rigorous test? No, no! His doubts vanish at the very sight of Jesus, like morning mists at sunrise. Even *before* the Risen One had laid bare His wounds, and uttered those half-reproachful, yet kind, sympathetic words, which evince intimate knowledge of all that had been passing through His doubting disciple's mind, Thomas is virtually a believer; and *after* he has seen the ugly wounds and heard the generous word, he is ashamed of his rash, reckless speech to his brethren, and, overcome with joy and with tears, exclaims, 'My Lord and My God!'[1]

Don't mistake these words, "My Lord and my God!" They were not a startled, ejaculatory cry to the Father in heaven, but they were "said to him," to Jesus, in recognition of Him. In this confession, Thomas made the most complete expression of the deity of Christ which any of His apostles made in the days of His flesh.

We must learn that the blessings of Christianity—redemption, revelation, and fellowship with Christ—come by *believing* Jesus, not by *agreeing* with Him. He brings a revelation of things foreign to our natural mind. His supernatural pronouncements must be believed upon demonstration of supernatural credentials. He has worked all the signs necessary to show His authority and establish faith in every one who "willeth to do the will of God" (John 7:17). We do not need to see them done over again. "Blessed are they that have not seen and yet have believed" (John 20:29). Blessed are they who receive the testimony of those through whom these things are confirmed unto us.

---

[1] A. B. Bruce, *The Training of the Twelve,* 3rd ed. (New York: Harper and Row, n.d.), p. 510.

For Further Study:

Bruce, A. B. *The Training of the Twelve,* 3rd ed. New York: Harper and Brothers, n.d. Pp. 33, 391-392, 506-510.

Butler, Paul T. *The Gospel of John,* Vol. II. Joplin, MO: College Press, 1965. Pp. 140-143, 243, 426-435.

Westcott, B. F. *The Gospel According to John.* Grand Rapids: William B. Eerdmans, 1881. Pp. 165-167, 293-297.

# 30

# WORKING FOR A CHRISTIAN WORLD

Why had Christ condescended to live on earth, to fulfill a ministry of humiliation, to endure grief and woe, to die a death of agony and shame? Surely it was not that after His departure all things might go on exactly the same as before!

Jesus saw the multitudes ill-housed, ill-fed, and oppressed by poverty. He saw them bound by prejudice and superstition, poisoned by hate and envy, ridden by disease. Surely He saw and He cared for all those things, but He saw them chiefly as "sheep without a shepherd" (Matt. 9:36), as children of God who knew not their Father, sitting in spiritual darkness. Jesus would be their light. I'm sure He could have introduced the products of our modern technology.

No one knows what He may have been tempted to do with systems of education and of government. But all that Jesus would do to improve the political, social, and cultural conditions of the world He left to be accomplished through the transforming effect of the gospel preached and believed. His was not a mere social gospel of soup, soap, and suffrage, but the divine gospel of salvation from sin, of eternal life through His own redeeming death and eternal priesthood, with power to regenerate the heart.

It is a very significant revelation of divine wisdom that, in view of all Jesus knew and saw and could do, still He concentrated all His interests and all His powers upon converting the individual. He would change society by changing the individual. He would transform the individual by the regeneration of the heart. He would reach the springs of action, desire, and will by presenting to the mind convincing testimony of those facts about Himself that would make men accept Him and lovingly submit to all that He commanded. It does make a difference what a man believes! It makes more difference than anything else does. "As a man thinketh in his heart so is he."

## *The Great Commission*

It would be very worth while if every Christian would memorize the four statements of the commission given by Jesus, as found in Matt. 28:18-20; Mark 16:15, 16; Luke 24:47, 48; John 20:21-23. This commission is a great climax in the revelation of God to man. With it begins the application to all the world of the salvation and light and blessing which had been in preparation in all former ages, and especially in Christ's personal ministry. All the preciousness of the redemption which Christ purchased with His own blood was hereby entrusted to His friends and consigned to His needy beneficiaries the world over. During the forty days after Christ's resurrection in which He appeared to the apostles at least five or six times (Cf. Acts 1:3), He spoke repeatedly of the work which they were to do. The four different statements in the accounts probably present His words to them on four different occasions, and they combine to make a remarkably complete statement of the plan of salvation and the mission of the church.

1. *The authority by which they were sent is stated—"all authority in heaven and earth."* The apostles knew by whom they were sent, and refused to heed rulers who commanded them not to preach in Christ's name (Acts 4:19; 5:29). We should realize that this work is commanded by the highest authority; it is not for us to question whether we agree with His plan, but to obey His order.

2. *The field of the service commanded is "all nations," "all the world," "the whole creation." The command is not obeyed as long as we discriminate against some or neglect any.* His gospel is to be preached at home as well as abroad, and in far countries as well as at home, "beginning in Jerusalem," but not waiting for complete success there before going elsewhere.

3. *The work to be done is definitely stated in summary.* They were not to do any work that was "nice" or popular, cultural or calculated to promote their institutions. *The command is to preach the facts about the death and resurrection of Christ, the fulfillment of the prophets, that men might receive Him as Saviour and yield to Him as Lord,* and to teach them to do all things that Christ commanded.

4. *The workers to whom this commission was first given were the eleven apostles.* To them *only* was promised the power from on high by the baptism of the Holy Spirit. Only with reference to their inspired pronouncements was it said: "Whose soever sins ye forgive, they are forgiven unto them; whose soever sins ye retain, they are retained" (John 20:23). Christ gave the commission only to the chosen agents, and commanded them to wait until they received divine power of inspiration, in order to make known the "faith once for all delivered unto the saints" and to give full assurance not only that the hope of pardon and eternal life through Christ's death and

resurrection are authorized to us, but also that the terms of salvation preached by the apostles are absolutely infallible and final.

However the work of carrying this message into all the world and to all generations has passed to the church as a whole. To all of us who consent to serve Christ, this commission gives instruction as to what service He wants performed. This is the work which He left for His friends. If we would be His friends we must do our part of it.

5. *The power for accomplishing so tremendous a task certainly did not appear to be in the apostles themselves; still the command is not futile.* A special endowment of power from on high was given (Luke 24:49; Acts 1:5, 8; John 16:13, 14; Acts 2:1-4). The words which the Spirit spoke through them are preserved unto us, and are still "living and active" (Heb. 4:12), "seed" of the kingdom (Luke 8:11), "the power of God unto salvation" (Rom. 1:16), "the sword of the Spirit" (Eph. 6:17).

### *The Apostles' Faithfulness and Success*

The success with which the apostles preached and converted men is really remarkable, especially in comparison with results we are achieving today. (See Acts 2:41, 47; 4:4; 5:14; 6:1, 7; 8:6, etc.). The effectiveness of their preaching is seen, not only in the number of converts, but even more in the character and conduct of the converts. (See Acts 2:42, 44-47; 4:32-37; 8:4, etc.) The work of the apostles furnishes us an excellent and challenging example of the kind of Christian work that pleases God and blesses many men. Remember that almost everything that we today consider necessary to success in the work was completely lacking when they started out to tell the world of Christ—they had no large company, no managing organization, no adequate funds or treasury, no prestige or political influence, no show of learning, no printing or publicity program, no mechanical aids. However, there were real reasons for their power and success, some of which are just as available to us today:

1. *Obedience.* "They went forth, and preached everywhere." They did not understand all about Jesus' plans and the coming kingdom, but they did just what He told them to do, and trusted God for results. They did not even turn aside from their preaching and teaching to manage organizaions and treasuries when these became necessary (Acts 6:1-7).

2. *Zeal and diligence.* At every opportunity, to one or many, to

friendly or hostile hearers, they preached. "And every day, in the temple and at home, they ceased not to teach and to preach Jesus as the Christ" (Acts 5:42). James and John had once asked for chief seats next to Jesus in the kingdom—they learned that no one sits in honor and ease simply watching the kingdom grow and prosper, but all must participate in the labors and sufferings of Christ.

3. *Knowledge and faith.* They knew what they had seen and whom they had believed. They preached with profound conviction, and acted in perfect harmony with the absolute truth and tremendous significance of their testimony.

4. *Their manner of preaching.* They knew and *emphasized* the *authority of the message,* that it was not theirs, but direct from God, and concerning the authority of God's Son. They preached with authority in tones that rang with it on every occasion. Theirs was the *witnessing of facts.* They knew whereof they spoke, not by reason or by guess, but by the most vivid and recent experience. They did not argue, or speculate, or ponder—they testified to things certain and tremendously important, adding also the testimony of the Old Testament. Their *purpose was to save.* They seemed to have no thought of consequences to themselves, but only bringing men to repentance. They knew all men needed to repent, and were not ashamed to preach it. They were completely surrendered to Jesus and expected every one else to be the same.

5. *A message definite and clear.* They promised pardon upon definite terms which all could fulfill; the same terms Christ specified in the Great Commission—faith, repentance, baptism, submitting to all that Jesus commands.

6. *Their unity in teaching, practice, spirit and fellowship.* All preached the same warnings of damnation, the same promises of salvation, the same commandments and conditions of favor. Their practice of unity and brotherhood had much influence upon the people.

7. *Their special qualifications.* They had complete understanding of the Scriptures (Luke 24:27, 45), the experience of eyewitnessing, and the baptism of the Holy Spirit. These gave great power in witnessing. The miracles wrought through them confirmed the word (Mark 16:20; Heb. 2:3, 4). This was the primary purpose of all Bible miracles in general. Such supernatural evidences were, in the

nature of the case, necessary to attest a supernatural message. When the message from God was once completely revealed and fully confirmed, the miracles were not needed.

For Further Study:

Foster, R. C. *Studies in the Life of Christ.* Grand Rapids: Baker Book House, 1962. Pp. 1353-1367.

Stott, J. R. W. "The Great Commission," *Christianity Today* (April 26, 1968), Pp. 723-725; (May 10, 1968), Pp. 778-782; (May 24, 1968), Pp. 826-829. Helpful article on the interpretation and application of the great commission.

# 31

## FRIENDS OF JESUS

The Scripture passages selected for this study are from various places in Mark, Luke, and John, recording the personal dealings or conversations of Jesus with persons of various ages, ranks, and nationalities. They are selected in order to show Jesus' customary attitudes toward all types of people. These incidents, as they are listed, are not in chronological order, and are not associated with one another. They simply are given in the order in which they occur in the New Testament as sample incidents from which we may study some general traits of the personality of Jesus. Each incident cited should be looked up and studied together with its context so that its story can be told briefly and clearly.

### *Some of Jesus' Personal Relationships*

1. *The little children brought* (Mark 10:13, 14, 16). Some loving parents sought that Jesus might lay His hands on their children and pray over them (Cf. Matt. 19:13, 14). Even some of Jesus' disciples thought He would not care to take time for the children, and they rebuked the parents. Jesus' life was very busy; He was continually dealing with the most important things of adult responsibilities, and the disciples thought the children would be an unnecessary annoyance, not worthy of His attention. But Jesus was indignant at seeing children despised. He loved the children, and He recommended some of their traits as good examples for adults; "Whosoever shall not receive the kingdom of God as a little child, he shall in no wise enter therein" (Mark 10:15; Matt. 18:1-6, 10).

> Not content with merely laying His hand on them, He took them up in His arms to do so, and blessed them. The tenderness which He manifested toward the little children should cause parents to more highly appreciate them, and to labor more assiduously to bring them up in the doctrine and discipline of the Lord.[1]

2. *The honorable councilor honoring Him in death* (Mark 15:43). Joseph of Arimathea was a member of the Sanhedrin or high court of the nation, but was a "good and righteous man . . . looking for

[1] J. W. McGarvey, *Matthew and Mark* (Delight, Arkansas: Gospel Light Publishing Company, 1875), p. 237.

the kingdom of God" (Luke 23:50-53). He was "a disciple of Jesus, but secretly for fear of the Jews" (John 19:38). The crucifixion of Jesus awakened his courage and revealed his true faith. When many formerly bold disciples had become timid and had fled, this formerly timid one "boldly went in unto Pilate, and asked for the body of Jesus." He used his high position to minister to his Lord in the hour of humiliation. He used the fruits of his wealth to furnish a fine new tomb for his Lord, who in death, as in life, had "not where to lay his head."

3. *The Twelve chosen* (Luke 6:13-16). After more than a year of public ministry Jesus had many disciples (i.e., more or less regular listeners and learners). From among them He chose twelve "whom also he named apostles." An apostle is *one sent* as a responsible messenger and representative. Before selecting them, Jesus had spent the night in prayer. They were indeed to be His friends, to whom He would entrust His message and His work on earth. Although He was the Master and they were servants, He was divine, they were human, and they honored Him as such; still He honored them as friends (John 15:15, 16), and loved them (John 13:1, 34; 14:1-3; 15:9-13). It is truly remarkable that Jesus was such an impartial friend to this group of men which included a traitor when He knew it would be so from the beginning (John 6:64).

4. *The women ministering* (Luke 8:1-3). Although Jesus always chose men for the responsible positions of public ministry, yet His personal regard and compassion and gracious ministry were as much for women and children as for men. He didn't judge men by the accidents of birth, and outward circumstances. He cared for all mankind; and every soul was and is precious in His sight for what it is and what it may be as a human soul (Gal. 3:28). Jesus' impartial friendship for all believers in every earthly condition often caused some unusual fellowship among them in serving Him. Among His apostles it brought together Matthew the publican (collaborator with Rome) and Simon the Zealot (advocate of violence against Rome) until all their differences were overshadowed in their common loyalty to Jesus. Among the women who helped support Jesus' ministry there was Joanna, the wife of Herod's steward, in fellowship with Mary, who had had seven demons.

5. *The publicans and sinners listening to Him* (Luke 15:1, 2). The common people heard Him gladly, and those who realized their

sinfulness and knew their needs sought Him with hope and were not disappointed. They did not seek Him as an associate in sinful or even frivolous pastimes, But they, with special reverence for His holiness, drew near to be pardoned and made clean. They found Him a willing and encouraging friend seeking to do good to them and to put away their sins and the memory of them. Jesus did not make Himself a sinner among sinners; neither did He keep Himself out of reach of sinners who could be brought to repentance. He actually sought them out, made them feel the convicting power of His righteous life and earnest words and the constraining power of His genuine love and helpful spirit.

6. *The fishermen seeking* (John 1:35-51). This happened before the beginning of Jesus' public ministry when Andrew and Peter first saw Jesus, and when John the Baptist bore his faithful testimony. Hearing John point out the Lamb of God, Andrew and a companion dared to follow Him. They found in Jesus' practice what He later said in His preaching: "Him that cometh to me I will in no wise cast out" (John 6:37).

7. *The ruler inquiring* (John 3:1, 2a). Nicodemus was a Pharisee and, although not as prejudiced against Jesus as other Pharisees, he was weak in faith and resolution. He seemed to lack the courage of his convictions, fearing the Jews and hiding his sympathies for Jesus. Nevertheless, he found Jesus ready to receive him and to teach him patiently.

8. *The woman of Samaria at the well* (John 4:6, 7). Jesus broke all the hidebound customs of hate and scorn to make way for the love of God. His love for souls was able to overcome great barriers in order to seek and to save the lost.

### *No Respecter of Persons*

A very practical way in which Jesus shows His deity is in the impartiality with which He invites, receives, and deals with all men on the same terms. Not only was He able to show Himself interested in all men during His earthly ministry, but the record of His life makes us all feel His interest in us centuries later. No one of us feels himself excluded from Jesus' circle of interest and friendship, unless it be by our limitation rather than His. He is accessible to all. "Come unto me, all ye that labor and are heavy laden" (Matt. 11:28), He says. And whosoever will may come. He is the true friend who loves at all times. His love is the boundless love of God who "so loved the world, that he gave his only begotten Son, that whosoever believeth on him should not perish, but have eternal life" (John 3:16). It seems hard for us to realize how much and how truly He loves us and loves all men, worthy or unworthy. "Greater love hath no man than this, that a man lay down his life for his friends" (John 15:13). He is indeed a friend to sinners—the best friend a sinner could ever have!

We need to understand and make quite clear the kind of friendship Jesus had for sinners. His practice was in perfect accord with James 4:4: "Know ye not that the friendship of the world is enmity with God? Whosoever therefore would be a friend of the world maketh himself an enemy of God." It is the Spirit of Jesus in the apostles which teaches us thus: "Be not deceived: Evil companionships corrupt good morals" (I Cor. 15:33); "What fellowship have righteousness and iniquity? or what communion hath light with darkness? . . . Wherefore, come ye out from among them, and be ye separate, saith the Lord, and touch no unclean thing; and I will receive you" (II Cor. 6:14-17). Jesus Himself was "holy, guileless, undefiled, separated from sinners" (Heb. 7:26). We must not become partakers of other men's sins. We must keep ourselves unspotted from the world. Yet we must love all and serve all, and be not only willing, but working, to uplift all that will look up to God for pardon and for purification.

Jesus tries to teach us true love and friendship for all men: "See that ye despise not one of these little ones" (Matt. 18:10). "Love your enemies, and pray for them that persecute you; . . . For if ye love them that love you, what reward have ye? do not even the publicans the same? And if ye salute your brethren only, what do ye more than others?" (Matt. 5:44-47). Compare James 2:1-9. The story of the good Samaritan illustrates perfectly how we are to try to be a friend, not just try to have friends. It is one thing to be a friend and another to have friends, although they usually go together; and many people want to have friends who are not willing to be friends.

Jesus was ready to be a friend to every one, but not every one was a friend to Him. Judas appeared to be a friend but proved untrue. Others were avowed enemies all the while. But don't overlook the fact that the great majority of the people who received the blessings of Jesus' teachings and miracles did not measure up to His standards for friendship to Him. "Ye are my friends, if ye do the things which I command you" (John 15:14).

Thank God, it remains forever true that He loves us—greater love there can not be. But it also remains forever true that if we love

Him we will keep His commandments. His commands are not grievous; but they are the way of life and the richest blessings. He has first loved us. He has sought us out and made a way for us to know Him, and serve Him, and love Him. If we are not His friend it is altogether our own fault.

For Further Study:

Lewis, C. S. *The Four Loves.* New York: Harcourt, Brace and Company, 1960. Pp. 87-127. Insights into the nature of friendship and love.

# 32

## EXPRESSING OUR FRIENDSHIP FOR CHRIST

A look at three incidents will reveal a beautiful friendship between Jesus and the sisters, Mary and Martha, and their brother, Lazarus. Their home was in Bethany, which was only about two miles from Jerusalem. There Jesus was received and entertained with great respect, but also with a naturalness and freedom of conversation and action that indicate familiarity and genuine mutual understanding and affection. Although the Gospel accounts are so brief that they tell only these three incidents, they clearly imply that Jesus had other associations with His Bethany friends. At the time of His first recorded visit with them, they were already disciples and full of faith. These events will be more easily associated and understood by us if we consider them in the order in which they happened (Luke 10:38-42; John 11; Mark 14:3-9. Cf. Matt. 26:6-13 and John 12:1-11).

### *"One Thing is Needful"*

Jesus was received in the home of Martha, Luke tells us. Nothing is ever said of the parents of Mary, Martha, and Lazarus, or of any husband to Martha, unless the guess is correct that Simon the leper was one or the other. Martha seems to be the mistress of the house and is called by Luke a "lady" ("Kuria," the feminine form of lord). Even Lazarus is not mentioned at this visit.

Her sister Mary "also sat at his feet and heard his word." The word "also" may be meant to indicate that that was not all she did. When Martha became so perplexed about much serving that she complained to Jesus that Mary did not help her, she said that Mary had "left" her to serve alone. Perhaps Mary had completed what she thought it her duty to do. It is suggestive to observe that at another feast for Jesus, (John 12:2) Martha served and Mary apparently did not. It appears that Martha was a good cook and "server," probably taking pleasure in her skill for preparing fine dinners. This time she seems to be overdoing it, to be bothered about unexpected guests, or something of the kind, for she becomes "cumbered with much serving," "anxious and troubled." She comes to Jesus and says, "Lord, dost thou not care that my sister did leave me to serve alone? Bid her therefore to help me." That Mary was not to be blamed for shirking is evident from Jesus' answer. Jesus' judgment of the merits in the case can certainly be relied upon; and

He defended Mary's "choice." However, His reproof of Martha was gentle and kindly: "Martha, Martha, thou art anxious and troubled about many things: but one thing is needful: for Mary hath chosen the good part, which shall not be taken away from her." It is easy to see where Jesus thought correction should be made. While Martha's service was probably unselfish and was intended to please Him, she had misjudged His interests and tastes. She had not realized *the one thing* that is always more needful in the Lord's sight than anything so temporal as food for the body. Martha was fretting and vexing herself over "many things" which were simply not worth it in themselves, but which especially were not worthy to interfere with the higher things of the Spirit—the hearing and heeding of the words of the Lord, the feeding of the soul.

Jesus' attitude here was just the same that He had tried to teach in Matthew 6:19-34 and Luke 12:22-34: "Seek ye his kingdom, and these things shall be added unto you." This was Mary's choice. While Jesus showed sympathy and love for Martha, He pitied and chided her, but for Mary He had only words of approval.

### *"He Whom Thou Lovest Is Sick"*

The first mention of Lazarus, the brother of Mary and Martha, was when he was sick with the sickness that caused his death. Although we do not know how much Lazarus had been with Jesus before, still his sisters knew that Jesus loved him, and John (11:5) reassures us that Jesus loved Mary and Martha and Lazarus. Jesus' friends knew His interest enough to send messengers to tell Him of Lazarus' sickness, even though Jesus was a long distance away—two of three days' journey, at least. Notice that the sisters did not ask Jesus to come heal Lazarus. They knew the danger that it would be to Jesus for Him to come near to Jerusalem. They probably knew well that Jesus could heal him with a word, without coming. They simply stated the facts in such a manner as to express their confidence in Jesus' love for Lazarus, and left it to Him to do what He would.

Jesus was certainly master of the situation. He announced to those with Him, "This sickness is not unto death, but for the glory of God, that the Son of God may be glorified thereby." He deliberately abode two days more where He was, then set out for Bethany. When He arrived, Lazarus had been dead four days. Jesus had known of his death, and had told His disciples of His purpose to come to awake him. When Martha heard that Jesus was coming, she went out to meet Him, and said, "Lord, if thou hadst been here, my brother had not died. And even now I know that whatsoever thou shalt ask of God, God will give thee." Even when Jesus said, "Thy brother shall rise again," Martha did not doubt, but confessed her faith in Him as the Son of God. Mary, too, was believing, but when Jesus saw her weeping, and the Jews also weeping who came with her, He groaned in the Spirit and was troubled, and shed tears Himself. The people said, "Behold how he loved him!" Together they went to the tomb, and Jesus called Lazarus from the dead.

After these experiences and expressions of great faith and of strong mutual affection, is it any wonder that when Jesus came again to Bethany for the Passover feast they made a feast for Him? Or that during those last trying days of storm and strife He spent the nights in Bethany?

### *"She Hath Done What She Could"*

After raising Lazarus, Jesus went away from Bethany to avoid the Pharisees, who were now more than ever determined to kill Him. But it was only a few weeks until the Passover, and six days before the Passover He came to Bethany. A supper was prepared for Him at which Martha served, Lazarus sat at meat, and Mary anointed Him (John 12:1-3). But the supper was in the home of Simon the leper (Matt. 26:6; Mark 14:3). Nothing else is known of this man Simon, but he must have been a close friend or relative of Lazarus and his sisters, possibly even their father or the husband of Martha. Surely he was not now a leper, but had been healed, if the text means that he was present at the feast. Perhaps his home was the same as Martha's house, and she was, or had been, mistress of it because he was away in a leper colony.

Here at supper together these friends who owed so much to Jesus, who believed so firmly in Him, who had felt so much of His love, were drawn to Him with many of the closest ties of spiritual affection. Now they even shared His danger, for the rulers in Jerusalem were seeking to put to death both Lazarus and Jesus (John 12:10). It is evident that the twelve disciples were at the supper, but we can not tell whether the local guests were many or few. Even if they were many, still in spite of their presence Mary carried out her expression of deep devotion.

While Jesus reclined upon a couch (as the custom was) before the table, Mary came with a sealed jar of very precious perfume. Breaking the jar, she poured the ointment on Jesus' head and also on His feet. And she wiped His feet with her hair.

This token of affection took the company by surprise. Lazarus and his sisters may have been in sufficiently good circumstances to admit of their making a substantial acknowledgment of their indebtedness to Jesus; and although this alabaster box of ointment had cost as much as would keep a laboring man's family for a year, this could not seem an excessive return to make for service so valuable as Jesus had rendered. It was the manner of the acknowledgment which took the company by surprise. Jesus was a poor man, and His very appearance may have suggested that there were other things He needed more urgently than such a gift as this. Had the family provided a home for Him or given Him the price of this ointment, no one would have uttered a remark. But this was the kind of demonstration reserved for princes or persons of great distinction; and when paid to one so conspicuously humble in His dress and habits, there seemed to the uninstructed eye something incongruous and bordering on the grotesque. When the fragrance of the ointment disclosed its value, there was therefore an instantaneous exclamation of surprise, and at any rate in one instance of blunt disapproval, Judas instinctively putting a money value on this display of affection, roundly and with coarse indelicacy declared it had better have been sold and given to the poor.[1]

When objection was made to the extravagance of Mary's act, Jesus said, "Let her alone . . . . She hath wrought a good work on me . . . . She hath done what she could. She hath anointed my body beforehand for the burying." It is hard to tell whether Mary, more than any other disciple, realized that Jesus would give up His life on the cross, and hence purposely anointed Him with reference to His death. It may be that Jesus made that application of her act beyond her conscious intention. But she ought to give her best in one unreserved act of devotion and honor to Him. *Nothing is too good for the Lord!* He desires and deserves our heart's fullest overflowing adoration.

We, too, may be friends of Jesus. He is as ready to love us as He was to love these friends at Bethany.

---

[1] Marcus Dods, *The Expositor's Bible: The Gospel of John*, Vol. II, (New York: A. C. Armstrong and Son, 1903), pp. 4-5.

For Further Study:

Edersheim, Alfred. *The Life and Times of Jesus the Messiah,* Vol. II. Grand Rapids: William B. Eerdmans, 1956 reprint. Pp. 145-147, 312-325, 358-360. Comment on narratives involving Lazarus, Mary and Martha.

LaSor, William. *Great Personalities of the New Testament.* Westwood, New Jersey: Fleming Revell Company, 1961, Pp. 60-69. Discusses Lazarus, Mary and Martha and their relationship with Jesus.

# 33

## CHRIST AND WOMEN

This outline is prepared to assist you in reading what Christ in the Gospels and through the apostles says about the place of women in salvation, in Christ's ministry, in the church, and in service for Christ.

### I. JESUS FREELY ASSOCIATED WITH WOMEN, MINISTERED TO THEM AND WAS HELPED BY THEM.

John 4:7-9, Jesus talked to the woman at the well. In 4:27, the disciples marvelled that He was speaking with a woman.

John 4:28-30, 41, 42, This woman had success in interesting the people of her village in Jesus.

Luke 7:37-50, A notorious sinner washed and kissed His feet. He said that she was forgiven and she loved much.

Matt. 15:21-28, In a foreign land, He granted a request for a Gentile woman and praised her faith. (Mark 7:25-30).

Matt. 19:13-15, He received little children when they were brought to Him, probably by their mothers, and taught, "See that ye despise not one of these little ones" (18:3-14).

Matt. 20:20-28, The mother of James and John dared come to Him and ask for her sons to sit in the chief seats in His kingdom.

Luke 10:38-42, He upheld Mary for sitting to hear His teaching when Martha wanted her to help with serving.

Luke 8:1-3, Some women traveled about with Him and provided for His entourage out of their own means.

Matt. 21:31, Jesus said the harlots would go into the kingdom ahead of the Pharisees, because they were willing to repent.

Matt. 14:21; 15:38, There were women and children in the crowds (5,000 and 4,000 men) which He fed miraculously.

Luke 11:27, 28, A woman dared to speak up in public to praise the blessedness of His mother. Jesus answered her, offering the same blessedness to anyone who would hear the word of God and keep it.

Mark 12:41-44, He pointed out the humble woman who had only two mites to give, and said she had given more than the rich men, for it was all she had. (Luke 21:1-4).

Matt. 26:6-13, He let Mary of Bethany anoint Him with precious ointment at a public feast and upheld her as doing a good deed which would always be remembered to her credit. (John 12:1-8; Mark 14:3-9).

Matt. 27:55, 56, There were women at the cross who had followed Him from Galilee and ministered to him. (Mark 15:40, 41; Luke 23:49; John 19:25).

John 19:26, 27, From the cross He assigned to John the care of His mother.

Luke 23:27-29, On the way to the cross He tried to comfort and warn the women who wept and mourned for Him in His sufferings.

II. JESUS ACCEPTED WOMEN INTO THE FAVOR OF GOD AND THE FELLOWSHIP OF THE FAITHFUL.

A. In His teaching, he showed sympathy and kindness for them. Sometimes He made them examples in His teaching.

Matt. 12:42, "The queen of the South will rise up in judgment with this generation and condemn it." (Luke 11:31).

Matt. 12:46-50, He offered to all women the privilege of being as important in His sight as His mother or sisters, if only they would do the will of His Father in heaven. (Mark 3:32-45; Luke 8:20, 21).

Matt. 24:16-21, In predicting the extreme hardships of the days of the destruction of Jerusalem, Jesus told the Christians to flee from the city; at the same time He expressed deep sorrow for the mothers with young babies and those about to be delivered. (Mark 13:14-17; Luke 21:20-23).

Matt. 24:40, 41, He speaks of women being chosen for rescue before the world's destruction in the same manner as men. (Luke 17:34, 35).

Matt. 19:4-6, Jesus emphasized the unity of man and wife, and the obligation of a husband to his wife as above that to his father. (Mark 10:6-9).

B. Later women received salvation in the same manner as men.

Gal. 3:25-28, All become children of God by faith and baptism into Christ, regardless of race, slavery, or sex.

Rom. 3:23-26, There is no distinction. All have sinned and are saved through the death of Christ and faith in the gospel.

Acts 5:14, Crowds of both men and women believed the gospel and were added to the Lord.

Acts 6:1-6, Foreign-born widows were numerous in the church very early.

Acts 8:12, Both men and women at Samaria believed and were baptized.

Acts 8:3; 9:2, Both men and women were persecuted and imprisoned for their faith.

Acts 16:14, 15, Lydia, a businesswoman, obeyed the gospel and furnished lodging to the preachers.

Acts 17:4, 12, At Thessalonica, many chief women believed and joined with the Christians.

Acts 17:34, At Athens, a woman was among the first few converts.

III. AFTER JESUS' DEATH AND IN HIS RESURRECTION APPEARANCES, WOMEN WERE MOST FAITHFUL AND HIGHLY FAVORED.

Matt. 27:61, Although two men who were prominent rulers of the Jews took charge of the body of Jesus and buried it, women disciples of His watched how it was done and determined to add their contribution toward completing the care of it. (Mark 15:47; Luke 23:55, 56).

Matt. 28:1, 5-8, Women came early on the first day of the week to the tomb, received from angels the first report of the resurrection, and were told to tell the apostles. (Mark 16:1-8; Luke 24:1-9; John 20:1, 2).

| | |
|---|---|
| John 20:11-18, | Jesus appeared first to Mary Magdalene. (Mark 16:9). |
| Matt. 28:9, | His second appearance was to the other women as they were obeying the angels' instructions to tell the apostles of His rising. |
| Mark 16:10, 11, | These women did deliver the message faithfully, although they were disbelieved. (Luke 24:10, 11, 22-25; John 20:18). |
| Acts 1:14, | The women continued in prayer and expectation with the apostles after Jesus had ascended, before the day of Pentecost. |

IV. JESUS CHOSE MEN, NOT WOMEN, TO BE SPIRITUAL LEADERS.

Jesus did not appoint any woman to be an apostle, or to be one of the seventy other miracle-working witnesses whom He sent out in Judea before His death (Luke 10:1-20). There is no indication that women received directly the great commission, on any of the several occasions when He gave it, or when He promised the divine powers and authority by which they would be empowered to carry it out. (Read John 20:21-23; 21:15-23; Matt. 28:18-20; Mark 16:15, 16; Luke 24:45-49; Acts 1:2-11.) There is no indication that any women received the outpouring of the Holy Spirit on the day of Pentecost, by which the apostles' message was attested. Of course, those who obeyed that day in repenting and being baptized in water, did receive the gift of the Holy Spirit which is part of the new birth of every Christian. But all of the following verses indicate that those who were baptized in the Holy Spirit and spoke in tongues on that occasion were apostles: Acts 1:26; 2:1; 2:7, 14, 37, 42. On Pentecost and following it, it was the apostles who bore the witness, worked the miracles, taught the people, bore the persecution, etc. Acts 3:6; 4:3, 33, 35; 5:12, 13, 18, 29, 40-42; 6:2, 6.

V. THE PLACE OF WOMEN IN THE EARLY CHURCH

A. N.T. passages which show service by women in the church:

1. Women workers:

| | |
|---|---|
| Rom. 16:1, 2, | Phoebe was a *deaconess* or *minister.* |
| Rom. 16:3-5, | Prisca (Priscilla) and Aquila, Paul's *fellow workers* deserve gratitude of many, and have |

a church in their home at Rome.

Acts 18:18, 19, Priscilla and Aquila had worked with Paul at Corinth and at Ephesus (I Cor. 16:19), and had a church in their house.

Rom. 16:6, "Mary worked hard among you." (R.S.V.)

I Cor. 11:5-16, Women were expected to pray or prophesy under the right conditions (but not in the main assembly; read I Cor. 14:26, 33-35).

Phil. 4:2, 3, Euodia and Syntyche "labored side by side with me." (R.S.V.)

Col. 4:15, Nympha had a church in her home.

Acts 21:8-10, Philip had four daughters who prophesied, but the message was given to Paul by Agabus.

Acts 5:1, 7-10, Sapphira shared with her husband in giving property to the church, and shared in the penalty for misrepresenting it.

Acts 12:12-16, Mary held a prayer meeting in her house, and Rhoda, a maid, kept the door and informed the Christians of Peter's arrival.

Acts 9:36-41, Dorcas served in good works and *almsdeeds* and was loved for it.

2. Instructions concerning women:

I Tim. 5:4-10, Dedicated women were supported by the churches if they had no family to support them and they had served well at home, in hospitality, benevolence, and every good work and continued in prayers day and night (and were at least 60 years old).

I Tim. 5:11-15, Younger widows are not likely to serve as well, but should marry, bear children, rule their household.

*Note: Women are to "rule their household" (I Tim. 5:14) in submission to their husbands (Eph. 5:21-33). God commands their husbands to love and honor them (I Pet. 3:7); and their children to respect and obey them (Eph. 6:1; Col. 3:18-20).*

I Tim. 3:11, Qualifications for women (either wives of elders, or women who serve somewhat as deacons serve).

Titus 2:3-5, The preacher is to instruct older women to train younger women in godliness and in exemplary family life, so that the word of God will not be spoken against.

Acts 2:17, 18, The powers of the Spirit, especially prophecy, are promised to daughters and handmaidens (not necessarily in the same degree or for all the same functions).

I Cor. 7:34, 35, An unmarried woman may be more careful for the things of the Lord than one who is concerned to please her husband.

I Cor. 7:39, 40, If a husband dies, the widow is free to marry another in the Lord, but may be happier to remain unmarried, under the circumstances of that time.

In general a Christian woman serves her Lord in serving her husband and children, but in many situations the demands made by her family may conflict with her highest ideals or desire for single-minded devotion to Christ. She can be holy, even with an un-Christian husband, but she could have less conflicts and distress in being holy without him. Yet, if she is married, she must live out her faith in that condition and not desert her family responsibility. (I Cor. 7:10-17).

B. Passages of the N.T. which direct and limit the area of service by women.

1. I Cor. 14:33b-37, Women are not to speak among the prophets in the public gathering of the whole church (see 14:26-33).

a. I Cor. 11:5-10, In the same book, conditions are stated under which they may pray or prophesy, evidently in some kind of private or semi-private situations.

b. I Cor. 11:3-12, The explanation for excluding women from speaking revelations for the church is found in the divine order of headship by which God's authority is graciously administered to us.

(1) Eph. 5:21-33, As verse 21 says, All of us are to be

subject to one another out of reverence for Christ. Wives are to be subject to the husbands because Christ has so designed for them to live in good order and to help their husbands practice the responsibility which is assigned to them by God and which is good for all the family. This works well when husbands love their wives "as Christ loved the church and gave Himself up for her." To acknowledge and follow God's wisdom in this divine order (of submission and responsible oversight) brings a blessing to the whole human family.

(2) Col. 3:18, 19, "Wives, be subject to your husbands, as is fitting in the Lord. Husbands, love your wives, and do not be harsh with them." (RSV)

(3) Gen. 3:16, "He shall rule over thee." This was probably what Paul referred to in "as also saith the law" (I Cor. 14:34).

(4) I Pet. 3:1-6, Women are to be in subjection to their husbands, live chastely, adorning themselves with a meek and quiet spirit.

Note on I Pet. 3:1-6 and Eph. 5:21-33:

When people are doubtful about the rightness of Christian wives being in subjection to ungodly husbands who expect them to participate in sinful deeds, they may be helped by reading Acts 4:19, 20 and 5:29. Notice that Peter taught Christians to be subject to every human institution as a general rule (I Pet. 2:13-17). But Peter himself set a good example of obeying God rather than men, when his rulers commanded him to disobey Christ (Acts 4:18-20; 5:29-32). And God upheld him and the other apostles in this resistance to authority (Acts 4:23-33; 5:17-25). Yet the apostles were submissive to the rulers in taking the punishment which their resistance brought on them. They bore the penalty patiently and without railing or retaliation.

2. I Tim. 2:8-15, Women are not to teach or exercise authority over a man.

a. Extent of teaching or leadership done by women.

(1) Acts 18:26, Priscilla apparently aided Aquila in "expounding the word of the Lord more perfectly" to Apollos, whether she took part in the discussion or just opened her home to him. Either way, it was done privately with no thought of domination over him.

(2) II Tim. 1:5, 3:14, 15, Timothy's grandmother Lois and mother Eunice were quite probably responsible for teaching him the "sacred writings."

Women certainly have the responsibility to teach and guide their own children, and that does not entirely cease at a certain birthday; yet the propriety and effectiveness of her teaching diminishes as the young man takes on the independence and responsibilities of a man. She should then rely upon her teachings of earlier years (and perhaps indirect or gentle reminders of them) and do her best to respect and use and build up the manhood of young men.

(3) Titus 2:3-5, "To train younger women to love their husbands and children, to be sensible, chaste, domestic, kind, and submissive to their husbands."(R.S.V.)

(4) I Tim. 2:12-14, It is not wrong for a woman to have information and to give it, but it is not well for her to assume the position of boss or director over men. This is a valid distinction, although either could be called teaching. There is a real difference between sharing knowledge modestly, and assuming authority in leadership, although the word "teaching" might be applied to either one. The women to whom Jesus appeared after His resurrection were told to tell the apostles that good news. But they were not given the position of apostles or leadership in the church. On the whole it seems that the Lord is not

trying so much to limit the rights of anyone as He is trying to teach a better order and to make known the relative duties He wants men and women to perform. It seems that I Tim. 2:12-14 connects the teaching a woman is not to do with serving in authority over a man, and with being a guide who may not always be reliable in times of moral crisis. ("The woman being beguiled hath fallen into transgression.")

(5) I Tim. 2:12. The meaning of "teach" is more than merely to give information; perhaps it means something more like setting standards for the church, or as in Titus 2:15: "These things speak and exhort and reprove with all authority. Let no one despise you."

The kind of situation which we have in a Sunday School class (or a home Bible study) is not described in the New Testament at all. It is hard to be sure whether or not it should be regarded as the assembly of the church in which a woman is not to speak, even to ask a question. (I Cor. 14:34, 35). Probably it is more like the situations in which Paul expected women to pray or prophesy (I Cor. 11:5), or to be active in training younger women and children. (Titus 2:3-5).

It is not fitting for us to make exact rules about what is permitted and what is not, where the Lord has not made it plain for us. But the principles of modesty, submission, and helpfulness must be put into practice.

In New Testament churches women ministered of their time, substance, hospitality, and labors in a variety of ways. Their part in the service of the church was appreciated and important, but it was not a leading part, not directive or managerial.

Although there is no distinction between Jew or Gentile, slave or slaveowner, woman or man in the matter of being welcomed into the family of God (Gal. 3:22-29), there is in God's sight a difference in the lines of service for which men and women are fitted and in which they make their best contribution to the whole family of God.

The most important thing to understand is this. The teachings of the Scriptures are not to be made a strict set of rules to set exact limits on a woman's activities, but to give the principles by which each Christian is to be guided in contributing the most to others in any situation.

The Christian woman must accept the fact that God has made her "for the man" (I Cor. 11:9). She was not created to be just like a man, but to be a helper and fill a need (Gen. 2:18-24).

She will be just as important and just as great in God's sight, without being as dominant or as much as public leader as the man. Jesus taught that the one who is servant of all is the greatest of all (Matt. 20:26-28; 23:11, 12; Mark 10:43-45). *Submission does not mean inferiority.* Jesus submitted to God and became a servant to all of us and God exalted Him for it (Phil. 2:5-11). Jesus would not consider a woman inferior because she is subject to her husband and is servant to her family. According to Jesus' teaching and example she will be exalted for it.

She must recognize man's God-given responsibility to lead in the family, in the church, and in society; and she should do her best to help him fulfill that responsibility.

Yet God, who established this order in the family of man and gave to women their greatness in a subordinate position, has shown in His word that women can sometimes serve outside their usual area of subordination. Consider the examples of Miriam (Exodus 15:20, 21); Deborah (Judges 4:4-10); Huldah (II Kings 22:14-20; II Chron. 34:22).

Is there really any need for a struggle between men and women to prove their importance, rights, or superiority? Should the man try to suppress the woman, or the woman resist her special calling and try to prove that she has unlimited rights and powers? Both must submit to the Lord Jesus.

Let both value each other, as God has valued every human being, and serve each other as it is His will for us to do: "in honor preferring one another" (Rom. 12:10). "For ye, brethren, were called for freedom; only use not your freedom for an occasion to the flesh, but through love be servants (slaves) one to another. For the whole law is fulfilled in one word, even in this: Thou shalt love thy neighbor as thyself. But if ye bite and devour one another, take heed that ye be not consumed one of another" (Gal. 5:13-15).

Let us accept the teachings and the challenges in the word of our loving Father that guide and stimulate each of us to fill a place that will richly bless us with the highest fulfillment of our God-given natures.

For Further Study:

Elliott, Elizabeth. *Let Me Be A Woman.* Wheaton: Tyndale Press, 1976. Response to those advocating a Christian feminism.

Ryrie, C. C. *The Role of Women in the Church.* Chicago: Moody Press, 1958. Basic study on the New Testament teaching concerning women.

# *Part Seven*

# THE KINGDOM

## 34

## THE KING OF KINGS

This is a study based upon two advance announcements of the coming of the Son of God to earth. One was through the prophet Isaiah more than seven hundred years before the event. The other was the message of the angel of God to Jesus' mother at the time of His conception (Isa. 9:2-7; Luke 1:26-80).

### *The King in Prophecy*

It was fitting that the hearts and minds of men should be prepared for His coming, made ready to realize His significance and to receive Him. All of God's dealings with men recorded in the Old Testament were preparation for His coming. But it was fitting that specific prophecies concerning Him, His person, character, offices, and work, should be given to arouse expectation and to lay a foundation for faith in Him. The prophecies furnished identification for Him when He came. They were part of the credentials of the Christ (cf. John 5:39, 46; Luke 24:25-27, 44-46).

Of course, the Scriptures chosen for this lesson do not by any means give a complete picture of the person and work of Christ. Other prophecies depict Him as the great prophet (Deut. 18:15-18; Isa. 61:1, 2), as the suffering servant and sacrifice for sins (Psalm 22; Isa. 53), and as the great eternal high priest (Ps. 110:4). These are selected to emphasize His authority to rule—to announce Him as King, Prince, and Lord.

In the past tense of prophecy, which speaks of the future as if it were already come to pass, He is promised as a "great light" and a bringer of joy to the nation. The will of the Lord revealed *is light.* It is according to truth and full of infinite wisdom. "The commandment of Jehovah is pure, enlightening the eyes" (Ps. 19:8). The whole world is in darkness and "the shadow of death" until Christ, the Light of the world, shines in the hearts of men (John 8:12; I John 1:5-7; 5:19, 20). The government of God is desirable. His goodness and mercy, His righteousness and majesty, bring the only true and lasting joy. "The precepts of the Lord are right, rejoicing the heart"

(Ps. 19:8). "Joy to the world, the Lord is come: Let earth receive her King!"

To emphasize His rulership it is said: "The government shall be upon his shoulder." He shall be called by terms which describe an exalted and divine ruler. His is an ever increasing government in never ending peace. "Of the increase of his government and of peace there shall be no end, upon the throne of David and upon his kingdom." He has a throne, "the throne of David." His kingdom shall be established and upheld with righteousness forever. All this was predicted in this one short passage in Isaiah. Other prophecies of similar import may be read in Genesis 49:10; Numbers 24:15-17; Psalm 2:1-9; 45:6, 7; 72; 110:1, 2; Isaiah 2:1-4; 11:1-10; 42:1-4; Jeremiah 23:5, 6; Daniel 7:13, 14, 27; Micah 5:2-4; Zechariah 9:9.

### *The King in the New Testament*

Luke 1 quotes the words of the angel Gabriel concerning Jesus: "The Lord God shall give unto him the throne of his father David: and he shall reign over the house of Jacob for ever; and of his kingdom there shall be no end" (Luke 1:32, 33).

Throughout the Gospels, Jesus is presented as King. This is especially apparent in Matthew, who records: (1) Jesus' royal lineage as the son of David; (2) the visit of the Wise-men to worship the newborn "King of the Jews"; (3) much teaching by Jesus about "His kingdom" (see especially Matt. 13:41 and 16:28); (4) "in the regeneration, the Son of man shall sit on the throne of his glory" (Matt. 19:28); (5) the request of James and John for chief places "in the kingdom" (Matt. 20:21); (6) Jesus' deliberate arrangements to fulfill (Zech. 9:9): "Behold thy king cometh" (Matt. 21:1-11); (7) the prediction of His throne of judgment before which "all nations" shall be judged (Matt. 25:31ff.); (8) Jesus' solemn affirmation in answer to Pilate's question: "Art thou the king of the Jews?" (Matt. 27:11); (9) the mockery of the soldiers and the sign on the cross, all of which emphasized that the real charge against Him was that He claimed to be king (Matt. 27:29, 42; Mark 15:18, 32; Luke 23:36, 37; John 19:19-22); (10) Jesus said, "All authority hath been given unto me in heaven and on earth" (Matt. 28:18).

Certainly, Jesus was a king, is King, and always will be "King of kings, and Lord of lords" (cf. I Tim. 6:15; Rev. 17:14; 19:16). It is true that He will deliver up the kingdom to the Father when all opposing power has been subdued (I Cor. 15:24, 25). He will complete and conclude His reign of intercessory and redemptive work, but He with the Father shall reign forever.

He is "Lord of both the dead and the living" (Rom. 14:9). He is risen "to rule over the Gentiles" (Rom. 15:12). He is at the right hand of God, "above all rule and authority," etc. (Eph. 1:20-22). His is the name above every name, "that in the name of Jesus every knee should bow," etc. (Phil. 2:10). Those who suffer with Him are to "reign with him" (II Tim. 2:12); for He will save them "unto his eternal kingdom" (II Tim. 4:18), "the eternal kingdom of our Lord and Saviour, Jesus Christ" (II Pet. 1:11). He is "ruler of the kings of the earth" (Rev. 1:5), "King of the ages" (Rev. 15:3); and "he shall reign for ever and ever" (Rev. 11:15; Heb. 1:8).

Still His kingship was not such as Herod imagined (Matt. 2:3), or such as the Galileans sought to make of Him (John 6:15): "they were about to come and take him by force, to make him king," or such as Pilate may have feared; for His kingdom "is not of this world" (John 18:36). His kingdom is not of this world, either in origin or nature; but it is in this world as well as in the next. It is to us in this world that all these Scriptures are written announcing Him as King. To us the beneficence of His rule is promised; and to us are the warnings and threats of His just wrath and vengeance upon those who are unwilling that He should rule over them. He came into this world to be a king (John 18:37; Matt. 2:2; Luke 1:32); yet He went out of it again to receive His kingdom (Luke 19:11-27); for His is a spiritual reign in the hearts of men who voluntarily accept it.

### *Exalting Him as King in our Lives*

We have seen above the testimony of the Scriptures to the ruling authority of Jesus Christ. That is what *God* thinks about the matter. "Let all . . . know assuredly that God hath made him both Lord and Christ, this Jesus whom ye crucified" (Acts 2:36). The trouble is that *men* do not recognize the appointment of God and accept Jesus as King. The one supreme tragedy, and the cause of all others in this world is that men do not exalt Christ as Lord. Although He is the "stone" that God has made "the head of the corner," He has been rejected by too many of the human builders. The fact that they reject Him does not alter the fact that He is their Master and Judge to whom they must answer. He has all authority and providential power over us, but *He does not force us now* to do His will. His rulership and His law are proclaimed unto men, and they are called upon to accept and obey Him, but He does not take away our power to choose or to refuse. He gives us liberty to sow as we will, *but He governs strictly what we will reap.*

God has made a plain and powerful revelation of His Son as Lord and Saviour, and of His will that all men should "honor the Son even as they honor the Father." He has set forth plainly His virgin birth, His eternal being, His divine Sonship, His divine attributes, His authority and power. God has made our attitude towards His Son the great issue of our lives. Any one who is not for Him is against Him (Matt. 12:30; 10:32, 33; Luke 12:49-59; John 3:16-18, 36; 8:24, etc.). Having revealed His Son and His will, God now "commandeth men that they should all everywhere repent: inasmuch as he hath appointed a day in which he will judge the world in righteousness by the man whom he hath ordained" (Acts 17:30, 31).

Christ should be exalted in the nation—our nation, and every nation. He was presented to the Jewish nation, an offer of righteous power and wisdom to bring them light, peace and joy. But they sought to exalt themselves, and turned Him down.

Any nation can have the great Redeemer for their own King if the people of that nation will enthrone Him in their hearts and do His will. His good will would be the law of our land tomorrow if we the people would just respect His authority and give heed to His commandment in His Word. If we would acknowledge *now* our Lord, before whom we shall some day be judged, we could have our nation freed from its greatest dangers and weaknesses—liquor, crime, greed, industrial strife, broken homes, and every form of sin. We would have the assurance of His power to preserve us and to prosper us; and we would have peace as only the Prince of Peace can establish it. But we can not exalt the divine Lord of our lives by such things as a commercialized and selfish celebration of Christmas, a formal resolution or official proclamation now and then, or by turning His church into a political pressure group that has exchanged the truth of His Word for the lies of modernism. We must exalt Him in the nation by personal and individual allegiance to Him. We must admire Him as "Wonderful," learn of Him as "Counsellor," worship and serve Him as "Mighty God," trust and love Him as "Everlasting Father," and follow Him as "Prince of Peace" with a loyalty greater than patriotism (Isa. 9:6). We must seek first His kingdom and His righteousness (Matt. 6:33).

For Further Study:

Geldenhuys, Norval. *The New Testament Commentary: The Gospel of Luke.* Grand Rapids: William B. Eerdmans, 1951. Pp. 74-98.

Leupold, H. C. *Exposition of Isaiah*, Vol. I. Grand Rapids: Baker Book House, 1968. Pp. 180-196.

Young, E. J. *The Book of Isaiah*, Vol. I. Grand Rapids: William B. Eerdmans, 1965. Pp. 325-343. Scholarly study of Isaiah 9:2-7 on the Messianic King.

# 35

## THE KINGDOM OF GOD AMONG MEN

The New Testament says much about the kingdom, mentioning it 140 times by the term "kingdom," besides the other terms and phrases used. The whole message of the great prophet, John the Baptist, was the importance of the coming kingdom and of personal preparation for it. Jesus taught more about the kingdom than He did about any other subject. He taught men to pray for the kingdom to come (Matt. 6:10). He said it was the greatest treasure in the world, one for which any one should joyfully sell all other possessions that he might gain the kingdom (Matt. 13:44-46). He told us all to "Seek first the kingdom of God and his righteousness; and all these things shall be added unto you" (Matt. 6:33). He made it more important than the food and clothing which are necessary to physical life. Surely it matters much whether we believe in the kingdom and know it, not only in theory, but in vital experience.

### *What is the Kingdom of God?*

It is not easy to give a definite and brief answer which would be satisfactory to all the Scriptural uses of the phrase. Its essential idea is the reign or government of God over the lives of men. Sometimes it comprehends the characteristics and advantages of the complete submission of an individual life to the rule of God. Sometimes it refers to the whole community of men who obey God on earth. Sometimes it has reference to heaven itself as a place where God reigns in perfect peace, wisdom, and glory. But regardless of all other circumstances, it is always essentially the rule of God in the hearts of men.

Other terms and phrases are used for the same idea, and are freely interchanged with "the kingdom of God." Matthew uses the words "kingdom of heaven" about 29 times, although it is not used in any other New Testament book (cf. Matt. 13:11 with Mark 4:11; and Matt. 13:31 with Mark 4:30, 31, etc.) It is also called "his kingdom (the son of Man's)" (Matt. 13:41; 15:28); "my kingdom" (Christ's) (John 18:36; Luke 22:29-30); "the everlasting kingdom of our Lord and Saviour Jesus Christ" (II Pet. 1:11); "the kingdom of God's dear Son" (Col. 1:13); "the kingdom of Christ and of God" (Eph. 5:5) "my (Christ's) church" (Matt. 16:18); the "church of God" (I Tim. 3:5, 15) "the church" (Eph. 1:22; 3:10, 21; 5:23-32); "the church of the first born (ones)" Heb. 12:23; or as congregations viewed distributively "churches of God" (I Cor. 11:16; I Thess. 2:14), and "churches of the saints" (I Cor. 14:33), and "churches of Christ" (Rom. 16:16).

These various expressions are not identical in their limits and points of emphasis, but they do overlap. All of them have reference to the realm of God's rule through Jesus Christ. That reign will someday be completed and unchallenged, and will continue so eternally; but it also exists now and has for many centuries in the midst of those who resist it or deny its present reality.

The kingdom is not represented as coming all at once fully formed and in its ultimate glory, but this term is used for the rule of God in different stages, and for the growing control of Christ over men through the gospel—"first the blade, then the ear, and then the full grain in the ear" (Mark 4:26-29). Study the other parables of the seed and of the leaven. Chiefly, of course, it looks forward to the glorious consummation, the complete subjection of all things to God, the eternal state of righteousness, peace, and blessedness that will result when God is given full control. Jesus came to establish the kingdom by revealing the righteousness, mercy, and goodness of God's will, and by winning the hearts of men to surrender themselves to Him—by redemption of sinners and reconciliation of their hearts to God, by putting the law of God into their minds and hearts through faith and love and regeneration of the Holy Spirit—(Heb. 8:10-11; John 3:5). The government of God is truly desirable. Pray that it may prevail upon earth as it does in Heaven. (See Psalm 19:7-14.)

As for the stages of the kingdom, there are (1) the kingdom of Israel when God was their true King, (2) the kingdom of grace, and (3) the kingdom of eternal glory: or, in other words, (1) the rule of God under the Mosaic law, (2) the rule of God through Christ and the church, and (3) the consummation of His rule and full assertion of His authority over all. There were "sons of the kingdom" (by fleshly inheritance) who were cast out (Matt. 8:12). Again, there was the kingdom which was come upon Christ's generation (Matt. 12:28) in the person of the king when the kingdom suffered violence from the days of John the Baptist (Matt. 11:12; Luke 16:16).

John the Baptist, Jesus, and the apostles (before the cross) preached that the kingdom was just at hand, to be expected and prepared for immediately. It was certain to come before that generation died (Matt. 16:28; Mark 9:1). In a sense it was already come (Matt. 12:28) in the person of the King, and it was suffering violence from the days of John the Baptist (Matt. 11:12; Luke 16:16). The rule of God and the principles of His realm were being presented in the preaching of Jesus, and Jesus could say, "Lo, the kingdom of God is in the midst of You" (Luke 17:21). This was said to the unbelieving Pharisees who did not have the kingdom in their hearts, but it was in the midst of them, in that its King was there proclaiming its laws and swaying His authority over them or at least some who were standing among them.

Now there is that stage of the kingdom which Jesus and John preached was "at hand" (Matt. 3:2; 4:17), which Jesus said would come before His hearers died (Mark 9:1), of which He spoke so much during the forty days after His resurrection (Acts 1:3), into which Paul says "we" have been translated (Col. 1:13), the kingdom formed of the redeemed while they are still among the wicked of the world (Rev. 1:6; 5:10). Then there will be the triumphant kingdom to come (II Pet. 1:11; II Tim. 4:1) in which not all church members will participate, but only those who are acceptable in faith and character unto the end (I Cor. 6:9, 10; Gal. 5:21; Cf. Matt. 13:47-50). These stages are frequently not distinguished: the word is used of life under God's control and care, both now and forever.

### *Characteristics of the Kingdom*

In Jesus' teaching on the kingdom in the Gospel accounts, the following characteristics of the kingdom are to be observed.

1. It springs from seed which is the word of God (Luke 8:11).
2. It comes by a process of continued growth (Mark 4:26-32).
3. Sons of the kingdom are the righteous (Matt. 5:20) growing in the world side by side with the wicked (Matt. 13:38-41).
4. The growing stage of the kingdom takes in some "bad" who are later to be eliminated and destroyed (Matt. 13:47-50).
5. It was "at hand" in the day of John and Jesus, to come before that generation died (Matt. 16:28; Mark 9:1).
6. Peter was to have the keys (Matt. 16:9).
7. Jesus taught His disciples to pray for its coming (Matt. 6:10).
8. It must be entered by a new birth of water and spirit (John 3:5).
9. It is the greatest treasure a man can find in this world; men will with joy sell all else to obtain it (Matt. 13:44-46).
10. It is not a kingdom of this world (John 18:36).
11. It does not come with a great demonstration of its power—"not with observation" (Luke 17:20).

12. The least in the kingdom is greater than the greatest born of woman (Matt. 11:11).

13. It is equivalent to "eternal life" and being "saved" (Luke 18:18, 25, 26).

Moreover, whenever it came to men, it was to come not with great demonstration of force, "not with observation," but as in inward growth (Mark 4:26-28). It was to spring from seed, which is the word of God (Luke 8:11), and to be brought about by preaching of the Word (Matt. 13:18-23). It was to begin small and grow to be very great (Matt. 13:31-33). During the growing stage it takes some "bad" as well as good, who have to be separated by the angels at the end of the world (Matt. 13:47-50). The sons of the kingdom are the righteous (Matt. 5:20), who grow in the world side by side with the wicked (Matt. 13:38-41). Yet it is not a kingdom of this world (John 18:36). It must be entered by a new birth of the Spirit (through faith in and submission to the word of the Spirit) and of water (baptism into Christ) (John 3:5; Eph. 5:26; Titus 3:5; I Pet. 1:23). And the least in the kingdom is greater than the greatest born of women (Matt. 11:11). Having part in it is equivalent to having "eternal life" and being "saved" (Luke 18:18, 25, 26).

One thing is evident—that Jesus did not mean to set up a worldly, materialistic, or military kingdom. The devil offered Him the kingdoms of the whole world, but He refused them (Matt. 4:8-10). The Jews and even the apostles wanted that kind of kingdom, but Jesus disappointed them. After the feeding of the five thousand, they sought to take Him by force and make Him king, but Jesus refused. The very next day He preached a sermon on the spiritual and eternal purposes of His ministry which was so unacceptable to them that multitudes went away and followed Him no more (John 6). This same idea presents itself at the time of the Triumphal Entry, when the people in all the clamor and excitement of a mob, gathered together as a whole nation at Jerusalem for the Passover, and welcomed Jesus into the city as "the King that cometh in the name of the Lord" (Luke 19:38), and as bring in the kingdom of His father David (Mark 11:10). If he had wanted a kingdom of force, or of material wealth, or of political organizations, He could have had it (see Matt. 26:53; John 18:36-37). Because of materialistic ambitions of the people regarding the Messiah, Jesus avoided telling plainly that He was the Christ, and He had to teach of His life's purpose and His kingdom by parables in order to hold their ambition and to try to make plain the unwelcome message of a spiritual kingdom, instead of temporal.

*Ways of Speaking of the Kingdom*

One group of passages represents the kingdom under the figure of a place. This is the case in all expressions involving the act of entering into the kingdom (Matt. 5:20; 7:21; 18:3). It is better to enter into the kingdom of heaven with one eye than, having two, to be cast out (Mark 9:27). Men are said to be near or far from it (Mark 12:34). Those who enter are those who are reborn and who do the will of God, who have by relationship with the Saviour and by their characters a certain fitness for it (Luke 9:62; Matt. 7:21; John 3:5). But after entrance has been secured, it is a place of enjoyment, as in Matthew 25:34, and a place where even Jesus Himself eats and drinks as in Matthew 26:29.

In a second class of passages the kingdom is represented as a possession. It is said to belong to the poor in spirit and to those persecuted for righteousness (Matt. 5:3, 10; Luke 18:16). It will be taken from the Jews and given to a nation bringing forth the fruits thereof (Matt. 21:43). It is the gift of God (Luke 12:32). It is the most valuable of possessions, and it is the height of wisdom to seek and the summit of prosperity to secure it (Matt. 6:33; Luke 12:31).

A third class of passages represents the kingdom as an organization constituted of a certain class of men. It is a body politic, growing from small beginnings into large proportions and power (Matt. 13:31; Mark 4:26, 27). Its members are the children of the kingdom (Matt. 13:38). Like every human organization, this, too, must have its offices and officers; but to suppose that these are to be appointed without reference to their character and on the same principle as in the political sphere—in order to lord it over their fellow members—is a grievous error. They rule in the very act of serving their brethren (Matt. 20:21-28; Luke 9:48).

A fourth class of passages designates the kingdom as an order of things, or a dispensation. Especially the Old Testament prophets announce the coming of this new order, first in Jerusalem and then to the whole world, under the dominion of the Messiah (Dan. 2:44; 7:14, 27)—a kingdom of the saints (holy ones). It shall be the final and everlasting dispensation, characterized by righteousness, justice and truth, by peace and perfect harmony, by prosperity and security (Isa. 9:6, 7; 11:1-10; 65:17-25; Micah 4:1-4). It was this that John and Jesus announced the approach of—God's rule in the transformed hearts of men. Jesus taught His disciples to announce the kingdom, to pray for it, and to prepare for it (Matt. 6:10-13; 7:23-27; Luke

12:35-48). The new feature of the dispensation thus announced is its spirituality. Its members are in it by choice and by their perfect willingness to do God's will. Thus its law is written on their hearts and in their minds (Heb. 8:10-12; Rom. 12:1, 2). It is a kingdom whose members share a common faith which dominates the life, and common gratitude for grace received, and common experience of self-renunciation or repentance, bringing all things into subjection to God and His Son, Jesus Christ. It is not brought about by outward coercion or characterized by external regulation. Its reality and power are constituted by inward transformation. One must be born anew to see it properly (John 3:3). "For the kingdom of God is not eating and drinking, but righteousness and peace and joy in the Holy Spirit" (Rom. 14:17).

The kingdom did come in the generation of the apostles as Jesus said it would (Mark 9:1). It did come with power on the day of Pentecost after His resurrection. Peter was given the keys (Matt. 16:19). Paul went everywhere preaching the kingdom of God (Acts 20:25), although he determined to know nothing save Jesus Christ and Him crucified (I Cor. 2:2). Philip preached the kingdom of God, and the faith of the Samaritans caused them to be baptized into Christ and become members of the church (Acts 8:12). Paul says God "translated us into the kingdom of his dear Son" (Col. 1:13), and John says "he made us to be a kingdom" (Rev. 1:6). The church is a kingdom. Today, in our dispensation, it is THE kingdom. It is certainly not a democracy as to its nature. Christ is the absolute monarch over all things pertaining to the church (Eph. 1:22).

The Scriptures examined in this study emphasize what participation in Christ's kingdom demands of the individual. Jesus wants us to count the cost of discipleship. He deliberately discourages the careless follower (Luke 9:58). He strictly demands undivided allegiance of those who want to do something else first (9:59-62). We must not permit ourselves to allow anything to become an excuse for resisting the command of Christ. The blessings and benefits of the kingdom depend upon the absolute rule of God; divine wisdom and goodness must have their way and have our fullest co-operation. In the very nature of the case, our participation of God's kingdom demands absolute unconditional surrender of ourselves to Him, and presents to us the cross by which we are crucified unto the world and the world is crucified unto us (9:23). He that would save himself from such surrender will lose everything, even what he saves. He that will give himself up to God's control is assured of God's everlasting care.

For Further Study:

Campbell, Alexander. *The Christian System.* Cincinnati: Standard Publishing Company, 1835. Pp. 107-152. Comprehensive study of scriptures relating to the kingdom.

Ladd, G. E. *Jesus and the Kingdom.* Waco, Texas: Word Books, 1964. Scholarly exposition of classical premillennialism. Summarized in Ladd's article, "Kingdom of God," *Zondervan Pictorial Bible Dictionary,* ed. M. C. Tenney. Grand Rapids: Zondervan Publishing House, 1963. Pp. 466-467.

Marshall, I. H. "Kingdom of God," *The Zondervan Pictorial Encyclopedia of the Bible,* Vol. III. Grand Rapids: Zondervan Publishing House, 1975. Pp. 801-809.

Stott, John R. W. *Basic Introduction to the New Testament.* Grand Rapids: William B. Eerdmans, 1964. Pp. 4-22. Summarizes Jesus' teaching on the kingdom.

Stevens, G. B. *The Theology of the New Testament,* 2nd ed. London: T. and T. Clark, 1906. Pp. 27-40. Helpful insights concerning the Kingdom of God.

# 36

## THE WISE AND GODLY MAN
(Outline of the Sermon on the Mount)

Sermon Purpose: To describe true righteousness and true success

I. THE WISE AND GODLY MAN IS BLESSED EVEN WHEN IT MAY NOT SEEM SO. Matthew 5:3-12

Who is really well off? Being blessed is a matter of being wise and godly, not of circumstances. Wisdom not of this world.

A. The poor in spirit (who know their need) have the kingdom. v. 3
B. The mourning (who see and feel this world's grief) shall be comforted. v. 4
C. The meek (who are not wilful, but submissive) shall inherit the earth. v. 5
D. Those hungering for righteousness will be filled. v. 6
E. The merciful will receive mercy. v. 7
F. The pure in heart will see God. v. 8
G. The peacemakers will be called sons of God. v. 9
H. Those persecuted for righteousness have the kingdom. v. 10
I. Those suffering for Jesus are richly rewarded, and are most joyful. vs. 11-12

II. THE WISE AND GODLY MAN IN RELATION TO THE WORLD. Matthew 5:13-16

A. As salt: worthless without salting effect. v. 13
B. As light: not to be hid, but to shine to all men, that God may be praised. vs. 14-16

III. THE WISE AND GODLY MAN IN RELATION TO THE LAW OF THE O.T. Matthew 5:17-48

A. Jesus does not destroy the law, but fulfills it; for it must be fulfilled. vs. 17, 18
B. Attitude toward God's law determines place in the kingdom. v. 19
C. In the kingdom righteousness exceeds that of the Pharisees. v. 20
D. Old time views of the law contrasted with true righteousness. vs. 21-48

CONDUCT AND CHARACTER:
1. The law about killing. vs. 21-26
   a. Killing compared with anger and contempt: MURDER AND MALICE. vs. 21-22
   b. The duty of seeking reconciliation promptly. vs. 23, 24
   c. Danger of being brought to judgment with differences unsettled. vs. 25, 26
2. The law about adultery. vs. 27-30
   a. Adultery and lust: the act compared with desire. vs. 27, 28
   b. Danger of tolerating temptation and living with lust: remove the cause of sin at all costs. vs. 29, 30
3. The law about divorce. vs. 31, 32
   a. Obligation to give a divorce certificate. v. 31
   b. Divorce and adultery: all divorce is wrong in some way. vs. 32
4. The law about oaths. vs. 33-37
   a. Oaths must be performed. v. 33
   b. Oaths are ineffective and presumptuous. vs. 34-36
   c. Oaths are unnecessary and tending to evil. v. 37
5. The law about retaliation or just revenge. vs. 38-42
   a. Punishment must be equal to the crime. v. 38
   b. Do not fight back at all. v. 39
   c. Return good for evil. vs. 40, 41
   d. Give to them that ask. v. 42
6. The law about loving your neighbor. vs. 43-47
   a. Love limited so as to encourage hate. v. 43
   b. Love your enemies and be like God. vs. 44, 45
   c. Love for friends only is no more than the worst men do. vs. 46, 47

E. True righteousness is unlimited, perfect, like God. v. 48

IV. THE WISE AND GODLY MAN'S MOTIVES IN RELIGION. Matthew 6:1-18

A. Righteousness is done for God, not to be seen of men. v. 1
B. Give alms not for glory of men, but in secret, and God will repay. vs. 2-4
C. Pray not to be seen by men, but in secret, and God will answer. vs. 5, 6
D. Pray not with empty words, but directly and sincerely, after this manner: the model prayer given. vs. 7-15

E. Fast not to be seen by men, but in secret and God will honor it. vs. 16-18

V. THE WISE AND GODLY MAN IN RELATION TO WEALTH AND WORRY. Matthew 6:19-34

A. Have your treasure not on earth, but in heaven; for your heart will be with it. vs. 19-21
B. Divided aims will fail: you cannot serve God and money. vs. 22-24
C. Be not anxious, for God will provide for you. vs. 25, 26
   1. God feeds the birds and will feed you, vs. 25, 26
   2. Anxiety accomplishes nothing. v. 27
   3. God clothes the flowers and will clothe you. vs. 28-30. He knows your need.
   4. Therefore, do not worry like the Gentiles; God knows your needs. vs. 31, 32
   5. Seek His kingdom and righteousness, and all will be supplied. v. 33
   6. Don't borrow trouble from tomorrow; today has enough of its own. v. 34

VI. THE WISE AND GODLY MAN IN RELATION TO JUDGING OTHERS. Matthew 7:1-6

A. Judge not, for as you judge you will be judged. vs. 1, 2
B. Why see and correct flaws in others when you have greater faults yourself? vs. 3-5
C. Don't entrust treasures to those who cannot receive them. v. 6

VII. THE WISE AND GODLY MAN AT PRAYER. Matthew 7:7-11

A. Ask, seek, and knock; such efforts will be rewarded. vs. 7, 8
B. Even a man will give good things to his children when they ask; how much more will God do it! vs. 9-11

VIII. THE GODLY MAN'S GOLDEN RULE OF CONDUCT TOWARD OTHERS. Matthew 7:12

IX. THE WISE AND GODLY MAN AND DANGER TO BE AVOIDED. Matthew 7:13-23

A. The broad and popular way leading to destruction. vs. 13, 14
B. False prophets coming in disguise but known by their fruits, as any tree is. vs. 15-20

C. False professions and false hopes. vs. 21-23
   1. Only those who do God's will shall enter the kingdom. v. 21
   2. Many will claim mighty works in Christ's name, yet they will be cast out. vs. 22, 23

X. CONCLUSION: THE WISDOM OF OBEYING CHRIST ILLUSTRATED BY TWO BUILDERS. Matthew 7:24-27

A. The wise man hears and does what Christ says. vs. 24, 25
B. The foolish man hears but does not obey. vs. 26, 27

For Further Study:

Barclay, William. *Gospel of Matthew,* Vol. I. Philadelphia: Westminster Press, 1956. Pp. 78-300. Helpful on word meanings, illustrations and application.

Fowler, Harold. *The Gopsel of Matthew,* Vol. I. Joplin, MO: College Press, 1968. Pp. 203-442. Extensive comment.

Hendriksen, William. *New Testament Commentary: Matthew.* Grand Rapids: Baker Book House, 1973. Pp. 258-383. Helpful comment.

Lloyd-Jones, Martyn. *Studies in the Sermon on the Mount,* 2 vols. Grand Rapids: William B. Eerdmans. Indepth exposition of the Sermon on the Mount.

Thomas, Leslie. *Outlines on the Sermon on the Mount.* Nashville: Gospel Advocate Company, 1958. Practical studies on the Sermon on the Mount.

# 37

# STANDARDS OF THE KINGDOM

Isn't it surprising? We do not have any extensive records of Jesus' teaching. Apparently it was always remarkably brief and simple. Although He taught the people informally day after day instead of just on special occasions, and although they sometimes pressed upon Him and kept Him from having time to eat and sleep normally, still the records of His teaching are very short. The longest single record of a sermon or teaching session in the New Testament is the Sermon on the Mount (Matthew 5, 6, and 7).

## *Setting for the Sermon*

Jesus' sermon recorded in Luke 6 is usually identified with the Sermon on the Mount found in Matthew 5, 6, and 7. At least it is very similar to parts of that longer account. The "level place" to which Jesus came down (Luke 6:17) may be a small plateau somewhat below the mountaintop but still on the mountain. There are several places like this on the mountains not far from Capernaum. Jesus had spent the night in prayer on the mountain and first named twelve of His disciples to be His apostles. Only Luke tells us that the naming of the apostles preceded this sermon (Luke 6:12-16). All the Gospel accounts are so very brief that they must omit many things that Jesus did and said.

It was summer, in the first half of Jesus' second year of ministry, right in the middle of the fifteen or sixteen months which He spent in Galilee. Great crowds had been coming to Jesus for miracles and to hear Him. A considerable multitude of them had become His "disciples" (i.e., learners who followed Him more or less regularly). From them (see Luke 6:13-17) He now chose twelve to be missionaries, ones to be sent out with some responsibility.

This magnificent sermon on true righteousness was delivered primarily to the crowd of disciples (Luke 6:20; Matt. 5:1, 2); yet there was also present a vast throng of people from various places up to a hundred miles away (Luke 6:17).

The Sermon on the Mount was spoken to Jews who lived under the law and the old covenant, but who also were disciples of Jesus. He had been teaching multitudes about the kingdom that was at hand, and exhorting people to repent and seek the will of God as preparation, part of the privileges and obligations of the kingdom. In this sermon He described the nature of the godly life and the kind of person who receives the favor of God. It was not a sermon on the gospel of God's grace or how God provides salvation for men; but it did first point out that the ones who feel poor and needy, who are sorrowing and seeking, are really well off because of what they may receive from God. He told what inner questions and motives must accompany religious deeds, such as praying, fasting, and giving. He urged men to seek the kingdom of God and His righteousness rather than things that mean "security" and "success" in this world. He exhorted them to seek, ask, and expect to receive, to enter in by the narrow door.

He warned of four great dangers in the way of life: (1) taking the broad way with the crowd, (2) listening to false teachers, (3) trusting in phony religion that is not doing the will of God, and (4) hearing the truth and not doing it.

Both Jesus and John the Baptist had been calling the people to repentance: that is, to turn their minds and hearts to do God's will. This sermon gives some of Jesus' explicit instruction about the way of living that is really righteous and pleasing to God. It describes what the mind is like which has been changed in repentance and is functioning by a genuine faith in God, with a good knowledge of the love and goodness of God. Although these words were spoken to Jews while they were still under the law and before the converting power of the gospel was fully established, they do not describe the actions of the flesh under the constraint of the law as much as they do the fruit of the Spirit in men set free from sin and filled with the newness of life in Christ.

### *Significance of the Sermon*

R. C. Foster characterized the sermon:

> The Sermon on the Mount is the greatest statement ever made on the general subject of religion and morals. It is at once profound and practical. It offers full and final discussion of some of the most elemental and persistent problems concerning our relation to God and to our fellow men. However, in regard to some of these problems it gives only a preliminary statement. The gospel is based upon the divine person of the Son of God and the divine program of redemption through His death and resurrection. Quite obviously, all of this could not be clearly stated as yet. Peter's sermon at Pentecost offers the necessary

> complement to the Sermon on the Mount. It is not intimated in any way that Jesus has given a complete statement of His message in this opening sermon. It is not to be isolated from the rest of the teaching of Jesus, but must be joined inseparable with it.[1]

> The Sermon on the Mount presents the highest ideals of living the world has ever received in the most beautiful language ever conceived. It opens with a series of sayings which sum up the ideal life of the Christian, and it closes with a passionate appeal to the world to accept and follow these ideals and thus build on the rock instead of the sand. . . . It should enable us to see clearly the absolute perfection of Jesus' teaching, the universality of its application to every life, the universal failure of mankind to attain to these ideals and our dependence upon God's love for forgiveness and help.[2]

Some say the church is not necessary if you just follow the Sermon on the Mount. They often think that a luncheon club using principles of the Sermon on the Mount can do the work of the church and render the church unnecessary. A person can adopt much of Jesus' teaching and still not believe in Jesus. There are many in the church because they agree with much of Jesus' teaching. Yet they are motivated by selfishness. "I love me. I'm the most precious guy. I want to save me so I'll join the church to save myself." Some like Ghandi have preached more of the ideas of the Sermon on the Mount than many preachers. But Ghandi was no Christian.

Some try to apply the teaching of Jesus to society and not to the individual. The Sermon on the Mount is not for society but is for Christians. Any attempt to enforce Christian standards or righteousness on unbelievers and non-Christians will not get the job done! The church should not attempt to enforce on society Jesus' standards. Christians must practice them and do their best to make believers out of non-Christians.

Many consider Jesus not as Lord and Master, but as a reformer and example, the highest man, the supreme teacher. This is "damning with faint praise." Any praise that considers Jesus less than God is not enough. When Nicodemus called Jesus teacher, Jesus gave him a test

---

[1] R. C. Foster, *Studies in the Life of Christ* (Grand Rapids: Baker Book House, 1938). P. 466.

[2] *Ibid.*, p. 467.

to see if his obedience would prove that he really considered Jesus as a Teacher sent from God. (John 3).

*Relation to the Law and Gospel*

The Sermon on the Mount is not the gospel. It is not a philosophy on what one ought to be. The Gospel is stated in I Corinthians 15:1-4. J. S. Stewart emphasizes that the early preachers declared that in the death and resurrection of Christ the kingdom of God had broken into human history with great power. He objects to the vague, non-doctrinal perversion of Christianity:

> The Gospel is regarded as a codification of human ideals and aspirations; religious instruction means teaching the ethic of the Sermon on the Mount; Jesus is the noblest pattern of the good life. This, it is assumed, is basic Christianity: anything which goes beyond it is 'sectarian theology,' mere debatable theory. What this view fails utterly to realize is that the Christian religion is not primarily a discussion of desirable human virtues and qualities—not that at all—but a message about God: not a summary of the ways men ought to act in an ideal society, but an account of the way in which God has acted in history decisively and for ever.[3]

Paul warns against preaching another gospel (Gal. 1:6-9). The Sermon on the Mount preached as a way of life with redemptive qualities apart from the covenant of grace through Christ's death is preaching another gospel. It is not the Sermon on the Mount in you the hope of glory but *Christ* in you the hope of glory (Col. 1:27).

The more you study the Sermon on the Mount the more you realize that it is not really good news. The better we understand it the less rejoicing it causes. Studying this sermon can make you feel bad. If you don't feel guilt in your conscience, you are dead or dulled. If it is the gospel, we are still under law. Though its precepts are spiritual ideals—higher than the Old Testament laws—they are still laws; and if such instruction is all we have or need for salvation, then salvation is by works, and Christ died in vain (Gal. 2:21; 3:21).

Its purpose is similar to that of the law of Moses: To bring us to Christ for righteousness by revealing true righteousness in precept for us to admire and desire, and that we might examine ourselves

---

[3] James S. Stewart, *Heralds of God* (New York: Charles Scribner's Sons, 1946). Pp. 65-66.

and repent. If it stood alone, without a sacrifice for sins, we would also despair. It examines men in the light of God's holiness, and no man passes the examination. It stirs our conscience and makes us glad to accept the gift of righteousness from the author of such standards. It sets forth elements of the 'perfection' to which we 'press on' (Heb. 6:1) and particulars of "the measure of the stature of the fulness of Christ" unto which we are called to attain through the full ministration of the church (Eph. 4:11-13). It lets us know the great goal of man, implies the need of help and introduces the help for attainment.

When men killed Christ they expressed their rebellion to righteousness, hatred against God, falsehood against truth, selfishness against service, hypocrisy against sincerity. Men hated the law of God. They would not endure God living among them. The world does not like the bright light of holiness and the demands and implications of it. Paul said, "All that would live godly in Christ Jesus shall suffer persecution" (II Tim. 3:12). You cannot manifest the righteousness of Christ and get all men to think well of you.

In this sermon Jesus teaches His deity by direct claim (Matt. 7:21-24), by tone of authority (Matt. 7:29) and by demonstration of the divine quality of His teaching. Suffering in personal devotion to Him is made the highest blessedness and cause for the greatest rejoicing (Matt. 5:11, 12). Seeking the kingdom of God and His righteousness is made life's most urgent pursuit (Matt. 6:33).

If this sermon is not the plan of salvation, then why was it given to us? God loves us. He wants us to know the nature of righteousness. He came to this world not only to call us from hell but to call us to heaven; from unrighteousness to righteousness; from darkness to light. He calls us not just out of hell to a hellish life outside of hell. Christianity is not just a fire escape from hell.

The Sermon on the Mount will make us conscious of our unrighteousness. We see God better when we understand these standards of righteousness. This is true no matter how good we feel we are. Beware of these dangerous ruts: "I do enough." "I am good enough." "I give enough." "I pray enough." This attitude is next door to worshiping self.

This sermon shows us our need of the gospel. These high standards of righteousness make us aware of our need of God's righteousness.

### *Standards of Blessedness*

Reading the Beatitudes, we are immediately reminded of Isaiah

55:8, 9: "My thoughts are not your thoughts, neither are your ways my ways, saith Jehovah. For as the heavens are higher than the earth, so are my ways higher than your ways, and my thoughts than your thoughts." Jesus in the Sermon on the Mount contradicts all common thinking. He says the person who is really well off and is in the best circumstances is the one who is poor, mourning, etc. We are not the best off when satisfied with ourselves—that's one sure thing!

The source of happiness is not in one's personality, not in circumstances. We find happiness when we are put in a right relation with God. Christ tells us how to be as beautiful as God wished us to be when first He thought of us. We say we would be happy if we had things or if we were some place. Jesus spoke not of possessions or places, but of ourselves. Notice that the first seven blessings are pronounced upon states of mind or heart, and the only external circumstance mentioned as blessed is persecution—a thing that we are prone to fear and shun at almost any cost (Matt. 5:3-12). He says that those who know need and hunger for righteousness are well off, and that those who are lowly and mourning are happy. This shows that He did not mean a shallow happiness or gaity. This blessedness is more than just a happy feeling; it is the favor of God upon those described. Most of these sayings are just the opposite of the world's view, and we are too much conformed to the world. We need to study them much and often to "be transformed by the renewing of our mind, that we may prove what is the good and acceptable and perfect will of God" (Rom. 12:2).

The qualities which Jesus blesses are not those exalted by the Jewish teachers of the law. Alas, how often *we* fail to appreciate these and exalt other, even opposite traits! There is no self-righteousness here in Jesus' list; no Pharisee fits into the picture, no matter how orthodox in confession or how correct in forms of religion.

These have the favor of God and shall have the kingdom—its mercy, its comfort, its satisfaction, its fellowship divine, its adoption and its inheritance—because they are prepared in heart to receive it and abide in it. They are conscious of what they do not have, and are unsatisfied with the spirit they have attained (See Rev. 3:17, 18). They are grieved by sin and are moved by love and sympathy (Study II Cor. 7:9-11). They are not arrogant, willful and headstrong, but humble, gentle and docile (See examples of Moses, Num. 12:3; Jesus, Matt. 11:29; Cf. II Cor. 10; I Tim. 6:11; II Tim. 2:24, 25; Tit. 3:1, 2; James 1:21; I Pet. 3:15). They intensely desire true righteousness and will not be satisfied with anything less, yet they are forgiving (See Matt. 18:35). They are not hypocritical, with a divided heart harboring evil purposes, but they are "all of a kind," even to the secret depths consistent with their outward professions (See I Sam. 16:7; Ps. 24:4; Prov. 4:23). They seek and practice reconciliation (See Rom. 12:14-18), yet they will not compromise or forsake righteousness or Jesus Christ even to avoid persecution. All such are blessed. "Theirs is the kingdom." They are not perfect in works of the law, or rich and great in the sight of the world, but they are receptive to the grace of God which gave God's Son, and will "with him freely give us all things." Whom the Lord blesses is blessed indeed!

### *Standards of Active Righteousness*

Too many people appear not to realize that Christianity is much more than abstinence from certain disreputable deeds and odious evils. A stick or stone could be a good Christian if the ideal were absence of guilt. But innocence is part of righteousness, and we too commonly have an inadequate, if not wrong, idea of what is innocent.

Jesus indicates that not all that is legal is innocent. We are guilty when we have not formally violated the letter of the law (Matt. 5:21-42).

R. C. Foster points out:

> Jesus emphasized the inner life, making the thought and intent to do evil as sinful as the deed itself. It is not enough to avoid murder, but we must not hate. Adultery is to be shunned, but lust also must be crushed. Evil words and deeds rise out of the heart. We must guard the heart as the very citadel of life.[4]

The golden rule (Matt. 7:12) is not so much cause as it is effect. It is the result of being right with God. It is not how to do it as much as being the result of being in tune with God. Jesus said in John 15 that we can not do anything without Him. Righteousness is not merely negative. That is live and let live. But Christ demands positive service.

Christ offers a higher standard of righteousness and power to attain. Do for God and not for self. "And whatsoever ye do, in word or in deed, do all in the name of the Lord Jesus, giving thanks to

---

[4] R. C. Foster, *op. cit.*, p. 467.

God the Father through him" (Col. 3:17). The power one gains by serving Christ selflessly is greater than any self-righteousness.

Our righteousness must be in what we do, and not merely in what we don't do. Most of us realize that if we would do some terrible deeds (as a habit, anyway) we would lose all hope of salvation. But we all need to realize that nothing can more effectively cut us off from grace and from hope than the habit of doing nothing; that is, nothing by faith, in the name of Christ, or to the glory of God. Before we "accepted" Christ we sinned sins of omission. Now we must confess and be forgiven of sins that are hard to see and easy to excuse, because they are what we did not do. "To him that knoweth to do good and doeth it not, to him it is sin" (James 4:17).

We cannot excuse ourselves by saying that we have done as well as others, or all that the occasion deserved, or all that the law required. Christ's standard is "more than others." He asks that good deeds flow *out of the love in our hearts,* not from the requirements of the occasion or law or custom or force. Go the second mile. "Let him have thy cloak also." (Matt. 5:40-41). "Love your enemies" (Matt. 5:44). The good Samaritan is an example Jesus gave to teach how it is done (Luke 10:25-37).

The standard of active goodness Christ holds before us is always above us, because it is likeness to God in His perfection. Again, it is from a changed heart within, out of a known kinship with God and out of accepting gladly the privilege of being like Him, having the "love of God shed abroad in our hearts, through the Holy Spirit which was given unto us" (Rom. 5:5). Such standards direct us in the greatest possible growth in the character befitting children of God, and at the same time save us from complacency. They keep us worshiping Him and seeking His mercy, having no confidence in the flesh (Phil. 3:3).

Foster reminds us, "the person who can study the Sermon on the Mount without suffering distress of conscience had better look to his conscience."[5]

For Further Study:

Foster, R. C. *Studies in the Life of Christ.* Grand Rapids: Baker Book House, 1938. Pp. 462-487. Discusses the principles in the

[5] *Ibid.*, Pp. 484-485.

Sermon on the Mount and relates the sermon to the social gospel and the deity of Christ.

See books listed on page 186 for comments on Matthew 5.

# 38

## PURITY IN HEART AND LIFE

God made us "male and female," and endowed us with wonderful powers and great blessings in our relations with one another and with our children. For our good, and in order that we might not corrupt and pervert ourselves, He commanded strict control and right use of our nature. God who made us gave this command. He knows the good effects of right living and the disastrous results of wrong living. Some men, in their ignorance or willful blindness, may not see the wrong in adultery, but God's Word makes known its sinfulness and God's wrath against it. He plainly, openly, and repeatedly forbids and condemns perversion of the body in fleshly indulgence.

### *Adultery Forbidden and Condemned*

The New Testament again and again declares the terrible fate in eternity that awaits the violators of God's law of chastity. *They shall not enter into the kingdom of God* (read I Cor. 6:9, 10; Eph. 5:3-6). They are shut out of the city of God, away from the tree of life (Rev. 22:14, 15). The wrath of God is upon them (Col. 3:5, 6; Heb. 13:4). Their part shall be in the lake of fire and brimstone (Rev. 21:8).

Many other warnings and exhortations are given against the lusts of the flesh. They "war against the soul" (I Pet. 2:11). They enslave, corrupt, and defile a person (II Pet. 2:18-22). This kind of sin militates against the body itself (I Cor. 6:18), and brings upon it the worst kind of disease and debility (Rom. 1:26, 27). See also Acts 15:28, 29; Gal. 5:16, 17, 19, 21; Rom. 13:13, 14; I Thess. 4:3-8; I Tim. 1:8-10; Tit. 2:11, 12; Heb. 12:14-17; Rev. 2:14, 20, 22. This terrible sin destroys the beauty and blessedness of the home and breaks the bonds of the marriage union (Matt. 5:32; 19:9). It is not to be tolerated in the life of a church member; if he will not repent he must be expelled from the fellowship (I Cor. 5:1-11).

Wicked men may excuse this sin, may play with its enticements, may cherish it; but God hates it and condemns it. He can save us from it, but not in it. He says so much about it and against it in His Word; surely we must not condone it or appease it, but we must speak boldly against it. It will not be pleasing to the crowd and may bring strong persecution to condemn a sin which is so popular and which is committed by men in high places. John the Baptist lost his life because he preached boldly and plainly against the adultery of the king. But this generation certainly needs faithful and fearless preachers to point out its sin.

The law is the same for men and women. We are ready to speak with scorn about "fallen women"; what of "fallen men"?

### *Avoid the Path of the Wicked*

Proverbs 4:14-23 emphasizes the need of avoiding the influence of evil companions and of the observation of evil ways and doings. "Be not deceived: Evil companionships corrupt good morals" (I Cor. 15:33). "But fornication, and all uncleanness, or covetousness, let it not even be named among you, as becometh saints; nor filthiness, nor foolish talking. . . . Be not ye therefore partakers with them; . . . and have no fellowship with the unfruitful works of darkness, but rather reprove them; for the things which are done by them in secret it is a shame even to speak of" (Eph. 5:3-12). Lust arises from evil thoughts, which are gendered by enticing sights or suggestive words. If we are to keep our hearts pure and our minds on worthy and holy things, we must avoid, resist, and reprove evil.

As Alexander Pope in his "Essay on Man" said:

> Vice is a monster of so frightful mien,
>   As to be hated needs but to be seen;
> Yet seen too oft, familiar with her face,
>   We first endure, then pity, then embrace.

How can one frequent the movies or the dance, or read lewd literature, or give his ear to vile stories without disobeying God and defiling his soul? Just because everyone else in your school or social set is doing it is no reason why you must walk in the same pathway of darkness. Do I mean to say that movies are evil associations that lead to sin? I certainly do. Their advertisements and research indicate that movies specialize in that which is lewd, licentious, and immoral.

A few years ago a foundation employed university professors of sociology and social science (not noted for being prudish) to make a systematic investigation of American movies and their moral influence. They checked fifteen hundred separate pictures and found that the first principle theme in the movies is sex; the second is crime; and the third is a kind of promiscuous and unworthy love-making that is more sex than anything else. It is obvious that since this research the movies have become more openly immoral and pornographic. The programs and movies on TV show a similar preoccupation with sex and immorality.

George Rawlinson warns:

> He that dallies with temptation, he that knowingly goes into the company of the impure, he that in his solitary chamber defiles himself, he that hears without rebuking these obscene words, transgresses against God's law, and, unless he repents, cuts himself off from God.[1]

Jesus plainly teaches that entertaining evil desires in the heart is the same as adultery in guiltness before God. "Everyone that looketh on a woman to lust after her hath committed adultery with her already in his heart" (Matt. 5:28).

### *Purity of Heart*

Jesus said, "Blessed are the pure in heart: for they shall see God" (Matt. 5:8). In the Bible the word "heart" is used to mean all the inner, mental and spiritual nature of man and its functions—such as thinking, believing, feeling, willing, judging, etc. (Matt. 9:4; 13:15; 22:37; Mark 2:8; Rom. 10:10; II Cor. 9:7; I John 3:20, 21). Purity is the state of being unadulterated, unmixed. Think what makes pure soap or pure water. A pure heart is one not corrupted by opposition within itself, at least one that does not entertain or seek low things as well as high—one that has one dominating conviction, one all-subduing purpose. It is very similar to what Jesus meant when He said, "If thine eye be single, thy whole body shall be full of light. But if thine eye be evil . . . darkness. . . . No man can serve two masters" (Matt. 6:23, 24). Note the example of Paul: "One thing I do" (Phil. 3:13, 14). James clearly sets purity of heart in opposition to "double-mindedness," and twice indicates the ill condition of the double-minded (James 1:8; 4:8). Paul specifically warns against "youthful lusts" as corrupting a "pure heart" (II Tim. 2:22).

If the physical heart is vital to our life and welfare, the spiritual heart is even more so. Naturally, out of it "are the issues of life" (Prov. 4:23). It is the seat of our purposes and the spring of our actions (read Mark 7:21-23). No matter what a man may think on special occasions that he wants to be, he will be whatever he has in his mind and heart hour after hour and day after day; "for as he

[1] George Rawlinson, *The Pulpit Commentary: Exodus,* Vol. I. (Grand Rapids: William B. Eerdmans, 1961 reprint), p. 138.

thinketh within himself, so is he" (Prov. 23:7). No man can think down and live up. "Sow a thought, and reap an act. Sow an act, and reap a habit. Sow a habit, and reap a character. Sow a character, and reap a destiny." The center of the character is the will, but the center of the will is the attention.

Each of us has only so much mental space. What is filled with frivolity, foolishness, and filth cannot be filled with goodness and godliness. Memorize Phil. 4:8, "Finally, brethren, whatsoever things are honorable, whatsoever things are just, whatsoever things are pure, whatsoever things are lovely, whatsoever things are of good report; if there be any virtue, and if there be any praise, think on these things" and follow it.

### *Sacredness of the Body, a Temple of God*

The body is not in itself or of necessity evil. It can be a good instrument and servant of the spirit for righteous works. It must be kept in subjection (I Cor. 9:27). The evil is in letting it become enslaved to sin. "The body is not for fornication, but for the Lord; and the Lord for the body" (I Cor. 6:13). The Lord redeemed the body, as well as created it. It is "bought with a price" and belongs to Him. We have no right to misuse and corrupt it. On the contrary, we have a very real obligation to develop it and make it a fit and effective instrument for Christ's service.

Alcoholic liquors slowly poison the body. They immediately affect its co-ordination and control. They unnaturally stimulate some of its vital processes and cause perversion of its appetites. In nearly all cases the user of liquor is led to sexual sin, because the body is not only unnaturally aroused by it, but the conscience and sense of moral restraint are deadened. The homes of our land will be not only threatened, but viciously attacked, as long as liquor is commonly used among us. The young people who would be pure, who would know the joys of true love and honorable marriage, who would be parents of admirable children, and who would come to old age in health of body, peace of mind, and hope of soul must settle it in their minds utterly to refuse alcoholic drink. Let us also turn away from all inflaming of fleshly passions by immodest dress, unclean words, or suggestive acts.

If we will have the faith in Christ to take His perfect counsel in these things we will find that self-denial with Christ is far greater glory and joy than to "enjoy the pleasures of sin for a season." It will be greatly to our own advantage to keep our bodies clean and useful vehicles of our own personalities all our lifetime, rather than making them habit-bound battlegrounds and even diseased wreckage to burden our lives. But most of all, it is our crowning privilege and honor, as well as duty, to surrender our bodies to God and let Christ live in us and work through us His glorious works of righteousness and mercy, producing the fruits of the Spirit, blessing all around us, and preparing us for eternal life in a transformed body of glory like His own.

For Further Study:

Lindsell, Harold. *The World, the Flesh, and the Devil.* Washington: Canon Press, 1973. Pp. 95-109; 117-118; 159-180. Deals with the problems of sexual immorality and pornography and finds the power for purity in the life in the Spirit.

Lutzer, Erwin W. *The Morality Gap: An Evangelical Response to Situation Ethics.* Chicago: Moody Press, 1972. Attempt to develop a consistently Biblical ethic.

Ridenour, Fritz. *It All Depends.* Glendale, California: Regal Books, 1969. Analyzes situation ethics and the playboy philosophy in the light of Biblical morality.

Skornia, H. J. *Television and Society.* New York: McGraw-Hill, 1965. Critical look at the place of television in American society.

# 39

# CAPTURING THE IMAGINATION

In recent years juvenile crime has increased by alarming proportions. Many juvenile officials have described these teenage offenders as frustrated, confused, and mixed up mentally. The ungodly lives of adults as well as youth in our society grow out of confused and corrupt thinking.

Paul emphasizes the importance of thoughts and imaginations: "With eyes wide open to the mercies of God, I beg you, my brothers as an act of intelligent worship, to give Him your bodies, as a living sacrifice, consecrated to Him and acceptable by Him. Don't let the world around you squeeze you into its own mold, but let God remold your minds from within so that you may prove in practice that the plan of God for you is good, meets all His demands and moves towards the goal of true maturity" (Rom. 12:1, 2; J. B. Phillips)

### *Thoughts Make the Man*

Bishop Taylor Smith aptly observed: "You're not what you think you are, but what you think, you *are.*" Ralph Waldo Emerson said, "A man is what he thinks about all day long." But that was not original with him. Marcus Aurelius, wise man of ancient Rome said, "Our life is what our thoughts make of it." But before Aurelius said it, the wise man of the Bible said, "For as he thinketh in his heart, so is he" (Prov. 23:7).

Satan tries to captivate our minds. The secret is to "gird up our minds" (I Pet. 1:13; RSV). Cultivate spiritual thinking by meditation on the things of God. "Thou wilt keep him in perfect peace whose mind is stayed on thee" (Isa. 26:3; KJV).

The importance of our thoughts must not be denied or diminished. Proverbs 4:20-27 speaks of the vital need to keep true teachings within the heart, "Keep thy heart with all diligence, for out of it are the issues of life" (Prov. 4:23). Paul wrote to the Corinthians regarding the "war of the mind." "For though we walk in the flesh, we do not war after the flesh: for the weapons of our warfare are not carnal, but mighty through God to the pulling down of strongholds; casting down imaginations, and every high thing that exalteth itself against the knowledge of God, and bringing *into captivity every thought to the obedience of Christ*" (II Cor. 10:3, 4).

Jesus also said, "For from within, out of the heart of men, evil thoughts proceed, fornication, thefts, murders, adulteries, covetings, wickednesses, deceit, lasciviousness, an evil eye, railing, pride, foolishness: all these things proceed from within, and defile the man" (Mark 7:21-23). The responsibility for sin is in man, not in his environment, or his economic condition, etc., as much as these may furnish occasion for sin. The desires are harbored and the choices are made within the individual. *You cannot live up and think down!* The only real difference between the worst and the best is what a person thinks. Therefore the tastes we cultivate, the attitudes we hold, the principles we believe in, and the desires we cherish have more to do with our character than anything else. W. E. Hocking has truly said, "The changing of human nature is the changing of desires." What we fill our hearts and minds with just might make the difference between heaven and hell. What thoughts come to your mind hour after hour—what do you think about more than anything else—when you just relax and let your mind wander? What is your wishful thinking centered on? Has the dream of "moreishness" captured your wishful thinking? Do you think about the mini-skirted girl when your mind falls into its "day-dream"? Is your mind filled mainly with gloating thoughts of self-accomplishments?

The Bible uses the word "heart" to mean all the inner, mental and spiritual nature of man and its functions, such as thinking, feeling, believing, willing, judging, etc. (Matt. 9:4; 13:15; 22:37; Mk. 2:8; Rom. 10:10; II Cor. 9:7; I John 3:20, 21.) Naturally out of it "are the issues of life." For it is the seat of our purposes and the spring of our actions.

The character of our hearts is made by the way we think and feel about things: both our deliberate, fundamental thoughts and feelings about God and the world and ourselves, and the unguarded flow of thoughts and feelings that fill up every day. Those thoughts and feelings are very often conflicting. We must choose between them. Some of them become dominant. All of them leave their impression upon us! Those to which we give some expression gain the ascendancy over others in determining what we really are like in heart.

Therefore we must be careful of the words we speak (Prov. 4:24); for they not only reveal the inner man, but they help to make him what he is. "Let no corrupt speech proceed out of your mouth, but such as is good for edifying as the need may be, that it may give grace to them that hear" (Eph. 4:29). "But fornication and all uncleanness, or covetousness, let it not even be named among you, as becometh saints; nor filthiness, nor foolish talking, or jesting, which are not befitting . . . and have no fellowship with the unfruitful works of darkness, but rather even reprove them; for the things which are done by them in secret it is a shame even to speak of" (Eph. 5:3-12). James says that if we fully control the tongue, we are able to master the whole body (James 3:2).

### *Flee These Things*

Don't be fooled into thinking you cannot control your imagination—thoughts. That's exactly what Satan wants you to think, as he pours into your mind suggestive actions, images of luxurious living, forbidden experiences which you yet *do* experience vicariously. "This one thing I do, forgetting those things which are behind and reaching forth unto those things which are before, I press toward the mark for the prize of the high calling of God in Christ Jesus. Let us therefore as many as be perfect, be thus minded: and if in anything ye be otherwise minded, God shall reveal even this unto you" (Phil. 3:13-15).

What occupies our attention fills our heart, and what takes our time consumes our lives. We are no better than those things to which we give favorable attention. Do not give time and attention to the attractions of fleshly indulgence. "Take time to be holy." Our attention is very largely directed by our eyes. Hence the Bible warns us against letting our eyes wander to sinful things. What we see helps make us what we are through directing our thoughts; but what we are will help to determine what we see. The heart directs the eye, but in turn is fed by it. Job was able to say that he "made a covenant with his eyes concerning the way that they should look upon a maiden" (Job 31:1). David looked, and lusted, and then committed his most grievous sin.

The efforts of many women to expose themselves and adorn themselves so as to make men desire them are to be condemned with utter contempt and abhorrence. The glamor and sex-appeal so glorified by the world of entertainment is not elevating but degrading. Police officials have frequently cited the connection between scantily-clad females and sex offenses.

A few years ago an Association for Mental Health and the Iowa Council on Family Relations co-sponsored a program which discussed sexual promiscuity. The reasons given for the increase in this problem were: freedom of autos; constant bombardment with sex stimuli; the way women dress; steady dating; Junior High School dances. These reasons were offered by secular experts such as psychologists, doctors, educators, and social workers.

Jesus speaks clearly on the matter of lustful thoughts. Men are to look on women with a clean mind and wholesome thoughts. He says, "Everyone that looketh on a woman to lust after her hath committed adultery with her already in his heart. And if thy right eye causeth thee to stumble, pluck it out, and cast it from thee: for it is profitable for thee that one of thy members should perish, and not thy whole body be cast into hell" (Matt. 5:28, 29). Jesus uses this drastic figure of speech to underscore the seriousness of the sin of lustful thinking.

Christian women are instructed to take care and precaution that she dress herself in such a way as not to arouse the lustful thoughts of the male onlookers. "In like manner also, that women adorn themselves in modest apparel, with shamefastness and sobriety, not with braided hair, or gold, or pearls, or costly array; but (which becometh women professing godliness) with good works" (I Tim. 2:9). Peter says to Christian women, "Whose adorning let it not be that outward adorning of plaiting the hair, and of wearing of gold, or of putting on of apparel; but let it be the hidden man of the heart, in that which is not corruptible, even the ornament of a meek and quiet spirit, which is in the sight of God of great price" (I Pet. 3:3, 4).

It is impossible to treat this subject of pure hearts and lives thoroughly or practically without reference to the movies and magazines that specialize in stimulating ungodly lusts, and that hold up for admiration people who are practicing adultery. How can we pray sincerely, "Lead us not into temptation," and then seek for pleasure amidst the lust of the flesh, the lust of the eyes, and the vainglory of luxurious and worldly living? How can one frequent the movies, or the dance, or read lewd literature, or give his ear to vile stories without disobeying God and defiling his soul? The prevalence of immodesty, of foul stories, of lewd pictures, is evidence of evil hearts of men who produce, pay for, and enjoy such things. We do not deny that sinful things are done and real people are tragically infected with deep corruption of heart and life; but we do not need to consent that this is worthy of publication for others to think about. Especially we should not make sin, crime, and moral filth the entertainment of multitudes. This type of entertainment—whether movies, novels, pornographic magazines or unclean stories—has a very close connection with the increase of broken homes, divorce decrees, illegitimate children, venereal disease, insanity, and juvenile delinquency. It is the responsibility of parents and adult citizens to promote high moral standards, modest living, clean thinking; and to oppose all lewdness from that of the radio and newsstands to that of the organized business of vice and prostitution.

### *Imagination: Blessing or Curse*

The human eye, you see, can be a blessing or a curse. "If thine eye be evil, thy whole body shall be full of darkness," warns Jesus in Matt. 6:23, adding, in Mark 9:47, "If thine eye offend thee, pluck it out; it is better for thee to enter into the kingdom of God with one eye, than having two eyes to be cast into hell fire."

Imagination enables us to look mentally at things beyond the range of our eyes. It gives us the power to analyze things without actually taking them apart. It gives us insight into the workings of things we cannot actually watch with the eyes. It helps us to anticipate experiences and make choices without unguided practice of trial and error.

Imagination is one of the leading faculties of our life, personality, and character. It molds and determines most of our interests and action, determines the zeal with which we perform. As a small boy or man may lead about a large and powerful elephant, so *the power of your will is led about by your imagination.* The center of the character is the will, but the center of the will is attention. Drifting attention produces a derelict type of life.

It is a pretty sure thing that no man ever made a great new invention or a success of any significant kind without working it out in his imagination first. Similarly, no one ever made a big sinful mess of his life without practicing in imagination first.

There are various things which stimulate the imagination. Songs are made to do so. When you hear a song expressing something you like or seek, you turn your imagination on and let it run. What kind of songs do you find stimulating? What kind of songs do you just endure without being aware of what they say or suggest?

Certainly literature is written to arouse the use of imagination. Reading requires imagination to fill out the skeleton of thought given in the words being read. This is one of the very important values of the power of imagination, that we may receive much real experience of knowledge and feelings from the things which are written. But the good power of imagination and memory is perverted and made an evil curse when it is mis-used to fill the mind with thoughts of sin and sinful desires. Of such is Paul writing when he says in Romans 1:32, "(they) not only do things contrary to God's command, but have pleasure in those who practice them." II Thessalonians 2:12 warns of the wrath of God to come against all those who "had pleasure in unrighteousness." Why should we enjoy as entertainment what we know is sinful? One great danger of watching television (or movies, or books) is that we will use it to enjoy the experience of sin by proxy—as well as that it will stimulate the imagining of acts that we would not ordinarily approve.

James says God does not tempt us, but we are enticed and drawn away by our own lusts (James 1:13-15). God may make trial of our faith to test or prove us. But James means that God does not entice us to sin. Jesus was tempted of Satan, that He might be perfected through sufferings, to be able to help us that are tempted, and to be touched with the feeling of our infirmities (Heb. 2:10, 18; 4:15, 16). But the power of temptation is in our desires. "Lust" is just another word for "strong desires." By the lying promises and attractive appearances that Satan makes for sin, he seeks to stir up our desires, which lead to sin, and the sin brings death. The best protection against it all is to know the will of God and cultivate so strong a desire to please Him that Satan's lies can be readily answered with the word of truth, and sinful desires can be rejected with swift determination.

The desires that tempt or entice to evil will not entirely cease while we are in the flesh and in this world of evil; but they must be denied, ignored and caused to fade away, by our constant and conscious rejection of them. The Christian must not drift along easily, but be vigilant and vigorous in directing his thoughts, his desires and his life. He is not removed from the conflict, but is constantly forced to choose to walk by the Spirit or to exercise the desires of the flesh.

Our imagination may be controlled by the will, led by desire, or ruled by habit. Let's think about this. *Imagination can be controlled by the will,* especially by an undivided, stedfast will; but if the will is vacillating, inconstant, opposed by unconquered desires, imagination will be led by desires.

Imagination will conjure up both gratification and justification for desire. Its attempts to satisfy desire are unrealistic and may cause one to be unsatisfied with the realities of life. Selfish indulgence in imaginary pleasures or attainments may lead to disappointment, when the anticipation exceeds the realization.

### *Changing Desires*

Faith, true faith in Christ and in His judgments, His love and

His promises, changes our desires. The warnings, the promises and the goodness of God lead us to repentance—a change of heart and desire. The privilege of change that God so graciously holds out in calling us to repentance is no light matter. Repentance is a privilege; and once we present our "changed" mind to God, He proceeds to change it even more. Even then evil imaginations may continue to bother and tempt us because they have become a habit. It is in the power of the gospel and faith to change desire, to strengthen the will and to conquer habits. To change a habit, put a good habit in the place of the one to be eliminated. Become active in use of thought and imagination toward the goal of the prize of our high calling in Christ. Apply it to devising methods of doing Christ's will and extending His kingdom.

God gives us exceeding great and precious promises to motivate us, to help keep us "looking to the recompense of reward" to help us "set our minds on the things above, not on the things upon the earth," so that by these promises we may "become partakers of the divine nature, having escaped the corruption that is upon the earth through lust (desires)" (II Pet. 1:4).

The Christian faces vital choices in life: *choose! refuse! seek! flee!* What reading do you do? On God's law do I meditate day and night, (Ps. 1:1, 2). Is this true of your life? What pictures, programs, or stories do you allow to lead and use your imagination? Imagination is closely connected with dreams, and is often called day-dreaming. Some of the dreams we have at night are but the extension of the day-dreams we imagined in the daytime. Are you a passive victim of the devil's propaganda? You don't need to act as if you are hypnotized and in a trance unconsciously controlled by others. As a Christian you must not be so weak in purpose and will that the passing impulse of the flesh has control and determines what you do. As you use your mind, set your mind. From Ephesians 4:22-25 the Christian receives the direction of purpose to take: renounce the rule of desires born of deception (misconception), that leads to deceived, wishful thinking, and accept the discipline of truth. "Be transformed by the renewing of your mind in Christ" (Rom. 12:1); "Let Jesus come into your heart." Surrender your mind to Jesus Christ as God, as Savior, as the eternal Wisdom from on high and let His mind dwell in you.

Look into the things God has prepared for you (I Pet. 1:10-12, 13ff; 2:1-2; II Pet. 1:3-5). Let His word have sway in your mind. Treasure the promises that redirect our desires and remake our natures. Never forget that the changing of human nature is the changing of desires.

With this in mind let the expulsive power of a new affection—the love of God, of truth, of kindness and generosity and mercy, of good men and good actions, put to death evil intent. Love good and hate evil, Paul says in Rom. 12:9. Let God's love, received in our hearts, give us love for Him, and for all that is true to His nature. The classic THINK passage of Philippians 4:8 tells us what we are to fill our minds with: "whatsoever things are true, whatsoever things are honest, whatsoever things are just, whatsoever things are pure, whatsover things are lovely, whatsoever things are of good report; if there be any virtue and if there be any praise, THINK on these things."

Fill your mind so constantly with the Lord and the good that He wills for us, that you leave no room for evil thoughts to sneak in and take control of your life. MAKE CHRIST THE MASTER OF YOUR MIND.

For Further Study:

See books listed on page 200.

# 40

# TRUTH AND SINCERITY IN SPEECH

Even if lying were not forbidden by God's Word, it would be wrong. It corrupts the character of the liar; for it is base, cowardly, and contemptible. It introduces chaos in society. It opposes the reality of things as they are. Falsehood attempts to build the thought and feeling and action and character of men upon a fictional foundation in willful opposition to the universe of actual existence. What folly!

There is no middle ground between falsehood and the truth, but one falsehood conflicts with many others. There is no consistency in lies, no standard for harmonizing them. Therefore, the liar ensnares and condemns himself in the contradictions of his own falsehoods; for "No man has a good enough memory to make him a successful liar." On the other hand, all truth is consistent with all other truth; and a man can be assured of consistency of character and steady growth in the mastery of self and circumstances, simply by constantly adhering to the truth.

The absolute truth is not always easy to know. "It requires hard, patient toil to dig down beneath the superficial crust of appearance to the solid rock of fact on which truth rests. . . . Truth is fidelity to fact; it plants itself upon reality; and hence it speaks with authority."[1] It is probably impossible for a mere man to know always the absolute truth, but the virtue of truthfulness is possible to all. Practical truthfulness consists in speaking exactly what is in my mind—not consciously misrepresenting or denying the truth as we know it. God gives us the power of speech and of action to express the thought in our minds. When we lie by word or deed (actions speak louder than words) we frustrate the very power to communicate ourselves to others.

But God in His wisdom and mercy did not leave man to figure out by his reason alone what was right and what was wrong. He revealed Himself and His will for our enlightenment and for our salvation.

## *Lying Forbidden and Condemned in the Bible*

God's attitude toward this sin is clearly and strongly expressed in both Old and New Testaments. Lies are identified with Satan, and are said to come from him as "the father of lies" (John 8:44; Acts 5:3). Truth is identified with God (Isa. 65:16; 25:1) and with

[1] *Hyde's Practical Ethics.*

Christ (John 14:6). The Holy Spirit is the spirit of truth (John 16:13); and the Word of God is truth (John 17:17). It is impossible for God to lie (Titus 1:2; II Tim. 2:13; Heb. 6:18). Lying lips are an abomination unto the Lord (Prov. 6:16, 17; 12:22).

In the ninth Commandment of the Decalog (Ex. 20:16) God especially forbids false witnessing against a neighbor, as in a court of justice. Deuteronomy 19:16-21 speaks more particularly of the penalty for perjury. But the teaching goes much father than that; even to the point of condemning lying in favor of a neighbor, or lying to him in flattery (Prov. 26:28; Ps. 12:2). We are not to receive and carry gossip and scandal (Ex. 23:1; Lev. 19:16; Ps. 15:3; 101:5). Sometimes it is right to expose wickedness in high places; but if we speak anything disparaging another, revealing or denouncing his sin, we must make sure that we speak accurately, giving no false impression, and that we truly need to speak it for the good of society. In the New Testament we are frequently warned against being slanderers (I Tim. 3:11; Titus 2:3), tattlers and "busybodies" (I Tim. 5:13; II Thess. 3:11), meddlers in other men's matters (I Pet. 4:15). Deceivers, whisperers, backbiters, and slanderers are listed among the worst of sinners, on whom the wrath of God abides (Rom. 1:29, 30; II Tim. 3:3).

The righteous are called upon to hate lying (Prov. 13:15; cf. Ps. 119:163), to respect not those who lie, and to reject their company (Ps. 40:4, 101:7). "Putting away falsehood, speak ye truth each one with his neighbor" (Eph. 4:25). "Lie not one to another; seeing ye have put off the old man with his doings" (Col. 3:9).

The punishment that is to come upon liars is of the severest kind, and indicates that lying is one of the most terrible sins. According to Psalms 5:6, God "will destroy them that speak lies"; and Proverbs 19:5 says, "A false witness shall not be unpunished; and he that uttereth lies shall not escape." Liars are positively and absolutely excluded from heaven (Rev. 21:27; 22:15). *"All liars, their part shall be in the lake that burneth with fire and brimstone; which is the second death"* (Rev. 21:8).

The unregenerated human heart is deceitful (Jer. 17:19); lying is practically universal in some form or other (Ps. 116:11). We need to examine ourselves and say, "Lord, be merciful to me a sinner." Liars will be saved only if they repent and love the truth as it is in Christ Jesus. How we need the Lord to renew a right heart within us! "For out of the abundance of the heart the mouth speaketh" (Matt. 12:34).

In Matthew 5:33-37 Jesus teaches that we need to be so reliable that when we say "yes" or "no" people know we mean it. "Let your speech be, Yea, yea; nay, nay: and whatsoever is more than these is of the evil one" (Matt. 5:37). Our word should be as good as a bond.

We are inclined to say talk is "cheap" and unimportant. But "every idle word that men shall speak, they shall give account thereof in the day of judgment. For by thy words thou shalt be justified, and by thy words thou shalt be condemned" (Matt. 12:36, 37). Our power of speech can be very valuable, able to bless and to save men; or it can be very expensive, and cost us our soul's salvation. Words cast abroad are very hard to gather up again. True repentance for sinful speech will require us, as far as possible, to make amends for the harm done; but this may cost much labor and grief, or be impossible. Thank God that we may repent, and be forgiven by Him, and start anew the life of righteousness according to the truth!

### *Reasons for Restraining the Tongue*

1. *Because of the coming judgment of God,* in which we must give account of every word, and be justified or condemned by our words, under the stern laws and warnings cited above.

2. *Because if the tongue is not bridled, we have no religion at all,* says James 1:26.

3. *Because if the tongue is properly governed, the whole body can be brought under control* (James 3:2). What we permit ourselves to speak has much to do with the control of our minds and all the rest of our lives. The motives, determination, the watchfulness that will succeed in governing the tongue will be sufficient to go far in controlling the whole body.

4. *Because "we are members one of another"* (Eph. 4:25). In ordinary human society we are dependent upon one another, and no man lives to himself alone; but in the church we are even more members one of another, as members of the body of Christ. Lies sow discord among brethren, and set men at variance with one another; they tend to make society impossible. A lie breaks the golden rule of doing unto others as we would that they should do unto us. A lie works toward further tearing down of character. The full fellowship of Christians is not possible without mutual trust and love.

### *How to Rid Our Lives of Falsehood*

How shall we overcome all falsehood? Not by strict law alone. For we may speak the literal words of truth in such a way as to deceive; or we may lie by saying nothing at all. In fact, using the truth to deceive others makes the worst kind of lie—the most misleading, the hardest to detect. The practice of quoting the Bible to teach false doctrine is devilish indeed. We must have truth in the heart. God desires "truth in the inward parts" (Ps. 51:6). It needs to be ingrained in our being. A good and honest heart will bring forth honest words and deeds. In order to deal honestly with others and avoid the many forms of disguised deception, we must put away hypocrisy and deal honestly with ourselves and with God.

1. Realize the truth of Psalms 139:4: "For there is not a word in my tongue, but lo, O Jehovah, thou knowest it altogether."

2. Strive to please God rather than men. Truth is often not only hard to discover, but it may be costly to speak. Truth is frequently opposed to sacred traditions, inherited prejudices, popular beliefs, and material interests. To proclaim truth in the face of these opponents has cost many a man his life; and today it often exposes one to much disfavor and even abuse. Hence comes the temptation to conceal our real opinions; to cover up what we know to be true under some phrase which we believe will be popular; to sacrifice our convictions to please men because we falsely believe that to be to our interest.

3. Trust in God for support and protection so that fear of men, in times of crises or danger, will not cause us, like Peter, to hide behind a lie.

4. Especially when we have done wrong the temptation to cover it up with a lie is very great. Here we must remember to put character above reputation, to seek God's approval above all, to correct rather than conceal the fault.

5. Cultivate love for the truth and occupy the mind with seeking it. Many lies are idle talk of idle minds. Excuse no little lies. Uphold always the ideal and purpose to know and to tell the truth.

6. Put on the whole armor of God (Eph. 6:10-18), and join in the battle for right.

7. Maintain a good conscience.

8. Finally, "Love thy neighbor as thyself." "Love worketh no ill to his neighbor" (Rom. 13:10). Love will make us as careful for our neighbor's reputation as for our own. Love will help us to return not evil for evil, but overcome evil with good, so that we will not stoop to answer lies with lies.

For Further Study:

Lindsell, Harold. *The World, the Flesh, and the Devil.* Washington: Canon Press, 1973. Pp. 75-78. Strong case for honesty.

Murray, John. *Principles of Conduct.* Grand Rapids: William B. Eerdmans, 1957. Pp. 123-148. In a chapter entitled "The Sanctity of Truth" Murray discusses the problems of being truthful.

# 41

## PLAIN FACTS ABOUT HONESTY

There is a very close relation between truth and righteousness. Righteousness is action according to the truth—according to the reality of God and the actual relationships of men. God is a God of truth, whose word can be depended upon, who is always consistent with Himself, who can not lie.

Unrighteousness is built on falsehood, whether in sincere ignorance or intentional evasion or denial of the truth. The power of Satan is in deceit, to turn men away from the truth of God.

We should love the truth and seek it as blind men long for sight. How can falsehood be a guide to successful action in any matter? How can we hope to build an enduring life structure upon a foundation of fiction? It is a pity and a tragedy when a man with good intentions acts upon false information or false assumptions because he can not find the truth; but it is worse when he has the truth and covers it with a lie. It is practically impossible to know always the absolute truth. But it is possible to speak and act with truthfulness and honesty, in love for the truth to the best of our ability to know it.

God's Word provides for us the necessary truth concerning our lives, their responsibilities and their salvation. But it bears its fruit in good and honest hearts (Luke 8:15). When we speak and act sincerely according to the truth as we know it, we are ready to receive more truth when it is revealed to us. But if we evade or cover up the truth which we do know, we are preparing to avoid or reject further truth when it is offered to us. Departure from the love of the truth makes us open to many delusions and deceits. See II Thessalonians 2:10-12.

### *Honesty is Wise*

Instruction in practical wisdom for successful living, like that of Proverbs, necessarily includes urgent exhortations to be honest and truthful. Children and fools, being ruled by selfish and changing desires, are ready to use false statements or to get things by dishonest means, in order to satisfy present desire. But as men become *wise* (through the revelation of God's wisdom, or through keen observation and experience) they learn that other things are supremely and eternally to be desired, namely, harmony with God, a character of consistency and integrity, and a social order founded on honesty.

It is found to be very far better to subject ourselves to the principles of honesty with all their restraints than to attempt by dishonesty to satisfy momentary desires. Truthfulness has the sure victory and the greater reward. Falsehood leads to frustration.

Nothing is more important in determining the character and outcome of one's life than fundamental honesty. God's Word teaches in many places this basic essential. The Ten Commandments condemn stealing and false witnessing (Ex. 20:15, 16). Jesus warns against hypocrisy (Luke 12:1-3) and condemns the hypocrites (Matthew 23). Ananias and Sapphira were punished by death for lying (Acts 5:1-11). Christians are commanded to lie not to one another (Eph. 4:25; Col. 3:9). Christian speech should need no bolstering by oaths, but should let simply "yes" mean yes, and "no" mean no (Matt. 5:37). A good conscience is urged (I Tim. 1:5, 19; I Pet. 3:16). Liars are sentenced to eternal torment in hell (Rev. 21:8; 22:15).

Deceit is folly and failure. It is wrong and destructive. It is cruel and unloving. Falsehood, fraud, and all forms of dishonesty are of the nature and works of Satan. "Lying lips are abomination to the Lord" (Prov. 12:22). God hates lying and calls upon the righteous to hate it (Prov. 6:16, 17; 13:5; Ps. 119:163; Rom. 12:9).

### *Complete Honesty Is Too Uncommon*

In spite of all God's teaching and all the lessons of human experience, what we call "common honesty" is still all too uncommon. So often we desire to make a good appearance to be approved by men, when the real condition of things would not be approved, and we therefore permit ourselves to misrepresent the facts. The "root of all evil," the love of money, causes many to practice lying or other deception. We look to the immediate results of an act or statement instead of to its fundamental rightness. We practice one deception and then must tell another lie to cover it. It is a growing evil. Those who have been dishonest in one thing are more inclined to be dishonest in others. The only protection against it is to inculcate in our lives a firm faith in God and in the ultimate triumph of the truth, and to fear all the ways of dishonesty.

It is a sad revelation of the sinfulness of American people to see the reports of impartial investigators into dishonest business practices. In some lines of business and repair service more than 60 percent have been found to be dishonest; and there is no reason to believe these are much worse than many others. Politicians whose word can be strictly relied upon are notoriously scarce. Many people who pride themselves on honesty in paying debts, etc., will strike as hard a bargain as possible in any deal, taking advantage of the ignorance of others. Many who think they would not steal will nevertheless appropriate public property for private use, or take all they can get from any large corporation when they have no just right to it. A man is not strictly honest until he will not accept more than his just due for service rendered or property sold.

Some of the hidden but pernicious forms of dishonesty are dishonest preaching, dishonest praying, dishonest singing, dishonest confession of faith and profession of religion. Much trouble in the church would be greatly relieved if men would always be plain and truthful about their real convictions. The great curse of infidelity, known as "modernism," in the church could soon be dealt with if all the crooked politicians and religious racketeers would truthfully declare themselves for what they really intend to believe. Using the truth to deceive, using the words of faith to indicate unbelief, quoting the Scripture to promote false doctrine, these are devilish indeed. They make the worst kind of lie and the hardest to combat.

Any attempt to deceive or to produce false conclusions is lying, even if all the statements made are true to facts in some sense.

### *The Practice of Honesty*

A form of falsehood that easily overtakes us is not with premeditated intent to deceive, but through weakness and indifference, failing to carry out in action what we have too glibly professed in words. True honesty demands faithful following of the principles we know and claim to hold. We set for ourselves ideals which are higher than it is possible for us to practice at all times. That is not wrong in itself. But becoming accustomed to being short of our professed standard, we excuse ourselves when we honestly know that we have not done what we could and should have done. Sometimes we avoid knowledge which would place upon us responsibility which we wish to evade; but we can not then claim to be excused by ignorance when that ignorance was by deliberate choice, and was not a necessary limitation beyond our control. For example to make this plain, and to suggest an exhortation to preachers, consider the case of preachers who claim to believe the Bible and uphold the Lord's standards of righteousness, who claim to be much concerned about the increasing evil of disregard for God's laws concerning marriage, then to avoid embarrassment, unpopularity or loss of profit, they will unite in adulterous marriage people who have been un-Scripturally divorced. They commonly excuse themselves of responsibility in the matter because of ignorance, when they made no attempt to make the teaching of Scripture known to the prospective husband and wife or to ask them if their marriage can be contracted in harmony with God's revealed will.

"Happy is the man who is too honest to be fooled by his own alibis." It takes a character most practiced in complete truthfulness to avoid all the subtle ways in which we incline to deceive ourselves. "Honest confession is good for the soul." Sincere apology is often a noble thing and a great help to human relationships. But the practice of making excuses, trying to retain the favor of men when we have not earned it, tends very much to lying. How often both to men and to God we plead inability when the real trouble was not with our abilities, but with our desires. The lame excuses that people offer to themselves for not attending church, and for not giving unto the Lord a fair and reasonable portion of the property and income He has commited to us, have become notorious for the fact that they are just lies to cover up the real fact that we just do not want to.

Manifold forms of dishonesty are all around us so much, and the situations of life frequently become so complicated, that we all are very likely to be ensnared by this sin. It creeps unnoticed into the life of every one of us. We must watch the whole course of our lives to develop habits of strict honesty and not to overlook the "small" things. Slight inaccuracies of speech may seem to be insignificant; but they open the door for more serious forms of deceit by generating a habit of indifference to truth. Besides, even the least untruth is treason against the royal supremacy of truth.

We must be prepared to maintain honesty when we are severely tried and it is very hard to speak the truth or to do the fair thing. Sometimes it may cost a great sum, or the forfeiting of one's life, to be strictly honest: but because of the faithfulness of God, our great judge and Saviour, we can confidently choose the right and trust the outcome to be joyful victory and great reward. In such circumstances only the character that is morally sound and absolutely unwilling to depart from the truth will stand the strain.

For Further Study:

See the books listed on page 213.

# 42

## LOYALTY TO THE KINGDOM
(Matthew 6:19—7:29)

"Loyal" and "loyalty" are words not found in most versions of the Bible, yet the idea is taught throughout the Bible better than anywhere else. The idea of loyalty is strong, faithful, unshakeable allegiance. Love, which is so much stressed in the Bible, covers all of that and more.

Jesus does not in so many words ask us to "be loyal" to Him, but He does more: He asks us to love Him, abide in Him and let no family ties or personal interests interfere with or even compare with our devotion to Him (John 15:4-10 and Luke 14:25-33).

### *Authority of the King*

In this, as in all His teachings, He assumes and expresses supreme authority and divine majesty. He doesn't offer arguments to be studied or suggestions to be proved by experience. He taught principles to be practiced, but not to be experiments. His principles prove valid in practice, but our duty to practice them is not in order to prove them, and is no greater when they are so proved than when they are first startlingly enjoined. His directives, given out of knowledge of all eternity, can not be tested completely in this life only, and must be accepted because of their source which assures their outcome.

He demands allegiance. It takes faith to follow Him. But He altogether merits our allegiance and devotion, and our trust in Him will never be brought to shame or disappointment.

No wonder the people "were astonished at his teaching, for he taught them as one having authority" (Matt. 7:28-29). He naturally and continually identifies following His word with doing the will of God.

In the warnings and appeals that climax the Sermon on the Mount, Jesus challenges us to undivided allegiance to Him, to God's will, to "his kingdom." He calls for the fruits and works of a genuine faith.

To those who are not professing to follow Him it is a call to set their course of life Godward and to follow it with resolute decision, guided by the revelation of God's will in Jesus' words.

To those who are professing to have made the choice of their goal and to be in the way of life and glory, it is a challenge to check their course.

We will not drift into righteousness and the blessedness of fellowship with God. They must be sought. We must set our course and give strict attention to it.

### *Our First Concern*

"Seek ye first his kingdom and his righteousness" has been the theme of many sermons because we need so much and so often to be exhorted to put first things first. Jesus' whole ministry in both deeds and words emphasized the importance of spiritual things over temporal things—the significance of our standing with God above any other thing (Matt. 12:50; Mark 10:21; Luke 10:42, etc.).

In actual practice, what is our first concern—the things of self or the things of God? our souls or our bodies? the success of our private finances or the sound progress of the Lord's business? our private household or the household of the faith? the approval of God or the praise of men? What things command our energies, compel our attention and make other things wait? When there is conflict between school and church, which claims our allegiance? Between business and church? Between family reunion and church?

It is said that Jenny Lind, the "Swedish nightingale," was once invited by the king of her country to sing in the royal palace at a festival, but it was to be held on the Lord's Day. She refused to come. The king came in person and pleaded with her and her only response was, "There is a higher King, Your Majesty. I owe my first allegiance to Him." She put Christ first and made Him the real king of her life.

It is so common today for "good Christians" and "church people" to be much concerned for their children to get a secular education and make high honors and a "good living" in the world, but to do nothing and feel no necessity to teach them anything about the Bible, the life of faith and the service of Christ. Yes, they want them to be "members of the church" and law-abiding citizens, but they direct their lives into the service of mammon. Many who think they have resisted the temptations to put desire for treasure first, still are anxious for what they shall eat and wear to the extent that that is their master. Note the common remarks, "Well, a man must live," and "A person has to make a living," as they go to work through all the bad weather and indisposition and inconvenience that would be a perfectly good excuse (to them) for neglecting the kingdom of God.

*"Ye cannot serve God and mammon."* Why shouldn't Christ *come*

*first?* He is of first rank, personally. His service is of first quality, intrinsically. He must be put first in our lives or be denied His proper place and His explicit request. Nothing can be loyalty to Him except putting Him first. But in this sermon Jesus does not ask that we give first place to His program merely because of His rank and rights as Lord, but because it is the *primary necessity of our lives.* He does not urge it as a matter of sacrifice to divine prerogatives, but as a matter of practical wisdom for us.

He is our life and our only escape from eternal death and destruction. Don't forget that *fact* just because it isn't beautiful to the popular eye. Seeking His kingdom is of primary importance inasmuch as life itself is of basic importance and greater significance than any particular circumstances of life. "What shall a man give in exchange for his life?" (Matt. 16:26).

But listen! "Fear not, little flock; it is your Father's good pleasure to give you the kingdom" (Luke 12:32). It is not only necessary to serve God; it is also safe, prudent and profitable. To them that are faithful in allegiance to Him, He promises to be faithful in Fatherly providence: "All things shall be added unto you"; "your heavenly Father knoweth that ye have need of all these things." (Cf. Rom. 8:28; Phil. 4:19.) The favor of God is a real and lasting treasure worth striving for with the best efforts of our lives; whereas, the riches of this earth are deceitful, unreliable and fleeting. To serve God is not a sure way to a high salary on earth, but it is the only sure way to a real security and ultimately a *tremendous success!* To guarantee the provision for our *real needs,* here or there, serve God. To have a sure and permanent defense against all the storms that assail, hear and do what Jesus says. To be a child and servant of God is the greatest opportunity that life offers; in fact, it is the only one that is not vanity of vanities and bitterness of soul in the end. O that men would really read Ecclesiastes, and that they would also really believe our loving Savior!

### *How Shall We Attain Unto The Kingdom Of God and His Righteousness?*

The general answer of Matthew 7 is: By doing the will of the Father—doing the things that we hear Jesus say.

Jesus did not yet preach the whole story of the kingdom God was preparing and the "righteousness of God by faith" to be accounted unto those who believed and obeyed the full gospel (Rom. 1:17; 3:21; 4:22-25; Phil. 3:9). It remained for the Holy Spirit to guide the apostles into all the truth about the full particulars of the riches of grace. But Jesus pointed out the road that, faithfully followed, would lead to all those things; viz., just follow Him. Jesus' purpose in the Sermon on the Mount was to prepare the hearers for the kingdom which would be fully revealed soon enough. They must be made ready to receive it. We must not attempt to separate this sermon from the rest of the New Testament, either to make legalism of this sermon, or to make that grace a theology based on sand: empty hearing and vain faith (Matt. 7:26, 27; James 1:22; 2:14-26). The loyal heart of obedient faith is expounded here.

J. W. McGarvey states:

> Doing the will of God must be understood, not in the sense of sinless obedience, but as including a compliance with the conditions on which sins are forgiven. Whether under the old covenant or the new, sinless obedience is an impossibility; but obedience to the extent of our ability amid the weaknesses of the flesh, accompanied by daily compliance with the conditions of pardon for our daily sins, has secured the favor of God.[1]

Then what standards and tests does Jesus set for loyalty that befits the kingdom?

1. (Matthew 7:1-5.) We must not be censoriously and uncharitably judging others while hypocritically blind to our own sins, but we must give place to God and show mercy as we expect to receive mercy. This general principle must be understood in the light of specific teaching, as in Matthew 18:16, 17; Titus 3:10; II Thessalonians 3:6, 14; II John 10; Matthew 7:15, 16; Romans 16:17; I John 4:1; I Corinthians 5:11 and I Peter 4:17, 18.

2. (Matthew 7:7-11.) Pray persistently, with faith in the goodness of God.

3. (Matthew 7:12.) By the Golden Rule practice the goodness which we seek to share, to do God's will and to represent correctly our Teacher.

4. (Matthew 7:13, 14.) We must not follow the crowd. We must enter the narrow gate. We must be willing to separate from the world and live the limited and restricted life, confined to seeking and doing God's will.

5. (Matthew 7:15-20.) We must not believe every religious teacher,

[1] J. W. McGarvey, *Matthew and Mark* (Delight, Arkansas: Gospel Light Publishing Co., 1875). P. 73.

but weigh their words and their works in the balance of the word of God. We must study the Bible and know the difference between true and false religion (I John 2:18-29; 4:1; II John 9-11).

6. (Matthew 7:21-27.) We must do more than pray, and more than hear the word, and more than spectacular deeds of religion; we must be obedient in heart and obedient to the word of God's revealed will. Prayer and outward profession without practice are useless and will collapse in utter ruin.

May God give us grace to apply these divine canons to our hearts and not to think more highly of ourselves than we ought to.

For Further Study:

See books listed on page 186 for comments on Matthew 6:19—7:29.

# 43

## WHAT THE KINGDOM IS LIKE
(Matthew 13)

The chief emphasis in the preaching of John the Baptist was that the kingdom of God was close at hand and men should prepare to meet the King (Matthew 3:2-12). Then Jesus and His disciples went throughout the land teaching as if the chief aim in anyone's life was to enter into the kingdom (See John 3:3, 5; Matt. 4:17, 23; 5:3, 10, 20; 6:10, 33; 7:21; Luke 4:43; 7:28; 8:1).

Jesus had preached in Judea about eight months (until He was leading more to baptism than John was—John 4:1-3). After that, He had preached in Galilee at least eight months or more. About half of His entire ministry was past. Many miracles had been wrought. Great throngs of people were following Him, so that He had not time to eat and sleep. Some of the Pharisees were trying desperately to combat His popular influence. His family sought to take Him home for a rest. That was the time when Jesus taught the sermon all in parables about the kingdom (just before He left on a boat trip during which He was so tired that He slept right through a terrible storm).

The people were excited about the kingdom message, but they did not understand it. The Jews expected a kingdom of military power and material wealth. They were not listening well to Jesus' teaching about true religion and obedience to God. When Jesus taught them about the kingdom of God, they did not understand or even realize that He was talking about it. They thought of the kingdom as a form of national power, a relationship between their own nation and other nations. But Jesus thought of it as a relationship between each individual and God. They thought of it as the possession of material security and power to rule over others; but He spoke of it as the possession of God's word and as submission to God's rule over one's own life.

To help them overcome their habitual, mistaken ideas of the promised kingdom and to show how near it was to each of them, Jesus told these simple illustrations, which were called in Greek, "parables." Jesus is famous for His parables on various subjects. Some notable ones had been told before the time recorded in Matthew 13. But on this occasion He spoke nothing but parables! An immense crowd was gathered on the shore of Galilee, so that Jesus got into a boat in order to speak to them all. He taught "many things in parables," perhaps more than are recorded in the combined accounts of Matthew 13:1-53; Mark 4:1-34; and Luke 8:4-18. But all that are recorded are comparisons to describe and identify the kingdom. Instead of defining or explaining the kingdom in abstract terms, Jesus pictured it in concrete comparisons. They were pictures to show the characteristics of the kingdom which the Jews had not seen or had never expected it to have.

Jesus was asked by His disciples why He spoke only in parables to this crowd. He said it was because the crowd did not know the secrets which He had been revealing about the kingdom, as the apostles knew them. The "mysteries" of the kingdom meant simply the things about it that were revealed and which would not be known unless they were learned by revelation. Jesus had been revealing them in His teaching, but the people did not give as much attention or have as much faith as the apostles did, and their old mistaken notions were very much in the way. Even in this sermon, if He spoke in plain terms about the kingdom without parables, they would not perceive what He meant.

No doubt the picture stories which He used left many of the people wondering and unconvinced; but they also left them with some clear and easily remembered pictures to refer to frequently until their minds were able to accept the truths of the kingdom to which they pointed.

We are helped in understanding the parables by the explanations which Jesus gave of two of the most complex ones to His disciples that very day. His interpretations of the soils and the tares give us a guide to the meaning of all the parables. The interpretation is also helped by the fact that two or more parables point to the same feature of the kingdom. Two or three illustrations of the same thing make one more sure of the point of each illustration.

### *Like The Product Of Seed Growing In Soil*

The first parable shows that the kingdom is like the results obtained when seed is sown on various kinds of soil. In explaining this one, Jesus said, "The seed is the word of God" (Luke 8:11).

Some hearers of the word are like the soil of the beaten path, not receptive to the word, and Satan takes it away from their consciousness, as birds eat the seed off the roadway.

A second class of hearers is like the thin soil over a slab of rock. The word gets from them an immediate response. They make a good start in letting the word of God live in them. But when trials and hardships come because of the word, their citizenship in the kingdom immediately withers away. They are not the stable kind of people who endure stedfast in what they know is right, but are like plants without roots deep enough to endure when the sun is hot.

A third kind of hearer includes those who have too much else occupying their minds and affections. They are like good soil with the seeds or roots of thorns in it. The word is received, but the cares of this world and the enticements of riches soon outgrow the desire to do God's will. The Lord's control is choked out by other controlling interests as wheat is choked out by Johnson grass.

The fourth class of hearers is like the good soil that bears much fruit. They hear the word of the Lord, understand it, and hold it fast in a good and honest heart (See Luke 8:15); hence they bring forth the fruit of living faithfully according to the will of God.

Another short parable, which is recorded only in Mark 4:26-29, says that the kingdom is like the growing of seed in the ground. The sower, having sown the seed does no more work on it, and does not know how it grows. But the earth produces of itself, first the blade, then the ear (or head of wheat), then the full grain in the ear. So the kingdom does not come like a finished product delivered from the factory, or like ruling power is seized in a revolution, but it grows by the effect of God's word in each person's mind and heart.

### *Like Wheat in a Field With Weeds*

Again (in Matthew 13:24-30) the kingdom is pictured as good seed growing in a field, but an enemy has sown tares (weeds that look like wheat) in the same field. Some servants suggest pulling out the weeds. But the owner said that wheat might be pulled up with them; therefore both would be allowed to grow together until the harvest, when they would be separated and the weeds would be burned.

Jesus explained this parable, being asked by His disciples, so we do not have to guess at its meaning. The field is the world. The good seed, or the plants that grow from it, represent the people of His kingdom, planted in the world by Christ. The devil is the enemy that sowed the tares, which are the people who serve the devil. Jesus did not say who the servants were that suggested pulling the weeds; perhaps they might be men who propose to serve God by killing off wicked men. But in the harvest, which comes at the end of this age, the reapers will be the angels, who will gather all the wicked to be burned. Notice that He said they will be gathered "out of His kingdom!" He had said before that "the field is the world" and the plants from the good seed are the sons of the kingdom. Either this views the whole world as the realm of His rule, potentially His kingdom, or the angels are to gather some wicked ones from among those who were the kingdom.

Then the righteous shall shine as the sun *in the kingdom* of their Father, when the kingdom apparently will be free from all offenses and evils.

### *Like a Net Full of Fish. Good and Bad*

Another parable pairs with the one about the tares to picture the fact that some unacceptable persons are to be sorted out of the kingdom at the end of the age. In this one the kingdom is compared to a dragnet gathering all kinds of fish. It is brought to shore, and the bad ones are thrown out, which represents the work of the angels at the end of this age, separating the wicked from the just and casting them into the fire (Matt. 13:49, 50).

The parables reviewed thus far show that the kingdom is not national and material, but spiritual and individual; also that it is not all glory and success, but some people start in it and fail, some are cast out at last, and others are unaffected by it though in contact with it. These comparisons indicate that the kingdom is not a time when the Lord forces His rule upon all, but those who accept His word yield to His rule and are the kingdom while they live on this earth in the midst of the ungodly.

### *Like the Best Kind of Growers*

Jesus said the kingdom is like a seed of mustard and like leaven. Both of these picture its growth. The mustard seed, though very small, produces a large plant, sometimes fifteen feet high, in one year. The leaven may not look much alive and may be only a little bit hidden in a large batch of meal, but quietly and unnoticed it multiplies itself. Thus Jesus' kingdom, beginning with twelve humble men (or even 120, or 500), looked insignificant, but by a spiritual vitality put into it by the Lord it had power to grow and encompass the earth.

The parables were not intended to be prophecies, but illustrations. The parable of the leaven represents the growth of the kingdom without noise or show, by transfer of transforming faith from one person to another; it probably does not predict the complete transformation of the world by the growth of the church or (as some say who consider leaven always a symbol of evil) the complete corruption of the church by evil growing in it. There are predictive elements in Matthew 13:41-43 and 49, 50, but these are subordinate parts of comparisons which describe the nature of the kingdom in pictures rather than telling the high points of its history in predictions.

### *Like The Most Precious Thing Known*

Two other parables picture the kingdom as having greater value than everything else combined that any man can have.

It is like a treasure lying hidden in a field. Whoever finds it will joyfully sell all he has to buy that field.

It is like one priceless pearl so precious that the owner of a great collection of prize gems will give all that he has to buy it.

Whether to the poor laborer, working in another man's field, or to the rich merchant admiring his collection of jewels, to everyone the kingdom of God is the opportunity of a lifetime. Perhaps by this we should test the reality of our faith in Christ's words:—Are we eager to sell all else to have Him rule in our lives? And how great is our joy at the opportunity to make the transaction?

For Further Study:

Barclay, William. *The Gospel of Matthew,* Vol. II. Philadelphia: Westminster Press, 1957. Pp. 60-101. Good comment on the Matthew 13 parables.

Lightfoot, Neil R. *The Parables of Jesus,* Part I. Austin: R. B. Sweet, 1963. Well outlined studies with competent comment.

Taylor, William. *The Parables of Our Savior.* London: Hodder and Stonghton, 1887. Pp. 17-103. Helpful exposition with good application.

# 44

## TREASURES OF THE KINGDOM
### (Matthew 13:44-46)

> The kingdom of heaven is like unto a treasure hidden in the field; which a man found, and hid; and in his joy he goeth and selleth all that he hath, and buyeth that field.
>
> Again, the kingdom of heaven is like unto a man that is a merchant seeking goodly pearls: and having found one pearl of great price, he went and sold all that he had, and bought it. (Matthew 13:44-46)

Of all the precious things that the thoughtless crowd casts aside or ignores as valueless, none is so greatly and so generally underestimated as the kingdom of Christ. Not only the majority of Americans, who take no active part in any church, prefer a mess of pottage to their birthright in Christ; but a large percentage of church members canot tell what Christ means to them. Indeed their lives testify that He means less to them than many mundane things. How does it go in your personal market? Are you selling everything else to buy Him? And—(don't answer out loud)—how great is your joy at the opportunity to make the transaction?

Jesus told two parables to emphasize the fact that whether to the poor laborer, working another man's field, or to a rich merchant, admiring his great collection of prize gems, to everyone the kingdom of heaven is the opportunity of a lifetime—literally! No man has so many worthy attainments and personal powers, such great wealth, such varied and important interests that he should regret losing every one of them to be a humble disciple of Jesus. It is easier for the poor and oppressed to realize that in coming to Christ they have nothing to lose and everything to gain. The rich and self-righteous, the proud and powerful are very hard to bring to that realization. Even when they see value in Christ their hearts are often "joined to their idols." "How hard it is for them that trust in riches!" (Mark 10:24). "How can you believe, who receive glory one of another, and the glory that cometh from the only God ye seek not" (John 5:44). Those who are wise in their own conceits have these things "hid from them" (Matt. 11:25). Compare I Corinthians 1:26-31. Still it *is* true that *any man* giving up all to have Christ has *nothing to lose and everything to gain!*

In Philippians 3:4-14 Paul tells of his own experience as a "merchant seeking goodly pearls." Compared with others he had made a good showing of things gained outside of Christ, but he counted them all loss to gain Christ. He actually suffered the loss of all things but counted them mere rubbish compared with the excellency of Christ.

### *Let's Take an Inventory*

What are the treasures that the Savior sets above the sum of all that the best-favored life can assemble? What is the preciousness that so satisfies the great apostle and makes all his former attainments as rubbish? It is evident that many of us do not value the kingdom as Jesus and Paul did. Surely we have not known what riches abound there. Jesus spoke as if any man in his right mind would joyously part with everything he had to get that supreme treasure as soon as he saw it. Paul and many others did just that. But today people are putting off accepting Christ, and are afraid to part with anything to gain Him.

What makes Christianity precious? One thing—it costs an infinite price: time and sacrifices, life and blood, heartaches and struggles of men and of God. Nothing else in history compares with it. Another thing—it is rare, the only thing of its kind and nothing else approaches it or can substitute for it. But Jesus was thinking of its value to us for what we may find in it and receive from it.

It is possible to expect the wrong thing and, being disappointed, to turn away and lose all. The crowd that Jesus fed miraculously tried to turn His beneficent powers to political and material purposes. They would take Him by force and make Him their king to satisfy their own ambitions and desire, but Jesus would not consent (John 6:15). Then Jesus, the following day, rebuked them for seeking the bread that perishes and tried to give them the Bread of Everlasting Life, but they had expected the wrong thing and when they found it not they forsook Him (John 6:26-66). Paul writes of those, "corrupted in mind and bereft of the truth, supposing that godliness is a way of gain" (I Tim. 6:5). So do not follow those false prophets abroad today who promise all the material things you want if you buy their religio-psychology course. But Paul did go on to say: "But godliness with contentment is great gain: for we brought nothing into the world, for neither can we carry anything out; but having food and covering we shall be therewith content" (I Tim. 6:6-8). In the same letter he said: "Godliness is profitable for all things, having promise of the life which now is and of that which is to come" (I Tim. 4:8).

*For The Life That Now Is:*

(Note: Do read the scriptures cited. Look into the catalogue of the products of God's love with at least as much interest as you look at Montgomery Ward's catalogue of products of American industry. This is merely an index held to a minimum of space.) We should expect and find:

1. Justification, the burden of sin removed, conscience relieved (Rom. 8:1, 33, 34; I Cor. 6:11; Heb. 10:19-23).
2. The burdens we bear (e.g., responsibility) lightened by love and by the strengthening the Lord gives (Phil. 4:13; II Tim. 4:17; II Cor. 12:9).
3. A sure and stedfast hope (Heb. 6:17-20).
4. Peace (Rom. 5:1; John 14:27; Phil. 4:9) freedom from anxiety, fear and despair (Phil. 4:6; Matt. 6:33).
5. Self-mastery, Christ dwelling in us (Gal. 5:16; Eph. 3:14-19; James 1:2-4; Gal. 2:20).
6. True liberty (Gal. 5:13; John 8:32, 36).
7. The unshaken life (Matt. 7:25; Rom. 8:37-39; Heb. 12:28; I Cor. 15:58; Phil. 4:12).
8. The best of human fellowship, refinement of every social relationship (Col. 3:8—4:6).
9. Comfort (II Cor. 1:3-5; I Thess. 4:18).
10. Increasing joy and satisfaction out of life (Phil. 4:4; Gal. 5:22).
11. Partaking of the divine nature, its beauty and poise, its radiant righteousness (II Pet. 1:3, 4); chastisement (Heb. 12:5-11); correction, instruction (II Tim. 3:16, 17) improvement—the discipline of a loving Father, building us up to a wonderful and beautiful ideal (Eph. 4:13).

*For The Life That Is To Come:*

1. Eternal life (I John 5:11, 12).
2. Transformation (Phil. 3:20, 21; I Cor. 15:50-54).
3. Being with the Lord (John 14:3; II Cor. 5:8). Divine fellowship unhindered.
4. Being like the Lord (I John 3:1, 2).
5. Joint-heirs with Christ, Heir of all things (Rom. 8:17).
6. Divine power's sure victory (Gal. 6:9; II Tim. 2:12).
7. Rest (Matt. 11:28; Heb. 4:9-11).
8. New heavens and new earth, wherein dwelleth righteousness

(II Pet. 3:14).

9. The glory of God and of the children of God (Rom. 5:2; 8:18-20; II Tim. 2:10; II Cor. 4:17; I Pet. 5:10; Rev. 21:11).
10. A kingdom that cannot be shaken (Heb. 12:28).

### *Reflections*

*These treasures are chiefly personal.* "I am thy shield and thy exceeding great reward" (Gen. 15:1). They are not in things, but in the realm of spirit and persons. Therefore they are not seen and appreciated by the profane eye of Esaus. Even the practical providence is the Lord's personal care. He is able to provide for all out of little or nothing. The feeding of the multitudes, miraculously, demonstrates Jesus' teaching that God knows our needs and cares about them. He will add all these things if we seek first the kingdom (Matt. 6:33; Phil. 4:19). To have the Lord is to have everything! "The Lord is my shepherd; that's all I want," said the little girl who had the words mixed, but the idea exactly right. We may have Him who makes "all things work together for good" (Rom. 8:28) and who is "able to do exceeding abundantly above all we ask or think" (Eph. 3:20). His best gifts to us are what He creates in us personally, not material stores.

*Cleansing! Righteousness!* Priceless goal of the awakened soul! We who know not the curse and shame and defilement of sin do not appreciate the cleansing from sin. We who believe not the written sentence of doom and damnation upon sinners care not for deliverance. We are so prone to have such low standards, such trashy ideals, as to be satisfied with a little self-righteous respectibility of works of the flesh, even in pride; but Paul sought not a righteousness of his own, of law and flesh, but sold everything to gain the righteousness of God, given by faith in Christ through His blood.

*He is so precious to me!* In a burning building a fire escape is the most precious thing—no matter if the crown jewels of Russia and England combined be there. Dear Brother, are you ashamed of this phase of our precious faith?

*It is desirable to be healthy, wealthy and wise.* These proverbial prizes are the object of most of men's daily efforts. In Christ we have: *wisdom* exceeding the greatest education; *security* exceeding the greatest wealth, the *unspeackable riches* administered for us now by a loving Father and reserved for us unto the day of inheritance; *health* of mind and soul, rightly affecting the body, renewing within though the outward man decay, lasting beyond the putting off of the flesh.

*The greatest treasures are yet to come.* We "who have the first-fruits of the Spirit . . . groan . . . waiting for our adoption, to wit, the redemption of our body. For in hope were we saved" (Rom. 8:18-25). "If we have only hoped in Christ in this life we are of all men most pitiable" (I Cor. 15:19). "In due season we shall reap, if we faint not" (Gal. 6:9). "In the world ye shall have tribulation" (John 16:33). The whole New Testament emphasizes that we are to invest this life in securing that one which is final and eternal. The blessings of God we receive here are to prepare us for and to lead us to that limitless blessedness there. "A tent or a cottage, why should I care? They're building a palace for me over there."

### *What Does Christ Mean To Us?*

Are we living up to the privileges of the kingdom? A man paid for first class passage on a steamship and took along a lot of cheese and crackers to eat for the whole trip. One day another passenger, too sick to eat, found him off by himself eating his cheese and crackers. "If you can eat, why don't you go eat that fine fare they are serving in the ship's dining room?" He answered, "The ticket for this trip cost so much I couldn't afford to eat that kind of meals." "Man, you paid for it in your ticket. You are not getting all that's coming to you."

Are we continually living such rejoicing, thankful, and victorious lives that other people may see how valuable Christ is to us and desire what they see that we have?

For Further Study:

See books listed on page 227 for comments on the parables of the Hidden Treasure and The Pearl of Great Price.

# *Part Eight*

# OLD AND NEW COVENANTS

## 45

### THE OLD TESTAMENT ATTESTED BY CHRIST AND THE APOSTLES

I. The Testimony of the New Testament to the Genuineness (Authorship) of the Books of the Old Testament

A. *Jesus' Statements:*

Matthew 13:14: "And unto them is fulfilled the prophecy of Isaiah which saith 'By hearing he shall hear, and shall in no wise understand; and seeing ye shall see, and shall in no wise perceive.' "

Matthew 15:7: "Ye hypocrites, well did Isaiah prophesy of you, saying . . ."

Matthew 22:43: "How then doth David in the Spirit call him Lord, saying . . ."

Matthew 24:15: "When therefore ye see the abomination and desolation which was spoken of by Daniel the prophet, standing in the holy place . . ."

Mark 12:26: "Have ye not read in the book of Moses, in the place concerning the bush how God spake unto him, saying . . ."

Mark 12:36: "David himself said in the Holy Spirit, 'The Lord said to my Lord, Sit thou on my right hand, till I make thine enemies thy footstool.' "

Luke 24:44: "These are my words which I spake unto you, while I was yet with you, that all things must needs be fulfilled, which are written in the law of Moses, and the prophets, and the psalms, concerning me."

John 5:46: "For if ye believed Moses, ye would believe me: for he wrote of me."

B. *Statements By Others In The New Testament:*

Matthew 2:17: "Then was fulfilled that which was spoken through Jeremiah the prophet, saying, 'A voice was heard in Ramah, weeping and great mourning, Rachel weeping for her children; and she would not be comforted, because they are not.' " (From Jer. 31:15).

Matthew 3:3: "This is he that was spoken of through Isaiah the prophet, saying . . ." (Isa. 7:14).

Matthew 4:14: "That it might be fulfilled which was spoken through Isaiah the prophet, saying . . ." (Isa. 40:3).

Matthew 22:24: The Sadducees quote Deuteronomy 25:5, saying that Moses wrote it.

Luke 2:22-24: Luke quotes from Leviticus and Exodus in telling of the presentation of Jesus in the temple, and says that it was according to the law of Moses.

John 1:17: "For the law was given through Moses" says John.

John 1:45: "We have found him of whom Moses in the law, and the prophets, wrote," said Nathanel.

Acts 8:28, 32: "and was reading the prophet Isaiah . . . now the passage of the scripture which he was reading was this, 'He was led as a sheep to the slaughter, And as a lamb before his shearer is dumb, so he openeth not his mouth. In his humiliation his judgment was taken away [justice was denied Him]. His generation who shall declare? For his life is taken from the earth.' " (Quoted from Isa. 53:7, 8.)

I Corinthians 9:9: "For it is written in the law of Moses . . ." (The apostle quotes Deut. 25:4.)

II. The Testimony of The New Testament To The Authenticity (Truthfulness) of the Old Testament Accounts

A. *Jesus' Statements:*

Matthew 6:29: "yet I say unto you, that even Solomon in all his glory was not arrayed like one of these."

Matthew 12:3: Jesus cites as true what is written in I Samuel 21:6.

Matthew 12:40: "For as Jonah was three days and three nights in the belly of the whale; so shall the Son of man be three days and three nights in the heart of the earth."

Matthew 12:42: "The queen of the South shall rise up in the judgment with this generation and shall condemn it; for she came from the ends of the earth to hear the wisdom of Solomon, and behold, a greater than Solomon is here."

Matthew 15:3-5: Jesus quotes from the Law of Moses,

calling it the "commandment of God."

Matthew 22:32: "I am the God of Abraham, the God of Isaac, and the God of Jacob. God is not the God of the dead, but of the living" (Ex. 3:6).

Matthew 23:35: "that upon you may come all the righteous blood shed on the earth from the blood of Abel the righteous unto the blood of Zachariah son of Barachiah, whom you slew between the sanctuary and the altar."

Luke 4:25-27: Jesus cites as true the accounts of Elijah and the widow of Zarephath, and of Elisha and Naaman.

Luke 17:26-29: Jesus cites as true the accounts of Noah and the flood, and of Lot and the destruction of Sodom.

Luke 24:44: "Then he said to them, 'These are my words which I spake unto you, while I was yet with you, that all things must needs be fulfilled which are written in the law of Moses and the prophets and the psalms concerning me.' "

John 3:14: "As Moses lifted up the serpent in the wilderness, even so must the Son of man be lifted up."

John 5:39: "Ye search the scriptures, because ye think that in them ye have eternal life; and these are they which bear witness of me."

John 6:32, 49: Jesus refers to the wandering of the Israelites and the giving of manna as true incidents.

B. *Statements By Others In The New Testament:*

Luke 3 and Matthew 1: These genealogies verify those of the Old Testament.

Acts 7: Stephen's speech verifies many statements of the Old Testament.

Acts 8:28, 32: "Now the passage of the scripture . . ." (From Isa. 53.)

Acts 13:16-22: Paul refers to events which took place in the Old Testament.

Romans 1:16, 17: Paul quotes from Habakkuk 2:4: "But the righteous shall live by faith."

I Corinthians 10:1-13: Paul refers to specific incidents that happened to the Israelites as being authentic.

Galatians 3:16: Paul bases his argument on the singular form (rather than the plural form) being used in the promise recorded in Genesis 13:15 and 17:8.

Hebrews 2:1, 2: "For if the word spoken through angels

(the Old Testament) proved stedfast . . ."

Hebrews 10:30: The passage quotes Deuteronomy 32:35, 36.

Hebrews 10:37: The passage quotes Habakkuk 2:3, 4.

Hebrews 11: The entire chapter cites as true the Old Testament accounts of Cain and Abel, Enoch, Noah, Abraham, Isaac, Jacob, Moses, and many others.

Hebrews 12:5: The passage quotes from Proverbs 3:11ff.

Hebrews 12:16: Reference to the incident of Esau's selling his birthright.

Hebrews 12:18-21: Reference to Exodus 19:12-22.

James 2:8-11: James quotes from Leviticus 19:18 and Exodus 20:13, 14.

I Peter 3:20: "that aforetime were disobedient, when the longsuffering of God waited in the days of Noah, while the ark was a preparing, wherein few, that is, eight souls, were saved through water" confirms parts of Genesis.

III. The Testimony Of The New Testament To The Inspiration (Authority and Infallibility) Of The Old Testament

A. *Jesus' Statements:*

Matthew 4:4: "It is written, 'Man shall not live by bread alone, but by every word that proceedeth out of the mouth of God.' " (Quoted from Deut. 8:3.) In verses 7 and 10 Jesus again quotes from Deuteronomy in His answers to Satan's temptations as stating rules from God which bound His own conscience and conduct.

Matthew 5:17, 18: Jesus' statements that He came not to destroy the law but to fulfill, and that the law would remain in effect until all was fulfilled, declare the truth of the Old Testament prophecies and the authority of the law.

Matthew 5:21, 27; 15:4; 19:18, 19: Jesus quotes five of the ten commandments on at least three different occasions: in the Sermon on the Mount, in argument with the Pharisees, and to the rich young ruler.

Matthew 19:4: "Have ye not read, that he who made them from the beginning made them male and female, and said, For this cause shall a man leave his father and mother, and shall cleave to his wife; and the two shall become one flesh?" Jesus affirms of Moses' statement in Genesis 2:24 that God said this.

Matthew 21:42: Jesus quotes Psalms 118:22, 23, referring

to it as "scripture."

Matthew 22:31: "But as touching the resurrection of the dead, have ye not read that which was spoken unto you by God, saying," and He quotes Exodus 3:6.

Mark 7:8-13: Jesus refers to the commandment, "Honor thy father and thy mother" as being the commandment of God. He concludes in verse 9: "Full well do ye reject the commandment of God that ye may keep your traditions."

Mark 12:36: "David himself said in the Holy Spirit," and Jesus quotes Psalms 110:1.

Luke 16:17: "But it is easier for heaven and earth to pass away, than for one tittle of the law to fall."

Luke 18:31: "And he took unto him the twelve, and said unto them, 'Behold, we go up to Jerusalem, and all the things that are written through the prophets shall be accomplished unto the Son of Man.' "

Luke 22:37: "For I say unto you, that this which is written must be fulfilled in me, 'And he was reckoned with transgressors' for that which concerneth me hath fulfillment." Jesus quotes Isaiah 53:12.

Luke 24:25, 26: "O foolish men, and slow of heart to believe in all that the prophets have spoken! Behooved it not the Christ to suffer these things and to enter into his glory?"

Luke 24:44: "All things must needs be fulfilled, which are written in the law of Moses, and the prophets, and the psalms, concerning me."

John 10:35: Jesus says, "The scripture cannot be broken" referring to Psalms 82:6.

John 13:18: "that the scripture may be fulfilled, 'He that eateth my bread lifted up his heel against me.' " Jesus quotes Psalms 41:9.

*True prophecies, those which never fail to come to pass, are from God. Jesus' insistence that the Old Testament prophecies are sure to be fulfilled amounts to testimony that they are from God.*

B. *Statements By Others In The New Testament*

Matthew 1:22: "Now all this is come to pass, that it might be fulfilled which was spoken by the Lord through the prophet . . ." quoted from Isaiah 7:14. The same terminology—"that which was spoken by the Lord through the prophet"—is used in Matthew 2:15 in quoting from Hosea 11:1.

Matthew 21:5: Matthew says Jesus fulfilled Zechariah 9:9, that "which was spoken through the prophet . . ."

Luke 1:55: "As he (God) spake unto our fathers," indirect quote by Mary alluding to Genesis 17:19.

Luke 1:67, 70: "Zacharias was filled with the Holy Spirit and prophesied, saying . . . As he (God) spake by the mouth of his holy prophets that have been from of old."

John 19:36, 37: "For these things came to pass that the scripture might be fulfilled . . ." John quotes Psalms 34:20 and Zechariah 12:10.

Acts 1:16: "Brethren, it was needful that the scripture should be fulfilled, which the Holy Spirit spake before by the mouth of David concerning Judas."

Acts 3:21: "Whereof God spake by the mouth of his holy prophets that have been of old."

Acts 3:22: "Moses indeed said, 'A prophet shall the Lord God raise up unto you from among your brethren, like unto me: to him shall ye hearken in all things whatsoever he shall speak unto you.' "

Acts 3:24: "Yea, and all the prophets from Samuel and them that followed after, as many as have spoken, they also told of these days."

Acts 4:24, 25, 31: The apostles and Christians prayed, saying, "O Lord, thou . . . who by the Holy Spirit, by the mouth of our father David thy servant, didst say," quoting Psalms 2:1, 2.

Acts 13:34: "He (God) hath spoken on this wise, 'I will give you the holy and sure blessings of David.' " (Quotation from Isaiah 55:3.)

Acts 28:25: "Well spake the Holy Spirit through Isaiah the prophet unto your fathers, saying," quoting Isaiah 6:9, 10.

Romans 1:2: "Which (the gospel) he promised afore through his prophets in the holy scriptures."

Romans 3:2: "First of all, that they (the Jews) were intrusted with the oracles of God."

Romans 9:25: "As he (God) saith also in Hosea," quoting Hosea 2:23.

Galatians 3:16: "He saith not, 'And to seeds,' as of many; but as of one, 'And to thy seed,' which is Christ." (Quotation from Gen. 13:15; 17:8.)

Galatians 3:18: "God hath granted it to Abraham by promise," referring to Genesis 22:17, 18.

II Timothy 3:15, 16: "And that from a babe thou hast known the sacred writings which are able to make thee wise unto salvation through faith which is in Christ Jesus. Every scripture inspired of God is also profitable for . . ."

Hebrews 1:1: "God having of old time spoken unto the fathers in the prophets by divers portions and in divers manners." (All the first chapter bears witness to the inspiration of the Old Testament.)

Hebrews 2:2: "For if the word spoken through angels proved stedfast,"

Hebrews 3:7: "Wherefore even as the Holy Spirit saith," quoting the words of Psalms 95:7ff.

Hebrews 8:8-12; 10:15-17: These passages affirm the divine source of Jeremiah 31:31ff.

Hebrews 12:26: "Whose voice then shook the earth: but now he hath promised, saying 'Yet once more will I make to tremble not the earth only, but also the heaven." (Quotation from Haggai 2:6.)

Hebrews 13:5: This passage affirms the inspiration of Deuteronomy 31:6 and Joshua 1:5.

I Peter 1:10, 11: "Concerning which salvation the prophets sought and searched diligently, who prophesied of the grace that should come unto you; searching what time or what manner of time the Spirit of Christ which was in them did point unto, when it testified beforehand the sufferings of Christ, and the glories that should follow them."

I Peter 3:19: This affirms the inspiration of the preachers in the days of Noah: "But made alive in the spirit; in which also he went and preached unto the spirits in prison that aforetime were disobedient when the longsuffering of God waited in the days of Noah."

II Peter 1:21: "For no prophecy ever came by the will of man: but men spake from God, being moved by the Holy Spirit."

II Peter 3:2: "That ye should remember the words which were spoken before by the holy prophets."

For Further Study:

France, R. T. *Jesus and the Old Testament.* Downers Grove: Inter-Varsity Press, 1971. Extensive study on Jesus' use of the Old Testament.

Pinnock, Clark. "The Inspiration of Scripture and the Authority of Jesus Christ," *God's Inerrant Word,* ed. by J. W. Montgomery. Minneapolis: Bethany Fellowship, 1973. Jesus teaches a trustworthy and inerrant scripture.

Tasker, R. V. G. *The Old Testament in the New Testament.* Grand Rapids: Wm. B. Eerdmans, 1946. Pp. 19-38. Jesus' use of the Old Testament.

Wenham, John. *Christ and the Bible.* Downers Grove: InterVarsity Press, 1972. Pp. 11-37. Jesus accepted the Old Testament as historically true, inspired by God and divinely authoritative.

# 46

## LAW OR GRACE

"The Law was given through Moses; grace and truth came through Jesus Christ" (John 1:17).

The New Testament plainly teaches what every Christian needs to know, that the religion which is by faith in Jesus Christ is separate and distinct from the Old Testament. It is not only a new covenant in place of the old one; but it is also one of a different kind. Even the Old Testament plainly declared that it would be so. Read Jeremiah 31:31-34 and the comments on it in Hebrews 8:1-13.

### *Christ Fulfilled the Law*

Jesus came not to destroy the law but to fulfill it (Matthew 5:17); and *He did fulfill it!*

He fulfilled it as a promise or note is fulfilled when it is paid in full. He brought, or did, or was, what the Old Testament promised and predicted.

He fulfilled it as a set of blueprints is fulfilled when the house is completed. He established what the Old Testament outlined and fore-patterned in type and shadow.

He fulfilled it as the apple fulfills the apple blossom. The Old Testament was as necessary in preparing for Christ and the gospel as the blossom is in preparing for the apple. But, as the apple blossom disappears when the apple comes on, not being destroyed or made void, but being fulfilled and validated by the apple which displaces it, so also the law is not destroyed but is made valid by the Christ who furnishes, and is, what it prepared for.

He manifested in His life the righteousness which the law described.

He bore in His death the punishment which the law inflicted. He fulfilled the sentence which it pronounced against sinners. Thus He upheld the validity of its demands and established its divine authority; but at the same time, He satisfied its claims and dismissed its charge against us. He nailed it to the cross (Col. 2:14).

### *A New Covenant*

After the death of Jesus, a new will (or testament) was proclaimed from heaven; and by it the former will is made obsolete and no longer binding.

In the book of Acts we see the new covenant in effect. We also see some men trying to perpetuate the old covenant even in the church. They tried to mingle together the rule of Christ and the rule of the law. But God revealed that they do not mix.

First, the benefits of the gospel were proclaimed to all in Judea without regard to how well they had kept the law. Then God expressly directed that it was to be preached to Gentiles without the law (Acts 10:1 to 11:18). Still later, when some tried to lay upon the Gentile Christians an obligation to the law, the will of the Lord was revealed that it was not to be so (Acts 15:1-31).

Still in many places and often the problem arose, for the advocates of the law were not easily convinced, and human nature is inclined to legalism. So the truth and grace of Christ versus the bondage and failure of the law, as a way of life and righteousness, was often discussed in Paul's epistles: especially in Romans, Galatians, Colossians, and Hebrews, but also in others.

Note some of the many ways in which the Spirit of God says that the law came to an end and was displaced by the gospel of Christ—"Ye are not under the law" (Gal. 5:18; 3:23-25). "Ye are not under the law, but under grace" (Rom. 6:14). "Ye also were made dead to the law . . . that ye might be joined to another" (Rom. 7:4). "I died unto the law, that I might live unto God" (Gal. 2:19-21). "Ye have been discharged from the law, having died to that wherein ye were held" (Rom. 7:6). "It is done away in Christ" (II Cor. 3:14). He "abolished . . . the law" (Eph. 2:14, 15). He "blotted out" the law, "and he hath taken it out of the way, nailing it to the cross" (Col. 2:14). He "made of necessity a change of the law" (Heb. 7:12). "There is a disannulling of a foregoing commandment, because of its weakness and unprofitableness" (Heb. 7:18, 19). "He taketh away the first (covenant) that he may establish the second" (Heb. 10:9, 10).

There can be no doubt that some law was abrogated; but there is often disagreement as to what it was. In II Corinthians 3:1-14 the old covenant which was done away is expressly stated to be that which was written on tables of stone when Moses' face was shining (i.e., the ten commandments). According to the letter of the apostles and elders in Acts 15:22-29, the Gentile Christians were not expected to observe anything of the Jewish law or customs except to abstain from blood, idols, and fornication. In Galatians 2:3; 5:2, 3, 6 and I Corinthians 7:18, 19 circumcision is especially mentioned as a key element of that which was no more binding upon men and circumcision was given to Abraham long before Moses' time. Paul says that if anyone accepts circumcision, as a religious obligation, he becomes obligated to do the whole law (Gal. 5:3); thus he makes it all a unit. Although we may regard part of the law as ceremonial and other parts as moral law, such a distinction is never made or even assumed in scripture.

Several passages, such as Romans 6:14, 15; 10:4; Galatians 2:16, 19, 21; 5:18, 23 use no article, "the," with the word "law" in the original language; thus they say that we are not under law any more, speaking of law in general as a principle or method by which God deals with men. They probably refer to the Mosaic law as the outstanding example of law, but they speak broadly of the nature of any legal system.

*The Christian is simply not under anything but Christ.* Read Colossians 2:8 to 3:17. Christ is the end of law (no article) for righteousness to everyone that believeth (Rom. 10:4). Compare Philippians 3:3-12.

### *A New Kind of Covenant*

The gospel of Christ is not simply another law or a better law; it is something different from law. The gospel did not introduce a new system of right and wrong, but a new way of dealing with it. The rule of Christ is not a reign of law, but the manifestation of a new creature, the product of a new spirit, the working of Christ in us through faith and love (Gal. 5:6, 13-18, 22-25; 6:15, 16; Rom. 14:17).

The written record of the law is still valuable. It is useful to reveal sin in its deadly sinfulness, and to show man's need for salvation under some system other than law. It helps to bring us to Christ (Gal. 3:24; II Tim. 3:15). It bears a powerful testimony to the divine origin of the gospel which it predicts and prefigures in so many ways.

But the law, as a covenant under which we have our standing before God, cannot continue in force over those who are in Christ. If Christians were to try to be justified by the law, then they would be fallen away from grace, and Christ would become of none effect to them (Gal. 5:1-6). In the very process of coming into Christ men are made dead to the law. By grace men are brought into *a new and different relationship with God, a new condition of heart, and a new kind of control in Christ.*

### *A New Relationship With God*

Under law man stands in a legal relationship with God; the law stands between man and God. One's acceptance or condemnation before God is determined rigidly by how he has kept the law. He stands as one who merits all that he receives, boasting before God (a sad distortion of goodness!). Or rather, actually, through lack of merit, he is unable to stand at all. The standards of God's law are perfect, and they allow for no deviation at all. Cursed is everyone who does not do all the law all the time (Gal. 3:10; James 2:10). By works of law no man can be justified before God (Rom. 3:19, 20; Gal. 2:16; 3:11; Acts 13:39). Under law anyone who feels justified can do so only by blinding himself to the meaning of the law and the condition of his own heart and life. The law can be nothing else than a "ministration of death" and "condemnation" (II Cor. 3:7, 9); for it can only declare the guilt and pronounce the doom of sinners. It cannot make alive. The law makes a just and righteous demand upon men; but it does not enable them to do and be what is demanded.

Under grace our relationship with God is quite different, not on the basis of how we have kept the law, but on the fact that we have become united with Christ and are living in Him. It is an entirely personal relationship, by which we accept His offer of loving favor by personal trust in Jesus and by accepting His death, His life, and His leadership for our redemption from sin, our way of life, and our reason to be. By His death on our behalf He fulfilled the sentence of the law against us. We acknowledge the guilt of our sin, accept His death as our death, count ourselves as crucified with Christ, and henceforth live no longer unto ourselves, but unto Him, in Him, and for Him. He is our righteousness before the judgment of God and He is our way of life here upon the earth. In Him we stand; without Him we perish! The best law keeper in the world is just as lost as the worst sinner in hell; but any man who will can have eternal life and the fruits of righteousness in Christ. Under law no one is worthy even to continue in this earthly life. But through yielding in faith and love unto Christ, we are being prepared to share with Him His own infinite and eternal inheritance. This is the power and the glory of God's grace!

### *New Creatures In Christ*

"If any man is in Christ, he is a new creature; the old things are passed away; behold, they are become new" (Read II Cor. 5:14-19). "For the law [principle] of the Spirit of life in Christ Jesus made me free from the law [dominion] of sin and of death . . . that the ordinance [or requirement] of the law [God's will] might be fulfilled in us, who walk not after the flesh, but after the Spirit . . . They that are in the flesh cannot please God. But ye are not in the flesh but in the Spirit, if so be that the Spirit of God dwelleth in you . . . If by the Spirit ye put to death the deeds of the body, ye shall live" (Rom. 8:1-14).

Coming to Christ for salvation, we surrender our defiled and condemned selves to death, we are buried with Him through baptism into His death, and rise to newness of life, in which it is not we that live, but Christ that lives in us (Rom. 6:3-5; Gal. 2:20).

In Christ we exercise and express the righteousness accounted to us by grace and the Spirit planted in us as a gift. The righteous will of God is not lowered; it makes no less demands upon us because we are in Christ; but through Christ we are enabled to meet the demands. Grace does not excuse us from doing the will of God, but it is part of God's way of enabling us to do His will.

We claim no merit for ourselves. He is our righteousness and our life. We live by His word to show our faith in Him, not to show our sufficiency as keepers of the law. Any good fruit produced in our lives is not for us to boast of or to receive credit for; but it is the product of Christ's working in us. Any deeds which we do in obedience to Jesus (whether moral or ceremonial) are not done as our deeds worthy of reward, but as His works in us. They are done in love for Him to the glory of His name, not ours. They are the result of regeneration, not the ground or condition thereof. We give thanks to Him for them.

When we have done all that we know of His will, we are still unprofitable servants and need to ask in faith for the mercies of His grace (Luke 17:10). But under grace we need not despair at our inability to know and do all of His will, because we are made to stand in His sufficiency (See Heb. 7:25; I John 1:8-10; 2:1, 2; Rom. 8:31-39; 14:4). Yet we cannot be self-satisfied or indifferent to the highest standards of His perfect pattern of goodness. Our works are never sufficient to be acceptable. We must live by faith. And faith working through love, seeking not to live our own lives but to let Him live in us, always impels us to do all things to His glory. We look not at ourselves either to excuse or defend ourselves, but we look at Him in admiration and loving imitation. The farther we advance in our efforts to be like Him the more we realize that we cannot attain such a goal in this life; yet we believe it is His purpose to give us this high character if we reach for it, believing in Him.

If we do not accept His control and let Him work in us, we do not accept His grace. No one is under grace until he has died to sin and self, and has become alive unto God in Jesus Christ.

For Further Study:

Campbell, Alexander. "The Sermon on the Law" in *Historical Documents Advocating Christian Union,* ed. by C. A. Young. Rosemead, Calif: Old Paths Book Club, 1955. Pp. 217-288. Argues that what the law could not do Christ did. The complete law of Moses was nullified and superseded by the gospel of Christ.

Stevens, G. B. *The Theology of the New Testament.* New York: Charles Scribner's Sons, 1899. Pp. 17-26, 362-374. Discussion of what Jesus and Paul taught about the law and the gospel.

Davis, John J. *Moses and the Gods of Egypt.* Grand Rapids: Baker Book House, 1971. Pp. 196-210. Studies the Ten Commandments in the context in which they were given and gives New Testament teaching on their meaning in the age of grace.

Dungan, D. R. *Hermeneutics.* Delight, Ark.: Gospel Light Publishing Co., n.d. Pp. 106-155. Discusses the necessity and principles for distinguishing between the covenants.

Fields, Wilbur. *Exploring Exodus.* Joplin: College Press, 1976. Pp. 413-421. A study of the Ten Commandments and their significance to Christians, who "are not under the law."

Ford, Harold W. "On the Law and the Gospel," *Christian Standard* (July 16, 1955), Pp. 686. Helpful essay on the relationship between the law and gospel.

Johnson, Ashley S. *The Two Covenants.* Delight, Ark.: Gospel Light Publishing Co., reprint of 1899 ed. Thirteen sermons on the relationship between the two covenants.

# 47

# JESUS' ATTITUDE TOWARD THE LAW

Jesus' teaching and practice reveal His attitude toward the law. In Christ was abrogated the entire Old Testament law, including the Ten Commandments, as a covenant or legal code. Jesus taught that the abiding moral principles revealed in the covenant God made with Israel are still binding on us today.

We certainly need more respectful knowledge of God's moral laws in this generation. Study of God's laws reveals sin and brings people to repentance. Probably our preaching of pardon would be more effective if people were made to see clearly the commandments of God they have broken. Certainly the church needs to learn to observe all things whatsoever Christ has commanded, in order to adorn the doctrine (Titus 2:1-10), to bear fruit to His glory, and to make our calling and election sure (II Pet. 1:5-11).

Jesus warned the disciples, "Beware of the leaven of the Sadducees" (Matt. 16:5-12). In studying about the law, we must not fall into the popular error of deciding by reason or by custom or personal taste how far these commandments are binding upon us, but we must view them as decrees of God and determine their force and perpetuity by the study of His Word in which they are revealed. We must not consider Jesus as a rabbi explaining, or even purifying, the law; but we must distinguish clearly between the old covenant which has passed away and the new covenant which is God's will for us, of which Jesus is the supreme lawgiver. We must avoid thinking of the words of Christ quoted in the four Gospels as the full expression of Jesus' will and teaching for us. All the New Testament is the word of Christ, made known through the Holy Spirit. The apostles taught and wrote what they received; their teaching is not theirs, but Christ's (John 16:12-15).

## *The Law of God Through Moses*

Read Exodus 20 and Deuteronomy 5 and 6 concerning the giving of the Ten Commandments. God gave to Israel not only this basic law or constitution, but also all her national system, institutions, and officers, memorial feasts, and all the forms of worship in detail; because all these things were preparation and patterns for the Christian covenant. They were not enforced as the will of Moses or the will of the people, but the will of God. All love and respect for God was measured by the keeping of the law. All infraction and neglect of the law was sin against God and was punished by Him.

Israel was strictly charged to lay up in their hearts all the words and laws of God, and to teach them diligently to their children, talking of them morning, noon, and night, at rest and at work, and keeping them before their eyes in writing (Deut. 6:4-9). But through indifference and preoccupation with other things, the homes failed in this all-important task, just as they do today. The law was neglected. The customs of pagan neighbors were adopted, and great calamities were brought upon the disobedient people. By Jesus' day, synagogue services were held every Sabbath, in which the law and the prophets were read. But the people were taught chiefly by Pharisees, who perverted their practice by hypocrisy and vain formalities, and their teaching by the great place given to opinions and the traditions of the elders.

### *Not to Destroy but to Fulfill*

Jesus, in the Sermon on the Mount declared: "Think not that I came to destroy the law or the prophets: I came not to destroy, but to fulfill. For verily I say unto you, Till heaven and earth pass away, one jot or one tittle shall in no wise pass away from the law, till all things be accomplished" (Matt. 5:17, 18). Jesus upheld and promoted the keeping of the law, but not with the same emphasis that the Pharisees had, and with total rejection of their traditions. Hence He was often regarded as a lawbreaker. He was also promulgating the principles of spiritual righteousness and freedom belonging to the new covenant, and His teaching went beyond the law. He spoke with authority of His own greater than that of the law. He was aware that these things might create the impression that He would destroy the law; that is, set it aside as of no force or value. The conflict between Him and the Pharisees, the chief exponents of the law, would suggest that He was opposed to the law itself. Therefore Jesus denied that He would destroy the law; and, more than that, He affirmed in the strongest manner His conviction that the entire Old Testament was from God and could not pass away unfulfilled. Not the smallest part of it could be regarded as fruitless (Matt. 5:17-19).

McGarvey explains:

> The term destroy is here used in antithesis, not with perpetuate, but with fulfill. To destroy the law would be more than to abrogate it, for it was both a system of statutes designed for the

ends of government, and a system of types foreshadowing the kingdom of Christ.[1]

Jesus was bringing new teaching and preparing a new covenant, but it did not destroy the law, for it was the very thing the law and the prophets were designed to prepare for. The law was a set of blueprints and patterns of the permanent house that Christ would build. The prophets were a stack of promissory notes which Christ would retire by paying them in full. If the fulfillment had not come, they would have been proved void, would have been destroyed. When the fulfillment came, the promises and patterns were no more in effect; they passed away, but they were not broken. When the fruit and seed are formed the bud and flower have passed away, but they have not been destroyed; they have been fulfilled.

Jesus also fulfilled the law in regard to its legal requirements, in its judicial demands upon the sinner. His death accomplished that which the continual sacrifices under the law could not do (Heb. 10:1-18). He accomplished the moral purpose of the law—His teaching, which took its place, is productive of righteousness superior to that of the law. He did not set aside the law and bring in anarchy, but He brought a better rule, filling up what was lacking in the law to govern the lives and spirits of men, and filling up what was lacking in it to express all God's holiness and His perfect will for man (e.g., the law of divorce, etc.). Righteousness apart from the law is witnessed in the law, and justification by faith apart from the works of the law does not make void the law but establishes it. (Study Rom. 3:21-31 and 8:4).

It is plainly affirmed in both Testaments that the old law and covenant would end in fulfillment and give way to a new and better system. A new lawgiver (Deut. 18:15-18), a new priesthood (Ps. 110:4), a new covenant (Jer. 31:31-34), a new sacrifice (Isa. 53), a universal kingdom including the Gentiles (Isa 2:2-4) are all predicted in these and many other passages. Christians are "not under the law" (Rom. 6:14), "were made dead to the law through the body of Christ," are "discharged from the law" (Rom. 7:1-6), are under a new covenant and the old covenant, which was written on stones when Moses' face shone, "is done away in Christ" (II Cor. 3:1-14). The law has fulfilled its purpose in bringing us to Christ; we are no

[1] J. W. McGarvey, *Matthew and Mark* (Cincinnati: Standard Publishing Company, 1875). P. 52.

longer under it (Gal. 3:17-29). Christ abolished the law (Eph. 2:13-22). Return to the weak and beggarly rudiments of the law and observance of days and seasons commanded therein is a very dangerous error (Gal. 4:1-11; 5:1-18).

### *Righteousness and the Law*

Surely Jesus did not mean to declare that in His kingdom men would be perpetually obligated to do and teach every least commandment of the Old Testament law. Rather He meant that the relative greatness of persons in the kingdom would be in proportion to their respect for and conscientious observance of the commandments of God which are intended for them. Inasmuch as He was then speaking to men who still lived under the old covenant, their characters were then judged by the laws of that covenant.

> The man who would break what he considered the small commandments of God under one dispensation, would be portionately disobedient under a better dispensation . . . To the great commandments, as men classify them, even very small Christians may be obedient; but it requires the most tender conscience to be always scrupulous about the commandments.[2]

The righteousness of Christians must "exceed the righteousness of the scribes and Pharisees" (Matt. 5:20). The scribes were the most advanced scholars of the law, and the Pharisees were the most zealous in its observance. Their "righteousness" was characterized by self-righteous pride in observance of minute regulations while they omitted the great and weighty matters (see Matt. 23:1-28). Their hearts were corrupted by their confidence in formal and ritual acts of righteousness as a substitute for being righteous in heart. Their satisfaction with their appearances made them not hunger and thirst after a pure heart and the will of God. We must continually hunger and thirst after the true righteousness of God, or we will not be filled.

"If righteousness is through the law, then Christ died for nought" (Gal. 2:21). If we are to stand blameless before God, it must be by the death of Christ and His merit imputed to us through our faith in Him. Commandments of God give the instruction by which an obedient spirit must live, but they will not produce that spirit of perfect submission. Only the heart that is won through true faith

---

[2] *Ibid.*, P. 53.

and grateful appreciation to whole-hearted love for God and His righteousness will have the spirit of real righteousness and will use the law to glorify God rather than self.

For Further Study:

Fowler, Harold. *The Gospel of Matthew,* Vol. I. Joplin, Mo.: College Press, 1968. Pp. 242-259.

See books listed on page 246.

# 48

## GOD'S LAW IS FOR OUR GOOD ALWAYS

When Moses was about to end his career as the leader of Israel, and Israel was preparing to enter the promised land, he spoke to his people a series of addresses reviewing the laws God had given them. He said, "The Lord commanded us to do all these statutes . . for our good always, that he might preserve us alive" (Deut. 6:24).

Moses repeated the Ten Commandments (Deut. 5), and in verse 29 we read God's fervent wish: "O that there were such an heart in them, that they would fear me, and keep all my commandments always, that it might be well with them, and with their children forever!"

We, as did ancient Israel, need to be convinced that God's government is most desirable. Men set up governments in order to provide wise leadership, strength for security and peace, and stability of society among other things. God's rule is the wisest, surest, and best obtainable. He has more personal, loving concern for all of us than any human government could have.

The laws that God has given are expressions of His love and His wisdom for our good. The idea that God's laws are killjoys that take all the fun out of life is a notion of unbelief and misunderstanding. In the long run obedience to God gives us more joy and peace than the transient pleasures of sin.

God knows how we are made and He gives His laws to fit our needs. We are made free and responsible to choose our actions. His laws give guidance to the choices we must make. Weakened and corrupted by sin, we choose inconsistently, first one way and then another. We need to feel and accept His authority expressed in His laws.

The ultimate purpose of God's will for us is to help us to be like Him, and to live according to His wisdom and goodness. His laws indicate His will in a concrete way. They illustrate the basic principles of His character and make known to us the divine nature that He wants us to share (see II Pet. 1:3, 4).

God's goodness makes His laws good. His love makes His decrees beneficent. Anyone who wants to be wise and good treasures the commandments and statutes of the Lord (see Ps. 19:7-14; 119:97-105).

### *Perverse Legalism*

Some of the Pharisees in Jesus' day thought they loved God's law. In reality they loved the self-satisfaction, power, and prestige that stemmed from their pretending to do God's will. They were ensnared in legalism and hypocrisy, not because they had respect for the law but because they desired to excuse themselves from duties and yet defend and exalt themselves as obedient to the law. Their desire to judge and command others rather than examine and control themselves led them further into legalism. They emphasized the outward appearance and sought the approval and praise of men more than the approbation of God.

Such legalism overemphasizes certain chosen symbolic actions. Whenever we forget that the righteousness of God's commandments is primarily a righteousness of inner character, when we lose sight of the fact that character produces conduct, when we ignore the character and the motive behind the conduct and value the form of the deed above the heart out of which it is performed, then we are caught in the trap of legalism.

The first chapter of Isaiah shows that God was not pleased with outward performance of commanded duties when the heart was not in the state that the commanded actions were meant to express.

### *The Greatest Benefit of the Law*

The great purpose of the law is that it shows up the sinfulness of sinful deeds and announces the punishment they bring. This helps to guide and to fortify the will of those who wish to do right. It eventually works to eliminate those who do not wish to do right. It restrains and tempers the madness of many. But best of all, it shuts up all men to judgment and shows that the only way of escape from condemnation is by faith in Jesus Christ. The law prepared for Christ by showing all men's absolute need for Him.

> The law requires righteousness and shows the sinner the depths of his sin, not to leave him in despair, but rather to lead him humbled and penitent to Christ, that God may receive him through faith. Paul's philosophy of the law is most succinctly set forth in Galatians 2:19: 'For I through the law died unto the law, that I might live unto God.' The apostle died to the law ethically; he broke off all relations to the law as a supposed means of salvation. Compare Romans 7:4, where death to the law is illustrated

> by the dissolution of the marriage-bond by the death of one of the parties. But how did he die to the law by means of the law? The answer is found in full in Romans 7:7ff. The law had shown him his sin and his guilt. It had put him to death ethically. It had slain his self-righteousness. This was a severe, but in its ultimate result, a saving process. The law had prepared him to receive Christ. It had taught him the inadequacy of all his 'works,' and had led him to accept a gracious salvation. He thus broke off all relations to the law and fled to Christ for salvation, and it was the law itself which, when he clearly saw its requirements, proved a powerful incentive urging him to do this. Thus the law, by showing him his sinfulness and helplessness, was a means of driving him to Christ. Hence, through the law, he became as a dead man to the law—ceased to regard it as a saving institute—and was pointed to the spiritual life graciously offered in Christ, in whose fellowship he found joy and peace. The law had slain him, but it was only that Christ might make him alive. He forsook the law forever, but only that he might become 'under the law to Christ' (I Cor. 9:21).[1]

What the law could not do because it was weak through the flesh, or rather, because human flesh was too weak to keep the law, God has done for us through the grace of Christ and the conversion of our hearts. Under the law alone we cannot have righteousness that will stand approved in God's judgment. Only the righteousness of Christ, accounted to us through faith, can make us acceptable to God. But the law certainly works for our good if it bring us to Christ.

### *Christ Fulfilled the Law*

Jesus showed great respect for the written law in the Old Testament. He quoted from it frequently as the word of God, and taught men to obey it. When His teaching went beyond it or corrected the inadequate concepts of righteousness that men derived from it, He said, "Think not that I came to destroy the law or the prophets: I came not to destroy, but to fulfill. For verily I say unto you, Till heaven and earth pass away, one jot or one tittle shall in no wise pass away from the law, till all things be accomplished" (Matt. 5:17, 18).

[1] George B. Stevens, *The Theology of the New Testament* (New York: Charles Scribner's Sons, 1899), p. 372.

Jesus' life and teaching, His redemptive ministry, and the way of salvation that He brought to men did fulfill the ideals, purposes, promises, patterns, and prophecies of the old covenant. His life was the perfect embodiment of the righteousness that the law described.

When Jesus suffered for sinners the death that the law decreed, He upheld the validity of its demands and established its divine authority (Rom. 3:31); but at the same time He satisfied its claims and dismissed its charges against us. He nailed it to the cross (Col. 2:14).

Many particulars of the law of Moses were by nature only temporary, imposed until a time of fuller revelation and a time of men's new relationship with God through Christ. Some of it was given so that it would have to be changed when the priesthood of Christ was revealed and ratified (Heb. 7:12).

Many passages of the New Testament state plainly that the old covenant, which was based upon the law, has been superseded by a new and better covenant based upon a better sacrifice and better promises. In Hebrews 7:11-22 we read of "a change also of the law" (v. 12), "a disannulling of a foregoing commandment" (v. 18) and the bringing in "of a better covenant" (v. 22, American Standard Version). In Hebrews 9:8-15 the old and new covenants are compared and contrasted. Hebrews 10:9 says, "He taketh away the first, that he may establish the second."

Second Corinthians 3:1-14 tells of the "ministers of a new covenant; not of the letter, but of the spirit" and affirms that "the old covenant . . . is done away in Christ" (American Standard Version). This old one is identified as written on stones and coming with glory when Moses' face was shining. The reference is clearly to the Ten Commandments.

Even the Old Testament prophesied that God would make a new covenant, not like the one He made with Israel when He brought them out of Egypt, but He would put His law in their inward parts and write it in their heart (Jer. 31:31-34).

The whole Old Testament, in all its parts, was fulfilled by Christ; and all its elements that are of permanent value and validity have been made a part of the teaching of Christ and the New Testament. The law for Christians, then, is not the Old Testament legislation, not the Ten Commandments, but the New Testament teaching of the will of Christ.

## *Conclusion*

The law made a just and righteous demand upon men; but it did not enable them to do and be what it demanded. Under grace we still have commandments. But the moral demands of Jesus presuppose a changed nature in man; they imply a previous conversion. The obedience that He expects is the result of a religious transformation. We obey Him not by the force of penalties and rewards of law, but by the motives of a heart united with Him in an experience of death and new birth, a heart filled with trust and love and with a genuine purpose to glorify Him.

We do His commands not to prove ourselves so worthy that we do not need His righteousness imputed to us or His Spirit implanted in us; but we obey Him because we accept Him as Lord as well as Saviour, and we love Him because He first loved us.

"For this is the love of God, that we keep his commandments: and his commandments are not grievous" (I John 5:3). The demands of Christ are greater and more constantly upon us than those of the law. But He gives us His Holy Spirit to bear the fruit that is not against any law and to give us power over the flesh (Gal. 5:13-25; Rom. 8:1-15). By keeping in fellowship with Christ we realize more than ever that His commands are not grievous, but are for our good always.

For Further Study:

Fowler, Harold. "The Law of Christ," mimeographed essay available from Ozark Bible College Bookstore, Joplin, Mo. 10 pages. A critique of the view which perverts the New Testament pattern into legalism and a plea for the control of the Spirit in which the commands of Christ and the apostles are honored yet freedom is given in areas of opinion.

Ketcherside, W. Carl. "Analysis of Legalism," *Mission Messenger* (August, 1960) Pp. 1-10. Bound in the volume entitled *Covenants of God* (*Mission Messenger, 1959-1960*). Critique of legalism.

Mansur, A. V. *Let My People Go!* Galt, CA: author, 1967. Pp. 1-14. A chapter entitled, "Law or Liberty; Not Both!"

See books listed on page 246.

# 49

# JESUS TEACHES THE RIGHT USE OF THE SABBATH

Jesus and all His generation until Pentecost after His resurrection lived under the law and covenant which was given through Moses at Mount Sinai. Without question they were obligated to keep the Sabbath—the seventh day of the week—by ceasing from labor.

Jesus' teaching about how to keep the Sabbath all arose out of His own practices and the violent objections to them raised by the Pharisees. The Jews, especially the Pharisees, were given to rigid observance of external ceremonies, such as purifications and Sabbath regulations, at the expense of the true spiritual principles and significance of God's laws (See Matt. 23:3-5, 23-28; Mark 7:1-23). It seems that Jesus purposely violated such traditions in order to teach against them and to set forth the right attitude toward God's laws. He deliberately sought to work miracles of healing on the Sabbath; and ate without washing His hands. In the controversies which followed, He commonly asserted His own supremacy over the Old Testament and its institutions (cf. "greater than the temple"; "Lord even of the Sabbath"; and John 5:16-18).

Jesus did teach that the Pharisees were perverting the Sabbath and using their traditions to defame and resist the righteousness of God in Christ. He did teach the true and just interpretation of the Sabbath law. But remember: He taught the right use of the Sabbath for Jews who were obligated to keep the Sabbath, not for Christians who have no part in keeping the Mosaic law.

### *Christians Not Under the Law, But Under Christ*

Read and study the meaning of the following passages of the New Testament which were written to Christians concerning the covenants and regulations binding upon Christians. (1) "Ye are not under law, but under grace" (Rom. 6:11-18). (2) "Ye were made dead to the law through the body of Christ . . . We have been discharged from the law, having died to that wherein we were held" (Rom. 7:1-6). (3) "And to the Jews I became as a Jew, that I might gain Jews; to them that are under the law, as under the law, not being myself under the law, that I might gain them that are under the law" (I Cor. 9:20). (4) "A new covenant"—the old one, written on stones "is done away in Christ" (II Cor. 3:14). (5) Paul and Peter, who were once Jews under the law, when Christians, lived as Gentiles free from the law

(Gal. 2:14-21). "now that faith is come we are no longer under" the law (Gal. 3:7-14, 17-29). (7) Observance of days and seasons indicates confidence in fleshly works of the Old Testament law, and makes the apostle afraid that his labor of preaching Christ to them was lost or wasted (Gal. 4:1-11). (8) "Ye are severed from Christ, ye who would be justified by the law . . . If ye are led by the Spirit, ye are not under the law" (Gal. 5:1-18). (9) "Christ abolished the law of commandments contained in ordinances" (Eph. 2:13-22). (10) "having blotted out the bond written in ordinances that was against us, which was contrary to us: and he hath taken it out of the way, nailing it to the cross" (By all means, read Col. 2:6-23 in full until you understand it). (11) "a change also of the law," "a disannulling of the foregoing commandment . . . and bringing in of a better covenant" (Heb. 7:11-22). (12) The Old Testament itself predicts the displacement of the covenant made with Israel when they were brought out of Egypt. It promises a new and better covenant, of a different kind, putting the laws of God into the hearts of men (Heb. 8:6-13). (13) The old and new covenants contrasted. "He taketh away the first that he may establish the second" (Heb. 9:8-15; 10:9, 10).

The Ten Commandments were an inseparable part of this law which was "abrogated," "done away," "disannulled," "abolished," "taken away," and "nailed to the cross." They are no more binding on any one today, as a legal code, than any other part of the Old Testament. They were not given as a whole to any nation other than Israel but were a covenant made expressly with Israel alone (Deut. 5:2-5; Exod. 31:12-17, etc.). The Decalogue, or any part of it, is never in any way distinguished from the Mosaic covenant which was abrogated. Specifically, II Corinthians 3:1-14 describes the old covenant which was done away as that which was written and engraved on stones, which was given when Moses' face shone and was veiled (see Exodus 34:29-35). The Ten Commandments were the basis of the covenant which God made with Israel when He brought them out of Egypt. They were placed in the "ark of the covenant." Both Old and New Testaments declare that it was that very covenant which was superseded by Christ and taken away that He might establish another (Jer. 31:31-34; Heb. 8:7-10).

Some things commanded in the old law are now commanded in Christ, but we are to do them because God commanded them, not because they were in the old law. Once Kansas was a territory, governed by territorial law. Some of the same things were forbidden by territorial law that are now forbidden by state law. But present residents of Kansas can not be held accountable to territorial law. They are not under it. We who are under the rule of Christ as Christians are no more under the law which God gave to Israel at Mount Sinai than we are under the law of the old Roman Empire. We are not to obey the Ten Commandments, but to obey Christ. And do not let any one lead you to anything apart from Christ (Col. 2:8—3:17).

The Sabbath is one of the shadows of things to come (see Col. 2:16, 17; Heb. 9:8-10; Heb. 10:1-9). Its typical significance is explained in Hebrews 4:4-11, where it is treated as a predictive ceremony and not as an eternal reality in itself. It is not a type of the Lord's Day, but of the rest of eternity in heaven.

It is urged that the Sabbath was commanded to be kept "for ever" (Exod. 31:16, 17). But many, many laws which all admit to be abrogated in Christ were said to be an ordinance forever (see Exod. 12:14, 17, 24; 27:21; 28:43; 30:21; 29:28; Lev. 6:18; 7:34; 10:15; 16:29; 23:31; 17:7; 23:14, 21, 41; 25:46; Num. 19:10; Deut. 15:17; 23:3; etc.).

### *Christ Did Not Perpetuate the Sabbath*

If Christ in the New Testament commanded the observance of the Sabbath or set an approved precedent for the church, we would be obligated as Christians to observe the Sabbath, but not otherwise (Matt. 28:18-20). But in all the record of His words and of the teaching of the apostles, who spoke for Him by the inspiration of His Spirit, there is no indication that Christians are expected to keep the Sabbath. Some New Testament passages have been misinterpreted and forced into service by Sabbatarians to appear to indicate indirectly that the Sabbath was to contine forever, but one needs only to read all of them in their own context and without preconceived notions and he will see that they do not do so.

(1) "The Son of Man is Lord even of the Sabbath" (Matt. 12:8; Mark 2:28). It is claimed that this means that the Sabbath is Christ's commandment and is perpetuated under His rule in the new dispensation. Rather, He is saying to the Jews that He had authority equal with God, including authority over the law of the Sabbath, under which law they were trying to convict Him of sin. He showed that He claimed to be Lord of the temple also; but that does not make the temple in Jerusalem a perpetual part of the New Testament order.

(2) Jesus entered the synagogue on the Sabbath (Luke 4:16). This was under the law. There was where the people were. He went there

to teach just as He went to the temple or the marketplace to teach. Jesus lived and died as a Jew under the law, although much of His teaching was advance promulgation of the principles of the new covenant.

(3) "Pray that your flight be not on the Sabbath" (Matt. 24:20). It is claimed that this indicates that the Lord would always prohibit Sabbath travel, and therefore when He warned Christians to flee He told them to pray that it might not be on the Sabbath Day, so that they would not be prohibited from carrying out His orders. Without displaying the inconsistencies and difficulties of this whole idea, I would point out that Jesus had reference to the coming destruction of Jerusalem by the Roman armies under Titus, in 70 A.D. (This is evident from a comparison of Matt. 24:15-20 with Luke 21:20-24). History (particularly Josephus in *Wars of the Jews,* Book vi) records the fulfillment of this prediction and the fact that the believers remembered the prophecy and fled from the city, saving themselves from the terrible seige that followed. The Sabbath would have hindered their escape because the Jews would still be enforcing the Sabbath (plus their traditions) and persecuting Christians who broke it (or their idea of it) just as they persecuted Jesus for healing on the Sabbath. Early in His ministry they sought to kill Him for that one thing (John 5:10, 16, 18; Mark 2:23—3:6).

If the Sabbath is to be kept today because it is commanded in the Old Testament law, then it should be kept according to the instruction of the law. But the law, including the Decalog, was done away. We are not under law but under Christ.

If the Sabbath is to be kept today as a matter of obedience to Christ, then it should not be kept at all, because Christ did not command Christians to keep it, but rather indicated its removal.

### *The Early Church Did Not Perpetuate the Sabbath*

These facts stand quite clear: (1) The Gentile churches were not instructed to keep the Sabbath, but were taught to meet, worship, and make offerings on the first day of the week (Acts 20:7; I Cor. 16:2). (2) The letter of Acts 15:22-29 omits the Sabbath from the "necessary things" for Gentiles out of the Old Testament law. No precept about any particular "day of rest" is to be found among all the varied moral directions given in the whole New Testament. (3) Quite on the contrary, this observance of a given day as a matter of divine obligation is denounced by Paul as a forsaking of Christ (Gal. 4:10), and requiring sabbath-keeping is even forbidden (Colossians

2:16). (4) The esteeming of any day above another is a matter of liberty, not of necessity (Rom. 14:5, 6). (5) The early Christian writers, just after the days of the apostles, record the general practice of the church carrying out the apostolic teaching. They show that Sunday, as the day of Christ's resurrection, was kept as a Christian day of worship and commemoration, and was called "the Lord's Day." The following four brief quotations will serve to underline this point:

Ignatius (before A.D. 125 at the latest) in his epistle to the Magnesians says: "No longer keeping the Sabbath, but living according to the Lord's Day, in which our Light arose."[1]

The Epistle of Barnabas (not likely to be a genuine work of the New Testament Barnabas, but certainly written between A.D. 90 and 120) says: "We keep the eighth day with gladness, the day on which Jesus rose again." This epistle goes on to distinguish that observance of Sunday from Sabbath-keeping, which it considers an error in Christians.[2]

Justin Martyr (A.D. 100-166) wrote and published a formal defense of Christianity about A.D. 140. In it he says: "And on the day called Sunday, all who live in cities or in the country gather together to one place." Then he describes the reading of the Scriptures, preaching, praying and partaking of the Lord's supper.[3]

The Gospel according to Peter (falsely so-called, but widely circulated before A.D. 200) says: "The Lord's Day began to dawn" (in telling Matt. 28:1) and "early on the Lord's Day" (in retelling Luke 24:1).

### *The Lord's Day Different From the Sabbath Day*

Sunday was sharply distinguished from the Sabbath. One was the day on which worship was offered in a specifically Christian form; the other was a day of ritual rest to be observed by all who were subject to the law of Moses. Nothing is said anywhere in the Bible about Sunday being a day of rest; it is distinguished only as a day of worship. People who criticize others for working on Sunday and themselves do not attend worship have things just backwards and are in danger of setting aside the Lord's revealed will by their traditions. How much better it would be for Christians to spend the day in service to Him and others than in the ways so common to many.

---

[1] Ignatius, *The Epistle of Ignatius to the Magnesians*, ix.

[2] *The Epistle of Barnabas*, xv.

[3] Justin Martyr, *The First Apology of Justin*, lxvii.

Let us hold to the liberty and simplicity that is in Christ, and fulfill the law in love to God and in taking thought for things honorable in the sight of all men.

For Further Study:

Robinson, F. E. "Sabbath" in *Dictionary of Christ and the Gospels,* Vol. II, ed. by James Hastings. New York: Charles Scribners Sons, 1908. Pp. 540-542. Deals with incidents involving sabbath and teaching about it in the Gospels and in the early church.

Waterman, G. Henry. "Sabbath" in *The Zondervan Pictorial Encyclopedia of the Bible.* Grand Rapids: Zondervan Publishing House, 1975. Vol. I, Pp. 181-189. Comprehensive examination of Biblical and historical data concerning the Sabbath.

Wilson, Seth. "Should Christians Keep the Sabbath?" Mimeographed paper, Ozark Bible College Bookstore. More complete study on the Sabbath.

# 50

# JESUS DEMANDS LOYALTY TO GOD

The first law of all in the basic commandments of the covenant between God and the Hebrews was the law about every individual's relation and attitude toward God. In all times and in every land the first of all fundamentals in the lives of men is always this: their acknowledgment of God as supreme and their constant and complete faithfulness to that profession. See Proverbs 9:10.

> To the Christian the first Commandment takes the form which our Lord gave it—'Thou shalt love the Lord thy God with all thy heart, and with all thy soul, and with all thy mind. This is the first and great commandment' (Matt. 22:37, 38). Not merely abstract belief, not merely humble acknowledgment of one God is necessary, but heart-felt devotion to the one object worthy of our devotion, the one being in all the universe on whom we may rest and stay ourselves without fear of His failing us. He is the Lord our God—not an Epicurean deity, infinitely remote from man, who has created the world and left it to its own devices—not a Pantheistic essence spread through all nature, omnipresent, but intangible, impersonal, deaf to our cries, and indifferent to our actions—not an inscrutable 'something external to us making for righteousness,' in the words of the religious Agnostic—but a being very near us, 'in whom we live, and move, and have our being.' who is 'about our path and about our bed, and spieth out all our ways,' a being whom we may know, and love, and trust, and feel to be with us, warning us, and pleading with us, and ready to receive us, and most willing to pardon us—a being who is never absent from us, who continually sustains our life, upholds our faculties, gives us all we enjoy and our power to enjoy it, and who is therefore the natural object of our warmest, tenderest, truest, and most constant love.[1]

### *The Sin of Godlessness*

Too many Americans consider their freedom of worship as if it were both political and moral freedom from all worship. Every man

[1] George Rawlinson, *Pulpit Commentary: Exodus* (Grand Rapids: Wm. B. Eerdmans, 1961), p. 136.

has a moral right to obey God rather than men in matters of religion, and our constitution guarantees him the political right to do so within broad limits, but he does not have an equal right to disobey God and live in spiritual anarchy. Only God has the authority to tell men where, when, and how they shall worship Him. God has not delegated authority to the political government to enforce worship. Very few, if any, of us would wish to authorize even elected public officials to enforce their ideas of right worship upon all men. But that does not mean that men "have a perfect right" to ignore God.

God must be reckoned with. We can not do justice without recognizing Him. We can neither find the truth apart from Him, nor have power to resist and overcome sin. He holds the power of life, the light of man's spirit, the eternal truth, the sources of liberty and joy. "But he answered and said, It is written, Man shall not live by bread alone, but by every word that proceedeth out of the mouth of God." (Matt. 4:4).

The best efforts at moral order (whether individually or socially) which disobey or ignore God are fundamentally anarchy and rebellion, rather than control and submission. The individual who abuses his religious liberty and lives a godless life becomes a danger and a poison to his community and really commits a crime against society.

### *The Sin of Having Rival Gods*

Vast multitudes say: "We do not ignore God. We believe in Him and worship Him—some. Other things take so much time and attention—they are necessary, practical, important things."

Sometimes I wonder how God looks upon our whole generation and our national customs. Does He find any of us who really puts Him first and alone upon the throne, and who lets none of the things of the world, of physical affairs, of personal ambitions or comforts—or "necessities"—command our lives and time and energies and take first place in our attention? What things command our energies, compel our attention, and make other things wait?

It is said that Jenny Lind, the "Swedish Nightingale," was once invited by the king of the country to sing in the royal palace at a festival, but it was to be held on the Lord's Day. She refused to come. The king came in person and pleaded with her, and her only response was, "There is a higher King, your Majesty. I owe my first allegiance to Him."

Oddly enough, the Bible never uses any form of the word "loyalty," yet it inculcates and demands the highest loyalty. It uses the word "love," "faithfulness," "obedience." Anyway, it makes it quite plain that any one who would be a servant of the true and living God must have no other gods, must serve no other master, must obey God only, and must love Him supremely. "We must obey God rather than men." (Acts 5:29). We must obey God rather than self. We must obey God! He is a jealous God. The lukewarm (Rev. 3:15-17) the limping and vacillating (I Kings 18:21) can not serve Him. "And Joshua said unto the people, Ye cannot serve Jehovah; for he is a holy God; he is a jealous God; he will not forgive your transgression nor your sins. If ye forsake Jehovah, and serve foreign gods, then he will turn and do you evil, and consume you, after that he hath done you good" (Josh. 24:19, 20).

This matter of doing right is not an impersonal matter of roles or principles about which we can meditate abstractly and have different opinions. It is a personal matter of personal love and submission to God or else personal affront, rebellion and enmity toward the maker of us and of all good things.

"Thou shalt have no other gods before me" (Exod. 20:3). "No other gods before me" really means in the Hebrew "besides me" or "in addition to me." Having a secondary god is disobedience to God. A second master is disqualification for true and acceptable service to the first Master. "No man can serve two masters: for either he will hate the one, and love the other; or else he will hold to one, and despise the other" (Matt. 6:24). This shouts condemnation against the idea that various gods of various religions can be all good and acceptable to some degree, at least. If Jehovah is to be the God of any people, all other gods must be renounced and opposed (Josh. 24:23).

When the Israelites worshiped Jehovah and also frequented the high places of Baalism, even while they considered Jehovah supreme and called on Him for relief from national distress, and while they had a different and lower conception of Baal, still they flagrantly violated God's command, all truth, and their own best interests.

No worthy husband wants his wife to consider him her lover, and also at the same time to have other lovers besides him. Our relation to God is even that personal, if it is right. If it is not marked by such personal, single devotion, then we suffer affliction within and loss without—internal conflict, confusion, and barrenness of spirit, the insecurity and want of the sinful woman who is without home and husband and the natural ties that bring peace and joy.

It was said in utter condemnation of the Samaritans that they feared Jehovah and served other gods (see II Kings 17:28-41). But how many church members are like them? Only God is competent to judge all others, but each of us can examine himself concerning whom we really serve.

"Now there went with him great multitudes: and he turned, and said unto them, If any man cometh unto me, and hateth not his own father, and mother, and wife, and children, and brethren, and sisters, yea, and his own life also, he cannot be my disciple. Whosoever doth not bear his own cross, and come after me, cannot be my disciple" (Luke 14:25-27). Notice how Jesus put Himself on exactly the same plane as God, demanding the same absolute devotion to Himself that belongs to God. Yet in His own life He set a perfect example of denial of self and of serving God alone in all things. He was to God a lowly servant—He is to us the King of kings with supreme authority. He was to God a perfect man—He is to us an absolute God.

He offers more of love and deserves more of respect than parents do. To Him we owe more than to all the generations of our ancestors. He is, or can be and should be, nearer and dearer than husband or wife. He sets before us more of hope, of challenge, and of call for loving service than our children do. He gives a more profound brotherhood than brothers or sisters can. He is more than all of physical life and earthly opportunity put together. In His service there is more of majesty and importance, more of fruitfulness, helpfulness, and goodness, than in all other things that occupy the mind, the body and the heart. Look again, my brother, and see—there is no such thing as a valid excuse for refusing, neglecting, or forsaking the service of Christ.

### *The Sin of Revising God*

The second Commandment was that they should not make any image to represent God. "Thou shalt not make unto thee a graven image, nor any likeness of any thing that is in heaven above, or that is in the earth beneath, or that is in the water under the earth: thou shalt not bow down thyself unto them, nor serve them; for I Jehovah thy God am a jealous God, visiting the iniquity of the fathers upon the children, upon the third and upon the fourth generation of them that hate me" (Exod. 20:4, 5). They must not devise and express in this way their own ideas of God. Any material representation would be false; they must strive to apprehend the true and spiritual representation that He makes of Himself.

Israel at Sinai, with Aaron as their leader, shortly after hearing this law, violated it by making a golden calf and worshiping it as Jehovah who brought them out of Egypt. They did not take to themselves a new God, but they sinned against God by disobeying His command and by falsely representing Him. Again, four or five hundred years later, Jeroboam led the northern tribes of Israel in worship, as he said, of Jehovah, but they worshiped an image falsely named and by ceremonies of his own devising contrary to the law of God.

Today those who refuse to recognize Christ as the full and accurate revelation of God, but make for themselves theoretical "images" of the "supreme Being," are idolaters of the same sort. Jesus said: "He that hath seen me hath seen the Father" (John 14:7-9; Cf. John 10:30; Matt. 11:27). When we say, "This is Jesus," by the same token we are saying, "This is our God." And any one who makes God to be different from Jesus and all the revelation of God's will which Jesus approved is guilty of making his own idol and falsely labeling it as the living God.

For Further Study:

Lewis, C. S. *The Four Loves.* New York: Harcourt, Brace and Company, 1960. Pp. 163-192. Perceptive comments on loving God.

Lockyer, Herbert. *Everything Jesus Taught,* Vol. I. New York: Harper and Row, 1976. Pp. 43-80. Sets forth Jesus' teaching about God: nature, love, holiness, sovereignty, and fatherhood.

Moser, K. C. *Attributes of God.* Austin, Texas: Sweet Publishing Co., 1964. Thirteen well-outlined lessons showing the Bible's teaching on the characteristics of God.

Tozer, A. W. *The Knowledge of the Holy.* New York: Harper and Brothers, 1961. A study of the attributes of God and their meaning in the Christian's life.

Torrey, R. A. *What the Bible Teaches.* London: James Nisbet and Co., Ltd., n.d. Pp. 13-67. Directs the reader to scripture which teaches about God.

# 51

# JESUS AND THE LAW OF LOVE

The greatest of the fundamental laws of the Old Testament is the principle of love, which Jesus said was the basis of all the law. Concerning the commands to love God and to love our neighbor Jesus said: "On these two commandments the whole law hangeth, and the prophets" (Matt. 22:40).

The apostle Paul, inspired by the Holy Spirit, said that love is the most excellent gift and fruit of the Spirit of God in those who are born anew through the word of the Spirit (I Cor. 12:31—13:13; Gal. 5:22), that "love is the fulfillment of the law" (Rom. 13:10), and "is the bond of perfectness" (Col. 3:14). James says that the law of love is the "royal law" (James 2:8). Peter says that it is to be practiced "above all things . . . for love covereth a multitude of sins" (I Pet. 4:8). John bears witness that "He that loveth not knoweth not God; for God is love" (I John 4:8). There can be no question about this—the Bible teaches that love is both basic and supreme in the realm of righteousness; it is the foundation and the pinnacle. Love is what the law requires; and with perfect love the law is quite satisfied.

## *The Love of God's Law*

Psalm 119, the longest chapter in the Bible, is a hymn of meditation and prayer in praise and devotion to the law of the Lord. It is a great acrostic poem, full of passionate love and longing for mastery of the ways of life and attainment of the ways of God's eternal righteousness. Any one who can read it and enter sincerely into its expressed yearnings and prayers is blessed; for "Blessed are they that hunger and thirst after righteousness; for they shall be filled" (Matt. 5:6). The psalmist realizes that the character and attainment that he seeks is to be found in God, and that God ministers unto us through His word of truth and commandment. In God's testimonies, precepts, statutes, commandments, and ordinances are to be found perfect wisdom and purity and power to attain unto lasting life, peace, security, tranquillity, joy, and satisfaction of soul. "Therefore I love thy commandments above gold, yea, above fine gold" (v. 127). Compare with this long and variegated meditation of this psalm the clear and concise parallel in Psalms 19:7-14; then let the spirit and feeling of it leaven the heart until its words haunt the memory. How can we appreciate the righteousness of love until we know the love of righteousness? Do our prayers express a yearning for God's will to envelop ours, His governing control to be over all our affairs, and His laws to fill our minds?

God's government is most desirable! All the reasons that cause men to set up human governments, seek teachers, and honor parents should cause them to seek the instruction and control of God. His wisdom is infinite. His justice is incomparable, perfect. His stability, dependability, and power to defend His own are vastly superior to all the empires of men. His laws are for our good always. His love and mercy are more tender and enduring than those of a mother for her afflicted child. Even His chastening is with the hand of love and "yieldeth peaceable fruit unto them that are exercised thereby, the fruit of righteousness" (Heb. 12:7-11). There is every reason to trust Him. Our lives are dependent upon Him. Apart from Him we grope and blunder and stumble; we accomplish nothing and end in corruption. But in Him is light and life, wholeness and health, peace and eternal victory. Surely we ought to love His law of righteousness—not resisting, but inviting its restraints; not avoiding, but pursuing its sacrifices of self in service to others. It is the way of God, and God crowns it with glory.

The life of Jesus is a very helpful example for us in many ways, but most of all in this respect—the way He loved and sought the will of God. He treasured God's word and used it to overcome temptation. He lived by it rather than by bread (Matt. 4:4); for His food was to do the will of His Father (John 4:32-34). He taught men to pray "Thy will be done" (Matt. 6:10); and by that prayer He gained the victory is His hour of severest trial—"nevertheless not my will, but thine, be done" (Luke 22:42).

### *God's Law of Love*

Even in the Old Testament, God definitely commanded "Thou shalt love the Lord thy God" (Deut. 6:5), and "Thou shalt love thy neighbor" (Lev. 19:18). Jesus said to the Twelve, "This is my commandment, That ye love one another, as I have loved you" (John 15:12). All through the New Testament, love is considered a commandment and an obligation to be consciously assumed (Luke 6:35; Rom. 12:9, 10; Eph. 5:2; Col. 3:15; I Thess. 4:9; I Tim. 1:5; I Pet. 1:22; 3:8; 4:8; II Pet. 1:7; I John 3:11, 23; II John 5). Now, it is often discussed and argued whether love can be commanded, or whether it is an involuntary effect. But the fact remains that God commands it and expects us to obey.

What then is love? The word "love," like the man who went down from Jerusalem to Jericho, has fallen among thieves who have battered and bruised it and stripped it of its meaning. It is used to name feelings and motives which range all the way from the real thing (giving of self for the good of others) to the very opposite, including some of the worst forms of selfishness and abuse of others. Louis Evans said it well:

> Love, whether used of God or man, is an earnest and anxious desire for, and an active interest in the well-being of the one loved. Different degrees and manifestations of this affection are recognized in the Scriptures according to the circumstances and relations of life, e.g., the expression of love as between husband and wife, parent and child, brethren . . . friend and enemy.

Love is not an abstraction to be had without doing anything. It is not a distant, impersonal, general tolerance of everybody, like indifference. It is eager and active concern for the good of those loved. Such a thing is not accidental or hereditary, but voluntary—a matter of character. It is not a matter merely of likes and dislikes, tastes and preferences. The Lord expects us to love people who are not pleasing, not likable, and offensive to our tastes, who do not love us and do not want us to love them. That is the main point of Matthew 5:43-48. Our love ought to come from the character of our hearts, not from the nature of the persons with whom we have to do. God shows the same character toward all men, good and bad. If we love only those who love us, we do no more than the worst of men. Christian love as such appears only when we begin to love those whom we would not love if we were not following Christ. We prove our Christianity not in those good things we do which are equaled by the non-Christians, but in those things which surpass all non-Christians. While God does good to all, He does not show in all things the same favor to all men unconditionally, and He does not expect us to treat all exactly alike. For love is not universal indulgence or a spineless sentiment of approval for everything. A parent who admonishes or punishes his child may love him not less but more than one who does not. The strict teaching and admonishment which Paul gave to the church at Corinth was out of much love and a heart "enlarged" toward them (II Cor. 2:4; 6:11; 7:3).

How is love manifested? It is active and manifests itself in actions that seek the good of others; it just does not exist in passivity. The

Christian should love God first and supremely (Matt. 22:37), and show it in keeping His commandments (I John 5:3; John 14:15), in hating evil and the things of the world (Ps. 97:10; I John 2:15, 16; James 4:4), and by loving our brethren (I John 4:19-21).

We are to love our brethren "without hypocrisy" (Rom. 12:9), "unfeignedly" (II Cor. 6:6; I Pet. 1:22), and "fervently" (I Pet. 1:22; 4:8)—showing it by "serving" (Gal. 5:13; John 13:1-5; Phil. 2:4-7); seeking not our own but our neighbor's good (I Cor. 10:24); pleasing not ourselves (Rom. 15:1-3); bearing one another's burdens (Gal. 6:2); avoiding all occasions of stumbling and seeking things that edify and make peace (Rom. 14:15-21; I Cor. 8:1-13); preferring others in honor above ourselves (Rom. 12:10); giving of our means to help them in their need (II Cor. 8:8, 24; I John 3:17); rebuking them that sin in order to save them (Lev. 19:17; Prov. 27:5, 6; Eph. 5:11; Matt. 18:15-17; Tit. 1:12, 13; Heb. 3:13); forgiving the penitent, restoring gently the fallen, encouraging the fainthearted (II Cor. 2:7, 8; Gal. 6:1; I Thess. 5:14; Eph. 4:2, 32); praying for them (James 5:16; Eph. 6:18); and in laying down our lives for others (I John 3:16; John 15:13).

The ingredients of love are stated by Paul in I Corinthians 13, and are analyzed by Drummond as follows: "Patience—'love suffereth long.' Kindness—'and is kind.' Generosity—'love envieth not.' Humility—'love vaunteth not itself, is not puffed up.' Courtesy—love 'doth not behave itself unseemly.' Unselfishness—love 'seeketh not her own.' Good temper—love 'is not easily provoked.' Guilelessness—'thinketh no evil.' Sincerity—'rejoiceth not in iniquity, but rejoiceth in the truth.' "[1] These are things that can be practiced continually by all of us, and by them the great gift of love is made up.

Love is indeed the "Greatest Thing in the World" and the greatest thing in the Christian life. It is the delightful fruit for which the seeds of doctrine are planted and the plant of faith is cultivated. It is the supreme test of our abiding in God and God in us (I John 4:12, 16), the crowning grace of godlikeness.

"Beloved, let us love one another: for love is of God" (I John 4:7).

For Further Study:

Barclay, William. *New Testament Wordbook.* London: SCM Press

[1] Henry Drummond, *The Greatest Thing In The World* (Philadelphia: H. Altemus, 1898). P. 24.

Ltd., 1964. Pp. 17-29. Explanation of the meaning of *agape* (love).

Lewis, C. S. *The Four Loves.* New York: Harcourt, Brace, and Company, 1960. Pp. 163-192. Perceptive comments on loving God and our neighbor.

Marshall, L. H. *The Challenge of New Testament Ethics.* London: Macmillian & Company Ltd., 1947. Pp. 102-107; 12-15. Explains the two great commands as the dynamic for the highest ethical life.

# Part Nine

# MONEY AND MATERIAL THINGS

## 52

## THE CHRISTIAN AND MONEY MATTERS

> In the administration of his money the Christian finds for the character of his profession *both a test of sincerity and a means of culture.* Here is an unmistakable revelation of the sentiment of his soul. 'Money talks.' Its use speaks a message, the meaning of which verbiage can not conceal. Hereby he tells truly what he would hesitate to express with his tongue. *This reveals the range of his vision and the goal of his desire.* It proclaims the character of his emotions, his attitude to society, and the object of his devotion. It testifies to the world concerning the virility of his faith and the vitality of his hope.[1]

A great portion of our time, energies, and attention is given over to money matters. Christian motives certainly can not dominate our lives without entering into our economic affairs.

A Christian's real character—the state of his love for God and his love for man—is shown in (1) the way he gets money, (2) the way he feels about what he has and what others have, and (3) the way he uses his money. A Christian in money matters seeks to follow these principles:

### *He Recognizes God as the Owner of All Things*

Just as Moses warned Israel in Deuteronomy 8, we need to beware lest we forget God, the giver of every good and perfect gift. Especially as we get enough wealth that we do not feel our dependence upon prayer and providence, we are likely to forget the real source and owner, and consider it all our own. The Christian gives thanks for all he receives, and respects God's ownership in the uses that he makes of it.

---

[1] E. Lynwood Crystal, *The Christian and His Money.*

### *He Serves God and not Mammon*

We must not lose sight of the things that are far more valuable than much gold or silver. Certainly, 'money isn't everything.' There are precious things that money can not buy, which are too important to have their value estimated in money. The book of Proverbs repeatedly declares that wisdom and understanding are more precious than gold, silver, or rubies (Prov. 3:13-15; 8:11, 19; 16:16). It also says that a good name is rather to be chosen than great riches, and loving favor rather than silver or gold (Prov. 22:1). The instructions and commandments of God are more to be desired than much fine gold (Ps. 19:10). Steadfast faith in Christ is more precious than gold (I Pet. 1:7; II Pet. 1:1). Jesus taught that the kingdom of heaven and the righteous life are a great treasure to be sought above the daily food and clothing of the body (Matt. 13:44; 6:33). What does it profit a man to gain the whole world and lose his own soul or life? (Matt. 16:26).

What is often called 'good business' or 'strictly business policy' may not be the will of God. The Christian will have to choose between the kind of dealing that makes the most money and the kind that serves God to His glory. There should be no uncertainty or hesitation in his choice. Money is not an end in itself, but a means to an end. For the Christian it is an instrument to be used or sacrificed freely to serve the purpose of God. Alas, that there are men who will use and sacrifice the things of God to serve money interests!

We must take heed not to serve mammon rather than God. "No servant can serve two masters . . . Ye cannot serve God and mammon" (Luke 16:13). It is not necessarily wrong for a man to have wealth. Indeed it is right if he is using it for the Lord. But it is wrong and tragic for the wealth to have the man. Whenever we get enough property that we can not easily let go of it, we are in great danger, however little or much that is. Consider the case of the rich young ruler in Matthew 19:16-24. We must guard against the tendency to consider wealth as an end or good in itself, to seek after it for its own sake and lose the desire to use it according to God's will. The service of riches is deceitful. We think we are going to serve God, but actually withhold doing His will to get more wealth. We plan what we would do if we had enough, but refuse to do right with what we have.

The riches of this world are temporal, even fleeting, and are not worth the sacrifice that many people make for them (Prov. 23:4, 5).

People place too high a value upon the getting of money; then, strangely enough they commonly squander it for nothing of value.

When we use or give up the temporal wealth of this world to gain the kingdom of God and the inheritance of Christ, it is no sacrifice.

Getting and holding property is not as necessary as we seem to think; but what we do with what we have is very important. "Not what you would do, if riches should e'er be your lot, but what you are doing today with the dollar and a quarter you've got."

Putting money first in haste to get rich is foolish and hurtful even in regard to this life alone (Prov. 11:24-28). Men spend their health getting wealth, then have to spend their wealth trying to get their health again. They lose precious things of personal culture, family life, Christian service, and freedom from care, who sell themselves to the task of getting rich. Moreover, the more they gain the more they want, and they are never satisfied. And the more they increase possessions the more they increase cares and expenditures (Eccl. 5:10, 11).

*He Depends on God as True Security, not on Wealth*

The riches of this world are unreliable; it is folly to trust in them. "He that trusteth in his riches shall fall" (Prov. 11:28).

"How hard it is for them that trust in riches to enter into the kingdom of God!" (Mark 10:24). A Christian cherishes the promise of God above gold. He loves God, the approval of God's word and of a good conscience, more than he loves money. He knows that if he seeks "first the kingdom of God and his righteousness, all these things shall be added" unto Him (Matt. 6:33). "Ill fares the land (or family), to hastening ills a prey, where wealth accumulates and men decay!"

We must set our affections on things that are above (Col. 3:1-5). We must fill our minds and direct our desires with the precious and exceeding great promises, that through these we may become partakers of the divine nature, having escaped from the corruption that is in the world through wrong desire (II Pet. 1:4). Thus let us be diligent in the greater 'business' of making our calling and election sure, in securing to ourselves the spiritual treasures of godliness (II Pet. 1:5-11; I Tim. 4:7, 8); and let us not be so much engrossed in obtaining the riches of this world, even those that are fairly earned by honest labor (see Luke 12:15). We must learn to live the life of trust, and by trust be free from overanxiety about material needs (Matt. 6:25). Riches do not remove anxiety, but increase it. Cast your care on Him who cares for you (I Pet. 5:7; Phil. 4:19). Trust Him for the supplies for today and the necessities of tomorrow (Matt. 6:34). It is better to serve God and have His loving care, than to serve mammon and have even a great store of goods.

### *He is Strictly Honest and Trustworthy*

The New Testament goes so far beyond mere honesty in enjoining goodness, generosity and godliness that it does not have to speak directly of honesty in the common sense. It condemns hypocrisy, lying, and stealing, which are involved in any financial unfairness. It commands us to "render to all their dues," to meet our obligations, and "owe no man anything save to love one another" (Rom. 13:7, 8). There is certainly no excuse for a Christian to be in any degree a 'sharp dealer.' In all things he should be 'fair and square.'

It is stealing to make capital of the misfortunes of others, to charge a high profit not for service rendered, but merely because of the other man's necessity to buy, to obtain money under false pretenses, to take advantage of the ignorance of others, to borrow without definite intention to repay, to leave debts unpaid needlessly long (see Rom. 13:8). It is a similar evil to injure or depreciate the value of another's property, either by deliberate act or by culpable negligence. Many people who will not steal directly from an individual, especially an acquaintance, will boldy appropriate public property. Just because it belongs to the public and to no one individual does not make the taking of it any less stealing. Accepting in silence a mistake in price-marking, bookkeeping, or changemaking is deliberately taking the property of another while he isn't looking, just as if he were shoplifting. Gambling is robbery by mutual consent, and is no less a crime. Every desire and every attempt to get the possessions of others for nothing, or without full value in exchange, is a symptom of the same soul disease, the same idolatry, covetousness (Col. 3:5).

The virtue of real honesty is by no means as common as some suppose. "All men are sure to steal in one way or another, who are not possessed by the spirit of honesty, who do not make it the law of their life to be ever doing to others as they would that others should do unto them." It behooves us to examine ourselves. Are there none to whom *we* should make restitution? We must fortify ourselves against this universal temptation. We must put away covetousness from our hearts; we must realize that the very desire to possess the property of others is *wrong*.

### *He is Neither Wasteful nor Miserly*

The Christian realizes that he is a steward, a keeper and administrator of the property of another. He does not throw away what does not belong to him. Because it is not his own he does not hoard it, or refuse to use it according to the will of God. It is a sin to be as stingy as most of us are toward the Lord's work in the church and world-wide evangelism, and toward helping the needy. At the same time it is a shame the amount that we waste and squander for no good purpose.

### *He is Generous*

The New Testament is full of injunctions and examples of cheerful liberality. The Christian is to do good to all men, especially the household of the faith (Gal. 6:10). Those who have are to share with those who have not (Luke 3:11; Matt. 5:42; Luke 6:38; Acts 11:28, 29; I John 3:17; Rom. 12:8, 13). We are to give generously even to enemies (Rom. 12:20). We are commanded, not only to use what we have but also to work that we may have wherewith to give (Eph. 4:28).

The Christian way of giving is by principle, not just by impulse; it springs from the love and liberality in his heart and not just from the special demands of the occasion. "As a matter of bounty, and not of extortion . . . Let each man do according as he hath purposed in his heart: not grudgingly, or of necessity: for the Lord loveth a cheerful giver" (II Cor. 9:5-7).

It is to be in fair proportion to what we have, and with regularity, faithfully (I Cor. 16:2; Luke 16:10-13). The New Testament does not say directly that we must give at least a tithe, because it gives so much higher and more spiritual standards and appeals (II Cor. 8:9), and because any real believer should realize that we owe the Lord much more than the Jew did. Any one who seeks a law of necessity commanding the tithe is not seeking how much he can give, but how little he must give, and that attitude is contrary to the spirit of the new covenant in Christ. We must realize that we are not our own, but bought with a price (I Cor. 6:19, 20), and first give ourselves (II Cor. 8:5), then work to have as much as possible to give (Eph. 4:28).

The complete safeguard against robbing our neighbors is this: such a love for them that our hearts desire to see them prosper, until we seek to give to them rather than to take anything from them. We must be regenerated, transformed through the renewing of our minds in Christ Jesus (Rom. 12:2; Phil. 2:5), and made free from self-seeking and become *givers* rather than *getters* (Acts 20:35).

### *He Wisely Invests in the Eternal Securities*

We must make our treasures the non-depreciating ones laid up above. Any man is a fool who lays up treasures on earth and is not rich toward God (Luke 12:15-21). Hence, a believing disciple does not measure life and success by the amount of money laid up on earth. But he has a use for money so worthy, so excellent, so rewarding that he seeks to put to use all that he can get.

He uses it (1) to fulfill his obligation to God to provide for his own (I Tim. 5), (2) to serve Christ and save the world through the church and its agencies of evangelism, and (3) to help the needy in the name of Christ—or, as Jesus stated it, to "make to yourselves friends by means of the mammon of unrighteousness; that, when it shall fail, they may receive you into the eternal tabernacles" (Luke 16:9; see 16:1-13). Jesus commended the wisdom of any one who would seize the opportunity of using our present control over God's property to lay hold on grace, to make good our faith, and to make our calling and election sure; thus obtaining eternal life and a great inheritance by the way we choose to use God's goods in this world.

It is the Father's desire to give us the kingdom, but we must make it our all-pervading desire to gain it, lest we should depart from it by losing our hearts to worldly things. We must guard against trusting in riches (Mark 10:24) and put away the desire to be rich (I Tim. 6:9, 10), and spend the treasures of this world to gain the treasures in heaven, for where our treasure is our heart will be (Luke 12:33, 34).

It is not the money in itself that is evil, but the wrong use of it or improper trust in it. The Lord gives us the right to possess property—His property, as a stewardship for Him. There is a place of service for Christian money-makers, if only they are strong enough in faith and spiritual purpose to withstand the temptations and to keep money in subjection to the will of God. Just as the preacher should use his opportunities to exalt Christ and serve the people unselfishly, so the Christian money-maker should not make money for his own luxury but for the glory of Christ and the service of men, especially the household of faith (Rom. 12:1-8; Gal. 6:6-10).

Money is a powerful instrument for good; through it we can extend our influence and assist in many, many forms of godly service. Let us study the following passages on the right use of money: (1) to care for one's dependents (I Tim. 5:8); (2) to pay taxes (Mark 12:17; Rom.

13:6, 7); (3) to support faithful teachers of Christian doctrine (Gal. 6:6-8; I Cor. 9:11-14); (4) to give to the poor (Mark 10:17-22; Acts 11:27-30; II Cor. 8, 9); (5) to make restitution of wrong (Luke 19:8); (6) to provide hospitality (Heb. 13:2; Rom. 12:13); (7) to do good to all men (Gal. 6:10; Eph. 4:28; Heb. 13:16); (8) to show forth the goodness of God (Matt. 5:16, 43-48); (9) to cultivate the fellowship of perfect Christian love (Phil. 2:4, 5; Gal. 5:13-15; I John 3:16-18).

"Honor the Lord with thy substance, and with the first-fruits of all thine increase" (Prov. 3:9); because it is not our money that we give to God but God's money that we keep for ourselves.

The necessities of life are not the things which keep body and soul together. The real necessities of life are the things which keep the soul and God together.

For Further Study:

Banker, John C. *Personal Finance for Ministers.* Philadelphia: Westminster Press, 1973. Practical advice on money management.

Bowman, George M. *Here's How To Succeed with Your Money.* Chicago: Moody Press, 1960. Practical advice on how to live within your budget, provide for the future and honor the Lord with your income.

Ford, George L. *All The Money You Need.* Waco, Tx: Word Books, 1976. Biblical principles on the use of money.

Lockyer, Herbert. *Everything Jesus Taught,* Vol. III. New York: Harper and Row, 1976. Pp. 44-64. What Jesus taught about money (poverty and riches).

Macartney, Clarence. *What Jesus Really Taught.* New York: Abingdon Press, 1958. Pp. 81-88. Exposition and application of Jesus' teaching about money.

Speer, Michael L. *A Complete Guide to the Christian's Budget.* Nashville: Broadman Press, 1975.

# 53

## THE PERILS OF COVETOUSNESS

This is a study for the heart; let us take it to heart. The tenth commandment forbids the evil and selfish thoughts and desires, just as the seventh, eighth, and ninth forbid the outward acts that express selfishness and lack of regard for others. The tenth commandment reveals (1) that God judges the motives behind our acts; (2) that many an act that appeared good to men has been rotten by reasons of the lust from which it sprang; (3) that God may condemn a man who is blameless in the sight of men; (4) that sinfulness is not determined only by outward effect of an act in harm to society, but by the state of a man's heart in relation to God and to His will. If only dishonest getting of money were sin, then covetousness would be only a dangerous state that might lead to sin; but coveting itself is sin—a state of distrust, dishonor and rebellion toward God—idolatry.

The law against covetousness is clearly and repeatedly stated in both the Old and New Testaments.

> A very great part of the Jewish law—such as its regulations regarding duties toward the poor, toward servants, concerning gleaning, usury, pledges, gold and silver taken during war—was introduced and intended to counteract the spirit of covetousness.[1]

This sin was frequently rebuked by the prophets; e.g., Isaiah 57:17; Jeremiah 8:10; Micah 3:11; Malachi 3:8-10. God's great displeasure at this sin, its evil effects and severe punishments are shown in such examples as: Achan, in hiding the treasure from Jericho (Josh. 7:1-21); Eli's sons (I Sam. 2:13-17); Saul, saving booty from the Amalekites (I Sam. 15:9-19); David, coveting Bathsheba (II Sam. 11:2-5); Ahab, desiring Naboth's vineyard (I Kings 21:2-16); Gehazi, taking a gift from Naaman (II Kings 5:20-27).

### *Keep Yourselves from all Covetousness*

John the Baptist preached that repentance should be expressed in sharing what we have with those in need, being content with our wages, no profiteering, and no extortion (Luke 3:10-14). Jesus taught

---

[1] William Evans, "Covetousness" *International Standard Bible Encyclopedia,* Vol. II, edited by James Orr (Grand Rapids: Wm. B. Eerdmans, 1939). P. 733.

that the man whose chief concern is with material possessions is a fool (Luke 12:15-21); that the service of money as a master makes it impossible for one to serve God (Matt. 6:24); that "the cares of this world, deceitfulness of riches, and the lust of other things" choke the life out of the faith of many who otherwise would bear much fruit for God (Mark 4:19); that to have possessions and to refuse to share with the needy merits eternal torment in flame (Matt. 25:31-46; Luke 16:19-25); that the indispensable essence of Christian discipleship is self-denial (Matt. 16:24; Luke 14:33). The urgent command of Christ is that we love one another (John 13:34, 35; 15:12, 13; Matt. 5:43-48; 7:12). Christian love is just the opposite of covetousness (Rom. 13:8-10; 12:9-15).

Covetousness is classed with the most gross and glaring sins (Eph. 5:3-5), and, like them, is a shameful thing to talk about except as in the Scripture it is "named" in order to teach and warn against its sinfulness. It is called idolatry (Col. 3:5). It excludes men from heaven, and because of it "cometh the wrath of God upon the sons of disobedience" (I Cor. 6:10; Eph. 5:5, 6; Col. 3:5, 6). It is "a root of all kinds of evil" (I Tim. 6:10), causing some to be led astray from the faith, causing many foolish and hurtful lusts (I Tim. 6:9), causing some to teach false doctrines (Titus 1:11; II Pet. 2:1, 3).

The New Testament requires the church to recognize the symptoms of covetousness in its members and to take account of it with great seriousness. An elder must be "no lover of money" (I Tim. 3:3). Elders or deacons must be "not greedy of filthy lucre" (Titus 1:7; I Tim. 3:8). It is one of the sins specified for which a man must be separated from the church if he can not be brought to repentance (I Cor. 5:11). The paragraph in II Thessalonians 3:6-15 discusses how the church should deal firmly with idlers, "spongers" or parasites, even when they have a pious pretext for their "disorderly" conduct.

### *Just What is Covetousness?*

Since it is so far-reaching in its effects, so important to our eternal welfare, we need to know as definitely as possible *what covetousness is,* what to resist and what to avoid to keep from covetousness. But it is especially dangerous at this point, because it is a subtle thing, deceptive and insidious. It transforms itself into an angel of light, and calls itself "prudence" and other deceptive names. "It is said that St. Francis de Sales received at the confessional a greater number of persons than were ever known to visit one confessor besides, but that he did not remember a single instance in which covetousness had been confessed. No wonder that church censure for covetousness is exceedingly rare," wrote E. S. Prout. Yet who will say that the sin itself is exceedingly rare? Croskery wrote on this subject: "It is a solemn thought that the most common of all sins is the most serious in God's sight."

New Testament words for covetousness mean literally: "Desire to have more," "set the heart on," "desire strongly," "love money," and "reach after." Covetousness is a wider concept than "love of money" alone, but that "root of all kinds of evil" is the most common and glaring form of it. Covetousness is selfish desire in general.

But some things are rightly desired, sought after, and longed for by the Christian (Be sure to read I Cor. 12:31; I Pet. 2:2; I Tim. 3:1; Matt. 5:6; Col. 3:1, 2; Phil. 3:12-14). Covetousness is desire for the wrong things: (1) Desire for the possessions of a neighbor. So far from wishing gain at another's expense, we are to seek and to rejoice at the gain of a neighbor as really as if it were our own (Rom. 12:15; 15:2; I Cor. 10:24, 33; II Cor. 12:15). (2) Desire for worldly possessions for their own sake, to the neglect of higher things, or with the result that we will not use them to serve spiritual ends. It is eager anxiety for wealth without regard to God's glory or our own spiritual good. In Matthew 6:19-34, Jesus was not talking about any form of stealing or seeking gain at a neighbor's expense, but he was rebuking the man who is concerned chiefly or only with making a living, however honestly. The sin of the rich fool in Luke 12 was not in what he did as much as in what he did not do! Thus covetousness is "desire for proper things carried to an improper degree." It is also desire to gain anything in an improper manner. Christians are commanded to work for their food (II Thess. 3:10), to provide for their own households (I Tim. 5:8), and to work to have wherewith to do good (Eph. 4:28). But in seeking these good and proper material things, we must still put the service of God and spiritual interests first; we must keep our hearts from loving the possessions themselves; we must live in trust, knowing that God Himself has promised to supply our needs (Matt. 6:33; Phil 4:19; especially Heb. 13:5, 6). Covetousness is a perverted sense of values.

Covetousness is misplaced trust, as it is misplaced desire. A covetous man is an idolater simply because he loves, trusts, and serves money more than he does God; he transfers to riches the love, desire, joy, trust, and labor that he ought to have toward God, and makes money his god. The sin is all the worse because he knows it is no god. We are getting into this terrible sin (1) whenever we think more about how to get money than how to please and glorify God; (2) when we rejoice more in increase of possessions than in righteousness or progress in the kingdom of grace; (3) when our contentment and comfort depend upon worldly success (Phil. 4:11-13; I Tim. 6:6-9); (4) when we will take time off from Christian work or worship to make money, but will not take time off from making money to serve Christ or help ourselves grow spiritually; (5) when we seek the treasures and luxuries of this world, and do not treasure the promises of God concerning the inheritance of the saints; (6) in short, when we seek our own and not the things of Christ.

One of the most shameful forms of covetousness is withholding (hoarding) wealth (little or much) and refusing to use it for good works. This dishonors God who gave the wealth; it distrusts His promises to replenish; it defies His command to put it to use in His name (Luke 12:33; 16:9-13; Mark 16:15; I Cor. 9:14; II Cor. 9:6-11; Gal. 6:6; Rom. 12:13; I Tim. 6:17-19). It is a terrible thing, for which we all need to repent, that the average church member is stingy, selfish, inhospitable, and without conscience in the matter.

### *How Shall We Flee These Things?*

Pray that you enter not into temptation. Pray that God may help you to remove covetousness from your heart, to cure it of the obsession to receive, and to learn the real truth of Christ's saying: "In all things I gave you an example, that so laboring ye ought to help the weak, and to remember the words of the Lord Jesus, that he himself said, It is more blessed to give than to receive" (Acts 20:35).

The right use of the money we have is one of the very best ways to teach ourselves to be unselfish about the possessions others have. Seek ways of self-denial (in little things, without boasting or praise) and of fruitful giving. Give—give until it hurts—give until it stops hurting—give until it feels good and leaves one calmly assured that the needs of the future will be met, whatever they may be. Sell what you have and give alms, lay up treasure in heaven. Become ashamed to wish for wealth—don't talk about it.

"Dug from the mountain side, washed in the glen,
Servant am I, or master of men;
Earn me, I bless you; steal me, I curse you;
Grasp me and hold me—a fiend shall possess you.
Lie for me; die for me; covet me; take me;

Angel or devil, I am what you make me."
—Author unknown

For Further Study:

See books listed on page 279.

# 54

## TRUE VALUES AND MATERIAL THINGS

Our sense of values is of very great importance because it gives direction to all our life's abilities and efforts. It determines how we will spend our money and our lives.

Just what things do we esteem highest and best? What do we love most? Let us test ourselves a little right now, using this opportunity to see whether we are most like the average American citizen, the foolish farmer of Luke 12, the rich young ruler, the penitent publican, or the apostle Paul. What do we seek after? wish for? dream about? glory in?

What is it that we value so highly that we actually and gladly give it our time and attention and energies? We hear so many excuses for not attending church and for not taking part in the stewardship of life and time—excuses which show that commercial interests, guests, hobbies, lodges, secular society, and personal pleasures are constantly exalted above Christian service by nominally Christian people. Alas, we put temporal ease above eternal life. We find time to do a thousand needless things, not knowing or not regarding the infinitely greater value of the Christian works from which we excuse ourselves. Our homes put more value on present happiness (so-called) than on moral faithfulness and devotion to duty; not knowing that happiness comes by self-denial and by serving others. As a nation we can mobilize millions of men and spend many billions of dollars for war to destroy nations that threaten our temporal interests, but can not send even a few thousand messengers of Christ and ministers of mercy to give life and to build the foundations of peace.

A perverted sense of values is one of the most obvious and disgusting phenomena to be observed in our land today. A nation of spoiled children and adults without ability to choose good rather than evil puts movies and TV above church; liquor above education; the things of shame, degradation, debauchery and corruption above those things that serve the eternal welfare of the individual and the race. Are we civilized when we will not restrain present desires in order to direct our lives to the attainment of the higher values to which we pay lip service?

### *Test of Character*

A surprising portion of God's word is given to instructions and commandments regulating our economic affairs. The temptations to sin in the matter of possessions are so universal, so frequent, and take so many forms that the wisdom of the loving Father speaks frequently and variously on this subject.

The right attitudes and principles regarding getting and using wealth are of greatest importance: (1) Because these matters occupy a large portion of the time, attention, and energies of our daily lives; (2) because they involve so many temptations and dangers; and (3) because being right in these things involves faith and faithfulness toward God, who will reward us with the true and eternal riches.

Charles Brooks shows how our use of money represents how we view our lives:

> Making money is a process by which we exchange our life's energy, our skill, our brains, our heart, our reserve force for what should be their equivalent. We are 'coining our life' when we work. That is what makes the matter of spending money so important. *We are spending our life.* If we waste our money, we are wasting our life. If we fritter it away, we are frittering away our life. If we invest it wisely, we are making a wise investment of life. 'You are not your own,' so you have no right to squander your life. Spending money is one of the highest tests of character.

In earning and spending we *test* and *express* and *develop* our characters. In these things we also have a very great effect upon the realtions of men in society. No wonder the scripture is filled with much admonition on the subject in both Old and New Testaments. Can we say that we are dominated by Christian motives if our dealings with money are not according to the teachings of Christ and the Bible? At least, we who believe in the goodness of God and who know we shall be judged by Him, should be ever seeking to know His will. We should welcome the instruction of His wisdom in these matters in which so much of our lives are concerned.

As part of the life of responsibility and righteousness which we are to live as creatures made in the image of God and set over the lower creation, we have given to us the *right* to hold possessions and the *duty* to use them as an expression of righteousness in the heart. Our constant activity in getting, preserving, managing, and especially spending money gives us a continual exercise of the morality or immorality in our hearts, and a great occasion for influence upon others through this expression of our own character. The use of property puts us to the test. It also gives us the power of extending ourselves and our influence.

The necessity of obtaining supplies for our physical lives puts all of us in relation to property and ownership, and practically forces every human being to get and to use property in some manner. Hence the regulation of these matters to a greater or less extent is found everywhere in customs or laws against stealing, etc. The great sinfulness and lawlessness of men is shown in the ways in which such laws are constantly being openly violated and secretly evaded. It is not at all surprising that God should give us laws and regulations pointing out the wrong to be avoided and the right attitudes and actions which please God and bless all concerned.

### *God and Our Wealth*

In business affairs we take into account such things as wars, depressions, inflation, bank failures, famines, federal laws, etc. Surely then God should be taken into account, He is a far more important factor in our business than all the others. He is the owner of all the wealth. He is the providential controller of all the other factors. He is able to impoverish or to enrich. To Him we shall finally give account of all our stewardship. *God is the most significant fact to face in business.*

Wealth does not protect us against God's claim upon our lives. Any amount of wealth does not make us independent of His overseeing care. The more wealth we have the more responsibility we have to use it according to His will for the welfare of His people and the glory of His name. The possession of riches actually creates responsibility to serve through them; but too commonly it is made the occasion for sinful indulgence of self, for disregard of God, and even for oppression of others through the power of wealth.

### *The Curse of Unbelief*

Overconcern with physical and temporal affairs to the neglect of righteousness and eternal life is a natural effect of unbelief in Christ, the gospel challenge, judgment to come, and eternal life. Worst of all is the fact that many put the matters of diet above morals, and housing above religion while claiming to be the offical spokesman for Christianity and to be "building the kingdom of God." The "social gospel" is urged as all important with only contempt for the gospel of eternal life. This is done in spite of the repeated teachings of Christ and the apostles which urge the exact opposite. (Read Matt. 6:25-33; Luke 12:22-34; John 6:27; Phil. 4:11-14; Col. 3:1-3;

I Tim. 6:5-10, 17-19; II Tim. 2:3, 13). In no other respect do we show ourselves so unbelieving and unwilling to follow the instructions of Jesus as in this matter of the relative value of earthly wealth versus being rich toward God. He indicated that we all have proved ourselves unrighteous stewards of the things God has given us, and we are about to have the stewardship taken away from us—hence, the only shrewd thing to do is to make use of the things in our possession (though they are not ours) to win friends who will gladly welcome us into eternal dwelling places. This is our one great opportunity for investment of what the world calls wealth. (Study Luke 16. Even then men scoffed at Him, seeking to justify themselves in their love of money.)

Parents who are nominally Christian seek for their children a life of commercialized material prosperity steeped in paganism, rather than a life of real devotion and self-spending service to the Lord. They think their foolish choice is the expression of love for their children when it is only the evil fruit of blindness and unbelief, choosing evil rather than good. Hear what Jesus said to Mary and Martha: "one thing is needful; Mary hath chosen the good part, and it shall not be taken away from her" (See Luke 10:38-42).

### *Who is Rich?*

The farmer in Jesus' parable thought he had wealth and security, but God called him a fool (Luke 12:19, 20). The prosperous men think they are blessed, but Jesus said, "Woe unto you that are rich" (Luke 6:24; cf. James 5:1-6; Rev. 3:17; I Tim. 6:9, 10). "What shall it profit a man if he gain the whole world and forfeit his life? Or what shall a man give in exchange for his life?" (Matt. 16:26). All things have value in proportion as they contribute to life. We simply have wrong ideas of what things are necessary to life. It is not food for the body, clothing, and shelter, but righteousness before God that is essential to life. That can be had only from Jesus Christ, who is our redemption and our righteousness (Rom. 3:21-26; I Cor. 1:30). He came that we may have abundant, eternal life.

"A man's life consisteth not in the abundance of things which he possesseth" (Luke 12:15). The true riches are not temporal but eternal, not outward but inward—"righteousness, joy, and peace in the Holy Spirit." The only real and permanent possession that we have is what we are. We can't call anything else our own or take anything else with us from this world. "Godliness . . . is great gain" (I Tim. 6:6; I Tim. 4:8). Jesus said, "sell what you have and give alms; make for yourselves purses which wax not old, a treasure in the heavens that faileth not, where no thief draweth near, neither moth destroyeth. For where your treasure is there will your heart be also" (Luke 12:33, 34). The exceeding great riches of heaven are not to be scoffed at merely because they are future. They are an inheritance undefiled that fadeth not away, reserved in heaven for you, who are to be joint-heirs with Him who is appointed heir of all things. Enemies of our faith do scoff at the promises but we are called in hope (Rom. 8:17-25) and the word of the Lord is faithful and sure. Be patient; we shall reap in due season. Indeed the riches of grace are not all far off in the future but "now and in this time" a hundred fold return is promised us for all that we give up for Christ (Mark 10:29, 30). Who would trade the humblest Christian life for the greatest worldly treasure?

The story is told of a certain rich man who died in ripe, old age. After his death, a group of his acquaintances were discussing his wealth, and one asked of the others, "How much did he leave?" One member of the group, wiser perhaps than the rest, answered, "Everything he had." The same will be said of every one of us.

For Further Study:

Crossley, Robert. *We Want to Live.* Downers Grove: InterVarsity Press, 1967. Pp. 7-22, 78-95.

See books listed on page 279.

# 55

## SCRIPTURES CONCERNING MONEY

"It is written, Man shall not live by bread alone, but by every word that proceedeth out of the mouth of God" (Matt. 4:4; Cp. Luke 4:4).

"And if any man would go to law with thee, and take away thy coat, let him have thy cloak also." "Give to him that asketh thee, and from him that would borrow of thee turn not thou away" (Matt. 5:40, 42).

"Lay not up for yourselves treasures upon the earth, where moth and rust consume, and where thieves break through and steal: but lay up for yourselves treasures in heaven, where neither moth nor rust doth consume, and where thieves do not break through nor steal: for where thy treasure is, there will thy heart be also" (Matt. 6:19-21).

"No man can serve two masters: for either he will hate the one, and love the other; or else he will hold to one, and despise the other. Ye cannot serve God and mammon. Therefore I say unto you, Be not anxious for your life, what ye shall eat, or what ye shall drink; nor yet for your body, what ye shall put on. Is not the life more than the food, and the body more than the raiment? Behold the birds of the heaven, that they sow not, neither do they reap, nor gather into barns; and your heavenly Father feedeth them. Are not ye of much more value than they: And which of you by being anxious can add one cubit unto the measure of his life? And why are ye anxious concerning raiment? Consider the lilies of the field, how they grow; they toil not, neither do they spin; yet I say unto you, that even Solomon in all his glory was not arrayed like one of these. But if God doth so clothe the grass of the field, which today is, and tomorrow is cast into the oven, shall he not much more clothe you, O ye of little faith? Be not therefore anxious, saying, What shall we eat? or, What shall we drink? or, Wherewithal shall we be clothed? For after all these things do the Gentiles seek; for your heavenly Father knoweth that ye have need of all these things. But seek ye first his kingdom, and his righteousness; and all these things shall be added unto you. Be not therefore anxious for the morrow: for the morrow will be anxious for itself. Sufficient unto the day is the evil thereof" (Matt. 6:24-34; Cp. Luke 12:22-32).

"Heal the sick, raise the dead, cleanse the lepers, cast out demons:

freely [without pay] ye received, freely give" (Matt. 10:8).

"And he that was sown among the thorns, this is he that heareth the word; and the care of the world, and the deceitfulness of riches, choke the word, and he becometh unfruitful" (Matt. 13:22; Mark adds "lusts of other things" 4:19; Luke adds "pleasures of this life" 8:14).

"And he answered and said unto them, Why do ye also transgress the commandment of God because of your tradition? For God said, Honor thy father and thy mother: and, He that speaketh evil of father or mother, let him die the death. But ye say, Whosoever shall say to his father or his mother, That wherewith thou mightest have been profited by me is given to God; he shall not honor his father" (Matt. 15:3-6; Cp. Mark 7:8-13).

"For what shall a man be profited, if he shall gain the whole world, and forfeit his life?" (Matt. 16:26; Cp. Mark 8:36; Luke 9:25).

"Jesus said unto him, If thou wouldest be perfect, go, sell that which thou hast, and give to the poor, and thou shalt have treasure in heaven: and come, follow me. But when the young man heard the saying, he went away sorrowful; for he was one that had great possessions. And Jesus said unto his disciples, Verily I say unto you, it is hard for a rich man to enter into the kingdom of heaven. And again I say unto you, It is easier for a camel to go through a needle's eye, than for a rich man to enter into the kingdom of God" (Matt. 19:21; Cp. Mark 10:21, 22; Luke 18:18-25).

"Tell us therefore, What thinkest thou? Is it lawful to give tribute unto Caesar, or not? But Jesus perceived their wickedness, and said, Why make ye trial of me, ye hypocrites? Show me the tribute money. And they brought unto him a denarius. And he saith unto them, Whose is this image and superscription? They say unto him, Caesar's. Then saith he unto them, Render therefore unto Caesar the things that are Caesar's and unto God the things that are God's" (Matt. 22:17-21; Cp. Mark 12:15-17; Luke 20:22-25).

"For from within, out of the heart of men, evil thoughts proceed, fornications, thefts, murders, adulteries, covetings, wickednesses, deceit, lasciviousness, and evil eye, railing, pride, foolishness; all these evil things proceed from within, and defile the man" (Mark 7:21-23; Cp. Matt. 15:18-20).

"And Jesus looked round about, and saith unto his disciples, How hardly shall they that have riches enter into the kingdom of God! And the disciples were amazed at his words. But Jesus answereth again, and saith unto them, Children, how hard it is for them that trust in riches to enter into the kingdom of God! It is easier for a camel to go through a needle's eye, than for a rich man to enter into the kingdom of God" (Mark 10:23-25).

"Peter began to say unto him, Lo, we have left all, and have followed thee. Jesus said, Verily I say unto you, There is no man that hath left house, or brethren, or sisters, or mother, or father, or children, or lands, for my sake, and for the gospel's sake, but he shall receive a hundredfold now in this time, houses and brethren, and sisters, and mothers, and children, and lands, with persecutions; and in the world to come eternal life" (Mark 10:28-30; Cp. Matt. 19:29; Luke 18:28-30).

"And he sat down over against the treasury, and beheld how the multitude cast money into the treasury; and many that were rich cast in much. And there came a poor widow, and she cast in two mites, which make a farthing. And he called unto him his disciples, and said unto them, Verily I say unto you, This poor widow cast in more than all they that are casting into the treasury; for they all did cast in of their superfluity; but she of her want did cast in all that she had, even all her living" (Mark 12:41-44; Cp. Luke 21:1-4).

"And he [John the Baptist] answered and said unto them, He that hath two coats, let him impart to him that hath none; and he that hath food, let him do likewise. And there came also publicans to be baptized, and they said unto him, Teacher, what must we do? And he said unto them, Extort no more than that which is appointed you. And soldiers also asked him, saying, And we, what must we do? And he said unto them, Extort from no man by violence, neither accuse any one wrongfully; and be content with your wages" (Luke 3:11-14).

"And he lifted up his eyes on his disciples, and said, Blessed are ye poor: for yours is the kingdom of God. Blessed are ye that hunger now: for ye shall be filled. Blessed are ye that weep now: for ye shall laugh. Blessed are ye, when men shall hate you, and when they shall separate you from their company, and reproach you, and cast out your name as evil, for the Son of man's sake. Rejoice in that day, and leap for joy: for behold, your reward is great in heaven; for in the same manner did their fathers unto the prophets. But woe unto you that are rich! For ye have received consolation. Woe unto you, ye that are full now! For ye shall hunger. Woe unto you, ye that laugh now! For ye shall mourn and weep" (Luke 6:20-25).

"But I say unto you that hear, Love your enemies, do good to them that hate you, bless them that curse you, pray for them that despitefully use you. To him that smiteth thee on the one cheek offer also the other; and from him that taketh away thy cloak withhold not thy coat also. Give to every one that asketh thee; and of him that taketh away thy goods ask them not again. And as ye would that men should do to you, do ye also to them likewise. And if ye love them that love you, what thank have ye? For even sinners love those that love them. And if ye do good to them that do good to you, what thank have ye? For even sinners do the same. And if ye lend to them of whom ye hope to receive, what thank have ye? Even sinners lend to sinners, to receive again as much. But love your enemies, and do them good, and lend, never despairing; and your reward shall be great, and ye shall be sons of the Most High: for he is kind toward the unthankful and evil. Be merciful, even as your Father is merciful" (Luke 6:27-36; Cp. Matt. 5:43-48).

"Give, and it shall be given unto you; good measure, pressed down, shaken together, running over, shall they give into your bosom. For with what measure ye mete it shall be measured to you again" (Luke 6:38).

"And Jesus said unto him, The foxes have holes, and the birds of the heaven have nests; but the Son of man hath not where to lay his head" (Luke 9:58).

"And he said unto them, Take heed, and keep yourselves from all coveteousness: for a man's life consisteth not in the abundance of the things which he possesseth. And he spake a parable unto them, saying, The ground of a certain man brought forth plentifully: and he reasoned within himself, saying, What shall I do, because I have not where to bestow my fruits? And he said, This will I do: I will pull down my barns, and build greater; and there will I bestow all my grain and my goods. And I will say to my soul, Soul, thou hast much goods laid up for many years; take thine ease, eat, drink, be merry. But God said unto him, Thou foolish one, this night is thy soul required of thee; and the things which thou hast prepared, whose shall they be? So is he that layeth up treasure for himself, and is not rich toward God" (Luke 12:15-21).

"Fear not, little flock; for it is your Father's good pleasure to give you the kingdom. Sell that which ye have, and give alms; make for yourselves purses which wax not old, a treasure in the heavens that faileth not, where no thief draweth near, neither moth destroyeth. For where your treasure is, there will your heart be also" (Luke 12:32-34).

"And he said to him also that had bidden him, When thou makest a dinner or a supper, call not thy friends, nor thy brethren, nor thy kinsmen, nor rich neighbors; lest haply they also bid thee again, and a recompense be made thee. But when thou makest a feast bid the poor, the maimed, the lame, the blind: and thou shalt be blessed: because they have not wherewith to recompense thee; for thou shalt be recompensed in the resurrection of the just" (Luke 14:12-14).

"So therefore whosoever he be of you that renounceth not all that he hath, he cannot be my disciple" (Luke 14:33).

"And he said also unto the disciples, There was a certain rich man, who had a steward; and the same was accused unto him that he was wasting his goods. And he called him, and said unto him, What is this that I hear of thee? Render the account of thy stewardship; for thou canst be no longer steward. And the steward said within himself, What shall I do, seeing that my Lord taketh away the stewardship from me? I have not strength to dig; to beg I am ashamed. I am resolved what to do, that, when I am put out of the stewardship, they may receive me into their houses. And calling to him each one of his lord's debtors, he said, A hundred measures of oil. And he said unto him, Take thy bond, and sit down quickly and write fifty. Then said he to another, And how much owest thou? And he said, A hundred measures of wheat. He saith unto him, Take thy bond, and write fourscore. And his lord commended the unrighteous steward because he had done wisely: for the sons of this world are for their own generation wiser than the sons of light. And I say unto you, Make to yourselves friends by means of the mammon of righteousness; that, when it shall fail, they may receive you into the eternal tabernacles. He that is faithful in a very little if faithful also in much: and he that is unrighteous in a very little is unrighteous also in much. If therefore ye have not been faithful in the unrighteous mammon, who will commit to your trust the true riches? And if ye have not been faithful in that which is another's, who will give you that which is your own? No servant can serve two masters: for either he will hate the one, and love the other; or else he will hold to one, and despise the other. Ye cannot serve God and mammon" (Luke 16:1-13).

"Now there was a certain rich man, and he was clothed in purple and fine linen, faring sumptuously every day: and a certain beggar named Lazarus was laid at his gate, full of sores, and desiring to be fed with the crumbs that fell from the rich man's table; yea, even the dogs came and licked his sores. And it came to pass, that the beggar died, and that he was carried away by the angels into

Abraham's bosom: and the rich man also died, and was buried. And in Hades he lifted up his eyes, being in torments, and seeth Abraham afar off, and Lazarus in his bosom. And he cried and said, Father Abraham, have mercy on me, and send Lazarus, that he may dip the tip of his finger in water, and cool my tongue, for I am in anguish in this flame. But Abraham said, Son, remember that thou in thy lifetime receivedst thy good things, and Lazarus in like manner evil things: but now here he is comforted, and thou art in anguish" (Luke 16:19-25).

"And he entered and was passing through Jericho. And behold, a man called by name Zacchaeus; and he was a chief publican, and he was rich. And he sought to see Jesus who he was; and could not for the crowd, because he was little of stature. And he ran on before, and climbed up into a sycomore tree to see him: for he was to pass that way. And when Jesus came to the place, he looked up, and said unto him, Zacchaeus, make haste, and come down; for today I must abide at thy house. And he made haste, and came down, and received him joyfully. And when they saw it, they all murmured, saying, He is gone in to lodge with a man that is a sinner. And Zacchaeus stood, and said unto the Lord, Behold, Lord, the half of my goods I give to the poor; and if I have wrongfully exacted aught of any man, I restore fourfold. And Jesus said unto him, To-day is salvation come to this house, forasmuch as he also is a son of Abraham. For the Son of man came to seek and to save that which was lost" (Luke 19:1-10).

"And when they were filled, he saith unto his disciples, Gather up the broken pieces which remain over, that nothing be lost" (John 6:12).

"Work not for the food which perisheth, but for the food which abideth unto eternal life, which the Son of man shall give unto you: for him the Father, even God hath sealed" (John 6:27).

"Mary therefore took a pound of ointment of pure nard, very precious, and anointed the feet of Jesus, and wiped his feet with her hair: and the house was filled with the odor of the ointment. But Judas Iscariot, one of his disciples, that should betray him, saith, Why was not this ointment sold for three hundred shillings, and given to the poor? Now this he said, not because he cared for the poor; but because he was a thief, and having the bag took away what was put therein. Jesus therefore said, Suffer her to keep it against the day of my burying. For the poor ye have always with you; but me ye have not always" (John 12:3-8).

OTHER SCRIPTURES: Acts 2:42-47; 4:34-37; 5:1-10; 8:18-23; 11:27-30; 20:33-35; Rom. 8:32; 12:8, 9, 11, 13, 20, 21; 13:1, 6, 7, 8; 14:21; I Cor. 4:2; 9:4, 5; 5:10, 11; 6:10; 10:31, 32; 16:1, 2; II Cor. 8:1-24; 9:1-15; Gal. 6:6-10; 2:10; Eph. 4:28; 5:3; 6:5-8; Phil. 2:4; 4:6, 11-13, 19; Col. 3:5, 22-25; I Thess. 2:7-9; 4:11, 12; II Thess. 3:6-15; I Tim. 3:3; 5:3, 4, 8, 16; 6:5-10, 17-19; II Tim. 3:2; 4:10; Titus 1:10, 11; Heb. 13:1-3, 5, 6; James 2:1-7; 4:2, 3, 13-17; 5:1-6; I Pet. 1:7, 18, 19; 3:3, 4; II Pet. 2:15; 3:10-13; I John 3:17, 18; III John 2, 5-8; Jude 11; Revelation 3:17, 18; 18:11-19.

# *Part Ten*

# OBJECTIONS AND OBSTACLES

## 56

### CONTROVERSIES AND OBJECTIONS IN JESUS' MINISTRY

*FIRST PASSOVER* Cleansing temple in Jerusalem (John 2).

Jewish officials challenge His authority to do it: "What sign have you to show?" (v. 18-20).

Does Nicodemus' coming at night indicate that Jesus was a controversial figure?

*Beginning of Galilean Ministry* 8 or 9 months after 1st Passover.

At Nazareth. Sermon in synagogue, illustrations of Gentiles, pushed to the cliff (Luke 4:23-30).

At Capernaum. Paralytic forgiven and healed; scribes and Pharisees thought it blasphemy to announce forgiveness of sin (Matt. 9:2-8; Mark 2:1-12; Luke 5:18-26. Note Pharisees from Jerusalem following).

At Matthew's house. Feast after his call; Pharisees said, "Why does he eat with publicans and sinners?" (Matt. 9:10-13; Mark 2:15-17; Luke 5:29-32).

Objection implied in the question of John's disciples, "Why do we and the Pharisees fast, but your disciples do not fast?" (Matt. 9:14-17; Mark 2:18-22; Luke 5:33-39).

*SECOND PASSOVER*

At pool in Jerusalem. Healed lame man on Sabbath; controversy on Sabbath work and making Himself equal with God; Jesus accused Pharisees of not believing Moses or seeking the glory of God; first mention of definite effort or desire to kill him (John 5, esp. v. 18).

In grain fields. 2nd Sabbath controversy; healed withered hand after challenging the watching Pharisees; Jesus looked upon them with anger, grieved at their hardness of heart (Matt. 12:9-14; Mark 3:1-6; Luke 6:6-11).

Capernaum (?). After the question from John; Jesus rebuked the unbelief and poor judgment of many; "Kingdom of heaven suffered violence"; "This generation like children," stubborn and inconsistent against both John and Jesus (Matt. 11:7-19; Luke 7:24-35). Rebuke of cities which did not repent after many miracles (Matt. 11:20ff).

In house of Simon the Pharisee. Simon's mental objections to Jesus' letting the sinful woman touch Him (Luke 7:36-50).

At Capernaum. Very busy with great crowds; dumb demoniac healed; Pharisees claim He is possessed by Beelzebub; "You brood of vipers! . . . how can you speak good, when you are evil?" (Matt. 12:22-37; Mark 3:22-30). Demand for a sign; "an evil and adulterous generation . . . no sign." "Men of Nineveh shall condemn this generation" (Matt. 12:38-45). His family attempts to interfere, seeming to object to the strenuousness of His ministry (Matt. 12:46-50).

East side of Galilean sea, land of Gadarenes. Casts out demons; people ask Him to leave (Matt. 8:34; Mark 5:17; Luke 8:27).

At Nazareth. Last visit recorded; general unbelief (Matt. 13:54-58; Mark 6:1-6).

*THIRD PASSOVER NEAR.* Fed 5000; sermon on the Bread of Life at Capernaum, "What sign do you do?" "Give us this bread always." "How does he now say, I have come down from heaven?" "How can this man give us his flesh to eat?" "This is a hard saying, who can receive it?" They forsook Him (John 6).

General Condition: "After this, Jesus went about in Galilee; he would not go about in Judea, because the Jews sought to kill Him" (John 7:1).

Capernaum. Jerusalem Pharisees publicly criticize Jesus for His disciples' eating with unwashen hands; Jesus counterattacks against their traditions which set aside the law of God (Matt. 15:1-20; Mark 7:1-23).

At Magadan. Pharisees and Sadducees test Him with a demand for a sign from heaven (Matt. 15:39; 16:1-4; Mark 8:10-12).

At Caesarea Philippi. Peter's objection to the first plain prediction of Jesus' death (Matt. 16:21-26; Mark 8:31-38; Luke 9:22-26).

At Capernaum (?). Jesus' unbelieving brothers object to His staying in seclusion and urge Him to go to the feast of Tabernacles (John 7:3-9).

*FEAST OF TABERNACLES* (*Six months before His death*). At the feast before Jesus came, many were looking for Him, but no man dared to speak openly about Him (John 7:11-13).

Jerusalem during the Feast. Jesus accused the rulers of seeking to kill Him. They answer, "You have a demon" (John 7:14-24). Some of the people said, "Is not this the man they seek to kill?" "We know where this man comes from" (John 7:27). They sought to arrest Him (John 7:30). The Pharisees heard the people muttering about Him, and they sent officers to arrest Him (John 7:32); but they did not (John 7:45, 46). "Is the Christ from Galilee? He comes from Bethlehem" (John 7:40-44). "You are bearing witness to yourself; your testimony is not true." "Will he kill himself, since he says, "Where I go you cannot come?" "Who are you?" (John 8:21-29). Dispute over their freedom and fatherhood (John 8:31-47). "Are we not right in saying you are a Samaritan and have a demon?" Vehement objection to the promise that believers will never see death: "Whom do you make yourself to be?" "Before Abraham was I am." So they took up stones to stone Him (John 8:48-59).

Jerusalem. The man born blind healed on the Sabbath. The healed blind man investigated and berated and excommunicated. Brief exchange between Jesus and the Pharisees on blindness and guilt (John 9:1-41). Dispute among the Jews about the Sermon on the Good Shepherd. Some: "He hath a demon" (John 10:19-21).

Judea. Another dumb demoniac healed and again some said, "He casts out demons by Beelzebub" (Luke 11:14-26). Jesus rebuked the demand for a sign (Luke 11:29-36).

Dining in house of a Pharisee. Jesus did not wash His hands; Pharisee astonished. Jesus rebuked the self-righteousness of the Pharisees for (1) outward cleansing, inward filth; (2) tithing herbs, neglecting justice, etc.; (3) loving pre-eminence; (4) hypocrisy; and included lawyers for (1) harsh legal burdens; (2) persecuting prophets and apostles; (3) perverting God's message, neither accepting it nor letting others accept it (Luke 11:37-54). They press Him hard to catch something for which to accuse Him.

To great multitudes Jesus gave a warning against the hypocrisy of the Pharisees (Luke 12:1). "I come to cast fire on the earth . . . To bring . . . not peace . . . but division" (Luke 12:49-53).

In a synagogue on Sabbath. Healing a bent woman; ruler of synagogue indignant (Luke 13:11-17).

*FEAST OF DEDICATION* Jerusalem. Jews ask Him to tell plainly if He is the Christ. Jesus said, "I told you" and appealed to His works, saying, "I and the Father are one." They took up stones to stone Him. He answered from scripture (John 10:22-33). They say, "You blaspheme." Again tried to arrest Him (John 10:34-39).

*DEPARTURE TO PEREA* (Three months before His death, John 10:40).

In Perea. Pharisees say, "Get away from here; for Herod wants to kill you," "I go on my way today and tomorrow and the next day; for it cannot be that a prophet should die outside Jerusalem (Luke 13:31-35).

In home of Pharisee on Sabbath. Man with dropsy: "Is it lawful to heal on the Sabbath?" Jesus healed the man and silenced the Pharisees (Luke 14:1-6). Jesus reproves guests for seeking chief places, and for inviting only those who might repay the favor (Luke 14:7-14).

Publicans and sinners come to Jesus. Pharisees murmur, "He receives sinners and eats with them." Parables of seeking the lost (Luke 15).

Teaching in Perea. "You cannot serve God and mammon." The Pharisees, who were lovers of money, scoffed at Him. Jesus rebuked them, "You justify yourselves before men, but God knows your hearts." Story of rich man and Lazarus (Luke 16).

After raising Lazarus from death. The chief priests and Pharisees gathered the council and said, "What are we to do?" Caiaphas said, "It is expedient that one man should die in place of the whole nation." So from that day they planned how to put him to death (John 11:43-54).

On last journey to Jerusalem. Pharisees tested him by asking, "Is it lawful to divorce one's wife for any cause?" and "Why then did Moses command one to give a bill of divorcement and to put her away?" (Matt. 19:1-9; Mark 10:1-12).

At Jericho. Zacchaeus received Jesus, the people sneered, "He has gone to lodge with a sinner" (Luke 19:1-10).

A few days before the Passover. People looking for Jesus and wondering, "Will he come to the feast?" For the chief priests and Pharisees had given orders that anyone knowing where Jesus was must report Him so they could arrest Him (John 11:55-57).

At a feast in Bethany. Judas objected to Mary's anointing Jesus, "Why this waste?" (Matt. 26:6-13; Mark 14:3-9; John 12:1-8).

*TRIUMPHAL ENTRY.* Crowds praising Him. Pharisees said, "Teacher rebuke thy disciples" (Luke 19:37-40).

Next day (Monday). Cleansed temple again; said, "You have made it a den of robbers" (Matt. 21:12-17; Mark 11:15-19; Luke 19:45-48).

Healing in the temple. Children praise Him; chief priests and scribes object (Matt. 21:14ff). They sought a way to destroy Him, but feared Him and the crowds.

Next day (Tuesday). In temple, Jesus authority challenged by priests, scribes, elders. Counter question about John's baptism; no answers (Matt. 21:23-37; Mark 11:27-33; Luke 20:1-8). Parable of two sons (Matt. 21:28-32). Parable of wicked husbandmen (Matt. 21:33-46; Mark 12:1-12; Luke 20:9-19). A trap question about tribute to Caesar (Pharisees with Herodians. Matt. 22:15-22; Mark 12:13-17; Luke 20:20-26). The Sadducees' question about marriage in the resurrection. The lawyer's question about the greatest commandment. Jesus' question about David's son being David's Lord (Matt. 22:23-46; Mark 12:18-37; Luke 20:27-44). Disciples warned against the Pharisees and their hypocrisies (Matt. 23).

Late Tuesday or Wednesday. Reflections about the coming of Greeks to Jesus, "Who is this son of man that must be lifted up?" Hardened unbelief; many believed but would not confess for fear of the Jews. Jesus said, "The word that I have spoken will judge on the last day" (John 12:20-50).

Thursday night. Trials before Annas, Caiaphas, Sanhedrin, Pilate, Herod, Pilate. Mockings and charges at the trials and at the Crucifixion.

For Further Study:

Foster, R. C. *Studies in the Life of Christ.* Grand Rapids: Baker Book House, 1938, 1962, 1968. Pp. 426-439, 445-6, 455-461, 655-674, 690-698, 868-879, 1125-1183. Comment on some of the controversies in which Jesus was engaged.

Harrison, Everett. *A Short Life of Christ.* Grand Rapids: Wm. B. Eerdmans, 1968. Pp. 123-135. Discusses Jesus' conflicts with the Pharisees.

Stott, John R. W. *Christ the Controversialist.* Downers Grove: Inter-Varsity Press, 1970. Discusses how Christ answered His critics.

# 57

## NOTES ON DEMON POSSESSION

One of the four following conclusions must be true concerning the reality of demons as mentioned in the Gospel accounts. No other is possible, and only one of these can be true.

Either, 1, Jesus did cast out real demons as represented; or, 2, Jesus did no such things but the accounts are entirely false; or, 3, Jesus did go through the motions and the pretense of casting them out, while He knew there were no real demons; or, 4, Jesus was as ignorant and superstitious on this subject as the people and honestly thought He cast out spirits in healing sickness.

Which of these views fits the facts and the testimony? The true meaning of a word or an expression may be put into its place in any account; and the definition will fit as well as the word it defines. Just read the accounts of Jesus' intelligent conversations with demons, supplying the word "disease" as the explanation for the word "demon."

### I. MEANING OF THE WORD "DEMON"

1. Not the same as the Greek word for "devil." There is only one devil but many demons.
2. Oldest meaning: divine power, deity. Homer (c. 850 B.C.) used it interchangeably with the word God.[1]
3. A being between man and God. Plato attempted to fix this definition. He used it in both a good and bad sense. Plato held that they included departed spirits of good men. Socrates spoke constantly of his "demon." Ignatius says that Jesus told His disciples after the resurrection, "I am not a disembodied demon."[2] This shows his way of expressing what Luke 24:37-39 says. See also Luke 4:33, "spirit of an unclean demon."
4. Elsewhere in the New Testament demons are always evil spirits, messengers and ministers of Satan.
   a. Heathen deities (Acts 17:18; I Cor. 10:20; Rev. 9:20).
   b. Ones who believe and tremble (or bristle) but are lost

[1] Josephus, *Wars of the Jews,* i. 2.8. See Acts 17:18 and Alexander Campbell's, *Popular Lectures and Addresses* (Nashville: Harbinger Book Club, 1861), Pp. 379-397 for older uses.

[2] Ignatius, *Epistle to Smyrna,* iii. 2.

(James 2:19).

c. They recognize Jesus as Son of God (Matt. 8:29; Mark 1:23, 24, 34; 3:11; Luke 4:41).

d. Agents of Satan (Matt. 12:24-26; Luke 10:17, 18; 11:15-22).

## II. EVIDENCES THAT THEY ARE IMMATERIAL, INTELLIGENT BEINGS, NOT TO BE CONFUSED WITH DISEASES OR FIGURES OF SPEECH.

1. The Old Testament legislation proceeded upon the assumption that there is such a thing as a "familiar spirit" (Lev. 19:31; Deut. 18:9-14).
2. In the New Testament they are regarded as personalities (for example, James 2:19, believing; Rev. 16:14, working signs). Jesus founded a parable on their conduct, (Luke 11:24-26).
3. Jesus distinguished between them and diseases. So did His disciples (Matt. 10:8; Luke 10:17-20).
4. Jesus addressed them as persons and they answered as such (Mark 5:8, 9; 9:25).
5. They manifested desires and passions (Mark 5:12, 13).
6. They showed superhuman knowledge of Jesus (Mark 1:24, 34; Matt. 8:29, and of His apostles, Acts 16:16, 17; 19:15).

## III. VIEWS OF THEIR IDENTITY AND ORIGIN

1. Plato: departed men, some good.[3] Josephus: spirits of evil men who have died.[4] Alexander Campbell held firmly to the view that they are (or were) the ghosts of dead men. He said all pagan writers, the Jewish historians, and the Christian fathers expressed this opinion. He thought it was implied in Scripture (I Tim. 4:1).[5]
2. The *Book of Enoch* says demons are fallen angels. Consider II Peter 2:4 and Jude 6 on "angels who sinned." Matthew 25:41—"the devil and his angels." Ephesians 6:11, 12—"We wrestle not against flesh and blood, but against principalities, against powers, against rulers of the darkness of this world, against spiritual wickedness in high places" (See Eph. 3:10; Col. 1:16; Rom. 8:38; Col. 2:15). Their immediate

---

[3] Plato, *Symposium.*

[4] Josephus, *op. cit.*, vii. 6.3.

[5] Campbell, *op. cit.*, Pp. 384-389.

recognition of Jesus might indicate former acquaintance with Him or supernatural knowledge. In the Bible they do not seem to be confused with ghosts; but in the one case of a dead man reappearing (I Sam. 28:11-19) he does not act as a demon.

3. Other spirits, neither human, nor of the rank of angels. (See Judg. 9:23; I Sam. 16:14; 18:10; 19:9; I Kings 22:19-23).
4. The word might be used of a combination of all of these.[6]

## IV. RATIONAL SUPPOSITIONS OF PROBABILITY.[7]

1. Any non-materialistic (idealistic or spiritual) view of the universe makes it likely that man is not the only product of the cosmic process.
2. Experiences of missionaries may be best explained by assumption of demon possession.
3. Lack of experience with demons in Christian countries may be explained.
4. The mysterious hinterland beyond surface consciousness is hardly known at all; so we cannot rule out the possibility of spiritual intelligences being able to affect it by entry from without.
5. It is common experience (as well as teaching of scripture) that the powers of darkness and evil do influence our moral freedom. Then it is just possible that they may act through man's physical nature upon his rational, or vice versa.
6. It is a well-ascertained fact physiologically that the conditions of a man's mental and spiritual nature exert influence upon the body and are influenced by the body: e.g., fever produces delirium; dyspepsia produces despondency; etc.
7. If effects between man and man can be produced by animal magnetism or by hypnotism, so might demons influence and disturb both the physical and rational natures.

## V. EFFECTS OF POSSESSION, OR ACCOMPANYING CIRCUMSTANCES

1. Physical ills or diseases.
   a. Matthew 9:32, 33, "dumb man" spoke when the demon

---

[6] J. Hering, "Demons", *A Companion to the Bible,* ed. by J. J. vonAllmen, (New York: Oxford University Press, 1958). Pp. 83-85.

[7] See R. C. Foster's comments on Balmforth's observations on the reality of demons, *Studies in the Life of Christ* (Grand Rapids: Baker Book House, 1968). Pp. 416-417.

was cast out.

b. Matthew 12:22, "blind and dumb."

c. Matthew 17:15, "epilepsy"; but Mark 9:25, "deaf and dumb spirit."

d. Mark 5:15, wildness.

e. Mark 7:25; Matthew 15:22ff, "grievously vexed," literally, "badly demonized" with no specific disability indicated.

f. The woman "whom Satan had bound" (Luke 13:16) "had a spirit of infirmity" but is not said to have been possessed. Deformity of the back.

2. There are some cases in which no physical ill is attributed to the demon (Mark 1:21; Luke 4:31ff). Jesus was charged with demon possession when no malady was apparent, but simply because of His speech and mental attitude, John the Baptist was similarly charged because of his manner of life (John 7:21; 8:48, 52; 10:20; Matt. 11:18).

Note that all these same physical ills, except the being "bowed together" are represented in the Gospels as separate from demon possession in other cases: deaf and having impediment, Mark 7:32; dumb, Matthew 15:30, 31; blind, Luke 18:35ff; John 9; epilepsy (KJV,lunatics), Matthew 4:24, literally "moonstruck," meaning epileptic, not insane.

3. Effects other than disease.

a. Superhuman knowledge (Mark 1:24; 5:7; 3:11, 12; Luke 4:41; Acts 16:16-18).

b. Fear of torment (Luke 4:33, 34; 8:28-31; Matt. 8:29).

c. Conversation as of third person (Mark 1:24, 25; Luke 4:34, 35).

d. Manner of departing (convulsions) (Mark 1:26; 9:20; Luke 4:35).

e. Extraordinary strength (Mark 5:3, 4; Acts 19:13-16).

f. Fierce wildness (Matt. 8:28; Mark 5:4, 5; Luke 8:29; cf. John 10:20).

g. Desire to enter into some body (Mark 5:12, 13; Matt. 8:31; Luke 11:24, 25).

h. Multiplicity (Mark 5:9; 16:9; Luke 11:26; 8:30).

## VI. NATURE OF PERSONS POSSESSED

1. Mostly grown men, but two were children (Matt. 17:15; Mark 7:25-30; 9:21; Matt. 15:22). Some were women (Mark 16:9; Luke 8:2, 3).

2. Some made very faithful helpers of Christ after they were released (Mark 5:20; Luke 8:2, 3).
3. They always appear to be pitied rather than blamed, treated as unfortunate rather than immoral. Jesus was interested in the persons, not the demons. At least their demons are something else than unbreakable bad habits.

## VII. OTHER REFERENCES TO THE WORKING OF DEMONS

1. I Timothy 4:1, doctrines of demons and seducing spirits.
2. James 3:5, factious wisdom is demoniacal ("devilish," KJV).
3. Revelation 16:14, "working signs" and going "forth unto the kings of the whole world, to gather them unto the war of the great day of God."
4. I Corinthians 10:14-22, involved in idolatry and heathen worship.

For Further Study:

Alexander, W. Menzies. *Demon Possession in the New Testament.* Joplin, Missouri: College Press, reprint of 1902 edition. Investigation of the historical, medical and theological aspects of the topic.

Chalk, John Allen and others. *The Devil You Say?* Austin, Texas: Sweet Publishing Company, 1974. Seeks to guide one to a Biblical perspective on understanding demons and the occult.

Edersheim, Alfred. *The Life and Times of Jesus the Messiah,* 8th edition. Grand Rapids: Wm. B. Eerdmans, 1900. Vol. I, Pp. 479-485; 607-613; and on Jewish nations and traditions, Vol. II, Pp. 755-763; 770-776. Good background on Jewish views.

Osterley, W. O. E. "Demon, Demoniacs," *Dictionary of Christ and the Gospels,* ed. by James Hastings. New York: Charles Scribners Sons, Vol. I., Pp. 438-443.

Sweet, Louis Matthews. "Demons" and "Exorcism," *International Standard Bible Encyclopedia,* ed. by James Orr. Grand Rapids: Wm. B. Eerdmans, 1939. Vol. I, Pp. 827-829; 1067-1068.

Unger, Merrill F. *Demons In the World Today.* Wheaton: Tyndale Press, 1971. A study of spiritual forces behind the present world unrest.

# *Part Eleven*

# JESUS TEACHES CONCERNING HIS IDENTITY

## 58

### JESUS' CLAIMS AND CREDENTIALS (John 5)

Jesus' teaching is not what made His person important; but His person makes His teaching important. The appeal of Christianity is the appeal of Christ. The power of Christianity is the power of Christ. The authority of Christianity is the authority of Christ. Christianity is Christ. The crucial question is "Who is Jesus of Nazareth?"

Careful study shows that Matthew, Mark, and Luke as well as John describe a Jesus of divine claims and supernatural deeds. We must make a decision concerning the divine claims of Jesus. He was crooked, crazy, or Christ. Because of the reliable historical records in our New Testament testifying to undeniable facts concerning Jesus we can come to put our trust in Him. We can accept the supernatural deeds which Jesus performed as credentials authenticating His claims. It is because we believe in Jesus as deity that we accept the infallibility of the Bible. The faith that saves you is not faith in the infallibility of the Bible, but faith in Jesus as Lord and Savior. He guarantees the truth and authority of both Old and New Testaments. Saving faith is a trust in the person of Jesus and a willing surrender to His authoritative control over you. We can not prove by reason or science everything Jesus said is true. But we can on reasonable, historical evidence come to a firm faith that Jesus is the Son of God and trust Him without reservation. We preach not a philosophy of what ought to be; not a theory of what may be; but we preach Christ and what He is.

During Jesus' first year of ministry He began to teach concerning His identity and work miracles as an evidence of His divine nature. A paralyzed man was brought to Him, and Jesus said, "Son, thy sins are forgiven" (Mark 2:5). Some thought He blasphemed, because they knew that only God could forgive sins. But Jesus healed the paralytic to show "that the Son of man hath authority on earth to forgive sins" (Mark 2:10).

When He had continued in Galilee for about four months, it was Passover time again; and Jesus went to Jerusalem. The text in John

5:1 does not name the feast but if the four months till harvest of John 4:35 be taken literally then Tabernacles (in October) and Dedication (December) would not be the feast of John 5:1. It was probably the Passover feast.

### *Authority Demonstrated*

By a pool in Jerusalem, Jesus found many people waiting to be healed by getting into the water after it was disturbed. The pool is still there, and a syphon in the underground water stream that feeds it causes the water to rush into it at intervals. The people superstitiously believed that an angel stirred the water and that it would heal the first one to get into it after each disturbance. Evidence from early manuscripts of the book of John show that John 5:4 is missing from all the earliest and best Greek manuscripts. Apparently it was added to the text centuries later by a scribe as an explanation of the people's attitude, but it should not be considered a scriptural statement that the water was moved by an angel.

One helpless man who had been lame for thirty-eight years was singled out by Jesus and healed there on the Sabbath day. Apparently, Jesus' purpose was to precipitate the discussion which followed; for He avoided healing others of the multitude of sick and disabled people who were in the place. Jesus hunted up the man healed, because he was being persecuted for carrying his bed on the Sabbath. At least, on that occasion, Jesus did not want to be known as a healer to the crowd of sick persons, but sought to make Himself known to the healed man and to admonish him to "sin no more, lest a worse thing come unto thee" (John 5:14).

In this miracle Jesus demonstrated His authority over nature by healing a man who had been lame thirty-eight years. By doing this miracle and commanding the man to carry his bed on the Sabbath, He implied authority over the Sabbath, at least the authority to interpret and apply the law differently from the way the Jews did. Jesus apparently violated their ideas of the Sabbath in order to set forth His claims of deity and to get them seriously considered and widely published.

### *Authority Disputed*

Here in John 5, in harmony with John's usual meaning, "the Jews" refers to those who were opposed to Jesus, the religious leaders who were the chief representatives of the traditional Jewish attitudes (John 1:19; 7:1; 9:22). The scribes and Pharisees had multiplied rules for Sabbath keeping until they were ridiculous and impossible to keep. They placed much emphasis upon enforcing Sabbath observance. It appears that Jesus purposely did this miracle on the Sabbath in order to challenge their additions to the word of God.

These Jews informed the healed man that it was illegal to carry his bed or mat. Carrying any burden was considered work that was forbidden on the Sabbath (Jer. 17:21-27; Neh. 13:19). But for one who had been lame so long to carry his light mat home was not the same as carrying burdens to market for ordinary business. The man responded that the one who healed him told him to carry his bed. After Jesus had exhibited the power to heal him, the man had not questioned His authority to command him to take up his bed. He made the best defense he could. They demanded to know who told him this. But he honestly did not know. It was not wrong for them to seek the one who commanded the act; but they showed not the slightest regard for the great miracle or for the man's release from affliction.

Later after the healed man had spoken with Jesus in the temple he went to the Jews and told them it was Jesus who had healed him. He probably thought it was his duty to tell them, since his own actions depended upon Jesus' command. Notice that he told them that Jesus healed, emphasizing the miracle that they ignored. It is likely that Jesus wanted him to tell the Jews.

They were persecuting Jesus because He did this on the Sabbath day (John 5:16). The Greek verb indicates continued action: they kept up their continual hostile activity against Jesus. This stream of opposition against Jesus went on for two years and ended in the crucifixion. Stoning was the punishment for Sabbath-breaking (Ex. 35:2; Num. 15:32-36). But the Jews were not permitted by the Romans to carry out the death sentence (John 18:31), although it seems that they were sometimes willing to do it against the rule of the Romans. They often threatened to stone Jesus (John 8:59; 10:31; 11:8), and they did stone Stephen (Acts 7:58, 59).

Jesus boldly claimed, "My Father worketh even until now, and I work" (John 5:17). Jesus' defense was that He was doing God's work all the time. Our Lord's words here are rather mysterious. What work is God doing? He keeps the universe in order. He provides for men salvation, divine providence, and answers to prayer. Idleness is not holiness. Idleness was not the true essence even of the Sabbath. But the main point is that Jesus did what He did by the authority of God. His defense angered the Jews and they "sought the more to kill him, because he not only brake the sabbath, but also called God his own Father, making himself equal with God" (John 5:18). They became more determined to put Him to death. They saw in His words another crime worthy of death, blasphemy. The statement of Jesus was not blasphemy, but it would have been if He had not been the Son of God, actually doing God's work in all that He did. Jesus was, and always had been, equal with God (Phil. 2:6; John 1:1-14). But the Jews did not know that, and they would not accept His testimony about it.

His demonstration of His authority in the healing was condemned by the Jews because they would not acknowledge any authority different from their own in matters of the law and of God. They completely disregarded the divine power manifested and sought to kill Jesus as a sinner without considering the possibility that He might have authority to do as He did.

### *Authority Defended*

Jesus' defense was a bold claim that He acted always with the full authority of God. He affirmed the full agreement and sweet fellowship between the Father and Son because of intimate friendship and fondness of each for the other. He left nothing to be guessed at but explicitly enlarged upon the claim that all the works of God were His and all the honor that was due to God belonged to Him. The Son could give life (physically—Luke 7:12-15; 8:49-55; John 11:39-44 and spiritually—Eph. 2:1-5; Col. 2:13) and execute judgment concerning the eternal destinies of all men (John 5:21-22, 27). Since Jesus is equal with God and is creator and judge of all men, He certainly should be honored and revered in every way, as God is. "He that honoreth not the Son honoreth not the Father that sent Him" (John 5:23). One cannot be morally good and deny the authority and truth of Jesus' words. No man who rejects Christ can be acceptable to God. Christians should refuse to participate in any worship which refuses to honor Jesus. In His defense Jesus declared His equality with God and His authority to raise the dead and to judge man's destinies (John 5:17-29).

Jesus went on to cite witnesses that would establish His claims: John the Baptist, His own miracles, the Father Himself, and the Scriptures (John 5:31-39). Jesus charged that the Jews did not believe Him because they did not have the love of God in them, because they sought honor from men but not the honor of God, and because they did not believe Moses (John 5:42-47).

The real issue in this controversy between Jesus and the Jews was not how the Sabbath should be kept, but who Jesus was. Christ was the issue, and He is the issue today whenever men dispute His teachings. When His authority is fully accepted, most questions about the will of God are easily settled. Settling the issue of Christ's authority is no mere academic question. It is a matter of basic importance and intensely practical.

In this controversy someone was seriously wrong. In order to learn the lesson intended in John's record, it is necessary to see clearly who was right. If Jesus is not God in the flesh, then the Jews were right in condemning Him. He cannot be merely a man and be a good and wise man. But if He had all the authority He claimed, then the Jews made the mistake of their lives; and all who ignore Jesus are making themselves enemies of God.

For Further Study:

Butler, Paul. *The Gospel of John,* Vol. 1. Joplin, Missouri: College Press, 1961. Pp. 171-220. Good comment; useful outline; special studies relating to Jesus' claims.

Geldenhuys, Norval. *Supreme Authority.* Grand Rapids: Wm. B. Eerdmans, 1953. Pp. 13-43. Discusses the authority of Christ as proclaimed in the New Testament and recognized in the early church as it relates to the authority of the Bible.

Morris, Leon. *The Lord From Heaven.* Grand Rapids: Wm. B. Eerdmans, 1958. Pp. 9-43. Discusses the claims of Jesus as presented in the Gospels.

Stott, John. *Basic Christianity,* rev. ed. Grand Rapids: Wm. B. Eerdmans, 1971. Forceful exposition of the direct and indirect divine claims Jesus made.

Wenham, John. *Christ and the Bible.* Downers Grove: InterVarsity Press, 1972. Pp. 43-83. Discusses the authority of Jesus as a teacher and answers objections to His divine claims.

# 59

## JESUS, THE BREAD OF LIFE (John 6)

A whole year elapsed between the healing of the lame man (John 5) and the feeding of the 5,000 (John 6). John says, "the Passover, a feast of the Jews, was nigh" (John 6:4). This would be two years after the first cleansing of the temple and one year before the crucifixion. John's account shows that he certainly is not ignorant of the passage of time. He is not unaware of the large gaps in his account of Jesus' doings. He speaks of the many, many events which are not written (John 20:30; 21:25). He makes the notes of time that give us the understanding we have of the chronology of Jesus' ministry (John 2:1, 12, 13, 23; 4:3, 35; 5:1; 6:4; 7:2; 10:22, 40; 12:1). In the first five chapters John tells mostly of Jesus' ministry in Judea, but in the sixth he tells of Jesus in Galilee in a situation that presupposes extensive campaigning and great success in impressing the multitudes. He shows his knowledge of the intervening year of Galilean ministry by telling the result of it in the great crowd of followers so enthusiastic about Jesus that they would not let Him go away from them, even in a boat.

### *Year of Activity*

Matthew, Mark, and Luke inform us of the many incidents of this year of Galilean ministry. Controversies over His activities on the Sabbath continued. But the common people heard Him gladly and gathered in great crowds from far and near to follow Him. From among many disciples Jesus chose twelve to be apostles (ones sent out to do His work, Luke 6:12-16). He preached the Sermon on the Mount (Matt. 5-7; Luke 6), the great sermon in parables (Matt. 13), and many other sermons. He worked many miracles, including stilling the tempest (Luke 8:22-25) and raising at least two from the dead (Matt. 9:24, 25; Luke 7:11-17). He forgave sins, gave hope to sinners, and led many to repentance. He taught many times about the coming kingdom.

The crowds became so great and pressing and Jesus' life so busy, that His family thought He had gone beyond the limits of reason, and they sought to take Him home for rest. But they could not get to Him. The Pharisees became desperate in their desire to destroy His influence, and they charged that He was doing His work by the power of the devil.

In His travels in Galilee Jesus saw the multitudes in need of guidance and care, like sheep without a shepherd. Three or more general tours of Galilee by Jesus are indicated in the accounts of His ministry there (Matt. 4:23-25; Luke 4:44; 8:1-3; Matt. 9:35—11:1). He told the apostles to pray for laborers; then He sent them forth two by two to work miracles and to preach repentance and announce that the kingdom was at hand (Matt. 10). Six pairs of apostles and Jesus went about through all the cities and villages of Galilee. In an area as small as Galilee (not more than thirty miles square) these miracle-workers proclaiming the coming kingdom would naturally cause extraordinary feelings and expectations.

The interest of the people in Jesus and in the kingdom reached its peak at this time. It was really a state of excitement when Jesus and the twelve came together again at Capernaum that thousands of men, women, and children neglected daily duties and ignored personal discomforts to follow the wonderful Teacher and Healer. Their excitement was probably heightened by the news that John the baptizing prophet had been beheaded by Herod. So it was that when Jesus and the twelve went away across the sea in a boat, the multitudes went around by land to be with Him on the other side. Having spent the day with Him, they were in need of food; and He fed them miraculously. John records this incident and the sermon on the bread of life which brings to a climax Jesus' Galilean ministry.

### *Turning-point*

This incident was a turning-point in His ministry. Its importance seems to be emphasized by the fact that all four Gospel accounts record it (Matt. 14:13-21; Mark 6:30-34; Luke 9:10-17; John 6:1-14). This is true of surprisingly few incidents.

Many interesting points worth pondering are found in the accounts of the feeding of the five-thousand—Jesus' purpose in leaving Capernaum (probably to give rest and private teaching to the twelve); the mind of the crowd, their expectations and purposes; Jesus' compassion shown in not fully eluding them, but giving them of His time, patient teaching, and healing power; His merciful consideration for their physical needs; His ability to supply; His use of all that men had to offer, multiplying it to fill the need; the abundance of the Lord's supply; His economy with the remains, "that nothing be lost"; the intentions of the crowd to make Him king "by force"; their confidence in His value and power to serve their purposes, but their unwillingness to trust Him to lead them according to His purposes.

Despite the interest we find in all these and other points, still it is well that we understand the importance of Jesus' sermon on the next day. Jesus used this occasion and setting to teach one of His greatest lessons, a "hard saying" that caused many hundreds of people to turn away and follow Him no more. A knowledge of the "feeding" and the circumstances that led up to it help us to understand the Lord's sermon; but if we have a clear conception of the setting, let us hasten on to the study of the sermon itself.

After the feeding of the 5,000 and refusing their bid to make Him king, Jesus sent away the multitude and the disciples (Matt. 14:22, 23), and went up into a mountain to pray. After about eight hours the disciples were struggling against a contrary wind when Jesus came unto them walking on the water in the stormy night (John 6:18).

### *"Meat Which Endureth"*

When it was day and Jesus and the disciples were again at Capernaum, the people were seeking Jesus again. They wondered how or when He had come over from the place of the feeding, because they knew He had no other boat in which to come and that they had watched for Him on the land. Who would think of walking on the water for a few miles in the stormy night? Jesus did not answer the question about how He had come across the lake, but rather began to rebuke their materialistic motives and to teach them about better food than the loaves and fishes—"meat which endureth unto everlasting life" (John 6:27). In the old English "meat" meant any food. Jesus did not mean that it was wrong to work that we may eat; but He said, "stop spending all your efforts for food that perishes; instead, work that you may receive from God everlasting life."

A rather long and lively discussion followed in which Jesus made increasingly clear that we must live by partaking of His life as the only source of life, while the Jews became more and more skeptical and unreceptive toward His teaching. Jesus said they should work for the food that endures. He as the Son of Man bearing God's official authorization is the only one capable of giving eternal life.

Falsely assuming that certain works that God required were the entire means of obtaining life, they asked, "What shall we do, that we might work the works of God?" Jesus says, "This is the work of God, that ye believe on him whom he hath sent? (John 6:28, 29). Believing God is the one work that any man owes to God. Believing is not merely consenting to an idea to the extent of not arguing against it; but believing is accepting something as true and acting upon it with complete confidence. Believing on Christ is not a single act of the mind, but it is a continuous state of trusting His truthfulness, authority, and power so that we follow and obey Him regardless of the cost or the consequences. The only works that save are the works of faith; and the only faith that saves is the faith that works (James 2:14-26).

The people had seen the great miracle of the feeding of the five thousand men besides women and children from five small loaves and two small fishes. Most of the crowd, at least, had seen many other miracles done by Jesus (John 6:2). Now they ask, "What sign shewest thou then, that we may see, and believe thee? Our fathers did eat manna in the desert" (John 6:30, 31). They refused to see the miracles that Christ had worked as reason for accepting and following whatever He taught. His miracles aroused in them desires for materialistic blessings to be divinely supplied, but they did not cause them to surrender their wills and opinions for His divine plans. Refusing to acknowledge His power and authority they suggest that Jesus feed them all continuously somewhat as Israel was fed manna in the wilderness.

Jesus said, "The bread of God is that which cometh down out of heaven, and giveth life unto the world. They said therefore unto him, Lord, evermore give us this bread. Jesus said unto them, I am the bread of life: he that cometh to me shall not hunger, and he that believeth on me shall never thirst" (John 6:33-35). In their state of poor understanding and unbelief, it was probably a disappointment to them to hear His answer. They had asked something from Him, and He gave only Himself. They asked something more, and He offered only what they already had, if they would receive it. The great gift was already theirs, if they only knew it. He had satisfied their physical hunger once, and they wanted Him to do so again. But if they really believed in Him and came to Him by faith, they would be satisfied completely and permanently with spiritual sustenance.

Jesus reminded them that seeing is not believing when they were unwilling to believe because their hearts were set on something else. They had seen Jesus' miracles, but many refused to believe in spite of the testimony of their own eyes. Jesus stressed both God's side and man's side in our salvation, "All that which the Father giveth me shall come unto me; and him that cometh to me I will in no wise cast out" (John 6:37). No one is worthy to stand before God as acceptable to Him in human merit; but God has chosen to save those who are receptive to His grace. Christ will receive all who really come to Him; but this does not say that none of them can go away again. This should not be taken to contradict Matthew 7:21-23; 22:11-14; I Corinthians 9:27; 10:12; Revelation 3:16; John 15:2 or other passages that warn of falling from Christ. It was God's will that Jesus should save all whom His grace could reach—all who believe and follow Him. Jesus is ready, willing, and able to do this; but He cannot help a person who will not believe and come to Him.

The people refused to believe that He came down from heaven, saying they knew His parents. He went on with His teaching, explaining that He was living bread, and would give His flesh that men might eat and never die. But they rejected such statements contemptuously. If they had searched His words for meaning, with due respect for them, they might have understood more, although the sayings were very strange to them.

### *The Only Source of Life*

Jesus declared, "It is the spirit that giveth life; the flesh profiteth nothing: the words that I have spoken unto you are spirit, and are life" (John 6:63). Many refused to believe Him and forsook Him and followed Him no more. Jesus turned to the twelve and said, "You do not want to go away also, do you?" Simon Peter answered Him, "Lord, to whom shall we go? You have words of eternal life" (John 6:66-67, New American Standard Bible). His words were strange and their meaning hard for the twelve also, but they recognized His extraordinary claims and powers, received the promises to those who believe Him, and waited for more light and further explanation.

In Jesus' teaching, the main point was this: that He was divine and had the power of life, to give to any and all who would receive it eternal life, and that life can not be had by men apart from Him and His gift of His body as a sacrifice to and for them. The apostles thought they did not understand, but they did believe that He was divine and had the power of life eternal, and that there was no other source of life. In fact, they got the point of the lesson pretty well.

Didn't Jesus foreknow that this sermon would discourage and disperse a great crowd of very enthusiastic and promising followers? Was He guilty of putting a stumblingblock in their way? This was a lesson of fundamental importance. They could not go on with their wrong purposes—trying to turn His ministry to serve their plans. If He could not get them to forsake their fleshly ambitions and seek first for everlasting life by the way of faith and submission to the

Savior, then they were not His followers at all, and they would not do themselves any good by being in His crowd.

Do we believe Him? Are we willing to receive this "hard saying"? Can we see by the eye of faith the conception that Jesus had of one important thing to work for in life? Just look at the difference between the crowd at a church dinner and the crowd at a prayer meeting! Just look about at the people you see every day and count how many are really working consciously and earnestly for the necessities of everlasting life in heaven more than they are for the food of this perishing flesh! Most of us have no higher ambitions than to satisfy the flesh and maintain it a few months here upon this earth. Are we able to take the Lord at His word and work not for a living, but for an everlasting life?

Christ is our life (Col. 3:4; John 14:6; 11:25). God has given to us eternal life, and that life is in His Son; he that has the Son has the life, and he that has not the Son has not life (I John 5:11, 12).

At His temptation, when Jesus was almost starved to death, He quoted, "Man shall not live by bread alone, but by every word that proceedeth out of the mouth of God." Jesus understood perfectly what are the real necessities of life. He gave the multitudes physical bread to show His interest in their welfare and to furnish a basis for faith in His words when He would offer them something more important than bread.

Jesus is the only Savior from guilt and death. He is also the essence of the new life into which we enter when our sins are forgiven. We are baptized, not only to receive forgiveness through His sacrifice, but we are baptized into Him, being made alive by His Spirit within us. Without a vital relationship with Him, we would become dead in new trespasses and sins, even though the old ones were blotted out. We need not only to be released from condemnation, but also to be filled with the Spirit of Christ, the life of Christ in us (Rom. 8:1-13; Gal. 2:20; 5:13-25).

He will raise us up at the last day. The bread that Jesus offered was not to provide physical sustenance in this life, for He emphasized the life after the resurrection. It is only in the future life that we really never hunger or thirst. Still in this present world Jesus satisfies men's deepest needs and longings if they come to feed on Him, not merely on things that He supplies.

### *Meeting the Test of Faith*

The miracles in the presence of all the multitude furnished a *basis for faith* in the divine power and personal reliability of Jesus. The sermon, with its strange sound and spiritual emphasis, refusing more physical aid but offering Himself as everything men need, supplied a *test of their faith.* The crowd *failed the test of faith.* They murmured against His words and turned away disappointed. They showed that they did not trust His words when they could not understand them and agree with them. They would not give up their hopes and ideas to take the spiritual realities He offered. The apostles did not understand Jesus' saying, but they *met and passed the test of faith.* What faith the disciples had! "To whom shall we go? Thou hast the words of eternal life" (John 6:68). We need such faith in Him.

For Further Study:

Barclay, William. *Jesus As They Saw Him.* New York, Evanston, London: Harper & Row, 1962. Pp. 258-262. Background information on the Bread of Life title.

Bruce, A. B. *The Training of the Twelve,* 3rd ed. New York: Harper and Brothers, Publishers, n.d. Pp. 120-154. Helpful interpretation and application of John 6.

Butler, Paul. *The Gospel of John,* Vol. I. Joplin: College Press, 1961. Pp. 221-262. Exposition of John 6.

Foster, R. C. *Studies in the Life of Christ.* Grand Rapids: Baker Book House, 1968. Pp. 149-183. Discusses the events and teaching in John 6.

# 60

## JESUS, THE CHRIST (Matt. 16:16)

Jesus is more than John the Baptist. He is more than one of the prophets. He is the Messiah promised in the Old Testament. This identity was never questioned in the early church.

> Now when Jesus came into the parts of Caesarea Philippi, he asked his disciples, saying, Who do men say that the Son of man is? And they said, Some say John the Baptist; some, Elijah; and others, Jeremiah, or one of the prophets. He saith unto them, But who say ye that I am? And Simon Peter answered and said, Thou art the Christ, the Son of the living God (Matt. 16:13-16).

I. What does Messiah mean?

A. Messiah means the anointed (Messiah is the Hebrew or Aramaic. Christ is the Greek translation).

1. The ceremony of anointing kings. Saul—(I Sam. 9:16; 10:1); David—(I Sam. 16:13); Solomon—(I Kings 1:39); Jehu—(I Kings 19:16); Hazael—(I Kings 19:15); Jehu—(II Kings 9:2, 3, 6); Joash—(II Kings 11:12); Jehoahaz—(II Kings 23:30).
2. The ceremony of anointing priests. (Lev. 8:12, 30; 4:3, 16; Exod. 29:7, 21; 30:30).
3. Instruction to Elijah to anoint Elisha as a prophet and Jehu and Hazael as kings (I Kings 19:15, 16).

B. What *conceptions of the Messiah* were *presented in the Old Testament?*

1. Conception of powers conferred by the anointing. David received the Spirit of the Lord (I Sam. 16:13). Especially responsibility and dignity were conferred, with a high degree of assurance that God would enable them to perform according to His will all their official duties. The anointed one becomes an agent of God, an implement to carry out the divine will (e.g., Jehu, II Kings 9:1-10).
2. Holy anointing oil, a special compound (Exod. 30:22-33). Even objects were anointed to sanctify them: altar of sacrifice (Exod. 29:36); tabernacle, ark of testimony (Exod. 30:26); table and its vessels, candlestick and its vessels

(Exod. 30:27); altar of burnt offering, the laver and its foot (Exod. 30:28).

3. The special majesty of God's anointed to come (Heb. 1:9; Ps. 45:6-8). "God has anointed me to minister" (Isa. 61:1-3; Luke 4:17-21).
4. Appointed priest with an oath, after the order of Melchizedek (Ps. 110:4; Heb. 5:10; 2:17; 7:15-17, 21, 28).
5. The stone which the builders rejected, made the keystone, or chief cornerstone (Ps. 118:22; Matt. 21:42; I Pet. 2:7).
6. David's Son to reign forever (Ps. 132:10-12; Jer. 33:15-17).
7. A prophet and law-giver like Moses (Deut. 18:15-19).
8. The picture in Isaiah. Judge among the nations, rebuke many people (2:4); born of a virgin, God with us (7:14); a light in Galilee (9:1, 2); of the increase of his government and of peace no end, upon the throne of David to establish it with justice forever (9:6, 7); a branch out of the roots of Jesse (David's father, 11:1); the Spirit of the Lord upon Him, of wisdom, might, knowledge and godly fear, to judge righteously, and to rule effectively the whole earth with the strength of His words, the rod of His mouth and the breath of His lips (11:2-5); a root of Jesse, a sign for the nations, unto Him shall the Gentiles seek (11:10); "Great is the Holy one of Israel in the midst of thee" (12:6); victory over death, over tears of bereavement (25:8); in Zion a precious cornerstone, a sure foundation, cf. I Peter 2:6, 7; (28:16); God's Servant, with God's Spirit upon Him, to bring forth justice to the Gentiles. The manner and success of His ministry, cf. Matthew 12:18-21, for a covenant of the people and a light to the Gentiles (42:1-9); Christ sent to the Gentiles, and the greatness of His deliverance by His reign, "salvation unto the end of the earth" (49:1-23); God's Servant exalted, greatly marred, startling many nations (52:13-15); the suffering Servant in His atoning death and ultimate triumph, cf. Acts 8:32-35; 55:3-5. An everlasting covenant, even the sure mercies of David; the commander and leader of the peoples; nations shall run into Israel for the Holy One of Israel (53:1-12); The Judge who was men's Savior, afflicted in all their affliction, the Angel of the presence who saved them and redeemed them; but when they rebelled He turned to be their adversary (63:1-10).
9. The dynasty of David would be restored in the person of the

Messiah (Isa. 11:1; Jer. 33:15). The Messiah was to the Son of David and king, ruling in power and righteousness. The Messiah was to be deliverer of Israel and restorer of national prominence.

10. Summary: Jesus' messiahship expresses:
    a. His relation to God who sent Him and whom He served.
    b. His relation to the Old Testament as revelation and preparation of His coming.
    c. His relation to the people whom He led, taught and delivered.

II. What conceptions of the Messiah existed among the Jews of the 1st century? (See Luke 2:29-32; Matt. 2:1-5; John 12:34; 4:25; 7:27, 31, 42; Luke 24:21, 26-46).

The Jews of the first century expected the Messiah to be a supernatural figure, restoring Israel miraculously. He would be preceded by a messenger of God (Elijah) who would purify Israel (Mal. 3:1-3; 4:5; Matt. 17:10-13). He would restore the nation and rule with military power. They certainly did not expect Him to be a wandering prophet. Peter's perception of Jesus as the Messiah is remarkable. It was not a product of the ideas of his generation but was given by revelation of God (Matt. 16:17).

III. How did the apostles understand this title?

The Messiah was definitely a real man, sent from God, with divine qualities and powers (Acts 2:22; 10:38), the prophet of Deuteronomy 18:15-18 (Acts 3:22; 7:37); superior to death (Acts 2:24); exalted to the right hand of God (Acts 2:33). He was more than a prophet. At least twelve times in Acts, Jesus is identified as the Messiah without any political implications (Acts 5:42, the constant emphasis of the apostles); (Acts 9:22, Paul at Damascus). He is called the Servant (may also be translated *child*) of the Lord (Acts 3:13, 26; 4:27, 30). It was fitting and necessary for Him to suffer (Luke 24:46-48; Acts 17:3; 8:26-40; I Pet. 2:21-25; 3:15—4:1). He is called Lord more than any other title in Acts (2:36; 7:59; 3:15; 4:12). He is described as a glorious and triumphant figure, coming again on the clouds with power and glory (I Thess. 4:16; Phil. 1:10; 3:20, 21). Jesus is Lord (Rom. 10:9; I Cor. 12:3; Phil. 2:11). Yet He was really man, sharing human experience (John 1:14, 18; Phil. 2:5-8), born of the seed of David (Rom. 1:3). His teachings establish a norm for all the church (Acts 20:35;

I Cor. 7:10, 11). He was the object of intense personal devotion (Phil. 1:21, 23; II Cor. 5:6-10; Phil. 3:8-14; Gal. 2:20; 6:14). As redeemer and savior of those who believe, He is the hope of all men (II Cor. 5:14-19; I Pet. 1:18, 19; 2:24; 3:18; Heb. 13:12). Other apostolic descriptions include: existing in the form of God and equal with God, creator of all things (Phil. 2:6; Col. 1:15-18; 2:9, 10; II Cor. 8:9; Gal. 4:4; John 17:5); exalted to the highest place of rule and of judgment (Eph. 1:20-23; 4:10; Heb. 8:1); the supreme messenger of God (Heb. 1:1-4; 2:1-4); the great deliverer (Heb. 2:9, 15, 18; 4:1-16); the one great High Priest (Heb. 7:1-28); mediator of the new and better covenant (Heb. 8:6; 9:15; 12:24).

IV. Did Jesus actually claim to be "the Christ"? Yes, in these ways:

1. His heavenly origin (John 8:23).
2. His relation to God (John 14:9; Matt. 11:27; John 10:14-18; 17:3-5).
3. Divine prerogatives (Matt. 28:18; Mark 2:10; John 5:28, 22; 15:26; 16:7).
4. Oneness with the Father (John 10:30; 14:23).
5. The Way to God (John 14:6; Matt. 10:32, 33).
6. Sinlessness (John 8:46).
7. Lordship over the spirit world (Matt. 13:41; 16:27; Luke 11:20).
8. His redemptive gift of Himself for others (Mark 10:45).
9. The demand that His followers sacrifice for Him (Matt. 10:18, 37, 39, 40).
10. Offering eternal life as His own gift (John 10:28, 29; 6:40, 51, 54).
11. He offers rest to the soul (Matt. 11:28, 29).
12. Called for faith in Himself (John 6:29; 14:1; 8:24).
13. His triumphal entry into Jerusalem as King, like Solomon (Matt. 21:4, 5; Mark 11:9, 10; Luke 19:37-40; John 12:13, 19).

*How Did God Reveal the Messiahship of Jesus to Peter?*

1. Testimony of John the Baptist. John the Baptist identified Jesus as the lamb of God, the Son of God, the one baptizing in the Holy Spirit and in fire, the one bringing in the Kingdom of God and ruling over it (Matt. 3; John 1; 3).
2. Teaching and claims of Jesus
   a. Lesson at Nazareth (Luke 4).

b. Samaritan woman (John 4).
c. Sermon on the mount (Matt. 5-7).
d. Sermon in John 5.
e. Sermon on the Bread of Life (John 6).
f. Teaching about the kingdom of God (John 3).

3. Prophecies fulfilled.
4. Miracles of Jesus
   Healing of the paralytic and claimed to forgive sins (Mark 2).
   Casting out demons (who testified that He was the Holy One of God).
   Calming the sea.
   Raising the dead.
   Giving miracle-working power to the twelve.
   Knowing the thoughts and hearts of men.
   Feeding the multitudes.
   Walking on the water.
5. Jesus' plans and promises.
   His purposes and motives, thoughts and attitudes.
   a. His God-consciousness.
   b. His clear and confident view of the future constantly dominant.
   c. His understanding of human needs and compassion to all.
6. One of the earliest and most significant evidences was the impact of His character upon the disciples. The greatness, wholeness, purity and power of His personality testified to His Messiahship.

*The Chief Evidences of the Christ*
*How the Messiahship of Jesus is Made Clear To Us*

1. His claims:
   A. To be a special representative of God—the supreme prophet.
   B. To be the fulfillment of many prophecies of the Old Testament.
   C. To bring the Kingdom of God and to rule over the domain of God.
2. The Old Testament Scriptures.
3. The testimonies of the apostles.
4. To Him God bore witness.
   A. By John the Baptist (John 1:29-34).
   B. By His special audible voice.
      1. at Jesus' baptism (Matt. 3; Mark 1; Luke 3).
      2. at the transfiguration (Matt. 17; Mark 9; Luke 9).
      3. at the last public teaching before the cross (John 12).
   C. By wonders, signs, and mighty works (Acts 2:22).

D. By His resurrection (Rom. 1:4; I Cor. 15:3-12).

For Further Study:

Barclay, William. *Jesus As They Saw Him.* New York: Evanston, London: Harper & Row, 1962. Pp. 93-159. Extensive study of the Old Testament, intertestament and New Testament material about the Messiah and His Kingdom.

Crichton, James. "Messiah," *International Standard Bible Encyclopedia,* ed. by James Orr, Vol. IV. Grand Rapids: Wm. B. Eerdmans, 1939. Pp. 2039-2044. Also treats views of the Messiah in the Old Testament, intertestament literature, and the New Testament.

Edersheim, Alfred. *The Life and Times of Jesus the Messiah*, 3rd ed. 2 Vols. Grand Rapids: Wm. B. Eerdmans, reprint of 1886 ed. Vol. I, pp. 160-179; Vol. II, pp. 72-88. Background information on Jewish ideas of the Messiah and exposition of Matthew 16:13-20.

Foster, R. C. *Studies in the Life of Christ.* Grand Rapids: Baker Book House, 1968. Pp. 699-727. Discusses the various interpretations of Matthew 16:13-20.

Jocz, J. "Messiah," *Zondervan Pictorial Encyclopedia of the Bible,* ed. by Merrill C. Tenney, Vol. IV. Grand Rapids: Zondervan Publishing House, 1975. Pp. 198-207. Summary of the various views in Biblical and non-Biblical writings.

# 61

## JESUS, THE LIGHT OF THE WORLD (John 7-9)

Jesus preached on the bread of life after feeding the five thousand in Galilee at Passover time. Six months later at the feast of Tabernacles in Jerusalem Jesus taught that He was the Light of the World.

During the six months between the two events, Jesus avoided Galilee and all the places where He was well-known. He took the apostles away from the politically minded Galileans into Gentile territory around Tyre and Sidon for private teaching and rest. He healed the daughter of one Gentile woman who made a persistent plea in great faith. Then Jesus and His disciples went to the area east of the Sea of Galilee and ministered among the people enough to stir up a crowd that followed Him unto the third day without food. Again He multiplied food miraculously to feed a multitude, this time four thousand men (Matt. 15:21-39). Even in strange places and in Gentile territory "He could not be hid" (Mark 7:24). The remarks of His brothers (John 7:3, 4) indicate that they considered Him to be strangely avoiding manifesting Himself to the people.

He went up the Jordan valley to Caesarea Philippi. Here Peter said, "Thou art the Christ, the Son of the living God" (Matt. 16:16). Then Jesus began to tell them plainly that He must die. A week later Jesus took Peter, James, and John up on a high mountain, probably Mount Hermon, and was seen by them in a blaze of divine glory talking with Moses and Elijah about His coming death at Jerusalem. From these and other events recorded of this six month period it appears that Jesus was concentrating on training the twelve to prepare them to accept His death and to bear their responsibilities as apostles.

When the feast of Tabernacles began in Jerusalem the people were filled with supressed excitement. They dared not speak openly of Jesus for fear of the Jews, but they could not forget Him. They were divided in their opinion of Him, whether He were good or bad, from God or not; but they were all generally interested in whether He would dare to come and preach publicly at this feast. For more than a year and a half there had been spasmodic attempts to destroy Him. The rulers were known to be bitterly opposed to Him.

Into this atmosphere Jesus and His disciples came to Jerusalem for the feast of Tabernacles, but they avoided the crowds going to it and arrived late. In the midst of the feast of eight days Jesus began suddenly and dramatically to teach in the temple. He made startling claims to absolute supremacy in their lives. With a calm and deliberate boldness He challenged their desire to kill Him (John 7:16-19). They could not defend their hostility and only falsely denied it. He kept on presenting Himself and His words as sent forth from heaven, to bring light and life to men. Instead of heeding the moral force of His words and acknowledging the divine testimony of His miracles, the Jews determined to resist Him and their own conscience. Hence they sought any little thing about which to quibble and to object. Still, many were amazed at His understanding and His prophetic utterances, and some believed on Him.

Day after day Jesus faced bitter opposition. The religious leaders sent soldiers to arrest Him, but they returned with empty hands to the chief priests and Pharisees with no other explanation for their failure than simply to say, "Never man so spoke" (John 7:46). In the midst of the scornful invective which the Pharisees poured upon the officers, Nicodemus injected the suggestion that a man was not condemned by the law until he had been heard and tried. Their answers to Him, as well as to the officers, reveal the unreasonable hatred and the groundless scorn which their hypocritical hearts held toward Jesus and anybody that was even partly fair toward Him.

In chapters seven, eight, and nine of John's gospel we can study the kind of teaching that Jesus did in the face of such unbelief and opposition, when He knew that His time to teach on earth in person was growing very short. Jesus' wonderful claims convinced some, amazed others, and angered many. Though Jesus spoke very convincingly and answered His adversaries very skillfully, they were completely unwilling to reconsider their false judgment of Him. Jesus's claims to divine authority and unique importance certainly demanded attention—either worshipful acceptance or firm resistance.

### *Jesus Taught About Himself*

"We preach not ourselves, but Christ Jesus as Lord; and ourselves as your sevants for Jesus' sake" (II Cor. 4:5); but Christ had to preach Himself! It is the person of Jesus that makes His teaching important, not primarily His teaching that makes His person important; He is the personal and perfect expression of God's being, God's revelation, God's truth, and God's righteousness. In Him we find wisdom, redemption, righteousness and eternal life. "In Him dwelleth all the fulness of the Godhead bodily" (Col. 2:9). To reveal truth and love, holiness and redeeming grace, God manifested His Son. And Jesus had no greater lesson to teach than this: that men should believe on Him whom God sent into the world for the enlightenment and salvation of the world.

How could men ever accept and grasp the lessons of spiritual truth and righteousness, if they would not accept or could not recognize the source from which, or of whom, alone those lessons could ever be learned? In the first place, obviously, it was more necessary for men to accept Him than it was for them to accept His teaching; for to reject Him was to reject the greater part of His teaching and to turn away from the only light to be had. Any moral and practical teachings of Jesus which can be followed by men without faith and reverence toward Him personally are not able to redeem and to regenerate men in themselves, and as far as they are practiced must be motivated by something in the natural heart, which, whatever it is, will be far less effective than the motive power furnished by Christ in the hearts of those who truly believe Him. But, of course, one cannot accept Him and continue to reject or ignore His teaching.

### *Jesus Taught That He Was Sent From God*

It was not Himself alone that He was exalting, apart from God; but it was the will and purpose of God that He served as the messenger of God. Once before (John 5:31) Jesus had said that if He bore testimony of Himself (alone and apart from God) His witness would not be true. Indeed it wouldn't. He must bear witness of God's will, judgments and grace; He must declare the Father's purposes and participation in all His deeds in order to tell the truth. Now the Jews tried to misapply His words and turn them against Him (John 8:13). Jesus' words were not false just because they concerned Himself, because He did faithfully proclaim Himself as God's messenger. He made all His deeds God's deeds. He came not in His own name, but in the name of God. Yet they rejected Him. Others who came in their own names were received. Such is the perversity of those who hate to surrender to the sovereignty of God (Cf. John 5:43, 44).

His coming from God made His words dependable and made them binding, obligatory upon all men. The gospel of Christ has its promises that cannot fail or disappoint one who believes the whole and follows it; but it also has its commandments which no man can disobey without rebelling against God. We may trust Jesus. We must hearken to Him. We can not "take it or leave it" with impunity. God says, "This is my Son; hear ye him" (Matt. 17:5). Jesus truly says, "He that receiveth me receiveth him that sent me" (Matt. 10:40); "He that heareth my word, and believeth him that sent me" (John 5:24); and "He that honoreth not the Son, honoreth not the Father which hath sent him" (John 5:23). No man can reject the Son of God and have reverence for God or serve God. "This is the work of God, that ye believe on him whom he hath sent" (John 6:29).

### *Jesus Taught That He Is Sufficient For The Needs Of All Men*

He offers light, life, and liberty unto all (John 6:47-51; 8:51; 8:12; 8:31, 32). He has promised to satisfy spiritual hunger and thirst, to give rest to the soul, to dispel its darkness, to set us free indeed, and to give us life for ever and ever. His claims are indeed great—too great to be ignored or to be deceitful. They manifestly are supernatural and require a supreme supernatural character to carry them out. He either is all and more than all else to us, or He is the most false and the most preposterous liar that ever was.

Nevertheless, He does not fail. He makes good His word. He raises the dead with a word, and gives sight to the man that was born blind. Therefore we should trust Him, although we can not see or understand all about Him and the means and ways by which He can satisfy every human need. Still He very plainly shows Himself to be from God and in possession of the power of God over life and death, and over the physical and moral universe.

Christ gives a new vision to see life in the view of all eternity, not merely the earthbound present. To us who were dead in trespasses and sins He gives a new life, making us dead to sin and alive unto God for evermore. He sets us free from the chains of guilt that bound us to the penalties of our old sins, and from the bonds of habit, lust and weakness that made us slaves of sin continually. Whereas in our natural mind of unbelief we feared the binding restraints of God's will and called ourselves free in doing our own will, we actually find that when we walk by faith in Christ we are truly free to fulfill our true destiny and our highest ambitions as children of God and heirs of the eternal realms of righteousness. We actually find burdens lifted and bonds broken. All these things are ours in Christ if we trust and obey Him, if we abide in His words and walk in the light that He gives to the way of life.

If we try to walk without Him and grope along in our own way we shall stumble in the darkness. We have not life in ourselves (John 6:53). We shall die in our sins (John 8:24). We can not come unto the Father except by Him (John 14:6). As light is necessary to the eyes, Christ is necessary to the character and immortal soul.

*Jesus Taught His Authority By Demonstration*

Jesus healed another well-known beggar on the Sabbath, this time a man born blind; He sent Him to wash his eyes in the pool of Siloam. When the man came back seeing, the Pharisees asked him how he received his sight. They wished to deny the miracle, and so they made a thorough investigation of it. They even called the blind man's parents to determine whether it was he that was born blind. The parents would not say how he was healed because they knew that anybody who said anything favorable about Jesus would be persecuted (John 9:1-23).

The Jewish officials were concerned about the man's opinion of Jesus. They reasoned that Jesus broke the Sabbath; therefore, He was a sinner and could not be used by God for such a miracle. They had to admit that the miracle happened; but they wanted the former blind man to think that Jesus' actions and commands had nothing to do with it. They insisted that he could thank God for his sight and reject Jesus. The healed man responded, "One thing I know, that, whereas I was blind, now I see" (John 9:25). This man recognized the power of a fact. He would not deny facts on the basis of doubtful judgments of men. The Pharisees set their judgment and pride of authority against facts.

The leaders questioned him again on how he could see. They had investigated all this before. They seem to be baffled by the man's clear thinking and courageous testimony. They apparently were trying to appear interested in getting the facts while really seeking to catch come inconsistency in his testimony. He was somewhat disgusted with the Pharisees for not accepting the force of the evidence presented. Because of their stubborn opposition to Jesus he knew very well that they were not seeking to be his disciples. He seems to be sarcastic, taunting their confusion in his question, "Would ye also become his disciples?" (John 9:27).

The Jews abused the man with scornful language insisting that they followed Moses who spoke with the authority of God, but in slurring reference to Jesus, said they did not know by whose authority He came and spoke. The man responded by pointing out how unreasonable it was for them to know the fact of the miracle and not see the evidence of Jesus' authority as one coming from God. He insisted that only God could do what Jesus did. His reasoning was clear and unanswerable: Jesus should be regarded as pleasing to

God and representing God simply because He was doing such works of divine power. The Pharisees were defeated in argument; they could not answer the facts and clear reasoning of the healed man. So they resorted to abuse and made a personal attack upon him as one born under a curse. For such a man to offer them instruction hurt their pride; and for him to foil them so completely was insufferable. They drove him out of their presence and probably excommunicated him (John 9:28-34).[1]

Some people charge that the ancients believed events to be miraculous which a scientific age would explain by natural law and that they accepted reports of miracles without requiring real evidence. The healing of the man born blind was investigated by the group of intelligent and educated men who were determined to disprove it, but they could not. They established the identity of the man who was healed and the fact that he had been born blind. They could easily perceive that now he could see. They could not shake his testimony about the way he was healed when he obeyed Jesus. What more could a modern scientific commission do to test the reality of the miracle?

The fact of the miracle is a clear demonstration that Jesus spoke and acted with the authority of God. We do well to accept Him as the source of light, and to rely on anything that He says. A clearer vision of His will will be ours.

### *Follow The Light*

Light enables us to see and know. The most important light is that which enables us to know God. In the Bible the word light is used to signify the revelation of God, with the wise manner of life and the true hope that it brings. By contrast, darkness signifies ignorance of God, especially as shown in sin and its consequences. Jesus is the source and the means of all spiritual knowledge. Man by human wisdom does not know God (I Cor. 1:21; 2:7-9). The only adequate revelation of God is in Christ.

As Jesus enabled the man born blind to see, so also He enables everyone of us who believes and obeys Him to see spiritually. But too many of us are like the Pharisees; we think we already have understanding without divine light. We are tragically ignorant of our

---

[1] The statement "God heareth not sinners" (John 9:31) was the opinion of the man formerly blind. It is well supported in the sense that he meant it (Ps. 66:18; Prov. 15:29; Isa. 1:15; Micah 3:4 and others). But this verse should not be misapplied as proof that God refuses to hear the prayers of all non-Christians.

ignorance. We may have much information on many subjects and still be like some people whom Paul described as ever learning but never able to come to a knowledge of the truth. Just as the Pharisees did not realize how blind they were, so many scholars of today do not realize how blind they are to real truth. We will either follow Jesus Christ or remain in the dark! Those who admit human blindness and let God reveal himself to them get the true light of life. But those who suppose that they see without God become ever more blind and enveloped in spiritual darkness from which there is no recovery. Thank God that He has "called you out of darkness into his marvellous light" (I Pet. 2:9).

For Further Study:

Barclay, William. *Jesus As They Saw Him.* New York: Evanston, London: Harper & Row, 1962. Pp. 262-268. Studies the Old and New Testament usage of referring to God in the imagery of light. Extra-Biblical literature is cited as refering to God as light as well.

Butler, Paul. *The Gospel of John,* Vol. II. Joplin: College Press, 1965. Pp. 13-104. Exposition. Study Questions. Expository Outlines.

Edersheim, Alfred. *The Life and Times of Jesus the Messiah,* Vol. II. Grand Rapids: Wm. B. Eerdmans Publishing Co., n.d. Pp. 148-187. Helpful information on the Jewish background for the Feast of Tabernacles and the events in John 7-9.

# 62

## JESUS, THE GOOD SHEPHERD (John 10)

Having come to Jerusalem for the feast of Tabernacles, six months before His crucifixion, Jesus remained in the parts of Judea, apparently until the feast of Dedication, which was about three months later (John 10:22). We should like to know more about His activities during those trying days. Only the accounts in John 7-10 and in Luke 10:1—13:21 tell us of His works and teachings in that period. These chapters are almost entirely records of sermons. They do not satisfy our curiosity concerning where Jesus was spending His time, or what great miracles He worked, or how He met or avoided the attempts of the hostile Jews to kill Him. But the things that are important are recorded for us. The important thing is that we realize who He is and what He means to the lives of all men, including our own.

Jesus simply and significantly declared "I am the good shepherd: the good shepherd layeth down his life for the sheep" (John 10:11). He is teaching about Himself. The background of all that He says is the unqualified claim that He is the only hope of mankind, that He is the Lord of all and necessary to all. This portion of His teaching implies the assumption of complete and unrivaled authority; yet it emphasizes not that men must serve Him, but that men must be served by Him. It tells in striking manner of the great and sacrificial things He is to do for His people, as the shepherd laying down His life for the sheep. This was the utterance of the Lord from heaven, Master of all, but who "came not to be ministered unto, but to minister, and to give his life a ransom for many" (Matt. 20:28). The paradox of it, and the strangeness of it to proud, self-sufficient, and unbelieving ears caused many to call Him mad, and to say that He had a demon (John 10:20).

"Earnestly, tenderly Jesus was pleading" for men to trust Him and receive the benefits of His leading and His care, His power to redeem and to give life abundantly. With what longing and sorrow He must have been filled, as He, who came from heaven to seek and save the lost, looked out upon the afflicted and perishing souls of men and offered His power and wisdom and gentle love to help them, but they would not believe and heed His call! This was one of the frequent times that He would have gathered the children of Jerusalem unto Him as a hen gathers her chickens under her wing, but they would not (Matt. 23:37). We are reminded of the pleadings of Jehovah toward Israel in the Book of Isaiah: "The ox knoweth his owner, and the ass his master's crib: but Israel doth not know, my people doth not consider" (Isa. 1:3; see Isa. 1; 52; 53; 54; and 55).

### *"All We Like Sheep Have Gone Astray"*

Turning to our own ways we wander in the paths of death and destruction. Like sheep without a shepherd, we lose our way and can not find the way to return to safety. We are filled with fear and confusion. We follow the "herd" even though it be over a precipice. We fall victim to ravenous beasts of prey. We can not preserve our own lives. Oh, if we would only realize how foolish, vulnerable, and helpless man is in the realm of spiritual life, in the face of fierce powers of wickedness in high places! If we would only see and acknowledge how badly we need a shepherd! If we would only recognize the shepherd's voice and follow Him that we might learn how much better things He has for us!

We can't see over the hills and into the fold. We won't learn to escape or overpower the violently destructive powers of sin. All the "lessons" of history do not make us wise unto life and righteousness. The hope of this whole race of men is not education, but faith; not training in self-sufficiency to meet the dangers and fulfill the needs of life, but trust in the shepherd to heed His voice and follow Him who supplies every need and protects all His own. Man is spiritually blind until He has Christ for light. He is lost in the wilderness until Christ is the Way in which he walks. He has no hiding place of security until He finds the door of the sheepfold, which is Christ Jesus. He is a wounded and dying sheep until Christ the great shepherd finds him and restores life and strength.

### *"One Door, and Only One"*

The two comparisons which Jesus made of Himself, the door and the shepherd, both teach the necessity of Christ for every man. He is the door of access to the Father (Eph. 2:18). He is the door of heaven itself (John 14:2), the way, the truth, and the life; no one cometh unto the Father but by Him (John 14:6). The door and the way are open to all. Whosoever will may come. But there is no other way. Whoever climbs up another way is a thief and a robber. There is one mediator between God and man (I Tim. 2:5). There is no other name wherein we must be saved (Acts 4:12). It is a narrow door admitting only those who follow closely the way of faith. He is the open door to safety, satisfaction, and sustenance; yet men refuse to enter in, but they batter at the walls to make "another way." Oh, the perversity of unbelief!

Christ is the only entrance requirement. "By me if any man enter in," whether he has been Jew or Gentile, rich or poor, learned or ignorant, good or bad, He can come in through Jesus Christ, by coming into Christ.

*The Shepherd and the Sheep*

"1. He goes before them. Like an Oriental shepherd, Christ does not drive His flock from Him; He draws them to Him. This he has done in the whole tenor of His human life—in His circumstances, His character, His toils, His sufferings and death, His glory.

"2. He calls them by name. This implies individual knowledge of all the sheep, whom He not merely marks, but actually names. Thus He denotes His property in them, His interest in their welfare.

"3. He leads them out into green pastures, and calls them to follow Him thither. His command takes the form of invitation. The attraction of His love induces His sheep to follow Him. He conducts them to the pastures where He feeds them, to the fold where He protects them.

"4. They hear and know His voice. Christ's tones, when He speaks to His own, are gentle and kind; His language is compassionate and encouraging. His voice is, therefore especially suited to the timid, the feeble, the helpless. To all such it is sweet, cheering, and comforting. The people of Christ are deaf to other voices, but are attentive to His. Its charm is felt, its authority is recognized. They have heard it before; they know it and love it; they distinguish it from every other. Gratefully and gladly do they hear the voice of the beloved.

"5. They obey and follow Him. The voice is enough. The true sheep do not wait for the crook, the staff; they are obedient to the shepherd's word of gentle authority. It is enough for them that the way in which they are led is His way. 'He that followeth me,' says Christ, 'shall not walk in darkness.' There is no questioning, no hesitation, no delay; the sheep follow whither the shepherd leads. Thus they have rest and peace. They fear no danger and no foe while their pastor watches over them and defends them. They need not ask why such a path is marked out for them, for they have perfect confidence in their divine leader. They need not ask whither they are going, for they are satisfied if they are in the pasture and the fold of Him who is the shepherd and bishop of their souls."[1]

In the midst of this world of many voices and conflicting calls, with confusing and frightening sounds abounding, it is necessary to know the shepherd's voice. To examine all things for ourselves and to determine the true origin and motive and degree of liability of every voice would be a prodigious task—much more than we could ever do. It is a wonderful relief, comfort, and security to know the voice of the divine shepherd. To know Him is eternal life (John 17:3), whether we know much else or not. When we have determined that He is the shepherd from God and that He has spoken a clear direction to us, then it is not necessary for us to hear and analyze the other voices. If Jesus said it, I believe it, and that settles it. Jesus knew what He was talking about. No one ever revealed the nature and works of God as He did. All the lines of rational and supernatural evidence unite to mark Him as God's appointed prophet and redeemer of man. To be our everlasting guide, God raised Him from the dead.

### *Laying Down His Life For The Sheep*

The works of Christ convince us, but the love of Christ constrains us. He gave His infinitely valuable and flawless life for our cursed and corrupted lives, because He loved us. He is not a hired time-server, but the sheep are His own and dear to His heart. "Greater love hath no man that this" (John 15:13). Surely such a demonstration of unlimited love and devotion of Himself to us should make us trust Him as a true shepherd and follow with joyful confidence wherever He leads, doing whatever He commands. Having such a shepherd, why should we follow any other voices?

It is a marvelous thing that He has the power to lay down His life for us and to take it up again to go on before us, ever living to be our shepherd and intercessor. His resurrection proves that His death was not a defeat or a failure, but a voluntary offering of Himself. He who encountered death and came off victor surely will not be overpowered and robbed of His flock by another adversary—"Neither shall any man pluck them out of my hand" (John 10:28).

---

[1] J. R. Thomson, *The Pulpit Commentary: Gospel of John*, Vol. II. (Grand Rapids: Wm. B. Eerdmans, 1962 reprint), p. 58.

For Further Study:

Barclay, William. *Jesus As They Saw Him.* New York, Evanston, London: Harper & Row, 1962. Pp. 187-200, 269-272. Information on Jesus as the Good Shepherd and as the Door.

Butler, Paul. *The Gospel of John,* Vol. II. Joplin: College Press, 1965. Pp. 105-135. Basic and practical exposition.

Morris, Leon. *New International Commentary: the Gospel According to John.* Grand Rapids: Wm. B. Eerdmans, 1971. Pp. 498-523.

# 63

## THE LORD OF LIFE AND DEATH (John 11)

Jesus boldly declared, "I am the resurrection, and the life: he that believeth on me, though he die, yet shall he live; and whosoever liveth and believeth on me shall never die" (John 11:25-26). Jesus claimed to be the author of life, the conqueror of death and the restorer to new life. He not only claimed this but He demonstrated it as well.

### *The Lord In Action*

Jesus had been teaching in the region across the Jordan River when He received news that His friend Lazarus of Bethany was sick. Jesus delayed two days; then He informed the disciples of Lazarus' death and His plan to go to Bethany (John 11:1-16).

Martha first met Jesus expressing anguish that Jesus had not been there so He could have prevented Lazarus' death. Her words do not blame Jesus, but express her faith in Him. She expressed her complete confidence in Him and His power, "I know whatsoever thou shalt ask of God, God will give thee" (John 11:22).

Jesus promised Martha, "Thy brother shall rise again" (John 11:23). She said she knew he would rise in the general resurrection. She knew this from the Old Testament. As a disciple of Jesus she had heard His teaching on the resurrection (John 5:28, 29; 6:39, 40, 44, 54).

Jesus said to her, "I am the resurrection and the life" (John 11:25). He does not merely teach the resurrection and promise life; He *is* both. All who are in Christ are abiding in life. Resurrection and life were not only future; they were present in person in Him. Martha was not only to trust in a future event, vague and remote to her; but she was to trust fully in the living person Jesus whom she knew and loved. Jesus had, then and there, all the power that produces resurrection and life. "He that believeth on me, though he die, yet shall he live" (John 11:25). To the believer in Christ, physical death is not the end of life. It is the entrance into a greater and better life (Phil. 1:23; II Cor. 5:1-4; 4:17; Col. 3:4; Rev. 7:14-17; Rom. 8:18-23). Even the dissolution of the body will not be death to them. They will never be separated from God, or from conscious enjoyment of Him or from doing His will. Jesus asked Martha if she believed this. She responded, "Yea, Lord: I have believed that thou art the Christ, the Son of God, even he that cometh into the world" (John 11:27). The Greek expression means, "I have come to a settled conviction."

Martha called Mary. Many mourners went out with Mary. And Jesus went with them to the tomb. Jesus shed tears of sympathy. As Jesus started toward the tomb, common-sense Martha spoke up, "Lord, by this time the body decayeth; for he hath been dead four days" (John 11:39). Jesus reminded her that He told her if she believed she would see the glory of God. The Lord then gave thanks to God for hearing Him. He did this in order to glorify God in the minds of the onlookers. Jesus came not in His own name, but to do God's will and to reveal God to men. He wanted to make sure that men saw that this miracle was from God (John 11:40-42).

"Jesus spoke with a loud voice, Lazarus, come forth" (John 11:43). Sound does not raise the dead. But the loud voice made everyone in the crowd cease wailing and give heed and see that the dead responded to Jesus' call. This event shows that the departed one was able to hear and respond immediately. The one who had died came out of the tomb. The entire body was wrapped around with linen cloths. Perfumes and spices were usually placed in the layers of the wrappings. Jesus asked that they "Loose him and let him go" (John 11:44). Lazarus needed some help, since he could not use his hands to uncover his face or loosen the windings. The people needed to face the fact that he was actually alive. It was a dramatic moment, but Jesus was matter-of-fact about it.

*What Lazarus could tell us!* Some may wish that Lazarus had written a description of his experience to give us interesting and valuable information about death and what follows it. Yet the one who wishes for a message from Lazarus is not much interested in what Jesus reveals about death and the life to come. This somehow seems characteristic of the attitudes of unbelief. Man prefers to glory in knowing all the answers as a matter of human knowledge that he can use or ignore as he chooses; but he does not care to trust the Lord who really knows and tells us what to do.

The experience of Lazarus does tell us that Jesus is the Lord of life! His voice raises the dead! To know Christ is better than to know the secrets of the universe. It is to Christ and His Word that we must turn if we want answers to our questions about life and death.

### *Jesus, the Author of Life*

John tells us that He who became Jesus in the flesh is also He who made all things and "in Him was life" (John 1:3, 4, 14, 17).

Paul says, He is "Lord of lords; who only hath immortality" (I Tim. 6:15, 16). He is one with the Father, "who giveth life to all things" (I Tim. 6:13; Acts 17:25, 28).

We do not know what life is, but we see it work and know that we have it. We do not know how He had life in Himself, or how He made us to live; but we see Him able to give life on earth before the eyes of men. In our helplessness and our inability to comprehend life, we are the more assured that He who has the power of life and death is indeed our superior, our Master, and our greatest benefactor.

What more tremendous claim could Jesus make than that which He made in the discussion with the Jews after He healed the lame man on the Sabbath, when He said, "Even so the Son giveth life to whom He will" (John 5:21)? In what greater way could He assume equality with God? Yet He made good His words by the act of raising the dead and giving them life at least three times.

It is an even greater thing, to those who can see it, that He gives to men who trust and obey Him spiritual life after the divine nature—life of the Spirit, which is so much more significant and glorious than the mere animal life of the body. He is indeed the bread of God "which cometh down out of heaven, and giveth life unto the world" (John 6:33).

### *Christ, the Conqueror of Death*

All the conquerors of the world have had to surrender to death. All the mighty lords of earth have been subject to death and had no control over it. But Jesus conquered death, and death is ever subject to His command. He called back the dead when and where He pleased. He took our death upon Himself and came forth victor over the grave. He will completely destroy death at last (II Tim. 1:10).

The Son of God came in the flesh to take our death upon Himself and to overcome the powers of death. "Since then the children are sharers in flesh and blood, he also himself in like manner partook of the same; that through death he might bring to nought him that had the power of death, that is the devil; and might deliver all them who through fear of death were all their lifetime subject to bondage" (Heb. 2:14, 15).

He defied death to hold Him: "I lay down my life, that I might take it again. No man taketh it from me, but I lay it down of myself. I have power to lay it down, and I have power to take it again" (John 10:17, 28). He also said, "The hour cometh, and now is, when the dead shall hear the voice of the Son of God; and they that hear shall live" (John 5:25). And the brief record tells of three times that He entered death's domain and rescued victims: Jairus' daughter (Matt. 9:25), the son of the widow of Nain (Luke 7:14, 15), and Lazarus of Bethany (John 11:43, 44). Then He submitted to the stroke of death Himself for our sins (I Cor. 15:3). But "it was not possible that he should be holden of it" (Acts 2:24). He demonstrated His power over death by His own resurrection (Acts 1:3; Rom. 1:4; 6:9). He is alive for evermore and has the keys of death and of Hades (the name the Greeks used for the entire realm of the dead) (Rev. 1:18). He will call all men from the grave unto life eternal and blessedness, or unto judgment and punishment (John 5:28, 29; Rev. 20:12, 13). All that die through Adam shall be raised from the dead through Christ (I Cor. 15:22). Then He will completely destroy death at last (I Cor. 15:25, 26; Rev. 20:14; 21:4).

Nothing short of this tremendous consummation of His rule over life and death can fulfill Jesus' claims and the prophecy of Isaiah "He will swallow up death in victory" (Isa. 25:8). We have full assurance that such an end shall be reached because He has fulfilled in His miracles and in His own resurrection so large a portion of His claims and the prophecies such as Psalms 16:10.

### *Jesus, The Restorer of Life, Health, and Wholeness*

Whether we are in danger of immediate death, or living a helpless and unsatisfactory life, or are already dead, Jesus can restore life and give us wholeness.

The sins of men have corrupted and disrupted their lives. Both directly and indirectly sin causes weakness, pain, and death. Christ by His miracles showed that He could overcome the effects of sin and make men new. But He was not content to restore physical health and leave men in sin. In each case He used the physical demonstrations to give men faith in Him and to draw them to Him that they may have life eternal. With each miracle of healing the body He sought to heal the soul, to give new life of faith and vital relationship with God, the source of life.

He came to give "life . . . abundantly" (John 10:10). That abundant life, He said, does not consist in the abundance of things which a man possesses (Luke 12:15). The life from God, to be found in Christ, is not life that can be supplied by any of the kings, wise men, or politicians of the earth; it comes from neither financiers nor physicians, psychologists, nor sociologists. "She [or he] that liveth in pleasure is dead while she liveth" (I Tim. 5:6). Men who are dead in sin do not know life such as Jesus gives. He "brought life and immortality to light through the gospel" (II Tim. 1:10). He is the life (John 11:25; 14:6). Except we believe Him we shall die in our sins (John 8:24). Except we eat His flesh and drink His blood we have not life in ourselves (John 6:53). He is the bread of life and the water of life.

Such statements as these may be hard to comprehend, but they should at least make it plain to us that all who trust and follow and feed on Jesus have something important and enduring and wonderful in store for them—something which can be had in no other way than by having Jesus come into their lives to renew them and to perpetuate them.

Jesus had sympathy for our physical needs, but He did not come to satisfy all our physical wants. On the contrary, He came to beget in us the life of the Spirit by which we put to death the deeds of the flesh (Rom. 8:13; cf. 8:4-12; Gal. 5:16-25). He used His ministry of miracles to show two things: (1) That He is Lord of life and death with power to do whatever He promises; and (2) that He had deep compassion and loving mercy for us in our distresses. He needed to win both our minds and our hearts to trust and to love Him so that we could come to Him and receive life that is life indeed.

"And the witness is this, that God gave unto us eternal life, and this life is in his Son. He that hath the Son hath the life; he that hath not the Son of God hath not the life" (I John 5:11, 12).

"Blessed be the God and Father of our Lord Jesus Christ, who according to his great mercy begat us again unto a living hope by the resurrection of Jesus Christ from the dead, unto an inheritance incorruptible, and undefiled, and that fadeth not away, reserved in heaven for you" (I Pet. 1:3, 4).

To know Christ in actual experience as the Lord of one's life is eternal life (John 17:3), for He himself is the life (John 14:6; I John 5:11, 12). Without Him there is neither resurrection nor life. Life is not a chemical process that can be generated according to a formula. Life is a gift from God through Jesus Christ; it originates in Christ. Let us not forget this when we listen to the arrogant and ignorant men who talk presumptuously as if all life were the product of accident and evolution in a material realm.

The way of life is not merely a moral process or a reward for quality of character. It is union with Jesus Christ, who is our life (John 3:36; 6:53; 8:24). Character and good conduct cannot raise a man from the dead; they cannot be good enough to claim the right to be raised up by God. Christ came from God that all who will may have life in Him. He can and will raise up those who accept Him as their life. Because of what He is, those who by faith are in Him shall live and never die. Believe in Christ, the Lord of your life. Be baptized into Him, being buried into His death and made alive in Him (Rom. 6:1-11). Let Christ live in you as one who has died unto sin and is alive unto God forevermore.

For Further Study:

Barclay, William. *Jesus As They Saw Him.* New York, Evanston and London: Harper & Row, Publishers, 1962. Pp. 284-291. Biblical use of terms resurrection and life.

Butler, Paul. *The Gospel of John,* Vol. II. Joplin: College Press, 1965. Pp. 136-163. Expository comment and outlines.

Foster, R. C. *Studies in the Life of Christ.* Grand Rapids: Baker Book House, 1968. Pp. 968-985. Expository comment on John 11:1-54.

Hendriksen, William. *New Testament Commentary: the Gospel According to John,* Vol. II. Grand Rapids: Baker Book House, 1954. Pp. 135-182. Detailed exposition.

Morris, Leon. *New International Commentary: The Gospel According to John.* Grand Rapids: Wm. B. Eerdmans, 1971. General comment as well as attention to technical issues.

## *Part Twelve*

# DEMANDS OF DISCIPLESHIP

## 64

### GREATNESS IN THE KINGDOM (Matt. 18)

In Matthew 18 Jesus taught about the heart of God and the attitudes that must be in those who are children of God. People need to learn to live together. All the nations of the world need to learn to live together. Successful home life is mostly a matter of learning to live together in mutual love and to the mutual advantage of the various ages and types of persons in the home. The general principles of this chapter have broad application to life in society as well as teaching concerning church polity, piety before God, salvation, judgment, and eternity. Remember that it is the Lord teaching us (not ourselves making a political or business philosophy, however good) and that His teaching here sets forth His will concerning the fellowship of *believers*, of Christians in the church.

In training the apostles for leadership Jesus taught basic principles and attitudes that should guide us in our relationships with one another.

#### *Humility*

The disciples had been disputing with one another about who was greatest among them (Mark 9:34ff; Luke 9:46ff), possibly provoked by the special blessing and promise given Peter (Matt. 16:16-18), the transfiguration seen by three but not even to be reported to the others (Matt. 17:1, 9), and the failure of the nine to cast out the demon (Matt. 17:14-20). They became so bold in their ambition that they asked Jesus, "Who is the greatest in the kingdom?" (Matt. 18:1). This question started this marvelous chain of teachings in which Jesus tried to transform their minds.

God's thoughts and God's ways are not those of men (Isa. 55:8, 9). Probably in no other respect do the ways of natural and sinful men differ from the ways of God more than in this matter of their opinions of men—how they classify "great" men, "inferior" men and "forgotten" men. It is hard for us to attain to the Lord's attitude. Ambition, envy and contempt arise again and again, and at the most inappropriate times (Luke 22:24). The danger is constantly with us and very great—the danger that we shall seek to save or to exalt ourselves and care nothing for others.

Jesus told the apostles that they would have to turn away from their sin of personal ambition and humble themselves as a little child in order to enter the kingdom at all. Their attitude was wrong. It was one of exalting self to the neglect of others, or even at the expense of others. Jesus told them, "Except ye turn, and become as little children, ye shall in no wise enter into the kingdom of heaven. Whosoever therefore shall humble himself as this little child, the same is the greatest in the kingdom of heaven" (Matt. 18:3, 4).

Jesus wanted His disciples to have the unique and heavenly spirit of true godliness—the spirit that so loves that it takes thought for others to serve and protect them, even the least honorable, the least significant of them. This attitude alone can protect us from the poisons of selfishness. Selfish ambition always brings strife among brethren and many occasions of stumbling. Selfish pride leads us to climb over others, trampling them down; but the love of God in our hearts makes us willing to stand on the bottom and push them up. So Jesus taught the disciples to be concerned not about the position they would hold, but about the needs of the little and weak ones for whom God cares. They should be doing their thinking and planning on how to avoid occasions of stumbling both to others and to themselves and be willing to cast off even that which was precious to them.

The greatest person is humble (Matt. 18:4). Such persons must not only consent to be lowly, they must look up to the lowliest they know, receive them with honor, taking care lest they stumble (Matt. 18:5, 6). What Jesus says seems to be the expression of strong feelings coming from the depth of His heart—the great heart of heaven, infinite, awe-inspiring, the object of the wondering worship of all men who ever catch a glimpse of it. Feel His sadness as He sees the woe of a world filled with occasions of stumbling. The loving heart of God, distressed at the callous indifference of men, teaches them better with love's own patience and gentleness.

Jesus pleads, "See that ye despise *not one*" (Matt. 18:10). This word "despise" (either in Greek or English) does not mean hate, but to have a low opinion of, to consider as worthless, to ignore or treat with indifference. Alas, we do despise some, but God doesn't. "It is not the will of your Father who is in heaven, that one of these little ones should perish" (Matt. 18:14). If "one of them be gone astray" He leaves the ninety and nine and seeks that one that is wandering and rejoices over every one (Matt. 18:12-13). He who counts our hairs much more counts us. God is no respecter of persons, but He respects man. Jesus does not attack their conceit by showing how poor and insignificant is the greatest of men, but by showing how valuable to God is the least of men. Men are precious in God's sight, objects of His angels' care, redeemed by the immeasurable ransom—the life of His unique Son—not because of what is peculiar to one or some, but to all. "See that ye despise not one" (Matt. 18:10).

Jesus' feelings and words were beyond the apostles at this occasion; their selfishness was not immediately overcome, but it is certainly a joy and a source of hope to us to see how grandly they did learn the lesson eventually, to see how self-forgetful and self-effacing they did become, and how they attained a great place in the kingdom. Notice how it was preached and practiced by Paul: "Let no man seek his own, but each his neighbor's good" (I Cor. 10:24. See also I Cor. 8:13; 10:33; 13:5; Rom. 12:10; 14:15; 15:1-7; Gal. 6:1-3; Phil. 2:2-5, 14, 15; Col. 3:12-14).

### *Love*

Of all men, those who sin against us are most likely to be lightly esteemed by us. We nurse our supposed grievances and readily resign our offenders to a state of guilt for which we feel no responsibility, often no regret, and sometimes even glory in the wrong, which makes us feel above them. Such is distinctly ungodly! All of us sin against God, yet God gave His dear Son to make a way to forgive us. Love for the offender causes us to care for his salvation as much as for our own; thus it sends us out to seek a reconciliation with Him.

The law of love is the basis of church discipline. Sin estranges and destroys. Love seeks and serves and tries to win to perfect accord. God is love. Love is the law of His kingdom (Rom. 13:8-10). He seeks peace, blesses peacemakers and commands us to seek a settlement of all wrongs and estrangements (Matt. 5:23-25; Rom. 12:16-21). Love is necessary to the godly character. Actions that are in themselves commendable are not truly good without love. It is indespensable to Christianity. Any pretense of Christianity without love is as unorthodox as it would be without Christ Himself (I Cor. 8:1; 13:1-3; I John 3:14; 4:7, 8, 20, 21).

The spirit of love pervades all that Jesus teaches on disciplining sinners. Indifference to guilt and estrangement is not love, any more than indifference to the state of the health and welfare of our families would signify special affection for them. Jesus knew the deadliness of sin, and His love could not consent to leave men subject to it. What good doctor will willingly ignore the presence of deadly infections that can be remedied! Neither is it godly fellowship or true love for our brethren to ignore in them the presence of sins that can be confessed, forgiven, and blotted out. The fellowship in the church was designed by the Lord to help save us from sin; and it could be a most powerful instrument if we would obey all that the Lord taught concerning the practice and withholding of that fellowship. Love dictated the goal and every step to be taken in the discipline of the offender. The object, of course, is not revenge, but reconciliation, not to crush and humiliate him, but to win and forgive and restore him. The method must be kind and generous, "in a spirit of gentleness" (Gal. 6:1). First, of course, there must be the fact of a real offense, not imaginary or merely suspicious.

We are to see the offending brother alone. This is just the very last thing some people will do. In pride and fear they shun the very person they should seek. They refuse to speak to him when it is their duty to be frank with him. Yet, too often, they talk of the matter to their neighbors and the train of gossip is started. It is better to speak to him than to brood over the wrong. But speak to him privately, as far as possible avoiding embarrassment and making it easy for him to acknowledge the wrong and repent. If he will not, take witnesses to establish all matters of fact and make another appeal. If he will not hear them, tell it to the church. The church must have reliable testimony of the fact. The church must exhort and expect the man to repent. The church also must refuse fellowship to a known offender who will not repent and accept genuine reconciliation. Heaven has laid a responsibility upon the church and has given her significant authority in such matters (Matt. 18:18). The church that will not heed her Lord in the solemn and sacred duties of discipline is not wiser and better than He, but merely cares less for the souls of men. Carrying out such instructions will never be lording it over one another or exercising undue authority, for when these words are properly obeyed it is by the authority of Jesus and not of men.

Such rigor, though pitiless in appearance, is really merciful to all concerned. It removes from the church a source of trouble and spreading infection which imperils the whole body. It is the best way to bring about the salvation of the offender, because forgiveness must be based upon repentance, and united disfavor of the entire congregation is intended to impress upon him his guilt and need of repentance. Paul said "Deliver such a one unto Satan for the destruction of the flesh, that the spirit may be saved in the day of the Lord Jesus" (I Cor. 5:5). The Corinthians did as Paul commanded, and it worked. See II Corinthians 2:5-11. Today the presence of many sectarian congregations glad to receive any member from another congregation hinders much of the effect of scriptural church discipline, but the will and the word of the Lord still stand.

### *Forgiveness*

Peter saw that the Lord's teaching all pointed to the goal of forgiveness and laid an unprecedented stress upon it; therefore Peter asked, "How many times shall I forgive? Until seven times?" (Matt. 18:21). According to the Rabbis, an erring brother should be forgiven three times. Peter must have thought seven times a larger number. The ordinary man falsely thinks he has a right to resent an injury or to demand full payment of every debt. Such an attitude considers forgiveness a special foregoing of one's own rights, and naturally thinks there is a limit beyond which we can not be expected to exercise such forbearance. Jesus' answer states that there is no limit and shows why there should be none. All Christians have asked and accepted from God unlimited forgiveness, and we have no right to refuse forgiveness to those who ask it of us.

Jesus told the parable of the unforgiving servant (Matt. 18:23-35). In the story, one man owed his lord a million times as much as the other man owed him, yet after he had been forgiven all of his enormous debt he refused to have mercy upon the poor man that owed him so little. He treated his debtor worse in every way than his lord had treated him. Although his conduct was outrageous, it was not different from that which we find among church members who, when they deal with their fellow servants, forget the great mercy of the Lord in the cleansing of their sins. Jesus' story was a cutting satire on Peter's suggestion of seven times, and no doubt it was startling to the disciples. It is new and strange to most of us, too. We are not likely to think of seven times as Peter did, but like the unmerciful servant we will not forgive once.

Jesus' words at the close of the parable are conclusive and fearful. There is no duty on which the Lord insists any more strenuously than this duty of forgiveness, and He always connects closely our forgiving with our being forgiven (See Matt. 6:12, 15; Mark 11:25; Luke 6:36, 37; James 2:13; Eph. 4:32; Col 3:13). This commandment concerns personal forgiveness and not social or judicial mercies.

God ordained governments for vengeance on evildoers on His behalf (Rom. 13:1-7). Furthermore, true forgiveness must be both given and received; it must be conditioned upon repentance, and this instruction does not tell us to forgive unconditionally. But we must take care that we have the desire to forgive in our hearts and work for a reconciliation. Jesus said we must forgive "from your hearts" (Matt. 18:35). It is easy enough to grant forgiveness with the lips, but to do it from the heart is confessedly hard for most of us. If it seems to us hard and unnatural, then that is evidence that we need our hearts changed. Above all, the forgiveness must not be grudging, for it must be seeking to take effect. It must be the outflow of love. If Christ lives in us until "it is no more I that live, but Christ that liveth in me" (Gal. 2:20), then the love of Christ that forgave me much should easily forgive my brother a little—nay, eagerly! "But if any man have not the Spirit of Christ, he is none of his" (Rom. 8:9).

Jesus said, "For if ye forgive men their trespasses, your heavenly Father will also forgive you. But if ye forgive not men their trespasses, neither will your Father forgive your trespasses" (Matt. 6:14, 15). Does this statement, resting our forgivenss upon our forgiving others, set aside or modify the terms of pardon as authorized in His great commission and as preached by the apostles—faith, repentance and baptism? No, it simply helps to show what the full force of our faith and the fruit of our repentance should be and must be. Repentance is the mental determination to accept and obey God's will. This lesson is instruction concerning what is God's will. Baptism is the first crucial test of faith by which we come into the mercy of Christ, but our salvation is constantly conditioned upon a continued, living (obedient, James 2:14-26) faith. Baptism is not its only test.

We must be willing to be forgiven and also willing to forgive. We must seek forgiveness from God with all the life and spirit that goes with it. We must also seek to forgive in the true spirit of Christ. For we are the debtors who can not pay.

The humble, loving, forgiving spirit is the secret of living together with others. This is the spirit of greatness. One with this attitude seeks what is best for others because he genuinely cares for them. "Love suffereth long, and is kind; love envieth not; love vaunteth not itself, is not puffed up, doth not behave itself unseemly, seeketh not its own, is not provoked" (I Cor. 13:4, 5). When the sons of Zebedee were seeking chief places for themselves, they probably felt it a noble ambition, but they were forgetting to care as they should for their brothers in the apostleship. They were not preferring others in honor above themselves (Rom. 12:10; Phil. 2:3). When the ten heard it and were moved with envy, they, too, were minding their own ambitions and were lacking in love that seeks to serve rather than to be served. The right kind of ambition to be truly great can be holy and noble: "Blessed are they that hunger and thirst after righteousness; for they shall be filled" (Matt. 5:6). But we are usually so wrong in our ideas of greatness. Christ wants to change our ideas of greatness. He wants to build within us true greatness.

Greatness in the kingdom is service to others. That is the way we serve God. These same qualities are found in the greatness of Christ. Isn't it a part of His greatness that He wants to share them with us?

For Further Study:

Bruce, A. B. *The Training of the Twelve,* 3rd ed. New York: Harper and Brothers, n.d. Fine study of Jesus' teaching in Matthew 18 under the chapter heading "Training in Temper."

Hayden, William, *Church Polity.* Chicago: J. J. Clarke, 1899. Pp. 97-126. Discussion of the necessity, purpose, manner and method of church discipline.

Lightfoot, Neil. *The Parables of Jesus;* Part I. Austin, Tx: R. B. Sweet Company, 1963. Pp. 48-54. Helpful exposition of the parable of the unmerciful servant.

Taylor, William M. *The Parables of Our Savior.* Grand Rapdis: Kregel Publishing, 1975 reprint. Pp. 95-103. Good application of the unmerciful servant parable.

Williamson, Chester. "The Church Should Practice Discipline," unpublished mimeographed essay available from Ozark Bible College Bookstore, 5pp. Very practical.

# 65

# THE SPIRIT OF TRUE WORSHIP—LOVE FOR GOD

Though we admit that God exists—even if we acknowledge that the Bible reveals the one true and living God—what does that profit if we do not worship and serve Him in our inmost spirits and according to the truth? To know of God and then neither glorify Him, nor submit to His will, would seem to be a more guilty wrong and a more violent rebellion than the blindness and folly of saying there is no God! In Romans 1, Paul says that the being of God is manifested in the things that are seen, "being perceived through the things that are made, even his everlasting power and divinity; that they may be without excuse." All men are responsible for giving to God reverence and honor. The great sin and degradation of much of the human race is discussed by Paul in Romans 1:20-32.

## *Need For True Worship*

To neglect to worship and give thanks to God is a very serious matter and a basis and beginning of gross evils, because it indicates a state of heart that cares not for all the goodness and truth which God embodies. And "out of the heart are the issues of life" (Prov. 4:23). Then the affection, admiration, and idealism, which should be fastened upon God, will soon be turned to some unworthy thing which is exalted to the place which God should occupy in the heart.

Far too many people think they can live normal and noble lives without any more worship or respect for God than a distant and occasional recognition of Him. They do not realize that (1) they are committing a direct affront and insult against God personally, refusing to accept His proper dominion in all the universe; (2) they are choosing not to exalt and abide by the good and pure and true, preferring darkness and corruption. The (apparently) moral man who is irreligious is one who violates the highest law, who despises the source and essence of righteousness, who resists the best interests of himself and his fellow man "Thou shalt worship the Lord thy God" (Luke 4:8). It is right. It is reasonable. It is natural. It is necessary. It is commanded by the supreme ruler and final judge of all men. Thou shalt love the Lord with all thy heart, soul, mind, and strength is the first and greatest commandment on which hangs all the law and prophets, all righteousness and life (Matt. 22:37-40). A character that is right toward every person and thing can be described simply as one that fears God; and the person who fears not God can not be expected either to respect good or to restrain evil. This contrast in characters is even more vividly implied in the simple statement that one man loves God, while another hates God.

Of all the perils that can assail a nation, there can be no greater danger than that of forgetting God. It seems always true of individuals and of nations that when they are satisfied and feeling no great need of help they forget God. They want Him chiefly for assistance. God, through Moses, warned Israel lest, when they became settled and comfortable, well-fed, and feeling secure, they should forget God (Deut. 8). Every sin we can name begins when we begin to forget God. And America today is showing that the hearts of her people are turning away from God, but we do not realize it as we need to. We must not be indifferent to it, for that very indifference is part of the lack of reverence and concern for the will of God.

The fullness of God's being and character dwells in Jesus Christ, and all God's authority and rule of the universe is given to Christ. All the obligation of man toward God demands that we actively worship and serve Jesus Christ in and through the church. The indifferent and disrespectful attitude of people toward the church, including the non-attendance of members, is indication of forgetting God.

The common acceptance of lowered standards in the home, increase of divorce, disobedience of children, immodesty of dress, salacious literature, impurity of speech, licensed and lavish flow of the liquors of lawlessness, and the almost universal devotion to the lust-laden motion pictures and T.V. programs: all are indications of how our people are forgetting or defying the law of God. America is suffering from trashy ideals.

"Exchanging the truth of God for a lie" and changing the glory of God for the glory of men and material things, ceasing to worship and thank God from the heart, will bring the same results in America today that it brought in other lands and in other times—darkness, lusts, uncleanness, vile passions, and corruption (Rom. 1:20-26). "Even as they refused to have God in their knowledge, God gave them up unto a reprobate mind, to do those things which are not fitting; being filled with all unrighteousness, wickedness, covetousness, maliciousness; full of envy, murder, strife, deceit, malignity, whisperers, backbiters, boastful, inventors of evil things, disobedient to parents, without understanding, covenant-breakers, without natural affection, unmerciful; who, knowing the ordinance of God that they that practice such things are worthy of death, not only do the same, but also consent with them that practice them" (Rom. 1:28-32). Are not all these things too much with us?

What then is the true worship which will save us from these things?

### *True Worship Is From The Heart*

It is more than mere form and ceremony. It is more than the place where it is performed, or the posture assumed, or the motions executed. "God is a Spirit: and they that worship him must worship in spirit and truth" (John 4:24). "Thou shalt love the Lord thy God . . . And to love him with all the heart, and with all the soul, and with all the strength, and to love his neighbor as himself, is more than all whole burnt-offerings and sacrifices" (Mark 12:33). This last sentence was spoken by an uninspired Jewish scribe, but Jesus approved it and said other things to the same effect. Worship is an attitude of spirit expressed by the attitude of body and accepting the forms and ceremonies which God prescribes. It is reverent adoration. It is love in the spirit of God. In the strictest sense it is not the outward activity of the body, but the inward attitude of active exaltation of God above everything else. It is such an adoration as belongs to God alone, and must not be given to men or angels.

I fear that we attend many "worship services" in which we do not actually do much worshiping. Singing may express worship, but it is likely to be done without worshiping; we may have our attention on the tune or the time or the persons present. Reading the Bible and listening to sermons are not in themselves worship. Prayer should be accompanied by worship in the heart turned toward God, but we may be occupied in thanksgiving by thinking of the things we have received, or in petitions by thinking of the things we need and desire. Worship is a soul's bowing down in adoring contemplation of God Himself. (Study Exod. 4:31; Josh. 5:13, 14; II Chron. 7:3; 29:29).

Formal "worship" in the place and ceremonies which God commanded is not acceptable to Him if it is without a repentant and submissive spirit, if it comes out of evil hearts satisfied in disobedience. Such pretense in attempting to flatter and deceive God is the height of presumption and irreverence. No wonder it is so very offensive to God, who says: "Your new moons and your appointed feasts my soul hateth; I am weary of bearing them. I have had enough of your sacrifices, bring no more vain oblations. I will not hear; your hands are full of blood" (Selected statements from Isa. 1:11-17;

cp. Amos 5:21-27; Josh. 7:6-15; Hosea 6:6).

*True Worship Is According To The Truth Of God's Nature and God's Revealed Will*

No matter what the spirit and intention, God will not be pleased to be worshiped with the use of images and idols. He positively forbade His people to make unto Him any image of anything in heaven or earth (Exod. 20:4). Images completely misrepresent Him and would lead the people away from the true worship and away from the true knowledge of God into the errors of polytheism and into the terrible depravity of sensuous indulgence and perversion that has always been connected with idol worship.

Worship is more than some ceremony or program that pleases us, that stirs, thrills, or moves our spirits to fervent feelings and longings—it is addressed to a God of truth, and must be according to the truth, not just a free expression of our feelings. It matters to God how we worship. "Obedience is better than sacrifice, and to hearken than the fat of rams. For rebellion is as the sin of witchcraft, and stubborness is as idolatry and teraphim" (I Sam. 15:22, 23). Perhaps Cain's sacrifice was more valuable to him than Abel's was, but since it was not according to God's revealed will (being not according to faith, Heb. 11:4) it was not accepted. The most gorgeous and costly and fervent display is not true worship if it rejects the will and word of God. The best way to exalt Him, to show love to Him and to reverence Him is to do what He asks. There can be no more spiritual worship than literal obedience performed with the whole heart and eager willingness. "If ye love me, ye will keep my commandments" (John 14:15).

Certainly the spirit of true worship is in that which glorifies God and not us. Any "religious" acts which cause us to boast or to be quite satisfied with ourselves are not truly worshipful. The wholehearted participation in the Lord's Supper is a most excellent act by which to express and to stimulate the spirit of true worship to the glory of Christ and humbling of ourselves. Every Christian should take advantage of each Lord's Day's opportunity to gather about the table.

For Further Study:

Campbell, Alexander, R. Richardson, Moses Lard and others. *The*

*Pioneers on Worship.* Kansas City: Old Paths Book Club, 1947. Essays calling for a restoration of worship of God as taught in the New Testament.

Torrey, R. A. *What the Bible Teaches.* London: James Nisbet & Co. Ltd., n.d. Pp. 471-478. Good outline summary of the Bible's teaching on worship.

Turnbull, Ralph G., ed. *Baker's Dictionary of Practical Theology.* Grand Rapids: Baker Book House, 1967. Pp. 364-372. Deals with the New Testament teaching concerning worship.

# 66

## THE CHRISTIAN WAY OF LIFE—LOVE FOR OTHERS
(Luke 10:25-37)

Jesus taught that love for God was the first and great commandment and the second commandment was love for one's neighbor. These fundamentals form the basis for all of God's laws (Matt. 22:34-40). During the third year of Jesus' ministry, Jesus used a lawyer's question as an opportunity to teach the lesson of love for others (Luke 10:25-37).

### *"This Do and Thou Shalt Live"*

A scholar of the Old Testament law asked Jesus, "What shall I do to inherit eternal life?" It was a large inclusive question well calculated by the official clique to test Jesus as a religious teacher.

Jesus replied with a question indicating that the answer was to be found in the word of God: "What is written in the law?" This does not mean that we should go back to the same law to find life after God has given us a new and better covenant (Heb. 8-10) and has "taken away the first that he may establish the second" (Heb. 10:9). The only way of life for any one is obedience to the will of God, the author of life, under the terms of whatever covenant God addresses to him—the Jew under the law, the Christian under Christ.

But to obtain life by doing the law one had to do all its requirements perfectly (Gal. 3:10; James 2:10), and no one, except Jesus, ever did accomplish the keeping of the law (Rom. 3:20; Gal. 2:16). Therefore, since the law could not save, through the weakness of the flesh, God, in grace, sent forth His Son that we might be saved through Him. The grace of God and the sacrifice of Christ blot out our sins on the condition of our faith and obedience toward Christ (Mark 16:16; John 3:36; Heb. 5:9; I Pet. 1:22). Under the new covenant of grace we are expected to fulfill the law of love as far as is possible. Love is even a test of our faith, without which we can not claim the promise of grace (I John 3:10-24; 4:7-21; Matt. 25:31-46). "If any man love not the Lord Jesus Christ, let him be anathema" (I Cor. 16:22). Our love to God and to man is not the cause of the salvation provided for us by Christ, but it is a required result. Love is the basis of all righteousness, and the essence of the "newness of life" in those who have been "made free from sin, and become servants of righteousness" (Rom. 6:4, 18-22). It is the spirit of those who have been born anew of "water and the Spirit" (John 3:5). Love must be in us if "it is not I that live, but Christ that liveth in me" (Gal. 2:20). Thanks be to God that we have the Savior and do not depend upon unbroken perfection of works of righteousness of our own for our salvation (I John 1:8, 9). Still, supreme love to Christ is the condition of Christian discipleship (Matt. 10:35-38; Luke 14:26).

### *"Thou Shalt Love"*

Can love be commanded? Some folks consider Jesus' command that we love everybody, including our enemies, impracticable or utterly impossible. But it is plain that the Lord does command it and expect it (John 13:34; 15:17; I Tim. 1:5; I John 3:23). The believer, therefore, must accept its possibility and practicability, and set out to do his Lord's will. Then what is the love that can be and is commanded?

R. A. Torrey described love:

> Love for another is a desire for and delight in their good. Love is not mere fondness for another or pleasure in their society. The character of another may be hateful to me and his society disagreeable, but still a real desire for his welfare is love.[1]

Torrey cites Matthew 5:43, 47; and I John 3:14, 16, 17 as the basis of his conclusion.

Jesus says, "Greater love hath no man than this, that a man lay down his life for his friends" (John 15:13). Surely, love is giving of ourselves in the interests of others, and the greatest love is the giving of our whole lives for the benefit of others.

Love belongs to the emotions and motives of the heart. It is not an act in itself, but the cause and spirit of many actions. Like all the virtues of the Christian life, it can not be obtained merely in the abstract and held in passivity. The reality of love is measured by the deeds it produces, or at least by the extent to which it struggles to express itself when its true desires are beyond the range of possibility. While the scripture speaks of love as an internal quality, motive, or attitude necessary to the true righteousness of even beneficial deeds (I Cor. 13:1-3), it usually recognizes love in its outward manifestations.

---

[1] R. A. Torrey, *What the Bible Teaches*. (London: James Nisbet, n.d.), p. 393.

Love is not theory but practice, whether toward God or men. Love is much misunderstood. Few words have ever been more abused than "love." It is used to name feelings and motives that range all the way from the genuine giving of self for the good of others to its very opposite, including some of the worst forms of selfishness and abuse of others. Still it is not what we don't know about love that should bother us as much as what we do know and don't practice.

### *How Love to God (or Christ) Is Manifested*

1. "This is the love of God, that we keep his commandments" (I John 5:3). "If a man love me, he will keep my word" (John 14:23; See also Exod. 20:6; II John 6; Deut. 10:12; John 14:15, 21; 15:10).
2. By hating evil (Ps. 97:10; Rom. 12:9) and by not loving the world (I John 2:15; James 4:4).
3. By loving God's children, our brethren (I John 4:20, 21), feeding His lambs and shepherding His sheep (John 21:15-17).
4. By worshiping Him with humility and gratitude (Luke 7:44-47).
5. By longing for His appearing and desiring to be with Him (II Tim. 4:8; Rev. 22:20; II Cor. 5:8; Phil. 1:23).

### *How Love to Man Is Manifested*

1. By doing no injury to others (Rom. 13:10), but good, even to enemies (Luke 6:27; Gal. 6:10).
2. By becoming a servant to others (Gal. 5:13; John 13:1-5; Phil. 2:4-7).
3. By seeking not our own, but our neighbor's, good (I Cor. 10:24); pleasing not ourselves (Rom. 15:1-3); bearing one another's burdens (Gal. 6:2).
4. By forgiving and comforting the penitent, restoring gently the fallen, encouraging the fainthearted, admonishing the disorderly, etc. (II Cor. 2:7, 8; Gal. 6:1; I Thess. 5:14; Eph. 4:2, 32).
5. By avoiding that by which a brother stumbles, and by doing things which make for peace and which edify (Rom. 14:15-21; I Cor. 8:1-13).
6. By giving of our means to help another's need (II Cor. 8:24; I John 3:17).
7. By preferring others in honor above ourselves (Rom. 12:10).
8. By praying for them (Matt. 5:44).
9. By rebuking them that sin in order to save them (Lev. 19:17; Prov. 27:5, 6; Eph. 5:11; Matt. 18:15-17; Titus 1:12, 13; Heb. 3:13).
10. By loving God and doing His commandments (I John 5:2).

11. By laying down our lives for others (I John 3:16; John 15:13).

12. "Love suffereth long, and is kind; love envieth not; love vaunteth not itself, is not puffed up, doth not behave itself unseemly, seeketh not its own, is not provoked, taketh not account of evil; rejoiceth not in unrighteousness, but rejoiceth with the truth; beareth all things, believeth all things, hopeth all things, endureth all things" (I Cor. 13:4-7).

The Jewish lawyer, in order to justify his own limited practice of love, sought to limit the scope of its application. Most of us are very much like him. Love patterned after the love of God must cross boundaries. Love regulated by opinion is merely love of our own opinion.

God, our teacher and example in love, does recognize some distinctions among men; He does not act the same toward all kinds of men; His wrath falls upon the sinner that will not forsake sin, but all God's acts are prompted by and carried out in love. He separated Himself from men because of sin (Gen. 3:23, 24), but He "commendeth his love toward us, in that, while we were yet sinners, Christ died for us" (Rom. 5:8). In like manner, we, too, can and must refuse to be joined to unbelievers and idolaters; we can and must have no fellowship with the unfruitful works of darkness (II Cor. 6:14-18; Eph. 5:11), but still sacrificial love must dominate our hearts continually toward those even from whom we must withhold our approval and partnership.

In commenting on Romans 13:8 David Lipscomb says:

> Love, then, beyond all doubt, is doing good to a person. When we do him good we love him, it matters not whether the good we do pleases or displeases him. Do to him what the divine law commands, and we do him good. It frequently will offend him. Be it so. Love demands that we should help him, even if he persecutes us for it. That was the love of Christ to man. He loved him, although His love excited the wrath and enmity of man.[2]

Love that is real and heartfelt will also strive in all ways honorable, though sacrificial, to avoid offending and displeasing (see I Cor. 10:31-33; 9:19-22). As in the case of the good Samaritan, love may be expensive. Christ's love for you and me was very expensive to Him!

Much has been written and said in this world concerning the

---

[2] David Lipscomb. *A Commentary on the New Testament Epistles: Romans.* (Nashville: Gospel Advocate Co., 1943). p. 238.

excellency of love—"The Greatest Thing in the World." The Bible itself is full of the subject with superlative emphasis on its pre-eminence.

For Further Study:

Hendricks, Howard. *Say It With Love.* Wheaton: Scripture Press, 1972. Empasizes love in our telling and living the gospel.

Lewis, C. S. *The Four Loves.* New York: Harcourt, Brace & Co., 1960. Lewis discusses with good insight four Greek words for love: romantic love, family love, friendship love, love that unselfishly acts in the other's best interest.

Lightfoot, Neil R. *The Parables of Jesus: Part I.* Austin, Texas: R. B. Sweet Co., 1963. Exposition of the parable of the good Samaritan.

Schaeffer, Francis. *The Mark of a Christian.* Downers Grove: Inter-Varsity Press, 1970. Strong appeal for the necessity of love in our relationship with others.

# 67

## EVERYONE'S RESPONSIBILITY TO RESPOND TO GOD'S MESSAGE (Outline of Luke 12)

Introduction

A. The time and circumstances.
   1. Many thousands gathered together, so that they trod on one another, to hear Jesus, or to accuse Him, or just to see the parade.
   2. Pharisees in vigorous opposition—Luke 11:53, 54 (jealousy, hatred, prejudice).
   3. Loyal friends of Jesus, no doubt: apostles, women from Galilee, Lazarus, Mary, Martha.
   4. Many who had heard the seventy, had seen miracles. See John 7, 8, 9, 10.
   5. Many, no doubt, just stood back and watched, avoided a decision, like the parents of the man born blind (John 9), like the rulers (John 12:42), secret disciples?

B. Relevance of the sermon.
   1. Imagine yourself in that mighty crowd. In which group would you belong? Bitter enemies? Loyal friends? Weak and silent believers? The undecided?
   2. The same groups exist today. Many are undecided for various reasons. Many really believe Jesus must be right, but will not make a definite and open decision to be all out for Christ and to lay hold of the kingdom of life and righteousness.

C. Goal of the sermon.
   1. In this sermon Jesus calls for men to (1) *Decide* who's right and what's important; (2) *Choose* the real aim and dependence of their lives; (3) *Live* in service and in expectation of His coming.
   2. In making this call, Jesus answers many of the reasons or excuses that hold men back. He offers understanding advice and divine help according to each man's need.

## I. RESPONSIBILITY TO DECIDE (Luke 12:1-12).

Between favor of men and favor of God.
Between fear of men and fear of God.

A. Beware of Phariseeism (12:1-3).

*Help for those hiding from reality and denying truth.*

1. Some think, "I stand well enough among men; that's the main thing." Others think, "I'm not such a bad sinner; I don't want to act like I had to forget everything else to get forgiveness by following Jesus."
2. Jesus' answer: failure of hypocrisy, and triumph of truth. All will out.

B. Fear God, not men (12:4, 5).

*Help for the fearful in face of opposition.*

1. Some think, "I'd be put out of the synagogue." "I'd lose business." "Rome will crush this kingdom before it gets started." "I'm afraid to be for Jesus."
2. Jesus' answer: men can't really hurt you much or for very long; but God's wrath destroys body and soul in hell.

C. Trust God and fear not (12:6, 7).

1. God's infinite knowledge and care, even for birds.
2. Don't be afraid that God will not care for you.

D. Acknowledge Jesus, and beware of rejecting God's Spirit (12:8-12).

*Assurance to those who confess Him.*

1. Promise to those who confess Jesus before men, and warning to those who deny.
2. Warning to avoid blasphemy by denying God's divine messengers.
   a. Blasphemy of Jesus now may be repented of and forgiven when more light comes.
   b. But blasphemy of the full and final revelation of the Spirit will not. Do not defame the latest and greatest manifestation of divine power, authority and grace—do not reject the last offer of

help (miss the last boat).

3. Promise of help by the Holy Spirit to meet persecution when they stand for Jesus.

II. RESPONSIBILITY TO CHOOSE (Luke 12:13-34). Subject of money brought up by one in the crowd but turned by Jesus as important part of His teaching to all. All must choose what they value most, what they rely upon and are most concerned about (Luke 12:13, 14).

A. Materialism is foolish—love of riches is vain (12:15-21).

Help for those greedy for gain.

1. Life does not consist of possessions (deceitfulness of riches vs. 15). (See I Timothy 6:6-11, 17-19; Mark 4:18, 19; 10:23-26, 29-31; Phil. 4:10-13).
2. Riches take wings and fly away, or must be left behind, not worth the candle (vs. 16-21).
3. Men satisfied with temporal wealth are likely to be very poor indeed before God (vs. 21).

B. Trust God and be free from anxiety for things (12:22-30)

Help for those worred about "necessities of life."

1. Realize that life is more than things.
2. Notice how God takes care of His creatures.
3. See that anxiety doesn't accomplish anything, can't add a step to your life.
4. Have faith and be free from slavery to material needs: God knows your needs.

C. Put first things first and place your treasure in heaven (12:31-34).

Assurance for those who put God's service first.

1. Seek the supreme value, God's kingdom; and all else will come with it.
2. God desires to favor and care for those who seek His will. He does not command us to do something and not enable us to do it.
3. Instead of holding to possessions, use them up in God's service, and gain treasure

in heaven. It's safer that way. Act according to faith.

4. Your heart will be where your treasure is.

III. RESPONSIBILITY TO LIVE (Luke 12:35-53). Through all of life, in every way, against all odds, to live according to the truth of God.

A. Be stedfast, always looking for the Lord (12: 35-40).

Challenge for wavering followers.

1. The Lord's coming is certain—but the time is uncertain (vs. 35, 36, 40).
2. He will honor and reward those who are ready at His coming (vs. 37, 38).
3. Example of householder and thief (vs. 39).

B. Be faithful in service (12:41-48). (Peter's question does not change the course of the sermon, vs. 41).

Charge to stewards tempted to be selfish.

1. Everyone who has received any commitment from the Lord must be a faithful steward—stewardship of life (vs. 42).
2. Rewards await the faithful stewards (vs. 43, 44. See Luke 17:7-10; 19:17, 18).
3. Punishment is sure for the unfaithful servants (vs. 45, 46).
4. Accountability varies, and judgment will be according to responsibility (vs. 47, 48).
   a. Even the ignorant will suffer for not doing God's will.
   b. To whom much is given, of him more will be required.

C. Be standing for Jesus, uncompromising and unmoved by opposition (12:49-53).

Call to arms for any who love peace more than righteousness.

1. Christ is a burning issue; His presence demands division over right and wrong (vs. 49).
2. Christ must face the issue to the point of complete submergence of self in suffering for righteousness and God's gracious purpose: He cannot turn aside, is pressed to that end (vs. 50).

3. Believers must be willing to "take sides" over Him, and suffer division from family or friends. Christ is the issue over which the world is split (vs. 51-53).

Conclusion: APPEAL AND DEMAND FOR THE DECISION WHICH WILL LEAD TO THE CHOICE AND LIFE OF FAITH (12:54-59).

A. You *can* decide! You can tell the signs of the weather; then you can tell the evidence of Christ's authority and truth (vs. 54-56).
B. Why not judge for yourselves what is right?
C. You *must* decide! Settle with God now, before you are dragged before His judgment seat, convicted, and sentenced where you can never get out! Make use of this day of opportunity for a peaceful and gracious settlement of your unpayable debt to God. You cannot be excused because people have differences of thinking over religion, Christ, and the kingdom; you must decide who is right and then follow with action.

Read the challenge in Joshua 24 and in I Kings 18.

For Further Study:

Geldenhuys, Norval. *New International Commentary: The Gospel of Luke.* Grand Rapids: Wm. B. Eerdmans, 1951. Pp. 348-369. Exposition of Luke 12.

Plummer, Alfred. *International Critical Commentary: The Gospel According to St. Luke,* 5th ed. Edinburgh: T. & T. Clark, 1922. Pp. 316-339. Scholarly comment on Luke 12.

# 68

## THE COST OF DISCIPLESHIP

The price we must pay to be disciples is not the cost of our redemption. What it has cost to prepare the gospel feast can not be calculated. To bring Christianity and its manifold treasures to us has cost an unparalleled array of rare materials and sacrificial services, such as the time, life, services, and suffering of chosen men who prepared the way for Christ; and even greater number of lives (beginning with the apostles) who have labored and suffered, spending and being spent that the message of Christ might be carried even to us. However, the real price of our salvation has been paid by God and Christ —the Christ who "emptied himself" (Phil. 2:7), "humbled himself" (Phil. 2:8), "became poor" (II Cor. 8:9), "suffered" (Heb. 2:18) and "bore our sins in his own body" (I Pet. 2:24). By these the kingdom has been prepared and is offered to us. The things required of us are merely terms of individual participation.

### *The Price Is High*

To follow Christ and share in His salvation we must surrender all to Him. The price is all that any man can pay. There is no standard amount that any man could possibly render and still have something left over to call his own. The young ruler had kept the commandments as he understood them, and appeared to men to be godly enough. But Jesus knew where to test him and reveal whether he exalted God above every other thing. In spite of all the good points in his favor (and he had many), one thing caused him to turn away in sorrow. In effect, he had another god. It is not wrong for a man to have money, but the money must not have the man. It must be subject to the command of Christ. Jesus does not command us all to put away all money immediately, but He warns us all that we "cannot serve both God and mammon" (Luke 16:13). He actually requires of all what He required of the ruler (Luke 14:33)—to renounce all that we have. The Lord seemed to realize that money, more than any other thing, was likely to rule men and keep them from serving God wholly. (See I Tim. 6:9, 10, 17-19; Matt. 6:19-34; Eph. 5:5.) But any other thing that holds us in its grip and does not yield to Christ is just as deadly. Your heart's idol may be a small one, legal and respectable, but if it causes you to disobey Christ, it is quite as fatal as the greatest sin on earth.

"How hard it is for them that trust in riches to enter into the kingdom of God!" (Mark 10:24). The Lord deemed it necessary to warn us thus. He knew the reality of the danger. Most of us refuse to see it or believe it. A vast number of unfaithful preachers "having itching ears" (and palms) have tried to explain away the force of these plain Bible statements. The idleness, self-pleasing and confidence in economic security that go with a "high American standard of living" although they become general and are not called riches, still have all the dangers that Jesus ascribed to riches. What could great wealth do for a man in Jesus' day that ordinary "comfortable means" can not do for one today, materially and spiritually? What if Jesus should put to the test today all the seekers after eternal life? How many church members today would readily give up all their earthly possessions at His command? He does require us to put all that we are and have into His service. Are we doing it? What doth it profit a man (or a nation of men) to gain the world's highest standard of living and lose his own soul? (Matt. 16:26).

No other discipleship on earth is so exacting as Christian discipleship. To accept Christ is (1) to renounce all other masters and (2) to give ourselves wholly to His service. To have God we must have no other gods. To have righteousness we must resign sin. To enthrone Christ we must renounce every other rule, including self-rule. "If any man cometh after me, and hateth not his own father, and mother, and wife, and children, and brethren, and sisters, yea, and his own life also, he cannot be my disciple" (Luke 14:26).

### *Self-denial*

"Then said Jesus unto his disciples, If any man would come after me, let him deny himself, and take up his cross, and follow me" (Matt. 16:24). To deny ourselves, that is the crux of the matter. We are willing to deny some things to ourselves, but then we seek to compensate ourselves by some other indulgence and call the whole thing "self-denial." The world, the flesh and the devil constantly urge us, "Assert yourself," "Suit yourself," "Avenge yourself," "Exalt yourself." Self-denial is such a continuous business it can not be accomplished once for all and forgotten about. In the motivation of every act throughout life there is the choice between our will and God's will. We must set our wills to do only God's will until, as Paul says, "It is no more I that live, but Christ that liveth in me" (Gal. 2:20). It is the saddest rejection of Christ for any one to say, "My life is mine and I'll live it to suit myself." "Ye are not your own; for ye were bought with a price" (I Cor. 6:19, 20). We just do not realize what a mess we make of things when we do as we please. We bring on sin and death and eternal destruction, besides all the miseries due to sin upon this earth. God would heal our lives, tune them in harmony, set them in beautiful order, make them fruitful and transform us into glorious children of His, to wonder at His love forever; but we must let Him have His way with us.

Such a complete surrender may seem hard to us, but it is no more than the sovereign Son of God has done first. Jesus submitted to the Father's will perfectly in all things, setting us an example and showing the wisdom and triumph of surrender to the love and righteousness of God. His example helps show His meaning in this text. He does not ask us merely to empty our lives, but to fill them with things divine, fruitful and glorious. A person might renounce all kings of idols, eschew wealth, "hate" his family ties and "his own life also," and yet not be a Christian. He must take up the cross and follow Jesus. Christianity can never be merely in things we do not do, but must be in a positive life of active holiness.

### *Cross-bearing*

We are much inclined to overemphasize the wealth that Jesus asked the young ruler to abandon, and we forget the life of service that Jesus aksed him to adopt (Matt. 19:16-22). Likewise, we probably at all times think too much of the self we are required to deny and the way we must forsake, and think not enough of the cross we are to take and of the following of Jesus.

What did the cross mean? To Jesus it meant condescension, humiliation, reproach, suffering and death. We should be willing that it mean all that to us. But Jesus did not mean that our cross should be merely extraordinary sorrows or misfortunes; the cross is for every disciple. "Whosoever does not bear his cross and come after me, cannot be my disciple" (Luke 14:27). Jesus' cross was the burden of the world. In bearing it He spent Himself completely for the salvation of others. He gives to every one of us the challenging call to take upon ourselves real concern and responsibility for the needs of others, especially, their salvation. The cross constrained and straitened His whole life (Luke 12:50; Matt. 20:28; John 12:27). The true disciple of Jesus has the same burden upon his soul (Rom. 9:1-3; 10:1; I Cor. 9:22). He "will most gladly spend and be spent for your souls" (II Cor. 12:15). We neither bear the cross nor follow Jesus if we do not feel the need of lost men and use ourselves up, a living sacrifice, for their salvation. The great commission definitely and plainly assigns to us the cross we are all to bear.

*The Price Is Low*

The price is low. Anybody can pay it! It must be low in price if all or any can obtain salvation. God paid the cost. He asks of us what little (very little) we have. It is well said: "It does not take a great man to be a Christian, but it does take all there is of him." The Lord gives us the new and divine and eternal life; He merely asks us to turn in the old wreck.

The price is low compared to what we gain as disciples of Jesus. Consider some of the blessings and values of being a Christian. We escape our condemnation (Rom. 8:1); we have peace that passeth understanding (John 14:27; Rom. 5:1; Phil 4:7); we have an inheritance in the family of God as sons (Rom. 8:17; I Pet. 1:4); we have a Father in heaven who loves us, (Phil. 4:19), who hears our prayers (I Pet. 3:12), who does not forget our labor (Heb. 6:10), who chastens (Heb. 12:5, 6); we have a hope that is sure and steadfast (Heb. 6:19), a new and worth-while purpose in life (Phil. 1:21), a new and satisfying view of death (Phil. 1:21, 23). Being a Christian brings us all the joys of that eternal home that Christ has gone to prepare (John 14:3; Rev. 21 and 22). These are values no one can afford to miss. There is no other way or place to obtain them. The yoke of Jesus is not a burden, but a bargain. Is it a sacrifice to invest a nickel in an oil well?

The price of following Jesus is certainly low compared with the cost of not following Jesus. When we refuse to follow Jesus we not only lose all of the above-named blessings, but we incur the wrath of God (John 3:36), exclude our names from the book of life and must look forward to the lake of fire (Rev. 20:15). "What doth it profit a man to gain the whole world, and forfeit his life?" (Mark 8:36).

We don't actually pay the price. The lord returns many times what He asks of us (Matt. 19:29). He knows our needs and grants us the use of much of what we devote to Him. "It is the Father's good pleasure to give you the kingdom" (Luke 12:32). He makes a special blessing of every sacrifice we are called to make. "The toils of the road will seem nothing when we come to the end of the way! Well, not exactly; for it is likely that they will seem like a very blessed part of the gift.

For Further Study:

Bonhoeffer, Dietrich. *The Cost of Discipleship.* New York: Macmillan, 1963. Ringing challenge to be totally committed to Christ regardless of the cost. Critical of 'cheap grace'—wanting salvation without surrender to Christ.

Bruce, A. B. *The Training of the Twelve,* 3rd ed. New York: Harper & Brothers, n.d. Pp. 262-271. Deals with the account of the rich young ruler under the theme of the rewards of self-sacrifice in the kingdom.

# 69

## MARRIAGE, DIVORCE, AND REMARRIAGE

Introduction: This is intended to be a brief summary of what is revealed of God's will on this much disputed subject. An effort is made to present every pertinent passage of scripture and to bring to consideration every permissible interpretation. But space is not given to refute or to support every interpretation.

I. Marriage

A. Marriage Was Instituted and Blessed by God.
It was a part of God's design in the creation of man, and is central or basic in His will for human society (Gen. 1:27, 28; 2:18-25). Marriage is honorable for all, or is to be kept honorable by all (Heb. 13:4). To forbid marriage is a doctrine of demons or conscienceless men (I Tim. 4:1-3).

B. The Positive Rule of Marriage for Life.
"Leave father and mother and cleave unto his wife" (Gen. 2:24). Jesus quoted Genesis 2:24 and added, "What God hath joined together, let no man put asunder" (Matt. 19:5, 6; Mark 10:6-9). A wife is bound by law to her husband while he lives (Rom. 7:1-3). A wife is bound for so long time as her husband lives (I Cor. 7:39).

C. Remarriage Permitted After Death of a Spouse.
"If the husband be dead, she is free to be married to whom she will; only in the Lord" (I Cor. 7:39, cp. Rom. 7:3). Paul recommends marriage for younger widows (I Tim. 5:14).

II. Adultery

A. Prohibition of Adultery.
"Thou shalt not commit adultery" (Exod. 20:14). Adultery comes from the heart and defiles the man (Mark 7:21). An adulterer cannot enter the kingdom, but can be justified (I Cor. 6:9-11). "Fornicators and adulterers God will judge" (Heb. 13:4). No fornicator . . . hath any inheritance in the kingdom of Christ" (Eph. 5:3-5). Adultery is frequently included in lists of sins in the New Testament (Gal. 5:19-21; I Thess. 4:3-8). The word translated "fornication" includes adultery and is not distinct from it. It is used in I Thessalonians 4:3-8 apparently of married persons, and seems to include adultery in I Corinthians

6:18; Colossians 3:5; Ephesians 5:3-5; Galatians 5:19; and Revelation 21:8.

B. In the Old Testament Adulterers Were to be Put to Death. "And the man that committeth adultery with another man's wife, even he that committeth adultery with his neighbor's wife, the adulterer and the adulteresss shall surely be put to death" (Lev. 20:10; cp. 11-21; Deut. 22:21-24). Adultery is a very serious matter. How can one who believes God's word take it lightly? It nullifies God's plan for the very important relations and responsibilities of the family unit. It defies His will and disrupts lives. It takes what God made holy and makes it common and profane. It degrades the soul of a being made in the image of God. What was made to be enobling and a means of spiritual strength is diverted to the practice of self-gratification. It is a crime against individual persons, against society, and against the wise will of God.

III. Divorce

A. Teaching Against Divorce.

While divorce was permitted in the Mosaic law, Jesus said that it was only because of the hardness of men's hearts and was not God's will even in the Old Testament society (Matt. 19:8). Deuteronomy 24:1-4 was given for the protection of the woman who was cast out, and to prohibit wife-swapping back and forth. In this text the first three verses furnish a protasis (condition) for the fourth verse, which is the law under these conditions. (This is evident in these translations: Revised Standard Version; New American Standard Bible; New English Bible; Modern Language Bible; An American Translation; New American Bible; and Jerusalem Bible.) The passage implies that men will put away their wives, but it does not so much give permission to put one away as it prohibits taking one back who has been married to anyone else. God says, "I hate divorce" (Mal. 2:16). Some would point out that the context emphasizes the treachery of Israelites putting away their wives.

B. Dealing with the Divorced.

1. Avoid disputes about words to no profit, questionings and strife (II Tim. 2:14-26; I Tim. 1:5-11; 6:3-5; Titus 3:9, 10).
2. Avoid being unnecessarily judgmental (Matt. 7:1-5; Luke 6:37-42; Rom. 12:16-21; 14:10-13; James 2:1-13; I Cor. 5:7-13), for we are sent to serve people more than we are to sort

them for the Lord.

3. Continue studying God's word to apply it with true spiritual understanding, and avoid accepting a dogmatic and legalistic church position or traditional view without discerning God's will. Try not to "go beyond what is written" (I Cor. 4:6).
   a. Always realize and teach that:
      (1) God does not want divorce.
      (2) That every divorce represents some spiritual failure.
      (3) That divorce and remarriage is not unforgivable.
      (4) That these as well as other evils can be overcome, even prevented if we give God's word its place in our hearts.
   b. Too often church people are studying only superficially, if at all, or trying to apply old opinions or unscriptural phrases, to determine how to judge divorced people, rather than how to save them and serve them.
4. We must be more concerned to succeed in helping them than we are to find excuses for our failure or for finding someone to blame for it (cp. Matt. 17:14-20; Mark 9:24-29). It should not be our aim to defend ourselves or make a name for ourselves in the minds of the unbelievers and the leaders of our society.
5. We must *communicate* to all God's grace and love, His truth, authority and righteousness, His reality and trustworthiness.
   a. Not merely discourage, but encourage them.
   b. No only with words, but with what we are and do. Let Christ live in us and work through us.
   c. Not to shirk, but to fulfill our responsibility to Christ.
   d. Not to excuse the sin, but to cure and heal the sinners.
   e. The cross shows that sinners are not worthless (Rom. 5:8); the cross of Christ draws men to Him (John 12:32); if we bear the cross we will draw more people, too.
6. We must fulfill our calling as God's new creatures and ministers of reconciliation, knowing no one from a merely human point of view (II Cor. 5:11—6:1). Try our best to represent Christ and all the transforming power of His love and truth.

IV. Adultery and Divorce

A. Scriptural Statements.

1. General — "And he said unto them, Whosoever shall put away his wife, and marry another, committeth adultery against her: and if she herself shall put away her husband, and marry another, she committeth adultery" (Mark 10:11, 12). "Every one that putteth away his wife, and marrieth another, committeth adultery: and he that marrieth one that is put away from a husband committeth adultery" (Luke 16:18).
2. Exception — "but I say unto you, that every one that putteth away his wife, saving for the cause of fornication, maketh her an adulteress: and whosoever shall marry her when she is put away committeth adultery" (Matt. 5:32). "And I say unto you, Whosoever shall put away his wife, except for fornication, and shall marry another, committeth adultery: and he that marrieth her when she is put away committeth adultery" (Matt. 19:9).

B. Exception Interpreted. Various views of this exception and of conclusions drawn from it.

1. Some think this applied only to Jews under the law, and it is not to be considered for Christians at all. The law decreed death for adultery, so of course a man could put away an adulterous wife and remarry because she would be executed. If he put away any other (an innocent wife) he would be guilty of adultery and cause anyone who married her to commit adultery.
2. Some think this term fornication applied only to sex before marriage, and she could be put away because the marriage was not a genuine one. Commentaries and lexicons generally agree that fornication in these passages includes and probably specifies the sin of adultery.
3. Does the fornication refer to any illicit sex, homosexuality, etc.?
4. Does the sexual unchastity of a mate make the other obligated to divorce, or is it better to forgive and to restore the sinful mate?
   a. Some think that an adulterer becomes one flesh with even a harlot, so that the original wife must divorce him or she will be living in a "polygamous union" (I Cor. 6:16).

b. Some think that since the law decreed death for adulterers that they are unforgivable. But didn't Jesus know that the Samaritan woman at the well was unforgivable (if that be so)? See John 4:10—what would Jesus give her, if she knew who He was? Does John 6:37 really mean to leave out as exceptions at least 1/10th of the people because of divorce or adultery, when Jesus said, "Him that cometh unto me I will in no wise cast out"? Why did Jesus say, "harlots go into the kingdom" (Matt. 21:31)? Why did Paul write (I Cor. 6:9-11) that adulterers were washed and justified and sanctified? Compare Ephesians 2:1-9 and 4:17-19.

c. Divorce on the ground of fornication may be permitted, but it is nowhere commanded or even recommended.

5. Does this exception contradict Paul's statement "a wife is bound to her husband as long as she lives" (Rom. 7:2; I Cor. 7:2; I Cor. 7:39)? Does it contradict Mark 10:6-12?
   a. Jesus' statements in both Matthew 5:32 and 19:9 are complete, clear and specific. There is no manuscript evidence to support any doubt about their being an original part of the book of Matthew.
   b. A simple statement of a general truth cannot contradict limitations on or exceptions to that truth when they are given on equal authority elsewhere.
   c. Paul's purpose in Romans was not to teach all about divorce and remarriage, but to illustrate the fact that Christians have been discharged from the law to be joined to Christ. In Corinthians also he states the general rule without having any reason to deal with a possible exception under bad or abnormal conditions.
6. How does one who divorces a wife, not for the cause of adultery, make her an adulteress (Matt. 5:32)?
   a. He gives her his permission to be joined to another, and it will seem to the woman that she has a legal right to marry; also it may become a necessity to find a way of living.
   b. Some think this only means that she will be made to bear the stigma of an adulteress, or appear to be an adulteress.

V. Is Remarriage Adultery?

A. Divorce under the law explicitly gave permission to marry someone else (Deut. 24:1-3). If no one has a right to remarry, why did Jesus state an exception to the rule that one who puts away a wife and marries another commits adultery? If divorce and remarriage, except for the cause of fornication, constitutes adultery, then divorce and remarriage for that cause does not amount to adultery.

B. Then why does Jesus say that anyone marrying her that is put away commits adultery? Is there an exception *implied* in this statement to conform to the exception *stated* in the preceding statement? Does this mean that only the sexually faithful spouse who puts away an unfaithful one may marry another? Some think that if the marriage bond is really broken for one of the pair it can no longer be binding upon the other, but of course the guilty one has already committed adultery to be forgiven or punished. Since the Jews in Jesus' day did not have the power under Roman rule to execute the death penalty upon adulterers, divorce was the only way of escape for innocent parties to intolerable marriages to immoral mates. Did Jesus give His consent to this kind of statement? If the person who puts away a faithful spouse remarries, then the innocent partner has no chance of reconstructing that marriage and can consider the divorce valid in God's sight, and hence can remarry. One whose companion has given himself (or herself) over to sexual immorality can divorce that person and marry another without being guilty of adultery. If this is not true, then the only exception to remarriage being adultery is when the unfaithful mate is executed for adultery.

C. Summary of Possible Conclusions:

1. All marriages of divorced persons are adulterous.
2. All marriages after a divorce where fornication was not the cause of the divorce are adulterous.
3. An innocent spouse who has been put away not for fornication may not marry just because he or she is put away; but if the mate who got the divorce marries, then the divorce may be considered valid in God's sight because there is no chance of that marriage being reconstructed.
4. If a marriage has been dissolved, even the one who committed adultery may repent and be forgiven, and later marry again. (If this be so, how then does anyone who marries a divorced person commit adultery?) It may be

granted that neither party is married any longer after a divorce for fornication has been secured; but it is not necessarily true that any unmarried person has an automatic right to marry.

D. Is divorce merely a legal separation under human law for protection of property and personal freedom or preservation of peace?
   1. The Old Testament spoke of divorce as permitting remarriage. The Jews seem to have always had that concept, and asked Jesus with that in mind. There is no evidence that any ancient society had a practice of legal separation from bed and board without the right of remarriage.
   2. If that is all Jesus intended divorce to mean, it would be unlikely that He would state only one cause for which it would be permitted. I Corinthians 7:11 seems to allow a Christian wife to depart from her husband but to remain unmarried or else be reconciled to her husband.

E. Does I Corinthians 7:27 say that a divorced person may marry without sinning? The person who was "loosed from a wife" might have been loosed by the death of the wife? It seems possible that Paul may have used the perfect passive of the verb to refer to a state of singleness without referring to any past action by which they became loosed. Therefore, it is a doubtful text to prove that one divorced may marry innocently.

F. Does I Corinthians 7:15 say that a marriage is dissolved if a non-Christian (unbelieving) husband is not willing to live with his Christian wife? If the non-believer departs, how is the Christian brother or sister "not in bondage in such cases"? Does the bondage here refer to the marriage contract? Or does it refer to a bondage in which a Christian would have to yield to any demands by the pagan mate in order to get him or her to live with the Christian and not depart?
   1. Some say that Paul uses the same word "bound" in reference to the marriage contract and its responsibility in Romans 7:2 and I Corinthians 7:39. But there is some difference between being "bound" as by a contract and being in bondage of slavery to a manner of life? Paul does not use the same word in Greek in both of these expressions. The fact is that in I Corinthians 7:15 he used a verb which means to be enslaved. It could refer to the total bondage

of a life that could not separate from the unbeliever. It does mean at least that much. It is doubtful whether it was intended to mean that the Christian is set free to be remarried to anyone else.

2. Many believe that "not in bondage" was intended to include dissolution of the marriage obligation in every sense. If the unbeliever who departs subsequently commits adultery or marries someone else, many would conclude that the believer's obligation to the marriage was certainly broken.

G. Did the apostles ever teach anything about divorce and remarriage? What did they do about people who wanted to become Christians after they had divorced and remarried not according to God's law? If the apostles required everyone who was not still married to their first spouse to break up the marriage they had and live without marriage, does it seem reasonable that no mention is ever made of such drastic teaching?

1. Some think that non-Christians were not subject to any of Christ's teaching for they could not be responsible to any law they had not been taught. Then it is inferred that at baptism their old sins and marriage bonds are blotted out; they are simply to live faithfully in the marriage in which they are involved when they become Christians. Others are afraid that this means that the non-Christians had no sin in any of his actions that were against Christ's teaching, which He did not know.

3. When a pagan accepts Christ as Lord, does he not accept Christ's standards in judgment over his past life as well as for direction of his present actions? Thus he repents and is forgiven, and serves under the rule of Christ as well as he can in the state in which he was called. He does not try to escape the responsibility for his former sins; neither can he change them. Our problem arises from the assumption that God could not forgive him and let him live with a second wife.

4. Is it God's purpose to punish all who married contrary to His law by making them remain unmarried all their lives? Or is it His purpose to make new creatures who will live according to His will in family relationships?

5. It is true that one should not plan to profit by sin. A Christian should not lust after a different woman and plan to commit adultery by divorce and remarriage then expect to

repent and be forgiven and be able to keep the second for which he lusted. But how do we know that no one can repent of a wrong marriage without breaking it up? The Bible does not use the phrase "living in adultery." Neither does it say that a man who has divorced and remarried "has two living wives." Do we distort our thinking by using expressions that beg the question? In I Corinthians 6:9-11 Paul mentions adultery along with other sins which were forgiven. In Corinth there were probably many who had been involved in divorces and remarriages. Paul can see them as former adulterers, but ones who are now cleansed and forgiven. There is no indication that they had separated from all illegal partners. For a Christian to marry an unbeliever is a sin by New Testament standards; yet those who are married to unbelievers are taught to continue faithful to their marriages where the unbeliever is willing. One who tries to apply an Old Testament example (see Ezra 10:3) might conclude that a Christian must put away the unbelieving spouse. But Paul says not to (I Cor. 7:12, 13). John the Baptist did tell Herod that it was not lawful for him to have his brother's wife. This close relationship was expressly forbidden in Leviticus 20:21.

6. Does the rule of I Corinthians 7:24 state a principle broad enough to apply to a second marriage?
7. Do the instructions of I Corinthians 7:2-9 not apply at all to persons who have been divorced?
8. If the first marriage cannot be restored (see Deut. 24:4) what command of God is served by sinning against the second wife or husband? The remarried husband is not bound to his first wife, if adultery is just cause for breaking up the marriage (Matt. 19:9). If the first marriage was not broken up by fornication before, then it was after the second marriage. And God forbids it to be reformed after a second marriage (Deut. 24:4).
9. Was the sin of adultery in breaking the vows and the union of the first marriage, or is it adultery to live faithfully with a second partner after one has a real change of heart? Must the sinful attitudes and actions that destroyed the marriage be continued? Or if their damage cannot be fully repaired, can they be repented of and forsaken in the context of a marriage of forgiven sinners?

10. Does forgiveness of the sin of divorce and remarriage become the same thing as approval of adultery, as if it were no sin at all? Does the church which welcomes repentant thieves to forgiveness admit that thieves did no wrong? Does a man who forms a legal, business partnership for bad motives have to break his contract, or can he change his sinful purposes and live up to his contract in a righteous way?

H. What shall we do in actual practice of marrying people?
   1. Shall we act as an agent of state law without reference to morality of the marriges performed?
   2. Shall we refuse to marry any divorced persons?
   3. Shall we marry only the "innocent party" of a broken marriage?
   4. Shall we teach the words of the Lord to each couple and lay upon them the responsibility to decide whether their marriage is in obedience to God?

VI. Concluding Observations

1. Let us beware of striving to be strict in interpreting and applying the words of scripture in order that we may feel merit in holding a more perfect legal standard. God may want to teach a kind of character in men more than a strict set of limitations on the legal status of a marriage.
2. Let us beware also of looking for loopholes to allow a lenient application of God's statements. Our leniency may be used to help men feel relieved of obligations to do what God wants.
3. Let us leave judging to God, as far as possible. When we try to decide exactly how men should be judged, we need to ask questions why we want to settle the matter. Did God intentionally leave His word so that it was not easily settled and so that we hesitate to judge others? Teach God's will against divorce; but we may not be sure how God will judge those who who have been guilty.
4. Preach God's mercy, repentance as needed, and forgiveness as available.
5. Expect the fruit of repentance in the continued seeking of God's will and in obedience to it as we can determine it. But beware of going beyond what is written in decreeing harsh terms as necessary fruit of repentance when God has not given a hint of such application in the word.

6. If divorced and remarried persons can become accepted and active members of the church, does that make the church teach that there is nothing really bad about divorce and remarriage? Does it need to? Let's not let it.
7. Let us make far greater efforts to teach so that Christians will avoid divorce.

For Further Study:

Duty, Guy. *Divorce and Remarriage.* Minneapolis: Bethany Fellowship, Inc., 1967. Balanced study on the interpretation and application of the relevant Biblical texts.

Meredith, Maurice. *The Divorce Question.* Bound together with Alva Hovey's *The Scriptural Law of Divorce.* Rosemead, Cal.: Old Paths Book Club, n.d. Both very fine works but are now out of print.

Schubert, Joe D. *Marriage, Divorce, and Purity.* Abilene: Biblical Research Press, 1966. A study guide on the Bible's teaching in regard to the whole area of marriage, divorce and sexual purity.

Stott, J. R. W. *Divorce.* Downers Grove: InterVarsity Press, 1971. Brief booklet which carefully deals with the problems in interpreting the texts on divorce.

# 70

# THE PRACTICE OF NEIGHBORLINESS

What does God expect of us concerning our treatment of the stranger, the poor, the homeless, and the helpless? The total teaching of the Old Testament on this subject is not different in principle from the teaching of the New Testament. Although some difference between the Testaments may be noted in matters of detail or emphasis, the principle of the Golden Rule plainly underlies both. The motives inculcated in the Old Testament are as high and as closely related to the character of God as are those in the New Testament. Jesus said the weightiest obligations under the law included mercy along with just dealing and faith toward God (Matt. 23:23).

### *Oppression Prohibited*

It seems that human nature is inclined to hold an unfavorable attitude toward people who are foreign to us, or who by any marked difference are distinguished from us, and who do not come within our circle of fellowship. "From the mythical gentlemen who excused himself for not saving a drowning man because he had not been introduced to him, to the Yorkshire native, who, seeing a strange face in his hamlet, cried, 'Let's heave a brick at him!' how common it is for people to limit their kindness to persons of their acquaintance!" It is a universal and persistent problem how to overcome the ill will and prejudice that men of one class hold toward men of another class or race. How common it is to despise and look down upon foreigners, and even to lay aside honesty and mercy in dealing with them! Immigrant laborers, especially if transient, are often considered as hardly human. Men of weak scruples will take advantage of a stranger which they would not take of an acquaintance. "Taking in" strangers has in modern slang, and in too much modern practice, a meaning quite contrary to Christian hospitality.

As we might expect, the law of God was against all oppression, mistreatment, and fraud, whether to strangers or any one else. It went beyond this, and commanded the Israelites not to glean their fields, not to strip their olive trees clean, etc., but to leave some of the fruits of the earth for the poor and needy to gather. (Read Exod. 22:21-23; Deut. 24:14, 15, 17-22.)

In several connections the Lord ordered them to have one law for both the native Israelites and the sojourner among them (Lev. 24:22;

Num. 15:15, 16, 29) with no respect of persons (Deut. 1:17; 10:17; etc.). Yet they were permitted to charge interest to foreigners and not to their own brethren (Deut. 23:19, 20).

### *Kindness and Service Commanded*

Israel was commanded not only to do no wrong to a stranger, but also to "love him as thyself" (Lev. 19:33, 34; Deut. 10:17-19). Strangers were to share in the benevolent giving of Israel—a special tithe of the increase every third year went to strangers, widows, orphans, and Levites (Deut. 26:12, 13). Every seventh year they were not to farm their land, but whatever grew of itself was for servants, strangers, and beasts (Lev. 25:3-7). Further extensive hospitality and generosity were commanded in Leviticus 25:35-38 and Isaiah 58:6, 7.

Christianity is more than mere neighborliness, or even brotherly kindness and social welfare but it certainly includes unselfish service to others. Many who promote utopian social and economic schemes have no higher object than a high physical standard of living. In Christianity the prime object is righteousness in the heart through reconciliation with God. In Christ "we preach not ourselves, but Christ Jesus as Lord, and ourselves as your servants for Jesus' sake" (II Cor. 4:5).

Jesus, the Lord, commands and exemplifies service. He "came not to be ministered unto, but to minister" and "went about doing good." He said, "Whosoever would be first among you shall be your servant" (Matt. 20:25-28). Confucius said men should not do to others what they would not want others to do to them. But Christ set us to active service with His rule: "All things therefore whatsoever ye would that men should do unto you, even so do ye also unto them" (Matt. 7:12). With general rules that are truly amazing He boldly outlines a life of overflowing goodness that we might not make for ourselves a place to stop in selfishness. He tells us to give to the man who has robbed us, to go willingly a second mile after we have been forced to go one, to lend without hope of receiving again, to do good to enemies, and to show kindness to all men. He assigns to us the most menial tasks of benefit to others: "Ye also ought to wash one another's feet" (John 13:14).

Too often we forget that our Christian life must be one of active service as well as worship and separation from the practices of sin. We are tempted to remain aloof from the needy world and pride ourselves on our separation when He has sent us to do a work for Him. The only way we can serve Him is to serve men, for Jesus does not need us to serve Him directly and immediately. He says, "Lovest thou me? . . . Feed my sheep" (John 21:15-17). He has placed us in His creation to do good to His wayward and lost creatures—His weak, starving, and homeless ones—just as a ranch owner has men who serve him by looking after his flocks and herds. Hence, Jesus said, "Inasmuch as ye have done it unto one of these my brethren, even these least, ye have done it unto me" (Matt. 25:40). It is a very dangerous temptation for us to be so much concerned about orthodoxy of opinion, so satisfied with ourselves for forsaking certain popular evils, and so interested in forms of worship, that we never get ourselves busy in His needy world to do the things that He has commanded us to do there. We can be condemned as much for the good we do not do as for the evil we do (James 4:17; 1:22-27; Matt. 25:41-45).

### *Hospitality*

The Greek word translated "hospitality" in the New Testament is a compound of simple words meaning "love for strangers." Christians are commanded to provide for their own household (I Tim. 5:8), to do good especially to the household of the faith (Gal. 6:10), to love their brethren fervently (I Pet. 4:8), "communicating unto the necessities of the saints" with tender affection one toward another (Rom. 12:10-13). But in immediate connection with these instructions there is added the command to "forget not to show love to strangers" (Heb. 13:2), to be "given to hospitality" (Rom. 12:13), to do good to all men. Brotherliness must not become exclusiveness. Gaius is commended for charity to both brethren and strangers (III John 5, 6). A deserving Christian character is marked by "hospitality to strangers" (I Tim. 5:10). Elders must be lovers of hospitality (I Tim. 3:2; Titus 1:8).

Christian hospitality should be performed not grudgingly, not merely as an obligation, but for the love of it. There is usually some one in each congregation who has grown in this grace and is ready to share and enjoy serving unselfishly. With what tender affection we remember them! But it has been so easy for many, many others to excuse themselves for selfishness and indifference that they do not recognize this duty or its rich rewards. Those who have the most are commonly the least ready to share it with others—the truly poor are generally the most hospitable, and the truly poor are those whom Jesus calls "blessed" in Matthew 5:3—"the poor in spirit."

### *Judgment: Faith and Works*

All men have sinned and deserve condemnation (Rom. 3:20-23; 6:23). They can be saved only through the grace of Jesus Christ, which is granted to them that believe. But the judgment of our faith will be by our works (James 2:14-26). Our faith in the mercy of God must work in us appropriate deeds, or it is mere sham. The New Testament constantly speaks of salvation according to grace through faith, but of judgment according to works. It makes plain that no man can blot out his own sins by good works alone. It is just as plain in stating that faith alone can not save (James 2:23). Baptism saves, but not baptism alone—or may other requirements for salvation alone (I Pet. 3:21). Many things are required.

Jesus' teaching in Matthew 25:34-46 does not mean that men may be saved by works of mercy without confessing Christ, for He Himself taught differently (John 6:53; 14:6; 8:24; Mark 16:16, etc.) He did not intend this picture of judgment to nullify the greater part (or any part) of the New Testament.

> The lesson taught in the passage is this: works of Christian benevolence, as we have opportunity to perform them, constitute one of the conditions of our acceptance in the days of judgment. They are, indeed, but the outgrowth of faith and love, and their absence proves that our faith is dead, and that love has not been born within us.[1]

Give as you would to the Master,
If you met His searching look;
Give as you would of your substance
If His hand your offering took.
—Author unknown

The way we are treating every needy soul along the way is the way we are treating Him. The finest gift we can give to men is the gift of Jesus Christ as their Lord and Saviour.

For Further Study:

Cairns, Earle E. *Saints and Society.* Chicago: Moody Press. A church historian gives examples, such as Wilberforce, of Bible-believing

[1] J. W. McGarvey, *A Commentary on Matthew and Mark* (Delight, Arkansas: Gospel Light Co., n.d.), Pp. 220-221.

Christians who led the way to social justice.

Henry, Carl F. H. *A Plea for Evangelical Demonstration.* Grand Rapids: Baker Book House, 1971. Calls for social action that takes the truth of the Bible seriously.

Lightfoot, Neil. *Parables of Jesus,* Part II. Austin, Texas: R. B. Sweet Co. Pp. 82-87. Exposition of the parable of the sheep and the goats.

# Part Thirteen

# THE FINAL WEEK

## 71

## THE TRIUMPHAL ENTRY OF THE KING

The accounts of the last week and resurrection occupy just about one-third of the total pages of the four Gospel accounts as a whole. Matthew gives more than one-third of his gospel record to the story of the last week and the resurrection. Doesn't this show that the Holy Spirit and the apostles attached greatest importance to this part of Jesus' ministry? The lessons of the final week deserve special study and special emphasis!

This kingly entry of Jesus into Jerusalem as the dramatic opening of the last week is reported rather fully in all four Gospels, and each adds some significant details to the record. See Matthew 21:1-11; Mark 11:1-11; Luke 19:28-44; John 11:55—12:19.

Jerusalem, a compact and populous city, was normally what we would consider very crowded. Now it was certainly crowded with Jews from every province and from many countries who had come for the Passover, the chief religious festival of the year.

### *Excitement and Expectancy of the People*

The people from the provinces knew Jesus, not only from His preaching and miracles which He had done among them in their villages, but also from His prominence at former feasts. At the Passover three years before, He had cleansed the temple (John 2:13-23). At the Passover two years before, He had been persecuted for Sabbath-breaking, and the Jews had sought to kill Him, even then, for "making himself equal with God" (John 5:18). At the feast of the tabernacles, six or seven months before, He had been a center of subdued excitement even before He appeared (John 7:11-13, 30, 32, 43-48). His continued ministry in Judea at that time only continued and increased the tension between Him and His enemies, as well as between the people themselves, who were sharply divided in opinion concerning Him (John 8:37, 40-45, 59; 9:16, 17; 10:19-21). At the feast of dedication, about four months before, they had taken up stones to stone Him (John 10:31). On all of these occasions Jesus had made some disciples.

Since the feast of dedication, Jesus had stayed in out-of-the-way sections of the country, except for one trip and master miracle, when He raised Lazarus from the dead at Bethany, less than two miles from Jerusalem. That mighty work was done in the presence of a multitude, and was so great in its effect upon the people that the rulers sought to kill both Lazarus and Jesus (John 11:45-53; 12:10). The priests and Pharisees had formally decided that Jesus must be put to death, and had given a public order that any one knowing Jesus' whereabouts should reveal it that they might take Him to destroy Him (John 11:53, 57).

It is understandable, then, that the crowds who came early to purify themselves for the Passover excitedly speculated whether Jesus would appear at the feast. They were curious regarding the outcome of the conflict between the rulers and Jesus. Yes, Jesus was coming, causing fear and amazement to His disciples as they observed the determined set of His face and His calm expectation of death as He walked straight into such danger (Mark 10:32). As He came into the highways and towns teeming with people going to the feast, the multitudes thronged about Him for healing, for pardon, and for teaching (Luke 18:35-43; 19:1-28).

Now just use your imagination to picture how things developed. Jesus came in to Bethany "six days before the passover" (John 12:1), which would seem to be Saturday, the Sabbath. A tradition of the Pharisees limited Sabbath travel to about seven-eighths of a mile, but there is no indication that Jesus ever kept the tradition. However, this could well have been Friday evening that He arrived at Bethany and stayed in the house of Lazarus and his sisters over the Sabbath (John 12:1-8). Common people came to see Him, and to see Lazarus, who had been dead, but was raised by Jesus.

Then the next day "a great multitude" heard that He was coming forth into the city, and Jesus, knowing all these things, took advantage of the time and made the arrangement Matthew describes about obtaining the ass's colt that had never been ridden (Matt. 21:1-7). In solemn dignity He rode into the city as a king in triumphal possession as if to claim the city for His own.

### *Why Did Jesus Enter the City Thus?*

Matthew says, "That it might be fulfilled which was spoken by the prophet" (Matt. 21:4). This same manner of speech must often be understood to mean "with the result that it was fulfilled." The prophecy was given because the event was to take place. The event did not take place just because of the prophecy. Solomon had announced his taking over the kingdom of David in this manner (I Kings 1:32-40). Zechariah had prophecied that thus the great Messiah King should come (Zech. 9:9, 10). "People . . . took branches of palm trees, and went forth to meet him, and cried, Hosanna: Blessed is the King of Israel that cometh in the name of the Lord" (John 12:12, 13). "And a very great multitude spread their garments in the way" (Matt. 21:8 K.J.V.).

This entry into the city by Jesus constituted His one public and dramatic claim to be the Christ. The Jews' expectations of the Messiah's work were so thoroughly political and militaristic that Jesus had avoided claiming openly that He was the Christ (Matt. 16:20; Luke 4:41; Mark 8:30). He had preached Himself as sent from heaven, the Son of God, Judge of the world, Shepherd of God's people, Light of the world, etc. He had spoken of the kingdom in such ways as to imply that He was the King, but He had never acted as they expected a king to act, and He even resolutely refused to be made a king. Such actions caused even John the Baptist to question Him, whether He were the "one that cometh" (Matt. 11:3). The Jews who considered Jesus more or less favorably were continually in uncertainty whether He was the Christ (John 7:26, 27, 31, 41; 8:53; 10:24). Note the perplexity of His own brethren about His claims and conduct (John 7:4). Jesus knew that the Jews of this generation were ready to revolt violently against Rome under the leadership of anybody they could get to be a "Christ." He had avoided revolution, and until this last week He had avoided the final conflict between Himself and the chief priests and Pharisees.

Jesus indicated often that He had a fixed plan for His work and a particular time and place to die. (See Luke 13:31-33; John 7:6, 8, 30; 8:20; 10:17, 18.) Earlier in His ministry there were times when He stayed away from those who would kill Him (John 7:1), when He "hid himself" and "went forth out of their hand" from the danger of being stoned (John 8:59; 10:39). But now He has come to Jerusalem to die, and He removes all doubts concerning His claim to be the promised King. He lays claim to the allegiance of those who believe, in a manner to approve and strengthen their faith just before it is to be so severely tested by His death.

It was God's will that He should be so acclaimed in this city that their rejection might be without cause. It was an answer to the doubts of the vacillating and unconvinced. It was a challenge to the power and authority of the corrupt rulers who were so hostile toward Jesus.

The Pharisees ordered Jesus to rebuke His disciples and stop the tumult, but He said, "I tell you that, if these shall hold their peace, the stones will cry out" (Luke 19:40).

It was indeed a stirring scene. As the people see Jesus ride from Bethany, permitting those around Him to acclaim Him King, more and more of them join the throng. Mixing their admiration for His tremendous miracles with their fabulous hopes of Messianic splendor, they praise Him for the past and rejoice for the future.

As He came over the top of the Mount of Olives and saw the city spread in full view below Him with the magnificent temple nearest Him, Jesus wept. The word used to describe His weeping at Lazarus' tomb (John 11:35) means to "shed tears"; but the word used in Luke 19:41 means to "sob and cry audibly like a child." He was shaken with grief in the midst of the joyous throng because He knew how shallow their faith, and how false their hopes, and how unreal their professed allegiance. Clearly He foresaw the latter part of the week and the tumultuous clamor: "Crucify, crucify him! Give us Barabbas!" Beyond that He saw what made Him weep in pity—the terrible misery in that city forty years hence, when the armies of Rome would bring upon it God's judgment for rejecting Him (Luke 19:41-44). See also Luke 21:5-24; 23:27-31; Matthew 23:33-36; Deuteronomy 28:44-57. All these things did come upon that generation as one may read in particular in Josephus' *Wars of the Jews.* Jesus said all this would happen "because thou knewest not the time of thy visitation." What a visitation of blessings has been given to us! How shall we escape if we neglect so great a salvation?

### *Enter: The King*

As He came on to the city "all the city was stirred, saying, Who is this?" (Matt. 21:10). Often men had asked that question concerning Him. He even pressed the question upon them Himself: "Who say ye that I am?" (Matt. 16:15). "The Christ, whose son is he?" (Matt. 22:42). It was to show who He was that He came into the city in such manner that day. In the face of Jerusalem skeptics and officials, the testimony of the multitudes was mild and weak, saying, "This is the prophet, Jesus" (Matt. 21:11). Yes, He wore His royalty, even on this occasion, with the simplicity of a prophet. But here was a prophet with the authority of a King, not a mere teacher of doctrines who could be ignored. From now on Jerusalem must do one of two things—crush Him, or bow to Him.

Mark's account makes it plain that Jesus did not cleanse the temple until the next day. Now He "entered into Jerusalem, into the temple; and when he had looked round about upon all things, it being now eventide, he went out unto Bethany with the twelve" (Mark 11:11). It sounds as if He were taking charge of the place as His own and looking it over to plan improvements, and no one dared to challenge Him. We wonder how early in the day it had all started, but now it is evening, and with majestic calm He retires to Bethany. The next morning, having withered a fig tree on the way, He came in and asserted divine authority over the house of God, cleansing it as He had at the very beginning of His public ministry.

Then and there He worked more miracles, healing the lame and blind. Thus began the week of plots, controversies and traps that were directed against Jesus by the envious rulers who dared not take Him openly, but grew ever more fanatically determined to put Him to death. How shameful and how revolting that their object was accomplished by the help of a traitor among His own disciples!

Still no one could take His life from Him. He laid it down of Himself. He went to Jerusalem to die for you and for me. This power and authority He showed not to avoid death, but to show us He died that we might believe and live.

For Further Study:

Edersheim, Alfred. *Life and Times of Jesus the Messiah,* Vol. II. Grand Rapids: Wm. B. Eerdmans, 1956 (reprint of 1886 ed.). Pp. 363-373. Helpful discussion of the Triumphal Entry.

Foster, R. C. *Studies in the Life of Christ.* Grand Rapids: Baker Book House, 1962. Pp. 1086-1102. Good harmonized study of Matthew 21:1-11; Mark 11:1-11; Luke 19:29-44; John 12:12-19.

# 72

## JESUS FACES THE CROSS (John 12)

The raising of Lazarus in the presence of a multitude, and next door to Jerusalem, had great effect. It caused many to believe on Jesus and strengthened the faith of many others. The report of it spread, causing excitement in Jerusalem and among the crowds that came to the Passover a few weeks later. The enemies of Jesus became more and more determined to kill Him (John 11).

Therefore Jesus went away to an obscure place called Ephraim (John 11:54). Then He went along the border of Samaria and Galilee, crossed over into Perea, and journeyed toward Jerusalem for the last Passover and the crucifixion. On that journey, He taught His disciples about the coming of His kingdom, prayer, and again predicted His death. Six days before the Passover He arrived at Bethany again, and at a supper in the home of Mary and Martha, Mary anointed His head and feet with precious ointment.

Multitudes who had come early for the Passover heard that Jesus was at Bethany and came to see Him. On the following day He made His triumphal entry into Jerusalem, and on the next day He cleansed the temple. On the third day, probably, Tuesday, there were many questions and controversies between Jesus and the rulers of the Jews. He told parables concerning God's judgment upon them and gave them a long rebuke and denunciation. It was most likely on that same day that a group of Gentiles who had come to worship at the feast sought an interview with Jesus.

### *"We Would See Jesus"*

A group of Gentiles who had accepted Jewish worship had come to the Passover. They were not merely Greek-speaking Jews. They were not necessarily from Greece, for all non-Jews were called Greeks. They were proselytes, converts to the Jewish religion (cp. Acts 2:10; 6:5). The Old Testament made provision for them to bring sacrifices (Lev. 22:18) and to pray to God in the temple (I Kings 8:41-43; Isa. 56:6, 7). In Jesus' time a very sharp distinction was made between Jew and Gentiles, and even proselytes were looked down upon as inferior to a born Jew. They were strictly forbidden to enter any part of the temple except the court of the Gentiles.

The Greeks came to Philip. Philip's name was of Greek origin, and his home city of Bethsaida was a city where Greeks as well as

Israelites lived. Perhaps these Greeks had a former acquaintance with Philip.

They requested, "Sir, we would see Jesus" (John 12:21). This was a polite and formal request. Merely to look at Jesus would have been no problem. Evidently they wanted to talk with Jesus. Philip conferred with Andrew who was also from Bethsaida (John 1:44) and his name was also of a Greek origin. Philip did not take the Gentiles to Jesus immediately because Jesus' teaching ministry had been limited to the house of Israel (Matt. 10:5, 6; 15:24) and because a meeting between Jesus and Gentiles would excite the wrath of the Jews against Him, especially if held in the temple (cp. Acts 21:28, 29).

There is no indication that Andrew and Philip brought the Greeks to Jesus, but they brought the problem to Jesus. Jesus answered Philip and Andrew. Were the Greeks there? Did they ever get an interview with Jesus? The whole answer of Jesus must have surprised the disciples, and it may seem to us strange and off the subject, until we study it well. Jesus was moved with far-reaching thoughts and deep emotions. There was no time now for Him to become a teacher to the Gentiles, but His heart was much concerned about them (John 10:16). He was on His way to the cross (in two or three days) to be a Savior for both Gentiles and Jews. Death on the cross was the only way that He could help them.

### *"The Hour Is Come"*

Jesus answered, "The hour is come, that the Son of man should be glorified." (John 12:23). The time was right here for Jesus to die and rise and send forth the message of salvation to all men. Death was the way He was to be glorified (John 12:16; 13:31, 32; 17:1; Phil. 2:5-11). By His death He would draw all men unto Him (John 12:32).

When Jesus came to Jerusalem for the fourth Passover season of His public ministry He knew that the time had come for Him to lay down His life for the people as a sacrifice and sin-offering. He had foreknown from the beginning that He would be killed and the third day rise again (see John 2:19-22). He had known and referred to the many prophecies that foretold His sufferings and death (Luke 18:31-34; Mark 9:12; cf. Ps. 22; Isa. 53; Zech. 11:12, 13; 12:10; 13:7, and many others). He had indicated foreknowledge of the very time and place at which He would die (Luke 13:31-35; 12:50; Matt. 16:21). Indeed, He had known and serenely faced the fact that for two years numerous attempts had been made to kill Him, especially in Jerusalem (John 5:18; Luke 4:29; Mark 3:6; John 7:1, 19, 25, 32, 44; 8:37, 40, 59; 10:31, 39; 11:16).

Jesus gave a simple illustration of the universal principle which He had on His heart—as a grain of wheat must die to produce, so every life that is kept from sacrifice is useless and lost. "Verily, verily, I say unto you, Except a grain of wheat fall into the earth and die, it abideth by itself alone; but if it die, it beareth much fruit. He that loveth his life loseth it; and he that hateth his life in this world shall keep it unto life eternal. If any man serve me, let him follow me; and where I am, there shall my servant be: if any man serve me, him will the Father honor" (John 12:24-26).

Jesus applied His principle. "Life" is used here to mean "self," and loving it is holding it dear as an end in itself. Anyone who gives his life or allows it to be used up for others as if he hated it is really putting it in safekeeping with Jesus.

Jesus stated it as a fixed principle, for us as well as for himself, that one who saves his life for himself is losing it, while life is kept safe by one who gives it up. The one who lives for self is hardly alive. "She that liveth in pleasure is dead while she liveth" (I Tim. 5:6). Often a young person is told by worldly people that he is throwing his life away in service for others who do not deserve it or in working for an unattainable or unpopular ideal. Jesus, however, says that these are the ones whose lives are kept by the power of God. Jesus leads all who would serve Him into the way of self-sacrifice.

Our Lord's spirit was deeply disturbed. A combination of powerful feelings shook the heart of Jesus. The opposition of the Jews was reaching its climax and He was conscious of the terrible punishment yet to come upon the nation (See Luke 19:41-44; 21:20-24; Matt. 23:37-39; 24:2, 16-21). The grossness of sin that would accomplish the crucifixion filled Him with horror. The opportunity to send forth light and salvation to all the world, so long planned and worked for, was exciting in its near approach. The realization of the cross and bearing the sin of the world was just coming in full strength upon the human consciousness of Jesus. No wonder His soul was troubled!

The Son of God was one with the Father, eternal, Creator of all things (Heb. 1:2; Col. 1:16; John 1:3). Yet when He was made flesh, He was truly human—He felt hunger and weariness, knew temptation and godly fear, needed faith and prayer. His sufferings were real, and He faced the cross with dread. Jesus had known from the beginning that He must die and on the third day be raised up. Again and again Jesus faced the cross, understood its necessity, and overcame every temptation to avoid it; but here in John 12 we see Him deeply troubled by the nearness and the bitter reality of it. This manifests the real humanity of Jesus.

Jesus said, "Father, save me from this hour, but for this cause came I to this hour" (John 12:27). It may be that He was praying, as in Gethsemane (Luke 22:42), and answering himself immediately with "but for this cause came I unto this hour." Or He may have made it a question: "Shall I ask God to deliver me from this hour? For this cause I came," as in John 18:11. Certainly this did not express unwillingness to go to the cross, but acceptance of it as the very purpose of His life.

Jesus came into the world to be our Savior, to give His life a ransom for men. He was born to die. He was delivered up to death "by the determinate counsel and foreknowledge of God" (Acts 2:23), being foreknown indeed from the foundation of the world (I Pet. 1:20). Jesus' sacrificial death was the only basis on which God could forgive any sin from Adam until now.

Jesus had to die to fulfill the law and retire the old covenant God had made with Israel so that He might make a new and better covenant with men of all nations. In His death He nailed the law to the cross and took it out of the way (Col. 2:14, 15). His death bought redemption for the Gentiles, broke down the middle wall of partition, and made both Jew and Gentile one new man in Him (Eph. 2:11-18). Therefore when the Greeks sought Jesus, He meditated upon the great necessity of the cross. Being lifted up to die was the great condition upon which He could bring all kinds of men to himself for salvation, unity, and fellowship with God. It is still the message of the cross that draws men to Him, that reconciles them to God, and that unites them in Christian fellowship.

"Father, glorify thy name" (John 12:28) is His fervent and unqualified prayer. He knew the price to be paid, the manner in which God must be glorified through His own death on the cross. God immediately answered His prayer, so all could hear. "I have glorified it" seems most likely to be a compliment to Jesus' feelings, the Father answered the heroic prayer with the only assurance that would satisfy Jesus: "I have glorified it, Son; and I will again." Jesus' sufferings would not be in vain. Some heard the words well enough to say that an angel spoke to Jesus. Perhaps those who said it thundered were unwilling to admit a supernatural answer to Jesus' words. The words were addressed to Jesus; however, they came not only for His sake, but also for theirs.

Jesus felt Himself in the midst of the great struggle with Satan and fully confident of the outcome of it. By the influence of Satan the whole world and everyone in it had gone into sin; and by sin, into death and condemnation. By Jesus' death the universal power of Satan was broken—a method for forgiveness of sin, regeneration of men, and the inheritance of life was to be an established reality upon the earth.

### *"If I Be Lifted Up"*

Jesus claimed that the salvation of all men rested on His shoulders. We need to remember who it is that is speaking here. Jesus is usually praised for His lowly and unselfish manner of life, and rightly so; but when one lists together the stupendous claims which He made concerning Himself, His lowliness of life looks strange by contrast. He must surely be the infinite God condescending to self-sacrificing and self-effacing service for men; or else His claims are false, swelling words of vanity, and He is the most consummate egotist, the most unconscionable liar the world has heard of.

He repeatedly used expressions about Himself that could be said only of Deity: "The Son of man hath power on earth to forgive sins" (Mark 2:10). "The Son of man shall send forth angels, and they shall gather out of his kingdom" (Matt. 13:41). "All things are delivered unto me of my Father . . . neither knoweth any man the Father, save the Son" (Matt. 11:27). "He that came down from heaven, even the Son of man" (John 3:13). "Before Abraham was, I am" (John 8:58). "I am the resurrection, and the life" (John 11:25). "I am the way, the truth, and the life: no man cometh unto the Father, but by me" (John 14:6). "I am the bread of life . . . he that believeth on me shall never thirst" (John 6:35). "I came down from heaven" (John 6:38). "I am the good shepherd . . . I am come that they might have life" (John 10:10, 11). "I am the true vine . . . without me ye can do nothing" (John 15:1, 5). "I and my Father are one" (John 10:30). "He that hath seen me hath seen the Father" (John 14:9). "All authority is given unto me in heaven and in earth" (Matt. 28:18). "The Son of man shall come in the glory of his Father with his angels; and then he shall reward every man according to his works" (Matt. 16:27). In John 5:17-29, Jesus called God His Father, "Making himself equal with God"; called Himself "the Son of God"; said that He would raise all the dead and execute judgment upon all. Three times Jesus directly said, "I am the Son of God" (Mark 14:61, 62; John 9:35-37; 10:36). It was commonly recognized by the people, by the rulers, by the devil, and by the soldiers who crucified Him that He claimed to be the Son of God.

He represented God's will as being more concerned with men's acceptance of Him as Lord and Savior than with anything else, and as being fulfilled in those who believed and followed Him. He continually made Himself the center of importance for all men, more necessary than life itself, and the sum and source of all blessings and success. Who besides Jesus could make this statement: "And I, if I be lifted up from the earth, will draw all men unto myself" (John 12:32). He had the divine power, authority, and trustworthiness; He had the unbounded love and the willingness to pay the price to win the hearts of men. Notice the great condition upon which He would be able to draw and to bless all men—"if I be lifted up."

What did it mean to "be lifted up"? The same expression is used in John 3:14; 8:28; 12:32, 34. It refers to the crucifixion every time—His being lifted up on the cross to die. John explains definitely that He said this "signifying by what manner of death he should die" (John 12:33). The multitude understood Him to mean death. They thought the Christ could not die, and therefore asked who was to be lifted up. They knew of Psalm 110:4; Isaiah 9:7; Daniel 7:14, and similar passages. They could not see how He could die and still fulfill these. They correctly associated "The Son of man" (John 12:23) with the Christ.

Jesus answered them, "Yet a little while is the light among you. Walk while ye have the light, that darkness overtake you not: and he that walketh in the darkness knoweth not whither he goeth. While ye have the light, believe on the light, that ye may become sons of light" (John 12:35, 36). This is an appeal for them to follow what is revealed of God's will and plan without waiting for answers to all their questions. They had reason to believe Him; they did not need to judge Him in every detail. So it is with us; we should walk in the light we have, not asking to know everything before we obey.

Indeed, it is the loving sacrifice and the amazing mercy of the Christ that draws our alien, sinful hearts unto Him, and causes us to be reconciled to God. Without the cross and its power to redeem, Christ could command and threaten us from without, but He could not draw and transform us from within. The cross is the great condition of His Saviorhood. As both Lord and Savior, as Priest and Teacher of men, He was made "perfect through sufferings" (Heb.

2:10; 5:9). To preach the gospel of Christ is to proclaim the doctrine of the cross, which, though it seems foolish or unacceptable to some men, has a peculiar power to save and to transform others (I Cor. 1:18-25; 2:1, 2). It was for the crucifixion that Jesus came into the world; He was born in order to die on the cross for us (Matt. 20:28; I Tim. 1:15; 2:6).

For Further Study:

See comments on John 12:20-36 in the following commentaries:

Lenski, R. C. H. *The Interpretation of St. John's Gospel.* Columbus, Ohio: The Wartburg Press, 1942. Pp. 858-882.
Morris, Leon. *New International Commentary: The Gospel of John.* Grand Rapids: Wm. B. Eerdmans, 1971. Pp. 589-606.
Westcott, B. F. *The Gospel According to John.* Grand Rapids: Wm. B. Eerdmans, 1951 (reprint of 1881 ed.). Pp. 180-184.

# 73

## AN EXAMPLE IN HUMILITY AND LOVE (John 13)

Two days before the Passover Jesus again told His disciples that He was to be delivered up to be crucified (Matt. 26:2). That same day the chief priests and elders met and plotted how they could arrest Jesus by stealth and kill Him. They decided they could not do it during the feast because of the people. Then Judas came to them and offered to betray Jesus so they could take Him in secret; and they gladly paid him thirty pieces of silver to do it.

### *The Last Supper*

On the first day of unleavened bread, the day on which the Passover lamb had to be sacrificed, Jesus sent Peter and John to prepare the Passover meal for Him and His disciples. They made ready for it in the usual way and at the usual time in an upper room to which Jesus directed them (Matt. 26:17-21; Mark 14:12-16; Luke 22:7-13). Jesus met with them for that ancient and sacred memorial, knowing that it would be His last supper with His friends on earth before His death.

This had to be on the fourteenth day of the month Nisan; it could fall on any day of the week. The next day, the day on which Jesus was crucified, was called the Preparation, the day before the Sabbath (Mark 15:42; Luke 23:54-56; John 19:31). Hence the day of the last supper was Thursday (as we count it), but the beginning of Friday as the Jews count days from sunset to sunset.

The Sabbath mentioned must have been the regular Saturday Sabbath, for the special day of holy convocation in Passover Week (if it ever was called a Sabbath) was the *first* day of unleavened bread (Exod. 12:16; Lev. 23:6, 7) and would have been the day on which Jesus was crucified or even the day before, according to Mark 12:12, since Jesus was alive and free on the day on which the Passover lamb was killed and the leaven was put out of the houses of Israel. The next day he was killed. The next day was "the Sabbath." "And when the Sabbath was past" before the first day of the week. The accounts do not say that two Sabbaths passed before the first day of the week. Read Luke 23:54—24:1 and Mark 15:42—16:12.

### *Conflicting Emotions*

The account in John 13 undoubtedly describes the Passover supper if we believe Matthew, Mark and Luke. Some critics have said that John here contradicts the declaration of the first three Gospels that Jesus ate the regular Passover supper. The critics allege that John here says this meal was a meal before the Passover meal. The phrase, "Before the feast" (John 13:1), does not give the time of the supper; it modifies the verb "knew." The meaning is this: "Jesus, knowing before the Passover that His hour had come to depart out of this world to the Father, and having loved His own that were in the world, loved them to the end [or to the fullest extent]." As He approached the sorrows and burdens of this eventful and fateful night, He knew well that the hour of His sufferings and departure had come, but His heart was filled with love for His disciples. These companions and co-workers He was leaving behind in the world, exposed to the dangers and hardships. He knew that Satan had put it into Judas' heart to betray Him. This does not mean that Judas was helpless and overpowered by the devil without any fault of his own, but that Judas had allowed the devil to deceive and lead him into this sin. He knew that Satan had asked also for Simon "that he might sift him as wheat" (Luke 22:31-34). He knew that all would be bewildered and shaken by the fact that He would actually be delivered into the hands of His enemies; that they would be scattered as sheep when the shepherd is stricken (Matt. 26:31).

Jesus also knew that, instead of studying His sayings and the words of the prophets how that the Son and Servant of God must surrender Himself to death and give Himself a ransom for sin, they were thinking in the opposite direction how they were going to be exalted to chief places in the kingdom of divine glory which they imagined must soon appear out of the crisis that was evidently impending. It must have grieved Him and made Him feel lonely in this selfish world to know that they were quarreling with one another about their relative ranks and places of honor (Luke 22:24), in the very night when He was descending to the very depths of self-abnegation, claiming nothing of His own in order to bear the cross of shame to a criminal's death for the sake of those who wrongly thought they had rights and rank. Possibly this dispute began over the prestige connected with certain positions at the table. It has been suggested that Judas, who had already bargained to betray Him, took a place of honor beside Jesus and that Peter went all the way to the lowest place. The diners lay upon couches, each leaning upon his left elbow, three men to a couch, with Jesus at the place of chief honor, in the center of the head couch. John lay at (not upon) Jesus' breast: that is, just in front of Him or at His right side. To ask a question privately John leaned back upon Jesus' breast (John 13:25).

In full awareness of His divine majesty, He humbled Himself to wash the disciples' feet as a loving service, and without degrading or belittling Himself at all (John 13:3). He served in this humble fashion, not because He forgot His divine nature, but because He remembered it. Jesus could have abased and humbled the disciples into abject and cringing fear; but He loved them. He sought to teach them, not to coerce them. He wanted to draw them to Him, not to drive them from Him. He was not willing to debase and crush them into cravens. He was willing, rather, with infinite patience and love to give them example and teaching to build them up and elevate them to that true greatness which was like His own, i.e., which seeks opportunities to give of self in service to others because of love for them. He had taught them all this before (Mark 10:41-45); this wasn't their first offense in selfish pride. Still He didn't scold and criticize them, but taught the same things over again with added promises of their exaltation with Him in the future (Luke 22:23-30). The Lord knew that we do not always learn these things the first time we hear them, and agree to them, but need many lessons.

### *The Master, A Servant*

Jesus arose from the supper and put off His outer robe and belt, and perhaps a tunic, to worked dressed like a slave, He washed the disciples' feet (John 13:4). The disciples were perhaps taken aback by Jesus' abrupt action, but their consciences must have troubled them when they realized what He was about to do. Everything Jesus needed was there. The disciples should have washed one another's feet, but none was willing to take the place of a servant and treat others as so much superior. Jesus washed even Judas' feet. Pictures often show the disciples seated about a table, thus creating the wrong impression about this act. As the disciples lay on couches about the table, the water was poured over their feet into a basin; the feet then were washed and wiped. But why did Jesus do this? Not only for a lesson. It was a genuine act of loving service, an act of humble willingness to do the most lowly service for His friends, an act of practical courtesy which they had forgotten or avoided in their preoccupation with selfish pride.

In the land of Palestine the rough and dusty roads, the absence of stockings, the use of sandals, the habit of walking barefoot, the much greater amounts of walking than we do, all make it necessary to give the feet frequent washings. (Read Gen. 18:4; 19:2; 24:32; 43:24; Judg. 19:21; I Sam. 25:41; II Sam. 11:8). These passages show that washing the feet was the first act on entering a tent or a house after a journey. This is regularly done when entering a house, especially the better upper rooms which were usually carpeted. The shoes were never worn in the house. It was the common dictate of good manners to provide either water for the guests to wash their own feet, or a slave to do it. It became almost synonymous with hospitality (I Tim. 5:10). Jesus rebuked a Pharisee, in whose house He was entertained, for not providing water for His feet (Luke 7:44). From an early date, however, it was considered one of the lowest tasks of servants (I Sam. 25:41), probably because it was done by the youngest and least-trained servants, or because of the idea of defilement connected with the foot. Therefore, if rendered voluntarily, it was a symbol of complete devotion. The undoing of the latchet or thongs of the sandals (Mark 1:7; Luke 3:16; John 1:27) seems to refer to the same menial duty.

When Jesus came to Peter, that reverent but bold and impulsive disciple spoke out in amazement and objection to what seemed to him unfitting: "Lord, dost *thou* wash my feet?" This outburst of feeling set off a little discussion which brought out the symbolic meaning of Jesus' act. Jesus said, "What I do thou knowest not now; but thou shalt know hereafter." They certainly saw that He poured water on their feet and dried them with a towel, but that He did more than that they would understand later. Because he didn't understand, Peter said, "Thou shalt never wash my feet." Peter had good intentions, no doubt, in saying that he would never permit the Lord to be so abased for him; but it was as if to say, "I am too good and too fair to let my Lord be humiliated for me." It was a dangerous frame of mind. Jesus answered him with deep significance, "If I wash thee not, thou hast no part with me."

Every one of us must consent for Christ to do a much more humiliating and more difficult thing for us. He had to take our sin and our shame upon Himself, bear our punishment, serve our sentence of just condemnation. If I say, "Oh, no, I could never let Him take my punishment upon Himself," I have no part with Him. Yet we are often inclined to that attitude of veiled pride that seems to say, "I'd never permit Jesus to be humbled for me." But He was. We must admit that He bore our death that we might live. We must let unbounded condescension of His divine grace put to shame all our pride and humble us completely, while we confess that He, our Master and Lord, did for us what we were unworthy and unable and unwilling to do for Him or one another.

*"Ye Should Do As I Have Done"*

Jesus wanted the disciples to consider the spiritual meaning of what He had done. He made it clear that even though He was Lord and Master, their supreme superior, yet He was willing to serve. He reasoned with them, "If I have acted as a lowly servant for you, you ought to do such acts for one another." Our Lord's statement, "Ye also ought to wash one another's feet. For I have given you an example, that ye also should do as I have done to you" (John 13:14, 15), was not a positive command to observe a set form as a church ordinance. No evidence suggests that the early church so understood it. It is a moral lesson by example. As Jesus did a useful service in love and humility, so we also should do any useful service for one another in love and humility.

Truly, indeed, if He the Lord and Master, was willing to do such a service for men, we should be willing, also. He was teaching us to do in like manner. He gave us the example that we should do as He did (John 13:15). Whenever washing one another's feet is an act of practical courtesy and helpfulness, that we can perform in a true spirit of simple love and humble service, we ought to wash one another's feet. But when it is of no practical helpfulness, when it is performed as a public religious ritual to *display* our "humility," at special seasons, toward select persons, it does not seem to fit the pattern Jesus gave. "Ritualizing such an act of life absolutely destroys its meaning."

The Great Commission assigned to the apostles the task of teaching the believers to observe all things that Jesus commanded; but we have no teaching from them concerning foot washing as a ceremony in the church. They do teach, however, lowliness, subjection, and loving service (Rom. 12:3, 10, 16; Gal. 5:13; Eph. 4:2; 5:21; Phil. 2:3-8; Col. 3:12; I Pet. 5:5, etc.). There is no indication in the way that Jesus did the act at the last supper that He was instituting a form of worship or making it part of His death. It is not an act of worship to God, but of service to man out of the right kind of a godly heart of humility and love. Even those who urge it as a perpetual ordinance in the church teach that it "symbolizes humility and service." Exactly so: Jesus gave a very striking example and symbol of that manner of conduct and attitudes of heart that He wants us to have. *He does not want us to repeat the symbol, but to practice reality.* His example was clear, and no command of His is more direct or authoritative.

If the Master does not consider Himself too good to wash His servants feet, then the servants are not too good to wash feet. Christ was teaching them not to think that they were above any loving service to another. The person who practices this principle in life will experience the highest good and the deepest happiness (John 13:16, 17).

### *"A New Commandment"*

Jesus warned the disciples that one of them would betray Him. Being asked who it was, Jesus said it was the one to whom He would give a bite of bread after He had dipped it in the dish. Then He dipped one and gave it to Judas, and Judas went out of the room. Jesus told the disciples again that He would be leaving them in a little while (John 13:18-33).

Our Lord then told the disciples, "A new commandment I give unto you, that ye love one another; even as I have loved you, that ye also love one another. By this shall all men know that ye are my disciples, if ye have love one to another" (John 13:34, 35). A similar commitment had been given in Leviticus 19:18: "Thou shalt love thy neighbor as thyself." Jesus did not use the Greek word for "new" that especially means of recent origin, but one that means in new condition, possibly never used before, unmarred by age, or not outworn. The commandment, as He gave it with and according to His own example—*as I have loved you*—has a new quality and power, a new motive and scope. It was new in the sense that Jesus by His example had given a richer dimension to love. As a result love is not so much a duty imposed by commandment; it is more an inward power, active in self-giving for the benefit of others without limit. True love, rightly understood, includes so much (Matt. 22:37-40; Rom. 13:8-10) that it can really be a badge that will always identify Jesus' pupils and followers as His very own. Of course, this is not the only test of discipleship, but it is a critical one.

Love is supreme. To love God is the greatest commandment; the second like unto it is to love one's neighbor as himself. Jesus said that love is the mark of His disciples (Matt. 22:34-40; John 13:35). "Love is the fulfilling of the law" (Rom. 13:10), and "the bond of perfectness" (Col. 3:14). Peter said it is to be practiced "Above all things" (I Peter 4:8). John testified that "he that loveth not knoweth not God; for God is love" (I John 4:8). Love is not only the crowning attainment of mature Christians, but it is also an indispensable essential of any character that is Christian. "If any man love not the Lord Jesus Christ, let him be Anathema" (I Cor. 16:22). Love is a test of our faith and without it we are as unorthodox and un-Christian as we would be without faith in God. In view of the large amount of teaching in the Bible about love and the stress laid upon the importance of it, do you think the churches of today really do enough to teach and to require the practice of love among their members?

We must understand the true nature of love. Much of the inadequacy of teaching on love in the church may be related to the fact that love is often misrepresented and misunderstood. Many think it is opposed to justice, to correction, and to chastening. We are all likely to think of love too much as sentiment apart from the actions of love. Love is not theory, but practice. It is a matter of emotions and motives of the heart, but these are made real as they become the cause and the spirit of many actions. Love is giving of ourselves in the interests of others. It is active and eager concern for the welfare of those loved. It is directly opposed to indifference and neglect. If we do what is right in or own sight, indifferent to its effect upon a brother, we do not walk in love (I Cor. 8:1-13; Rom. 14:15). If we hope to be saved through the gospel, but will not do or give anything to save others, we have not love in our hearts.

Jesus brought to men a new understanding of love, a new appreciation for it, and an intensified motive for loving. He also gave us new power to love, through the gift of the Holy Spirit: "The love of God is shed abroad in our hearts by the Holy Spirit" (Rom. 5:5; Gal. 5:22). Love was not unknown in the old covenant, but it is revealed more fully in the new covenant, not because God became any more loving, but because the way was opened up by Christ for men to have a better and fuller fellowship with God.

For Further Study:

Bruce, A. B. *The Training of the Twelve.* New York: Harper and Brothers, n.d. Pp. 341-355. Helpful on the spiritual lessons in John 13:1-20.

Edersheim, Alfred. *The Life and Times of Jesus the Messiah.* Vol. II. Grand Rapids: Eerdmans, 1956 reprint of 1886 edition. Pp. 479-509. Excellent background information of the Last Supper.

Hendriksen, William. *New Testament Commentary: Gospel According to John,* Vol. II. Grand Rapids: Baker Book House, 1954. Pp. 219-241. Thorough treatment of the date of the meal and of the events and teaching in John 13.

Morris, Leon. *New International Commentary: The Gospel of John.* Grand Rapids: Eerdmans, 1971. Pp. 612-635. Thorough treatment of the passage.

# 74

## LAST INSTRUCTIONS AND PREDICTIONS BEFORE THE CROSS (John 14-16)

In this study we look at the sober scene of the Passover feast where Jesus was eating His last supper with the disciples. After He had washed His disciples' feet and had eaten the meal, probably accompanied by the usual psalms and ceremonies of the occasion, He sorrowfully warned them that He was to be betrayed and delivered into the hands of His enemies, and that He was going where they could not come. Jesus' prediction that one of them would betray Him caused them to ask each in turn, "Is it I?" Jesus indicated to Judas that He knew of Judas' infamous plot, and in a veiled manner which others did not understand He sent Judas out (John 13:21-30). Peter and the others (Matt. 26:35) asked why they could not go with Jesus, and professed willingness to dare and endure anything for Him; but they were warned that they would all stumble in faith and would flee, and, especially, Peter would deny the Lord (John 13:36-38).

Sometime in the midst of these events at the close of the ancient traditional supper, Jesus instituted the new supper of the broken bread and fruit of the vine in memory of His own body and blood given as a sacrifice for the sins of many. We can not tell whether or not Judas left before the Lord's Supper was instituted. Apparently it is not necessary for us to know.

### *Ties That Bind*

To Jesus this night was a time of tender feelings and a troubled heart. We can not know how much this was true! But we can see some glimpses. He had come into the world with love in His great divine heart to woo and to win the world, to serve and not to be served, to save and not to judge. For three years He had seen and borne with the folly and faithlessness, the hardness of heart and confirmed selfishness of men; He was "a man of sorrows, and acquainted with grief" (Isa. 53:3). Through all His labor and affliction of spirit these twelve men had been His companions (Luke 22:28-30; Matt. 19:28). They were "his own that were in the world"; He had loved them, and He "loved them unto the end" (John 13:1). They had become dear to Him personally, and they were precious to Him. He was to entrust to them the word of life for the world. To a great extent the results of His sacrificial death depended upon their faithfulness and spiritual stamina. He knew how great were the trials they would have to meet. He knew how weak and human they were.

On this night they seemed to be showing how weak and dull and undependable they were. He knew their selfish ambition—contending over who was greatest (Luke 22:24). He could not make them understand His departure or many things that He wanted to speak to them (John 16:1-12, 17-19). He knew they would not be able to watch and pray with Him in the hour of crisis and would forsake Him. Nevertheless, this was not a time of censure, but a time to speak with sympathy and patience gentle and hopeful words of encouragement and reassurance, lest their weakness and dullness cause them to be overcome by despair.

He looked upon them as "little children" (John 13:33). His words in these chapters (John 14-16) and the intercessory prayer that follows (chapter 17) are like the parting words of a wise and fond mother to her children gathered around her when she knows that death will soon take her from them. He spoke with great love and intimate and personal care for them, giving warnings and promises to help them meet the great trials that would come upon them. With these thoughts in mind read again, all at once, from John 13:31 to 17:26. No man can have greater love for his friends than that which Jesus proved Himself to have for His (John 15:12-15). No mother could have more deep and tender affections and longings for her children than Jesus had for His own. His heart was filled with sorrow on their account.

### *The Proof of Love*

In these paragraphs Jesus says many things that point out the proof of His love for the disciples.

1. His open and plain speech. "If it were not so, I would have told you" (John 14:2). "I have called you friends; for all things that I have heard of my Father I have made known unto you" (15:15). He wanted them enlightened and prepared for the things to come. He did not withhold from them His own feelings or the Father's purposes. He put confidence in them and took them into His plans and interests as fully as He could.

2. The promise to prepare a place for them. Love seeks the continued welfare and provision for those who are dear (14:2).

3. The desire to have them where He is to be. Love seeks not to be separated from, but present with, its own (14:3; 17:2).

4. The promise to hear their prayers and do what they ask of Him

and of God in His name. Love seeks to grant every reasonable request (14:13, 14; 16:23, 24).

5. The promise to give them the divine aid and fellowship of the Holy Spirit, another Companion in His place. This promise involved far more than they could then understand (14:16-18, 26; 15:26; 16:7, 13).

6. The desire to give them His peace, to comfort them in fullness of confidence in the Father and in Him, that they be neither troubled nor fearful (14:1, 27; 16:33).

7. The purpose to make full His joy in them—joy that no one could take away (15:11; 16:22, 24). It is the very nature of love to give, and to seek always to give true and lasting joy to those who are loved.

8. The way He prayed for them (17:6-19).

9. Most of all, the fact that He laid down His life for them—"Greater love hath no man than this" (15:13).

Jesus also stated that they should prove their love for Him—by keeping His commandments (John 14:21-23, 24; 15:10-14), especially that they should love one another (13:34, 35; 15:12, 17). He also told them that if they truly loved Him with understanding they would rejoice that He went as He did in obedience to the Father, who is greater than He (14:28).

Any one that does not keep Christ's words and obey Him does not love Him (14:23); but His words are the Father's, who sent Him 14:24). He that hates Christ hates the Father also (15:23). Hence no man can truly love and honor God unless He will receive and obey the words of Christ. We look at ourselves and the question arises: "How many of them?" Oh, alas, how we all fall short! Does I Corinthians 16:22 prove that we are all anathema? Let us all have humility when we start to profess how we love the Lord. Let us not judge our brethren too strictly. Let us ask for mercy and have faith in His mercy that we may do His will for love of Him and not in self-righteousness.

*The Deity and Necessity of Jesus*

The gentle and consoling words of Jesus in John 14 have become favorites of many people and have been applied to many situations; but we must consider the situation in which they were first spoken. The apostles were made sorrowful and troubled by Jesus' sayings about betrayal and death. If they had understood God's plan, they might have borne their sorrow more easily. Jesus' departure would have saddened them because of personal affections, but the outcome would have been worth it all.

In the midst of His sorrow and expressions of unselfish love Jesus is making Himself equal with God and indispensable to man. "Believe in God, believe also in me" (John 14:1) puts faith in Him and in God on the same plane. The real source of consolation was to be found in faith. There was really no cause to despair, because God and Christ would be depended upon. The Greek word for "believe" is the same in form both times, but it is a form that can be either indicative (a statement) or imperative (a command). In either case they were not accused of being altogether without faith, but were told to keep on believing.

"In my Father's house . . . I prepare a place" (John 14:2, 3), assumes proprietorship there. "If ye had known me, ye should have known my Father also: and from henceforth ye know him, and have seen him" (John 14:7) is a staggering claim, which provoked the request, "Show us the Father." Then Jesus made the unqualified statement of deity that can not be misunderstood or explained away. His answer to Philip would certainly be intolerable arrogance and blasphemy if it were any less than absolutely true. Here is Jesus; and by the same token here is our God! Any god we worship that is different from the character and teaching of Jesus is merely an idol, perhaps devised in our minds instead of fashioned with our hands, but a concoction of men. Jesus is the perfect manifestation of God to man. God is in Him. If you can't see it, believe it for the sake of the works of God which He did (John 10:37, 38; 14:10, 11).

He is the Way, the Truth, and the Life (John 14:6). To know God we must learn of Christ. To come to God we must come by Him. He is the Vine (John 15:1-9), the stem of all enduring and fruitful life. To bear fruit we must abide in Him. Apart from him we can do nothing! We stumble over the simplicity of these statements and others like them in the scripture. When will we surrender our theories and our logic that we may have Christ, the Truth, and the divine Wisdom? (I Cor. 1:30; 4:18-20). When will we cast off our self-righteousness to be found only in Christ and His righteousness?

*The Promise of the Spirit*

Jesus promised He would not leave the apostles desolate (John 14:18). Literally the word means "orphans." He had called them "children" (John 13:33); now He promised not to leave them fatherless. He would send "another comforter" (John 14:16). The idea of the Greek word is not easy to put into English. "Helper," "Advocate," "Counselor," and "Companion" are fairly close to it. The word "Comforter" was first used in translating this passage by Wycliffe six hundred years ago, when it meant "strengthener." But it has changed so much in use since then that it is misleading to modern readers. There is no New Testament teaching that the Holy Spirit is to make anyone comfortable, but rather that He is to make us strong, active, capable, and faithful in the Lord's service. Yet there is joy and peace in the soul as a result of living by His guidance. "Another" implies that the Holy Spirit was to be the one to take Christ's place as a permanent companion for the apostles.

He is a divine person, like Christ and God. He is called the Spirit of truth because His special mission to the apostles was to reveal the truth because this name describes His character. The world in its unbelief, its preference for darkness, its unwillingness to acknowledge God's perfect truthfulness and authority cannot recognize and accept the Spirit. Some men could not receive Jesus because they resisted the truth He told them; in like manner those who reject the Spirit's message (because it reveals their sinfulness and they prefer other ideas) cannot receive Him. They keep themselves from knowing Him. The disciples had Christ and His words then, which gave them the presence of the Spirit. "He abideth with you, and shall be in you" (John 14:17). The Spirit was to enter into their lives more completely and control them from within.

In the sad hours of farewell before His arrest, Jesus gave help and encouragement to His apostles. He warned them of trials they would have to meet. He promised them they would have the help of the Holy Spirit to guide them and assist them in their work of witnessing for Him (John 14:26; 15:26; 16:13-15). These promises apply to the apostles alone as the context in each case shows. The Holy Spirit inspired the apostles so they would remember Christ's words and reveal His truth to the world (John 14:17, 26). The Spirit teaches us these things through the words of the apostles as found in the New Testament. The Spirit would guide the apostles into all truth and enable them to predict the future (John 16:13). These promised powers were to qualify them as spokesmen for Christ executing His testament on the earth, and making known the faith once for all revealed unto the saints.

The workings of the Spirit that are listed in these passages were to prepare the apostles for their special work. They had a very important work to do in first delivering the word of Christ to the world.

Promises of power and authority through the Holy Spirit were given again in meetings Jesus had with them after the resurrection (Luke 24:49; John 20:22, 23; Acts 1:5, 8). These promises pointed to a definite event that happened on the Day of Pentecost (Acts 2).

Aren't you glad to know that the apostles were given their message directly from God by the miraculous working of the Holy Spirit? We know they did not speak their own ideas and could not be mistaken. Their teaching is "the faith which was once for all delivered unto the saints" (Jude 3). The truth and guidance that God gave to them are given to us through their words, which stand unchanged to the end of time. We do not need any inspired men today to reveal God's will to us.

What we need is God's Spirit dwelling in us through obedience to His Word. We should not apply to ourselves the promises that were made only to the apostles. All Christians are certainly not expected to have the infallible inspiration and full authority to speak for Christ which was promised to the apostles. However, we ought to claim for our own those promises that were made to all who love and obey Christ. Such a promise is found in John 14:23: "My Father will love him, and we will come unto him, and make our abode with him." Jesus had promised before that every believer would have the Spirit (John 7:38, 39). The apostles taught that the Holy Spirit is given to those who obey Christ (Acts 2:38, 39; 5:32). The Spirit is not just an extra, but a real and vital part of our salvation (Titus 3:4-7; Rom. 8:8-17). The Christian life is lived in the Spirit and bears the fruit of the Spirit (Rom. 14:17; Gal. 5:22-25). To all practical purposes, this is equivalent to Christ living in us and our living by faith in Him (Gal. 2:20; Eph. 3:16, 17).

Let Christ's thoughts fill your mind; surrender your will to His will; let love for Him rule every part of your life; and God will make you a new creature, made alive with Christ through His Spirit dwelling in you.

For Further Study:

Bruce, A. B. *The Training of the Twelve,* 3rd ed. New York: Harper and Row, n.d. Pp. 378-488. Forcefully shows Jesus' empathy with the apostles as He encourages them through His farewell instructions and promises recorded in John 14-16.

Butler, Paul. *The Gospel of John,* Vol. II. Joplin, Mo.: College Press, 1965. Pp. 239-321. Helpful comment on John 14-16.

# 75

## OUR LORD'S PRAYER FOR UNITY (John 17)

Jesus is our great high priest. He is the only one who is acceptable to God and worthy to make intercession for sinners. He made the one perfect sacrifice for sin, entered into the presence of God with His own blood, and sat down on the throne of mercy. Through Him Christians have access to the throne of God in prayer. On the eve of His sacrifice of Himself, at the last supper Jesus expressed His loving concern for His disciples as He tried to prepare them for the shock of His crucifixion.

Later the same night Jesus and His disciples went out of the upper room where they had eaten the Passover supper (John 14:31). He had much more to say to them, and so He continued His discussion as they made their way across the city toward Gethsemane. We do not know where they were during much of this discussion; but since the priests opened the gates of the temple to the people at midnight after the Passover supper, it is quite possible it was carried on in the temple courts.

Jesus offered His great intercessory prayer that the Father would glorify the Son (John 17:1-5), sanctify the disciples (John 17:6-19), and unify the believers (John 17:20-26). What unselfish purpose and loving concern, that in the face of agony and sorrow unto death, He prayed this fervent and farsighted prayer for us!

Before His prayer Jesus had said all that He could well say to the disciples, His thoughts naturally turned to God in prayer. He needed the companionship and support of God for the ordeal which He was facing, but He prayed chiefly for others. He was deeply concerned for sanctification of His intimate disciples and for the unity of all who believe on Him through the apostles' word. We simply cannot know how deep and strong were His heart's yearnings and how fervent His prayer on their behalf as He felt both His love for them and their great responsibility as He looked forward to seeing in them, and through them, the fruit of His own life and death.

First, Jesus prayed for Himself and His work (John 17:1-5), that having completed His work upon the earth He might be glorified, in God's way, even through the crucifixion, resurrection, and ascension, in order that He might glorify the Father. He had received from God authority over all things (Matt. 11:27; 28:18) in order to accomplish the Father's will for the redemption of men. He had kept

Himself within the Father's will and purpose and plan. He had dedicated Himself fully to the work. He had kept the Father's mind and spirit and work in Himself. Now, this very day, His life is to be expended utterly as the sacrifice for sin to bring righteousness to sinners.

The portion of the prayer concerning Himself is not selfish but is a plea to glorify God by the fulfillment of God's plans. It is also a yearning for the perfect fellowship with God that had been His glory in eternity.

Next our Lord turned His attention to the needs of the apostles (John 17:6-19). He asked that the apostles might (1) have His joy in themselves; (2) be kept safe from the evil forces of the world, both physically and spiritually; and (3) be pure in their devotion of their lives to God, made holy by the truth. He also prayed that they would be one.

Now He must entrust all His interests on earth to the apostles and leave them to be the embodiment and the carriers of the life-giving Spirit, and the way of salvation for all men. How He prayed for the apostles! Jesus was speaking to God in prayer apparently loud enough so that the disciples could hear Him and be strengthened by His words. He mentioned that the world hated the apostles because they were obeying the word of God. Rather than the easy option of taking the apostles out of this world, He prays for their spiritual strength for their task in the world (John 17:13-15).

Central in His concern for the apostles is that they must be dedicated—by God and by themselves. He prays: "Sanctify them in the truth: thy word is truth. As thou didst send me into the world, even so sent I them into the world. And for their sakes I sanctify myself, that they themselves also may be sanctified in truth" (John 17:17-19). Jesus asks God to set them apart for this task through the truth, the word which He had delivered to them. Through the agency of that potent word, as they kept it in heart and lived by it, God Himself was to be in them to direct, to speak, and to work in them His will. O that these apostles might be faithful and continue walking in the Lord and the Lord in them!

Sanctify means to make holy or to separate from ordinary things or uses and devote entirely to one worthy purpose. Jesus' statement "I sanctify myself" (John 17:19) shows the word does not mean primarily cleanse or purify. Jesus sanctified Himself by devoting Himself completely to the task of providing for our salvation. Jesus desired that every power and faculty of the apostles might be separated from worldly uses and consecrated to God's purpose. When the truth of God fills the mind and rules the heart, the whole man is made holy. One cannot be truly sanctified by any enforced control of conduct from outside himself, but he is consecrated by the effect of his being convinced of the truth and living fully in harmony with it. Jesus had called and prepared the apostles to be sent as missionaries to the world. The final commission came later, but the preparation was almost complete.

In the third part of His prayer Christ prayed that believers would (1) be united; (2) be perfected into one; and (3) come to be with Him and see His glory (John 17:20-26). Christ prayed "that they may all be one; even as thou, Father, art in me, and I in thee, that they also may be in us; that the world may believe that thou didst send me" (John 17:21). Christ's praying for all believers was somewhat like a man praying for his own body, that he might have good use of it in work that requires good co-ordination; but the church is Christ's body to do His work in the world, and He is crippled by its disunity. Believers must be perfected into one body and one spirit if they are to serve well the one Lord, stand fast in the one truth, and show the world the one divine Savior.

The unity for which Christ prayed is not just any kind of union, but a specified kind and on a specified basis. It is to be personal, every individual united. It is to be spiritual, a harmony of mind, heart, and soul, and not enforced from without. It is to be visible, so that the world will be strongly influenced to believe because of it.

Jesus desires the personal unity of each Christian with every other Christian. Such unity can be achieved only as each believer makes Christ the center of his faith and the authority for his life and religious matters.

O that the generations of believers that followed them might be perfected into one—they in the Lord and the Lord in them! Jesus' prayer was intensified by the fact that all His past labors, all His present sacrifice of Himself, and even His future joy, were involved in it. Who can read these outpourings of the deep and holy desires of our Savior without sadness and regret that we are so far from fulfilling His purpose and desire for us? Who can read without feeling that an unbelieving world is the dreadful price we pay for our sinful divisions?

Can we make ourselves and others desire unity of believers enough to pray for it like Jesus did and work for it like Paul? We are not likely to come near to accomplishing unity of Christians until we want it very much, even more than we want our own way, more than we want to exalt ourselves. I hear much talk about unity and the need for it, and about the problems of division. There is much written about it. Sometimes it seems almost to be another subject like the weather: "Everybody talks about it, but nobody does anything about it." In the prayers that I hear I do not discover that it is being prayed for very much; certainly not with the definiteness and fervent desire that Jesus expressed in His prayer. Brethren, let us learn to care, to pray, and to work that we "may be perfected into one; that the world may know that Jesus came from God" (John 17:23).

*Why Must We Have Unity of Christians?*

1. Jesus wants it that way. It should be enough that Christ prayed for unity of the church,' who gave Himself for her, who will claim her for His bride, who will give to her all His inheritance.

2. The Holy Spirit through the apostles urged unity (I Cor. 1:10; Eph. 4:1-6; Phil. 2:2; I Pet. 4:8-11).

3. The practice of division will condemn us (Gal. 5:20, 21; I Cor. 3:16, 17).

4. We are commanded to avoid or turn from those who cause division (Rom. 16:17, 18; Titus 3:10, 11; II John 9-11).

5. That the world may believe. Division among the churches makes it impossible for the schools to teach the certain truths of Christianity; and it gives to every common-school pupil the false impression that religion is not a matter of fixed truth, but only a matter of feelings and that every one makes his religion for himself, and it is just as respectable as any one else's religion. However much we may wish and agitate for the public schools to teach Christianity, they simply cannot do it while divisions continue to exist. The world discounts or disregards the testimony of a divided Christendom, just as we discount the so-called "scientific" conclusions which differ from and contradict one another while all are represented as "assured results." The less we care about contradictions in our testimony, the less the world cares about our affirmations. If it does not make any difference *what* one believes, it probably does not make any difference *whether* one believes. If one church is as good as another, possibly none is as good as any, since both statements rest upon the assumption that falsehood is as good as truth, disobedience as good as obedience.

6. Because division comes from putting human authority in the place of Christ. At least in some part it displaces Christ as the head of the church, and that is blasphemy (Eph. 1:20-23).

7. Because division comes from putting the words of men in the place of the infallible word of God. At least in some part it displaces the Holy Spirit as the revealer and spokesman of Jesus Christ and His covenant (I Cor. 2).

8. Because Christ is one and not divided. We cannot be perfectly united in and with Him without becoming united with each other. If we have the mind of Christ we will have the same mind, and so one through all the characteristics of the Christian which we receive from Christ Himself. Unity is natural and inherent in Christianity; and division among Christians misrepresents its nature.

9. Because division wastes and dissipates the energies and resources of evangelistic workers and supporters; furthermore, it turns a great bulk of religious effort from evangelism to party promotion and party regulation and party contentions. If all the printers' ink, if all the hours of study and conference, if all the money and men that have been employed to keep up human institutions had been used to bring men to their Savior, what glorious results might have been! As it is, five centuries of vigorous denominationalism leave the churches far from holding their own against the avowedly pagan world. "A house divided against itself cannot stand" (Matt. 12:25).

To sum up, all the causes of division are sinful; all the results of division are shameful; all the characteristics of division misrepresent Christ and despoil the godly character. Surely division is of the devil and is his best implement for hindering the church from victory. The faith, devotion, obedience and brotherliness that produce unity are godly. The practice of unity is sweet and blessed (Ps. 133:1). The results of unity are faith and its glorious victory. Its goal is that all should be perfected into one in Christ. Can any man doubt that unity is of God and is a prerequisite to a victorious church?

### *What Is the Unity For Which Christ Prayed?*

1. Jesus in His prayer describes it briefly, but exactly: "As thou, Father, art in me, and I in thee . . . that they may be one, even as we are one" (John 17:21, 22). This indicates the spiritual nature and extent of the unity He desires.

2. Such as the world can see: "that the world may believe" (John 17:21). To have this effect upon the world, unity would have to be visible. This does not mean that it would have to consist mainly of formal affiliation with religious organizations. Quite the contrary. A true unity in Christ will show in attitudes and practices without any organizational controls to centralize it. But it does mean it must

be more than a claim of invisible unity which outward actions deny.

Christ manifested the goodness and righteousness of God and made it possible for us to be partakers of the divine nature and be united in the divine kind of unity that exists between the Father and Son. Such converted lives, united in the glory of godlikeness, will show the world that Jesus was really from God and that the love of God abides both in them and upon them (John 17:21-23).

3. A fellowship of those who are called of God and set apart for His name, to do His work by His Spirit, using His Word—all in every place "that are sanctified."[1] This includes all who come to Christ through God's word and according to God's plan (John 6:37-40). Jesus had made known the real character of God so that His name was understood and appreciated. His purpose was not that His disciples might have the right name on their meetinghouse, but that they might have the love of God in them.

4. It is such a vital relationship as is described by figure of the members of the body in relation to the head (I Cor. 12; Rom. 12:4, 5), or of the branches to the vine (John 15:5).

5. Such as existed in the apostolic church when "the multitude of them that believed were of one heart and of one soul" (Acts 4:32).

6. Such as prompted the Gentile Christians to send help to Jewish Christians in time of need (II Cor. 8:1-9; especially verse 5).

7. Such as is indicated in the following words used in apostolic exhortations: "speak the same thing," "Be perfectly joined together," "same mind," "Like-minded," "same love," "of one accord," "preferring one another," and "with one accord and one mouth" (I Cor. 1:10; Phil. 2:2; Rom. 12:10, 16; I Cor. 12:25, 26).

8. Such as is characterized by "one Lord," "one faith," "one baptism," "one body," "one Spirit," "one hope," "one God and Father over all, in all and through all" (Eph. 4:1-6).

Can any man imagine that the state of Christendom today is the unity that pleases the Lord?

Note particularly that it was unity in faith, "the faith once for all delivered unto the saints." Jesus prayed that *those who believe* might be one. It was He that said, "but he that disbelieveth shall be condemned" (Mark 16:16). Paul, who so earnestly urged the Corinthian brethren to unity and love, closes his great letter of correction with

---

[1] Study the word sanctify and its other forms with a concordance. See the article "Sanctification" by H. F. Rall in *International Standard Bible Encyclopedia* (Grand Rapids: Wm. B. Eerdmans, 1939), iv, Pp. 2681-2685.

this: "If any man love not the Lord Jesus Christ, let him be anathema" (I Cor. 16:22). In Galatians 5:20-21 divisions under every name are condemned, but in Galatians 1:8, 9, Paul writes: "If any man preach unto you any gospel other than that which ye received, let him be anathema." In the first Epistle of John, Christian love and fellowship are upheld in their true nature and necessity, but in II John 9-11, Christians are strictly commanded to refuse fellowship to "anyone bringing not this teaching." Jesus commended the church at Ephesus because they could not endure evil men and did try false apostles (Rev. 2:2). He held it against the churches at Pergamos and at Thyatira that they had there some that held injurious teaching (Rev. 2:14-17, 20).

Unity of believers with unbelievers is so impossible that intermarriage of the two is not to be attempted (II Cor. 6:14—7:1). They could have a form of union, but not unity sanctified in Christ. "What portion hath a believer with an unbeliever?" "Or what communion hath light with darkness?" How can we hope to promote true unity in Christ while we disregard Christ's will and harbor unbelievers within the fellowship? Study and apply the following scriptures: Romans 16:17-19; Galatians 1:6-9; Titus 1:9-16; Titus 3:10; I John 2:18-26; 4:1-6; Jude 3, 4; II Corinthians 10:3-5; 11:13-15; I Timothy 6:20, 21; II Timothy 3:5; Ephesians 5:7-12.

### *How Shall We Attain Christian Unity?*

It can and should be attained among real believers. Unity is not unnatural to Christianity. Division is the unnatural, the abnormal state for Christians. Unity with rebels and unbelievers can never be accomplished. Hence, as long as the unbelievers pose as Christians it will not be possible for all nominal Christians to be united.

The description of unity implies the basis for it and the means of accomplishing it. Much study will be required for us to see all our misconceptions and remove all the hindrances and perfect all the details, but the general principles can be stated briefly and must be accepted before we can go further.

Unity must be in Christ. It is natural among those who accept Him and submit fully to His divine authority. Any other kind of unity is not only hopeless, but worthless. If all believe Him as He is revealed in the Spirit-inspired word of the New Testament, we will have "one faith." If all submit to Him, we will have "one Lord" (Eph. 4:4-6). The only way in which we can all "speak the same thing" is to speak what He has revealed in His word (I Cor. 1:10).

We can and will be all one body if we will let Him be the only Head of each of us and let His will and mind and purpose work in and through us. We do not need to have the same gifts and accomplishments, nor the same thoughts and opinions in the things of which He has not spoken, but we must have our lives surrendered and every thought brought into subjection to Him.

Keeping Christ as its head, solely and completely, the church will preserve authority and purity, and will require of everyone just what Christ requires. It will also preserve liberty and require nothing but what Christ requires. We must have as much patience and mercy for one another as Christ has for us. Now especially we need to study carefully the application of Romans 14. The basis of Christian unity is unity of each individual with God. What unites a repentant sinner with Christ unites him with all other persons who are thus united with Christ.

In all matters on which the Bible has spoken plainly we can all believe alike if we will believe what it really means to say. In all things which the word of God has commanded we will practice alike if we obey Him. In all matters of doctrine or practice of which the word of God does not speak, we have no right to lord it over one another; and each may have his own opinion. Differences in this realm of opinion should not hinder our love for one another. In *faith* (believing what the Lord has said) let us have *unity;* in *opinion* (deciding what the Lord has not decided for us) let us have *liberty;* in obedience to Him *loyalty* and *faithfulness:* in all things *love.*

"He drew a circle that shut me out,
Heretic, rebel, a thing to flout;
But love and I had a mind to win,
We drew a circle that took him in."

"There are circles large and circles small,
To shut men out or to include them all,
The making of circles goes on and on,
But what of the circle that God has drawn?"

For Further Study:

Campbell, Thomas, "Declaration and Address" in *Documents Advocating Christian Union,* ed. by C. A. Young. Chicago: The Christian Century Co., 1904. Pp. 71-210. Available in printed form from Lincoln Christian College Bookstore, Lincoln, Ill. Carefully thought out program for Christians to follow in seeking to fulfill the unity of the Lord intended and established. Recently paraphrased by Knofel Staton and available in booklet form from College Press, Joplin, Missouri.

Kershner, Frederick D. *The Christian Union Overture.* St. Louis: Bethany Press, 1923. Subtitle "An Interpretation of the Declaration and Address" of Thomas Campbell.

Reasoner, Norris Jacob. *Be One.* Joplin, Mo.: College Press, 1928. A humble and loving appeal for the kind of practice of Christianity which will promote the unity which the Lord established.

Wilson, Seth. *How to Have and Enjoy God's Gift of Christian Unity.* Joplin, Missouri: Mission Outreach, 1975. A study of Ephesians 4 suggesting a practical approach to the promotion of that unity established by Christ and His apostles.

# 76

# THE PRACTICE OF FELLOWSHIP AND UNITY

God wants peace and harmony in His universe. He will not surrender the world to the forces of evil in order to have immediate peace at any price, but His ultimate object is to overcome all strife and enmity. His will is, not only that we should "live and let live," but that we should live together in mutual helpfulness, sharing our lives. He desires unity and fellowship between Himself and man, as well as between man and man. The greatest commandments of the old covenant were that we love God with all our being, and that we love our neighbors as ourselves (Deut. 6:5; Lev. 19:18; Matt. 22:36-40). The new commandment that Jesus gave His disciples is that we love one another as Christ has loved us (John 13:34). We are to bear "one another's burdens, and so fulfill the law of Christ" (Gal. 6:2). "He that loveth his neighbor hath fulfilled the law" (Rom. 13:8-10; cp. James 2:8, 9).

It is wrong to think that we can be good Christians alone and indifferent to the lives and welfare of others, neglecting to come together in united expressions of faith and of worship to God through Christ. We are commanded to "consider one another to provoke unto love and good works; not forsaking the assembling of ourselves together, as the custom of some is, but exhorting one another" (Heb. 10:24, 25). We have a solemn request from Jesus, who died for us, that we participate in the breaking of bread in His memory, and that we all drink of the cup of the blood of the covenant (Matt. 26:27, 28). It seems that even nominally Christian people, those who think that they heed the Lord, just will not learn that He commanded us to worship Him and to love one another. The church makes a poor impression on the world while the majority of its members are notoriously indifferent to fellowship with Christ in His supper, and are torn by jealousy, strife, and faction, in which are "confusion and every vile deed" (James 3:16).

It is one of our fundamental failings, and the cause of many others, that we live so much by and for ourselves, forgetting God "in whom we live and move and have our being" (Acts 17:28), spurning our divine friend, who would share His whole life and glory with us and live in us, and despising our fellow men—and we are often actively engaged in rebellion against God and conflict with men.

*Understanding Fellowship and Unity*

Fellowship is communion, participation, sharing—having valuable and significant things in common—having, feeling, and doing things together in mutual interest. When two lives become one in an ideal marriage, that is fellowship. The fellowship Christ wants us to have is like that between Himself and the heavenly Father, each finding the fulfillment of Himself in the other.

It is a fellowship of faith based upon the word of truth (John 17:8). It is sharing the same convictions and principles by believing the same truth (I John 1:3). Men have always been brought into that fellowship by the hearing and believing of the testimony about Jesus. Jesus prayed for the unity, not of all men as such, but of all that believe on Him through the apostles' word (John 17:20-23).

Our fellowship is with God and Christ (I John 1:3; John 17:21; I Cor. 1:19). Indeed, it has its basis in the reconciliation of the sinner to God. The uniting of the individual with Christ is what brings about the unity between individuals in Christ. It is participating in the death of Christ, by which He died my death, and in His resurrection (Rom. 6:2-11; II Cor. 5:14, 15; Gal. 2:20; 6:14). It is receiving within ourselves the mind and spirit of Christ, receiving for our inheritance the unsearchable riches of Christ's inheritance, and, in turn, yielding to Him this life for Him to live in and to work through.

Christian fellowship is the fruit of a regenerated heart. While it is commanded, it can not be produced by the mere force of commandment. It is unity of the Spirit in the bond of peace (Eph. 4:3). It can not be accomplished by organization or by uniformity of ritual or tradition. Rather, it is the natural expression of love. It must come from the heart and its inner desires. Fellowship is unity, and unity is fellowship. One makes the other; neither can be had without the other.

New Testament fellowship had concrete expression: (1) In "breaking down the middle wall of partition" between races and classes (Gal. 3:26-28; Eph. 2:11-19); (2) in doing away with "respect of persons" because of wealth or worldly rank (James 2:1-9); (3) in effective co-ordination of the body in the work of building up itself "through that which every joint supplieth" (Rom. 12:3-7; Eph. 4:16); (4) in the important and difficult work of restoring or disciplining those who fall into sin (Gal. 6:1; II Thess. 3:6, 14, 15; I Cor. 5:11; II Cor. 2:6-11, etc.); (5) in giving and receiving material goods (Acts

4:32-35; Phil. 4:14-16; II Cor. 8:1-15; I Cor. 9:11-14); (6) in foregoing of rights and privileges for the protection of the weak, and in regard for the conscientious scruples of brethren (Rom. 14:13-20; 15:1-3; I Cor. 8:1-13); (7) in suffering persecution for Christ's sake and in ministering to those that were persecuted (Phil. 3:10; 4:14; Heb. 10:32-36; 13:3; I Pet. 2:21; 4:12-16; Rev. 1:9; II Tim. 2:10-12; 3:12; Rom. 8:17); (8) in public worship, praise, prayers, the Lord's Supper, and preaching—and in missionary reports.

Even on the night of His humiliation, in the hours of His great agony, Jesus' love directed His thoughts and prayers for others. He prayed for His apostles, who were with him, and for all who in any age believe in Him, for we all come to have our faith by their word (Rom. 10:17).

The earnest desire of the Lord, repeatedly expressed was that the believers might all be one, "as thou, Father, art in me, and I in thee, that they also may be one in us" (John 17:21). He sought a real unity, and a unity of spirit, purpose, and principle; not a potential or superficial unity, He didn't just say to the world of men, "Now get together and co-operate." He called them unto Himself, gave them a foundation of revealed truth, gave them His name, gave them the glory and dignity of sonship, as adopted into the family of God. He strictly commanded us that we should love one another as He has loved us.

The express purpose for which He prayed was "that the world might believe" and "know that thou hast sent me, and hast loved them, as thou hast loved me" (John 17:21, 23). The unity which He sought, then, is to show itself effectively to the world, and to help produce faith. We must confess with shame that instead of such unity today we have division that hinders faith notoriously.

Christ's prayer was that we might be united in Him—that all who believe Him should be perfectly one with Him and with one another in Him. He did not ask or intend that we should be joined together with unbelievers, or on any other basis than in Him. It is indeed pleasant and good for men to dwell together and work together in harmony, but the greatest, most blessed and really necessary unity is unity between a man and Christ. Shall we separate from God in order to unite with men? Or shall we not, rather, if necessary, separate from men to unite with God? He commands us to be holy and separated from the unfruitful works of darkness (Eph. 5:11); to be not yoked with unbelievers (II Cor. 6:14-18); to avoid false teachers (Rom. 16:17; II Tim. 3:5); to refuse the factious (Titus

3:10); to partake not in the evil works of those who abide not in the teaching of Christ (II John 9-11); to try leaders and reject those who are not of God (I John 4:1-6; II Pet. 2:1-18; Acts 20:29-32; Gal. 1:8, 9; Rev. 2:2; Rev. 2:14, 20); to come out of and have no fellowship with counterfeit religion and the apostate church (Rev. 18:4). The Lord commands unity, and He commands separation. Let us say with Joshua, "As for me and my house, we will serve Jehovah" (Josh. 24:15), even when it means total war with the Canaanites.

### *How the Apostles Handled a Threat to Unity*

When the Lord led some in preaching the gospel to Gentiles and adding them to Christ without the law of Moses, the contrary view of some others causes no small contention. It was a great threat to unity of the church of Christ (Acts 15). It often seems to me that if Paul and his co-workers averted division in their generation, we certainly ought to be able to do so today.

To attain and maintain untiy *we must care.* One great hindrance to unity is indifference to it. Let our complacency in division be gone! Let us heed Jesus' prayer, and join in it—fervently! Let us pray and seek and try to overcome the barriers and boundary lines that divide us. Unity is of the Spirit and of the heart. It will not come in full reality of expression until we want to draw near to one another in Christian love and fellowship—until we are pained at every discord.

Paul and Barnabas, and the others, were enough concerned to make long journeys and to examine the issue face to face with anyone to determine the Lord's will. They were not content to say, "I know I'm right. The others will have to come to me." As long as we are not enough concerned to take time, give thought, visit one another, and seek out the Lord's will together, we will not overcome the divisive issues that continually arise from ignorance and selfishness and unbelief.

Love is a necessity—with its expressions of mercy, forbearance, patience, preferment of others. Cold haughty exclusivism is as much misrepresentation and disloyalty to Christ as false teaching, and certainly a hindrance to unity. One form of it is officialism, which knows as brethren only those who submit to "official" oversight of men, and which co-operates only in contriving to "lord it over" the brethren. Those at the Jerusalem conference addressed their letter: "The brethren which are of the Gentiles" (Acts 15:23). Faith in Christ makes all men kind.

To have unity *we must all give our allegiance to one Lord.* First

He gave Himself that we might have one common object of strong devotion, or authority for ultimate appeal, one redeemer on whom our lives depend. By being bound to Him we are bound to each other. When we fasten our hearts upon Him, He directs our affections to one another. There can be no great unity of men without Christ as the focal center and co-ordinator of it. Without individual consecration to Him, co-operation is unlikely and insignificant. When we love Him, we love and cooperate with those who serve and exalt Him (I John 5:1).

A united structure must have one foundation. We must have a common center around which to gather and arrange ourselves. To maintain unity of purpose and endeavor in the midst of diversity of talent and opportunity we must be coordinated by one supreme authority—the authority of Christ (Matt. 28:18; Eph. 1:20-23; Col. 1:13-18; I Tim. 6:13-16). For this very reason we can not have unity in some council of churches among those who openly repudiate the authority of Christ and His word. The Jerusalem conference accomplished unity among these who accepted the will of Christ revealed through His apostles; but there were others who did not so accept the guidance of the Spirit in the apostles, and they are found later practicing division over circumcision and related matters of the law (Galatians).

To maintain unity *we must have a revelation of God's will.* The conference at Jerusalem was successful because the basis of their decision was this: "What has God revealed?" Peter presented the fact that God had sent His Spirit upon the uncircumcised, and "made no distinction between us and them, cleansing their hearts by faith" (Acts 15:8, 9). Paul and Barnabas rehearsed the signs and wonders God had wrought among the Gentiles through them. James showed that the scripture agreed. They were ready to accept the revealed will of God.

Even among men who acknowledged the same Lord, and who had a desire for unity, it was necessary for them to have clearly determined what the word of the Lord was regarding the matter that troubled them. Human wisdom is so diverse that the only way we could all speak the same thing is to speak the word of Christ just as He gave it. The letter sent from the Jerusalem meeting was not just their decision; it was the Holy Spirit's decision. This is of great importance. This conference does not set a precedent for us to meet and decide what we will without reference to the will of God.

God gave us His word that we might "speak the same thing" and "be of the same mind" (I Cor. 1:10). We can not have real unity in faith, teaching, and practice without the possession and full use of the infallible word of divine revelation on all matters in which we are to be in perfect accord.

We can have a common faith, a unity of faith, in the divine word. "Shall two walk together, except they have agreed?" (Amos 3:3). Men's opinions differ, but all opinions must be subject to the word of God (II Cor. 10:5), and opinions on other matters not expressly covered in the word of God do not have to be agreed one with another. The revelation of God covers all the essential principles and particular commandments necessary to bind our lives and our endeavors into one sweet symphony of harmony and peace, if we will accept it and keep opinions out of the way. Opinions and love of opinions is another great hindrance to unity, fostered by ignorance, selfishness and unbelief. The opinions that hurt most are those that rise in unbelief and should have been smothered by faith in the infallible word.

The threat to unity at Antioch was caused by (1) putting something else—traditions, human judgments—above Christ; (2) sincere zeal for God's word without proper understanding of it; (3) the tendency to set up themselves as a standard for others. Reverent heed to the Holy Spirit's revelation overcame all of these. But unbelief makes men fail to give full acceptance and obedience to Christ. They, then, are dependent on poor, fallible, variable human wisdom, and use it to separate from those who do believe and follow Christ.

Unbelief and ignorance may produce false convictions with all attendant zeal and firm resistance. These are often not so much from conscious rejection of the scripture as from misunderstanding or incomplete acceptance of it, on account of prejudice. Such convictions are common, are a real barrier to unity, and must be dealt with in overcoming division. Here we see the need of a humble spirit and constant study of the word of God, with special care not to go beyond the things that are written. Among believers who have accepted Christ upon His own simple terms, we must receive one another, "not for decision of scruples" (Romans 14). As long as men's opinions do not seriously hinder their submission to Christ and to the express requirements of His word, we may tolerate some of them that we can not approve. "To his own lord he standeth or falleth."

Intolerance can cause division, but tolerance alone can never bring unity such as Christ prayed for.

To maintain unity *we must keep central the redeeming work of*

*Christ.* He gave us His covenant of redeeming love, bought and sealed with His own blood, that we might have our hope and security in Him, might realize that we are helpless and condemned by ourselves, and might be humbled by the price that was paid for us.

He gave us a share in the glorious work and grave responsibility of bringing the men of the world to this salvation through faith in the Savior. He commissioned us to propagate this word of truth, not merely impersonally, but with personal concern for souls to be saved and brethren to be edified by it. In the work, we are to coordinate our diverse gifts and natures into one body, expressing not ourselves but the will of Christ and the power of His Spirit to regenerate and to sanctify. The discharge of our responsibility and the accomplishment of the Lord's purpose demand that we submit ourselves perfectly to Him, "subjecting ourselves one to another in fear of Christ" (Eph. 5:21), that His one Spirit may animate the one body to the glory of Christ and the saving of the world. A house divided against itself can not stand (Matt. 12:25). Our fellowship must not be marred by disunity; it must not be a matter of mere formal felicitation, or even of cooperation in only temporal and material interests. It must be real unity in Christ's special work of making men children of God by the new birth.

As a constant teacher and reminder of these things, He has given us the communion supper by which we express continually our participation in His death for us, and in which we may unite in genuine fellowship of faith and worship. It should so strengthen our allegiance to Jesus and our affectionate gratitude to Him that we will be drawn closer to our brethren in Him. It puts to shame all our pride and brings us all to one common level before the cross of redemption.

### *Principles for the Practice of Christian Unity*

I would summarize the most basic practices for the promotion of Christian unity:

1. Unlimited surrender to one Lord, Christ Jesus, the Son of God. As in international affairs some men are seeking to attain peace and united actions by the surrender of the sovereignty of nations to the United Nations, so in religious affairs some campaign for the surrender of local autonomy of congregations to the decisions (i.e., the rule) of centralized authorities in agency headquarters or conventions; and some plead for the surrender of everyone (from individuals to whole denominations) to the leadership of great councils of churches. It is my humble opinion that the nations would find a ready basis

for a just and lasting peace, if they would truly acknowledge the sovereignty of God and do His will. I am convinced that the people of all Christendom could find a sure basis for unity if they would seek it through obedience to Christ alone as Lord over all things pertaining to the church.

2. No glorying except in Him; no loyalty binding our hearts so that it can operate against His will or against the fellowship of His people. If this seems impossible, then our allegiance to Him must be so strong that it always overrules every other.

3. Love for all who are His, because He commands it, and because His love is shed abroad in our hearts. This does not mean that we always have to determine just who is His. We can love men for their intention to be His, and help them to fulfill it.

4. To make unity, make *believers* in Christ, but do not try to standardize them according to our opinions or human traditions. All our efforts to control them, confess our failure to convert them. Unity increases as we increase in genuine faith and the practice of it. Christianity is made to run on faith and love, as a Chevrolet is made to run on gasoline; and it will not run without them. Obviously this is not merely an affirmation of doctrine, but a faith that acts upon complete confidence in the Lord and His word. Let me say it this way: Faith is not holding to ideas regardless of our inability to prove them; but faith is following the Lord Jesus regardless of the consequences and in spite of our inability to see where He is leading us. We do this because He has proved Himself to be trustworthy, because of the evidence that He is the conqueror of death, the living Son of God, the Way, the Truth, and the Life.

5. Study diligently the Bible as the source of truth and light, as the way of life and felicity. God knows the commandments, the attitudes, and the practices that will lead men into unity. In fact, He has revealed them. Of course, this presupposes that the Bible is a revelation of the will of God, the wisdom and the truth which God gave to men. The Bible makes this very claim for itself in many statements and in many indirect ways. The Bible's teaching about unity is based upon the Bible's claim to authority. We cannot have one without the other.

6. A basic requirement for unity is an attitude of humility and love that seeks to help others instead of the judging attitude that withdraws from all whom we do not approve. Look again at Ephesians 4:2: "with all lowliness and meekness, with longsuffering, forbearing one another in love," is part of keeping the unity of the Spirit in the

bond of peace.

We must receive imperfect brethren. That is the only kind there is. We have no right to devise any tests of fellowship. We are not authorized to draw a line of fellowship: we must simply discover where Jesus drew the line. We must determine how Jesus identifies a man with Himself, how He calls one into the fellowship. Then we must receive our brothers in Christ as Christ receives us. We have no right to choose our brothers. Realizing our imperfections, let us humbly seek God's forgiveness and God's corrective guidance.

Romans 12 and Romans 14 have much important teaching for the promotion of peace and unity. First be fully consecrated to Christ. Think not too highly of self. Recognize the differing gifts of God in different brethren. Love not in word only. Feel family affection for one another. In honor prefer one another. Pray for one another. Be helpful and sharing in all circumstances. Send forth blessing even to those that oppose you. Don't retaliate if men disapprove you. Take care for the welfare and the good conscience of every brother. Unity is in the mind, in the way we think toward one another; and it requires humility. There is nearly always pride in division. Our life must be a confession of Jesus Christ, not a profession of our excellence or loyalty to Him.

There will be differences of opinion and practice. We must face them as brothers, not enemies. We must settle them as servants of the same Lord, following the same instructions from on high. Differences must be occasions for discussion and study, not for division. Regard division not as an instrument for purifying the church, but as a weapon for destroying it. Listen to one another, study together as equals with very much in common. No one has a right to despise another who is purchased by Christ's blood and born into the family of God.

7. II Timothy 2:14-26 teaches that we must shun vain disputes and foolish questionings, profane babblings and strife about words to no profit. "The Lord's servant must not strive, but be gentle towards all, apt to teach, forbearing, in meekness correcting them that oppose themselves." Yet the church is to be warned against false teachings. We need leaders in local churches who take seriously their responsibility to lead in teaching sound doctrine and rejecting false doctrines.

8. We need to act from strictly non-sectarian motives to do Christ's will. Fellowship is not only a matter of theory or of sentiment, but there is a very important realm of practice, participating together

in Christian works. Let us show that we belong to Christ, not to any party. Let us claim no other people but all of Christ's people. Let us recognize every work of Christ as our work, and participate in it for His sake as far as we have opportunity, without caring who gets the credit. If we judge that some work is not what Christ wants done, let us refrain from it, regardless of who urges us, not following human leaders as if we belonged to them, not compromising Christ's authority, His word, or our allegiance to Him for the favor of men or the promotion of human glory for anybody. "Whatsoever ye do, in word or in deed, do all in the name of the Lord Jesus, giving thanks to God the Father through Him" (Col. 3:17). Do all as His agents, taught by His word, impelled by love and devotion to Him, subject to His approval, His favor, and His help. Let Him over-rule our plans and modify our efforts wherever they fail to uphold the fellowship of His whole body or where they hinder other portions of His work.

When people who intend to be Christians are not of one heart and soul, it is because they have something else binding them other than Christ.

When Christ comes again to separate the sheep from the goats, to take the saints, living and dead, to dwell wth Him forever, we will all want to be in that one body. We are now too much interested in getting members in our congregations and organizations, but not enough concerned for all the saints who belong to Christ. Pray, work, and study; find the nature of our divisions, learn the causes of them for which we need to repent; develop a climate of repentance of the sin of division. Be honest in facing our own faults and the obstacles to unity. Set Christ's aims, spiritual aims for individual lives, far above institutional goals, or entirely in place of them, putting real Christianity above all kinds of conformity to human customs. Cultivate a desire for all the unity that is possible within the limitations of the revealed will of Christ, the Head of the Church.

For Further Study:

See books listed on pages 419-420.

# *Part Fourteen*

# SECOND COMING AND JUDGMENT

## 77

### THE COMING JUDGE

When Jesus was riding into Jerusalem on a donkey, surrounded by the excited throng shouting His praise, the people of the city asked, "Who is this?" And some of the crowd answered, "This is the prophet Jesus, from Nazareth of Galilee" (Matt. 21:11).

How far short their description fell! How little they really understood who He was!

Today, far too many people are thinking of Jesus as only a teacher or prophet from Galilee in the days of long ago. They think that He has had some interesting and important effects upon society. They may respect, somewhat, His teaching and His following, but they only think that they know Jesus.

No one knows Jesus who thinks that He belongs to the past, or who considers that we have to do only with the moral and social application of His teaching.

He is far more than a prophet in the past. He is a power in the present. And He is the most certain and significant of all the prospects for the future!

Jesus is living and reigning today at the right hand of the Father in heaven, offering His covenant of mercy and the new birth of the Spirit to all who will receive, calling out of the world a people for His own possession. He is coming again to earth to consummate this age, to receive His redeemed ones unto himself, to purify His kingdom, and to execute the righteous judgment of God upon all the living and the dead.

The gospel of Christ is a message of facts—facts of history, unchangeable as the past naturally is, and sure as historical records and testimony can make them. But they are not just ordinary facts such as may be found in every part of history. They are unique facts of men's experience with God when God came to men in human form in the person of Jesus Christ. They are the incomparable facts of His life and works, revealing His divine person and power and His eternal purpose for all men of every age. Thus the gospel is not merely a record of the past. It is even more than the truth regarding our present duty and welfare. It points inexorably to the future. It is most important as a preparation for and a promise of things to come. Predictions are an inseparable and most vital part of the gospel, giving meaning to its facts and purpose to its commandments. The promises and warnings of the Lord help to enlighten and to motivate every believer of His Word.

The most important prospects for the future for you and me and everyone are not the prospects of national prosperity or depression or war or conquest of space, but the certain coming of Jesus to end this age and to institute a new order of things.

### *We Can Be Sure of His Coming*

That He is coming is sure because He said so. We, of course, cannot know it or prove it any other way, except to take His word for it. But we can trust Him completely because of the undeniable facts of His first coming which clearly proved His divine character. To anyone who believes in Him as the Son of God, the predictions of His word are plain enough to make us very sure that He is coming back in person in visible form.

He said, "If I go . . . I will come again, and receive you unto myself" (John 14:3). "For the Son of man shall come in the glory of His Father with His angels; and then He shall reward every man according to his works" (Matt. 16:27). "When the Son of man shall come in His glory, and all the holy angels with Him, then shall He sit upon the throne of His glory" (Matt. 25:31). "They shall see the Son of man coming in the clouds of heaven with power and great glory" (Matt. 24:30b). Under oath in court, on trial for His life, Jesus said, "Hereafter shall ye see the Son of man sitting on the right hand of power, and coming in the clouds of heaven" (Matt. 26:64).

He made several parables for the purpose of emphasizing the importance of His coming and the need for one's being watchful and ready for it: "As the days of Noah were . . . so shall also the coming of the Son of man be" (Matt. 24:37-42; Luke 17:26-30); the householder and the thief; the faithful and the wicked servants (Matt. 24:43-51); the foolish virgins (Matt. 25:1-13); the parables of the talents (Matt. 25:14-30); and of the pounds (Luke 19:11-27).

Angels said, "This same Jesus, which is taken up from you into heaven, shall so come in like manner as ye have seen him going into heaven" (Acts 1:11).

Those whom Jesus sent to preach the gospel He also inspired by His Spirit to guide them into all truth and to make known to them things to come (John 16:13-15). Throughout their preaching and their writings they taught that Jesus was coming again in person. "For the Lord himself shall descend from heaven with a shout, with the voice of the archangel, and with the trump of God; and the dead in Christ shall rise first" (I Thess. 4:16. See also Acts 3:20, 21; I Pet. 1:7; 5:4; II Pet. 3:3, 4; James 5:7; Heb. 9:28; I John 2:28; Rev. 1:7; I Cor. 1:7; 4:5; 11:26; 15:23; Phil. 3:20, 21; Col. 3:4; I Thess. 1:10; 2:19; 3:13; 4:16-18; 5:1-4, 23; II Thess. 1:7-10; 2:1, 8; I Tim. 6:14, 15; II Tim. 4:1, 8; Titus 2:13). The apostolic writers not only speak plainly and directly of Christ's coming, but they also refer to His "appearing," "being manifested," His "presence," the "revelation" of Christ, and the "day of Christ" (for example Phil. 1:6, 10; I Cor. 5:5; II Thess. 2:2; Heb. 10:25).

Some men say they count 318 times that Christ's coming is mentioned in some manner in the 260 chapters of the New Testament. No doubt some of that number are obscure references, and of some it may be very doubtful whether they are interpreted correctly when they are applied to the second coming of Christ. But definite and plain predictions of that great event are made literally dozens of times in such manner that they could not be fulfilled in the conversion or death of individuals, in the beginning of the church, the coming of the Holy Spirit, or the judgment upon Jerusalem. They emphatically predict things which have not happened yet and they could not point to a secret or "spiritual" or invisible coming.

### *When? No One Knows*

When He is coming, we do not know, because He has not told us that (Matt. 24:36). He has continually emphasized the need to be ready at all times because no one will know when He is to come (see Rev. 16:15; I Thess. 5:2, 3; Matt. 24:27-51; 25:1-13). He will come as a thief in the sense that His coming will be unannounced, unexpected, and sudden. In the same sense it will be as travail upon a woman with child.

But He has assured us that when He does come it will be evident to all, with power and great publicity, as the lightning in the east is seen unto the west, with a great shout and the sound of the trumpet (Rev. 1:7; Matt. 24:26, 27, 30, 31; I Cor. 15:52; I Thess. 4:16).

### *Why He Wants Us to Know of the Future*

Our Lord wants us to know some things about the future. He wants us to be warned and prepared for crises that must come. He wants us to understand the nature of our salvation, and know that this world is not our hope or our permanent home. He wants us to look forward with hope and longing to His coming in glory and to our perfect union with Him whom we love. He wants us to realize that He himself is our destiny and our exceeding great reward. He wants us to have assurance and comfort in the afflictions and sorrows of life.

He would have us all to be as strong and steadfast as Paul, by having his kind of faith in the "far more exceeding weight of eternal glory" and by looking with him "not at the things which are seen, but at the things which are not seen." Read II Corinthians 4:16 to 5:11.

Daily consciousness of the imminent return of Christ will surely prompt more godly living, promote more sacrificial giving, produce more patience and even rejoicing under trials, and purify our motives in all that we do. We need to realize that we do all our works under His watchful eye, and we shall soon stand before Him to give account.

The heart of Christianity is the vital power of faith, hope, and love—all centered upon Jesus Christ. Anyone who does not believe His word enough to hope for His coming and to love His appearing will surely lack the personal force of Christ in his life.

The predictions of His coming should be even to the unbeliever an inducement to heed more seriously Christ's commands and claims, because His coming is a threat to the disobedient as well as a promise to the faithful.

### *What Will Happen When He Comes?*

The Lord has revealed only a few particulars and something of the general nature of the great events which will take place when He comes. No doubt there are many things in store for us that we have not been told, because we could not grasp or appreciate them now. Very likely some of the things predicted will not happen just as we imagine them. It is difficult, if not impossible, to tell in what order or how close together the following events will come to pass. But we are told that in connection with His coming or after it: the dead will be raised (I Thess. 4:16; John 5:28, 29); the saved will be with the Lord (John 14:3; I Thess. 4:17); the bodies of the redeemed will be changed into the likeness of the body of His glory (Phil. 3:21; I Cor. 15:52-54; Rom. 8:23-25); the world and the works therein will be burned up (II Pet. 3:11-13); a crown of glory will be given to the faithful (II Tim. 4:8; I Pet. 5:4); Christ will execute judgment upon all men (II Tim. 4:1; Jude 14, 15; Acts 10:42; 17:31; John 5:22-29;

II Cor. 5:10); He will reject many who thought they were saved (Matt. 7:21-23; 22:13, 14; Luke 13:25-27; compare Matt. 13:40-43 and 47-50); the door of salvation will be forever closed (Luke 13:25-28); there will be grief and terror in the hearts of many because they are unprepared to meet Him (Matt. 24:30, 50, 51; 25:30; Rev. 1:7; 6:14-17; Luke 13:28; I Thess. 5:3; II Thess. 1:7-9).

Whether or not all men are to be judged at one time, or whether there will be two judgments, or three or five, is relatively unimportant. Probably no man knows just how and when it will all be done, but the Lord will take care of it without our figuring it out. The important matter is to be ready for judgment by being in Christ, and to know that "We must all appear before the judgment seat of Christ; that every one may receive the things done in his body, according to that he hath done, whether it be good or bad" (II Cor. 5:10).

Let every sinner remember this fact, and contemplate what it will mean: Our Savior will be our judge! He who once served the sentence of death for us, who now makes intercession for us at the throne of God, who invites all to come to Him and be saved—it is He who will come in flaming fire, rendering vengeance upon all who know not God and obey not the gospel! (II Thess. 1:9).

For Further Study:

Allis, Oswald T. *Prophecy and the Church,* rev. ed. Philadelphia: Presbyterian and Reformed Publishing Co., 1947. Thorough dicussion of issues in the interpretation of Biblical prophecies.

Bales, J. D. *Prophecy and Premillenialism.* Searcy, Ark.: J. B. Bales Books. Expansion of his earlier work on "New Testament Interpretation of Old Testament Prophecies."

Hendriksen, William. *The Bible on the Life Hereafter.* Grand Rapids: Baker Book House, 1959. Deals with the whole range of questions regarding Biblical prophecy concerning the end of the age.

Hughes, Phillip E. *Interpreting Prophecy.* Grand Rapids: Wm. B. Eerdmans, 1976. Gives attention to principles of interpretation of prophecy.

Ladd, George E. *Jesus and the Kingdom.* New York: Harper & Row, 1964. Deals with Jesus' teaching on His Kingdom and the end of time from viewpoint of historic pre-millenialism.

Ludwigson, Raymond. *A Survey of Bible Prophecy.* Grand Rapids: Zondervan Publishing House, 1973. Brief, objective explanation of various viewpoints and terms involved in the study of Bible prophecies relating to last things. Former edition was entitled *Bible Prophecy Notes.*

Reese, Gareth. *Let's Study Prophecy.* Moberly, Mo.: Central Christian College of the Bible. Defense of amillennial understanding of New Testament prophecy.

Summer, Ray. *The Life Beyond.* Nashville: Broadman Press, 1959. Pp. 95-146. Discusses the certainty, manner and time of the second coming. Includes good practical discussion on the effect this doctrine should have on our lives.

# 78

## WHEN IS JESUS COMING AGAIN? (Matthew 24)

The purpose of this study is to outline, clarify, and emphasize what Jesus said about the future in His great prophetic discourse in Matthew 24, Mark 13, and Luke 21.

Charles F. Kettering, the famous inventor, said, "I'm interested in the future, because I expect to spend all the rest of my life in it."

Although many people are interested in the time of Jesus' second coming, and more should be, no one actually knows anything about it except what is recorded in the Bible. It is written there (Matt. 24:36) that no one knows the day or hour. Jesus said a good deal about it, without setting a time, because really it doesn't matter so much when He comes, as it does that we shall expect Him at all times and be ready.

Christians, especially evangelistic workers, are interested in pointing out the signs that precede that impending and momentous day, because they hope to make everyone heed the warnings, promises, and commands of the Lord and be ready. In their zeal to impress folk of little faith with the fact that Jesus is coming just any time now, some have tried to find more "signs" than Jesus actually gave.

I suppose no passage has furnished more phrases for popular misuse and misunderstanding than this discourse. How many people think that wars and rumors of wars, earthquakes, famine and pestilence are signs of Christ's coming! All Jesus ever said of these things is that they are not signs, even of the fall of Jerusalem, and the apostles were not to be troubled by them. Read the chapters for yourself and see!

Aren't we inclined to feel that prophecy is of uncertain meaning and therefore anyone is free to guess about it any way he wants to? It may become a matter of sad importance if we teach so many conflicting opinions and arbitrary assumptions that people lose respect for the very subject that we are trying to impress upon them.

The New Testament does teach in dozens of places concerning the second coming as a matter of great importance for us to know about. Christians should look forward to it with joy and longing. (Read Titus 2:13, 14; I Thess. 1:10; 4:13-18; 5:1-11; II Tim. 4:8; Heb. 9:28; John 14:1-3; Acts 1:11; Phil. 3:20, 21; I John 2:28; 3:1-3; I Pet. 1:7; 5:4; I Cor. 1:7, 8; James 5:7, 8; Rev. 22:20.) But it will bring judgment, and multitudes unprepared will have sorrow and terror (Matt. 16:27; I Cor. 4:5; I Thess. 5:2, 3; II Thess. 1:7-10; Luke 17:22-36; 18:8; Rev. 1:7; 6:12-17; Matt. 25:1-46).

A vivid expectancy of the Lord's appearance is profitable, because it prompts godly living, promotes sacrificial service, provides comfort for the suffering, produces patience and rejoicing under severest trials, and perfects watchfulness with prayer.

Matthew 24, Mark 13 and Luke 21 constitute one of the most important (and abused) sections of the Bible on this great subject. The following outline gives a whole view of these chapters and seeks to relate their parts properly to each other. They are not mere collections of prophetic puzzles with hidden double meanings, but clear records of Jesus' answers to His friends' questions about the destruction of the great stone buildings at Jerusalem and about a sign of His coming.

I. The Occasion and the Question (Matt. 24:1-3; Mark 13:1-4; Luke 21:5-7).

1. Observing the magnificent buildings of Jerusalem.
2. Jesus' dire prediction: "There shall not be left one stone."
3. The disciples' questions:
   a. "When shall these things be?" (Destruction of Jerusalem.)
   b. "What shall be the sign of thy coming, and of the end of the world?"

II. Answers to the Questions.

1. Answer to first question, concerning Jerusalem (Matt. 24:4-28; Mark 13:5-23; Luke 21:8-24).
   a. Warning of preliminary, unrelated troubles. "The beginning of travail." Beware false alarms (Matt. 24:4-14; Mark 13:5-13; Luke 21:8-19).
      (1) False Christs, wars, famines, earthquakes do not indicate the end; be not troubled or led astray.
      (2) Persecutions, apostasies, false prophets, shall afflict the church: "Take heed to yourselves"; endure to the end; trust God for help; the gospel testimony shall go into all the world. (Cp. Col. 1:6, 23; Rom. 1:8; 10:18; 16:19).
   b. The sign of Jerusalem's end, and how to escape the woes of that terrible time (Matt. 24:15-28; Mark 13:14-23; Luke 21:20-24).
      (1) "The abomination of desolation standing in the holy place" is "Jerusalem compassed with armies" (Luke

21:20.) "Then know that her desolation is at hand."

(2) Let those in Judea flee to the mountains without delay. Pray that the hardships of flight may be lessened; but the unprecedented afflictions of the city must be escaped at all costs. Believe no false prophets, signs or promises; I have forewarned you; the Christ will not come until He is seen from the east to the west.

(3) The tribulation shall be excessive, shall threaten extinction of the Jewish people, shall take them captive to other nations, shall leave Jerusalem to the Gentiles, "until the times of the Gentiles be fulfilled."

2. Answer to second question, concerning Christ's coming (Matt. 24:29-31; Mark 13:24-27; Luke 21:25-28).
   a. The time is purposely indefinite; but the event is to be watched for at all times ("Immediately" Matt. 24:29), after a terrible and extended (see Luke 21:24) tribulation.
   b. But the event itself shall be unmistakable; accompanied by tremendous sights and sounds in all earth and heaven, the Lord Himself shall be seen by everyone, coming in the clouds with power and great glory.
   c. The angels shall gather the elect from everywhere: look up, your redemption draws near.

III. The Answers Reviewed in Contrasting Summary (Matt. 24:32-36; Mark 13:28-32; Luke 21:29-33).

1. Parable of the leaves of trees: when spring begins you know summer is coming. Watch for "all these things"—wars, percutions, false Messiahs, the desolation of Jerusalem—to come to pass in this generation. (all of them did happen before A.D. 70.)
2. Solemn affirmation of the unfailing certainty of His words.
3. But "of that day"—Jesus' coming—no one knows. The time cannot be told, even by the Son of God.

IV. Parables and Exhortations to Be Ready at All Times (Matt. 24:37-51; Mark 13:33-37; Luke 21:34-36).

1. As in the days of Noah the flood came suddenly upon those who had been warned but believed not, so shall the coming of the Son of man be without any immediate forewarning signs.
2. In the midst of daily work, suddenly one shall be taken and another left; watch for ye know not the day. (The "elect" shall

be taken; compare Matt. 24:31; I Thess. 4:16, 17; I Cor. 15:52.)

3. Parable of a householder unprepared for a thief who came when he was not expected. Be ready, for when you think not, the Lord comes.
4. The servants of the absent Lord have each his own work to be faithful in till He comes. He may not come as soon as they imagine; but if they think that he tarries and can take advantage of His delay to indulge in sin; He will come when they least expect it and will punish them. "Watch at every season" (Luke 21:36).

Jesus continued these lessons in the twenty-fifth chapter of Matthew: (1) in the parable of the ten virgins waiting for the bridegroom, (2) in the parable of the talents committed to servants until the Lord's return, and (3) in the scene of judgment that shall take place when He shall come in His glory. In these He emphasizes that the servants must be prepared to wait patiently and to serve faithfully even though the Master may not come for "a long time." His coming will bring strict judgment and swift vengeance upon all who have not used the intervening time in His service.

For Further Study:

Foster, R. C. *Studies in the Life of Christ.* Grand Rapids: Baker Book House, 1962. Pp. 1154-1210. Comment on Jesus' predictions about the destruction of Jerusalem and the second coming.

See commentaries on Matthew 24, Mark 13, and Luke 21. Also see books listed on pages 435, 436.

# 79

## A SECRET RAPTURE CONSIDERED

I truly desire to see people awakened to the reality and tremendous significance of the second coming of our Lord. But to put all the emphasis upon a secret rapture and mysterious disappearance of the saved, as if that were certainly the nature of Christ's coming, is to teach as Bible truth what is at best a doubtful, speculative view of the implications of the Bible.

The Lord's coming is surely and clearly taught; so also is the separation of the saved from the unsaved, the resurrection of those in Christ, the transformation of the bodies of both the living and the resurrected saints, and their rising to meet Him, ever to be with Him. But after much restudy of the scriptures, I agree with R. A. Torrey's statement: "the doctrine of the secret rapture of believers does not seem to have much support in scripture."[1]

I have seen the Baptist motion picture on the rapture and have heard the idea for years. I have had no particular reason to oppose it, and have no feeling against, if that is what the Lord wants to do; but I just can't find that the scripture teaches it. I have the *Millenium Bible* by Biederwolf before me; and it makes the fullest study of all the implications which men have found in or read into every prophetic passage. It certainly favors a premillenial view with separate resurrections, a period of tribulation, etc.; but its comments on the rapture are divided, uncertain and confused, not at all strong for a secret rapture.

I Thessalonias 4:13-17 does indeed teach that the saved (both living and resurrected) will be caught up to meet the Lord in the air at His coming, but there is no indication that it is silent and secret so that it leaves the rest of the world mystified by their absence. It says that the Lord will come with a shout, with the voice of the archangel and the trumpet of God. How can we know that this coming to meet His saints is a different coming from that described in Revelation 1:7 where it says: "Every eye shall see Him, and they that pierced Him?" "For as lightning cometh out of the east and shineth even unto the west; so shall the coming of the Son of man be" (Matt. 24:26, 27; Luke 17:23, 24).

Those who hold that Matthew 24:30—"They *shall see* the Son of man coming on the clouds of heaven with power and great glory"—

---

[1] R. A. Torrey, *What The Bible Teaches* (London: James Nisbet & Co., n.d.), p. 199.

refers to a third coming (or to a second phase of His coming) seven years after He has taken the saved out of the earth, run into serious difficulties. They must make verse 31 refer to a group called "his elect" who are not of the church or the redeemed at His coming. The parable of the ten virgins surely does not indicate that those who are unprepared at His coming will be gathered in later. I Thessalonians 5:3 indicates that the coming of the Lord which brings sudden destruction upon the wicked is to be in a time when they are saying, "Peace and safety," which hardly seems to be at the climax of seven years of terrible tribulations after all the righteous have disappeared.

The Scriptures most cited as teaching this seven years of tribulation are from Daniel and Matthew 24:21, 29, which in their context refer to the Jews and the fall of Jerusalem. In Luke 17:22-37 Jesus told His disciples that they would desire to see one of the days of the Son of man, but would not be able to until He comes upon both the godly and the ungodly by surprise when they are buying, selling, planting and building, apparently unmindful of any impending judgments.

The Bible does not say that Jesus is coming once "for His saints" and again "with His saints." The passage in I Thessalonians 4:13-17, which is supposed to teach the former, says: "Even so them also that are fallen asleep in Jesus will God bring with him." If "to be absent from the body is to be at home with the Lord" (see II Cor. 5:8; Phil. 1:21-23) then, when the Lord comes to unite the dead saints with the living ones and to transform the bodies of both (see I Cor. 15:51; Phil. 3:20, 21), why wouldn't He bring the saints with Him? Isn't it also possible that Jude 14—"The Lord came with ten thousands of His holy ones" (This is the ASV and "saints" simply means holy ones) refers to the angels that come with him" (see also Matt. 16:27). Matthew 13:39-41 says He will send the angels to gather the wicked, and Matthew 24:31 also says that when He comes, He will with the sound of a great trumpet send forth His angels to gather His elect from all parts of the world.

The statements about one being taken and another left (Matt. 24:40, 41; Luke 17:34, 35) do not necessarily picture a secret rapture. The word which is translated "taken" in each of these verses is the same word exactly which is used in John 14:3 "I will come again and receive you unto myself." These verses may only say that of people who live and work together here, one will be received by the Lord and the other left out, when Jesus comes for His own.

When the Scripture says that His coming will be as a thief in the night, it explains that it means suddenly and unannounced upon those who are not looking for Him, but it never indicates that it means stealthily and unseen (see I Thess. 5:1-3; Luke 12:39-46; Matt. 24:42-44; Rev. 16:15). In fact, Peter says: "But the day of the Lord shall come as a thief; in the which the heavens shall pass away with a great noise; and the elements shall be dissolved with a fervent heat, and the earth and the works that are therein shall be burned up" (II Pet. 3:10). All this comes "as a thief!"

There may be some time between events that are associated with the Lord's coming, the resurrection of the saved, the resurrection of the wicked, the judgments of men, destruction of this earth, establishment of a new heaven and a new earth wherein dwelleth righteousness (II Pet. 3:13), etc. But the time tables which man offer on the "rapture," the "tribulation," the "revelation of Christ with the saints," the "millenium," the "judgment of the nations," etc. is all speculative. It is not found in the Scripture and the advocates of all these things cannot find grounds enough to agree among themselves concerning the order and timing of them.

Even the expression in I Thessalonians 4:16—"the dead in Christ shall rise first" does not necessarily depict a second resurrection. The contrast which is stated in the context is between the living believers and the dead believers. The living will not precede the dead, because the dead will be raised first, and then (next) the living will be caught up with them to meet the Lord in the air. Nothing at all is said about the resurrection of the unbelievers in the entire chapter.

I know that Revelation 20:5 says: "the rest of the dead lived not until the thousand years should be finished. This is the first resurrection." And I am not at all sure exactly what many verses of this chapter refer to, although their general intent is clear. But I do notice that it does not say, or even clearly imply, that the reigning with Christ for one thousand years is to take place upon the earth. And it does not say, or even clearly imply, that the thousand years of reign begins at the second coming of Christ. It says that John saw the "souls" of martyrs and of undefiled worshippers of Jesus reigning with Him. Jesus is reigning, even now, at the right hand of God, far above all rule, and authority, and power (Eph. 1:20-23). Long ago He told the church in a letter, that He had overcome and sat down on His Father's throne with Him (Rev. 3:21). Jesus said on earth that He was a king, and that His kingdom was not of this world (John 18:33-37). He also solemnly promised that the kingdom would come with power while many that heard Him speak were still alive (Mark 9:1). The apostles preached that the Christians of their day were in the kingdom of God's dear Son (Col. 1:13; Rom. 14:17), although they looked forward to the kingdom of the future also (II Pet. 1:11, and others). They considered that the universal gospel of their day fulfilled the prophecy of Amos 9:11, 12 about God's building again the tabernacle of David (Acts 15:15-18). Revelation 1:6 cites it as a fact in John's day that "He made us to be a kingdom and priests." They even speak (rather mystically) of the fact that He has raised us up with Christ and made us to sit with Him in the heavenly places (Eph. 2:6). The first resurrection of Revelation 20:5 could be the resurrection of the believer when he is "raised with Him [Christ]" and "made alive together with Him" (Col. 1:12, 13; 3:1; Eph. 2:5).

For Further Study:

Hendriksen, William. *The Bible on the Hereafter.* Grand Rapids: Baker Book House, 1959. Pp. 178-184. Rejects the view that the rapture will be secret and that it will be 1000 years before the resurrection of the wicked.

Ludwigson, R. *A Survey of Bible Prophecy.* Grand Rapids: Zondervan Publishing House, 1973. Pp. 133-160. Surveys various views on the time of the rapture—whether it is to be before or after the tribulation.

# 80

## JESUS' TEACHING ABOUT THE JUDGMENT

### *The Fact of Judgment*

All the revelation of God to man implies that man is responsible to God for what he does with life and the other gifts of God. Many direct declarations of the Word of God combine to make known to us that all men shall give account to God and receive a just judgment from Him before whom nothing is hid. There will be a day of reckoning for all men at one time or another (See John 5:28, 29; Luke 11:31, 32; Matt. 10:15; 11:22, 24; 16:27; 12:36-41; Acts 17:31; Rom. 2:6, 16; 14:10-12; II Cor. 5:10; II Thess. 1:6-10; II Pet. 2:9; 3:7; I John 4:17; Jude 6; Rev. 20:12-15; 22:12).

Many Bible students distinguish several different judgments. Indeed, some phases of God's judgment upon sin in this world have already been carried out and are being continually carried out (for example Gen. 3:14-24; John 16:11; Rom. 8:3; Gal. 6:7; John 3:18, 19). Moreover, God's sentence against this sinful world (as well as the guilt of all men) has already been announced (II Pet. 3:10-12; Rom. 2:12; 3:9-23; 11:32; Gal. 3:22). But the complete justice of God is yet to be revealed and the full severity of His sentence is yet to be realized upon those who are outside of the salvation in Christ. Some day He must make known the individuals who are accepted under the terms of that conditional salvation. Still, it is not so important whether there are to be three or five or seven judgments, as it is to be ready for our judgment when it comes.

When the apostles went out preaching the gospel of salvation, the announcement of judgment to come was prominent in their message (Acts 17:31; 24:25). The Holy Spirit was given them that through them He might convict the world of sin, righteousness, and judgment (John 16:11); and Peter testified that they were charged to preach Jesus as the Judge of the living and the dead (Acts 10:42). The fact that the preaching of judgment is not popular today is evidence of unbelief and unfaithfulness in a large proportion of preachers of this day, who fit the description Paul gives in II Timothy 4:3, 4: "For the time will come when they will not endure the sound doctrine, but, having itching ears, will heap to themselves teachers after their own lusts; and will turn away their ears from the truth, and turn aside unto fables." It shows the lack of courage to face the displeasure of men and the lack of love for lost souls to bring them face to face with that from which they need to be saved.

Don't be afraid of scaring someone into accepting Christ. Men are not much interested in salvation until they know that they are lost. Many souls were saved by the preaching of the apostles because they were made to tremble and fear and seek salvation. "The fear of the Lord is the beginning of wisdom" (Prov. 9:10). In one of the most evangelistic chapters of Jesus' preaching, He says: "Fear him, who after he hath killed hath power to cast into hell; yes, I say unto you, fear him" (Luke 12:5). Many do not accept the Savior because they do not accept the judgment and sentence which God has written against them for their sins. Sinners ought to be scared—not falsely—but with a realization of their true danger; at the same time they ought to see that they are loved and to realize God's desire to save them.

### *The Judge*

The same Jesus who was the lowly Son of man, who was the sacrifice for our sins, is now the Lord of lords. He must reign until His enemies become the footstool of His feet, and He himself will be the Judge of all (John 5:22, 27; Acts 10:42; Matt. 7:22, 23; 25:31-46). See also the second Psalm. Jesus shall return to the earth and call all men to judgment before Him. The last time, He will come to judge and to destroy those who will not receive His salvation (II Thess. 1:7-10). To the believers it is very comforting to know that He who will be our Judge is our Savior, the one who has suffered with us a Brother in the flesh (Heb. 2:10-12), and who has loved us so dearly that He died for us, who also has been a "merciful and faithful high-priest" for us. The unconverted should find it all the more fearful to contemplate that in the terrible day of judgment, the only one who might have been their Advocate and Savior will have become their judge. Now is the time to confess and claim Him as a Savior! Then every tongue will be impelled to confess Him as Lord to the glory of God (Phil. 2:10, 11), but not to the salvation of themselves; rather to their own condemnation for having resisted and rejected Him all through life.

### *The Law or Basis of Judgment*

In this account of the judgment (Matt. 25:31-46) Jesus draws a dramatic picture of a conversation with the two groups after their division, which indicates the basis of their fate. We need not suppose that such a conversation must actually take place at the judgment, or that this is the only matter that will be considered. Certainly the Lord does not mean for this to be used to deny any teaching found in the rest of the inspired scripture.

J. W. McGarvey observes:

> The acts here specified are all deeds of benevolence; all belong to the category of good works. We are not hence to conclude that good works alone can secure to us everlasting life, seeing that in the midst of our good works we commit sin, and before the beginning of our good works we lived in sin. Forgiveness for these sins must be secured by complying with the conditions thereof, or we will be condemned on their account, notwithstanding all the benevolence which we can perform. The lesson taught in the passage is this: that works of Christian benevolence, as we have opportunity to perform them, constitute one of the conditions of our acceptance in the day of judgment. They are, indeed, but the outgrowth of faith and love and their absence proves that our faith is dead, and that love has not been born within us.[1]

Matthew 25:31-46 does not mean that men may be saved by works of mercy without confessing Christ, for He Himself said, "No one cometh unto the Father but by me" (John 14:6), and "Except ye eat the flesh of the Son of man and drink his blood, ye have not life in yourselves" (John 6:53). See also I John 5:11, 12 and John 3:36. For other passages on those who will or will not inherit the kingdom, see Galatians 5:19-21; Ephesians 5:5; I Corinthians 6:9, 10; II Timothy 2:12; 4:8; James 2:5; Revelation 21:7; Romans 8:1-17.

It is fully and forcefully taught that no one will be saved by the perfect merit of his works, but by the sacrifice of Christ applied to the individual upon the condition of obedient faith in Christ (Rom. 3 to 8; Gal. 3; Eph. 2:1-10, etc.). That kingdom has been in preparation for us from the foundation of the world, and it is the gift of God (Luke 12:32). We do not earn it or create it ourselves; but God gives it on His own terms. Those terms might be summarized in the words "faith working through love" (Gal. 5:6). Hence at various points in the full revelation of the Christian covenant our salvation is attributed to, or conditioned upon, the following (at least):

1. Grace (Eph. 2:4-9; Rom. 3:24).

---

[1] J. W. McGarvey, *A Commentary on Matthew and Mark* (Delight, Arkansas: Gospel Light Publishing Co., n.d.) Pp. 220-221.

2. The Blood of Christ (Rom. 5:9; I John 1:7).
3. The gospel (Rom. 1:16; Acts 11:14; Rom. 10:13-17).
4. Faith (John 3:16; 3:36; 6:47; Rom. 3:28, 30; 5:1, 2).
5. Repentance (Luke 24:46-48; Acts 2:37, 38; 3:19).
6. Christian baptism (I Pet. 3:21; Acts 22:16; Gal. 3:27).
7. Works (by which faith is perfected) (James 2:24; Matt. 7:21-23).
8. Holiness or sanctification (Heb. 12:14; I Cor. 6:9-11).
9. Confession of Christ (Rom. 10:9, 10; I John 4:2, 3, 15; Matt. 10:32).
10. Love (I John 3:10-24; 4:7-21).
11. Obedience (Heb. 5:9; I Pet. 1:22; II Thess. 1:7-9).
12. Benevolent deeds (Matt. 25:31-46; Gal. 6:8-10).
13. Forgiving others (Matt. 18:35; Eph. 4:32; James 2:13).
14. Chastening (Heb. 12:6-11).
15. Remaining faithful until death (Rev. 2:10, 26; Heb. 3:6, 12; 10:23-31).

We are most often said to be saved by faith, but the predictions of judgment consistently say that we will be judged according to our deeds or works. The Lord does not recognize a faith that does nothing. Doctrine is fundamental and essential. Faith is necessary. But both faith and doctrine are in order to life. The Lord gives us doctrine as seed (Luke 8:11); and He gives worship and fellowship with exhortation as watering, cultivation and pruning; but we shall be judged by the fruit produced. See Hebrews 6:7, 8. We cannot produce good fruit without good seed, cultivation and care; but a garden is not praised for the amount of unsprouted seed it can show, or the rank growth of all kinds, but for the good fruit. The word of God is the seed; the plant is faith; the fruit is love working to the glory of God. Some acts of charity alone cannot take the place of the doctrine, regeneration, worship, etc. of true religion; but, on the other hand, all true religion must be or produce the practice of the two greatest commandments (See Matt. 22:37-40; Rom. 13:9, 10; I Cor. 13:1-3).

The first commandment orders unreserved and unlimited love to God, which included much indeed. "This is the love of God, that we keep his commandments" (I John 5:3), and "If any man love the world, the love of the Father is not in him" (I John 2:15).

God Himself does not need the services of our hands and possessions (Acts 17:25) but He commands us to serve Him by ministering to the needs of those around us since God cares for them, especially Jesus' "brethren" (Matt. 12:49, 50; 28:10; Gal. 6:10). The second commandment is really inseparable from the first; for "If a man say, I love God, and hateth his brother, he is a liar; for he that loveth not his brother whom he hath seen, cannot love God whom he hath not seen" (I John 4:20). The needs of men are always around us If we care not for the present, visible needs of man, it becomes evident that our lives are not ruled by love to God and to man. Jesus does not care more for service to men's bodies than to their souls; but He can test us by that which all can see the need of, and which all can help to supply, thus proving the reality and fullness of our love, and by that, whether we are begotten of God (I John 4:7, 8).

### *The Destinies*

The Lord always divides men into only two classes—lost or saved—heirs or outcasts—blessed or cursed. He never allows a middle class, and He never seems uncertain of the dividing line. There are just two ways to go—to heaven or to hell—into the kingdom prepared for you from the foundation of the world, or into the eternal fire which is prepared for the devil and his angels but shared in by those who rebel against God and make their choice to go to the devil, following his lies and his ways. Jesus says not only that the fire is eternal, but also that the punishment in it is to be eternal; and He used the same word concerning eternal punishment that He used concerning eternal life. One is as long as the other, and both as certain as the eternity of God. Jesus said more about hell than all the rest of the inspired messengers of God. The fate of the lost bore heavily on His heart. Jesus said some unpleasant things about that place of torment (Mark 9:43-48; Luke 16:23, 24; 20:18; Matt. 7:19; John 15:6; Matt. 13:31, 41, 42), but He laid down His life to make atonement for our sins so that we would not have to go there.

For Further Study:

Morris, Leon. *The Biblical Doctrine of Judgment.* Grand Rapids: Wm. B. Eerdmans, 1960. Surveys the Old Testament and New Testament teaching on the doctrine of judgment.

Summers, Ray. *The Life Beyond.* Nashville: Broadman Press, 1959. Pp. 147-182. Helpful study of the New Testament teaching about the agent, time, objects, basis and outcome of judgment.

# *Part Fifteen*

# HOLY SPIRIT

## 81

## INTRODUCTORY STUDY ON THE HOLY SPIRIT

*Evidence of the Personal and Practical Significance of the Holy Spirit*

A. The New Testament shows that the Holy Spirit is:
  1. A gift from God to be valued and enjoyed.
    a. Promised to everyone obeying the gospel (Acts 2:38, 39; 5:32).
    b. Jesus thought it a supreme gift to be sought by prayer (Luke 11:13).
    c. For every true believer in Jesus (John 7:38, 39).
    d. Dwells in our bodies (I Cor. 6:19; I Thess. 4:8; Rom. 8:11). (Compare Gal. 2:20; Eph. 3:17; Phil. 1:21; Col. 1:27; John 14:23; Phil. 2:13).*
  2. A necessity in order to be in Christ and be saved.
    a. We must be born of the Spirit as well as water (John 3:5).
    b. He is part of the means of salvation (Titus 3:5-7).
    c. Without the Spirit of Christ (and of God) we are none of His (Rom. 8:9, 10).
    d. Only those led by the Spirit are sons of God and heirs (Rom. 8:12-17).
    e. The essential reality and basis of a Christian life—or what the Kingdom of God really is (Rom. 14:17).
    (Compare Luke 17:20, 21; John 18:36; 6:63; 15:4-8; Gal. 5:6; 6:15; II Cor. 5:14-17; II Cor. 6:16; Col. 1:27).*
  3. A subject of commandments to Christians.
    a. "Be filled with the spirit" (Eph. 5:18).
    b. "Walk by the Spirit" (Gal. 5:16, 25).
    c. "Quench not the Spirit" (I Thess. 5:19).
    d. "Grieve not the Holy Spirit of God" (Eph. 4:30).
    (Compare Heb. 6:4-6; 10:26-30; Matt. 12:31-37).*

---

* Compare these passages which affirm the same reality but do not use the word Holy Spirit. Study these passages as commented on and explained by the other listed scriptures.

4. A help to victorious holy living.
   a. By the Spirit put to death the deeds of the body (Rom. 8:13, 14).
   b. Christian virtues are fruit of the Spirit (Gal. 5:22, 23).
   c. The love of God is in us through the Holy Spirit (Rom. 5:5).
   d. Strengthened with power through His Spirit in the inward man (Eph. 3:16).
   e. Sanctified by the Holy Spirit (Rom. 15:16).
   f. The Spirit helps us in prayer; intercedes for us (Rom. 8:26, 27).

   (Compare Phil. 2:12, 13; Eph. 1:16-20; 4:22-24; Col. 3:1-17; Eph. 6:10-18).*
5. A basis of our faith.
   a. The Spirit, speaking in the Old Testament prophets, prophesied and prepared for the coming of Christ (I Pet. 1:10, 11; II Pet. 1:19-21).
   b. Bore witness to Christ in visible form (Luke 3:22; John 1:32, 33).
   c. Filled Jesus, led Him, and assisted His works (Luke 4:1, 14, 18; Matt. 12:28).
   d. Led the apostles into all truth and brought to their memories what Jesus had taught them (John 14:26; 16:13; cf. 15:26; 16:8).
   e. Coming of the Spirit was testimony of the resurrection (Acts 2:32, 33; 5:32).
   f. Gifts and power of the Spirit confirmed the word (Heb. 2:4; I Cor. 2:4, 5).

   (Compare I Thess. 1:5, 6; 2:13; I Cor. 2:6-16).*
6. A guarantee of our hope for eternal perfection with Christ.
   a. Bears witness (through His word) with our spirits that we are children of God (Rom. 8:16).
   b. Is the earnest (guarantee payment) of our inheritance with Christ (Eph. 1:13, 14; II Cor. 1:22; 5:5).
   c. Proof of the reality of God's work in us and our participation in redemption and conversion (I John 3:24; 4:13).

   (Compare Rom. 5:5; John 13:35; I John 3:14, 15; 4:20).*

B. Do not the above statements show that the Holy Spirit is important to us?

---

* Compare these passages which affirm the same reality but do not use the word Holy Spirit. Study these passages as commented on and explained by the other listed scriptures.

C. What Paul asked twelve men at Ephesus (Acts 19:2) is a good question for you and me: *Did YOU receive the Holy Spirit when you believed?*

*Who or What is the Holy Spirit?*

I. The Holy Spirit is a person (a thinking, feeling, acting, responsible individual).

A. He is said to do what only persons can do.

1. He speaks (I Tim. 4:1; Rev. 2:7; etc.).
2. He testifies (John 15:26).
3. He teaches (John 14:26; I Cor. 2:13).
4. He searches and reveals (I Cor. 2:10).
5. He leads and forbids (Acts 16:6, 7).

B. He is said to have characteristics of a person.

1. Mind (Rom. 8:27).
2. Knowledge (I Cor. 2:11).
3. Affection, or love (Rom. 15:30).
4. Will (I Cor. 12:11).
5. Being grieved or vexed (Isa. 63:10; Eph. 4:30).
6. Being resisted (Acts 7:51).
7. Being lied to (Acts 5:3).
8. Being despised or scorned (Heb. 10:29).

C. Personal pronouns in the masculine gender are applied to Him, in close connection with the noun "spirit" which is neuter and should normally have all of its pronouns and modifiers in the neuter (John 15:26; 16:7, 8, 13, 14).

D. The Spirit is not a mere impersonal force or influence we somehow get hold of and use; but He is a personal being, wise and holy, who is to get hold of us and use us. He is one with whom we may have the closest friendship or fellowship (Phil. 2:1; II Cor. 13:14). He enters into our personalities, and we become new persons, with renewed minds, affections, desires and wills.

If we have trouble thinking clearly and distinctly about the Spirit of God, it probably is because we do not understand clearly our own spirits. But we can accept the fact that He is a person like Jesus Christ, except for the body Jesus used, or like ourselves in that He has the essential faculties that make us to be persons rather than material machines.

II. The Holy Spirit is a divine person, with deity like that of God and Christ.

A. He is said to have the attributes of God.
   1. He is eternal (Heb. 9:14). Was with God in creation (Gen. 1:2).
   2. Knows what God knows (I Cor. 2:10-11).
   3. He exerts the power of God (Luke 1:35; Acts 1:8; Micah 3:8; Judg. 14:6).
   4. He is everywhere present as God is (Ps. 139:7-10).
   5. He is holy, the Spirit of holiness (Rom. 1:4), Spirit of grace (Heb. 10:29), Spirit of truth (John 14:17; 16:13), Spirit of wisdom (Isa. 11:2).
B. The works of the Spirit are the works of God.
   1. Creation (Gen. 1:2; Job 33:4; Ps. 104:30).
   2. Giving life (Gen. 2:7; Rom. 8:11; John 6:63; John 3:5).
   3. Authorship of prophecies (II Pet. 1:21).
   4. Working of miracles (Matt. 12:28; I Cor. 12:9, 11).
C. The Holy Spirit is the Spirit of God, the Spirit of Christ, and is spoken of in such connection with God and Christ that it shows they are of the same divine nature (I Cor. 12:4-6; Matt. 28:19; Acts 5:3, 4; II Cor. 13:14).

The chart on the following two pages compares three spiritual gifts: Baptism in the Holy Spirit, the Miraculous or Special Gifts of the Holy Spirit, and the Indwelling of the Holy Spirit in every Christian. It shows how each gift was received and the purpose for which each was given.

Read and study the scripture passages cited to understand what God says about each of these gifts.

## THREE SPIRITUAL GIFTS COMPARED

*BAPTISM OF THE SPIRIT:* Administered by the Lord Jesus. Promised only to His apostles. Received by apostles on Pentecost; by some Gentiles about ten years later (Acts 2; 10). No other examples in God's Word. It was:

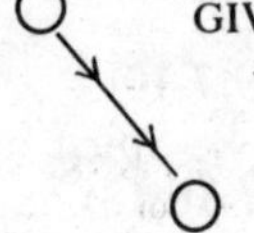

GIVEN BY GOD AND CHRIST

WITHOUT HUMAN INTERVENTION

TO MEN SELECTED BY GOD
(The apostles and the household of Cornelius)

This baptism could not be performed by men. It was not required for salvation; never commanded for anyone—it was promised to a select few.

PURPOSE: *A sign* from God that these Jewish teachers were delivering God's message when they declared that Jesus was the Christ. *A sign* later that non-Jews were fully eligible for God's grace without submitting to the law God gave for Israel through Moses.

* * * * * * * * * * * * * * * * * * * * * * * * * * * * * * * * * * * * * * * * * * * * * *

*OTHER MIRACULOUS GIFTS OF THE SPIRIT:* Administered to selected men by apostles of Christ and others empowered by God. Promised to none, other than through Old Testament prophecy. Received by many during early years of the Lord's church. Gifts included healing, speaking God's message directly, speaking or interpreting languages unknown to the person. These were:

GIVEN BY GOD AND CHRIST

THROUGH LAYING ON
OF THE APOSTLES' HANDS

TO MEN SELECTED BY
APOSTLES AND HOLY SPIRIT

These gifts were desired by many and given to few. Paul suggested that Christians should welcome the gifts and "desire" them. Not promised. Not commanded. Misuse of the gifts became a serious problem in Corinth.

PURPOSE: *To guide* the church in its infancy. *To further "establish"* that Christ's gospel really came from God.

* * * * * * * * * * * * * * * * * * * * * * * * * * * * * * * * * * * * * * * * * * * * * *

*INDWELLING OF THE SPIRIT:* Administered directly by the Lord. Promised to every person who accepted God's terms for pardon and obeyed them (Acts 2:38). This gift is:

GIVEN BY GOD AND CHRIST

AS A RESULT OF OBEDIENCE
TO GOSPEL COMMANDS BY
FAITH IN CHRIST

TO EVERY PERSON WHO IS SAVED

Essential for salvation. The Spirit dwells within each Christian who wants Him and welcomes Him.

PURPOSE: *To enable victorious Christian life.*

* * * * * * * * * * * * * * * * * * * * * * * * * * * * * * * * * * * * * * * * * * * * * *

*BAPTISM IN THE HOLY SPIRIT*

*Administered* by the Lord Himself (Matt. 3:11) to those whom He chose. (Read: Acts 1:4, 5, 6; 11:15-18; John 14:26; 15:26, 27; 16:12-15; Luke 24:46-49; John 20:21-23). The Holy Spirit proceeded directly from God's heavenly throne (Acts 2:1-4; 10:44-48). This manifestation of the Spirit was PROMISED, NOT COMMANDED, and not administered by men.

PURPOSE: As a SIGN from God to all on the day of Pentecost that the APOSTLES WERE AUTHORIZED from heaven to preach the terms of pardon. As a SIGN to the Jewish Christians that GENTILES COULD BE SAVED by Christ's gospel. (Read Luke 24:47; Acts 2:12-16, 33, 37; 11:1-4, 15-18; 15:8). The baptism of the apostles in the Holy Spirit on Pentecost was the initial coming of the Holy Spirit to abide in the church and to furnish the other gifts to all flesh—both Jews and Gentiles (Joel 2:28-32; Acts 2:17-21). By this coming, the Spirit gave the divine message by which all believers would be "born of the Spirit" (I Pet. 1:23; Heb. 4:12; Eph. 1:13; John 7:38, 39).

* * * * * * * * * * * * * * * * * * * * * * * * * * * * * * * * * * * * * * * * * * * * * * * * *

*THE MIRACULOUS OR SPECIAL GIFTS OF THE HOLY SPIRIT*

*Administered* by the twelve apostles through the laying on of hands upon those whom they or the Holy Spirit chose to help them in the initial proclamation and confirmation of the word of God, while the church of Jesus Christ was being established, before the written Word of God was fully revealed. (Read: Acts 8:18; 6:6; 8:14-17; 19:6; II Tim. 1:6; I Cor. 12:11; I Tim. 1:18; 4:14).

PURPOSE: To help the apostles during the initial work of proclaiming the word and establishing the church of the first century, God's Church, the body of Christ. Confirming, establishing, and providing the divine authority of the apostles and prophets as they revealed the word (Heb. 2:4). Miracles, wonders, and signs were for this express purpose, until the full revelation of God's word was completed and confirmed. These miracles, wonders, and signs caused faith in the word spoken (Read: Acts 5:12-16; 8:6-13; 13:9-12; I Cor. 14:22; II Cor. 12:12).

* * * * * * * * * * * * * * * * * * * * * * * * * * * * * * * * * * * * * * * * * * * * * * * * *

*THE GIFT OF THE HOLY SPIRIT TO BE AN ABIDING PRESENCE*

*Administered* by the Lord Jesus Christ for as many as the Lord our God shall call unto Him, through the gospel—even to those who are afar off—upon the OBEDIENCE OF FAITH. Available to all who will receive it. (Read: Acts 2:33-41; 5:32; 19:1-6; Rom. 8:9-16; II Cor. 1:21-22; I Thess. 4:8; Titus 3:5-7; I John 3:24; John 14:23; Eph. 3:16).

PURPOSE: To enable Christians to overcome the carnal human nature and put on the divine nature of Christ our Lord (II Pet. 1:3, 4). To dwell in them (I Cor. 6:19), sanctify them (Rom. 15:16), and make the church a temple of God (I Cor. 3:16; Eph. 2:21, 22). To put to death the deeds of the body (Rom. 8:13, 14). To produce the fruit of the Spirit (Gal. 5:16-25). To put God's love into us (Rom. 5:5; I Cor. 13:1-13) and give us joy and peace (Rom. 14:17; Gal. 5:22). To be a guarantee of our eternal inheritance (Eph. 1:13, 14; II Cor. 5:5; I John 3:24; 4:13).

* * * * * * * * * * * * * * * * * * * * * * * * * * * * * * * * * * * * * * * * * * * * * * * * *

For Further Study:

Crawford, C. C. *The Eternal Spirit,* 2 vols. Joplin, Missouri: College Press, 1972, 1973. The first volume discusses the person and power of the Holy Spirit and the second deals with the word and works of the Spirit. Scholarly and detailed.

DeWelt, Don. *The Power of the Holy Spirit,* Vol. I. Joplin, Missouri: College Press, 1963. Pp. 1-38. Discusses the personality of the Holy Spirit and how He helps each Christian. Further volumes with the same title deal extensively with Biblical teaching about the Holy Spirit (Vol. II, 1966; Vol. III, 1971; Vol. IV, 1976).

Ketcherside, W. Carl. *Heaven Help Us.* Cincinnati: Standard Publishing Company, 1974. First identifies the Spirit and then details how He helps us harmonize our lives with the divine will.

# 82

## WHERE TO READ ON GIFTS OF THE HOLY SPIRIT

Read what the Word of God says about the Holy Spirit and the workings or gifts of the Spirit.

Too many books and articles are circulated which state only the opinions, experiences and imaginings of people who are not really authorities on the subject. They show their liability to error by the way they differ from one another.

Too many times the Bible passages which are read are few, and are interpreted by man's experiences, when the experiences need to be understood by the revealed truth of God. Each passage should be seen in the light of all that the Bible has to say on this subject.

The following outline is not intended to set forth a doctrine of the Holy Spirit, but to help the reader to read all that God's word says about the Holy Spirit's work in the Christian era. *Do read the scriptures cited here.* This is only an index or listing of passages, arranged to suggest which ones are most closely related to each other or which deal with the same phases of the subject. Comments are minimal, being intended only to help the reader of the Bible passages to read what the author intended to say, perhaps to avoid some common misconceptions which have been associated with these passages when they have been taken out of context or have been read with doubtful presuppositions in mind.

If you will not read with this the scriptures, you probably do not really care enough to know God's truth on the subject. If you just want to keep your old opinions, you can suffer the consequences; but what of other people whom you influence? If you just want to look at the headings to see my opinions, they really do not matter that much and, in a sense, they are none of your business. Now get your Bible.

I. THE GIFT RECEIVED BY THE APOSTLES (called "baptism").

   A. Predicted in the Old Testament (Joel 2:28-32; Acts 2:17-21). Note: This passage was probably intended to prophesy not only the baptism on Pentecost, but also the continuing work of the Spirit including all the gifts listed below.

   B. Predicted by John the Baptist (Matt. 3:11; Mark 1:7, 8; Luke 3:16; John 1:33).

Note: John's preaching about fire as the destiny of those who do not repent (Matt. 3:8-10; Rev. 20:10, 14, 15; 21:8).

Mark does not quote John's prediction of punishment in fire or of baptism in fire (1:8). Jesus predicted baptism of the Holy Spirit without mentioning fire (Acts 1:5, 8; Luke 24:49; John 16:7-15). Peter, likewise, spoke of baptism in the Holy Spirit without any reference to fire (Acts 11:16). Acts 10:44, 45 says "the Holy Spirit fell" and was "poured out" upon the Gentiles, without referring to fire. The tongues that rested upon the apostles at Pentecost were not actually said to be fire but "tongues parted asunder (distributing themselves or being separated) like as of fire" (Acts 2:3).

John the Baptist didn't make his prediction to tell who would be baptized in the Holy Spirit but to identify Jesus as the one who had that divine power and prerogative. This is especially evident in John 1:31-34.

C. Promised by Jesus (John 14:16-18, 26; 15:26; 16:7-15; Acts 1:5-8; Luke 24:49).
   1. Another Helper-Companion (like Jesus) (John 14:16).
   2. To abide with them forever (John 14:16). Probable meaning: to abide throughout the church age in various gifts and ways of working.
   3. The Spirit of Truth (John 14:17).
   4. The world could not receive Him (John 14:17).
   5. The presence of Jesus to be in them (John 14:17, 18).
   6. What the Spirit would do for them (John 14:26—16:15).
      a. Teach them all things (John 14:26).
      b. Bring to remembrance all Jesus had said to them (John 14:26).
      c. Bear witness of Jesus (John 15:26).
      d. Would not come unless or until Jesus ascended (John 16:7).
      e. Convict (convince) the world of the sin of not believing in Jesus, of the righteousness of Jesus, and of judgment of the world (John 16:8-11).
      f. Guide them into all truth (John 16:13).
      g. Declare to them things to come (John 16:13).
      h. Glorify Jesus (John 16:14).
      i. Declare to them things of God (John 16:15).
   7. Reminders after His resurrection (John 20:21-23; Acts 1:5, 8; Luke 24:49).

   a. To come in Jerusalem, a few days after ascension (Acts 1:5; Luke 24:49).
   b. Would bring power from on high to them (Acts 1:8; Luke 24:49; John 20:22, 23).

D. To whom did Jesus promise these things?
   1. To the apostles, clearly. Read John 15:15, 16; 13:5-18; Luke 22:14, 28-30.
   2. He did speak a promise about any man who loves and obeys Him (John 14:23) aside from the discussion and promises addressed to the apostles.

E. Received at Pentecost (Acts 2:1-18).
   1. The pronoun "They" in 2:1 must refer to "the apostles" in Acts 1:26. The listeners said the ones speaking were *all Galileans* (Acts 2:7). "Peter, standing *with the eleven*" spoke (Acts 2:14). The church depended upon *the apostles' teaching* (Acts 2:42). *The apostles* worked signs and wonders (Acts 5:12, 13). *The apostles* were the ones persecuted (Acts 5:17, 18, 29). *Two apostles* walked to Samaria (forty miles) to confer works of the Holy Spirit on the believers there. What they caused Samaritans to receive was more than regeneration by the Spirit; (1) they had already believed and been baptized, and (2) the "Holy Spirit" given by the laying on of the apostles' hands was something that Simon could see and wanted to purchase (Acts 8:5-19). *It was the apostles to whom Jesus had promised baptism in the Holy Spirit* (Acts 1:5).
   2. Caused them to speak foreign languages recognized by people from about 15 nations (Acts 2:8-12).
   3. Came with sound of wind and visible tongues parted like fire (Acts 2:2, 3).
      Note: When Jesus told the disciples He was leaving, He promised to send the Holy Spirit as another Companion-Helper to stay with them perpetually (John 14:16). On Pentecost the Holy Spirit came to stay. The signs of His coming are naturally unique. The speaking in tongues occurred other times, yet it is not the purpose of the Holy Spirit to repeat Pentecost, but to do the work for which He came.
   4. Baptism of the apostles in the Holy Spirit marked the beginning of the church (Matt. 16:18, 19), the kingdom (Mark 9:1), the new covenant (II Cor. 3:5-14; Jer. 31:31-34; I Cor.

11:25; Heb. 8:1-13; 9:11-24; 10:11-29; John 16:7-15; 20:21-23; 7:38, 39; Eph. 2:13-22; Ezek. 37:26-28; Isa. 2:3), and the work of the Holy Spirit in the church.

F. The Apostle Paul evidently received much the same kind of gift.
   1. He received nothing from those who were apostles before him (Gal. 1:12, 13).
   2. He was to receive the Holy Spirit at the time of his conversion (Acts 9:17).
   3. He was told then that he was to be the Lord's messenger, even of things yet to be revealed (Acts 26:16-18).
   4. He conferred miraculous gifts by laying on his hands (Acts 19:6-12; II Tim. 1:6).
   5. He claimed the authority and the signs of an apostle (II Cor. 10:1-9; 11:5; 12:12).
   6. Apparently he had all the powers of anyone baptized in the Holy Spirit.

G. Workings and the results of the Holy Spirit in the apostles.
   1. Speaking in unlearned languages (Acts 2:4-11; I Cor. 14:18, 19).
   2. Working miracles (instant and unquestionable) (Acts 3:6-8; 4:16, 21; 5:12, 15, 16; 9:32-42; 13:9-11; 14:3, 8-11; 16:18; 19:11, 12; 20:9, 10; 28:4-9; II Cor. 12:12).
   3. Speaking boldly with unanswerable wisdom (Acts 2:22-36; 3:14-26; 4:8-12, 19, 20, 31, 33; 5:29-32; 14:3-17; 15:7-11; 17:22-32; Matt. 10:17-20; Mark 13:11; Luke 21:12-15).
   4. Speaking for God by inspiration, about things in heaven or in the future (beyond human knowledge) with confidence and accuracy (Acts 2:33, 38, 39; 5:3, 4, 9; 10:34, 35; 15:28, 29; 27:21-26; I Cor. 2:6-16; 14:37; 15:50-54; Gal. 1:11, 12; Eph. 3:1-9; I Thess. 2:13; 4:13-17; II Pet. 3:15, 16).
   5. Conferring gifts of the Holy Spirit by laying on of hands (Acts 8:14-20; 6:5, 6, 8; 8:5-7; 19:6; II Tim. 1:6).
   6. Receiving on occasion special instructions where and how to serve Christ (Acts 5:20; 10:9-20; 13:2; 16:6-10; 18:9, 10; 23:11).
   7. Preaching the gospel (I Pet. 1:12).

II. THE SIMILAR GIFT (called "baptism") of the Spirit, upon Cornelius and his household (Acts 10:44-48; 11:15-18).

Note: There is neither evidence nor reason to suppose that they received all the apostles did. As far as we know, it was only a temporary power to speak in tongues, as the apostles did in the beginning of their experience on the day of Pentecost. Note: Some think the prediction of John the Baptist (Matt. 3:11) was general in scope and used "baptize you in the Holy Spirit" to predict all the works of the Holy Spirit, especially the indwelling in every Christian. This could be; even so, we must distinguish clearly between the powers given to the apostles for their work and the regenerative indwelling of the Spirit received by every Christian.

Other Bible facts help us understand "Baptism of the Holy Spirit" and for whom it was intended.

A. The "baptism in the Spirit" received by Cornelius and his household came before they obeyed the gospel and was a sign that they should be permitted to be baptized into Christ (in water). Read Acts 10:44-48; 11:14, 15; Gal. 3:26, 27; Rom. 6:3-11; and I Cor. 12:13. Peter told believers at Pentecost to "repent and be baptized for the forgiveness of your sins; and you shall receive the gift of the Holy Spirit" (Acts 2:38). Their baptism was in water. See Acts 8:36-39 and I Pet. 3:20, 21. It was a "washing of regeneration"—being born again—accompanied by a "renewing of the Holy Spirit" (Titus 3:5, 6; John 3:3-7; I Cor. 12:13; Rom. 6:3, 4; Col. 2:12, 13).

B. I Cor. 12:13 does not say that all were baptized in (or by or with) the Holy Spirit in the sense that "baptize in (or with) the Holy Spirit" is used in Matt. 3:11; Acts 1:5 and 11:16. Paul in I Cor. 12:13 says that by the influence or with the impulse of the Holy Spirit all were baptized in their entering into the body of Christ, just as in I Cor. 12:3 he says that all who confess Jesus as Lord must do it in (or by the influence of) the Holy Spirit. Compare his use of "in the Holy Spirit" in Rom. 14:17 and Eph. 2:18.

C. Eph. 4:4-6 speaks of "one baptism" as a bond of unity, one significant experience in which all Christians participate. A close study of the New Testament shows that all believers, in that generation, were baptized in water, into Christ (Acts 2:38, 41; 8:12-16, 36, 38; 9:18; 10:47, 48; 16:15, 30-33; 18:8; 19:5; 22:16; Rom. 6:3-5; I Cor. 1:13-16; 12:13; Gal. 3:27; Col. 2:12, 13; Titus 3:5; Heb. 6:2; 10:22; I Pet. 3:20, 21).

D. The act of becoming a Christian was described as being "obedience of faith" (Rom. 1:5; 6:16; 15:18; 16:26; Heb. 5:9; I Pet. 1:2, 22). Condemnation is pronounced upon those who "obey not the gospel" (II Thess. 1:8; John 3:36 [any correct translation]; Rom. 10:16-21). *Baptism in the Holy Spirit was never commanded and cannot be obeyed.*

E. All Christians were to have the Holy Spirit in them (Rom. 8:9) through believing the gospel and obeying it (Eph. 1:13, 14; John 3:3-7; Acts 2:38, 39; 5:32; John 14:23; I Cor. 12:3, 13). But not all spoke in tongues—see I Cor. 12:29, 30. The Holy Spirit must have a part in their conversion, causing them to confess sincerely that Jesus is Lord (I Cor. 12:3), causing them to be baptized into His body (I Cor. 12:13), and thus to be "born of water and the Spirit" (John 3:5; Titus 3:5). The Holy Spirit did not have to add miraculous demonstrations.

F. *If* the indwelling of the Holy Spirit in every Christian is a fulfillment of "He shall baptize you in the Holy Spirit" (Matt. 3:11), then that baptism is *not* always (or even usually) indicated by speaking in tongues, and baptism in the Spirit is *not* the power to work miracles, and it is *not* something to be sought *after one's new birth in Christ.*

G. Many Bible passages speak of the gift of the Holy Spirit to Christians, or the Holy Spirit *dwelling* in Christians, or *filling* them, but no passage calls this "baptism in the Spirit."

H. The baptism of Cornelius' household was a sign that Gentiles were to receive the gospel and the grace of God the same as the Jews. As such, it was an exceptional case and never was repeated.

III. THE VARIOUS "SPIRITUAL GIFTS" RECEIVED BY CHOSEN LEADERS FOR SIGNS AND FOR GUIDANCE OF THE EARLY CHURCH (Heb. 2:3, 4).

A. Predicted by Joel 2:28-32, and by Jesus in Mark 16:17, 18.

B. Conferred by the laying on of the apostles' hands (Acts 8:14-25; 19:6; II Tim. 1:6).

1. Was there any other way of receiving such powers? Not that we know of for anyone except the apostles themselves.
2. God's giving the Holy Spirit to them that ask Him (Luke 11:13) may not be the same as giving miraculous powers. The power to work miracles is not exactly the Holy Spirit, but something the Holy Spirit can do. Jesus' apostles had

worked miracles for nearly a year before Jesus predicted that believers would have the Holy Spirit, and then "the Holy Spirit was not yet given because Jesus was not yet glorified" (John 7:38, 39; compare Matt. 10:1, 5-8; Mark 6:7, 13).

3. We do know that Timothy had a gift that was given "with the laying on of the hands of the presbytery," (I Tim. 4:14). The preposition in Greek means *in the company of* or *together with,* but does not mean *by means of;* and in II Tim. 1:6 Paul says that the gift was given to Timothy "*through* the laying on of my hands." The elders at Lystra probably laid hands on Timothy when he was committed to the work of Christian missions and joined Paul and Silas (Acts 16:1-4). Evidently Paul participated in the ordination and his hands conferred the spiritual gift at the same time.
4. The apostles at Jerusalem laid hands on seven men who were chosen by the congregation for ministry to the neglected widows, perhaps also for other responsibilities (Acts 6:1-6). Soon after this, two of them, Stephen and Philip, were working miracles, preaching with apparent inspiration, and receiving visions and messages from heaven (Acts 7:8, 10, 15, 55, 56; 8:6, 7, 13, 26, 40).
5. Peter and John were sent to Samaria, where they conferred some manifest gifts, so that "Simon saw that through the laying on *of the apostles'* hands the Holy Spirit was given" (Acts 8:14-25).
6. Philip had worked miracles there (Acts 8:4-7) but he did not impart any spiritual gift of this nature. Was it because he could not? Obviously, God was willing for them to receive it.
7. Did others than apostles lay on hands? Was the laying on of hands always for this purpose? Apparently not. At Antioch hands were laid on Barnabas and Saul to commit them to a new mission, after they had both been named among the prophets and had been responsible leaders and teachers for some years (Acts 4:36; 9:27; 11:22-26, 30; 13:1).
8. Although Ananias told Saul (Paul) that the Lord sent him "That thou mayest receive thy sight and be filled with the Holy Spirit," there is no indication that Saul's inspiration or powers as an apostle were conferred by the laying on of

the hands of Ananias. Read carefully Acts 9:10-19.

C. An offer to buy the power to confer these gifts was severely rebuked (Acts 8:18-24).

D. Not intended for all Christians; at least, no one gift was given to all (I Cor. 12:29, 30).

1. A failing attempt to imitate miracles drew attention to the special power of those who could do them (Acts 19:13-20).
2. *Who* chose the ones to receive such gifts? or *how* were they chosen? Paul said that prophecies led the way to Timothy (I Tim. 1:18) and that the gift was given by prophecy (I Tim. 4:14). He also wrote: "All these worketh the one and the same Spirit, dividing to each one severally even as He will" (I Cor. 12:11). Heb. 2:4—"by manifold powers, and by gifts of the Holy Spirit, according to His own will." The Holy Spirit picked Barnabas and Saul for the missionary journey (Acts 13:1, 2), but this is not necessarily the same. In Acts 6:3 the apostles told the crowd of disciples to pick men, according to the qualifications given through the apostles inspired by the Holy Spirit. Probably that was the manner in which the Holy Spirit made the elders of Ephesus overseers (bishops or pastors) (Acts 20:28), since qualifications are given by inspiration for men to follow (I Tim. 3:1-7; Titus 1:5-9).

   On the other hand, in I Cor. 14:1 Paul says: "Follow after love; yet desire earnestly spiritual gifts, but rather that ye may prophesy." And in I Cor. 14:13: "Let him that speaketh in a tongue pray that he may interpret." Evidently a Christian could choose a gift by praying for it under some circumstances, or at least could prepare himself for it to some extent.

E. Various gifts were given, as the Holy Spirit chose (Heb. 2:3, 4; I Cor. 12:1-30).

"God has set some in the church, first *apostles,* secondly *prophets,* thirdly *teachers,* then *miracles,* then *gifts of healing, helps, governments,* divers *kinds of tongues,*" (I Cor. 12:28).

"The *word of wisdom,* . . . the *word of knowledge,* . . . *faith,* . . . *gifts of healing,* . . . *working of miracles,* . . . *prophecy, discerning of spirits,* . . . various kinds of *tongues,* . . . *interpretation of tongues,*" (I Cor. 12:6-11).

In Eph. 4:11-16, the gifts of Christ for fully equipping the saints unto the work of ministering included, *apostles, prophets, evangelists, pastors* and *teachers.*

All these lists taken together include persons or positions of leadership, or powers to work visible signs, and functions of teaching and oversight.

Heb. 2:4 says that God bore witness with those who heard Jesus "by signs and wonders and by gifts of the Holy Spirit, according to His own will."

In II Cor. 12:12 Paul said, "The signs of an apostle were wrought among you . . . by signs and wonders and mighty works."

Yet some "gifts" listed for the serving of members in the body are not of a miraculous nature. Read Rom. 12:4-8 and I Pet. 4:10, 11.

Special gifts for teaching by revelation and for giving evidence of divine inspiration might naturally be temporary. Other gifts for serving in obedience to the revealed word might be expected to be more universal and permanent.

1. *Apostles* are listed among God's gifts to the church; but, of course, they were not made by the laying on of the hands of the apostles. To understand their place among spiritual gifts, read the following.
   a. Apostles were chosen by Christ Himself (Matt. 10:1-5; Mark 3:13-15; Luke 6:12-16; Acts 1:20-26; 9:15-18; 26:15-18).
   b. They were "clothed with power from on high" (Luke 24:49; Acts 1:8) to receive all the knowledge and abilities listed in part I, sections C and G (pages 458 and 460).
   c. The church was built upon apostles and prophets (Eph. 2:20; compare Rev. 21:14).
   d. Both apostles and prophets were instruments through whom the Lord made His revelation of the "faith once for all delivered unto the saints" (Jude 3; Eph. 3:5). They were guided "into all truth" (John 16:13), and we can have this same truth when we receive the message which they were directed to write for us in the books which have become our New Testament.
   e. The church continued in the apostles' doctrine from the beginning (Acts 2:42; II Tim. 1:13; 2:2). Their word had special authority. It was not theirs, but from Christ who gave it to them (John 20:21-23; 17:21; Gal. 1:12).
   f. The apostles were distinguished from the rest of the

church:

1. in working miracles (Acts 2:43; 4:33; 5:12, 13; II Cor. 12:12).
2. as witnesses of the resurrection (Acts 1:22; 2:14, 32; 4:35; 5:29-32; 6:2-4; I Cor. 9:1).
3. in oversight (Acts 4:34-37; 6:2-6; 8:14; 9:27; 11:1; 15:2, 4, 6; 16:4; I Cor. 4:9-13; 9:1, 2; II Cor. 11:5; 13:10; 10:1-9; 3:5, 6; 4:1-5).
4. in conferring miraculous powers or spiritual gifts (Acts 8:18; 19:6; II Tim. 1:6.
5. in making known the revelation of God (Gal. 1:11-17; 2:7-9; Eph. 3:5; I Thess. 2:6, 13; II Thess. 3:6, 14; II Tim. 1:13; 2:2; II Pet. 3:2, 15, 16; I John 4:6; Jude 17; I Cor. 14:37).
6. as the prime target of persecutions (Acts 5:18; I Cor. 4:9-13).

g. Paul resisted and exposed false apostles because it was important whom the church considered authoritative as the source of God's truth (II Cor. 11:13-15; Acts 20:29, 30; Gal. 1:7-9; 2:4; Titus 1:10, 11; see also II Pet. 2:1; Rev. 2:2).

h. Apostles were important gifts of Christ to the church, but they finished a work that is not to be repeated. They are still important in the church, continuing their work through the word they have left us.

2. The gift of prophecy.

a. Prophecy is not always prediction, but it is always speaking by direct inspiration of God. See Matt. 26:68; Acts 13:1, 2; I Cor. 14:3, 24, 25; II Pet. 1:20, 21.

Prophecy is not equivalent to preaching; it may be written. The manner of proclamation is not indicated in the word or its Biblical usages. But the divine origin is always indicated. All revelations from God are prophecies. Messages by men without divine inspiration are not prophecies in any true Biblical sense.

b. The foundation of the church includes prophets as well as apostles, as spokesmen for Christ, the ultimate and only foundation (Eph. 2:19-21; 3:5; I Cor. 3:11).

c. The New Testament writers Mark, Luke, James and Jude were prophets, as evidenced by the acceptance of their writings as inspired. One would expect that Luke, a co-worker with Paul, and Mark, who worked with Paul and Peter (I Pet. 5:13; II Tim. 4:11) and James, the most prominent leader of the Jerusalem church (Acts 12:17; 15:13; 21:18; Gal. 1:19; 2:9), had the apostles' hands laid on them, even as Timothy had (II Tim. 1:6).

d. Prophets and prophetesses in the New Testament (fulfilling the prophecy in Joel 2:28-32) included Stephen, Philip, Agabus, Barnabas, Simeon, Niger, Lucius, Manaen, Judas, Silas, and Philip's daughters (Acts 11:27, 28; 13:1, 2; 15:32; 19:6; 20:22, 23; 21:9, 10).

e. Read about the gift of prophecy in I Cor. 11:4, 5; 12:28, 29; 13:9; 14:1, 3-5, 24, 29, 31, 32, 37, 39; Eph. 4:11; I Tim. 1:18; 4:14.

f. Prophets could control themselves, deciding when to speak and when not, and speak only one at a time (I Cor. 14:29-33).

g. Paul wrote (I Cor. 13:8) that prophecies would "be done away." He was not saying that some prophecies would be false, but that prophecy by the Holy Spirit would cease to occur. The reason he gave was that "we prophesy in part." Prophecy by the gift of the Spirit was given piece by piece, some to one man and some to another. See Acts 20:22, 23; 21:10-12; I Cor. 14:26-33. But when the complete has come the giving of pieces will cease (I Cor. 13:9, 10). What was in part was revealed truth; what would become complete and take the place of the practice of prophesying would be completed revelation of God's word for everyone.

h. The New Testament warns about false prophets. There are many (I John 4:1; Matt. 7:15; 24:11, 24); Elymas the sorcerer whom Paul blinded for a time (Acts 13:6-8) the maid with "a spirit of divination" (Acts 16:16, 17). Many will sincerely think they prophecied in the name of Christ, yet He will reject them (Matt. 7:21-23).

3. Teachers (I Cor. 12:28; Rom. 12:7), "evangelists, pastors and teachers" (Eph. 4:11).

   a. Each of these did a kind of work that remains important in the church. However, before the New Testament books were available these teachers were in great need of the gifts of "knowledge" and "wisdom" (I Cor. 12:8).

   b. Teachers are mentioned in combination with prophets

in Acts 13:1, perhaps stating the main function of the prophets.

Again, teachers are combined in Eph. 4:11 with "pastors," as given to the church. *Pastor* is an old word for shepherd. Elders were commanded to shepherd the church (Acts 20:28-32; I Pet. 5:1-4; Heb. 13:17). Paul said the Holy Spirit made the elders to be overseers (Acts 20:28).

c. These are gifts, provided by Christ for the church, for work of a spiritual nature. But they are not necessarily signs or supernatural powers. They are to raise up other teachers, not by inspiration but by communication of what they had received (II Tim. 2:2).

False teachers were a real danger even in New Testament times (II Pet. 2:1; 3:16, 17).

4. Wisdom and knowledge (I Cor. 12:8; 1:5; 13:2, 8; 2:6-13; 14:6; II Pet. 3:15).

a. Paul contrasted the wisdom of this world which did not know God with the wisdom furnished by the Spirit of God who revealed "the deep things of God" (I Cor. 2:10). The Spirit taught the apostles the divine wisdom (I Cor. 2:6-13; II Pet. 3:15).

b. The gifts of divine knowledge and wisdom were limited to certain pieces of guidance and to special occasions. Even Paul was not given specific information on all matters.

c. The gift of knowledge was limited because it was in pieces or parts, but the revelation of God was to be completed to the point where the *pieces* of miraculous knowledge and prophetic utterance would be unnecessary (I Cor. 13:8-10).

d. These gifts must be distinguished from the wisdom and knowledge which all of us may acquire progressively. All Christians are told to ask for wisdom (James 1:5). This should not be considered a promise to give every petitioner a ready-made decision for those things he can decide for himself, but the ability to use his mind with right motives implying the basic truth given from God.

e. God wants us to use wisdom that comes from fear of the Lord (Prov. 9:10) and from faith's understanding and from possession of the Holy Spirit in making decisions; He does not want to make each decision for us (Col. 1:9; Eph. 1:17, 18; Phil. 1:9; Heb. 5:14; James 3:13-18).

Christ and the gospel give to everyone understanding and wisdom of superior value, progressively as we will receive it. This kind of help is called wisdom in James 1:5; Eph. 1:8, 17; Col. 1:9, 28; 3:16; 4:5; James 3:13; 3:17. It is mentioned as knowledge in Rom. 15:14; Eph. 4:13; Phil. 1:9; Col. 1:9, 10; 3:10; I Tim. 2:4; II Tim. 3:7; Heb. 10:26; II Pet. 1:5-8.

5. Miracles and healings

a. Miracles may be defined as events in the physical world worked by the direct power of God as a sign of God's approval. Study Mark's account of Jesus' healing of the paralyzed man to understand this definition (Mark 2:10).

Miracles were called "powers," "mighty works," and "works" emphasizing the power of God which produced the miracles. The term "wonder" called attention to the effect they created in those who observed. The purpose of miracles as divine credentials is seen in the term "signs."

Jesus worked various kinds of miracles: power over disease, power over nature, power over demons, power over death, superhuman knowledge.

Jesus worked miracles primarily to demonstrate His deity (Mark 2:10; Luke 7:18ff; John 5:36; 10:37, 38; Acts 2:22, etc.)[1]

b. Apostles and some others in the early church exercised the gift of working miracles.

Paul said he came not with words of human wisdom but "in demonstration of the Spirit and of power that your faith should not stand in the wisdom of men, but in the power of God" (I Cor. 2:4, 5; cp. I Thess. 1:5; Mark 16:20).

"Truly the signs of an apostle were wrought among you in all patience, by signs, and wonders and mighty works" (II Cor. 12:12). The ministry of the early missionaries was aided by miracles as evidence of the truth of their message (Acts 13:9-12; 14:8-11; 19:10-12). The miracles

[1] See "The Purpose of Miracles," pp. 57-61.

also gave to the church evidence of God's approval of the message preached by Paul (Acts 15:12).

Paul called attention to the working of Christ through him "in the power of signs and wonders, in the power of the Holy Spirit" (Rom. 15:19). Paul mentions the miracles God worked among the Galatians (Gal. 3:5). Signs confirmed the word of revelation, "God also bearing witness with them, both by signs and wonders, and by manifold powers and by gifts of the Holy Spirit according to his own will" (Heb. 2:4).

c. In addition to the evidential purpose of miracles they also revealed divine compassion (Matt. 20:34; Mark 1:41-44). However, they did not always serve as expressions of compassion on those whom they were wrought: Elymas blinded by Paul (Acts 13:11) and Ananias and Sapphira executed (Acts 5:1-11).

Miraculous powers included ability to exorcise demons (Acts 5:16; 8:7; 16:16-18; 19:12); ability to raise the dead (Acts 9:36), protection from snake bite (Acts 28:3-6), as well as the power to heal.

d. The miraculous power to heal (I Cor. 12:9, 28, 30) must be distinguished from healing from ordinary medical skill and from divine healing that comes as an answer to prayer and not through the exercise of the gift of healing.

Peter and John healed a lame man (Acts 3:11-16); many sick folk healed (Acts 5:12-16); Aeneas (Acts 9:34); Paul healed a cripple (Acts 14:8-10); other sick (Acts 19:11, 12), father of Publius (Acts 28:8).

e. Does God always want miracles? They were not always wrought or even expected, by the best of believing servants of God. Paul left Trophimus sick at Miletus (II Tim. 4:20). Paul told Timothy to take medicine (I Tim. 5:23). Paul prayed and was refused removal of "thorn" (II Cor. 12:8). All the apostles suffered death. When Peter was delivered, it was not expected (Acts 12:1-17). Later Peter was not delivered; both he and Paul were killed.

f. Does the faith to remove mountains mean a miracle-working faith? (Matt. 17:19-20; 21:21; Mark 11:23; Luke 17:6; I Cor. 12:9; 13:2).

g. We are warned about "lying wonders" and miracles to

deceive the elect (Matt. 24:24; II Thess. 2:9; Rev. 13:14; 16:14; 19:20).[2]

6. Tongues and interpretation of tongues
   Tongues are mentioned only in the following passages: Mark 16:17; Acts 2:4-12; 10:44-48; 19:6; I Cor. 12:10, 28-30; 13:1, 8; 14:2-28.
   a. Tongues were foreign languages not known by the speakers but recognized by men who knew those languages (Acts 2:4-12).
   b. Peter said what occurred in the house of Cornelius was the same thing (Acts 10:46; 11:15).
   c. Paul taught men at Ephesus about Christian baptism and baptized them into Christ when he found they didn't know anything about the Holy Spirit. After that he laid his hands on them, and they spoke in tongues and prophesied (Acts 19:1-7). There is no indication that they sought the gift of tongues or that tongues had any connection with their baptism.
   d. Tongues were for a sign to unbelievers (I Cor. 14:22), especially to unbelieving Jews (I Cor.14:21). This is the one stated purpose for tongues.
   e. Some think I Cor. 14:14 states another purpose for tongues, but Paul is arguing for the use of spiritual gifts to edify the church (I Cor. 14:14-19).

      One is not to speak in tongues in church unless he knows there is an interpreter present (I Cor. 14:28). When Paul says "he who speaks in a tongue edifies himself" (I Cor. 14:4), is he approving of this? Is he not really accusing them of misusing the tongue, not using a spiritual gift for the purpose for which it was given?

      Likewise in I Cor. 12:31 perhaps we should read a mild rebuke. It could just as accurately be translated, "But you are zealously seeking the greater gifts." In the second person plural of the present tense, indicative and imperative forms look exactly alike. The context and line of thought must indicate which it is. In view of the overall teaching of I Cor. 12-14, rebuking pride in some gifts, and expressing the same divine source for all different

[2] See discussion of current claims to miraculous demonstrations on pp. 474, 475.

gifts, and teaching "to each is given the manifestation of the Spirit *for the common good*" (I Cor. 12:7, R.S.V.), is it not more likely that Paul is disapproving of their desire for the greater gifts?

It seems clear that in these chapters he is teaching against both selfish pride in some gifts as greater and failure to use the gifts for others.

Paul lists miraculous signs and supernatural function and shows that no one of them is for everyone. Read I Cor. 12:28-30. "Are all apostles?" demands a negative answer. "Do all speak in tongues?" demands a negative answer. Members of the body should not all expect to be alike or all to have the same function (I Cor. 12:16-25).

f. Paul says tongues will cease (I Cor. 13:8). With this statement he explains why prophecies and the gift of miraculous knowledge would cease, but does not explain when or why tongues would cease. Is it not because tongues as a sign of revelation are not appropriate after revelations cease to be made (I Cor. 13:8-10)?

g. Paul says all the tongues in the world are of no value to expressing the working of the Holy Spirit if they are used without love (I Cor. 13:1, 8). Love is the greatest work of the Holy Spirit and the work of the Spirit which is for everyone and which never ends.

7. Helps and governments

Probably designates those who help those in need and those who are leaders in the church (Rom. 12:8; I Cor. 12:28). No explanation or examples are given. This should call to our minds for special attention I Pet. 4:10, 11.

8. The gift of the indwelling Spirit

Jesus promised the divine indwelling (John 14:23). The apostles taught that the Holy Spirit is given to those who obey Christ (Acts 2:38; 5:32). The gift of the Holy Spirit is a vital part of our life in Christ (Titus 3:4-7; Rom. 8:8-17). Our body is a temple for the Holy Spirit (I Cor. 6:19). The church as a group is a temple of God (I Cor. 3:17; Eph. 2:22). The Christian life is lived in the Spirit and manifests the fruit of the Spirit (Gal. 5:16-25). Christ lives in us (Gal. 2:20; Eph. 3:14-19). God works in us (Phil. 2:13). The Holy Spirit strengthens the inner man (Eph.

3:16). How grateful we must be for God's gracious gifts that have enabled us to "become partakers of the divine nature" (II Pet. 1:4).[3]

Conclusion:

Does the Bible indicate that the apparent experiences of miraculous gifts might be false or not from God? (Matt. 7:21-23). Some will declare that they have prophesied in Jesus' name but Jesus did not know them. Paul warns that the "man of sin" would deceive many with "lying wonders" (II Thess. 2:9-11). John predicted that the devil or agents of the devil "do great signs" and "deceive many" (Rev. 13:13-15; 16:13, 14). If the devil transforms himself as an angel of light, and his ministers pose as ministers of righteousness (II Cor. 11:14-15), Satan could be the author of apparent spiritual gifts which are not according to God's will.

Some ask, "Would the devil praise God, promote good desires, make people love one another?" The devil counterfeits religion (II Cor. 11:14-15); attacks to destroy (I Pet. 5:8); lies and promotes lies (John 8:44; Acts 5:3); produces corrupt doctrines in the church (I Tim. 4:1-3); takes advantage of the church (II Cor. 2:11); blinds spirituality (II Cor. 4:4); deceives with works that appear to be divine (Acts 8:9-11). The spirit of divination which the apostles cast out of the girl at Philippi was using supernatural knowledge to identify God's true servants, yet she was in the service of Satan (Acts 16:16-18). Demons did confess Christ (Matt. 8:28, 29; Mark 5:7). People who are deceived by Satan regarding wonders and revelations may praise God, not because Satan makes them praise God, but because they are deceived and think God did them. The devil would use any means, even praise to God, to deceive.[4]

"Prove all things; hold fast that which is good" (I Thess. 5:21).

---

[3] Study the scriptures listed in the "Introductory Study on the Holy Spirit" pp. 450, 451, 452.

[4] See "Studying The Works of the Spirit: Miraculous and Non-Miraculous" pp. 474-481.

# 83

## STUDYING THE WORKS OF THE SPIRIT: MIRACULOUS AND NON-MIRACULOUS

*An Investigation of Scriptures Relating to the Modern Claims of Supernatural Works of the Holy Spirit*

This is not to question *whether* a Christian has the Holy Spirit, or whether one must yield to His influence and seek a genuine fellowship with Christ through the Spirit and a fuller experience of His power (Eph. 3:16, 17; 5:18; Rom. 8:1-16).

But we are seeking answers to the following questions:

1. How should the Holy Spirit manifest Himself in every Christian's life?
2. How are we to seek to receive the fullness of the Holy Spirit?
3. How are the various manifestations of the Holy Spirit related to each other?

Note: This is not to put God on trial, or to subject the activities of deity to human judgment; but it is to seek to know God's will for us, and, if we may, to understand His ways.

*It Should Be Agreed By All That the Scripture Does Teach the Following:*

1. That the Holy Spirit is involved in the new birth of every saved person, and is connected with baptism into Christ (John 3:3-7; 7:38, 39; 14:23; Acts 2:38; 5:32; 19:3; Rom. 8:9-11; I Cor. 12:13; Titus 3:5-7; Heb. 6:4, 5).
2. That the fruit of the Spirit is exhibited in the personal transformation of mind and character (hence conduct) of each individual who grows in Christian faith as he should (Gal. 5:16-25, esp. 22-23; Rom. 8;2-4, 12-14; 14:17; I Cor. 6:9-11, 17-20).[1]

   Is not this work of the Holy Spirit equivalent to, or the same as, Christ in us? (Gal. 2:20; 4:19; Col. 3:1-17; Eph. 3:16-19). Compare also the dwelling or working of God in Christians (John 14:23; II Cor. 1:21; 3:17, 18; 6:16; Eph. 2:22; Phil. 2:13).

   This manifestation of the divine nature in us (II Pet. 1:3, 4) by

[1] For further study of this point read the scriptures cited on the "Evidence of the Personal and Practical Significance of the Holy Spirit," pp. 450-452.

reason of the personal indwelling of God's Spirit in place of, or in control of, our spirits is the ultimate goal of God's work with us. This is the end for which miracles were wrought. It is the object for which miracles can never be an acceptable substitute (I Cor. 12:31 to 14:1; I Tim. 1:5; II Pet. 1:3-11; I John 1:5-8; 3:1-6).

### *What Are We To Understand About Miraculous Demonstrations of Holy Spirit Power?*

Tongues, interpretation of tongues, prophecy, revealed knowledge, healings, and various other miracles were real and had a place in New Testament times. But what was that place? And do they have the same place today?

1. These are works or signs of the Holy Spirit, not the Holy Spirit Himself. They are related to the Holy Spirit as effects of which He is the cause. They have been found where the personal indwelling of the Holy Spirit did not occur. The apostles and the seventy disciples mentioned in Luke 10 worked miracles months before Jesus said, "He that believeth on me, as the scripture hath said, from within him shall flow rivers of living water." And John explained "But this spake he of the Spirit, which they that believed on him were to receive: for the Spirit was not yet given; because Jesus was not yet glorified" (John 7:38, 39; cp. Matt. 10:7; Mark 6:13; Luke 10:17-20).

   Consider the example of the messengers of Saul and Saul himself on a mission of murder against God's anointed; yet they were made to prophecy by the Spirit of God (I Sam. 19:18-24). So also Balaam's ass (Num. 22:25-30). This was probably the case with Samson (Judg. 14, 15, and 16). It was before the household of Cornelius was born of water and the Spirit, even before they were promised the gift of the Spirit, that they manifested the miraculous powers (Acts 10:44-48).

   It is evident that some men who are not pleasing to Christ at the final judgment will at least claim to have worked many miracles in His name (Matt. 7:21-23). If they speak that boldly to His face, does it not appear that they will be sincerely convinced that they have actually wrought such mighty works by His power? Is it possible that they did and still were outside of Christ and were unsaved at the last?

   The Holy Spirit Himself is a personality, a Divine Person, with a mind and character and will, equal with God, perfect and holy. He dwells in men to take control of mind and will and character and make it over, or rather replace the human nature with the Spirit and nature of Christ.[2]

2. It does not appear that such miraculous demonstrations are universal or necessary effects whenever or wherever the Holy Spirit dwells in men. A man who honestly says Jesus is Lord manifests the Spirit (I Cor. 12:3). Not everyone in the New Testament church had the gifts of miraculous knowledge; at least not all had any one sign (I Cor. 12:29, 30). Paul makes it clear that love is a more excellent way of manifesting the Spirit than all the miracles (I Cor. 12:31 and all chapter 13; cp. Rom. 14:17; Gal. 5:22, 23; I John 4). Acts 3, 4, and 5 seem to indicate that all the miracles were worked by the apostles although all the people received the gift of the Spirit and were said to be filled with the Holy Spirit. Acts 4:31 may refer to the apostles particularly.
3. Are the miraculous demonstrations ever the chief work that God wants the Spirit to do with men, or are they a means to another end? Such things were to confirm the faith in the message by showing that it had a supernatural origin. (Heb. 2:3, 4; John 20:31; 14:11; Mark 16:20). The word of God has the power to regenerate and to sanctify through faith which allows the Spirit of God to dwell within us (Eph. 3:16-19; I Tim. 1:5; Gal. 5:22-25).
4. Miraculous deeds did not guarantee a spiritual church, or a heart filled with the divine nature of the Spirit, or a life full of fruit of the Spirit. The Corinthian church "came behind in no gift" but was enriched "in all utterance and in all knowledge" (I Cor. 1:5-7); yet that church was notorious for errors in doctrine and evils in practice. The exercise of miraculous gifts among them did not produce such decency and order as God is supposed to be the author of (I Cor. 14:23-33; cf. II Cor. 8:7; I Cor. 8:1; 11:17-34). Remember Matthew 7:22.
5. Are not such miraculous powers likely to be abused, misunderstood, and put in a place of too much importance, in which they become a source of pride or of distrust and disunity among brethren? This appears to be at least a danger in the Corinthian church, in view of I Corinthians 14. This is emphasized by some who advocate tongues and miracles today.
6. Are such miraculous demonstrations always caused exclusively by the Holy Spirit? May some of the experiences and utterances be

[2] For further study of Who or What is the Holy Spirit, see pp. 452, 453.

caused by the workings of the subconscious mind, by something like hypnotic influences? Jesus and the apostles warned in the first century of the possibility of "lying wonders" (Matt. 24:24; 7:22; II Thess. 2:9; I John 4:1-6; Rev. 13:14; 16:14; 19:20). Even in the Old Testament we find warnings against false prophets with signs (Deut. 13:1-5; 18:22; Isa. 8:20). Moses faced sorcerers who imitated his miracles to some extent (Exod. 7:11, 12).

7. How can we test the "spirits" by an objective and sure standard rather than by our feelings or inward inclinations? What must we think of "prophets" and so-called miracle workers who teach and practice contrary to clear and fundamental parts of Christian doctrine? Must we give up trying to understand the word and follow the teachings of those who show signs today? Must the claims of those who profess miracles be tested by the New Testament? Or must our understanding of the New Testament be tested by the teaching of those who seem to show signs.

Isolated wonders do not necessarily prove a divine religion or a revelation from God, in the same way that Bible miracles prove that the Bible is from God. The Bible miracles were part of a coherent combination of many miracles and messages to which they were significantly related. Any unexplained wonder here or there must be tested by its coherence with the undeniable body of complete and coherent evidence in the miracles and prophecies which constitute the undoubted revelation of God. The extent and quality of miracles and revelations by the apostles and the Bible writers is different from the many various "miracles" and "prophecies" that have been claimed since the days of the New Testament. Even Pharoah could see or should have seen the difference between Moses' miracles and those of his magic men (Exod. 7). Philip's works at Samaria outclassed those of Simon Magus (Acts 8). Paul's record of the word of God stands forever against any contrary gospel, He said, "Though we or an angel from heaven preach unto you any other gospel than that which we preached to you, let him be anathema" (Gal. 1:8). "If any man thinketh himself to be a prophet, or spiritual, let him take knowledge of the things that I write unto you, that they are the commandment of the Lord" (I Cor. 14:37).

*Some Tests of the Spirits are Stated or Implied in the Scriptures*

1. When miracles are charged for or are made a means of gaining wealth they do not seem to represent the power of God nor are they

used according to the will of Christ (Matt. 10:8).

2. One does not have the Spirit of God who will not confess Jesus (I John 4:2, 3).
3. One is not approved by Christ if he refuses to hear, heed and keep the words of the apostles as they were guided by the Holy Spirit in the original Christianity of the New Testament (I John 4:6).
4. It is not God's Spirit if it does not cause love for brethren (I John 4:8; 3:10).
5. It is not the Spirit of God if it leads to indulgence of ungodly lusts, sensual living, "separation," etc. (Jude 17-23).
6. The Spirit of God does not cause men to be jealous and factious; but the wisdom from above is pure, peaceable, easy to be entreated, full of mercy and good fruits, without uncertainty, without hypocrisy (James 3:13-18).
7. The Spirit which God made to dwell in us does not lead us to lust and covert and envy (James 4:5).[3]
8. That which is really of the Spirit of God will harmonize with the true nature of the Spirit of Christ which is to be in us as described in these passages: Romans 12; Galatians 5:13-26; 6:1-9; Ephesians 4:17-32; 5:1-33; Philippians 2:1-15; Colossians 3:1-17.
9. The true Spirit of Christ must produce Christlikeness.
   a. He was guileless (I Pet. 2:22; Isa. 53:9).
   b. He was humble (Phil. 2:5-8; I Pet. 2:23; Matt. 11:29; John 13:3-9).
   c. He was compassionate (Matt. 9:36-38; Luke 19:10; Matt. 20:28; Rom. 9:3).
   d. He was resigned to God's will (John 4:34; Luke 2:42; John 18:11; 12:23-28).
   e. He sought prayer and fellowship with God (Mark 1:35; Luke 6:12; etc.).
   f. He was fervent and zealous (John 4:34; 2:17; 9:4; Matt. 21).
   g. He was forgiving (Luke 23:34; 7:48; etc.).
   h. He is faithful, loyal, steady, consistent (Heb. 13:5; John 13:1; 10:12-18).

*Some Important Questions to Consider About the Reality, Nature and Power of the Spirit.*

1. Can one be filled with the fruitbearing Holy Spirit by faith in the

[3] Some problems are encountered in the translation of this verse. It seems to teach this point which is also taught in other passages as well (Gal. 5:16-25, etc.).

word without any special striving for ecstatic experience or miraculous manifestations of the physical powers of the Spirit?
2. Are all who are without the physical signs of power deficient in faith or unwilling to be controlled by God?
3. Is the righteousness, joy and peace in the Holy Spirit which is the essence of the kingdom (Rom. 14:17) available only as a special attainment or special divine favor after justification, and always accompanied by special signs of physical power?
4. Do obedient believers in Christ who have no miraculous experiences or demonstrations have "righteousness, peace and joy in the Holy Spirit" only in a different degree, or do they have a false peace and joy and a false sense of participation in the righteousness of Christ? Do miraculous manifestations have any direct relation to righteousness, peace and joy in the Holy Spirit?
5. Are some Christians with the appearance of faith and Christian character still without the "earnest of the Spirit" (cp. II Cor. 1:22; 5:5; Eph. 1:13, 14) or is the earnest of the Spirit available without miraculous manifestations?

*How Is One To Know That He Has The Spirit?*

It is altogether clear in the New Testament that every Christian has and must have the Holy Spirit. How can we receive this gift from God?
1. Pray (Luke 11:13). For what? For tongues, or like David in Psalm 51:10, or Paul in Ephesians 3:16-19? Is this a promise of the person who dwells in us and transforms us, or of powers that may be misused and abused?
2. Repent and be baptized (Acts 2:38, 39). Be baptized (Acts 19:3). Obey (Acts 5:32). Believe (John 7:38, 39). Keep Christ's word (John 14:23).
3. Apostles' hands were laid on the person (Acts 8:18; 19:6; 6:6, possibly; II Tim. 1:6). But in I Timothy 4:14, Paul does not say by the hands of the elders, but together with the hands of the eldership. Evidently Paul's hands were laid on Timothy at the same time as the elders' hands (probably when Timothy left Lystra to be a missionary), and Paul's hands conferred a gift (by prophecy) at that time (cp. I Tim. 1:18).
4. By the hearing of faith, not by the works of law (Gal. 3:2; 3:14; Eph. 1:13; 3:17).
5. For the apostles, by tarrying in Jerusalem (Luke 23:49; Acts 1:5, 8; cp. John 20:22, 23). Should we all do likewise?

6. Does Paul set an example in this that we should expect to follow? (Acts 9:17; 22:16). Was this through the hands of Ananias? Or was it the every-Christian gift at his baptism? Or was he given the inspiration of an apostle as directly as those who received it at Pentecost? What conclusion can you draw from answers you cannot know?
7. Did the laying on of hands in Acts 13:1-4 confer any powers?
8. Why didn't Philip lay hands on the Christians at Samaria? (Acts 8:8-18).
9. Can we actually know of any way that anybody ever received a miraculous gift of miracle-working power except by the laying on of an apostle's hands, or by being an apostle and receiving it directly from heaven? The household of Cornelius (Acts 10). Was that a good example of regular procedure? Note they received this manifestation before baptism. What continuing effects did this have?

### *What Is Baptism In The Holy Spirit? Are All Christians To Be Baptized In The Spirit?*

1. John the Baptist said the One coming after him would "baptize you in the Holy Spirit" (Matt. 3:11). Does this say all, or indicate who? Just before His ascension Jesus told the apostles, "for John indeed baptized with water; but ye shall be baptized in the Holy Spirit not many days hence" (Acts 1:5). Here is a clear case of fulfillment of John's prophecy.
2. Peter described the coming of the Holy Spirit upon the household of Cornelius: "And as I began to speak, the Holy Spirit fell on them, even as on us at the beginning. And I remembered the word of the Lord, how he said, John indeed baptized with water; but ye shall be baptized in the Holy Spirit. If then God gave unto them the like gift as he did also unto us, when we believed on the Lord Jesus Christ, who was I that I could withstand God? And when they heard these things, they held their peace, and glorified God, saying, Then to the Gentiles also hath God granted repentance unto life" (Acts 11:15-18). How much does this have in common with the apostles on Pentecost?
3. What promises of Jesus were fulfilled by the coming of the Spirit on the apostles at Pentecost? Jesus promised that the Holy Spirit shall teach you all things, and bring to your remembrance all that I have said unto you" (John 14:26). Does this apply to us? Or does the context show that it was a promise only to the apostles?

Study in context John 15:26; 16:13; 20:22, 23; Luke 24:49; Acts 1:8; 2:4. Does everyone receive such physical manifestations of power when the Holy Spirit comes upon them?

4. "For in one Spirit were we all baptized into one body" (I Cor. 12:13). Does this mean that we must be or are all baptized in the Spirit? Compare closely Romans 8:9, 14; I Corinthians 12:3; Galatians 5:16; 5:25; Ephesians 2:22. Could it be used here in the sense shown in Galatians 6:1; I Corinthians 4:21; II Timothy 1:7; I John 4:6? Is Holy Spirit baptism the "real" baptism that all Christians must share? See Acts 10:46, 47; I Peter 3:21; Colossians 2:12; Galatians 3:26, 27; 4:19.

For Further Study:

Burdick, Donald W. *Tongues: To Speak or Not To Speak.* Chicago: Moody Press, 1969. Evaluates tongues speaking in the light of the New Testament.

DeWelt, Don. *The Power of the Holy Spirit,* Vol. I. Joplin, Missouri: College Press, 1963. Pp. 39-150. Discusses these two questions: Should I be baptized in the Holy Spirit? and Should I speak in tongues?

Gromacki, Robert Glenn. *The Modern Tongues Movement.* Philadelphia: Presbyterian and Reformed Publishing Co., 1967. Historical and Biblical study.

Pack, Frank. *Tongues and the Holy Spirit.* Abilene, Texas: Biblical Research Press, 1972. Gives historical background for modern claims of speaking in tongues. Careful study of New Testament teaching on the work of the Holy Spirit.

Staton, Knofel. *Spiritual Gifts Today.* Joplin, Missouri: College Press, 1973. Studies the New Testament teaching in seeking answers to current issues regarding spiritual gifts today.

# *Part Sixteen*

# DEATH OF CHRIST

## 84

### OUR CRUCIFIED KING

Did you ever have an almost unbearable job to do, or a very painful ordeal to endure? Yet you went ahead with it willingly, though dreading it, because you knew it had to be done or you loved someone enough to do it? When it was successfully completed, what a triumphant feeling—"That's over, and done right, too!" To have such an experience helps one picture and feel how Jesus went to the cross, willingly after agonizing dread, bore it in all its severity, then said, "It is finished!" (John 19:30).

After the last supper with the disciples and His intercessory prayer in John 17, Jesus made His way to Gethsemane, accompanied by the eleven. Here after His intense prayer He was found by Judas and the mob. The betrayer kissed Jesus. The mob came to take Jesus with swords and clubs; yet they fell backward to the ground when He stepped forward and identified Himself without fear. Jesus was then seized by the officers. Some of the apostles wanted to fight; but Jesus said He could call legions of angels if He wanted to. In the hours that followed Jesus was shuttled from one court to another. His case was heard by Annas, Caiphas, the Sanhedrin, Pilate, Herod, and Pilate again.

To avoid the possibility of interference by the people who believed Jesus to be a prophet the Jewish rulers sought to take Jesus in the night and to get rid of Him as quickly as possible. In their many trials and with many false witnesses the Jews were not able to make a case against Jesus (Matt. 26:59, 60). Finally, the high priest put Jesus under oath to tell whether He was the Son of God, and Jesus solemnly and plainly affirmed that He was. They considered this to be blasphemy, and they made it their "lawful reason" why He must die.

The final disposition of Jesus' case rested with Pilate, for he alone had the right to pronounce the death sentence. The Romans had forbidden the Jews to execute the death sentence (John 18:31). Pilate examined Jesus as thoroughly as he could and said repeatedly that he found no fault in Him. Pilate, realizing that Jesus was innocent, offered the Jewish crowd the choice of Barabbas or Jesus, but the mob, urged on by the religious leaders, demanded the life of Jesus.

The Jews made much use of Jesus' claim to be a king, although His kingdom was not of this world, and threatened Pilate with political troubles if he did not condemn Jesus. Pilate was not too well acquainted with truth and its obligations, so he tried to speak for Jesus, yet deliver Him up to the wishes of the Jews, and to renounce all responsibility in the matter. He went through the motions of washing his hands of it all, but instead of dismissing the case and freeing the prisoner, he claimed to dismiss the matter by turning Jesus over to the Jews to be crucified.

### *Jesus Gives His Life*

They heaped mockery, ignominy, and mistreatment upon our Lord. They laid upon Him the heavy wooden cross. Jesus started out carrying His own cross, but the effect of the scourging and other abuses made Him weaken under its weight. We cannot determine the exact place of the crucifixion, but it was outside the city; and as they went out the soldiers compelled a passer-by, Simon of Cyrene, to carry the cross (Mark 15:21; Luke 23:26). It is not known why it was called "the place of a skull" (John 19:17). The Latin word for skull, *calvaria,* gives us the word Calvary. A small hill just north of Jerusalem is thought to resemble a skull in appearance and to be a probable location of the crucifixion. Crucifixion was a form of punishment usually reserved for condemned slaves, traitors, or the worst criminals. The one on the cross died a thousand deaths, suffering long and terribly. The two men crucified with Him are described as "thieves" (Matt. 27:38) and "malefactors" (Luke 23:32). At first they joined in the mockery against Jesus; then one repented (Luke 23:39-43).

Matthew says the title on the cross was set over Jesus' head, which is the chief indication that the cross of Christ was of the traditional form with an extended upright beam above the crossarm (Matt. 27:37). The title Pilate had placed on the cross—"Jesus of Nazareth, the King of the Jews"—was written in three languages: Hebrew, Greek and Latin (John 19:19-20). Thousands of Jews were gathered for the Passover from every nation and province where they lived. Hebrew (the Aramaic dialect derived from ancient Hebrew) was no longer known by all of them. Greek was the international language; Latin was the official language of Rome.

Pilate's statement on the sign above Jesus seemed to uphold Jesus' claim and to accuse those who condemned Him, making them traitors.

The sign made the chief priests so uncomfortable that they tried to get Pilate to have it changed. Pilate firmly rejected their request (John 19:21-22). He seems to have been taking vengeance upon them for the bitterness and trouble that they had brought to him. He, too, was uncomfortable.

The crucifixion was performed by a squad of four soldiers. It is not likely that they divided each garment, but they probably made a four-way division of all His clothing—shoes, belt, head covering, and outer robe—perhaps casting lots to see who got each part (Mark 15:24; John 19:23). There was one other garment, a tunic or long shirt worn next to the skin, which was without a seam. It was not convenient to divide and was more valuable in one piece, and so they gambled for it. "That the scripture might be fulfilled" (John 19:24) does not mean that it was the purpose of the soldiers to fulfill prophecies about Jesus. The clause in the original Greek is in the form that is commonly used to express a purpose; and in our English version it is translated literally. Perhaps we should translate our text thus: "They cast lots, so that the Scripture was fulfilled." God predicted events because He knew they would happen; we should not think of Him as forcing men to do evil just because it had been predicted.

At the beginning of the crucifixion, someone had offered Jesus a drink of sour wine mixed with myrrh and gall, but He would not drink it (Matt. 27:34; Mark 15:23). Many believe that it was a stupefying drink provided by merciful people to deaden the pain. His cry, "I thirst" seems to have come after some six hours of suffering on the cross through the heat of the day. Great thirst was one of the worst agonies of crucifixion. Jesus did not say, "I thirst," just because it had been prophesied (John 19:28). A short stick from a bush called hyssop was used to reach Jesus' mouth with the sponge with vinegar on it. The cross was probably not high. Jesus did not refuse to drink as He did the one at the beginning (John 19:29-30). Probably it did not have gall and myrrh in it. It is very likely that even a mouthful of sour wine from a sponge was a real help to relieve His parched throat so that He could speak plainly and loudly the next two utterances.

Matthew and Mark mention a loud cry before He died, which may be the shout of victory: "It is finished!" (Matt. 27:50; Mark 15:37; John 19:30). His sufferings were about to end, but that does not seem to be the main significance of this cry. Prophecy is fulfilled! The law is perfected and abrogated! An age is brought to an end that a new age may begin. God's eternal purpose has been carried out. He delivered up His spirit unto God. He said, "Father, into thy hands I commend my spirit" (Luke 23:46), and He left the body, and it was dead.

The good shepherd laid down His life for the sheep according to the will of God. He laid it down, no one took it away from Him (John 10:18). Oh, the Jews wanted to take it; and they defiled themselves with the guilt of taking away His life; but they could not have done it without His willingness to go to the cross for us. Of course He submitted willingly to it all because He came into the world to give His life a ransom for sinners (Matt. 20:28).

While He was on the cross, they mocked and derided Him, claiming that He could not come down. He could, but He wouldn't. He stayed on the cross for us. "Not the nails, but His love, held Him there." Oh, what love!

Why did He bear such anguish and pain? The sufferings of crucifixion were real and terrible: the torn flesh, pulled tendons, stretched joints, inflamed sores (from scourging as well as nailing), the burning sun, the great thirst, and who knows how much more. But all of these were not the worst of His sufferings. We cannot know in this life the anguish of Jesus' soul when He felt himself made guilty before God of all the sins of men, when His soul was made to feel the unearthly pangs of the doomed being driven from God to hell. "The earth grew dark with mystery." How long and how great were the sufferings of His soul in that darkness! We can know only that it was enough to serve the sentence of the second death. Why all of this? Because a just sentence was written against you and me, and Jesus loved us enough to want to save us by fulfilling the law's demands in our place. He offered us an opportunity to accept His death as our own and to live a new life in union with Him. "Who his own self bare our sins in his own body on the tree, that we, being dead to sins, should live unto righteousness: by whose stripes ye were healed" (I Pet. 2:24).

### *Importance of the Death of Christ*

The death of Christ as a willing sacrifice for our sins is a subject all Christians should study—every Lord's Day at the Lord's Supper. It is a basic and indispensable fact of Christianity, the grounds of our redemption, the source of our sanctification. It merits our continual meditation and increasing appreciation. The Lord considered His death the climax of His life on earth, the greatest thing He ever did; and He requested us to keep it ever before our minds in worship to Him (Luke 22:19, 20; I Cor. 11:23-29).

The death of Christ goes back into the counsels of eternity (I Pet. 1:18-20). It was foretold by the prophets (Ps. 22; Isa. 53; I Pet. 1:11; Luke 24:44-46). Throughout the patriarchal and Jewish dispensations the dying Christ was kept before the world in the institution of animal sacrifices (Gen. 4:4; 8:20; Ex. 12:7-12; 29:38; Lev. 16:24). Of all the great and interesting things that Moses, Elijah, and Christ could have found to talk about on the Mount of Transfiguration, it was the death of Christ that they discussed (Luke 9:28-31). Jesus' death was attended by miraculous phenomena (Matt. 27:45, 50-54). It was to be preached to the whole creation (Mark 16:15; I Cor. 15:1-4). "The doctrine of the cross" is equivalent to the gospel of salvation in Christ, and it is the wisdom of God and the power of God whereby we are saved, in which we stand (I Cor. 1:18, 24; 2:2; 15:1-4).

The theme of heavenly worship is "The Lamb that was slain" (Rev. 5:9-12).

The death of Christ is typified, prophesied, proclaimed, or applied in every part of the scripture. It is one of the essentials that give to the sixty-six books of the Bible their organic unity, making them as one living organism whose lifeblood is the blood of Christ. Anywhere you scratch beneath the surface in the Bible you draw blood, the blood of redemption in the death of Jesus Christ. All that went before that fateful day of crucifixion was in preparation for it. All that comes after it was in order to apply it to us.

All the way through His ministry Jesus knew that the cross was the goal of His life, and He looked forward to it with steadfast courage and willingness (John 2:19-22; 3:14, 16; 6:51; 10:11, 18; 12:32; Matt. 16:21; Luke 24:26). It was God's will that He should be delivered up to die for us (Acts 2:23; John 10:17; Rom. 8:32); it was not "possible" to grant Jesus' request in Gethsemane that this cup might pass from Him (cf. Matt. 26:39).

### *The Necessity of Christ's Death*

Let it not be overlooked, or disregarded, that Christ had to die. There could be no other way. It was no mere matter of convenience, no accident. Certainly He could have escaped from the men who killed Him. But He could not come down from the cross, because of the inner and moral necessities of His own nature and mission. It helps us to understand His death in its deep meaningfulness and great value to us, if we study the question: "Why was it necessary for Him to die?"

1. He had to die to fulfill the purpose and promised plan of God; to complete the program begun in all the past ages and dispensations; to make good the word of the prophets and His own teachings; to confirm the truth of His Messiahship (Mark 10:45; Matt. 16:21; John 3:14-17; 12:23-33). All the animal sacrifices, the altars and offerings of the Old Testament were but shadowy promises of the efficacious death of the Christ. "According to the scriptures" He died (I Cor. 15:3); and according to the scriptures He had to die (Luke 24:26, 44-46).

2. He had to die to be true to His own righteousness. He knew He should do good, and to not do it would be sin (James 4:17). He expressed His own perfect character.

3. He had to die to conquer death and bring to nought him that had the power of death, and to free men from the fear of death (Heb. 2:13, 14).

4. He had to die to reveal fully the reality of God's love—the infinite love and grace and longing that God had toward men (John 3:16; 15:13; I John 4:9-11). Love must be "not in word; neither in tongue; but in deed and in truth" (I John 3:18).

5. He had to die to win the hearts of men, to induce us to love God and forsake sin, to reconcile us to God, to break our unbelief and resistance of the righteousness of God. The power of the gospel to regenerate and transform grows out of the cross of Christ, by which I am crucified unto the world and the world is crucified unto me (Gal. 6:14; 2:20; II Cor. 5:14-21).

6. The big reason that summarizes many of these, and more, too, is this: He had to die "for our sins." The wages of sin is death. To take away our sin, He had to take its death, our death, upon Himself (Rom. 4:25; Heb. 9:22; Isa. 53:5, 6, 8; Heb. 2:9; John 1:29; Gal. 1:4, etc.).

7. To demonstrate the righteousness of God—"that he [God] might be just, and the justifier of him that hath faith in Jesus" (Rom. 3:25, 26). God is a righteous and knowing judge. He cannot merely disregard sin. In order to call us righteous without making God a liar, Jesus took our sins upon Himself and bore the punishment on the condition that we would yield our lives to Him to be identified with Him, being found in Him and He in us by a fellowship of death. On our account he died for sin in love for us, that we might die to sin in love for Him.

The Lord wants the death of Christ proclaimed—in word and in the Lord's Supper—because the death of Christ so vividly proclaims several lessons which we must not forget: 1. the fact of sin and its severity; 2. the wrath of God against sin; 3. the wages of sin is death; 4. the futility of man's attempts to remove or minimize sin; 5. the nature of sin is selfishness; 6. the nature of righteousness is surrender and self-denial; 7. the only remedy of sin, the blood of Christ; 8. the love of God that seeks and sacrifices not to condemn, but to save us.

### *The Meaning of the Cross*

To Jesus, His death meant pain and sorrow, heaviness and woe, condescension, humiliation and shame, all of which He didn't deserve, and how deeply we cannot imagine! But it also meant glory and exaltation (Phil. 2:5-11)—first shame and suffering, then glory. "For the joy that was set before him endured the cross, despising the shame" (Heb. 12:2).

To us it means that He died our death; then our death is past. We are crucified with Christ (Gal. 2:20); it is not ours to live our own lives (Rom. 6:1-11). We died, and the lives we live we must live unto Him (II Cor. 5:14-17). He purchased our lives and must be allowed to live in them to His glory (I Cor. 6:19, 20). It means that if we accept His death for ours and surrender our lives to Him we shall suffer death no more, but He will live in us a manner of life that is good, true, beautiful, full, joyous, and successful—a life triumphant and eternal—partaking of His divine nature (II Pet. 1:3, 4; I John 5:11, 12; 3:1-5). It means for us fellowship in His sufferings and participation in His glory (Phil. 3:10, 11; Rom. 8:17)—for us, too, the cross and then the crown.

For Further Study:

Crawford, C. C. *Sermon Outlines on the Cross of Christ.* Murfreesboro, Tenn.: Dehoff Publishers, 1960. and *The Passion of Our Lord.* Joplin: College Press, 1968. Practical studies.

Denney, James. *The Death of Christ.* Downers Grove: InterVarsity Press, 1951. Classic work on the Biblical doctrine of the death of Christ.

Morris, Leon. *The Cross in the New Testament.* Grand Rapids: Wm. B. Eerdmans, 1965. Thorough study on the New Testament teaching relating to the death of Christ.

Warfield, B. B. *The Person and Work of Christ.* Philadelphia: Presbyterian and Reformed Publishing Co., 1950. Pp. 325-530. Scholarly essays on the work of Christ as redeemer.

# 85

## "GOD WAS IN CHRIST, RECONCILING"

In Jesus Christ God became flesh and dwelt among us, and we beheld his glory (John 1:1, 14). The prophet said, "They shall call His name Immanuel"; and Matthew explains that the name means "God with us" (Isa. 7:14; Matt. 1:23).

The brief records of Jesus' birth report that He was conceived by the Holy Spirit and hence was the Son of God most high (Matt. 1:20; Luke 1:32, 35). By the age twelve He expressed His own consciousness of His special relationship with God, gently correcting Mary, who had spoken of Joseph as His father (Luke 2:48, 49). Still He accepted the obligations and limitations of true humanity, and was subject to His earthly "parents."

When He was baptized, the voice of God said "Thou art my beloved Son, in whom I am well pleased." The Spirit of God in a visible form descended and rested upon Him. By that sign the prophet John knew that the message he had been given was confirmed, and he testified that Jesus was the Son of God (Luke 3:21, 22; John 1:29-34).

Jesus walked the earth as a man, was hungry, cold, and weary like any man. He was tempted, even as we are, yet without sin. All the while, in His spirit, personality, and character, there was the quality and nature of God. In His coming to earth, He somehow "emptied himself" of certain divine characteristics (Phil. 2:5-8). Nevertheless, He manifested on the earth a truly divine life, work, and purpose. He humbled himself to be a man, but humility is not beneath the dignity of divine excellence; and in all His humility He was still Lord and master.

### *He Did the Works of God*

He was master of the elements. He changed water into wine; stilled a temptest with a word; walked upon the wind-tossed sea; withered a fig tree; multiplied a few loaves and fishes to feed thousands of people; produced a net-breaking catch of fish where none had been found; and sent Peter to find a coin in the mouth of the first fish he caught on a hook.

He was master over death and disease. He called forth Lazarus from the tomb on the fourth day, after the body had begun to decay, still bound hand and foot with graveclothes. He raised two others from the dead before that: Jairus' daughter and a widow's only son.

He cleansed lepers with a touch; cured paralysis with a word, and even at a distance; made the blind to see; rebuked the burning fever; and granted the cure of a twelve-year hemorrhage for a woman who merely touched the hem of His garment.

He was victor over the forces of wickedness. The demons knew Him and cried out in fear and defiance. He commanded them to be silent and made them come out of their victims. A legion of demons could not resist His authority and power. The devil himself could not deceive or sway Him, but was driven from Him.

Jesus came to earth to serve men and to save them. He did not condemn and destroy, but He knew thoroughly their sinful hearts. He read the minds of friend and foe. He chided the ambitious secret thoughts of His apostles (Mark 9:33-37; 10:41-45; Luke 22:24-30). He knew all along the character and plottings of His betrayer. He answered the unuttered accusations of detractors (Mark 2:6-12), and showed them that He did not blaspheme when He pronounced the forgiveness of sins. He answered the mistaken mental judgments of Simon the Pharisee, and showed that He knew more than Simon expected Him to know about the hearts of those present (Luke 7:36-50). He saw through the motives of pretended praise offered by those who sought to ensnare Him with a question about the tribute money (Matt. 22:15-22). He knew Peter better than Peter knew himself, and predicted his denials specifically (see Matt. 26:33-35 and Luke 22:31-34).

Jesus did not overpower the minds of men, nor overthrow the freedom of their wills. But He completely understood them, and He fitted His words exactly to each one's needs. "He needed not that any one should bear witness concerning man; for he himself knew what was in man" (John 2:25).

The works of Jesus were the works of God, and the power that was in them was God's. The words of Christ were the words of God; His was the wisdom which they displayed. The plans and purposes of Jesus' life were the eternal purposes of God: He carried out God's predetermined plan on schedule. And Jesus' motives were the motives of God. He could truthfully say, "I and my Father are one"; "He that hath seen me hath seen the Father"; and "if ye had known me, ye should have known my Father also" (John 10:30; 14:9; 8:19).

He claimed divine appointment in Nazareth's synagogue, on the occasion of His first recorded sermon in Galilee: "This day is this scripture fulfilled . . . The Spirit of the Lord is upon me, because he hath anointed me . . ." (Luke 4:16-21). He declared His divine prerogatives in the face of the first fierce opposition of the rulers of Jerusalem, claiming to do all that the Father does; to have power to give life to the dead, to be judge of all men, to be destined to be honored by all men even as the Father is honored (John 5:19-29).

He offered Himself as all that any man needs and as a vital necessity for every man: "If the Son therefore shall make you free, ye shall be free indeed"; and "If ye believe not that I am he, ye shall die in your sins" (John 8:36, 24). "I am the way, the truth, and the life; no man cometh unto the Father, but by me" (John 14:6). "He that abideth in me, and I in him, the same bringeth forth much fruit; for without me ye can do nothing" (John 15:5). "I am the bread of life: he that cometh to me shall never hunger; and he that believeth on me shall never thirst"; and "Except ye eat the flesh of the Son of man, and drink his blood, ye have no life in you" (John 6:35, 53). "Neither knoweth any man the Father, save the Son, and he to whomsoever the Son will reveal him. Come unto me, all ye that labour and are heavy laden, and I will give you rest . . ." (Matt. 11:27-30).

### *As a Man among Men*

The Christ was also the Son of David, the seed of Abraham; and He usually preferred to speak of himself as the "Son of man." In order that He might be a perfect priest, to make intercession for men, and to inspire the confidence of men, it was fitting that He should be one of them and share in human experience. The word Christ is from the Greek word for the Old Testament word Messiah, which meant "anointed one." Prophets, priests, and kings were anointed; and the Messiah was to combine all three offices in one. As a prophet He was both a faithful messenger of God's word and a perfect representation of God in human form. As a king He was meek and lowly, seeking to serve rather than to be served, but winning the highest devotion and fullest obedience, because He is the king of love. As a priest He is the only one who lived a perfect, sinless life, who is worthy to stand in the presence of God, and who is able to offer the only adequate sacrifice for the sins of others. From His human experience and temptation He is able to know our need perfectly and to be touched with the feeling of our infirmity. Because of His divinity and sinlessness He is able to make full atonement and to abide at the mercy seat of God continually.

The gospel is the story of God, our Creator, living a human life on earth, in which He revealed Himself, expressed His love, accomplished men's redemption, and brought life and immortality to light for men. It is the story of God with us, in the midst of us, winning and restoring men to himself. He became man that He might make us partakers of His divine nature and share with us His own eternal glory and righteousness.

### *Reconciling Sinners to Himself*

God and men needed to be reconciled to each other, because they were separated by sin. Man's sin caused God to have a true complaint and a just sentence against men. The holiness of God could not accept men for full fellowship and blessing while their guilt remained and while the hearts and lives of men continued to be full of sin. The sinfulness of men caused them to be darkened in their understanding and vain in their reasonings, so that they did not really know God, and did not trust or love Him, but resisted His approaches to them and perverted the revelation that He had made to them.

Jesus understood that the greatest need of all men was to be set free from sin, from its doom, its guilt, its defilement, and its enticing delusion. In order to redeem men and restore them to full fellowship with God, He was willing, not only to associate with sinners, to show them kindness and teach them righteousness, but even to give His own life as a ransom for all.

To accomplish the reconciliation of sinners He had to do two great difficult works. One was to settle the just charge that God had against us by taking our sins upon himself and bearing them in His own body upon the cross, so that God might be just in blotting out the sentence against us on the ground of our union with Christ by faith and new birth in Him. The other was to change our attitudes toward God so that we would love and trust Him, willingly do His bidding, and let Him be the manager and keeper of our lives.

Jesus achieved these purposes of divine grace by accomplishing in His earthly life and ministry certain notable and necessary things. He manifested God's goodness and desire to save men from sin and its consequences. He demonstrated the power of God, showing His ability to do what He promises. He taught and exhibited true righteousness, which made clear man's sinfulness and need for pardon and cleansing from sin. He led men to hunger for righteousness they did not have, and to tremble for sin they had too much of. He himself made the atoning sacrifice for sin and opened up the new and living way of access to God. He took away sin's penalty by bearing it himself, and made it possible for any man to be cleansed and made acceptable to God through Him. He loved men until they began to love Him and wanted to let God have full sway in their lives.

He provided a source of spiritual life and overcoming power for men by giving the Holy Spirit of God to dwell in the lives and hearts of men, to bear the fruit of a changed heart and a right spirit before God (John 7:38, 39; 14:23; 3:5; Acts 2:38; Rom. 8:1-11; Gal. 5:16-25). When men accept His death as their own and cease to live unto themselves the old life of self-will, He makes them new creatures by the life of His Spirit within them, living unto Him a life that is reconciled to God (II Cor. 5:14-19).

In His resurrection and other miracles He laid the foundations of faith; He called and prepared the apostles as witnesses to the truth; so that we might have an honest conviction of truth concerning Him to support a lifelong trust able to withstand the winds and currents of thought and emotion. He gave us abundant evidence for making an intelligent, firm and wholehearted commitment unto Him.

Jesus' work of reconciliation was not altogether completed during His life on earth. Much of it was accomplished through His death and resurrection, and even after His ascension into Heaven. But all reconciliation of men with God is accomplished through Jesus Christ —through the finished work of His incarnation, through the effect of His message on those who hear, believe, and obey it.

He has given to us a glorious part in this continuing ministry of reconciliation (II Cor. 5:18-21). We should rejoice in it as Paul did. Let us be faithful and fervent in entreating men on behalf of Christ, beseeching them, "Be ye reconciled unto God."

For Further Study:

See books listed on pages 488 and 489.

# 86

# NEW LIFE THROUGH ACCEPTING JESUS' DEATH

"I have been crucified with Christ; and it is no longer I that live, but Christ liveth in me: and that life which I now live in the flesh I live in faith, the faith which is in the Son of God, who loved me, and gave himself up for me" (Gal. 2:20).

We need to meditate on the meaning of the cross. Brief periods of meditation during the serving of the Lord's Supper on Sundays are helpful. But also we need to give many an hour to serious meditation on what the cross means in our lives.

## *Jesus Was Crucified For Us*

The idea of sacrifice was not a human invention born of the superstitions and fears of men. God originated sacrifice! All the sacrifices made from the time of Cain and Abel and Adam and Eve until Jesus' death were promissory notes which were paid in full by Jesus' death on the cross. Why were all these sacrifices made? God required them as acts of obedient faith on the part of those who were seeking to please Him (Heb. 10:1-10).

In the Old Testament times God did not attempt to redeem man with the blood of bulls and goats. God did not try one thing and find that it failed. He planned from the beginning to give His Son. The other sacrifices were just the proclamation of the coming sacrifice of His Son. I think the Lord's Supper today does for us exactly what the animal sacrifices did for David, Moses, and Abraham. They both proclaim our sinfulness and need of a sacrifice and proclaim God's provision of a way of redemption. Only the Lord's Supper looks back upon the accomplished redemption by Jesus Christ; the animal sacrifices looked forward unto the sacrifice that would be acceptable unto God. Hebrews 10:6, 7 says that in sacrifices and burnt offerings God had no pleasure, and they were not acceptable unto Him; but He prepared a body for His Son that He might do His will. Jesus came to do God's will; but the old sacrifices did not accomplish God's will. God proclaimed the need of a sacrifice from the beginning. There has never been any way for any man's sin to be forgiven, except through redemptive sacrifice.

How could God be righteous and let Abraham get by with lying like he did? How could God be righteous and let Jacob get by with cheating like he did? (He charged an exorbitant price for a bowl of bean soup!) How could God be righteous and let David get by with murder like he did? One English philosopher-poet said, "Mercy but murders, pardoning them that kill." Think that through. The judge of all the earth knows right and He must do right. God cannot sit on the bench, so to speak, and have sinners like me brought before Him and say, "He is no sinner." If a judge pronounces the guilty guiltless, then the judge is guilty. God cannot do that! God knows! God is true! God cannot simply say a sinner has not sinned. He cannot ignore sin. It is absolutely morally impossible for God simply to forget about and overlook the sins of men. *How can He be righteous then and forgive sinners?*

God does not condone sin. He does not break His own word. "The soul that sinneth shall surely die" (Ezek. 18:20). He carries it out to the letter. But He provides out of His own heart's generosity, out of His own love and holiness, the means by which we may identify ourselves with the death of Christ, and may receive the gift of life in Christ—a life that is not our own but is dead to self. We come forth from baptism as newborn babes—born in the righteousness of God. Isn't it a tremendous truth which you read in the scriptures, "Him who knew no sin, God made to be sin on our behalf that we might become the righteousness of God in Him" (II Cor. 5:21). See I Peter 2:24-25; Matthew 20:28; Titus 2:11-14; Romans 3:23-31.

In anguish, in punishment, in torment on the cross, Jesus cries out, "My God, my God, why hast thou forsaken me?" (Matt. 27:46). I think He knew why; but He could not help the cry. Never had Jesus been out of harmony with His Father, out of joyful satisfaction of the Father's good pleasure, and complete devotion to the Father's will. Here in obedience to Him now He suffers as the guilty, suffers for all the guilt of the world, Even the feeling of God's great displeasure and wrath against sin was upon Him. It was almost more than He could bear. Perhaps this actually broke His heart physically. It is more than we can realize that He was willing to die in our place that we might be made the righteousness of God in Him, that we might return unto the Shepherd and Bishop of our souls, that we might let Christ put within us a new life, so that God could be just, in the passing over of the sin done aforetime (Rom. 3:25).

All the sins God had not punished yet from the Old Testament times, all the sins He seemed to wink at and to pass over and forgive, the sins of all those who had not been sent to hell made God appear guilty for condoning them, until Jesus' sacrifice fulfilled the purpose of God. At the same time Jesus' death justified them before

God by faith, and fulfilled the sacrifices by which God had foreshadowed the death of Jesus to them. By obeying in faith the sacrifices, they identified themselves with the death of Jesus. But they did not enter the kingdom the way we do. Though, like John the Baptist, they may be the best ever born of women, they are not up to the standard of the least that are born of the Spirit. We have the special privilege of knowing His death, and receiving the gift of His life.

### *We Are Crucified with Christ*

Why could Jesus die in our place? Why could nothing else be a suitable sacrifice for our sins? Some persons reject the idea that someone could suffer the penalty for another's sins and any kind of justice be made out of it at all. It seems so true that my sin is my sin and nobody else is accountable for it or can bear the punishment of it. How can another take away my guilt from me? How can Jesus' death mean anything to my guilt?

God declares that Christ died for my sins. I must accept His death as the evidence of God's love. I must accept His death as God's provision for my own death as the sentence I deserve and turn my own life over to Jesus. If Jesus gives me His death and I give Him my life, then it is a fair exchange. If I accept His death as mine so that my death is past, then He died my death, and it is no more my life that lives, but Christ lives in me. I am united with Him so that God sees Him in me, because He now lives in me, and sees me in Him. Then you can see how God is just and the justifier of those who have faith in Jesus.

I think that forgiveness of sins by God required something more than the arbitrary or technical transference of guilt from one being to another. This is something that it seems cannot be done in justice. There is no justice in it! But God does not do it that way. Read carefully Romans 3:21-31. Note first that salvation is to those who believe. This is one place where people misunderstand the gospel. They assume that people can be saved in unbelief. The gospel cannot be understood if it is applied to anybody but believers. Christianity cannot be consistently held if even its standards of morality are applied to anyone but believers. You cannot make a community Christian without making individuals believers. That is true from households to nations. International relations can never be on a Christian basis until the individuals who control those nations and conduct those nations are believers in Jesus Christ above all else.

Paul says, "whom God set forth to be a propitiation, through faith, in his blood, to show his righteousness because of the passing over of the sins done aforetime, in the forebearance of God; for the showing, I say, of his righteousness at this present season: that he might himself be just, and the justifier of him that hath faith in Jesus" (Rom. 3:25, 26). We do not put faith in the blood, but salvation must be by the means of the blood, through faith.

God himself could not be just, if He merely called a sinner guiltless. He cannot just forget about a man's sin. But by Jesus fulfilling the law of God and by the man being identified with Jesus before God, so that the Spirit of Christ lives in the man, and the death of Christ is accepted by that man on his own part, in a covenant of life and of death, God can justly forgive and forget.

Why is faith required? Why didn't God just make a sacrifice somewhere in the universe and then tell us the sacrifice is made? I had some vague idea like this in the first ten years I remember going to church—that Jesus died for sins; therefore sins don't matter anymore. A lot of people seem to think that Jesus took care of my sins without affecting me in any way. Jesus doesn't take care of your sins unless you die to sin. The sentence of death still applies to you and to me, not simply to Him. It is His death which we accept as our death. Romans 6:1-11 preaches "the doctrine of the cross" in your life:

> What shall we say then? Shall we continue in sin, that grace may abound? God forbid! We who died to sin, how shall we any longer live therein? Or are ye ignorant that all we who were baptized into Christ Jesus were baptized into his death? We were buried therefore with him through baptism into death: that like as Christ was raised from the dead through the glory of the Father, so we also might walk in newness of life. For if we have become united with him in the likeness of his death, we shall be also in the likeness of his resurrection; knowing this, that our old man was crucified with him, that the body of sin might be done away, that so we should no longer be in bondage to sin; for he that hath died is justified from sin. But if we died with Christ, we believe that we shall also live with him; knowing that Christ being raised from the dead dieth no more; death no more hath dominion over him. For the death that he died, he died unto sin once; but the life he liveth, he liveth unto God. Even so reckon ye also yourselves to be dead unto sin, but alive unto God in Christ Jesus.

It is not only that Jesus had to be crucified for our salvation; we must be crucified for our salvation by being crucified with Him. We must accept His death as our own death, so that the body of sin is done away and we are no longer under the dominion of sin. So we count ourselves dead unto sin and alive unto God for evermore.

The purpose of Jesus' death was to make salvation available for the whole world (I John 2:3). He "is the Savior of all men, especially of them that believe" (I Tim. 4:10). Yet His death does not accomplish the redemption of the whole world, only of repentant believers who are baptized into Him. That is why baptism is so important. That is why faith in Him is so important. That is why we must preach the gospel. That is what is lacking of the sufferings of Christ which may be "filled up on our part, for the sake of His body the church." In Colossians 1:24 Paul says, "How I rejoice in my sufferings for your sake, and fill up on my part that which is lacking of the afflictions of Christ in my flesh for His body's sake, which is the church."

How could Paul be so bold as to imply that Jesus didn't suffer enough on the cross? Jesus did suffer enough to accomplish the atonement for our redemption; but Jesus' suffering did not carry that redemption to every man. It takes the continuing body of Jesus, the church, to do it. It takes messengers of the cross like Paul, to fill up on their part what is lacking of the sufferings of Christ to reach all men. The message of the cross of Christ is God's plan of redemption for man. But the hearer must make the response of faith so he can receive its benefits.

The sacrifice of Jesus is not effective just because he died. Rather it is effective when you accept it as your death, when you are buried into His death, and when you rise to walk in the newness of life with Christ's Spirit dwelling in you. The scripture plainly says that if the Spirit of Christ does not dwell in you, then you are none of His (Rom. 8:9, 10). It is because of this union with Christ that His death is justly seen as your death, and your life is justly seen as His life, and your life is His liability which He has fully paid on the cross.

*We must accept the sentence of death in ourselves.* I think God exemplified this in the Old Testament in dealing with the people of Israel, when He gave them a law and a covenant, and told them they would perish if they didn't keep them. They didn't keep His law, and He said the nation of Judah must perish. Then when he had destroyed it, as soon as the sentence was carried out, He could begin to keep His word to bring it to life by grace for the sake of the promises

He had made. Note how Jeremiah bought a field before the nation was destroyed to show his confidence that God would raise up the nation after the sentence had been carried out (Jer. 32).

We are not in the new covenant if we have to be controlled by laws. If you have to be compelled to give 10% because it is the law of God, you aren't in the new covenant. If you have to be compelled to attend church because it is the law of God, then you are not in the new covenant. The only people that are in Christ are those who believe Him, who love Him, and who work, not by the laws of the old covenant, but in the freedom that is in Christ. They do not use their freedom as an occasion to the flesh, but by the Spirit put to death the deeds of the flesh, and live by faith working through love. Study Galatians 5 on this subject. The flesh cannot be reborn; the flesh must die! That's the point! By flesh we do not mean that the body in and of itself is evil, but we mean the self-will and fleshly mind that does things because I like it, because I want to, because I am the master of my life, because I sit on the throne, because I don't care about God. This must die! This whole attitude must die! The church has a hard time being the church when it is filled with carnal people who have the fleshly mind, who have their will and their way that must be satisfied, and who simply compromise with one another instead of surrendering unto God, unto a newness of life (Rom. 8:5-13; 6:1-11, 17, 18, 20-23).

*New Life In Christ*

II Corinthians 5:14-17 says, "For the love of Christ constraineth us; because we thus judge, that one died for all, therefore all died. [If He died our death, our death is past.] He died for all that they should no longer live unto themselves, but unto Him who for their sakes died and rose again. Wherefore we henceforth know no man after the flesh [i.e., from the merely human point of view, because we don't live to exercise our own minds and to have our own feelings and to think our own thoughts and to make our own judgments]." We simply don't have a life of our own anymore. It has been bought with a price, it has been taken over by Jesus, it has entered into His death. Even if we have known Christ (as Paul once mistakenly knew Him) from the human point of view, yet now we know Him so no more. "Wherefore if any man is in Christ, he is a new creature: the old things are passed away; behold, they are become new" [all things are become new]."

Paul describes his new life in Christ: "For I through the law died unto the law, that I might live unto God. I have been crucified with Christ; and it is no longer I that live, but Christ liveth in me: and that life which I now live in the flesh I live in faith, the faith which is in the Son of God, who loved me, and gave himself up for me" (Gal. 2:19, 20). That's the life we live: the life Christ gives to those who open their hearts to Him because they trust Him. They believe in God's judgment and in His grace. They accept the sentence of death upon self for sin; and they accept the gift of new life, which is Christ's life in us in place of our own.

The greatest mistake the Christian can make is to say "It's my life, and I'll live it," because that must reject our salvation. The *only* salvation there is for any sinner, is to give my life up to Jesus and to receive His death for mine. And any time anybody thinks "It's my life, and I'll live it," he has forgotten the cleansing from his old sins. He has forgotten his Savior, he has renounced his Master, and he has immediately taken all his sins upon himself afresh.

We are not saved simply by Jesus' death, but by our union with Jesus' death, by our entering into Jesus' death, by the applying of His death to us, by the reality of the fact that it is "no longer we that live but Christ that lives in us." This does not mean that our salvation depends upon our keeping a tense obligation to law constantly to keep ourselves saved. That is not the idea at all. It just means that with a complete confidence in Jesus, you simply quit running your own life and let Jesus open it up under new management.

The life that we have lived in our own bodies, we lived into an impossible state of debt and bankruptcy and guilt and degradation. But Jesus took the life that we had ruined, He closed out the old account, paying it off, and opened up our lives anew under new management. He lets us work here, and live here, and enjoy the better conditions. But He is the owner and the proprietor of your ears and your hair and your clothes and your car and your nose and your handwriting and everything. He is the proprietor. It is this union with Jesus that makes redemption effective.

I cease to live my sinful life, and I enter into covenant with God into a covenant relationship with Christ. The two lives are blended together and His Spirit fills me, and the guilt is upon Him, and I'm free. My sins are gone! Praise God, my sins are gone, deeper than the deepest sea, never to be remembered anymore because in Christ I've ceased to be. A man does not stand anymore before God in judgment by himself. He will be judged before the judgment bar of Christ according to the deeds done in the body whether they be good or evil (II Cor. 5:10). His deeds prove the reality of his faith. But we stand in Christ.

The biggest difference between men is whether they are in Christ or not in Christ, not whether they are rich or poor, white or black, modern or ancient, in East or West, educated or uneducated, but *in Christ or not in Christ!* "In Christ there is now no condemnation," Paul says in Romans 8:1 and expands it into a whole glorious chapter of assurance. Those outside of Christ are "without God and without hope in the world" (Eph. 2:12; see Eph. 4:17-19).

That is why our union with Christ is more permanent than marriage, and more significant. When we are joined to Christ, it is the most significant thing that ever happens to us. The sinners who have faith in Jesus can be justified by Him through their faith (Rom. 4 and James 2:14-26). We become a part of Him who becomes righteousness in us, and the requirement of the law is fulfilled in us who walk after the Spirit and not after the flesh. Not that God's law becomes ineffective; it is removed as a law, the ministration of death and condemnation; but the law is really established. "Do we then make the law of none effect through faith? God forbid: nay, we establish the law" (Rom. 3:31). "There is therefore now no condemnation to them that are in Christ Jesus. For the law of the Spirit of life in Christ Jesus made me free from the law of sin and death. For what the law could not do, in that it was weak through the flesh, God, sending his own Son in the likeness of sinful flesh and for sin, condemned sin in the flesh" (Rom. 8:1-3). What God could not do in the law, in that it was weak depending upon the flesh, He did through the gospel. In Jesus Christ He sent His Son and condemned sin in the flesh, that the requirement of the law might be fulfilled in us who walk after the Spirit and not after the flesh. For the flesh is not subject to the law of God; it is at enmity with God; but ye are not in the flesh but in the Spirit, if so be that the Spirit of Christ (God) dwelleth in you (see Rom. 8:4-11).

Regeneration is essential to the Christian life. We have sometimes concentrated upon baptism to the point of neglect of the regeneration of a man. We do not realize that one cannot just join a church and be saved. We must be born anew to be saved. To emphasize the significance of this, some people have tried to make it an overwhelming emotional experience, which they seek at some point to represent as a miracle from God; and then they minimize obedience to the gospel. On the other hand, we emphasize obedience in baptism and minimize the faith and repentance, the surrender of self, the taking up of a new relationship with Christ and the world, through the crucifixion of self. Then from these two extremes we both neglect the combination and reality in which they should unite. Trust and surrender to Christ in our hearts must be united with obedience to His word if we actually have the new life made available through His death.

"When I survey the wondrous cross
On which the Prince of Glory died,
My richest gain I count but loss
And pour contempt on all my pride.

Were the whole realm of nature mine,
That were a present far too small;
Love so amazing, so divine
Demands my soul, my life, my all."

—Isaac Watts

For Further Study:

Barclay, William. *The Mind of St. Paul.* New York: Harper and Brothers Publishers, 1958. Pp. 97-108. Explains Paul's teaching about the meaning of the death of Christ. Barclay adopts some liberal positions in some of his writings.

Byers, Melvert. "We Enter By Death." *Christian Standard* 91 (Oct. 13, 1956), Pp. 647. Stresses the need to crucify our self-centeredness.

Cottrell, Jack. *Being Good Enough Is Not Good Enough.* Cincinnati: Standard Publishing Co., 1976. Discusses salvation, redemption, justification and reconciliation in non-technical language. Shows the interpretation of Christ's death for us made by the apostle Paul in Romans and Galatians.

Chamberlain, William Douglas. *The Meaning of Repentance.* Grand Rapids: Wm. B. Eerdmans, 1943. Shows that repentance is not remorse but it is a complete renovation of one's mind from the mind of flesh to the mind of the Spirit.

Morris, Leon. *The Cross in the New Testament.* Grand Rapids: Wm. B. Eerdmans, 1965. Pp. 180-269. Extensive development of Paul's teaching on the cross.

# 87

## WAS JESUS CRUCIFIED ON FRIDAY?

When the question, "Was Jesus crucified on Friady?" is raised, it may be hard for you to find a clear and definite statement about it in the Bible. Good Christians may think He had to be in the tomb longer than the time from Friday afternoon to Sunday morning, because of the expression "three days and three nights" in Matthew 12:40.

It doesn't matter too much on what day Jesus was crucified; but it does matter how people use the scriptures and how they trouble the church over such questions. Any view that denies that Jesus ate the Passover meal at the regular time is in direct conflict with the plain statements of fact in three inspired books of the New Testament (Matt. 26:17; Mark 14:12; Luke 22:7). Yet such a view is often taken by people who think that they are upholding the strict accuracy of Jesus' words against centuries of false tradition.

This is merely a question of historic fact, not affecting our obedience to the commands of the Lord, and not essential to our reverent appreciation of Him. It should not be made a "test of fellowship" or source of contention. But as a matter of fact it makes all the better example for a study of how to get the truth of God's Word by considering all the facts and letting the passages which are definite and clear in meaning determine the interpretations of those which are not so sure.

### *What Does The Bible Say?*

This is a Bible study. Get your Bible and read the passages cited. Space will not permit quoting them.

All the Gospels say that Jesus was crucified and buried on the day called the *Preparation.* Read Mark 15:42; Luke 23:54; John 19:14, 31, 42; and Matthew 27:60-62. The word translated *Preparation* was used as a name for the day which we call *Friday,* and it is still the word for Friday in modern Greek.

John 19:14 says, "It was the preparation of the passover." Some have thought that this means the day on which the Passover lamb was prepared; but it can mean simply "Friday of Passover week." Comparison with all the facts will show that this is what it does mean. Beginning with the Passover sacrifice and supper, seven days of unleavened bread were observed; and the entire week was called the

Passover (see Luke 22:1; John 2:23; 18:39). Mark 15:42 explicitly states, "It was the preparation, that is, the day before the sabbath." The same meaning is shown in John 19:31. The regular weekly Sabbath was Saturday.

### *But Which Sabbath?*

The first day of unleavened bread might be called a Sabbath, because it was a day of rest according to the law (Lev. 23:7, 8), and so was the seventh, or last, day. Some suggest that the Sabbath immediately following Jesus' death was not Saturday, but the first day of unleavened bread, which could fall on any day of the week.

In the law (Lev. 23:4, 6), the seven days of unleavened bread were counted after the Passover meal, beginning Nisan 15. But all leaven was put out on the day the Passover was prepared, Nisan 14; so the day that the Lamb was killed came in time to be called the first day of unleavened bread. (See Mark 14:12 and Luke 22:7).

But if either of those days—the one just preceding the supper, or the one following it—was actually called a sabbath, still *neither of them could be the Sabbath day that followed the burial of Jesus. For Matthew 26:17-20; Mark 14:12-17; and Luke 22:7-16 all state with absolutely unmistakable clarity that Jesus was alive and eating the Passover supper in the evening following the first day of unleavened bread* when the lamb was sacrificed. If the day following the supper was the day of rest (or special Sabbath) it was still not the day after Jesus was buried, because it was the day of crucifixion.

Therefore, we see that, if there was in that week any day called a Sabbath other than Saturday, it had to be one that was past by the time Jesus was buried, and not the day following His burial. The day of preparation, then, on which He was crucified, could not be any day other than the day before the regular weekly Sabbath which we call Saturday.

One good brother has suggested that the *seventh* day of unleavened bread was the Sabbath which "drew on" as Jesus was buried. That would mean that Jesus was subjected to six or seven days of trials, mockings, and delays between the time He was arrested and the day of crucifixion. The Gospels do not show any intention of indicating that. The trials before the priests and the Sanhedrin were at night and dawn (Luke 22:66); that before Pilate was early (John 18:28); all happened in quick succession.

Moreover, no account gives any hint of more than one Sabbath between the burial of Christ and His resurrection on the first day of the week. Just turn and read how clearly Friday, Saturday, and Sunday are recorded in Luke 23:43 to 24:1. "And that day was the preparation, and the sabbath drew on. And the women also . . . beheld the sepulchre, and how his body was laid. And they returned, and prepared spices and ointments; and rested the sabbath day according to the commandment. Now upon the first day of the week, very early in the morning, they came unto the sepulchre." The word Sabbath here is singular.

### *Properly Read, John Agrees*

John's account agrees completely with these statements. John 13:1 does not say that the last supper was before the Passover, but that Jesus knew before the Passover meal that He must depart at this time. John 13:29 does not prove that the Passover meal was to come later. The disciples who supposed that Judas was sent to buy something for the feast may have had in mind the seven-day festival. Or if it was possible at that hour to buy provisions, that might have been for the meal now beginning. In John 13:2 the Greek does not say "supper being ended," but "supper being come."

John 18:28 does not prove that the Pharisees had not eaten the Passover meal, because they called all seven days connected with it "the Passover." Anyway, the Passover meal was eaten at night, and such defilement as they feared in Pilate's hall would end at sunset.

John 19:31 shows plainly that the preparation was the day before the Sabbath. Calling that Sabbath "a high day" does not make it other than a Saturday Sabbath. It only means that it was considered especially sacred because it came in Passover week.

Some who hold to a Thursday crucifixion insist that the Lamb of God had to be killed at the same time the Passover lamb was being killed. This would be Thursday afternoon before the Passover meal that night. Why must this be so? The antitype (Jesus) did not and could not have corresponded with the type (Passover lamb) in every respect. The time of the slaying of the Passover lamb had nothing to do with the time of Christ's death.

### *"Three Days and Three Nights"*

Since the history states so plainly the fact that Jesus was crucified on Friday, it is necessary to take the prophetic figure of speech about the sign of Jonah (Matt. 12:40) as an inexact expression intended to agree with the statement which is made a dozen times, that Jesus arose "on the third day." (See Matt. 16:21; 17:23; 20;19; 27:63, 64;

Luke 9:22; 18:33; 24:7, 21, 46; Acts 10:40; I Cor. 15:4; and Mark 9:31; 10:34 in the K.J.V.) "After three days" is used in Mark 8:31 (9:31 and 10:34 in A.S.V.) to mean the same as "on the third day." While those do not seem the same to us, it is evident that they did mean the same to the Jews. (See also II Chron. 10:5, 12; Esther 4:16; 5:1; Matt. 27:63, 64). "Three days and three nights" is just a fuller form for saying "after three days"; and both could mean in popular speech the same as "on the third day." Any expression means just what it is used to mean. The facts of the record show with what meaning the expression was used by Jesus. We must not put into it a meaning that will deny or disregard the facts; but the facts must control our interpretation.

For Further Study:

Andrews, Samuel J. *The Life of Our Lord.* Grand Rapids: Zondervan Publishing House, 1891. Pp. 455-481. Thorough study harmonizing chronological details. Accepts Friday crucifixion.

Geldenhuys, Norval. *New International Commentary: The Gospel of Luke.* Grand Rapids; Wm. B. Eerdmans, 1951. Pp. 649-670. Essay on the day and date of the crucifixion. Defends Friday as date of Jesus' crucifixion.

McGarvey, J. W. *Jesus and Jonah.* Cincinnati: Standard Publishing Co., 1896. Pp. 65-72. Deals with the interpretation of "three days and three nights."

Robertson, A. T. *A Harmony of the Gospels for the Students of the Life of Christ.* New York: Harper & Row, Publishers, 1922. Pp. 279-287. Concise discussion of evidence. Concludes that Jesus ate the regular Passover meal and was crucified on Friday.

Wescott, B. F. *The Gospel According to John.* Grand Rapids: Wm. B. Eerdmans, 1951. Holds that Jesus did not eat the regular Passover meal and was crucified the morning before the Passover.

## *Part Seventeen*

# RESURRECTION OF CHRIST

## 88

### THE RESURRECTION OF JESUS

Proclaim the good news! Tell the facts! Carry the message to all the world! Jesus has risen from the dead! This was the apostles' assignment; and to it they applied themselves as men possessed of a magnificent obsession. They knew by tremendous and triumphant experience the reality of the death and resurrection of Jesus. Of all the facts that support our faith, this is the most meaningful and the most certain.

Under the teaching of Jesus during His resurrection appearances, the apostles began to see the significance of these facts in the plan of God for all men. They began to feel the transforming power of this great manifestation of God's might and mercy. They felt the obligation to carry out Jesus' urgently repeated command to tell everybody these facts by which men are brought to salvation and new life and without which men have neither hope nor light in a world of darkness and death.

Far too much, we take it for granted that men do know these facts when in reality they do not. Many, many people have heard something about the resurrection of Jesus. But they think of it as a religious doctrine which some men believe. They do not actually know it as a fact. We must proclaim the resurrection of Jesus not as part of a philosophical ideal, nor as our opinion or a corollary of hopeful dreams for the future, but as a certainty of what God has done in the past. Jesus has commanded us to make it known "to the whole creation." For by this knowledge men are saved through believing and obeying the risen Lord.

#### *The Centrality of Christ and His Resurrection*

Christianity is Christ! It is confidence in Jesus Christ as the divine Son of God, having all authority and absolute trustworthiness. Christianity becomes a matter of doctrines and practices simply because Jesus taught and commanded. Its doctrines are His teachings; and its practices are obedience to His commands.

Our Christian faith is faith in Christ and the divine revelation of which He is the source and center. It certainly is not a philosophy or a system of reasonings about realms beyond our experience. It is following Him wherever He leads and trusting Him for all our needs. The whole validity of Christianity and of the Bible depends upon who Jesus is—upon His personal merit and power.

Because He put His stamp of approval upon the Old Testament, and said that it could not be broken (John 10:35) and that none of it shall pass away until all be fulfilled (Matt. 5:18; Luke 24:44), therefore we believe that the Old Testament scriptures are inspired, authoritative and divinely dependable. Because Jesus promised to give to the apostles the Holy Spirit to guide them into all truth as well as to remember all that He taught them (John 14:26; 16:12-14), we believe that the New Testament scriptures are inspired of God and possessed of divine accuracy and authority.

The evidence that Jesus is the Son of God is shown:

1. In many Old Testament prophecies (e.g., Isa. 9:6; Micah 5:2-4; Ps. 110:1; 45:6, 7, etc.);
2. In His supernatural birth;
3. In the direct testimony of angels (Luke 1:30-35);
4. In the witness of John the Baptist (John 1:33, 34);
5. In the confession of demons (Mark 5:6, 7);
6. In the testimony of the voice of God at His baptism and on the Mount (Matt. 3:16, 17 and 17:5);
7. In Jesus' sinless life, in which all His deeds and motives were of God;
8. In His superhuman wisdom and insight into the nature and needs of men;
9. In His miraculous works, showing both the power and the merciful character of God;
10. In His persistent and positive claims to be one with God (See Matt. 11:27; 28:18; Mark 2:10; Luke 22:69-71; John 8:58; 10:30; 14:6-11; etc.).

*But the death and resurrection of Jesus are the facts that reveal most clearly and conclusively His person and character, as well as His purpose and His ministry to us.*

In the New Testament the resurrection is made the chief evidence upon which faith in Christ is to be based. It is the fitting climax of every account of His life. The key-note of Peter's sermon on the day of Pentecost was: "This Jesus hath God raised up, whereof we are all witnesses" (Acts 2:24-32). "With great power gave the apostles their witness of the resurrection of the Lord Jesus" (Acts 4:33). It was the major item of testimony in all their preaching (See Acts 3:15; 4:2; 5:31, 32; 10:40, 41; 13:30-37; 17:31, 32; 26:8, 23; Rom. 1:4; I Cor. 15:1-18). It is continually emphasized in the epistles as the basis of our faith and hope, and as a motive to holy living (See Rom. 6:4-11; 8:34; I Cor. 15:58; Eph. 1:19-23; Phil. 2:9-11; Col. 2:12; 3:1-4; I Thess. 4:14; I Pet. 1:3-7; Heb. 13:20, 21).

Jesus Himself often predicted His own resurrection and considered it the greatest sign of His authority and truthfulness (See Matt. 12:38-40; 16:21; 17:9, 23; 20:19; John 2:19-21; 10:17, 18). His enemies noticed His predictions of His resurrection and even the time that He set for it (See Matt. 27:63). In their blindness they tried to stop the power of God with military might and the authority of a Roman seal. They only provided circumstances that contributed to the proof of the resurrection.

The guard they placed to watch the tomb stands guard today against false objections and foolish doubts that would try to explain away the empty tomb.

Many people who are misled by scientific talk of unvarying uniformity in nature and who therefore doubt miracles, speak in glowing praise of Jesus' teachings. But they overlook the fact that Jesus' teaching was much more than a set of rules for conduct. He taught much about the life to come and insisted that faith in Him is the only way to life. He taught men to put their trust in Him because of His works which demonstrated that the power of God was with Him. He emphasized the importance of the resurrection as the sign of His authority and dependability. There is no honest or intelligent way to separate something called "Jesus' Teachings" from His words recorded in the New Testament which emphasize repeatedly the supreme importance of every man's definite commitment of self to Him by faith and obedience to His authority (See Matt. 7:21-27; 10:32-38; 11:27; 12:30-42; 16:14-28; 21:37-45; 22:41-46; 26:63, 64; 28:18-20; John 3:36—as properly translated in most versions: "He who doth not obey"—; John 5:22-29; 6:29, 53-57; 8:24; 10:24-30; 12:46-48).

Confession of Christ and belief in the resurrection go together to obtain salvation: "Because if thou shalt confess with thy mouth Jesus as Lord, and thou shalt believe in thy heart that God hath raised him from the dead, thou shalt be saved" (Rom. 10:9). Denying the resurrection of Christ is the same as denying His authority and power to save: "If Christ hath not been raised, your faith is in vain; ye are yet in your sins" (I Cor. 15:17).

### *Direct Evidence For The Resurrection*

The resurrection of Jesus is not a matter of hope for what will happen, or a faith in what should happen, but knowledge of what did happen. It is not a compelling feeling, or reasonable philosophy, but it is a fact. If the events of the past, recorded as history can be known, then we know that Jesus arose from the dead. The fact of the resurrection is made known to us with certainty in exactly the same manner and by the same means in which we know of the American Declaration of Independence—by documentary testimony, standing results and necessary association with other facts independently established.

The chief proof of the resurrection is testimony. The testimony for Jesus' resurrection is the kind that all experience proves to be reliable—the kind that is acceptable to establish the truth in any court or in any matter of history.

The witnesses are *sufficient in number*—eleven apostles, five or six women (at least), some other disciples, James, Paul, and more than five hundred at one time. These saw Jesus alive after His death again and again, singly and in groups, indoors and outdoors, by day and by night. All were brought to one conviction. Their united, active witnessing and their convincing testimony produced thousands of believers within a few days in the very city where it happened, less than two months after Jesus was in the tomb. The testimony of some of them and the experience of all of them is recorded by at least six writers in different accounts that show all the variations of independent testimonies and all the harmony of truth.

The witnesses were *competent*—men of intelligence (read their classic writings) of mental balance before and after; well-prepared by long and intimate acquaintance with Jesus; of a mental attitude requiring proof; having personal interest in knowing the certainty of these things. They, at least the leading ones, repeatedly saw the risen Christ and listened to extensive teaching from Him, walked and talked with Him, touched Him, and saw Him eat in their presence, discussed His death and resurrection and plans for the future.

> "To whom also he showed himself alive after his passion by many proofs, appearing unto them by the space of forty days, and speaking the things concerning the kingdom of God" (Acts 1:3).

They even saw Him ascend into heaven. There was no mistaking His identify. They told of much detailed experience with Him. The circumstantial details of their accounts show that they were not trying to tell of an inner conviction but of real physical experiences. This destroys the supposition that they could have been honestly mistaken. If Jesus did not actually arise and appear as they said, then they knew their testimony was false.

But they were *honest men.* They had been trained in righteousness, in both reverent fear and loving devotion toward the God of truth. Their lives show no tendency to dishonesty. Their teachings and their examples have had the greatest power in the world to make other men honest. They had nothing to gain by spreading a false report; but rather suffered much affliction and even death for their witnessing. Some men might die for what they believed and be mistaken. No such group of men will devote years of life and accept death for what they know to be false. But these apostles lived and died for what they knew to be true; if it had been false they most surely would have known that it was.

But there was other testimony, of unusual quality and force, to support the testimony of the eye-witnesses. The prophecies of the Old Testament testify of the coming of this unique event in the life of the promised Messiah (Ps. 16:10; Isa. 53:10-12). As we have noted above, Jesus Himself predicted it, and it cannot be destroyed without destroying his integrity.

That Jesus was dead and buried, and that the tomb was empty the third day, are facts that His enemies established. His enemies through the last twenty centuries have tried either to deny His death or to explain the absence of the body. Their attempts have tested the accounts at every point and demonstrate both the facts and impossibility of explaining them by anything except the actual resurrection.

The disciples' unshakable conviction, the great change wrought in them, the faith of multitudes of Jews and "a great company of priests" (Acts 6:8), the transformation and ministry of Saul of Tarsus are all effects that must have an adequate cause, but for which no other cause can be found than the fact of Jesus' resurrection. No one has been able to deny that the apostles and the *early church honestly and firmly believed that Jesus* arose bodily from the grave. And no one has ever given a satisfactory explanation of how this firm and persistent belief could have arisen without the reality of the resurrection. Surely no one can deny that the church came into existence and Christianity became a force in the world, beginning with and growing because of the firm conviction and the convincing testimony of the resurrection.

The resurrection is confirmed by the *Holy Spirit,* who came upon the apostles as Jesus had promised (Luke 24:49; John 15:26; 16:7-14; Acts 1:5, 8), and who bore witness with them concerning the resurrection (Acts 2:33; 5:32).

The testimony is confirmed by *perpetual observances* which are based upon the fact of the resurrection. The form of baptism pictures both Christ's burial and resurrection, and their significance in our lives. The practice of worship on the first day of the week instead of the seventh, and that in a church which was at first Jewish, explicitly and pointedly commemorates both the resurrection of Jesus and its importance in their sight.

The resurrection of Jesus Christ from the dead is a fact made known to us by such an array of testimony and effects that it is more than what is usually called faith. Conviction based on testimony of facts frequently reaches the point at which it is called knowledge; for we speak of knowing many things that happened in the past which are made known to us through testimony and effects. The resurrection of Jesus is a matter of knowledge as much as any other fact in history is a matter of knowledge. At least, it is surely clear that to the eleven apostles the resurrection was not merely a belief, but knowledge of the greatest possible certainty. To us it is not only a part of the doctrine of Christ, but a proof of the authority of all His doctrine—not so much a belief, but a firm basis for faith in Him and hope of that which He has promised.

### *Consider Who It Was That Arose!*

The resurrection of Jesus was not merely an unexplained appearance of some unknown or ordinary man from the grave. His resurrection was in perfect harmony with His manner of life, His unique birth, His unparalleled works, His distinctive death, and with the prophecies that prepared the way for Him. The resurrection of Jesus is made both more readily believable and much more meaningful when we consider the following facts:

1. He fulfilled the promises and predictions of the prophets; His resurrection is a victory for revealed truth.
2. He is the One who lived in perfect righteousness; He arose as victor over great powers of wickedness.
3. He was the One who had raised others and promised to raise all men; His resurrection gives assurance that He still gives life to whom He will.

4. He is the One who predicted His own resurrection and claimed to speak the truth; it is proof that His words are infallibly true and all His claims are valid.

5. His death was declared to be an offering for our sins (Matt. 20:28; 26:28). His resurrection is our victory over sin and death if we join our lives with His. His rising proves that His death was adequate and acceptable for our redemption.

6. He is the One who said that all judgment was given unto Him and who read men's hearts with unerring accuracy. His resurrection is positive proof that we all shall stand before Him to be confessed by Him or to be condemned by Him.

We might be interested in what Lazarus would tell of his experience in four days of death and in living again, but we could not have much assurance that Lazarus could deliver the rest of us from death and all its terror. We should indeed be students of everything Jesus has to say; for He is the author of a divine covenant by which we all may have eternal life, and He is the judge to whom we all must give account.

We can be sure that Jesus is the Lord of life and death. Let us serve Him with glad assurance that our labor is not in vain in the Lord.

Let every man acknowledge Him as Lord—*admit* who He is, *submit* to His commands and the control of His Spirit, and joyfully *commit* to His keeping all that we are or hope to be.

We must either acknowledge and serve Him as our Lord here on earth, or confess Him as Lord hereafter to our everlasting shame and condemnation (Phil. 2:9-11).

For Further Study:

Anderson, J. N. D. "The Resurrection of Jesus Christ," *Christianity Today* (March 29, 1968), Pp. 628-633. Excellent essay. Presents evidence and answers recent attacks. Anderson, a British lawyer, summarized the evidence for the resurrection in a popular form in a booklet *The Evidence for the Resurrection of Jesus Christ*, (Inter-Varsity, 1966.

McDowell, Josh. *Evidence That Demands a Verdict.* San Bernadino, Calif.: Campus Crusade for Christ International, 1972. Pp. 185-273. Valuable collection of quotations and information on the resurrection. Well outlined and organized to make it usable.

Smith, Wilbur M. *Therefore Stand.* Grand Rapids: Baker Book

House, 1945. Pp. 359-437. Good chapter stating the case for the resurrection.

Sparrow-Simpson, W. J. *The Resurrection and the Christian Faith.* Grand Rapids: Zondervan Publishing Co., 1968 reprint of 1911 edition. Excellent work. Good on doctrinal meaning of the resurrection. His work is summarized in an article on "The Resurrection of Jesus Christ" in the *Dictionary of Christ and the Gospels,* ed. by James Hastings.

Stott, John R. W. *Basic Christianity,* rev. ed. Grand Rapids: Wm. B. Eerdmans, 1971. Pp. 45-60. Good refutation of the critical objections to the resurrection.

Tenney, Merrill C. *The Reality of the Resurrection.* Chicago: Moody Press, 1963. One of the best works on the fact and meaning of the resurrection.

# 89

## THRILLING SCENES OF THE RESURRECTION DAY

"Were you there when they crucified my Lord?" When someone sings it sincerely, your skin tingles. "Were you there when He rose up from the dead?"

We wish we could have been there to see the disciples' sorrow turn to joy, and to feel the surge of their assurance as their ebbing faith came back in full flood and rose to new heights—an irresistible force, a conviction that could not be suppressed.

Still it really isn't necessary to have been there for us to share in the certainty and the life-giving power of the fact of Jesus' resurrection. The thrilling scenes of the resurrection day can be seen in order by blending the records of Christ's resurrection.

I have visited the skull-shaped hill north of Jerusalem which may have been that "place of a skull" "called Golgotha." I took pictures of it and of the empty tomb nearby which many think is most likely to have contained briefly the body of Jesus. But if I could have been there with my camera when the angels said, "He is not here: for He is risen," or when Jesus said, "Mary," I could have photographed only a part of the events that are pictured so vividly in words for us in the various accounts of the New Testament. Each of the disciples of Jesus had only part of the thrilling experiences which are combined for us in the testimonies of the four Gospels, and Acts, and First Corinthians.

We can view the pictures which all of them left for us. And we can arrange the incidents in order as they happened in rapid succession on that eventful morning. When we do, we see the complete unity and agreement of all the different accounts of the various witnesses.

### *The Events of the Resurrection Morning in Order*

1. Very early on the first day of the week, while it was still dark, Mary Magdalene, Mary the mother of James, Salome, Joanna, and some other women, set out for the tomb of Jesus (probably from Bethany, at least half an hour's walk away). They were bringing spices to anoint His body. (Matt. 28:1; Mark 16:1; Luke 24:1; John 20:1).

2. Meanwhile, at the tomb, there was a great earthquake, as an agnel of the Lord came down from heaven and rolled away the stone. In fear the soldiers fell to the ground like dead men, and then fled

to report to the chief priests (Matt. 28:2-4; 11-15).

3. The sun was just rising as the women drew near the tomb (Mark 16:2). They questioned among themselves, "Who shall roll away the stone?" for the stone was very great (Mark 16:3). But, looking up, they saw that the stone was rolled back (Mark 16:3, 4; Luke 24:2; John 20:1).

4. Mary Magdalene immediately ran back to tell Peter and John (John 20:2).

5. But the other women came to the tomb and heard the angel say, "Fear not . . . He is risen, as He said. Come, see the place where the Lord lay" (Matt. 28:5, 6).

6. Upon entering the tomb they saw two angels who said, "Why do you seek the living among the dead? Remember how He told you in Galilee, that the Son of man must be crucified and on the third day rise. Go quickly and tell His disciples and Peter that He is going before you into Galilee. There you shall see Him, as He told you" (See Matt. 26:32). They departed quickly from the tomb with fear and great joy, and ran to bring His disciples word (Matt. 28:5-8; Mark 16:5-8; Luke 24:3-8).

7. Peter and John, hearing the alarming news from Mary, ran to the tomb. John arrived first, and paused to look into the vacant tomb. Peter came following John, rushed past him and went in. Then John also entered. They observed how the grave clothes were lying; the napkin which had been around His head was rolled up in a place by itself, apart from the linen cloths in which so many spices had been wrapped. John saw these things and believed. Up to now they had not understood the scripture that He must rise from the dead. Thoughtfully each went to his lodging place in Jerusalem (Luke 24:12; John 20:3-10).

At John's home there must have been someone overjoyed to hear his story (see John 19:27)!

8. Mary Magdalene, who had followed Peter and John back to the tomb, arrived after they left and remained near the tomb weeping. As she wept she stopped and looked into the tomb. She beheld two angels sitting, one at the head, and one at the feet, where the body of Jesus had lain. They asked her, "Woman, why are you weeping?" She said, "Because they have taken my Lord, and I know not where they have laid Him" (John 20:11-13).

9. Turning around she saw Jesus, but knew not that it was He. Jesus said to her, "Woman, why are you weeping? Whom are you seeking?" Supposing Him to be the gardener, she said to Him, "Sir,

if you have carried Him away, tell me where you have laid Him, and I will take Him away." Jesus said to her, "Mary." She turned and said, "Master." Jesus said, "Do not cling to me" (RSV).[1] "But go and tell my brethren that I am ascending to my Father and your Father, to my God and your God" (John 20:14-17; Mark 16:9).

10. Leaving Mary, Jesus then appeared to the other women who were still on their way to tell His disciples what the angels had said. Jesus greeted them with the usual greeting, which means literally, "Rejoice"; but the meaning was seldom as fitting as at this moment! They came and took hold of His feet and worshipped Him. Jesus told them, "Do not be afraid. Go tell my brethren to go into Galilee, and there they will see me" (Matt. 28:9, 10).

11. These women, as well as Mary Magdalene, told what had happened to them, to the eleven and to all the rest, as they mourned and wept; but they would not believe it (Mark 16:10, 11; Luke 24:9-11; John 20:18).

12. At some time that day Jesus appeared also to Peter (Luke 24:34; I Cor. 15:5).

### *Appearances Later in the Day*

In the afternoon He appeared to two disciples as they walked to Emmaus, about seven miles from Jerusalem; but they did not know Him. He talked with them and told them of the prophecies of Christ's suffering and death. When they arrived at the village, they invited Him to supper with them. At the meal He took bread and blessed it, and broke it and gave to them. Then they knew Him, and He vanished out of their sight (Luke 24:13-32).

That very hour they returned to Jerusalem. They found the apostles (except Thomas) and others gathered with them, and told them all that had happened. Some of them also told the two, "The Lord has risen indeed, and has appeared to Simon" (Mark 16:13; Luke 24:33-35).

As they spoke these things Jesus came and stood in their midst and said, "Peace be unto you." They were afraid, supposing that they beheld a spirit. He asked, "Why are you troubled? See my

---

[1] The verb translated "touch" in the common versions means basically "to fasten." The middle voice, present imperative, used here can mean "Do not keep on touching me" or "Do not keep on fastening yourself to me." The fact that the other women took hold of Jesus' feet in the next few minutes (Matt. 28:9) and that Jesus invited the apostles that evening to "Handle me and see" (Luke 24:39) show which translation should be adopted.

hands and feet; touch me and see, for a spirit does not have flesh and bones as you can see that I have." He rebuked some of them for their hardness of heart, because they had not believed those who had seen Him, He showed them His hands and His side. They still wondered, and disbelieved for joy. He said, "Have you anything here to eat?" They gave Him a piece of fish, and He ate it before them. They all were glad they saw the Lord (Mark 16:14; Luke 24:36-43; John 20:19, 20).

Jesus said again, "Peace be with you. As the Father has sent me, even so send I you." Then He breathed on them, and said, "Receive the Holy Spirit." Thus He reminded them of the promises He had made before His death concerning the Holy Spirit they were to receive to teach them all things and to bring all His teachings to their remembrance. Then He added, "whose soever sins ye forgive, they are forgiven unto them; whose soever sins ye retain, they are retained" (John 20:21-23).

### *Appearances After the Resurrection Day*

A week later He appeared to the apostles again with Thomas present, and all were convinced (John 20:24-29). They went to Galilee and Jesus kept His appointment there with them (Matt. 28:7, 10). He met with seven disciples by the sea (John 21). They had not forsaken Him to return to fishing, but were there at His command. On a mountain in Galilee He met all the eleven (Matt. 28:16-20) either before or after the breakfast by the sea; and it is possible at this time that He appeared to "about five hundred brethren at once" (I Cor. 15:7). At Jerusalem again He appeared to all the eleven and they saw Him taken up into heaven (Luke 24:50, 51; Acts 1:4-12).

Over this period of forty days He appeared to the disciples repeatedly, showing Himself alive by many convincing proofs, and speaking to them of the kingdom of God (Acts 1:3). In these appearances He spoke to them the great commission to tell these things to all the world to bring repentance and remission of sins to all people (Matt. 28:18-20; Mark 16:15, 16; Luke 24:46-48; Acts 1:8). He told them more about the power of the Holy Spirit which they were to receive in Jerusalem a few days after His ascension (Luke 24:49; Acts 1:4, 5, 8).

### *Importance of Various Accounts*

The gospel accounts of the resurrection of Jesus are so independent of each other, and so different in the details each chose to tell, that they are sometimes thought to be in conflict or to show some confusion about what really happened. But if we accept the fact that each writer did not tell all he knew, and if we see that when one account leaves out a name, or some other detail, the omission does not contradict another account which includes that item, we can fit them all together into a continous and harmonious narrative.

For example: Matthew names two of the women—"Mary Magdalene and the other Mary." Mark names the same two and adds Salome. Luke names the two Marys and adds Joanna "and the other women with them." John names only Mary Magdalene, but quotes her as saying, "We" (20:3). There are omissions, but no contradictions.

Some translations have in Matthew 28:1, "Late on the Sabbath" or "In the end of the Sabbath." The Greek preposition *opse* means "after" as well as "late." Properly translated it agrees perfectly with Mark 16:1; Luke 24:1; and John 20:1. If the women had gone to the tomb at sunset Saturday, would they not have seen the military guard there? But from Mark 16:3 it appears that they did not know about the guard or the sealing of the tomb. Surely there is no real conflict between going "to see the sepulchre" and going to anoint the body (Matt. 28:1 with Mark 16:1).

When John 20:1 says they went to the tomb "when it was yet dark" and Mark 16:2 says "at the rising of the sun," John may well be speaking of the start of their journey, and Mark of their arrival. Mark begins that same sentence with "very early in the morning." They may have bought some of their spices during that journey (see Mark 16:1), or may have gone to meet some of their group. To walk from Bethany to Calvary takes more than half an hour.

Such differences in the accounts really strengthen the evidence. The independent testimony of several good witnesses is surer than just one account given alike by all. The witnesses do not need to tell the same story, but they must support the main fact with details that do not discredit them.

The resurrection of Jesus is the most important fact in history. At least it is the most important fact for us all to know for sure. We can be sure of it because of the factual and convincing testimony of the New Testament witnesses who lived and died for their testimony in unshakable conviction.

We can be as sure as if we had been there—with cameras.

For Further Study:

McGarvey, J. W. *Evidences of Christianity.* Nashville: Gospel Advocate, reprint of 1891 ed. Part III, Pp. 132-162. Good on reconciling alleged contradictions in the gospel accounts of Jesus' resurrection.

See books listed on pages 514, 515.

# 90

## THE RISEN LORD AND HIS DISCIPLES

"Faith cometh by hearing, and hearing by the word of God" (Rom. 10:17). As Isaiah says, "Who hath believed our report? and to whom is the arm of the Lord revealed?" We receive the testimony of one (or more) who is trustworthy, and we accept it with such confidence that it gives us assurance of things hoped for, and conviction of things not seen (cf. Heb. 11:1). This conviction based on testimony of facts frequently reaches the point at which it is called knowledge; for we speak of knowing many things that happened in the past which are made known to us through testimony and effect—events outside of our personal experience of which we experience only the testimony and the fruits, but we "know" them, else there is no knowledge of history.

The resurrection of Jesus Christ from the dead is a fact made known to us by such an array of testimony and effects that it is more than a matter of faith. It is a matter of knowledge as much as any other fact in history is a matter of knowledge. At least, it is surely clear that to the eleven apostles the resurrection was not merely a belief, but knowledge of the greatest possible certainty. To us it is not so much a part of the doctrine of Christ, but a proof of the authority of His doctrine; not so much a belief; but a basis for faith and hope.

When Christ says that His death was for the remission of our sins, all we can do is believe it, taking His word for it (Matt. 20:28; 26:28; cf. Gal. 1:4; Rom. 4:25; I Pet. 2:24; John 1:29; Isa. 53); but we know that He died. When He says that He is coming into the world a second time to receive His own in glory and to judge the living and the dead, we simply believe because He said it personally and through His appointed and inspired spokesmen (Matt. 16:27; John 14:3; 5:26-29; I Thess. 4:13-17; Acts 1:11; Rev. 1:7; etc.). But of the facts of His first coming—i.e., that Jesus once lived in Palestine—we have more knowledge.

If we are willing to say that we know George Washington lived and led American armies, we may say that we know Jesus arose from the dead. If we may say we know that Abraham Lincoln lived and was president, let us say boldly that we know Jesus arose, flesh and bones. As for myself, I have much more real evidence of Jesus' resurrection than I have ever had concerning the existence of my grandfather Wilson.

To the apostles Jesus showed Himself by many proofs, appearing unto them by space of forty days, and speaking things concerning the kingdom of God (Acts 1:3). In the New Testament we have the recorded testimony of more than a sufficient number of witnesses, competent persons who were eyewitnesses again and again—under various circumstances eating with Him, walking with Him, discussing His death, His resurrection, His teachings, and plans for the future (Luke 24:15-49; Mark 16:14-18; Acts 1:3-8; John 20:19-29; 21:4-18). There could be no mistaking His identity. There could be no doubt of the purpose and fitness of His return from the grave. They were even permitted to see His departure from the earth, ascending into heaven. The resurrection had long since been prophesied (Ps. 16:10; 17:15; Isa. 53:10-12), and He Himself had predicted it (Matt. 16:21; 17:9, 22, 23; 20:17-19; 12:39, 40; Mark 9:9, 31; John 2:19; 10:17-18). It was confirmed by the Holy Spirit, who came upon the apostles as Jesus had promised (John 14:16, 17; Luke 24:49), and who bore witness with them concerning the resurrection (Acts 2:33; 5:32).

To us, the fact of Jesus' resurrection is further confirmed by the indisputable fact that the church exists founded upon faith in the resurrection and unexplainable without the reality of that event.

### *The Meaning of the Resurrection*

The resurrection is a fact, not only of great certainty, but of even greater meaning and power. It means Jesus is indeed the Savior from sin—that His death on our account was accepted by God. It supports His claims in full and proclaims Him the Son of God with power (Rom. 1:4). It is the heart of the gospel, and always has been (I Cor. 15:1-4). If the account of the resurrection were false, then all of Christ's claims are false; then the prophecies of Him were and are false, and Christian faith is a vain delusion. What kind of crazy world would it be that produced the greatest influence for truthfulness and righteousness out of deep deceit, fraud, and falsehood?

The resurrection means that Jesus lives to fulfill His promises, to make intercession for us (Heb. 7:25), to come again for His own, to bring all men to judgment—the resurrection means judgment! (John 5:28, 29; Acts 17:31). It means His likeness is our goal, and death is no hindrance to it.

It means that we have a greater goal than earth's best offers, that man has a greater concern than physical self-preservation, that there is a greater calamity than death.

We list without discussion some of the things which the resurrection assures:

1. He lives, hence we shall live (John 14:19).
2. The body was raised; our mortal bodies shall put on immortality (I Cor. 15:53; Rom. 8:11).
3. He was unique, divine in character (Rom. 1:4).
4. He has all authority (Matt. 28:18).
5. His righteousness correctly represents God (Acts 2:24, 33; 3:14, 15; 22:14).
6. His death is effective for our redemption (Acts 13:37-39).
7. He is Lord over death forever (Rev. 1:18; I Cor. 15:25, 26).
8. All shall be raised and judged (John 5:28, 29; I Cor. 15:22).
9. Christ will be the judge and the basis of judgment (Acts 10:40-43; 17:30, 31).
10. The terms of pardon proclaimed by His apostles are valid (John 20:23).
11. The apostles speak with all Christ's authority throughout the New Testament (John 14:26; 15:26, 27; 16:13-15; Acts 1:5, 8).

### *The Appearances to the Apostles, and Their Effects*

The apostles had feared that Jesus' enemies would try to kill Him (John 11:8, 16), and they had wanted to avoid Jerusalem, but they seemed never to think of His conquering death itself. In the Garden of Gethsemane, when Jesus was seized, they all turned and fled. Peter and John recovered enough to follow afar off, to enter into the court of the high priest, but there Peter denied His Lord boldly three times. It seems that only John dared to be near the cross. He and the women had such love that it overcame their fear and enabled them to bear the pain and sorrow of that dreadful scene. After the death of Christ the fears of the eleven seem to have become perhaps even a little worse, for they stayed in the house with the doors shut "for fear of the Jews."

The women, who were at the cross and first at the tomb on the first day of the week, were rewarded with the first appearances of the risen Lord. They (as Jesus commanded—Matt. 28:10; John 20:17) brought the good news to the disciples, "as they mourned and wept," but they believed not. Peter saw the empty tomb, but still did not understand; then Jesus appeared to him (John 20:2-10; I Cor. 15:5). Next, Jesus walked with the two disciples (not of the twelve) as they went to Emmaus. When He had taught them the

Scriptures concerning His suffering and death, and made Himself known to them, they hastened back to Jerusalem to tell the apostles. While they were speaking with them—Jesus came into their midst. It was the evening of the same day on which Jesus arose, and this was His first appearance to the group of the apostles. He upbraided them for their unbelief (Mark 16:12-14). They still disbelieved the testimony of the others who had seen Him, and they were terrified when they saw Him, supposing Him to be a ghost. He proved to them that He had flesh and bones.

Thomas was not present, and when told of it he still doubted. Because of this he is called "the doubter," but he doubted hardly any more than they all had. One week later Jesus came to them again when Thomas was present, and Thomas acclaimed Him, "My Lord and my God!"

The apostles went to Galilee at Jesus' command (see Matt. 28:10). While they waited there, seven of them fished for food (John 21:2, 3, 12). Peter is accused of forsaking all faith in Christ and giving up His service because of his suggestion that he go fishing. This idea is indeed grotesque in view of these facts: (1) that he had lately seen the risen Lord at least three times, (2) that he had been told by Him to come to Galilee, (3) that men may work for food while believing on the Lord, (4) that he was first to desert the boat and nets when Christ appeared on the shore, (5) that he professed his love for Jesus that very hour.

At least two more times and possibly many others Jesus appeared to the apostles, speaking to them things concerning the kingdom (Acts 1:3) and giving them the commission of their world-wide work for Him (Matt. 28:18-20; Mark 16:15, 16; Luke 24:45-49; John 20:21-23). From this time on they realized the power and presence of the Lord. They showed no more fear of men, but boldly in the face of vigorous threats they proclaimed the resurrection. They knew the certainty of the fact, and they understood its great importance and power to give anyone a victorious faith in Jesus. In all their preaching the apostles emphasized the resurrection as a central fact and the chief evidence of their gospel message.

For Further Study:

See books listed on pages 514, 515.

# 91

## FELLOWSHIP WITH THE RISEN LORD (Luke 24:13-35)

On the first day of the week after Jesus' crucifixion, in the afternoon of the very day on which He arose, two of His disciples were walking from Jerusalem to Emmaus. One of them is not named at all, and the other is called Cleopas (Luke 24:13-35). This name is not to be confused with Clopas (or Cleophas, in King James Version) in John 19:25. Nothing else is recorded of these men aside from this incident, but it reveals several things about them (cf. Mark 16:12, 13).

Evidently they were not of the twelve apostles (v. 33). They were well acquainted with Jesus and His works, and hoped that He would "redeem Israel." They knew that the women who had gone to the tomb that morning had reported finding it empty and seeing an angel who told them Jesus had risen. They knew also of the visit of Peter and John to the tomb. They were vitally interested and were talking earnestly about these things. Certainly they were close friends and companions of the apostles and the women who believed; for they called them "Of our company" and "them that were with us," and after their own experience with the risen Lord they went immediately to the apostles, and Jesus appeared to them all while they were together.

Jesus had seventy disciples whom He had sent out two by two with miraculous powers (Luke 10:1-20) whose names we do not know; and there were about a hundred and twenty in close fellowship of faith a few weeks later in Jerusalem. These two men may well have been of those groups. The fact that Jesus made this appearance to them marks them as valuable witnesses, men destined to responsible leadership in the church, or as particular friends of Jesus.

### *They Knew Him Not*

They did not recognize Jesus, not because they were not well enough acquainted with Him, but because He "was manifested in another form" (Mark 16:12) and "their eyes were holden" (Luke 24:16). Evidently, Jesus purposely kept them from recognizing Him by appearing without the marks of crucifixion and other characteristic marks, and by some supernatural influence over them.

The question suggests itself: Why did He not want them to know Him? "That they might see the resurrection of Jesus in the Scriptures before they saw it in reality," suggests McGarvey.[1] But why that? Jesus wanted to instruct them in the meaning of what they already knew or should have known. They should have believed without seeing, but there is more here than desire to rebuke their unbelief. He could use their questioning and meditative frame of mind to help them to understand the crucifixion, the atonement. The resurrection is merely a marvel of comparatively little meaning without the full force of the crucifixion. As the resurrection gives power and demonstrative certainty to the crucifixion, so the crucifixion gives depth of meaning and definite application to the resurrection. Cleopas and his companion had hoped that Jesus would "redeem Israel," by which they meant the wrong thing (Luke 24:21). To them to "redeem Israel" meant to free the nation from servitude to Rome, and to restore national independence, glory, and prosperity (cf. Acts 1:6). If they had been immediately assured of the resurrection of Jesus they would have had their minds filled again with these false material hopes.

### *A Lesson From the Scriptures*

Jesus opened to them the scriptures, while they were seeking for light, and showed to them that the suffering and death of the Christ did not lessen the hope of true redemption but assured it—that Jesus was not to be rejected because of His death, but all the more firmly believed on account of it. This divinely conducted Bible study, more than anything else, should have helped them to understand their own words—"he who should redeem Israel."

After leading them to tell what they knew and what they were thinking, the first thing Jesus (still unknown to them) did was to rebuke them for unbelief. He rebuked them not for disbelieving the women who reported the angel's saying, but for disbelieving the prophets; not for disbelieving what the prophets said about the resurrection, but "all that the prophets have spoken." The leading proposition of His instruction was put in the form of a searching rhetorical question: "Was it not necessary that the Christ should suffer these things and enter into his glory?" (Luke 24:26). Both the King James and American Standard Versions are weak here in saying: "Ought not" and "Behooved it not." Many other translations give the accurate, simple, and forceful reading: "Was it not necessary?"

[1] J. W. McGarvey and W. K. Pendleton, *The Fourfold Gospel* (Cincinnati: Standard Publishing, n.d.), Pp. 748.

or "Did not the Christ have to suffer?" Yes, He had to die—the shameful and agonizing death of the cross.

He began from Moses, and in all the prophets He interpreted in all the Scriptures the things concerning Himself (Luke 24:27). What a wonderful exposition of God's Word and God's plan of redemption that must have been! Their hearts burned within them as they heard this stranger who had seemed so ignorant of the crucifixion bring into focus before their attention passage after passage which they had overlooked, but which set forth clearly the fixed purpose that the Christ should suffer "these things" (Luke 24:32). Indeed, He was "delivered up by the determinate counsel and foreknowledge of God" (cf. Acts 2:23). No wonder their hearts "burned" as they were made to think of the wonderful fact of revelation, the suffering love of God making a sacrifice of His dearest and best for the redemption of His sinful creatures!

The prophets foretold the sufferings and crucifixion of the Christ many times in various ways: (1) by type or symbol (as the Passover lamb and other sacrifices); (2) by many brief or even indirect flashes (as Ps. 35:19; John 15:25; Zech. 11:12, 13; Matt. 26:14-16; 27:5-10; Isa. 50:6; Matt. 26:67; 27:26; Dan. 9:26; Mark 9:12; Zech. 12:10; John 19:37; Ps. 34:20; John 19:36; Zech. 13:1, etc.); (3) by the most direct and extended predictions, including many details with plain meaning (such as the entire twenty-second and sixty-ninth Psalms, and the fifty-third chapter of Isaiah). These last-mentioned three chapters yield a truly marvelous list of details of prophecy concerning the Messiah's suffering, death, burial, and resurrection. Do read them through and see what direct and clear predictions are made.

The resurrection is also plainly predicted in Psalms 16:8-11 (cf. Acts 2:25-31). All the predictions of His exaltation and eternal reign call for His triumph over the vicarious death predicted for Him elsewhere. In this way Psalm 22 and Isaiah 53 indicate the resurrection. See Daniel 7:13, 14.

This hour's instruction by Jesus on the way to Emmaus sets forth His attitude toward the Old Testament and the duty of His disciples to know it and to heed it. He distinctly approved the Old Testament as a revelation from God, and claimed it as an authoritative witness to Himself. "The scriptures . . . bear witness of me" (John 5:39). "If ye believed Moses, ye would believe me; for he wrote of me" (John 5:46). See in Luke 24:44-47 the account of a later appearance of the resurrected Lord, at which time He said, "All things must needs be fulfilled, which are written in the law of Moses, and the prophets, and the Psalms concerning me." Moses, the prophets, and the Psalms were in those days common terms designating the three great divisions of the Old Testament as the Jews arranged it.

These two disciples who were so sad and puzzled on account of the sufferings and death of Jesus did err, not knowing the Scriptures, and Jesus rebuked them for it. It seems that all of Jesus' disciples made this same mistake in spite of Jesus' plain teaching concerning His coming.

### *The Recognition and Certainty of His Resurrection*

At Emmaus the two disciples urged Jesus to come in and sup with them, for it was toward evening. As He broke bread and blessed it, He made Himself known to them, then vanished. They realized, then, why His exposition of the prophets had been so clear, masterful, and thrilling. They returned immediately to Jerusalem (about seven and one-half miles, or about two hours' steady travel, Luke 24:31-35). They knew where to find the apostles, and rehearsed all that had happened to them and to those "that were with them" (v. 33). The apostles also reported to the two that Jesus had appeared to Peter. Still the hearts of many of them were full of doubt (see Mark 16:13, 14), and when Jesus Himself appeared in their midst while they were talking, they thought He was a spirit (Luke 24:36, 37).

Jesus challenged them to see that He had flesh and bones and was not a spirit. To demonstrate further, He asked for food and ate before them (Luke 24:39-43). Their slowness to believe gives occasion for such proofs and tests as afford us the greatest possible certainty of the fact of the resurrection. They certainly were not deceived through any overwhelming desire to see Him alive again, but were most unready to accept even the best testimony and the first sight of Him.

The combined experience of several groups of disciples in repeated meetings with the risen Lord, by day and by night, indoors and out, alone and in groups, hearing Him at length as well as seeing Him, touching Him and watching Him eat fish, soon overwhelmed even their stubborn doubts and fully convinced them for all time. They gave themselves to the proclamation of the resurrection testimony and even gave their lives rather than deny it.

The resurrection is not a matter of faith, strictly speaking, but a matter of fact, one of the best attested facts of all history, which we may know as surely as we may know anything out of the past. It is supported both by credible witnesses and by undeniable consequences which can be explained in no other way than by the fact of the resurrection.

For Further Study:

See books listed on pages 514, 515.

# *Part Eighteen*

# GREAT COMMISSION

## 92

### ORDERS FROM THE COMMANDER-IN-CHIEF

In what is called the church today, there is a wide-spread defection from the divine mission of the body of Christ. To many it is just the same as if the Lord had not given the great commission. Do you know what He commanded, or where to find it?

*Evangelism Commanded by Christ*

The same day on which Jesus arose He appeared to ten of the apostles (and others with them, Luke 24:33-36) and said, "As the Father sent me, even so send I you" (John 20:21-23). Perhaps at the same occasion He said, "Go into all the world, and preach the gospel to the whole creation" (Mark 16:15, 16). He sent the apostles to Galilee and appointed a certain mountain for a meeting place. When Jesus came, some doubted. This suggests that a crowd of disciples had gathered, in addition to the apostles who had already seen the risen Lord from two to four times each (See I Cor. 15:6). Jesus said, "All authority has been given to me in heaven and on earth. Go, therefore, and make disciples of all the nations, baptizing them in the name of the Father and of the Son and of the Holy Spirit; teaching them to observe all things whatever I commanded you; and lo, I am with you always, even unto the end of the age" (Matt. 28:18-20).

Did the Lord give this assignment only to the apostles? How then was it to last to the end of the age? He also told them to "Pray to the Lord of the harvest that He raise up laborers for His harvest" (Matt. 9:38). He also sent Ananias to Saul to give this assignment to him (Acts 22:12-16). The Holy Spirit told the church at Antioch to send Barnabas and Saul into foreign evangelism (Acts 13:1-3). Paul told the church at Rome, "How shall they hear without a preacher and how shall they preach, except they be sent" (Rom. 10:13-15). And he told Timothy to train more preachers (II Tim. 2:2). The third epistle of John says of traveling preachers, "You will do well to send them on their way as befits God's service . . . So we ought to support such men, that we may be fellow workers in the truth" (III John 5-8).

In the great commission to the church, we have a Master with all authority; but most of us have not obeyed Him. We have a Message of pure truth, historic facts, clear evidence and convincing power; but have we really believed it? We have a Ministry of mercy—proclaiming repentance and remission of sins unto all men; but we have not cared enough to try.

What are you doing to carry out the work that the Lord gave us to do? Do you see the mission of the church as the Lord's body to carry His grace and truth to all men? We are the church. Is that really our mission in life? Some say they have not been called to spread the gospel. But haven't we all been sent?

### *Privilege and Priority of Evangelism*

In view of His orders to all believers, isn't it our responsibility to go with the gospel or else to show reasonable cause to believe that the circumstances in which He has placed us were intended by Him to keep us in some position of support from the home base?

What do you think God will say in the judgment about churches or individual Christians that commend themselves for keeping the Lord's Supper every week (because they see one statement of the example of one church in Acts 20:7) and yet these same loyal churches have no active program for carrying out the direct and repeated command to preach the gospel to all men?

Other works can be done in a Christian manner, but evangelizing is the one work that the Lord distinctly commanded us to do.

"How shall they believe in Him of whom they have not heard?" (Rom. 10:14). The world languishes and perishes while God waits for His people, for you and me, to tell the world of salvation.

My regret is that I have but one life to give to preaching the good news, the words of eternal life. I thank God that I can feel that I have extended my ministry by helping to send men and women to various places to tell the story. Yet, in my own feelings, I feel like asking God for a miracle of restoration of my youthful vigor and for Him to allow me to go to Europe, or South America, or Southeast Asia to spend another lifetime raising up laborers for His harvest. When I think of it, there are at least six continents and several islands where I would like to preach. If God gave me one more lifetime to do it, would I be satisfied? And why should I be granted this privilege and joy if you and you and you can be stirred up to see the challenging opportunity? Many more of God's children should have their share in the inexpressible pleasures of giving this treasure of faith and hope and love to the multitudes whose lives will be blessed and renovated by it. That is why I am rambling on like this and baring my private thinking and selfish feelings. May Jesus Christ be praised that He has shared this privilege with us!

Let us use our present resources and opportunities and influences to do the most essential thing for the glory of God and to supply every man's greatest need.

Issues of morality and truth in society, government and education must be faced. Many see a need for general and professional education in a Christian atmosphere. But we need Bible Colleges that exist for the primary purpose of raising up messengers of the cross who will take the gospel of Christ throughout the world. Nothing else is so important. Nothing else will do so much to correct social ills.

To be effective in maintaining the faith and instilling the faith in all the students who come to such Bible Colleges, the teachers, staff and workers of the college need to be devoted to preaching the word. Many men have been challenged to leave big salaries and top positions in business or education and have turned to the preaching of Christ. Someone else can collect the taxes or turn the wheels of industry, but the spread of the gospel is a truly unmixed blessing which all men need. "Thou foolish one, this night is thy soul required of thee; and all the things which thou hast prepared, whose shall they be?" Jesus said this, and He said it applies to everyone who lays up treasure for himself, and is not rich toward God (Luke 12:20, 21).

I have four sons. They have varied talents and good scholastic records. They look at various things they would like to do and be. They shrink a little, I think, from dropping into the slot of a preacher —as I shrank more than a little. But I would rather see each of them a mediocre but devoted proclaimer of the everlasting gospel than to see any of them a great success in the things that will all perish with this passing world. If they can use their various skills to pay the way or gain entrance so that they may preach the gospel, or edify the church and multiply its workers, then praise God for that. But what right do people have to ask the church to provide personal and professional education for them to use to their own enrichment while they keep sheltered from worse contaminations of the world and feel safe in Jesus while living for self and the world?

What about general education, vocational and professional training in "secular" fields, or a high degree of human culture? Use it for Christ, for eternity, for the salvation of men sinking now into hell! But do not spend the life of a believer to promote the passing interests of this present world for their own sakes, to be used as any unbeliever uses them!

*Relying On God's Power*

The church is the great divine missionary agency. The Great Commission is still the one supreme order of the supreme commander. This mission of the church rightly is the mission of every member of it. The apostles and members of the early church felt the burden and responsibility laid upon them. Why did the early church succeed so marvelously? It was not because of organization, publicity, institutions, political influence, buildings and equipment, large expenditures, or because of compromise of its doctrine with the popular ideas. They did not have the human resources and earthly means that we have today. Apparently, they did not need to depend on promoting human agencies and programs.

With plain, direct testifying to Jews and Greeks, to small and to great, they turned the world upside down. With much machinery and budgeting we do almost everything except the main thing. In Paul's lifetime, the gospel "was preached in all creation under heaven" (Col. 1:23, also v. 6). The early church took seriously our Lord's words: "We must work the works of him that sent me, while it is day; the night cometh when no man can work" (John 9:4). They sowed the seed and trusted God to give the increase (I Cor. 3:7). Their concern was "that the exceeding greatness of the power may be of God, and not from ourselves" (II Cor. 4:4-7; cp. Matt. 28:20).

In the work of evangelizing, the church is to go near as well as far. If we can not go across the world for Christ, that does not excuse us for refusing to go across the street in Jesus' name. But the Lord said "Go" (Matt. 28:18). Some have suggested "As you go" as the right translation since this is a participle in the Greek original. But in New Testament usage a participle which is connected with an imperative verb derives the imperative force from the verb.[1] The going is imperative. Not all Christians will go to a foreign field; but we need to go and tell the good news whether near or far. When we send workers out we must be careful that those we send are faithful to Christ.

Are you really sure you can't go take the gospel to those who haven't heard? A young missionary challenges us to answer this question:

[1] Kenny Boles, "Go," *Christian Standard*, CIX (October 27, 1974), p. 976.

"While vast continents are shrouded in almost utter darkness and hundreds of millions suffer the horrors of heathenism or of Islam, the burden of proof lies upon you to show that the circumstances in which God has placed you were meant by Him to keep you out of the foreign-mission field!"[2]

Let the believers belong to Him who purchased them. Let the church be the church. And let the will of the Lord be done! What are you doing to fulfill the imperatives of the Great Commission? Whatever you have or know, use it to obey Christ's command. Or are you A.W.O.L. from where the action is? Why should you not be shot for treason, for rebellion against the orders of the King of the Universe?

For Further Study:

Allen, Roland. *The Spontaneous Expansion of the Church,* rev. ed. Grand Rapids: Wm. B. Eerdmans, 1962. Seeks to present principles for world evangelism and attempts to correct hindrances to spontaneous growth.

Coleman, Robert E. *The Master Plan of Evangelism.* Old Tappan, New Jersey: Fleming H. Revell Co., 1963. A very practical and popular study of our Lord's strategy of evangelism.

Green, Michael. *Evangelism in the Early Church.* Grand Rapids: Wm. B. Eerdmans, 1970. Extensive history of evangelism in the church's first three centuries of existence.

Kane, Herbert. *Christian Missions in Biblical Perspectives.* Grand Rapids: Baker Book House, 1976. Pp. 34-49. What Jesus taught about missions.

McLean, Archibald. *Where the Book Speaks,* 2nd ed. Joplin, Missouri: College Press, reprint of 1907. Preachable sermons on missions in the Bible. Chapters IV through VIII have some outstanding messages on texts from the words of Jesus.

Tippett, Alan. *Church Growth and the Word of God.* Grand Rapids: Wm. B. Eerdmans, 1970. A study of the principles of church growth as rooted in the Old Testament and expressed and practiced in the New Testament.

---

[2] Basil Holt, *Christian Nurture,* (Cincinnati: Standard Publishing Co., 1943), p. 95.

# 93

## THE WORLD MISSION OF THE CHURCH

The Great Commission was one of Christ's most far-reaching commands. It is a task that can never be done and dispensed with. The evangelization of the world must always be in the process of being accomplished, but never completed and laid aside, until the Lord Himself shall come and take charge of the gathering of His own and the destruction of the wicked. It stands before us as a never ceasing test of our faith in Christ and our faithfulness to His command. Selfishness and indolence, littleness and pride, may be overwhelmed by the difficulty and magnitude of the task of winning the whole world. We may excuse ourselves for a time on the ground that we cannot do the job. But the fact remains that this is a major obligation of the follower of Christ. Evangelism is essential to the very nature of Christianity.

The follower of Jesus is a messenger for God to all the world. Jesus came from heaven to seek and save the lost (Luke 19:10) and to the same work He sends us (John 20:21; Mark 16:15). Nothing else so proves the love of God for man as His sending His Son to save us from sin. Nothing else so tests the reality of our love for God and for our fellow men as what we feel and do about the salvation of the souls of men. If we love the Lord we will keep His commandments (John 14:15; I John 5:3). If we love men we will carry to them the blessings of the gospel.

The world-wide mission of the church is not to spread democracy throughout the world—and to build a world council of humanitarian organizations and humanistic religions—not to spread the doubtful benefits of western civilizations, education, and mechanization. The world mission of the church is to save souls—to dispel the darkness of sin by bringing to men the Sun of righteousness—to bring eternal life and glory to those who are condemned to death and despair—for "His divine power has granted unto us all things that pertain to life and godliness through the knowledge of him who called us by his own glory and virtue" (II Pet. 1:3). The very purpose of the church itself is often misunderstood or perverted by false and selfish leaders. An observer of the activities of many churches might think that their chief purpose was to build fine buildings; or to celebrate Christmas and Easter; or to provide respectable entertainment; or to be a community unit for dispensing all sorts of propaganda, and for collecting funds for all sorts of campaigns and projects; or simply to provide a place to meet nice people and make friends. Now, whatever might be said in favor of any of the above activities, none of them, or all of them together, is not the essential purpose of the church. Other organizations might do all these things, and still the church would be necessary.

The real purpose of the church is to preach Christ, to serve Christ, and to perfect the rule of Christ in every heart of all mankind. The church is to build the kingdom of God: that is, to bring men to surrender to the rule of God in Jesus Christ, and to teach them to observe to do all that He has commanded (Matt. 28:18-20) until He dominates every word, thought, and act of their lives (see Col. 3:17; II Cor. 6:19, 20; 10:31). The great task before us is to evangelize and to edify, to recruit and train believers, obedient believers, in Christ, in order that in Him they may find peace, light, life, hope, love and innumerable blessings here and hereafter.

The mission of the church is evangelism. It is the same at home or abroad. Incidental conditions of home or foreign missions are secondary compared to the understanding of the mission on which we are sent by the Lord. When we understand and believe the gospel of Christ, then, by the very nature of it, we are compelled and constrained to take it to all men.

### *Compelled by the Command of Christ*

The Great Commission is the King's command. It is the marching orders of the army of the Lord. He sends and we must go. If the church serves Christ, who bought it and built it, who is head over all things pertaining to the church, then it must obey His command to go into all the world, preach the gospel to the whole creation, make disciples of all the nations, baptizing them, and teaching them to observe all His commands (Matt. 28:18-20; Mark 16:15, 16; Acts 1:8). This command was given with the express reminder that He had all authority in heaven and on earth.

This command was not given to the apostles alone. The fact that its provisions extend to the "end of the world" shows that its obligation rests upon the Lord's people as long as there are any of them here. It states the task committed to the church throughout all time. Each one of us who is part of the church at any time or place has his own part in fulfilling that assignment. "We are His disciples; we His work must do." To rephrase a famous couplet: "Ours is not to reason why; it is but ours to do or die!"

"Will the heathen be saved if we do not send them the gospel?" is a question of serious importance; but another of greater importance to me and you is this: "Will I be saved if I do not send it in obedience to the Lord's command?" One missionary said, "If I knew I would never again have a convert, I would go right ahead and preach the gospel unto all creation." Another said, "What have we to do with success—we have our marching orders—we must go forward."

The Lord exercises His power to save through the message of the gospel, and forgives men upon the condition of their faith in it. He has committed to us the task of carrying the message to all sinners. There are no Christians where the gospel has not been carried by men; and, to us, there has been revealed no hope for any to whom its blessed truth is not made known. (See II Thess. 1:7-9). In giving the Great Commission, Christ committed the work of saving the world into the hands of men. Since He has commanded us to do it, we must preach the gospel to all men in order that by being faithful servants of His we might save ourselves. Since it has pleased Him to commit this treasure to earthen vessels (II Cor. 4:7), we must be true to the trust in order to save others. Surely, if we care at all for the Lord's will, or for our brothers' welfare, we should be diligent in evangelizing the whole world.

Since Jesus commanded evangelism, we are not Christian if we are not evangelistic, and the work of evangelism is the same work at home and abroad. The logical order is to work at home and near-by fields first (see Acts 1:8), but the Lord also says "into all the world," "all nations," "unto every creature," "unto the uttermost part of the earth." Any one who doesn't believe in evangelism on the foreign field doesn't believe Christ. The Lord seems to desire haste in the establishment of Christian centers throughout the world. There was surely much evangelizing left to do in Judea and Samaria when "the hand of the Lord" promoted the mission work at Antioch. There was much more to be done at Antioch when the Holy Spirit commanded them to send Paul and Barnabas into still other foreign fields. Paul saw and planned to do much more evangelizing that needed to be done in Asia Minor when the Lord led him on to Europe (Acts 16:6-10).

### *Compelled by the Nature and Truth of the Gospel*

If any one does not believe in missions, He does not believe Christ, for Christ commanded it. But if there was no Great Commission, the gospel message itself impels universal evangelism. If it means anything to us, it must be true. If it is true, it is for all men. The gospel has the same light and salvation to offer to all men. All men are lost in sin (Rom. 3:19-23). "The whole world lieth in the evil one" (I John 5:19). There is only one Savior and plan of salvation (John 14:6; Acts 4:12). Christ died for all; His love and saving power are sent forth to all. The Lord is not willing that any should perish (II Pet. 3:9), and He is no respecter of persons (Acts 10:34).

The church does not belong to one nation, or race, or class, or age, but is the will of God and the gift of God for all mankind. All men have been made by God, and are responsible to God. All men are in need of the same grace. The gospel is not given to us to keep; but by the very nature of it, if we accept it as true, we accept the obligation to deliver it to others. If we are honest, we will deliver the precious truth to those for whom it is designated. We are too often guilty of criminal neglect in carrying around with us the serum of life but doing nothing for the thousands about us who are dying an eternal death. We look down upon unbelieving, un-Christian nations for their pagan barbarianism, while we live in luxury by embezzling what was consigned to them through us. How like the rich man in Luke 16 is the Christian who knows the gospel but selfishly refuses to share it.

Love and the gospel cross all the barriers and chasms of difference between men. God made the gospel to be universal. Jesus had predicted bringing the Gentiles into the fold to be one flock with the Jews (John 10:16); but the deep-seated Jewish prejudice against Gentiles was not easy to overcome. Barnabas was a good man who could see the grace of God and be glad. He had been one of the first to give his property to the apostles (Acts 4:36, 37), and to receive Saul the persecutor into fellowship after his conversion (Acts 9:27). He and Paul taught these Gentiles to give freely and beforehand to the saints of Judea when the famine was predicted. The nature of the gospel constrains us to overcome our enmities and send it to all men.

Some people do not tell the good news because they have nothing to tell. It is no longer a question whether Christianity is worth spreading; but it may be a question whether your Christianity is worth spreading. The fact that you don't spread it seems to indicate that it is not. A doctrine of doubts or of self-righteousness does not demand telling at any personal sacrifice. But if the gospel of Christ is true, it must be told. If we believe it, we are committed to telling it. If we accept it, we are no longer our own, but are bought with a price.

We have no life to live but the life of service to Jesus Christ in saving the world from sin.

Certainly, we should give ourselves diligently to missionary work because God has commanded it; because the Holy Spirit directed and blessed the first examples; because the world is lost; because of the worth of a soul; because of the love of the Savior; because of the fact of hell to be avoided; because of the glories of heaven to be gained; because Jesus has the right to full satisfaction with the results of His labors and suffering; because it is the most glorious, permanent, and far-reaching in its effects of any work that we could do. It is the great way, the necessary way, of love and obedience to God, of love and service to men.

### *Compelled by Need and by Love*

To do one's duty is good, and not to be minimized or despised. But to win the world to Christ is more than a duty. It is a privilege. If the church is filled with the Spirit of Christ, and has been imbued with the love of God, it will want to seek and save the lost—everywhere.

Very briefly and incidentally the Book of Acts records time after-time the great success of the early missionaries (Acts 2:41, 47; 4:4; 5:14; 6:7; 8:12; 9:31, 35, 42; 11:24; 12:24). The reasons for such uniform success are indicated in the book. "The hand of the Lord was with them" as He had promised (Matt. 28:20), for they were obeying His commission and all its terms. They preached "the word." They did not doubt their message, but testified powerfully the facts, the commandments, the warnings, and the promises of the gospel of Christ. It is the duty of a messenger to guard and preserve the message as well as to deliver it (John 8:31; I Tim. 4:16; II Tim. 1:13; Jude 3; I Tim. 6:20; II John 9). They were diligent and steadfast in prayer as well as in teaching and preaching (Acts 2:42; 4:23-31; 6:4; 12:12; 13:2). They were united in faith and in spirit, able to work together (Acts 4:32, 33; 12:1; cf. John 17:20-21). The multitude of believers carried the good news, not the apostles only (Acts 8:1, 3; 11:19). Moreover, they did not try to shield themselves, serve themselves, or exalt themselves; but they were willing to spend and to be spent in doing what Christ had given them to do. They counted their possessions not their own and their lives as not dear unto themselves (Acts 4:32-37; 20:24; 5:41).

Paul was first sent by the authority of Christ's command. Paul was attracted by the marvelous truth and character of the gospel message. But Paul came to be drawn more and more by the needs of men out of Christ, and was constrained by the love of Christ to beseech and entreat men (at all costs to himself) to be reconciled to God. His heart's desire and supplication to God was for the rejectors of the gospel that they might be saved (Rom. 10:1). For their sakes he had great sorrow and unceasing pain in his heart, and could even wish that he himself were anathema from Christ, if by that he could win their salvation (Rom. 9:1-13). When we realize that men out of Christ are "dead in trespasses and sins" (Eph. 2:1); "are without God and without hope" (Eph. 2:12); are blind, in darkness in the power of Satan, and need forgiveness of sins (Acts 26:17, 18); do not know God (I Thess. 4:5); have all sinned, and will perish by their sin without the law (Rom. 3:23; 2:12); cannot be saved by their self-righteousness (Rom. 3:19; 10:3, 4); will be punished (II Thess. 1:7-9) and cast into the lake of fire (Rev. 20:15); if we have any love in our hearts, we will eagerly do all we can to reach them with the gospel, which is able to save them all.

Do we love Him enough to go for Him, to speak for Him, to glorify Him and to bring Him His own that He may heal them? If we love Christ, we will keep His commandments (John 14:15).

For Further Study:

See books listed on page 535.

# HARMONY OF MATTHEW, MARK, LUKE, JOHN

*PLACES, TIME PERIODS, EVENTS, SCRIPTURE*

| Place | Event | Matthew | Mark | Luke | John |
|---|---|---|---|---|---|
| | **THE BEGINNING** | | | | |
| 1. | — Prologue and introductions | 1 | 1 | 1 | 1 |
| 2. Jerusalem | — Gabriel's announcement to Zechariah about a son | | | 1 | |
| 3. Nazareth | — Mary and Gabriel | | | 1 | |
| 4. Judea | — Mary, Elizabeth, & Mary's "song." | | | 1 | |
| 5. Nazareth | — Joseph informed about Mary, their marriage | 1 | | | |
| 6. Judea | — Birth of John, Zechariah's prophetic utterance | | | 1 | |
| | **THIRTY YEARS PREPARATION** | | | | |
| 7. Bethlehem | — Birth of Jesus | | | 2 | |
| 8. Jerusalem | — Presented in the Temple | | | 2 | |
| 9. Bethlehem | — Wisemen found Him | 2 | | | |
| 10. Egypt | — Fleeing from Herod's decree | 2 | | | |
| 11. Nazareth | — Boyhood home | 2 | | | |
| 12. Jerusalem | — Passover, age 12 | | | 2 | |
| 13. Nazareth | — Grew up until about 30 years old | | | 2 | |
| 14. Jordan in wilderness of Judea | — Immersed by John (Genealogy) | 1,3 | 1 | 3 | |
| 15. Wilderness | — Tempted by Satan | 4 | 1 | 4 | |
| 16. Bethany | — Pointed out by John, obtained first disciples (beyond Jordan) | | | | 1 |

| | | | | | |
|---|---|---|---|---|---|
| 17. Cana of Galilee | — Wedding, first miracle | | | | 2 |
| 18. Capernaum | — With family and disciples "Abode not many days" | | | | 2 |
| | **FIRST YEAR OF MINISTRY** | | | | |
| | *EARLY JUDEAN MINISTRY* (8 or 9 months) | | | | |
| 19. Jerusalem | — FIRST PASSOVER; cleansed temple (First *public* ministry on record) | | | | 2 |
| 20. Judea | — Period of about 8 or 9 months | | | | 3 |
| | Miracles ("no man can do these things. . . .") | | | | |
| | Preached to Nicodemus new birth and eternal life, Son lifted up | | | | |
| | Making and immersing more disciples than John | | | | |
| 21. Sychar in Samaria | — Woman at well; all city came out; abode two days (4 months to harvest) | | | | 4 |
| | *GALILEAN MINISTRY* (1 year and 3 or 4 months) | | | | |
| 22. Cana of Galilee | — Spoke the word and the nobleman's son at Capernaum was healed | | | | 4 |
| 23. Nazareth | — Read and taught in synagogue; first rejection there | | | 4 | |
| 24. Capernaum | — (1) Called four fishermen | 4 | 1 | 5 | |
| | (2) Healed demoniac in synagogue | | 1 | 4 | |
| | (3) Peter's mother-in-law, crowd in the street | 8 | 1 | 4 | |

| Place | Event | Matthew | Mark | Luke | John |
|---|---|---|---|---|---|
| 25. First Galilean tour | — (1) Great crowds, miracles | 4 | 1 | 4 | |
| | (2) Leper healed | 8 | 1 | 5 | |
| | (3) Paralytic through roof | 9 | 2 | 5 | |
| | (4) Call of Matthew, feast of publicans | 9 | 2 | 5 | |
| | (5) Controversies over eating and fasting | 9 | 2 | 5 | |
| | **SECOND YEAR OF MINISTRY** | | | | |
| 26. Jerusalem | — SECOND PASSOVER: Lame man at pool; controversy about Sabbath healing; sermon on deity and credentials | | | | 5 |
| 27. Galilee | — (1) Controversy over Sabbath reaping | 12 | 2 | 6 | |
| | (2) Healed withered hand on Sabbath in synagogue (Capernaum?) | 12 | 3 | 6 | |
| | (3) Thronging crowds from far and near, many miracles | 12 | 3 | 6 | |
| | (4) Named twelve "Apostles" | | 3 | 6 | |
| | (5) Sermon on the Mount | 5,6,7 | | 6 | |
| | (6) Healed centurion's servant in Capernaum | 8 | | 7 | |
| 28. Nain | — Raised widow's son | | | 7 | |
| 29. Capernaum | — (1) Question from John the Immerser; sermon on John | 11 | | 7 | |
| | (2) Condemnation of unrepentant cities; the great invitation | 11 | | | |

| | | | | | |
|---|---|---|---|---|---|
| | (3) In house of Simon the Pharisee; Penitent woman forgiven | | | 7 | |
| 30. Second Galilean Tour | — (1) Healed blind and dumb demoniac; charge of league with Satan | 12 | 3 | | |
| | (2) Sign sought; Sign of Jonah; Judgment of this generation | 12 | | | |
| | (3) Mother and brethren try to interrupt | 12 | 3 | 8 | |
| | (4) Sermon in parables | 13 | 4 | 8 | |
| | (5) Challenge of high cost to would-be followers | 8 | | 9 | |
| 31. On Sea of Galilee | — Stilled the tempest | 8 | 4 | 8 | |
| 32. Gergeaa | — Demoniacs and swine | 8 | 5 | 8 | |
| 33. Capernaum | — Healed woman with flow of blood, Raised Jairus' daughter | 9 | 5 | 8 | |
| | — Healed two blind men and dumb demoniac | 9 | | | |
| 34. Nazareth | — Apparently last visit; unbelief; some miracles | 13 | 6 | | |
| 35. Third Galilean tour | — Twelve sent out in pairs; | 10 | 6 | 9 | |
| | — Herod's fear of Jesus (Tour ends at Capernaum, multitudes greatly aroused.) | 14 | 6 | 9 | |
| 36. Across the Sea, near Bethsaida Julias | — THIRD PASSOVER NIGH — Day of teaching; fed 5,000; refused crown; night of prayer | 14 | 6 | 9 | 6 |

| Place | Event | Matthew | Mark | Luke | John |
|---|---|---|---|---|---|
| | **THIRD YEAR OF MINISTRY** | | | | |
| | *RETIREMENTS AND TRAVELS WITH THE TWELVE* (6 months) | | | | |
| 37. On the Sea | — (In the night) Walked on water; stilled tempest | 14 | 6 | | 6 |
| 38. Gennesaret | — Miracles | 14 | 6 | | |
| 39. Capernaum | — Sermon on the Bread of Life; Many forsake Him | | | | 6 |
| | — Controversy with Pharisees about traditions (washing) | 15 | 7 | | |
| 40. Phoenicia | — Retirement with apostles; healed demonized daughter of Syro-Phoenician woman | 15 | 7 | | |
| 41. Decapolis | — Healed deaf stammerer and many others | 15 | 7 | | |
| | — Fed 4,000 (considerable public ministry implied) | 15 | 8 | | |
| 42. Magadan | — Pharisees and Sadducees demand sign from heaven | 16 | 8 | | |
| 43. On the Sea | — Crossing in boat; warned disciples against influence of popular leaders and parties | 16 | 8 | | |
| 44. Bethsaida | — Healing of blind man | | 8 | | |
| 45. Caesarea Philippi | — Question of Jesus' identity; Peter's confession | 16 | 8 | 9 | |
| | — First plain prediction of His death | 16 | 8 | 9 | |

| | | | | | |
|---|---|---|---|---|---|
| 46. An exceeding high mountain (Hermon?) | — Transfiguration | 17 | 9 | 9 | |
| | — Healed demoniac boy | 17 | 9 | 9 | |
| | — Further prediction of cross | 17 | 9 | 9 | |
| 47. Capernaum | — (1) Peter and the temple tax | 17 | | | |
| | (2) Discussion of who shall be greatest | 18 | 9 | 9 | |
| | (3) The unknown worker of miracles | | 9 | 9 | |
| | (4) Discussion of stumbling blocks, mistreatment, forgiveness | 18 | 9 | | |
| | (5) Advice of His unbelieving brethren | | | | 7 |
| 48. Journey through Samaria | — Sons of Thunder would call down fire | | | 9 | |
| | *LATER JUDEAN MINISTRY* (about 3 months) | | | | |
| 49. Jerusalem | — (1) FEAST OF TABERNACLES: Confused opinions about Him; Attempt to arrest Him; Water of Life | | | | 7 |
| | (2) Sermon on the Light of the world; freedom; Abraham's Seed | | | | 8 |
| | (3) Healing the man born blind; controversy | | | | 9 |
| | (4) The Good Shepherd and the Door of the Sheep | | | | 10 |
| | (5) The seventy sent out; discussion on their return | | | 10 | |
| | (6) A lawyer's question; parable of good Samaritan | | | 10 | |

| Place | Event | Matthew | Mark | Luke | John |
|---|---|---|---|---|---|
| 50. Bethany | — Jesus and Mary and Martha | | | 10 | |
| 51. Place of Prayer | — Discourse on Prayer | | | 11 | |
| 52. Place Unknown | — Controversy about demons and league with Satan | | | 11 | |
| | — Signs and judgment of this generation | | | 11 | |
| 53. Pharisee's house | — Invited to dinner; Denounced Pharisaism | | | 11 | |
| 54. Before a multitude of many thousands | — Great evangelistic appeals | | | 12 & 13 | |
| | (1) Warning against hypocrisy & fear of men | | | | |
| | (2) Against covetousness: parable of rich fool | | | | |
| | (3) Against anxiety for worldly needs: trust God | | | | |
| | (4) Urged watchfulness and preparedness for day of account; parable of waiting servants and wise steward | | | | |
| | (5) Christ the burning issue; no neutrality | | | | |
| | (6) Settle with God "out of court" | | | | |
| | (7) No difference, *all* must repent | | | | |
| | (8) Parable of fig tree: 3 chances, one more, then cut down | | | | |
| 55. In a synagogue | — Woman bowed double; controversy about Sabbath healing | | | 13 | |

| Place | Event | | |
|---|---|---|---|
| | — Parables of the kingdom: mustard & leaven | 13 | |
| 56. Temple in Jerusalem | — Feast of Dedication; Attempts to kill Jesus for blasphemy; Jesus' claims: the door, the good Shepherd, one with God, the Son of God | | 10 |

*LATER PEREAN MINISTRY* (about 3 months)

| Place | Event | | |
|---|---|---|---|
| 57. Perea | — Retirement to place of His baptism | | 10 |
| 58. Cities and villages | — Journeys and discussions in Perea: few saved, Herod the fox | 13 | |
| 59. Home of a Phraisee | — On the Sabbath, healed dropsy and discussion; conduct at feasts: chief seats, whom to invite; parable of great feast, slighted invitation, excuses | 14 | |
| 60. Before a great multitude | — Sermon on cost of discipleship | 14 | |
| 61. Place Unknown | — (1) Parables of lost sheep, coin & son | 15 | |
| | (2) Parable of the unjust steward | 16 | |
| | (3) The rich man and Lazarus | 16 | |
| | (4) Stumbling blocks; forgiveness; unprofitable servants | 17 | |
| 62. Bethany | — Raising of Lazarus | | 11 |
| | — Rulers in Jerusalem plot to kill Jesus | | 11 |
| 63. Ephraim (city) | — "Tarried" with the disciples | | 11 |

| | | Matthew | Mark | Luke | John |
|---|---|---|---|---|---|
| 64. Trip through borders of Samaria, Galilee, and Perea to Jerusalem | — (1) Healing ten lepers | | | 17 | |
| | (2) Sermon on the time of the coming of the kingdom | | | | |
| | (3) Teaching on prayer: the unjust judge; Pharisee & Publican | | | 18 | |
| | (4) Teaching on divorce (in Perea) | 19 | 10 | | |
| | (5) Jesus and the little children | 19 | 10 | 18 | |
| | Rich young ruler; peril of riches | | | | |
| | (6) Apostles' reward | 19 | 10 | 18 | |
| | (7) Parable of laborers in the vineyard | 20 | | | |
| | (8) Plain prediction of the crucifixion | 20 | 10 | 18 | |
| | (9) James and John ask chief honors | 20 | 10 | | |
| 65. Jericho | — Blind men helped (Bartimaeus) | 20 | 10 | 18 | |
| 66. Road to Jerusalem | — Zacchaeus | | | 19 | |
| | — Parable of Pounds | | | 19 | |

*LAST WEEK IN JERUSALEM AREA*

| | | Matthew | Mark | Luke | John |
|---|---|---|---|---|---|
| 67. Bethany | — Reception: Mary anoints Jesus | 26:6-13 | 14:3-9 | | 12:1-11 |
| 68. Jerusalem | — "Triumphal" entry (probably on Sunday) | 21 | 11 | 19 | 12 |
| 69. Bethany | — Next day cursed fig tree on the way to Jerusalem | 21 | 11 | | |
| 70. Jerusalem | — Second cleansing of the temple (Monday?) | 21 | 11 | 19 | |
| 71. Bethany | — Night's lodging | 21:17 | 11:19 | | |

| | | | | | |
|---|---|---|---|---|---|
| 72. Jerusalem | — (Tuesday?) Day of discussions | | | | |
| | ( 1) Question of Jesus' authority | 21 | 11 | 20 | |
| | ( 2) Parable of two sons | 21 | | | |
| | ( 3) Parable of the vineyard | 21 | 12 | 20 | |
| | ( 4) Parable of the wedding garment | 22 | | | |
| | ( 5) Question of tribute to Caesar | 22 | 12 | 20 | |
| | ( 6) Question of the resurrection | 22 | 12 | 20 | |
| | ( 7) Question of the greatest commandment | 22 | 12 | | |
| | ( 8) Question about the Son of David | 22 | 12 | 20 | |
| | ( 9) Denunciation of Scribes and Pharisees | 23 | 12 | 20 | |
| | (10) Widow's mite | | 12 | 21 | |
| | (11) Sermon significance of life and death | | | | 12 |
| | (12) Predictions of end of Jerusalem and of the world; His second coming | 24 | 13 | 21 | |
| | (13) On judgment: ten virgins; talents; judgment scene | 25 | | | |
| | (14) Prediction of Jesus' death (Wednesday?) Judas' plot to betray Jesus | 26 | 14 | 22 | |

*FOURTH PASSOVER*

| | | | | | |
|---|---|---|---|---|---|
| | (15) Thursday, first day of unleavened bread; made ready the Passover | 26:17-19 | 14:12-16 | 22:7-13 | |
| | (16) (The Upper Room) after night (Jewish Friday) Passover meal; | | | | |

| | Matthew | Mark | Luke | John |
|---|---|---|---|---|
| feet washed; disciples warned; Judas departed; Lord's supper instituted; farewell discourse with the apostles | 26 | 14 | 22 | 13 & 14 |
| (Out in the night) Parting instructions and predictions: parable of the vine; Holy Spirit promised; | | | | 15 & 16 |
| Great intercessory prayer | | | | 17 |
| (18) (Gethsemane) Agony and prayer; angels came; betrayal and arrest | 26 | 14 | 22 | 18 |
| (19) (Court Rooms) Trials before Annas, Caiaphas, Sanhedrin, Pilate, Herod, Pilate; Tortures | 26 & 27 | 14 & 15 | 22 & 23 | 18 |
| (20) (Golgotha) Crucifixion and burial (Friday, day of Preparation) | 27 | 15 | 23 | 19 |
| *FORTY DAYS AFTER THE RESURRECTION* | | | | |
| (21) (In a garden outside the city) Sunday—the resurrection announced to women at the tomb | 28 | 16 | 24 | |
| — Appearance to other women | 28 | | | |
| — Appearance to Mary | | 16:9 | | 20 |
| (22) (Jerusalem) | | | | |
| — The women report to the apostles | | 16 | 24 | 20 |
| — The guards report to the chief priests | 28 | | | |

| | | | | | |
|---|---|---|---|---|---|
| | — Appearance to Peter | (I Cor. 15:5) | | 24:34 | |
| 73. Trip to Emmaus | — Appearance and teaching to two disciples | | 16 | 24 | |
| 74. Jerusalem | — (same night) Appearance to the ten | | 16 | 24 | 20 |
| | (8 days later) Appearance to the eleven | (I Cor. 15:5) | | | 20 |
| 75. Galilee | — Appearance to seven by the sea | | | | 21 |
| | — To the disciples on a mountain; Great commission | 28 | | | |
| | — To more than 500 brethren (I Cor. 15:6) | | | | |
| 76. Jerusalem | — Appearance to James; to the apostles (I Cor. 15:7; Acts 1) | | | 24 | |
| 77. Near Bethany | — The ascension (Acts 1; Phil. 2; Eph. 1) | | 16 | 24 | |

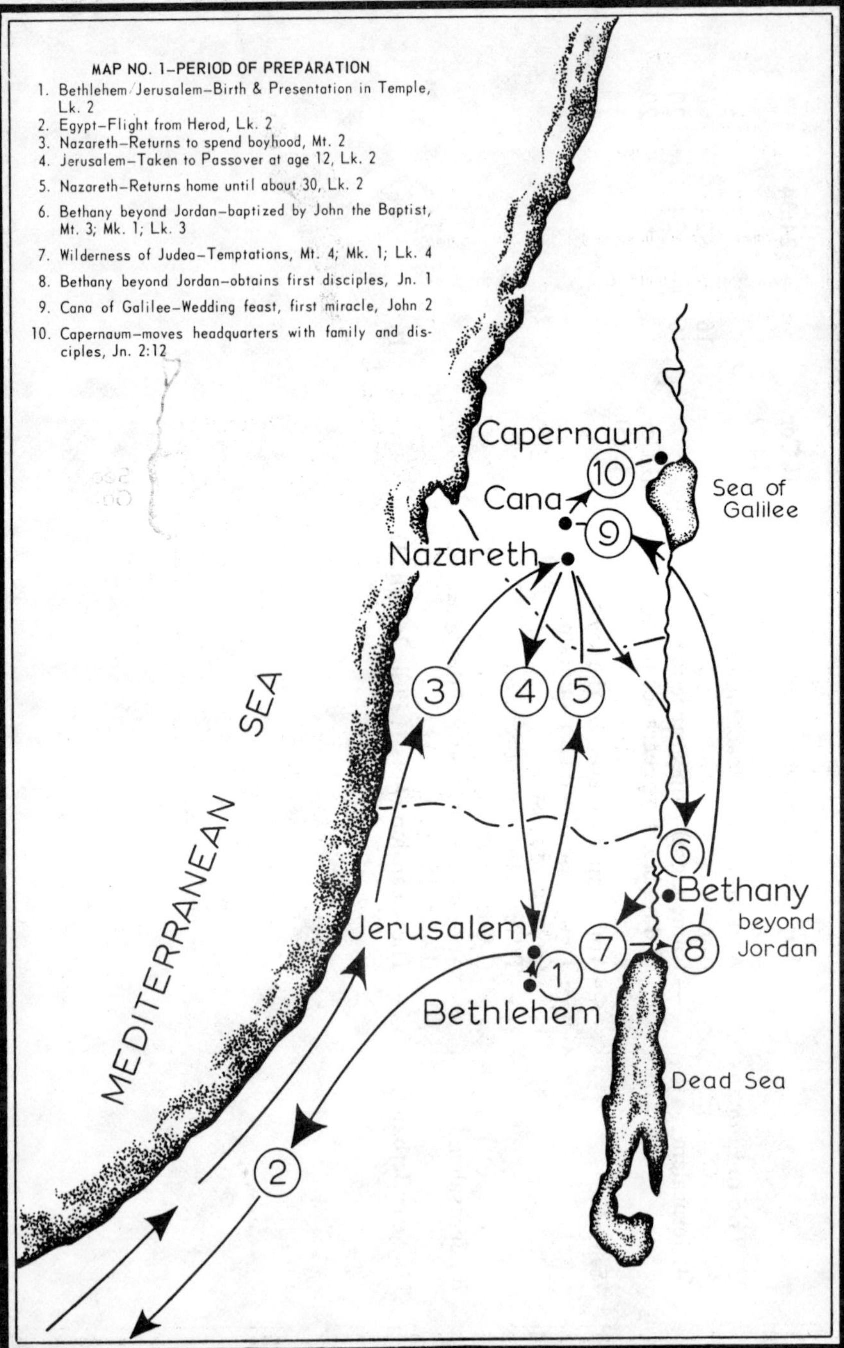
MAP NO. 1–PERIOD OF PREPARATION
1. Bethlehem/Jerusalem–Birth & Presentation in Temple, Lk. 2
2. Egypt–Flight from Herod, Lk. 2
3. Nazareth–Returns to spend boyhood, Mt. 2
4. Jerusalem–Taken to Passover at age 12, Lk. 2
5. Nazareth–Returns home until about 30, Lk. 2
6. Bethany beyond Jordan–baptized by John the Baptist, Mt. 3; Mk. 1; Lk. 3
7. Wilderness of Judea–Temptations, Mt. 4; Mk. 1; Lk. 4
8. Bethany beyond Jordan–obtains first disciples, Jn. 1
9. Cana of Galilee–Wedding feast, first miracle, John 2
10. Capernaum–moves headquarters with family and disciples, Jn. 2:12
Capernaum
Sea of Galilee
Cana
Nazareth
MEDITERRANEAN SEA
Bethany beyond Jordan
Jerusalem
Bethlehem
Dead Sea

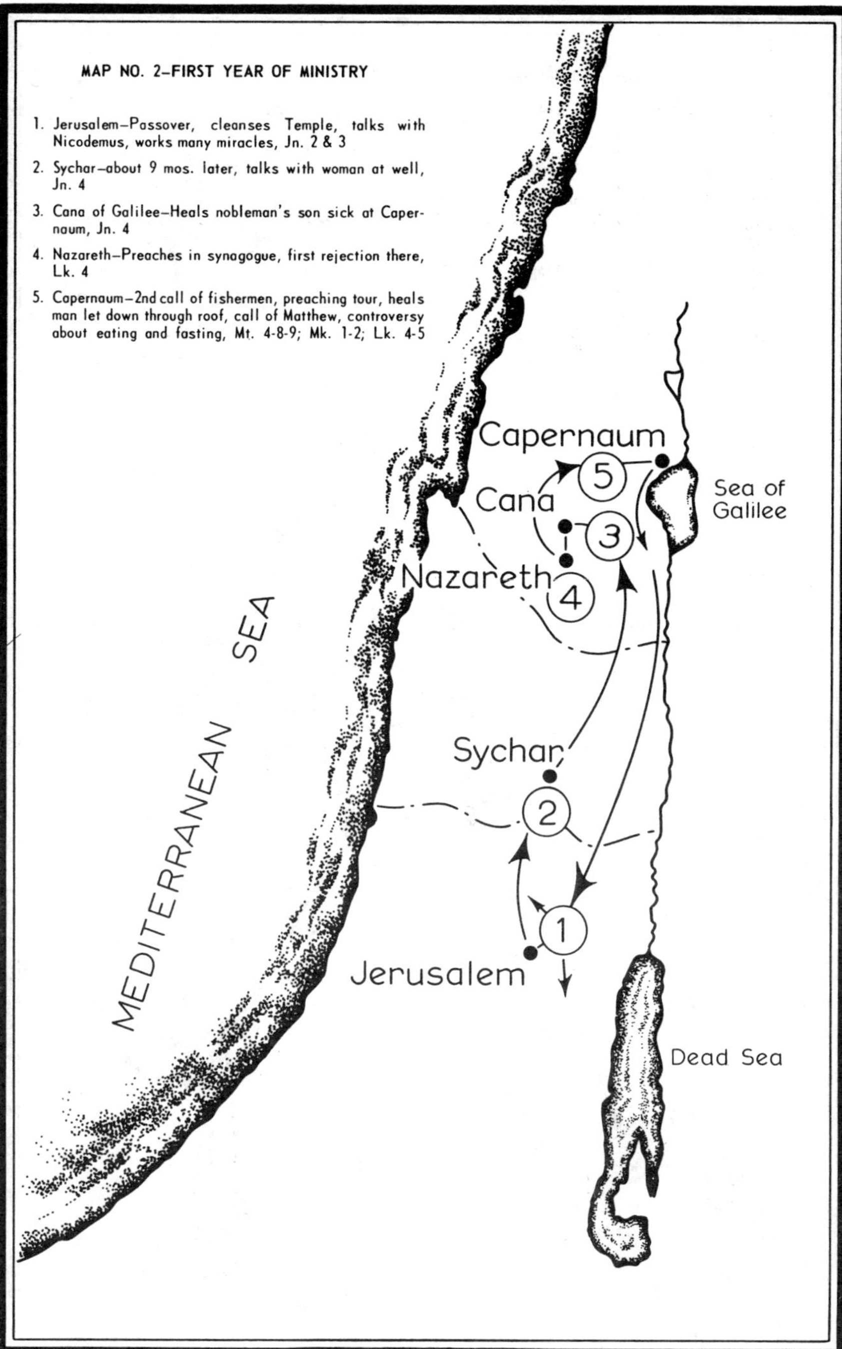
MAP NO. 2–FIRST YEAR OF MINISTRY
1. Jerusalem–Passover, cleanses Temple, talks with Nicodemus, works many miracles, Jn. 2 & 3
2. Sychar–about 9 mos. later, talks with woman at well, Jn. 4
3. Cana of Galilee–Heals nobleman's son sick at Capernaum, Jn. 4
4. Nazareth–Preaches in synagogue, first rejection there, Lk. 4
5. Capernaum–2nd call of fishermen, preaching tour, heals man let down through roof, call of Matthew, controversy about eating and fasting, Mt. 4-8-9; Mk. 1-2; Lk. 4-5
Capernaum
5
Cana
3
Sea of Galilee
Nazareth
4
MEDITERRANEAN SEA
Sychar
2
1
Jerusalem
Dead Sea

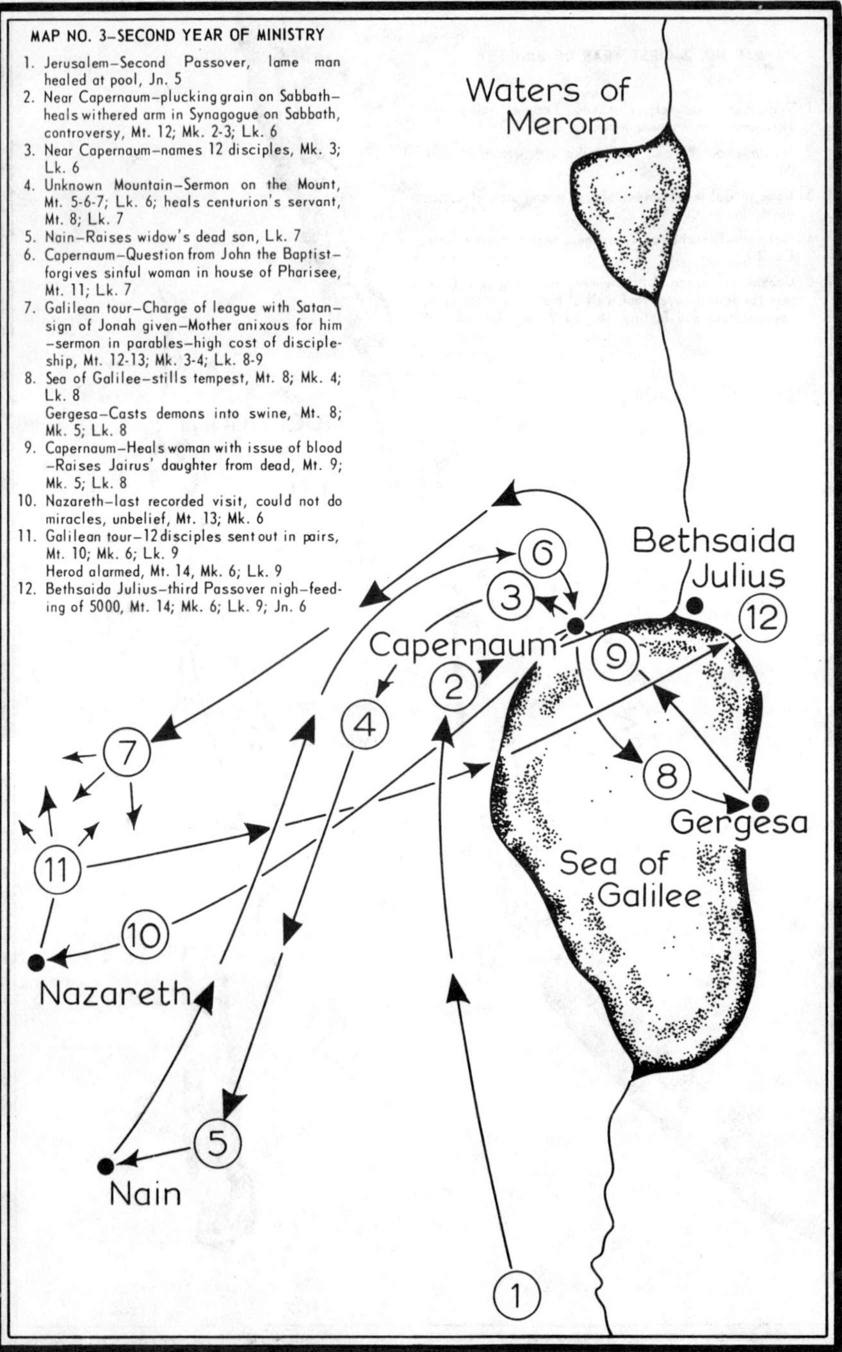
MAP NO. 3–SECOND YEAR OF MINISTRY
1. Jerusalem–Second Passover, lame man healed at pool, Jn. 5
2. Near Capernaum–plucking grain on Sabbath–heals withered arm in Synagogue on Sabbath, controversy, Mt. 12; Mk. 2-3; Lk. 6
3. Near Capernaum–names 12 disciples, Mk. 3; Lk. 6
4. Unknown Mountain–Sermon on the Mount, Mt. 5-6-7; Lk. 6; heals centurion's servant, Mt. 8; Lk. 7
5. Nain–Raises widow's dead son, Lk. 7
6. Capernaum–Question from John the Baptist–forgives sinful woman in house of Pharisee, Mt. 11; Lk. 7
7. Galilean tour–Charge of league with Satan–sign of Jonah given–Mother anixous for him–sermon in parables–high cost of discipleship, Mt. 12-13; Mk. 3-4; Lk. 8-9
8. Sea of Galilee–stills tempest, Mt. 8; Mk. 4; Lk. 8
Gergesa–Casts demons into swine, Mt. 8; Mk. 5; Lk. 8
9. Capernaum–Heals woman with issue of blood–Raises Jairus' daughter from dead, Mt. 9; Mk. 5; Lk. 8
10. Nazareth–last recorded visit, could not do miracles, unbelief, Mt. 13; Mk. 6
11. Galilean tour–12 disciples sent out in pairs, Mt. 10; Mk. 6; Lk. 9
Herod alarmed, Mt. 14, Mk. 6; Lk. 9
12. Bethsaida Julius–third Passover nigh–feeding of 5000, Mt. 14; Mk. 6; Lk. 9; Jn. 6
Waters of Merom
Bethsaida Julius
Capernaum
Gergesa
Sea of Galilee
Nazareth
Nain
1
2
3
4
5
6
7
8
9
10
11
12

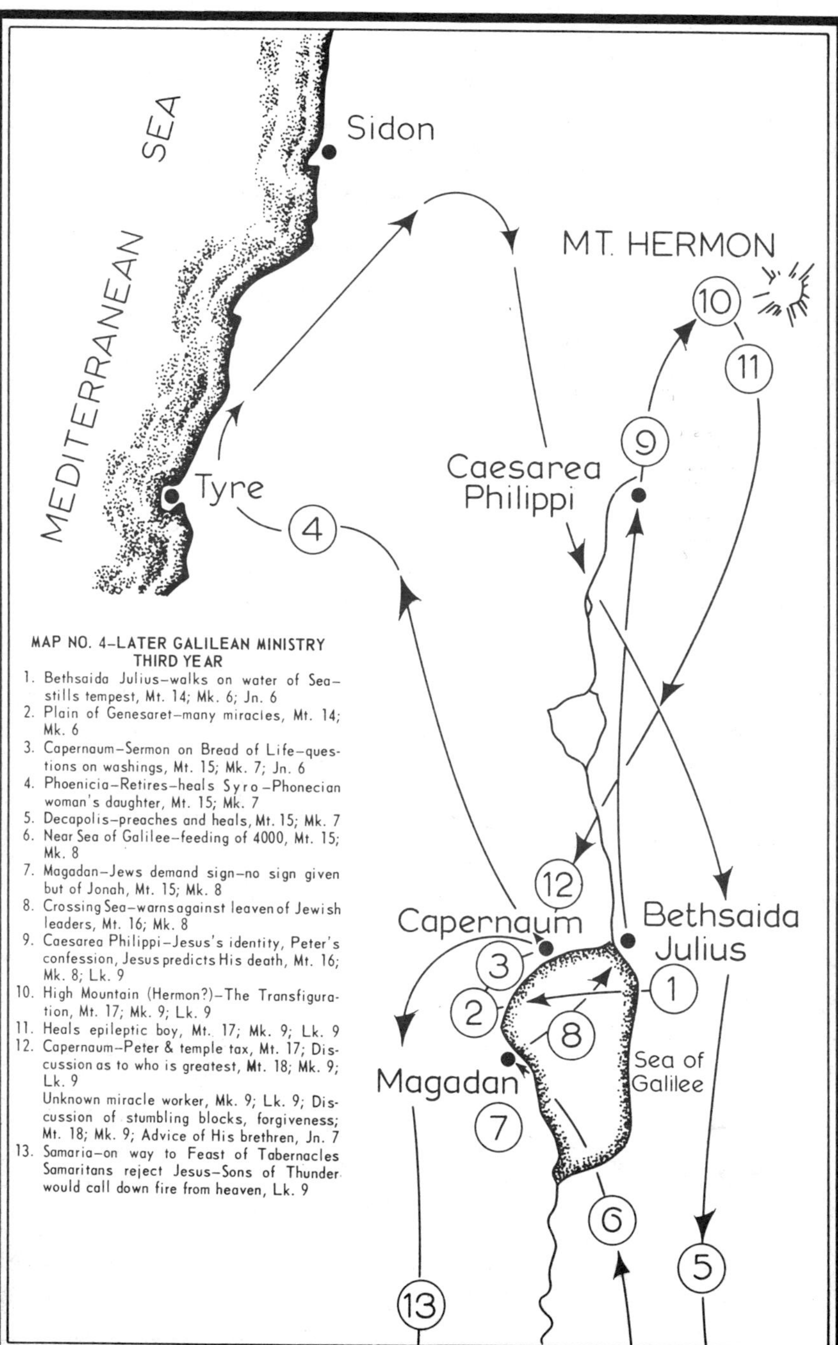
SEA
MEDITERRANEAN
Sidon
MT. HERMON
Tyre
Caesarea
Philippi
Capernaum
Bethsaida
Julius
Magadan
Sea of
Galilee
1
2
3
4
5
6
7
8
9
10
11
12
13
MAP NO. 4–LATER GALILEAN MINISTRY
THIRD YEAR
1. Bethsaida Julius–walks on water of Sea–stills tempest, Mt. 14; Mk. 6; Jn. 6
2. Plain of Genesaret–many miracles, Mt. 14; Mk. 6
3. Capernaum–Sermon on Bread of Life–questions on washings, Mt. 15; Mk. 7; Jn. 6
4. Phoenicia–Retires–heals Syro–Phonecian woman's daughter, Mt. 15; Mk. 7
5. Decapolis–preaches and heals, Mt. 15; Mk. 7
6. Near Sea of Galilee–feeding of 4000, Mt. 15; Mk. 8
7. Magadan–Jews demand sign–no sign given but of Jonah, Mt. 15; Mk. 8
8. Crossing Sea–warns against leaven of Jewish leaders, Mt. 16; Mk. 8
9. Caesarea Philippi–Jesus's identity, Peter's confession, Jesus predicts His death, Mt. 16; Mk. 8; Lk. 9
10. High Mountain (Hermon?)–The Transfiguration, Mt. 17; Mk. 9; Lk. 9
11. Heals epileptic boy, Mt. 17; Mk. 9; Lk. 9
12. Capernaum–Peter & temple tax, Mt. 17; Discussion as to who is greatest, Mt. 18; Mk. 9; Lk. 9
Unknown miracle worker, Mk. 9; Lk. 9; Discussion of stumbling blocks, forgiveness; Mt. 18; Mk. 9; Advice of His brethren, Jn. 7
13. Samaria–on way to Feast of Tabernacles Samaritans reject Jesus–Sons of Thunder would call down fire from heaven, Lk. 9

MAP NO. 5—THIRD YEAR, LATER JUDEAN MINISTRY (about 3 months)

1. Temple; Feast of Tabernacles; Sermons on Light of World; Freedom; Abraham's Children; Man born blind healed; Good Shepherd; 70 sent out to evangelize, Jn. 7-8-9-10 & Lk. 10
2. Bethany; Jesus, Mary & Martha, Lk. 10
3. Place of Prayer; Discourse on Prayer, Lk. 11
4. Place unknown; charged with being in league with Satan, Lk. 11
5. Dining in Pharisee's home; denounces Pharisaism, Lk. 11
6. Before multitudes of 1000's Great evangelistic appeals on Hypocrisy, Anxiety, Covetousness, Lk. 12-13
7. In a Synagogue; heals woman bowed double; controversy over healing on the Sabbath, Lk. 13
8. Feast of Dedication (December); Jews seek to kill Jesus, Jn. 10

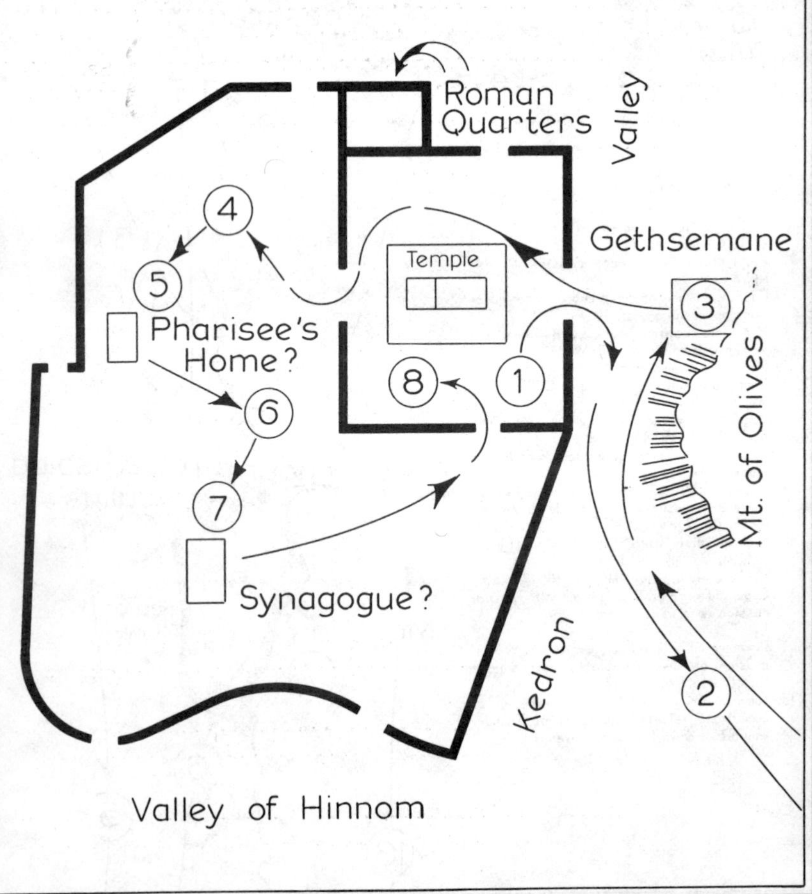

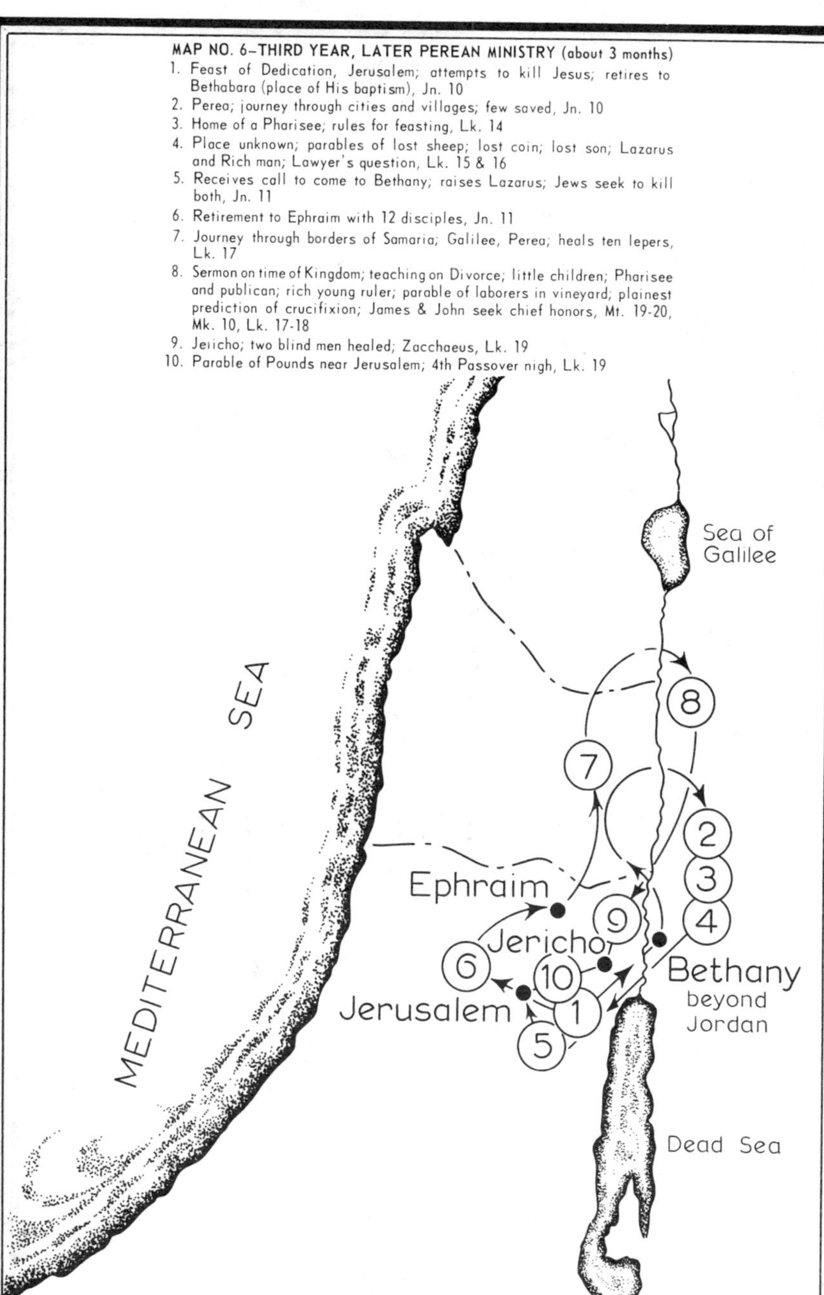
MAP NO. 6–THIRD YEAR, LATER PEREAN MINISTRY (about 3 months)
1. Feast of Dedication, Jerusalem; attempts to kill Jesus; retires to Bethabara (place of His baptism), Jn. 10
2. Perea; journey through cities and villages; few saved, Jn. 10
3. Home of a Pharisee; rules for feasting, Lk. 14
4. Place unknown; parables of lost sheep; lost coin; lost son; Lazarus and Rich man; Lawyer's question, Lk. 15 & 16
5. Receives call to come to Bethany; raises Lazarus; Jews seek to kill both, Jn. 11
6. Retirement to Ephraim with 12 disciples, Jn. 11
7. Journey through borders of Samaria; Galilee, Perea; heals ten lepers, Lk. 17
8. Sermon on time of Kingdom; teaching on Divorce; little children; Pharisee and publican; rich young ruler; parable of laborers in vineyard; plainest prediction of crucifixion; James & John seek chief honors, Mt. 19-20, Mk. 10, Lk. 17-18
9. Jericho; two blind men healed; Zacchaeus, Lk. 19
10. Parable of Pounds near Jerusalem; 4th Passover nigh, Lk. 19
Sea of Galilee
MEDITERRANEAN SEA
8
7
2
3
4
Ephraim
9
Jericho
6
10
Bethany beyond Jordan
Jerusalem
1
5
Dead Sea

### MAP NO. 7—LAST WEEK

1. Bethany—Feast, Mary anoints Jesus, Mt. 26:6-13; Mk. 13:3-9; Jn. 12
2. Jerusalem—Triumphal entry (Sunday) Mt. 21; Mk. 11; Lk. 19; Jn. 12
3. Temple, enters, looks around, says nothing, leaves, Mk. 11:11
4. Curses fig tree (Monday), Mt. 21; Mk. 11
5. Temple—cleanses 2nd time (Monday), Mt. 21; Mk. 11; Lk. 19
6. Temple courts?—Great day of discussions (Tuesday)—Mt. 21-22-23-24-25; Mk. 11-12-13-14; Lk. 20-21-22
7. Retirement to Rest?—(Wednesday), Judas plots to betray Jesus, Mt. 26; Mk. 14; Lk. 22
8. Upper Room—(Thursday), 4th Passover, Lord's Supper, Mt. 26; Mk. 14; Lk. 22; Jn. 13-14
9. Gethsemane—(Thursday night), Parting discourses, agony, betrayal and arrest, Jn. 15-16-17; Mt. 26; Mk. 14; Lk. 22
10. Trial before Annas and Caiaphas, Mt. 26-27; Mk. 14-15; Lk. 22-23
11. Trial before Sanhedrin, Jn. 18
12. Trial before Pilate
13. Trial before Herod
14. Trial before Pilate (2nd)
15. Golgotha—(Friday), Crucifixion, Mt. 27; Mk. 15; Lk. 23; Jn. 19
16. Garden—(Sunday), Resurrection, appears to Mary, other women, Mt. 28; Mk. 16; Lk. 24; Jn. 20

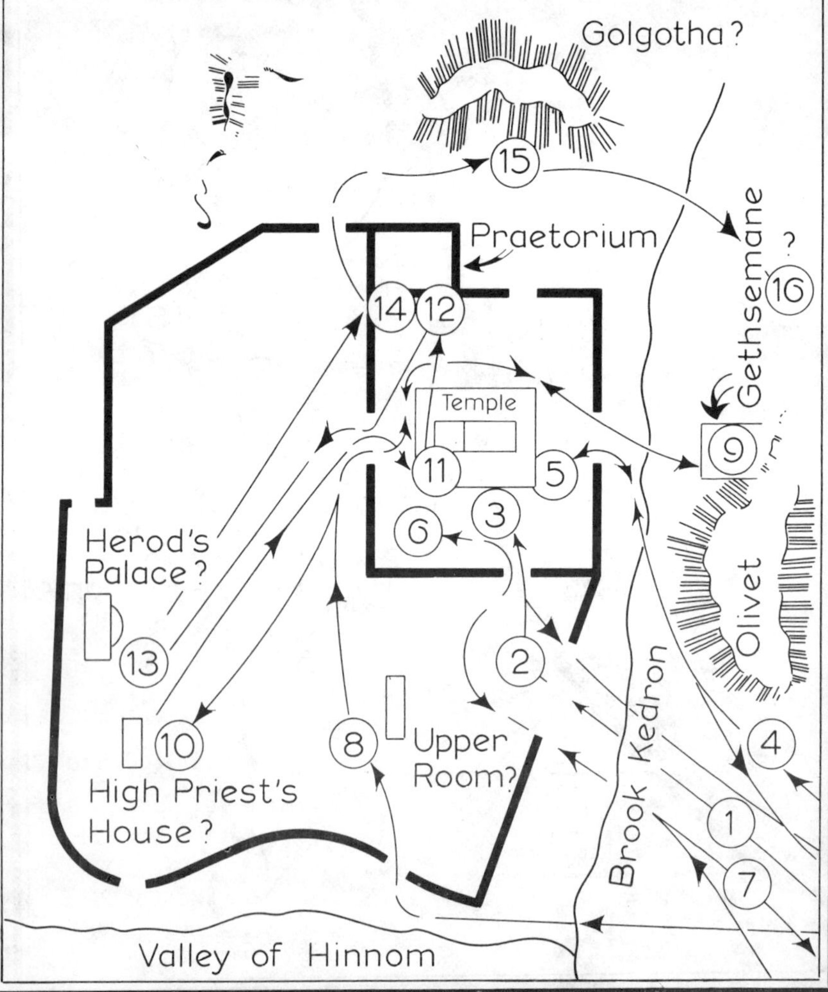

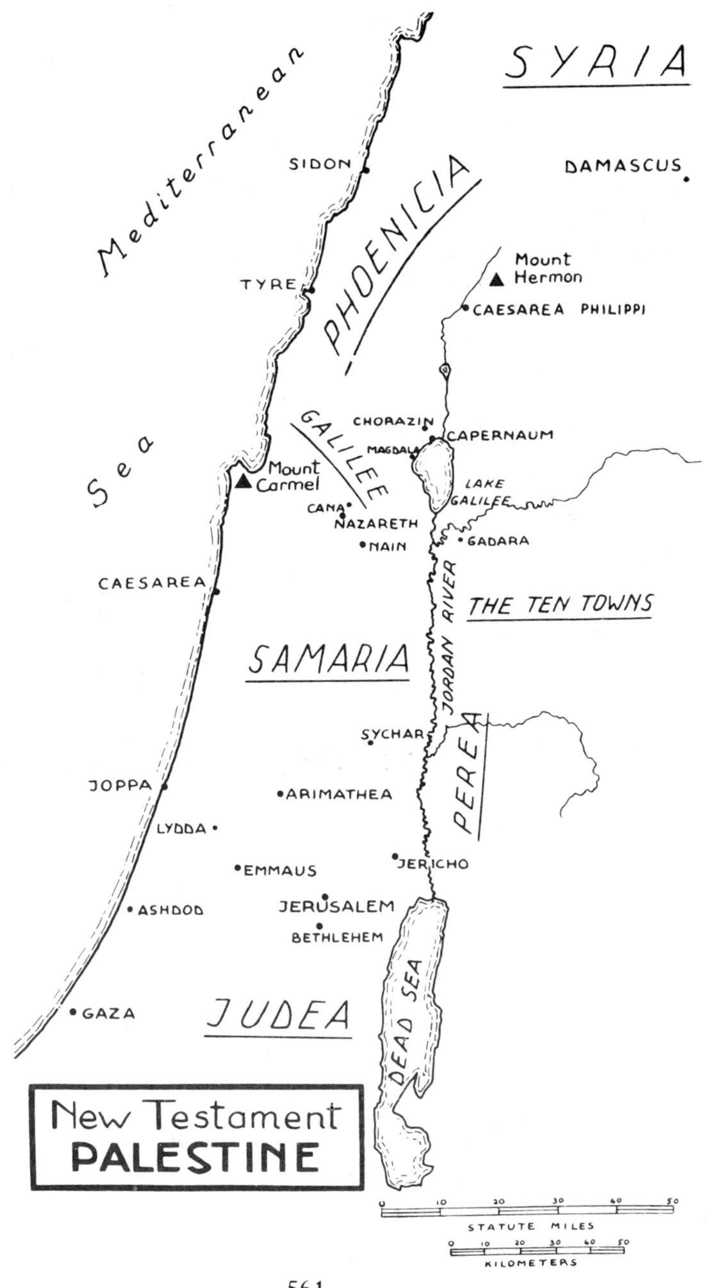
SYRIA
Mediterranean
Sea
SIDON
DAMASCUS
PHOENICIA
Mount
Hermon
TYRE
CAESAREA PHILIPPI
GALILEE
CHORAZIN
CAPERNAUM
MAGDALA
Mount
Carmel
LAKE
GALILEE
CANA
NAZARETH
NAIN
GADARA
CAESAREA
JORDAN RIVER
THE TEN TOWNS
SAMARIA
SYCHAR
PEREA
JOPPA
ARIMATHEA
LYDDA
JERICHO
EMMAUS
JERUSALEM
ASHDOD
BETHLEHEM
DEAD SEA
GAZA
JUDEA
New Testament
PALESTINE
0 10 20 30 40 50
STATUTE MILES
0 10 20 30 40 50
KILOMETERS

## BIBLIOGRAPHY FOR THE STUDY OF THE LIFE OF CHRIST

Harmonies of the Gospels:

Robertson, A. T. *A Harmony of the Gospel.* New York: Harper and Brothers Publishers, 1922. Based on A.S.V. (1901) text. Section or passage harmony.

Wieand, Albert C. *A New Harmony of the Gospels,* rev. ed. Grand Rapids: Eerdmans, 1950. Based on R.S.V. text. Phrases by phrase harmony.

*Harmony of the Gospels in Greek,* Synopsis Quattuor Evangeliorum, Stuttgart (American Bible Society).

Introduction to the Gospels:

Foster, Lewis. "Basis for the Historical Jesus," *Christian Standard,* (July 13, 20, 27, 1963). Pp. 427-428; 453-454; 471-472. Shows the inadequacy of the liberal views of Christ.

Foster, Lewis. "The 'Q' Myth in Synoptic Studies," *The Seminary Review,* Vol. X, No. 4 (Summer, 1964). Pp. 69-81. Shows lack of evidence for the "Q" source in the two-source theory.

Guthrie, Donald. *A Shorter Life of Christ.* Grand Rapids: Zondervan Publishing Co., 1970. Good on background. Summarizes various critical approaches to the life of Christ. Excellent bibliography.

Guthrie, Donald. *New Testament Introduction, 3rd rev. ed.* Downers Grove: InterVaristy Press, 1970. Up-to-date and scholarly.

Henry, Carl, ed. *Jesus of Nazareth: Saviour and Lord.* Grand Rapids: Wm. B. Eerdmans, 1966. Scholarly essays on key issues in Gospels study.

Kistemaker, Simon. *The Gospels in Current Study.* Grand Rapids: Baker Book House, 1972. Analysis and evaluation of contemporary views of Gospels from strongly conservative viewpoint. Rejects the two-source theory.

Marshall, Howard I. *Luke: Historian and Theologian.* Grand Rapids: Zondervan Publishing House, 1971. Analyzes current theories concerning Luke and upholds Luke's doctrinal presentation of Jesus as grounded in accurate history.

Martin, Ralph, P. *Mark: Evangelist and Theologian.* Grand Rapids: Zondervan Publishing House, 1973. Analyzes recent scholarly opinion on Mark's Gospel.

General Surveys of the Gospels:

Culver, Robert Duncan. *The Life of Christ.* Grand Rapids: Baker Book House, 1976. Helpful, brief harmonized study of the life of Christ.

Guthrie, Donald. *Jesus the Messiah.* Grand Rapids: Zondervan Publishing House, 1972. Basic, non-technical, harmonized survey of the life of Christ.

Sharp, C. J. *Life and Teaching of Jesus.* Cincinnati: Standard Publishing, 1970. Adapted from Sharp's, *The Christ of the Four Gospels* (1942) which was described by the author as "a brief simplified, but systematic, study of the four Gospels."

Tenney, Merrill, C. *New Testament Survey,* rev. ed. Grand Rapids: Wm. B. Eerdmans, 1961. Pages 123-228 survey the Gospels.

Wartick, Wallace and Wilbur Fields. *New Testament History: The Christ and the Inter-Testament Period.* Joplin: College Press, 1972. Survey of the life of Christ using explanatory notes, questions and special studies. Brief review of the history between the testaments.

Commentaries on the Life of Christ:

Edersheim, Alfred. *The Life and Times of Jesus the Messiah,* 3rd ed. Grand Rapids: Wm. B. Eerdmans, 1956 reprint of 1886 ed. One volume unabridged. "The standard, complete work on the life of Christ, interwoven with a history of the times in which He lived." This is preferred over the abridged volume, *Jesus the Messiah.*

Foster, R. C. *Gospel Studies,* Vols. I, II and III. Cincinnati: Cincinnati Bible Seminary, 1970, 1971, 1971. Very helpful question and answer studies through the life of Christ.

Foster, R. C. *Studies in the Life of Christ.* Grand Rapids: Baker Book House, 1938, 1962, 1968. Valuable study of introductory questions and expository studies on the entire life of Christ. Extensive.

Harrison, Everett F. *A Short Life of Christ.* Grand Rapids: Wm. B. Eerdmans, 1968. Studies on topics relating to the life of Christ—rather than a harmonized life of Christ.

McGarvey, J. W. and P. Y. Pendleton. *The Fourfold Gospel.* Cincinnati: Standard Publishing, n.d. Complete chronological life of Christ with comments interjected into the Biblical text.

Shepard, J. W. *The Christ of the Gospels.* Grand Rapids: Wm. B. Eerdmans, 1939. An exegetical study of the Gospels harmonized.

Commentaries on Matthew:

Broadas, John A. *Commentary on the Gospel of Matthew.* Philadelphia: American Baptist Publishing Society, 1886. Respected commentary by a Baptist.

Fowler, Harold. *Gospel of Matthew,* Vol. I & II. Joplin: College Press, 1968, 1972. Detailed study. Second volume covers through Matthew 12.

Hendriksen, William. *New Testament Commentary: The Gospel of Matthew.* Grand Rapids: Baker, 1973. Comprehensive commentary by conservative Calvinist.

Lewis, Jack P. *The Living Word Commentary: The Gospel According to Matthew,* Vol. I & II. Austin, Texas: Sweet Publishing Co., 1976. Brief exegetical comment. Based on the R.S.V. text.

McGarvey, J. W. *Matthew and Mark.* Delight, Arkansas: Gospel Light, n.d. Basic brief comment. Helpful.

Plummer, Alfred. *An Exegetical Commentary on the Gospel of Matthew.* Scribner & Sons, 1908. Helpful technical work on the Greek text. Liberal in places, e.g., denies Matthew's authorship and sees inaccuracies in the text but defends miracles and the virgin birth.

Commentaries on Mark:

Cranfield, C. E. B. *Cambridge Greek Testament Commentary: The Gospel According to Mark: Introduction and Commentary.* Cambridge: University Press, 1959. Technical, based on Greek text. Liberal.

Hendriksen, William. *New Testament Commentary: The Gospel of Mark.* Grand Rapids: Baker Book House, 1975. Extensive exegetical and expository work.

Hiebert, D. Edmond. *Mark: A Portrait of the Servant.* Chicago: Moody Press, 1974. Exegetical and devotional commentary.

Lane, William L. *New International Commentary: Commentary on the Gospel of Mark.* Grand Rapids: Wm. B. Eerdmans, 1974. Extensive work by an evangelical.

McGarvey, J. W. *Matthew and Mark.* Delight, Arkansas: Gospel Light, n.d. Basic, brief comment. Helpful.

Commentaries on Luke:

Arndt, William. *Gospel According to St. Luke.* St. Louis: Concordia Publishing House, 1956. Thorough. By conservative Lutheran.

Ash, Anthony. *The Living Word Commentary: The Gospel According to Luke,* Vol. I & II. Austin, Texas: R. B. Sweet Co., 1972. Based on the R.S.V. text.

Boles, Leo H. *A Commentary on the Gospel of Luke.* Nashville: Gospel Advocate Co., 1940. Based on the A.S.V. text. Clear, brief comments.

Geldenhuys, Norval. *New International Commentary: Commentary on the Gospel of Luke.* Grand Rapids: Wm. B. Eerdmans, 1951. Good, solid commentary.

Hobbs, Herschel. *An Exposition of the Gospel of Luke.* Grand Rapids: Baker Book House, 1966. Application of the text to our lives today makes this commentary useful to the preacher.

Morris, Leon. *The Gospel According to St. Luke.* Grand Rapids: Wm. B. Eerdmans, 1974. Brief, but of good quality.

Plummer, Alfred. *International Critical Commentary: The Gospel According to St. Luke,* 10th ed. Edinburgh: T. & T. Clark Publishing, 1914. Classic work based on Greek text.

Commentaries on John:

Barrett, C. K. *The Gospel According to St. John.* London: SPCK, 1955. Advanced work based on the Greek text. Liberal.

Butler, Paul. *The Gospel of John.* Joplin: College Press, 1961, 1965. Basic exposition of this Gospel.

Hendriksen, William. *New Testament Commentary: The Gospel of John.* Grand Rapids: Baker Book House, 1954. Comprehensive, by a Calvinist.

Lenski, R. C. H. *Interpretation of St. John's Gospel.* Columbus, Ohio: Wartburg Press, 1942. Comprehensive, by a Lutheran.

Morris, Leon. *New International Commentary: Commentary on the Gospel of John.* Grand Rapids: Wm. B. Eerdmans, 1971. Extensive work by an evangelical.

Westcott, B. F. *The Gospel According to John.* Grand Rapids: Wm. B. Eerdmans, 1951. On English text, a classic.

# INDEX OF SUBJECTS

# INDEX OF SCRIPTURE REFERENCES

LUKE



LUKE





LUKE







LUKE

LUKE



LUKE

JOHN



JOHN

JOHN



JOHN

ROMANS



ROMANS

ROMANS

ROMANS



I CORINTHIANS